Mark Siegel

Sailor Twain

or The Mermaid in the Hudson

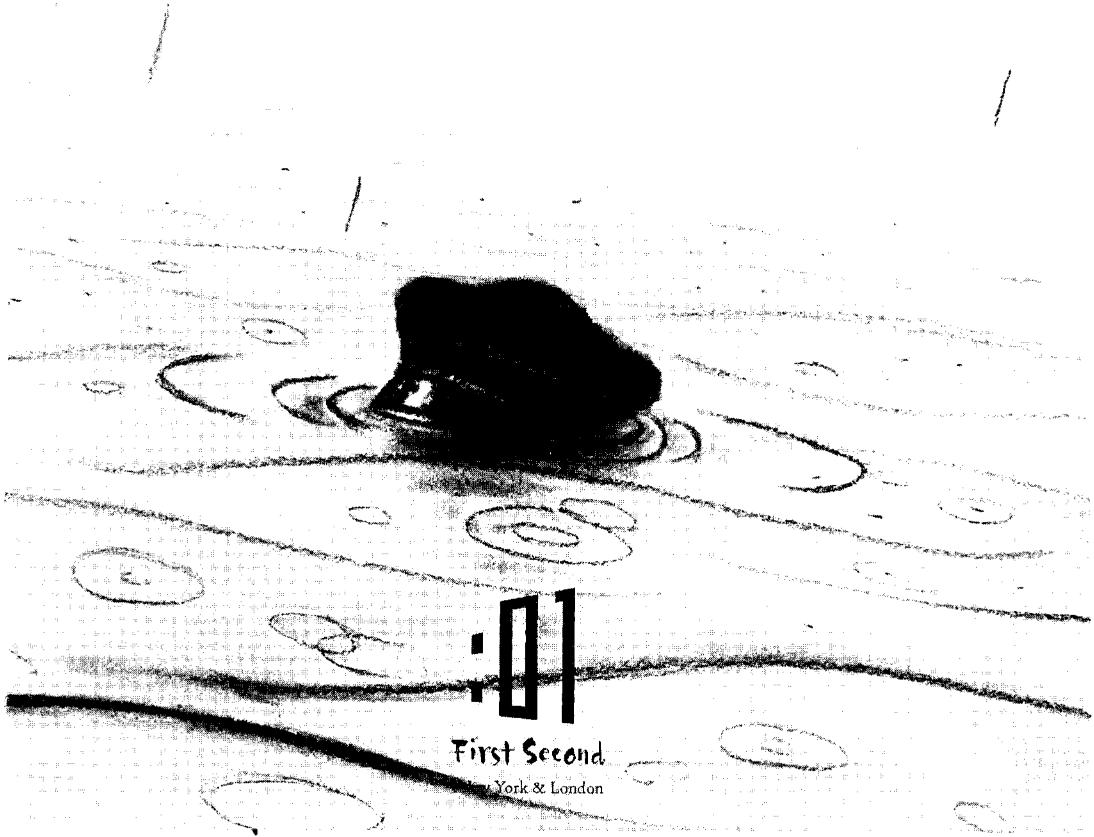

First Second
York & London

For Edward and Marie-Claire Siegel

Mon front est rouge encor du baiser de la Reine;
J'ai rêvé dans la grotte où nage la sirène . . .

Gérard de Nerval, *El Desdichado*

CONTENTS

PART II: CAMOMILLE

PART III: WORLD'S END

PART IV: SAILOR TWAIN

OVERTURE

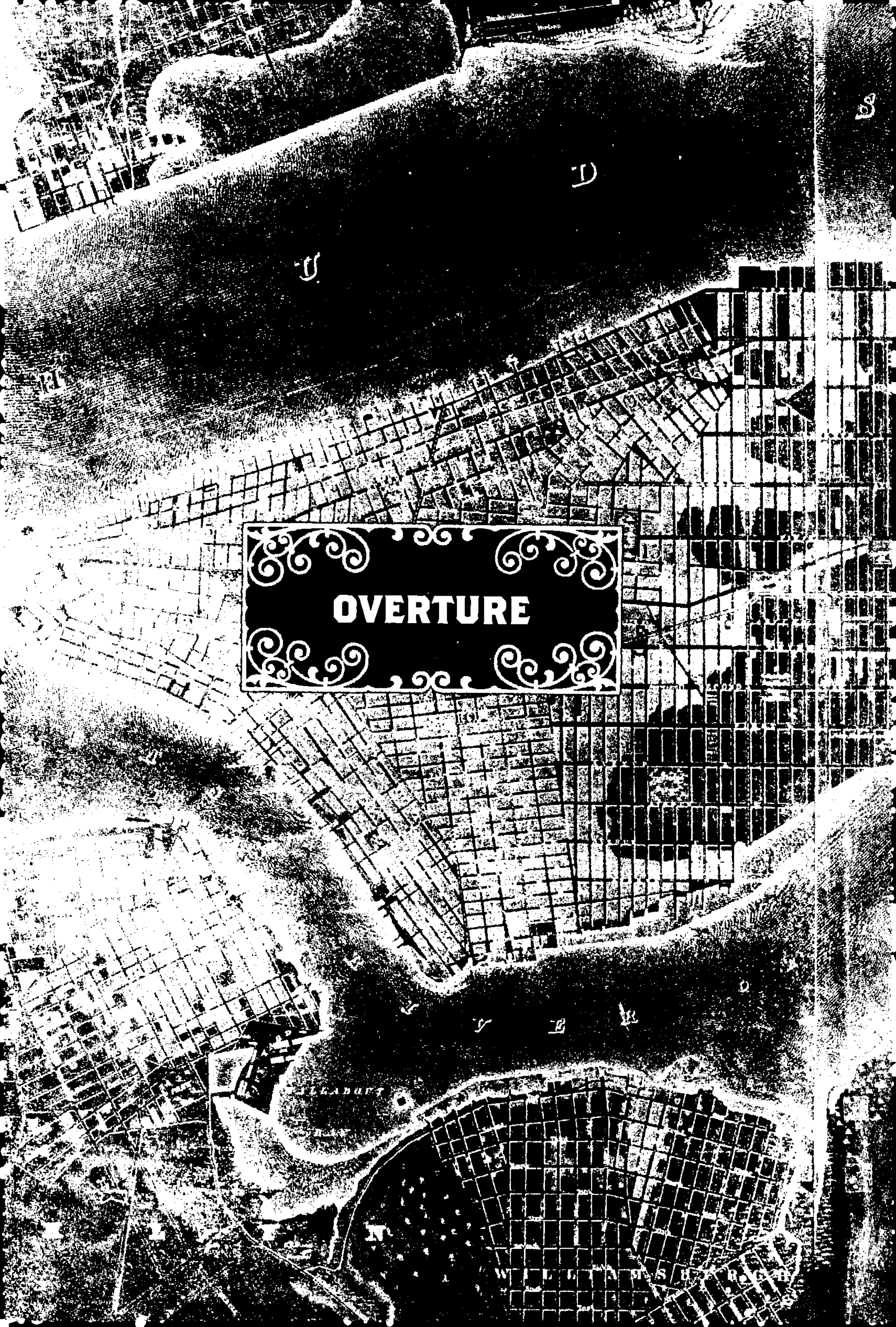

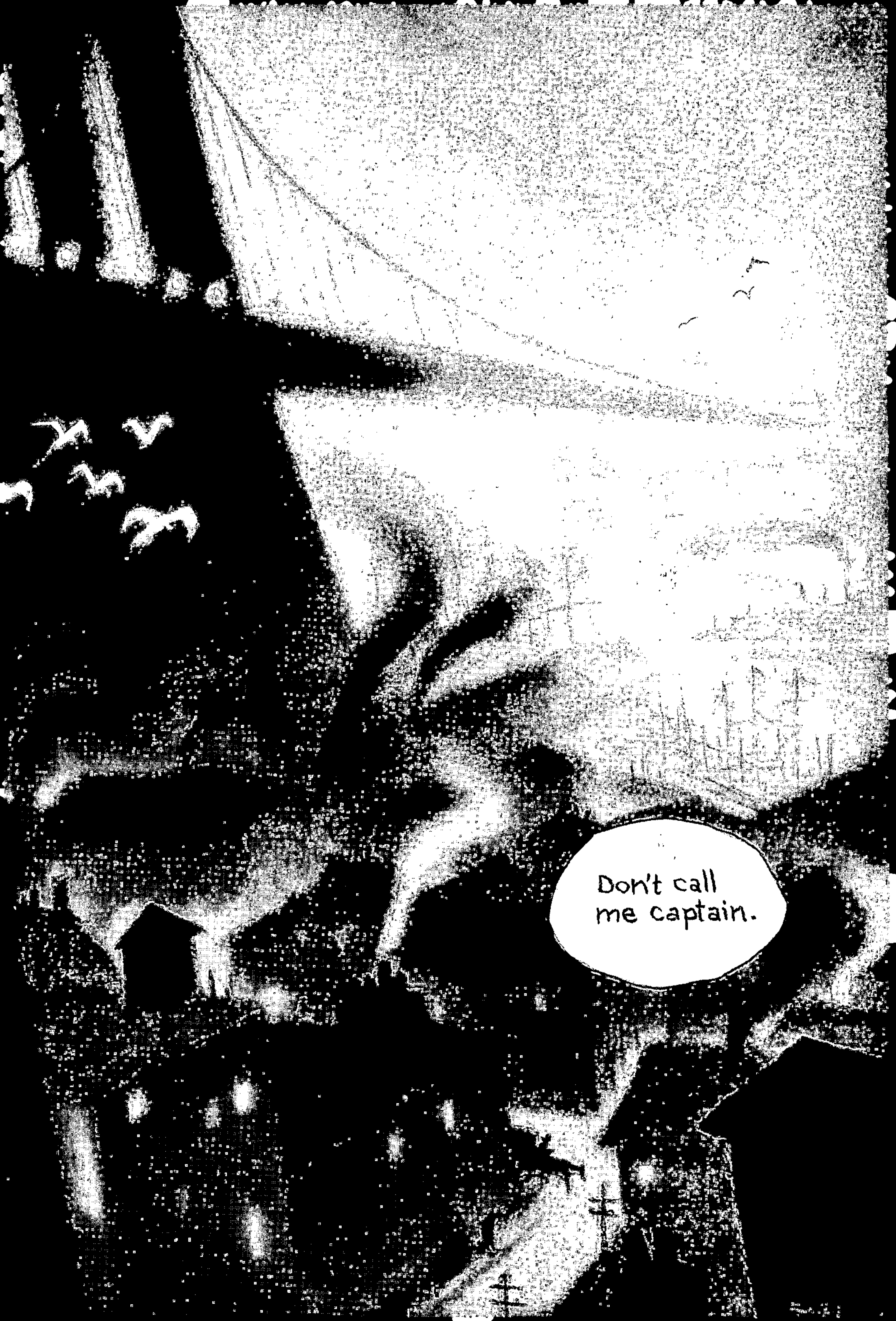
Don't call
me captain.

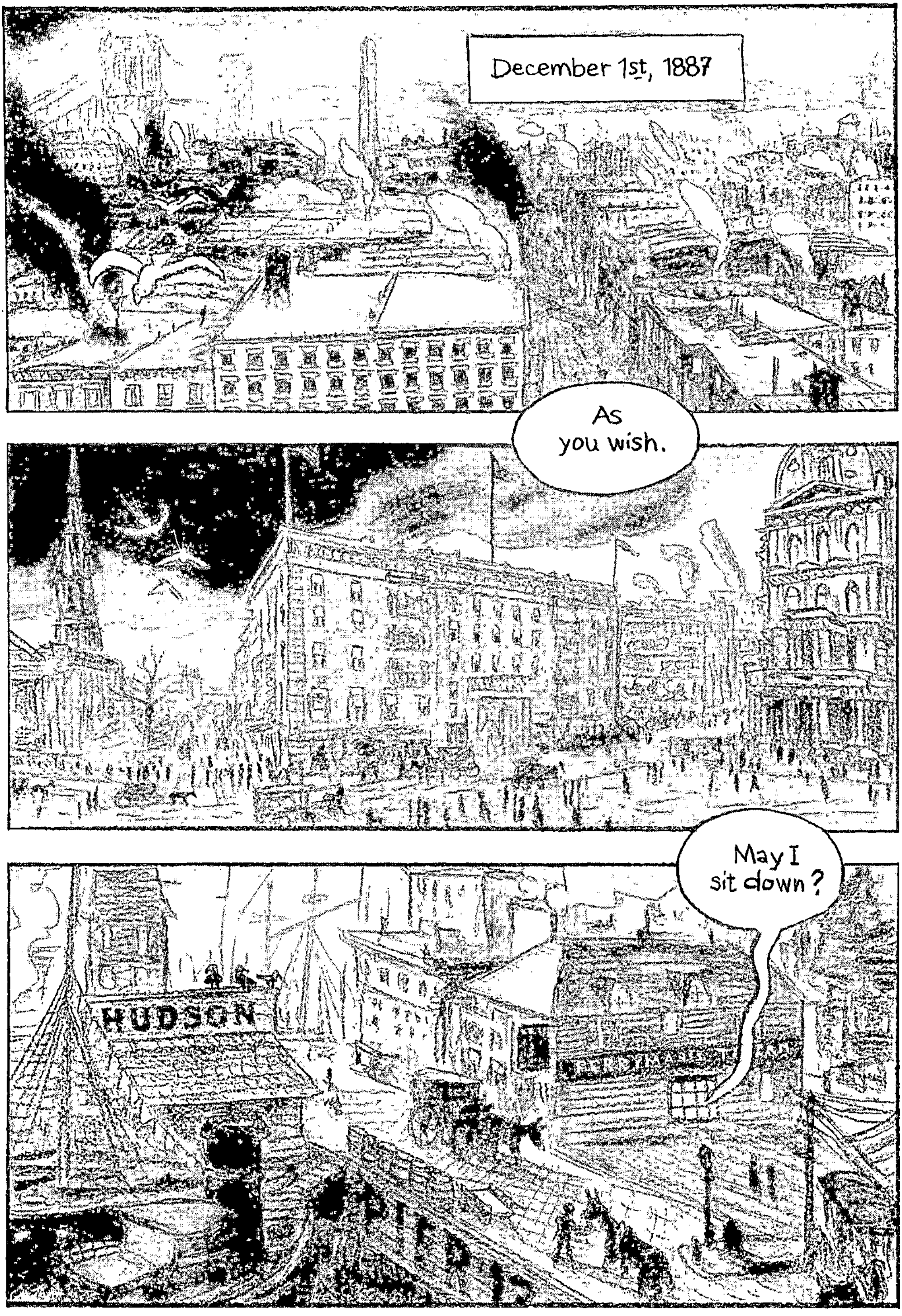
December 1st, 1887
As you wish.
May I sit down?
HUDSON

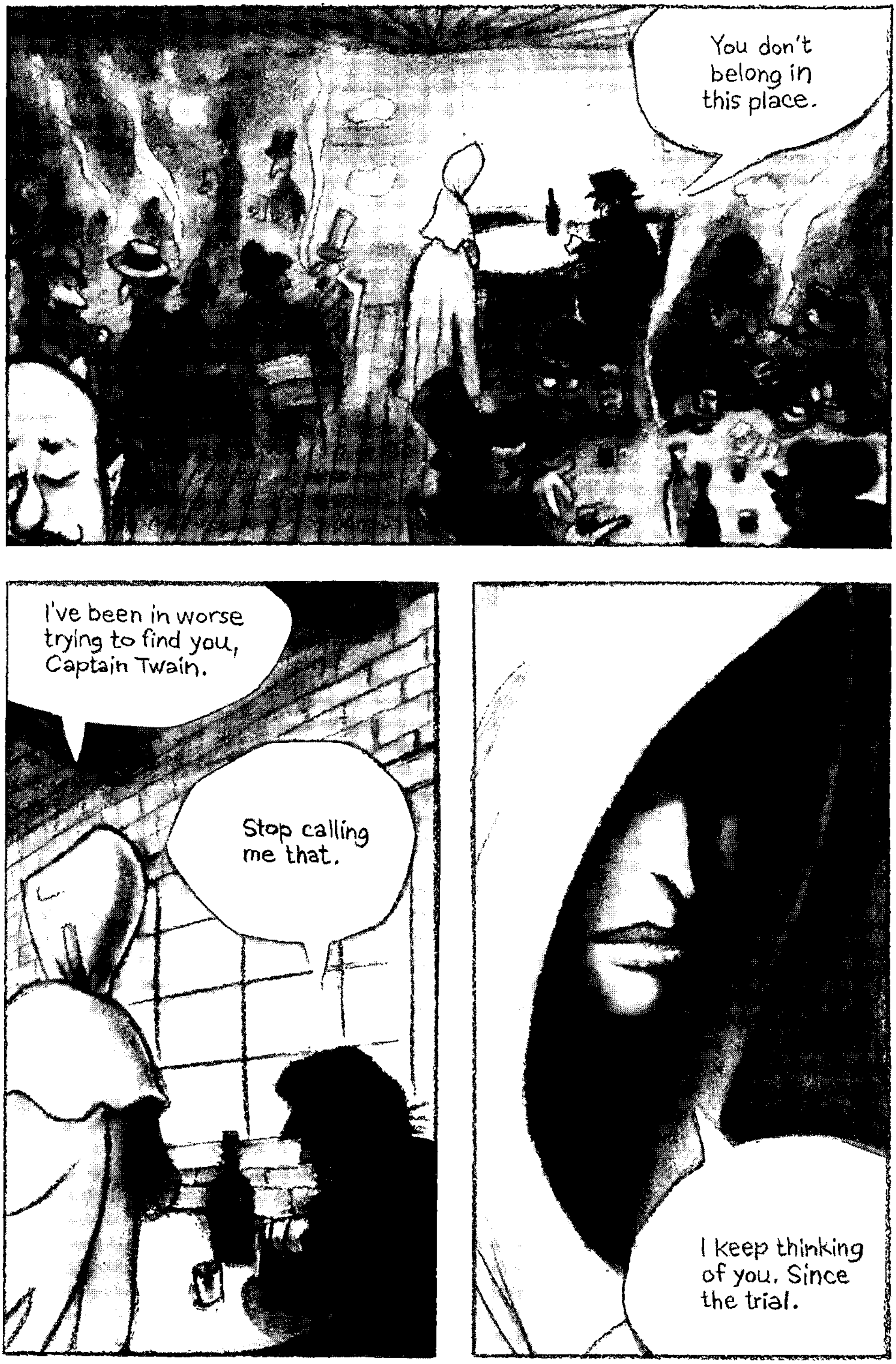
You don't belong in this place.
I've been in worse trying to find you, Captain Twain.
Stop calling me that.
I keep thinking of you. Since the trial.

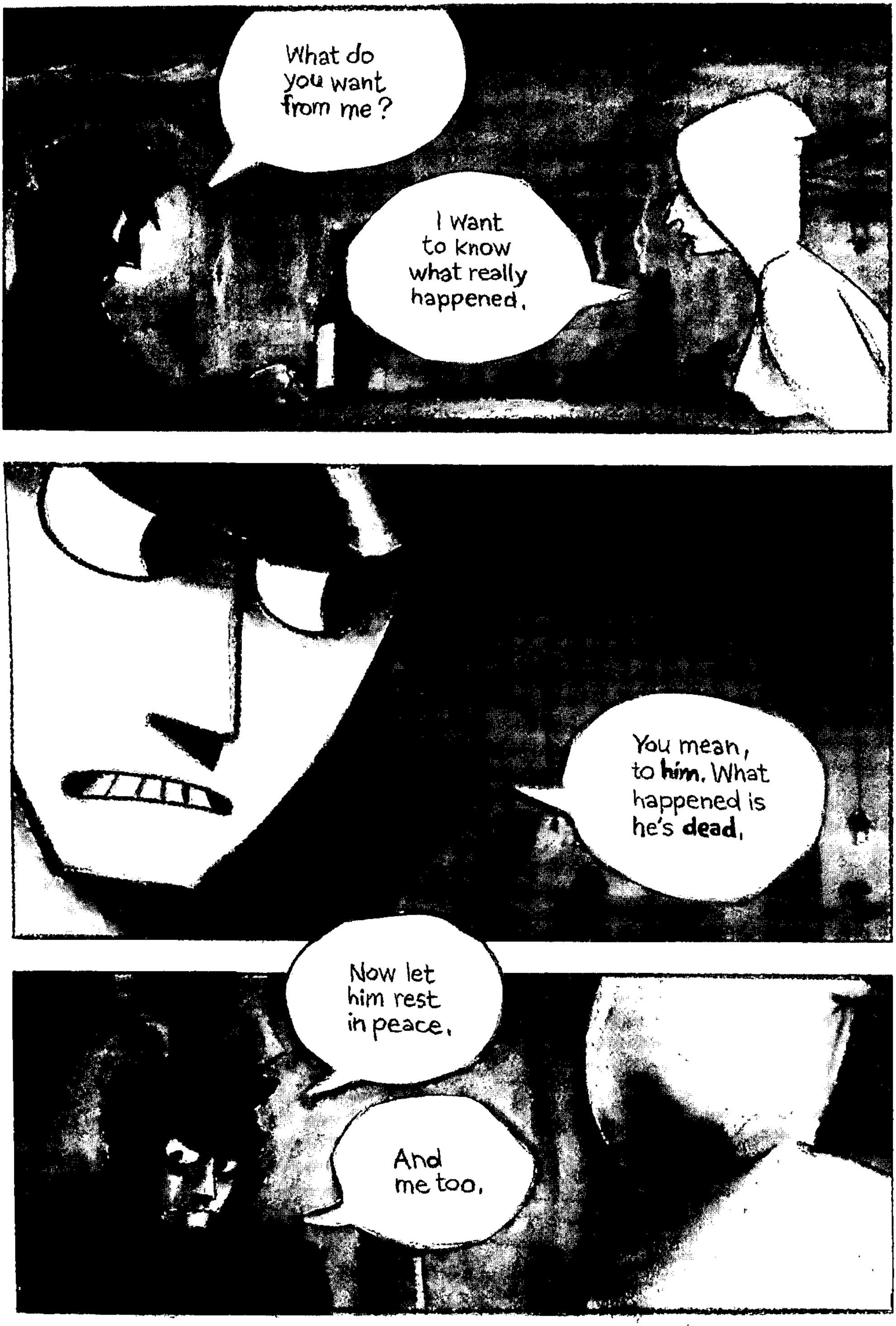
What do you want from me?
I want to know what really happened.
You mean, to **him.** What happened is he's **dead.**
Now let him rest in peace.
And me too.

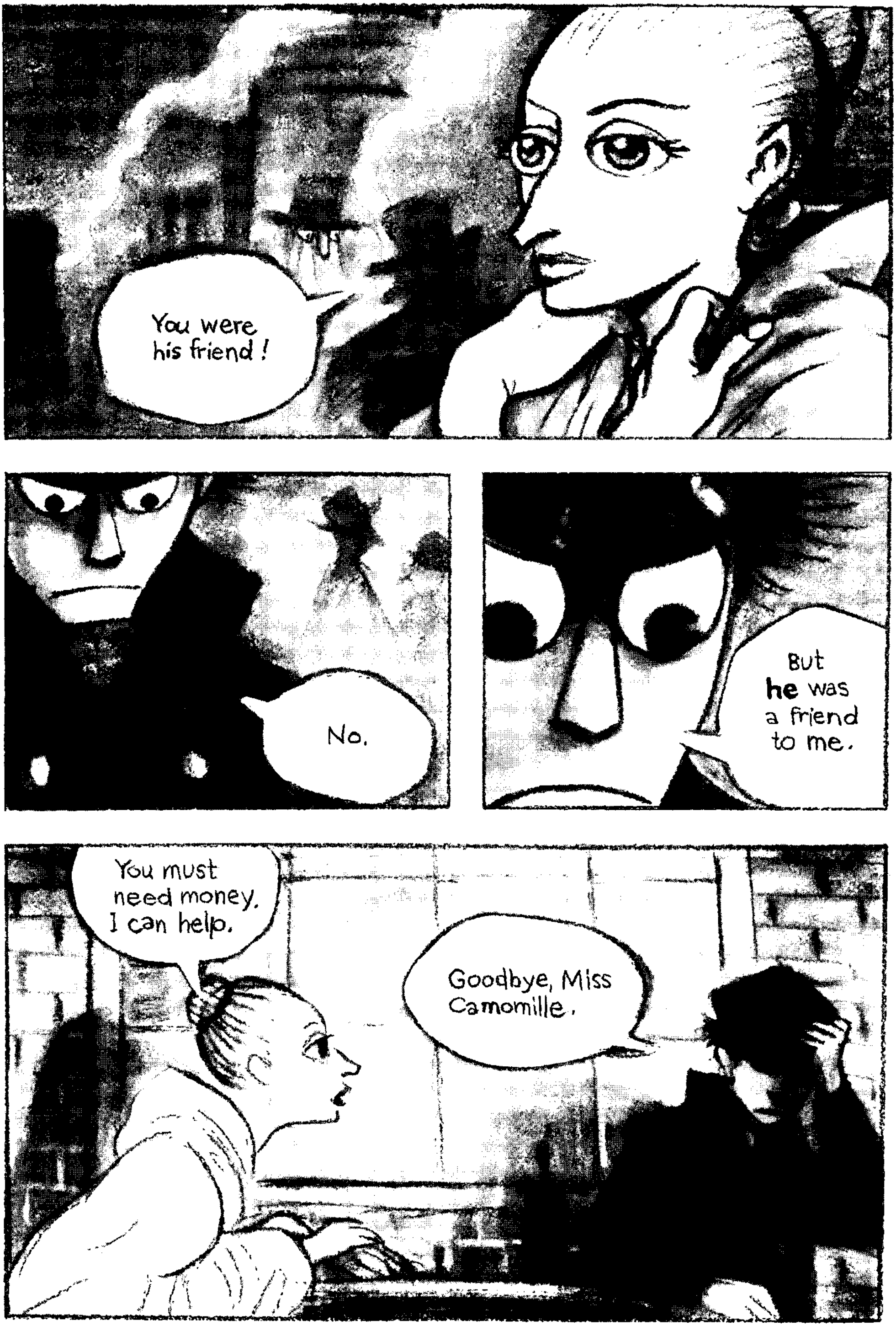
You were his friend!
No.
But **he** was a friend to me.
You must need money. I can help.
Goodbye, Miss Camomille.

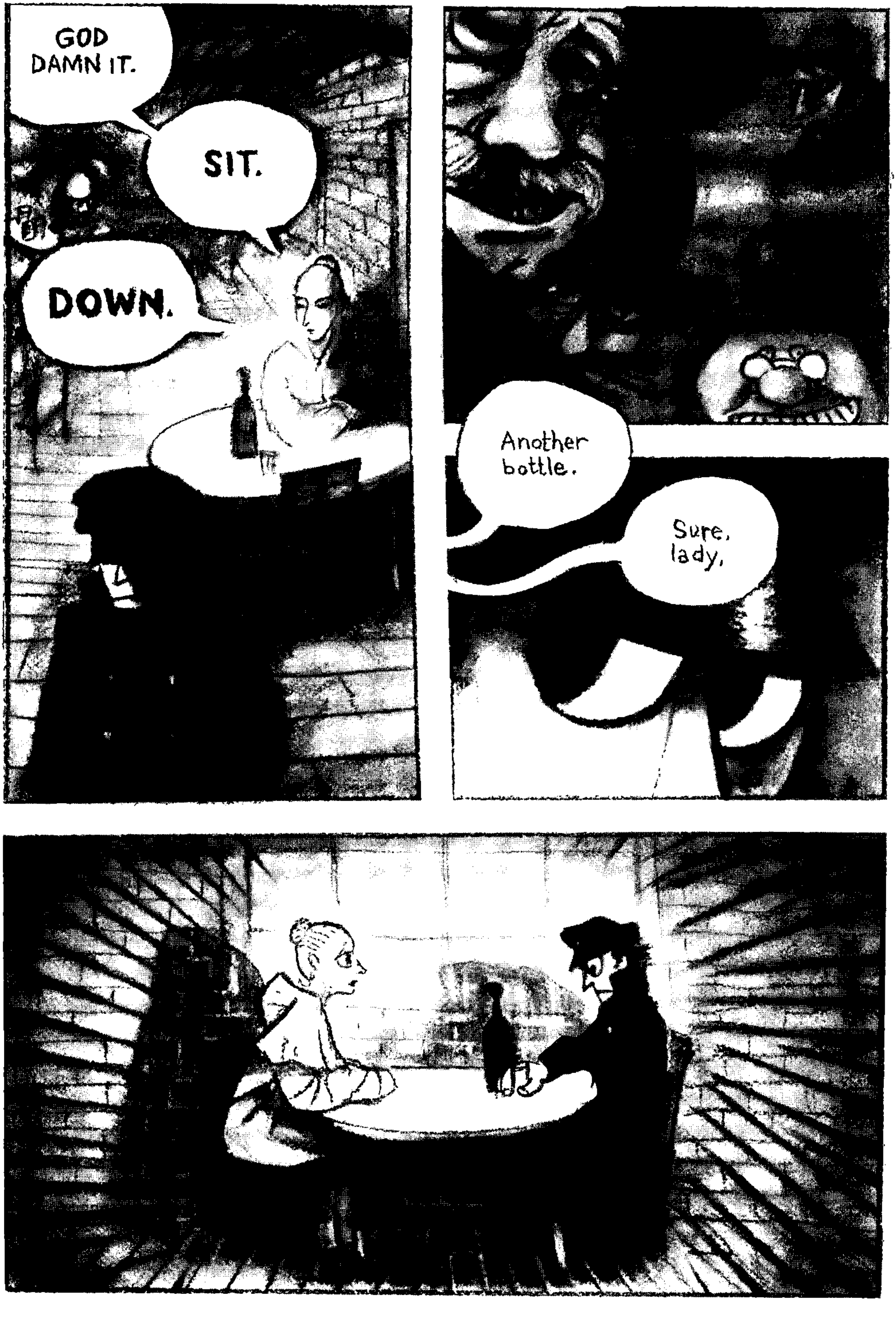
GOD DAMN IT.
SIT.
DOWN.
Another bottle.
Sure, lady,

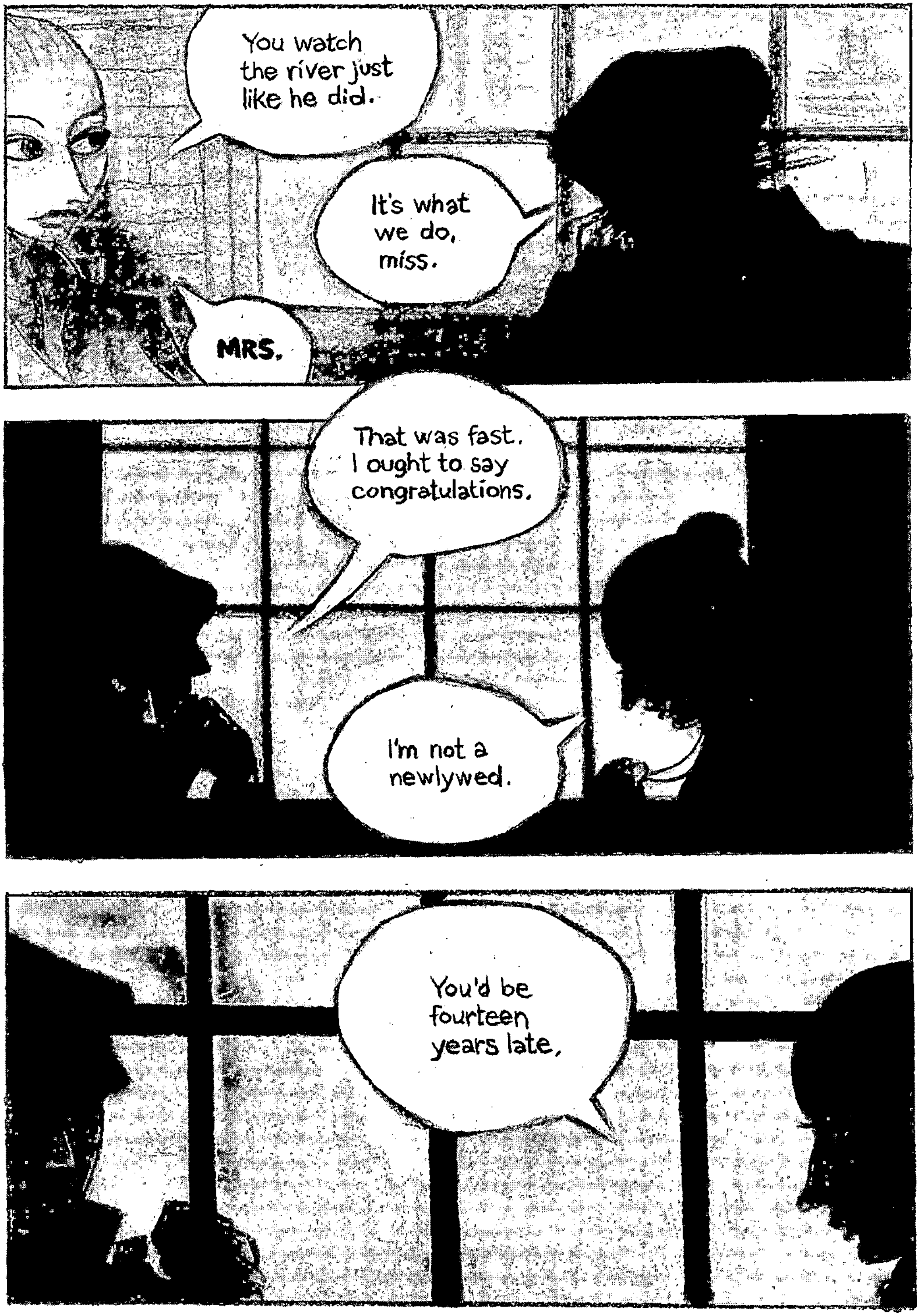
You watch the river just like he did.
It's what we do, miss.
MRS.
That was fast. I ought to say congratulations.
I'm not a newlywed.
You'd be fourteen years late,

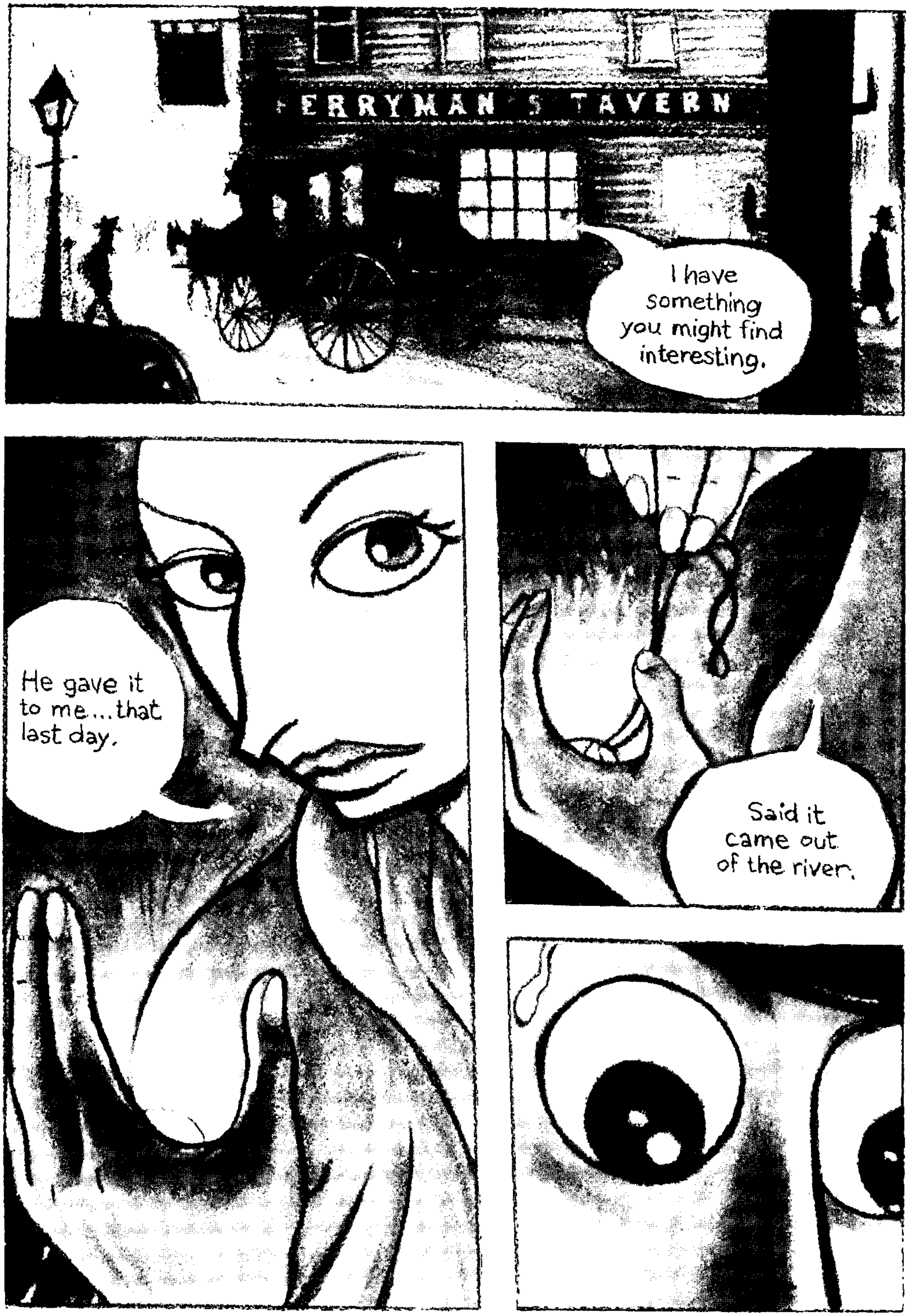
ERRYMAN'S TAVERN
I have something you might find interesting.
He gave it to me...that last day.
Said it came out of the river.

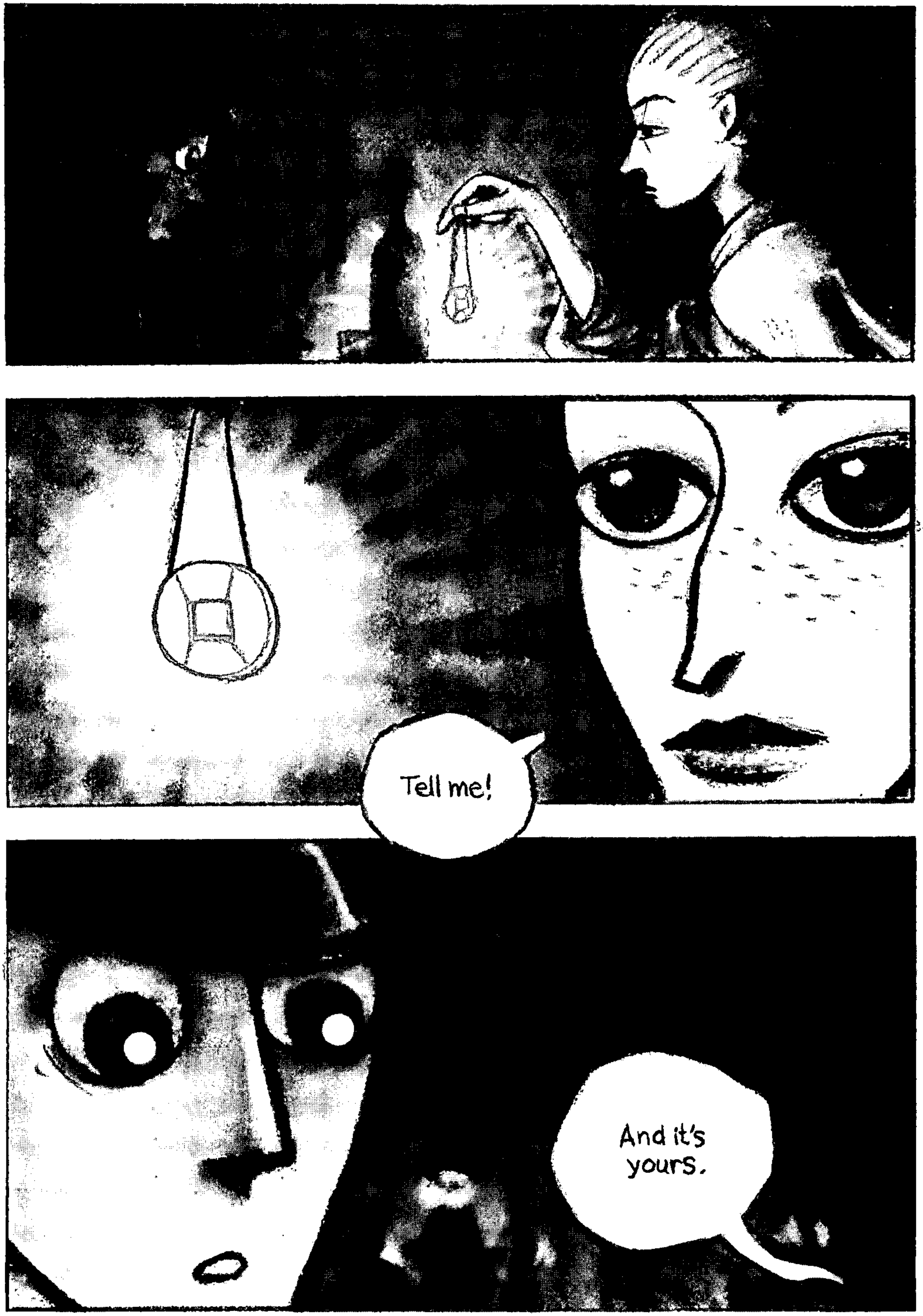
Tell me!
And it's yours.

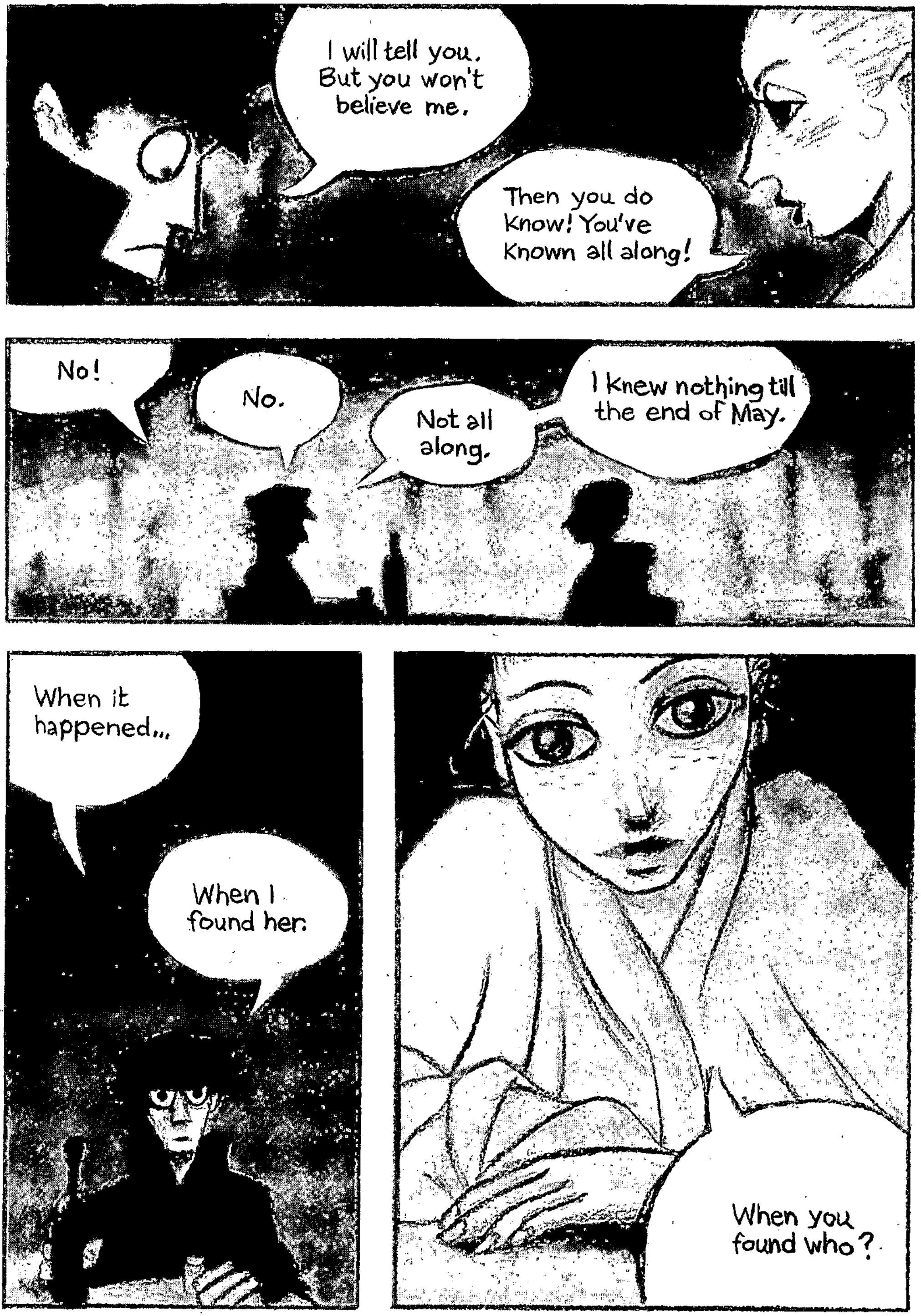
I will tell you. But you won't believe me.
Then you do know! You've known all along!
No!
No.
Not all along.
I knew nothing till the end of May.
When it happened...
When I found her.
When you found who?

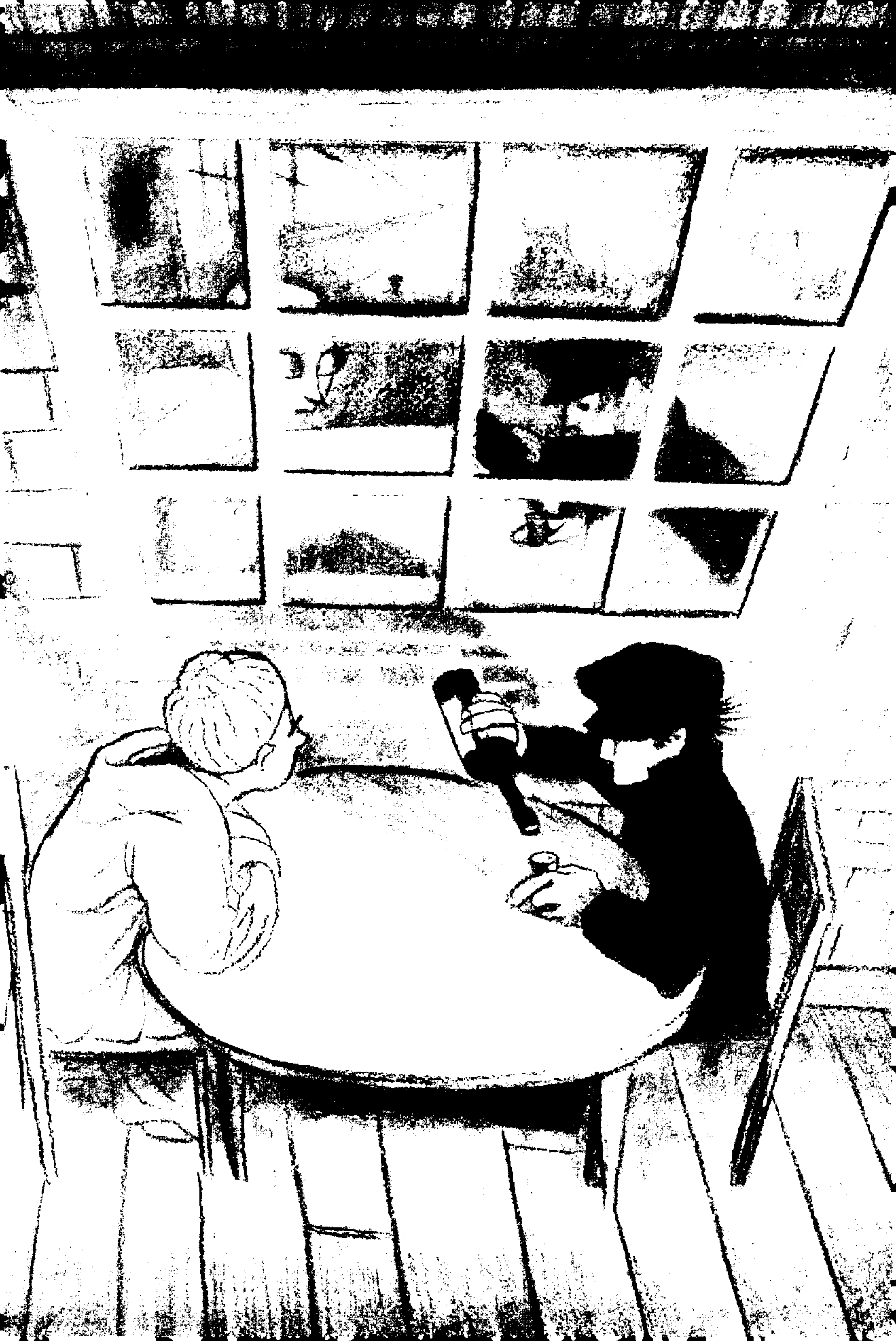

MYSTERIOUS DISAPPEARANCE OF STEAM SHIP OWNER

Friends & Acquaintances Fear Worst

COLD SPRING, N.Y.—The owner of the "Lorelei" steamship line has disappeared without a trace after several weeks of reportedly eccentric behavior.

Jacques-Henri Lafayette was last seen September 9 aboard his paddlewheeler in the waters off New York. In his absence, his brother and business partner, Donné Lafayette, has taken over their popular passenger line.

According to company information regarding to his brother, dead or alive.

The LORELEI plies the Hudson day and night, from Manhattan to Albany. The line has been in business since 1848, and has distinguished itself among Hudson river steamboats.

Its former chief officer was young Capt. Elijah Twain of Tarrytown, N.Y., the son of renowned Capt. Josiah Twain. Since the elder Lafayette's lavish hospitality and distinguished dinner parties have been well known...

Metropolitan Police are investigating Mr. Lafayette's last whereabouts and conducting interviews with his employees...

CROWDS FOR BEAVERTON

The slippery C.G. Beaverton has become a national phenomenon. This author—whose full name his tight-lipped publisher has never yet released—has risen to an unprecedented popularity with another unlikely, obscure and fantastical guidebook. Beaverton's peculiar blend of anthropology and make-believe now claims a throng of readers of all ages from coast to coast. These avid readers remind us of the most zealous followers of the late Dickens, when his "Great Expectations" drew crowds at every new installment. Even Samuel L. Clemens must be watching this Beaverton nervously from his family home in Hartford.

(Cont'd from p. 17)

They have been called 'imaginary books' and 'impossible travelogues.' Beaverton's writings defy a library's typical shelving methods. Take his 'Secrets & Mysteries of Aegypt and Chaldea', for instance, and its rich descriptions of the River Nile, interrupted by the author's culinary recommendation for travelers to the pharaohs and various delicate eats children playing on the shores of the done by his own hand. With hardly a transition, our guide in these foreign lands takes us to what is perhaps a dream, or an hallucination owing to too much sun, into an ancient temple, a conversation with a magical entity, rides inside of a desert wind. The book concludes with a packing list, replete with the kinds of hats and even underthings best suited for those wishing to travel there. Why are we so rapt by this fabulous journal? Perhaps because Beaverton gives us a world where iron and steel have not yet replaced magic, a childlike belief. Or perhaps we simply wish he would take us with him on his next journey.

New work from C.G. Beaverton outsells Mr. Dickens

New York City, N.Y., April 17.—Not since the last installment of "A Tale of Two Cities," have booksellers reported such lines outside their storefronts. The massive pre-orders of Mr. Beaverton's Secrets & Mysteries of the Hudson River, a fanciful account of Hudson Valley folklore, are merely a prelude to the book's official release later this month. Beaverton's previous book, "Secrets & Mysteries of Aegypt and Chaldea" boasted historic sales in the United States and in Europe. Notoriously private, the author Beaverton has intrigued readers and reporters alike by shunning all public appearances despite numerous invitations from colleges and speaking halls.

...New York Times, April 17, 1887

C.G. Beaverton's SECRETS AND MYSTERIES OF THE RIVER

Part One
TWAIN'S SECRET

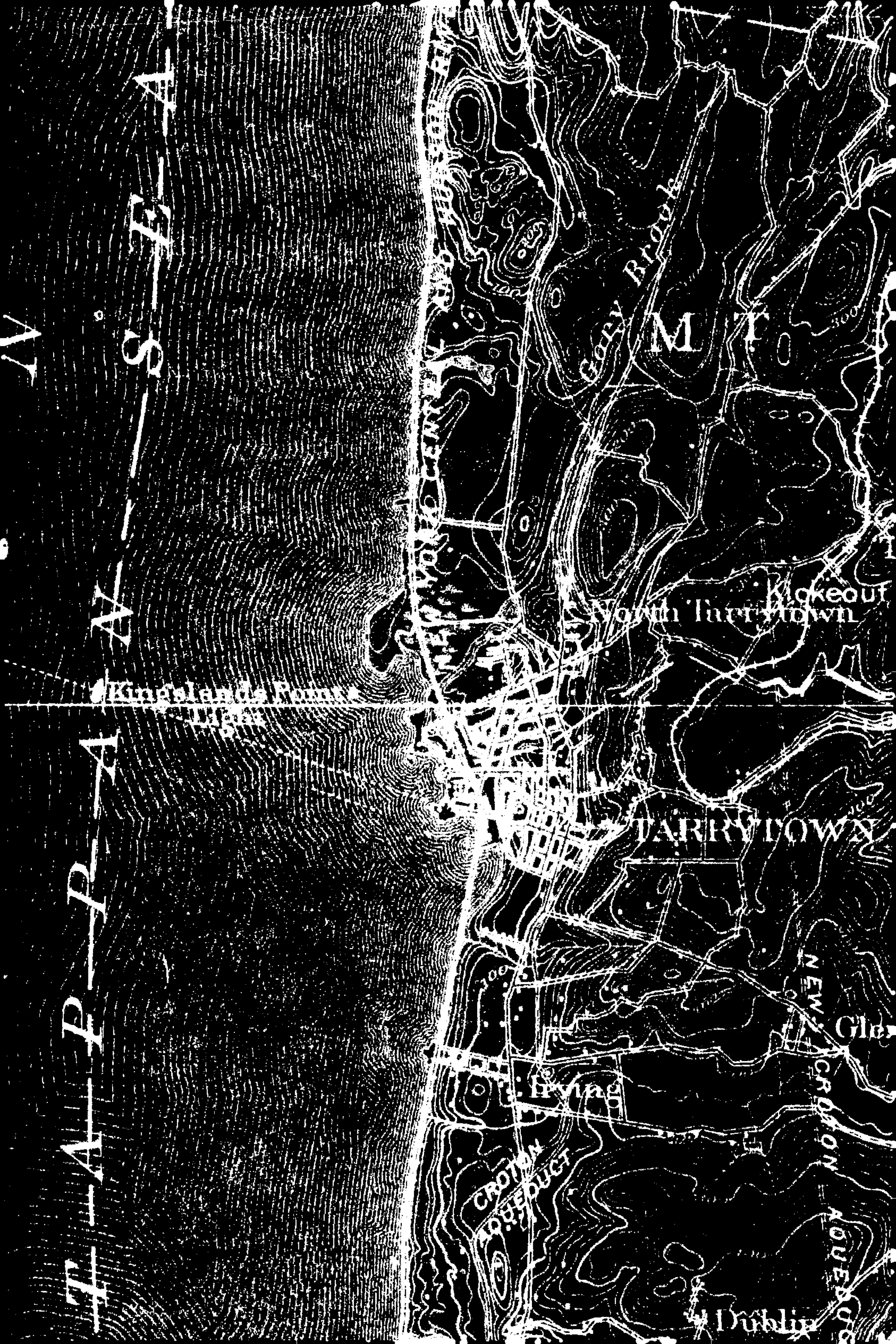
TAPPAN ZEE
Kingsland Point Light
North Tarrytown
Kickeout
TARRYTOWN
Irving
Dublin
Gory Brook
CROTON AQUEDUCT
NEW CROTON AQUEDUCT

Pt I, Chap.1

"THE FRENCHMAN'S STEAMBOAT"

Tappan Zee Crossing, 18 miles north of New York City, May 25th, 1887

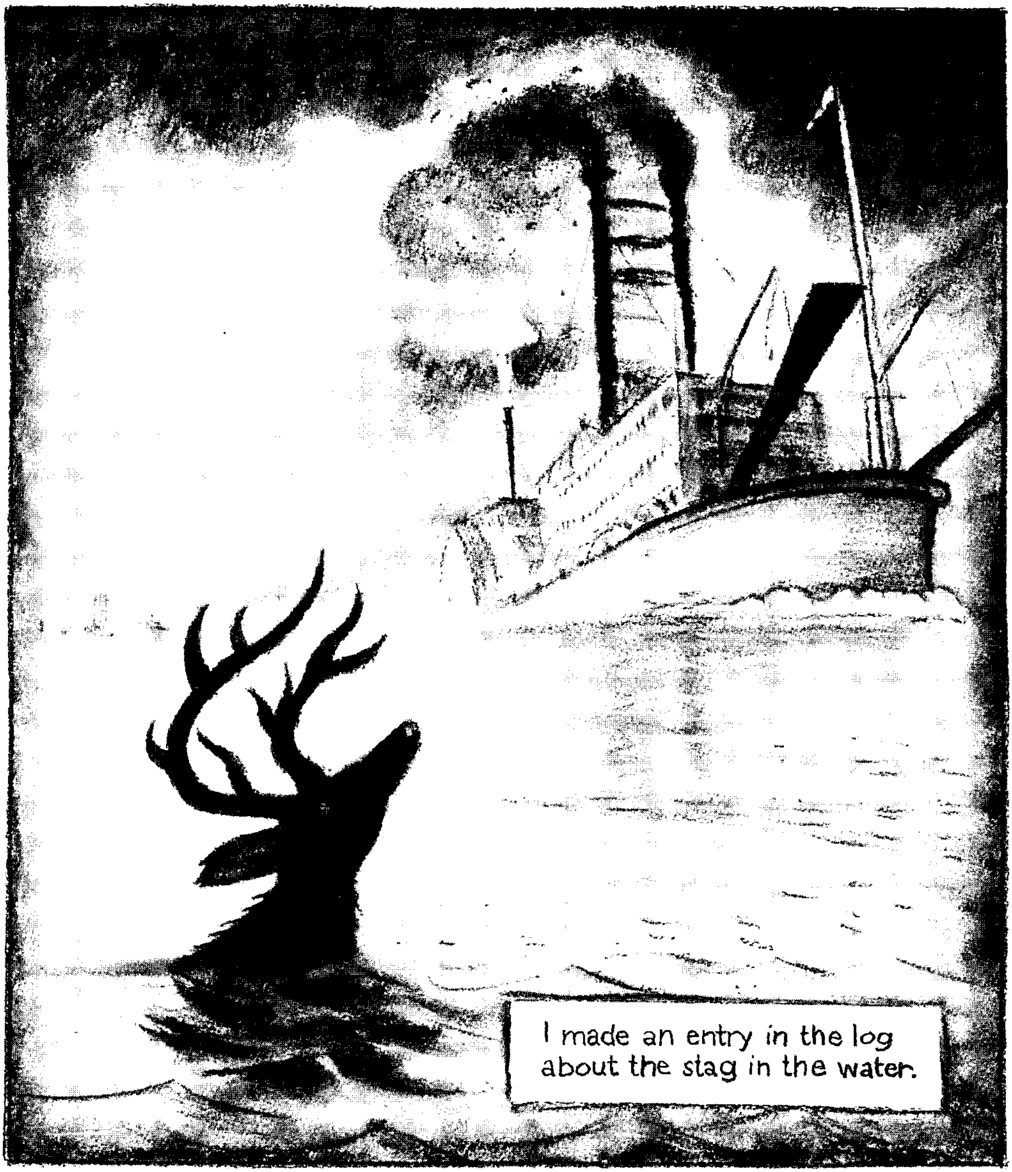
I made an entry in the log about the stag in the water.

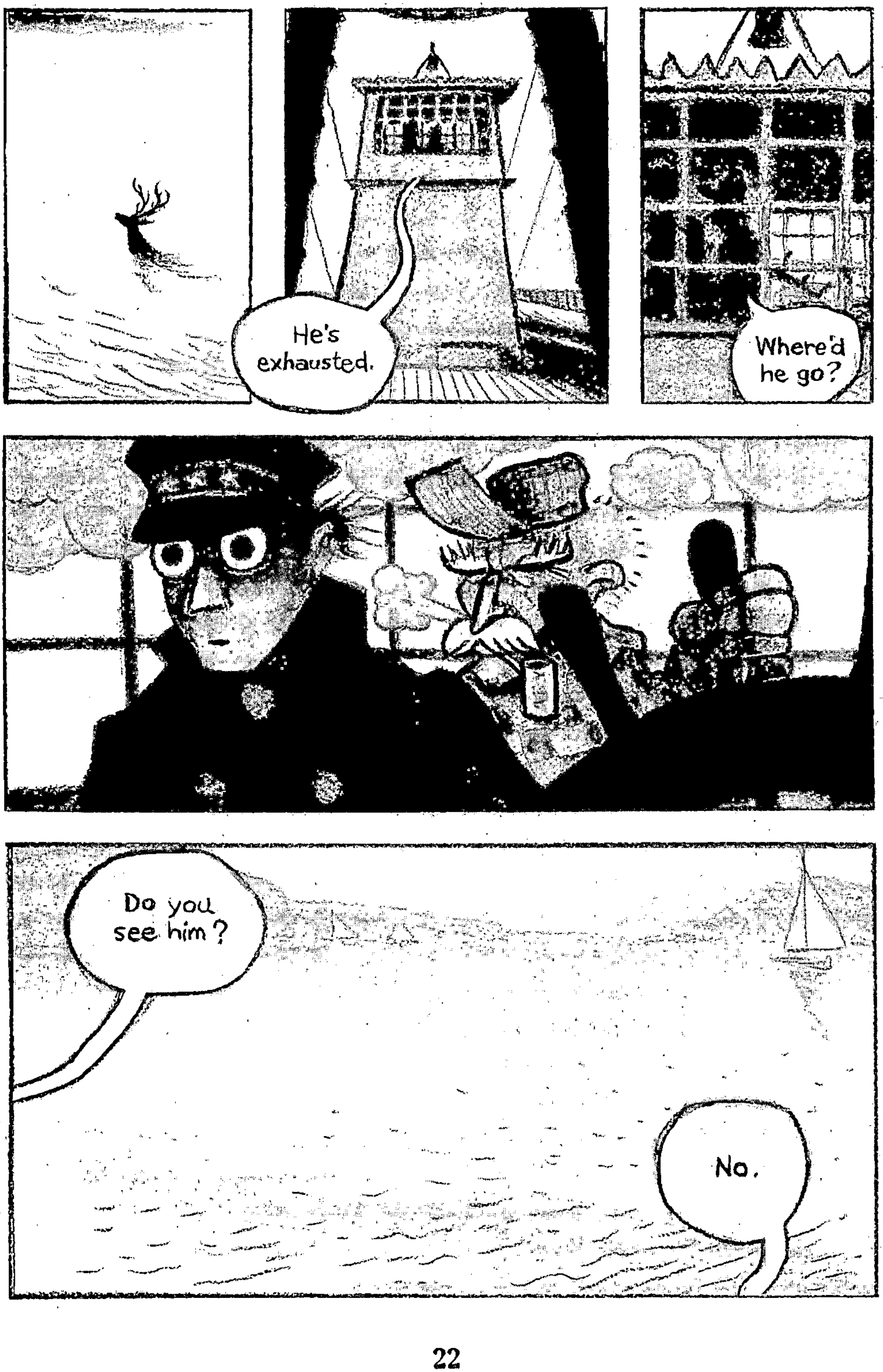
He's exhausted.
Where'd he go?
Do you see him?
No.

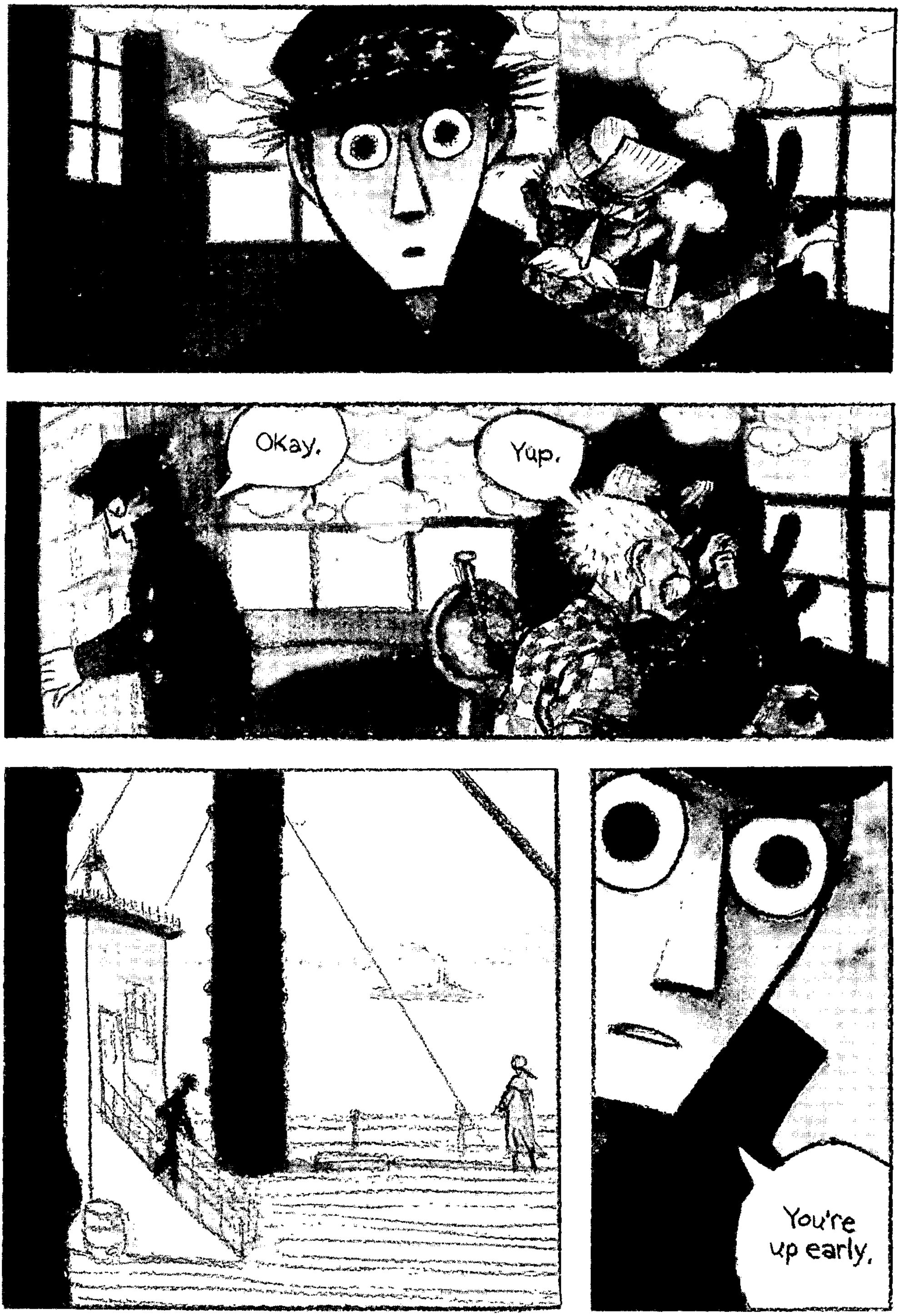
OKay.
Yup.
You're up early.

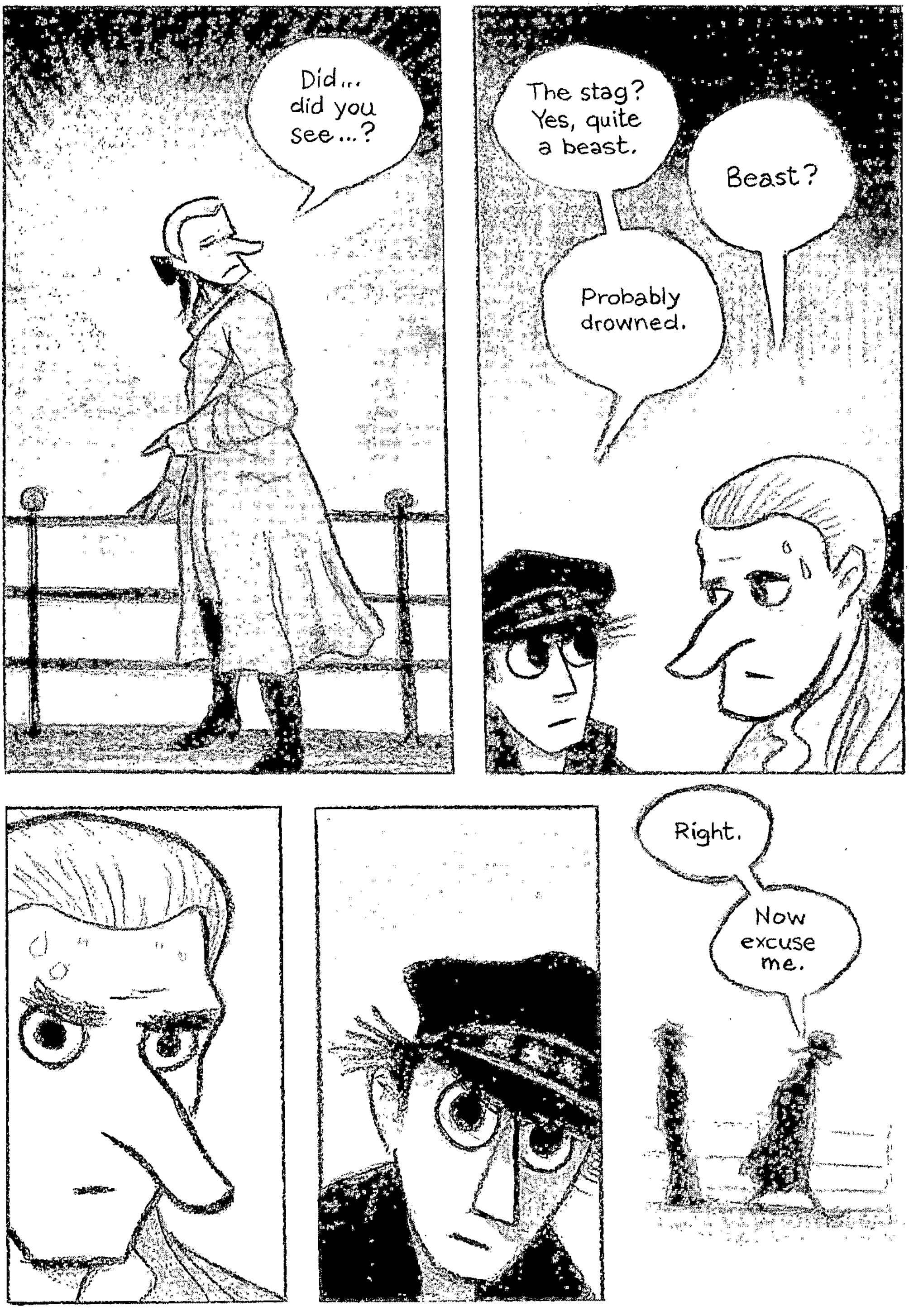
Did... did you see...?
The stag? Yes, quite a beast.
Beast?
Probably drowned.
Right.
Now excuse me.

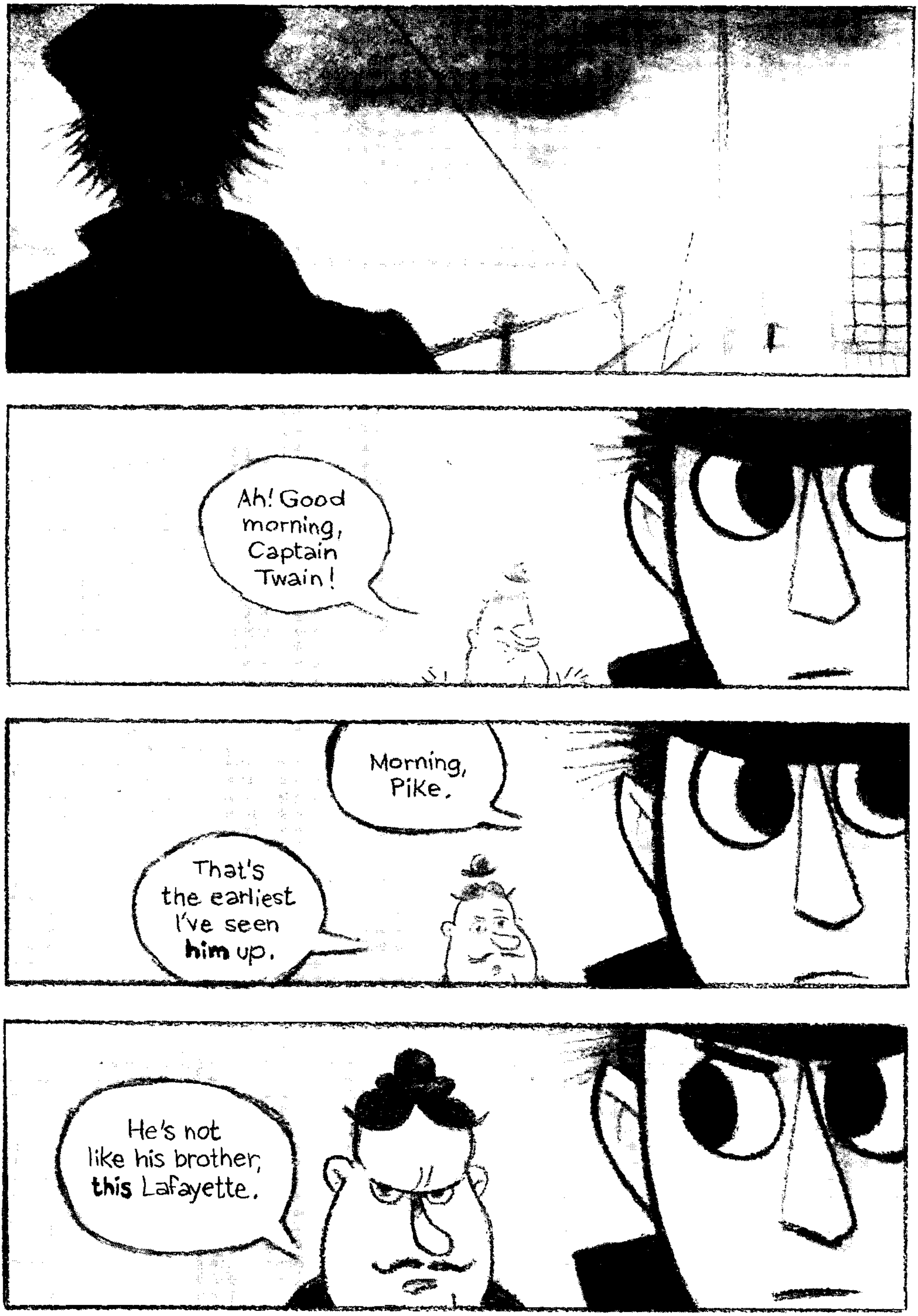
Ah! Good morning, Captain Twain!
Morning, Pike.
That's the earliest I've seen **him** up.
He's not like his brother, **this** Lafayette.

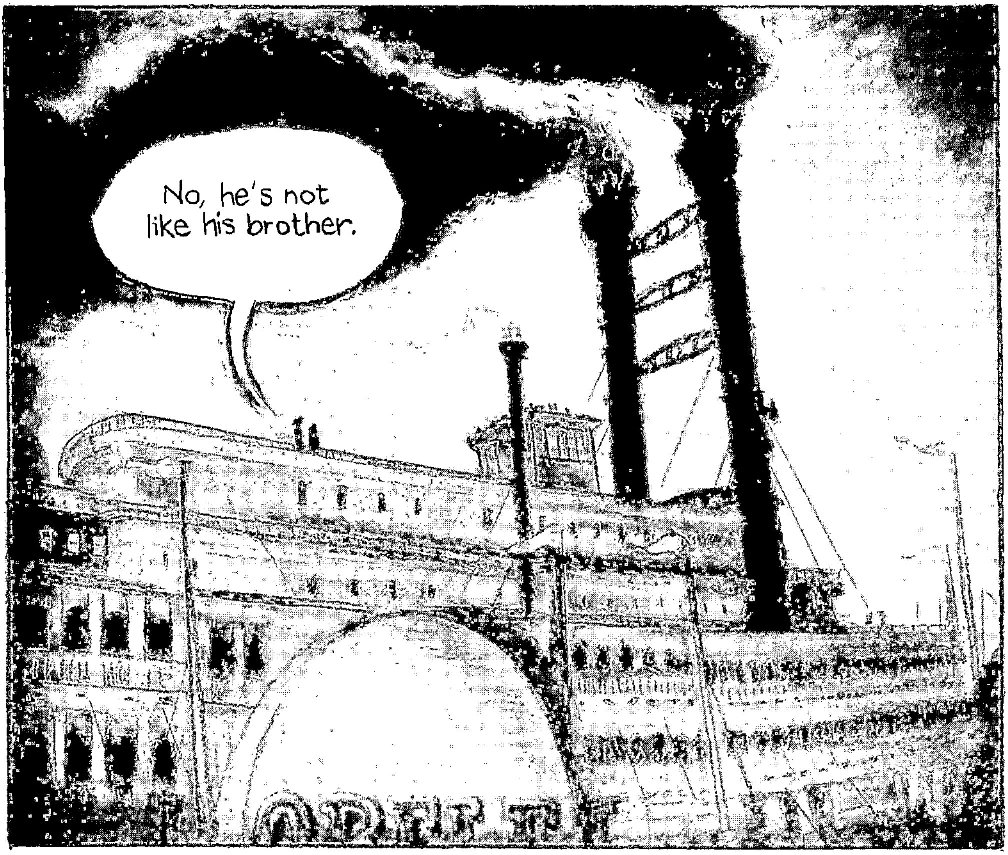
No, he's not like his brother.

Lafayette's older brother Jacques-Henri—now **he** was a businessman.

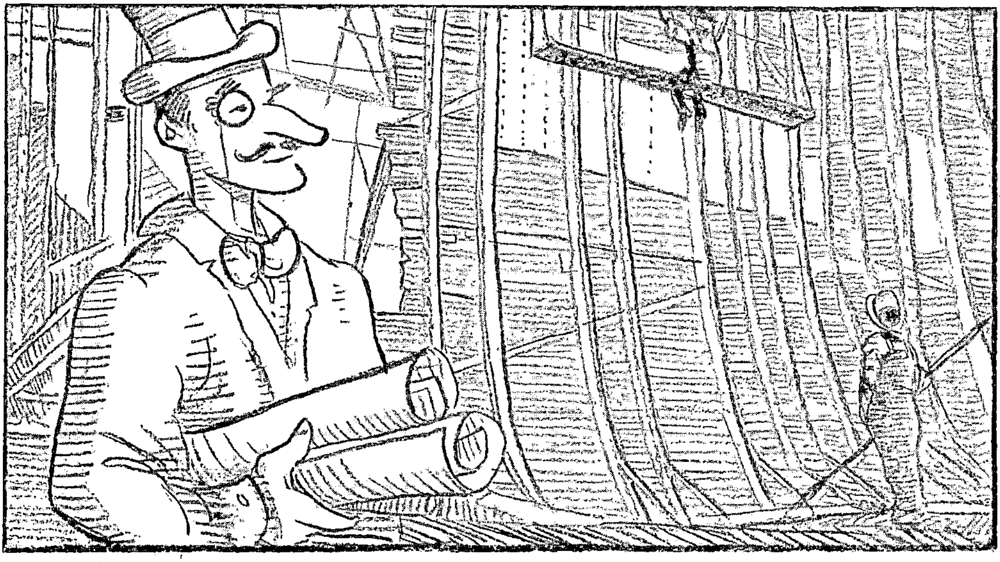

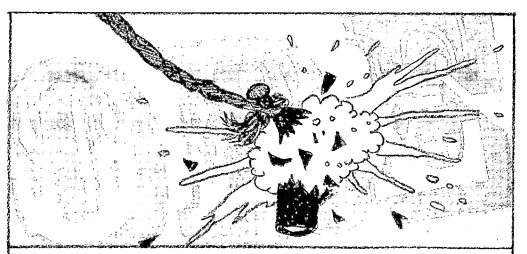

He had come from France in '77, with some capital and big ideas. The Hudson River Line and the Central Hudson Line had cornered the market in New York steamboating for over twenty years.

Everyone thought the new Frenchman in town would be minced meat in no time.

CLAP CLAP CLAP CLAP CLAP

By 1885, he had built his two steamboats, the LORELEI and the MELUSINE, a smaller dayliner. Together the steamers were raking in over $350,000 a year.

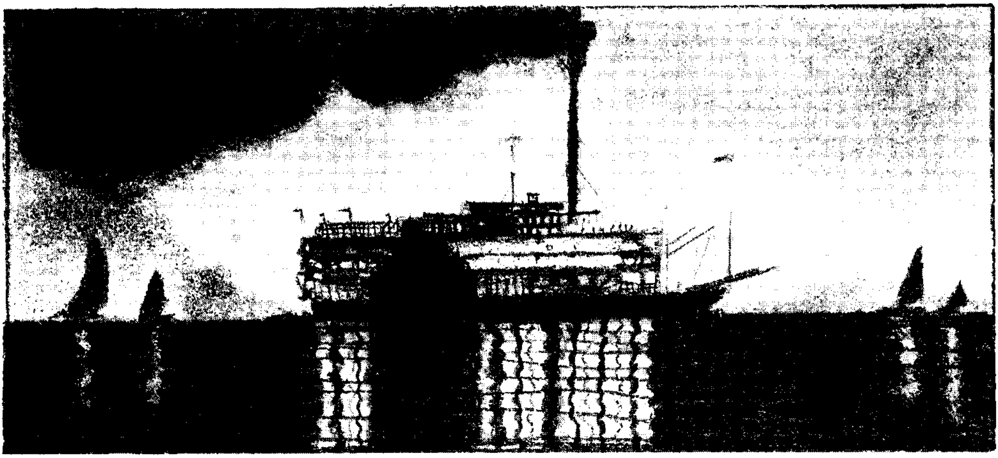

With its masked balls and dinner parties, the LORELEI never failed to draw Vanderbilts, Van Rensselaers, Astors, and Stuyvesant Fish out of their mansions.

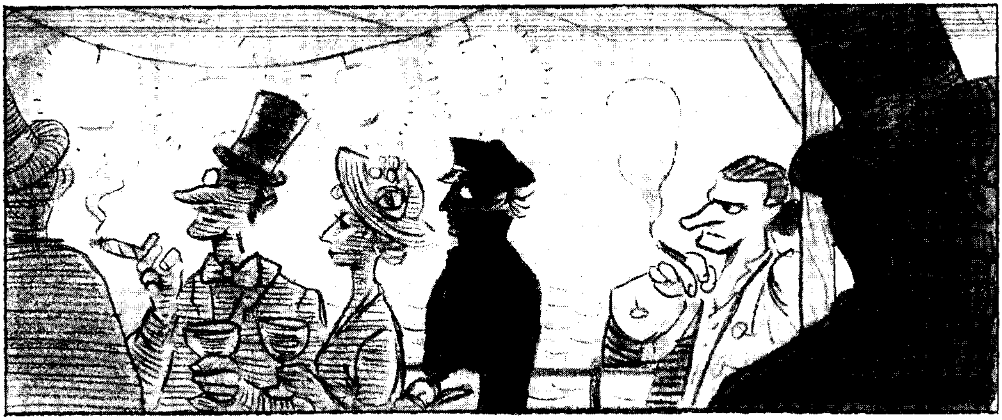

Jacques-Henri de Lafayette's younger brother Dieudonné, on their father's orders, arrived after some sordid mishap involving a duel in Paris.

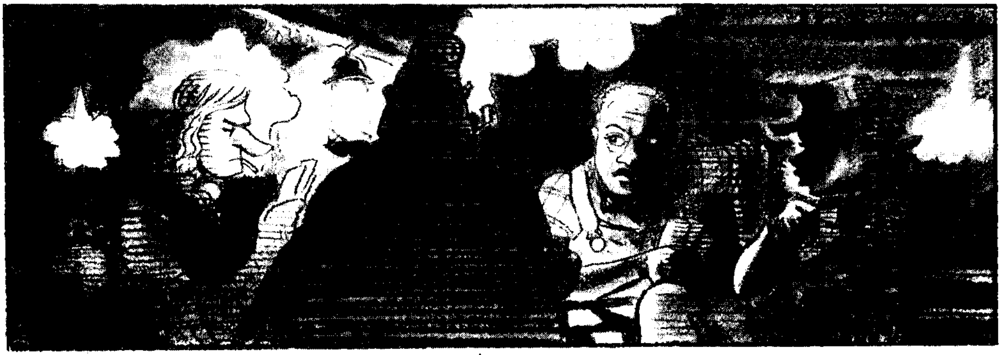

He joined his brother in the paddle-wheeling venture even though he didn't know the first thing about boating or life on the river.

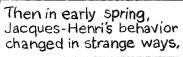
Then in early spring, Jacques-Henri's behavior changed in strange ways,

The ship gossip was that he had secretly been eating opium or drinking absinthe, but I never saw any evidence of it.

He would disappear for a few days at a time, returning sometimes in the middle of the night.

Then he vanished,

It was in the papers. There were search parties and detectives in three counties.
By year's end, it was thought he drowned or died somehow.
Lafayette didn't come out from his brother's quarters for days on end.
I gave him occasional reports.
He paid me little mind, and was usually poring over some of his brother's arcane books and journals. I thought he, too, was going mad.
AGAINST RARE SPELLS
Adriatic Tales
deep down
October
World's End below
sunken upside down
without any trace
Lilac Wine
alas that
she sang.

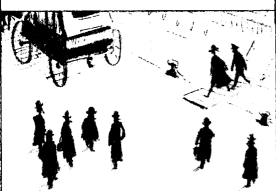

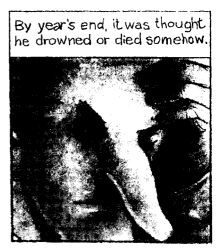

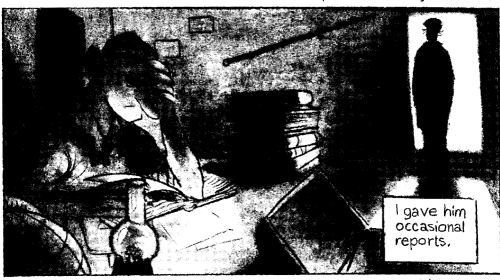

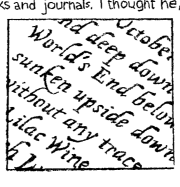

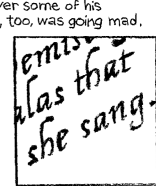

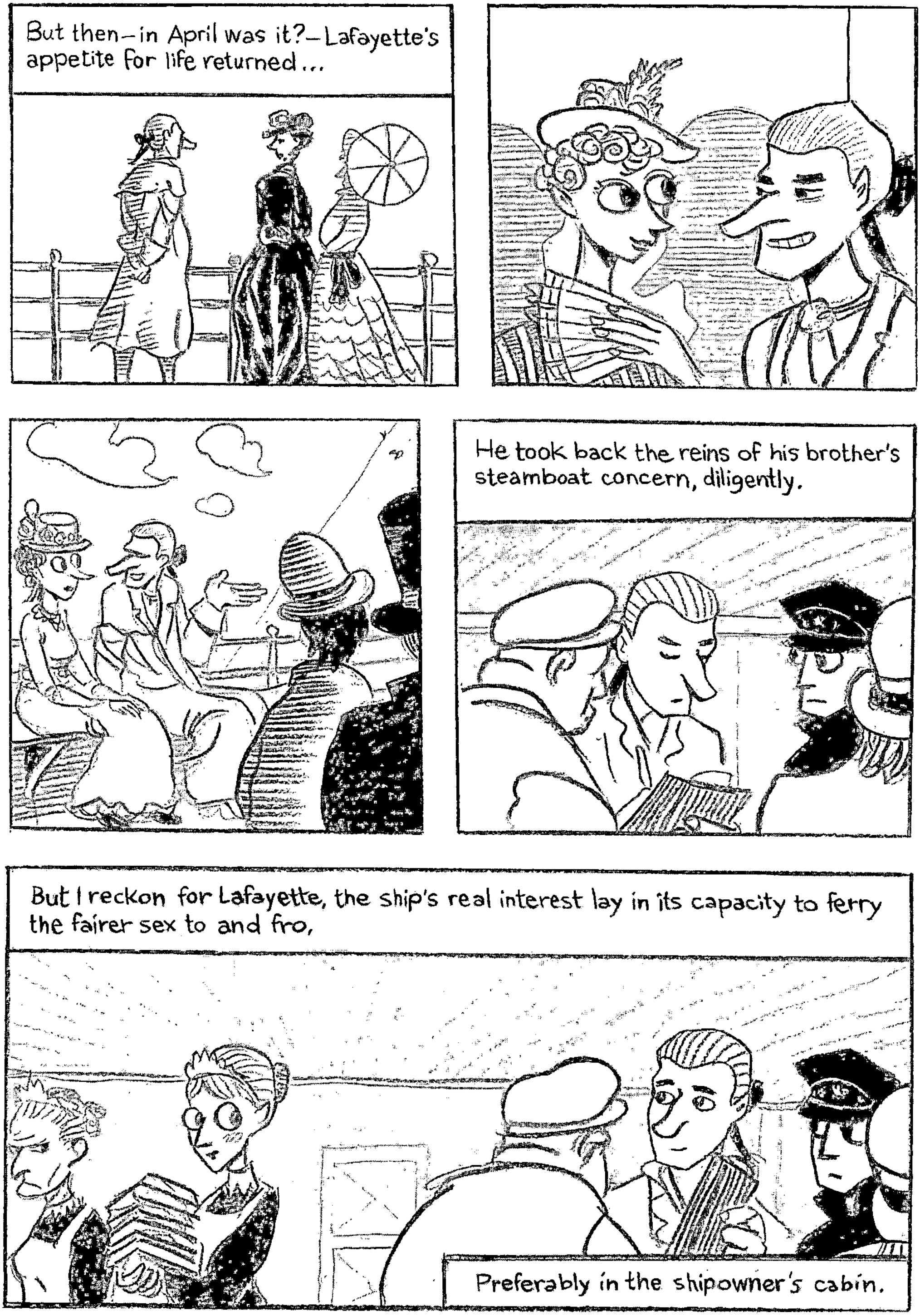
But then—in April was it?—Lafayette's appetite for life returned...
He took back the reins of his brother's steamboat concern, diligently.
But I reckon for Lafayette, the ship's real interest lay in its capacity to ferry the fairer sex to and fro,
Preferably in the shipowner's cabin.

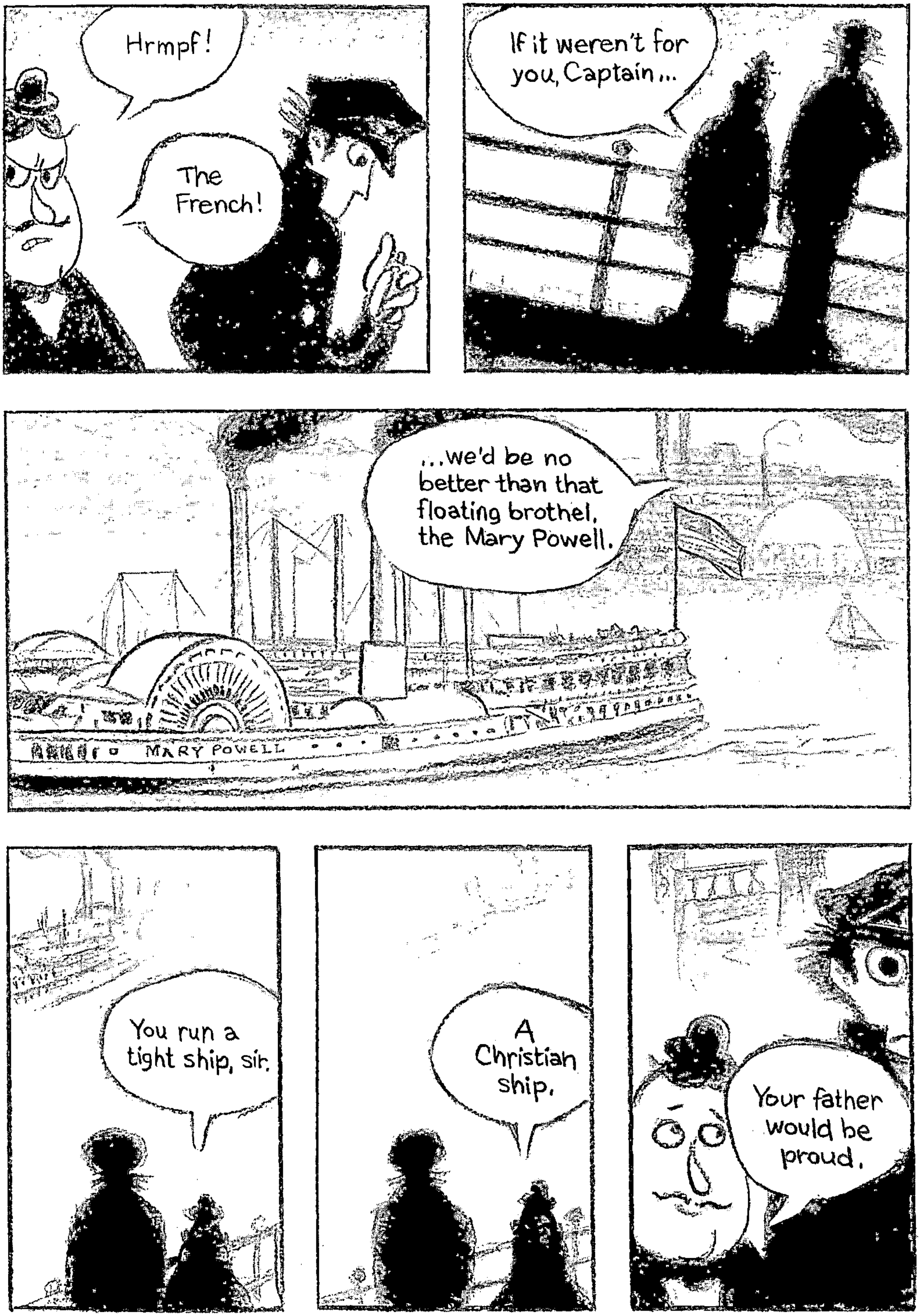
Hrmpf!
The French!
If it weren't for you, Captain...
...we'd be no better than that floating brothel, the Mary Powell.
MARY POWELL
You run a tight ship, sir.
A Christian ship.
Your father would be proud.

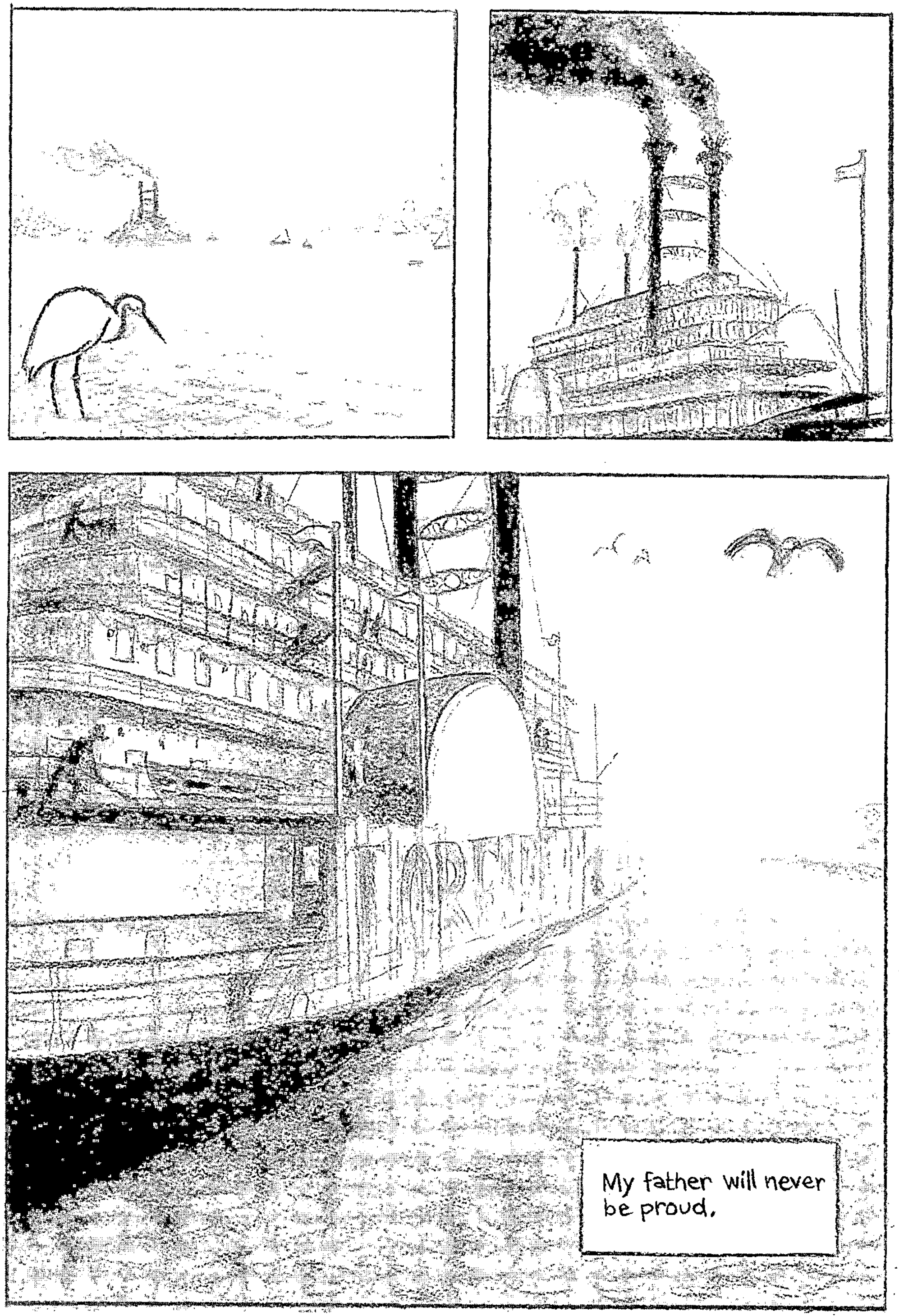
My father will never be proud.

Pt 1, Chap.2

"AN UNLIKELY SURVIVOR"

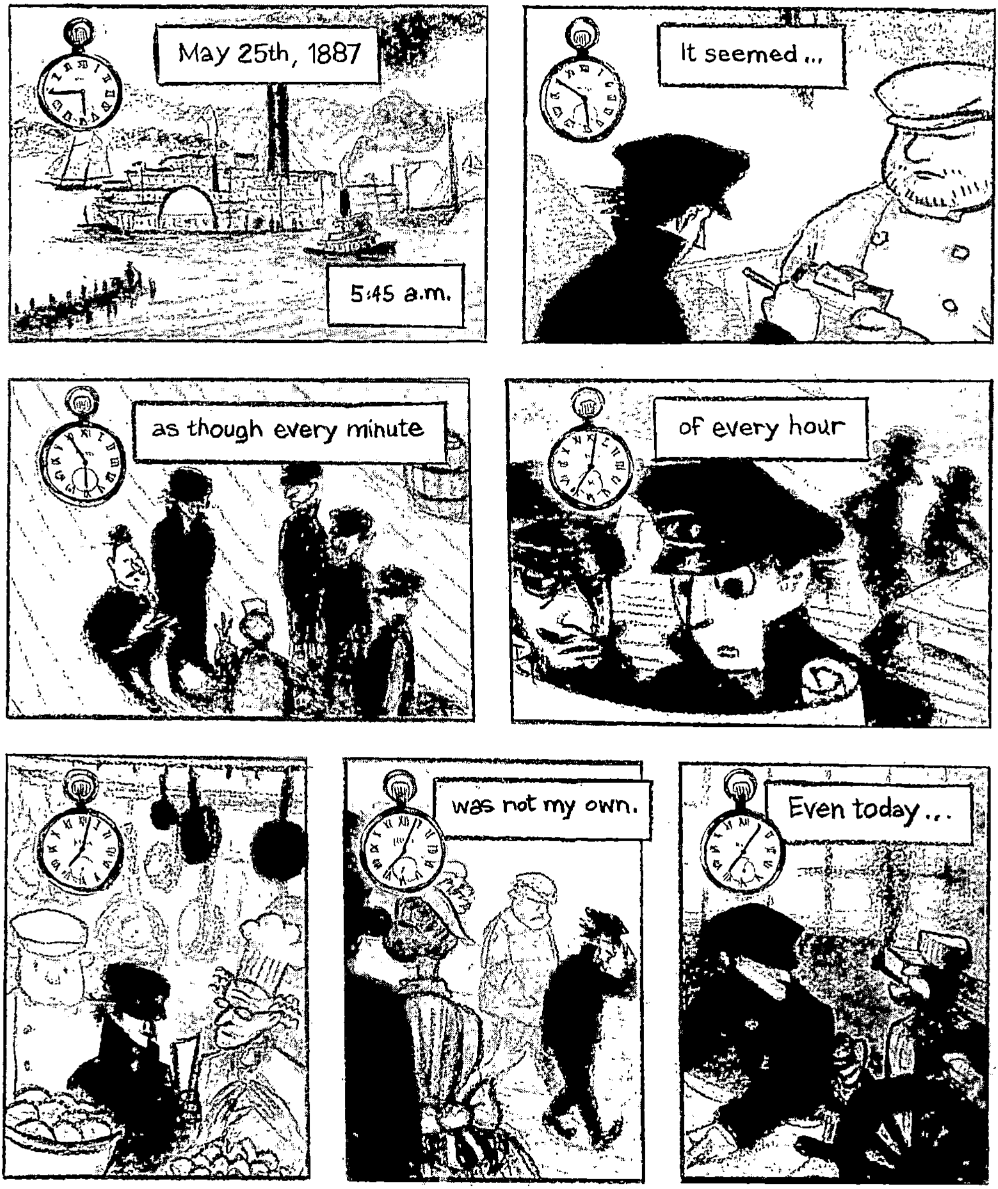
May 25th, 1887
5:45 a.m.
It seemed ...
as though every minute
of every hour
was not my own.
Even today ...

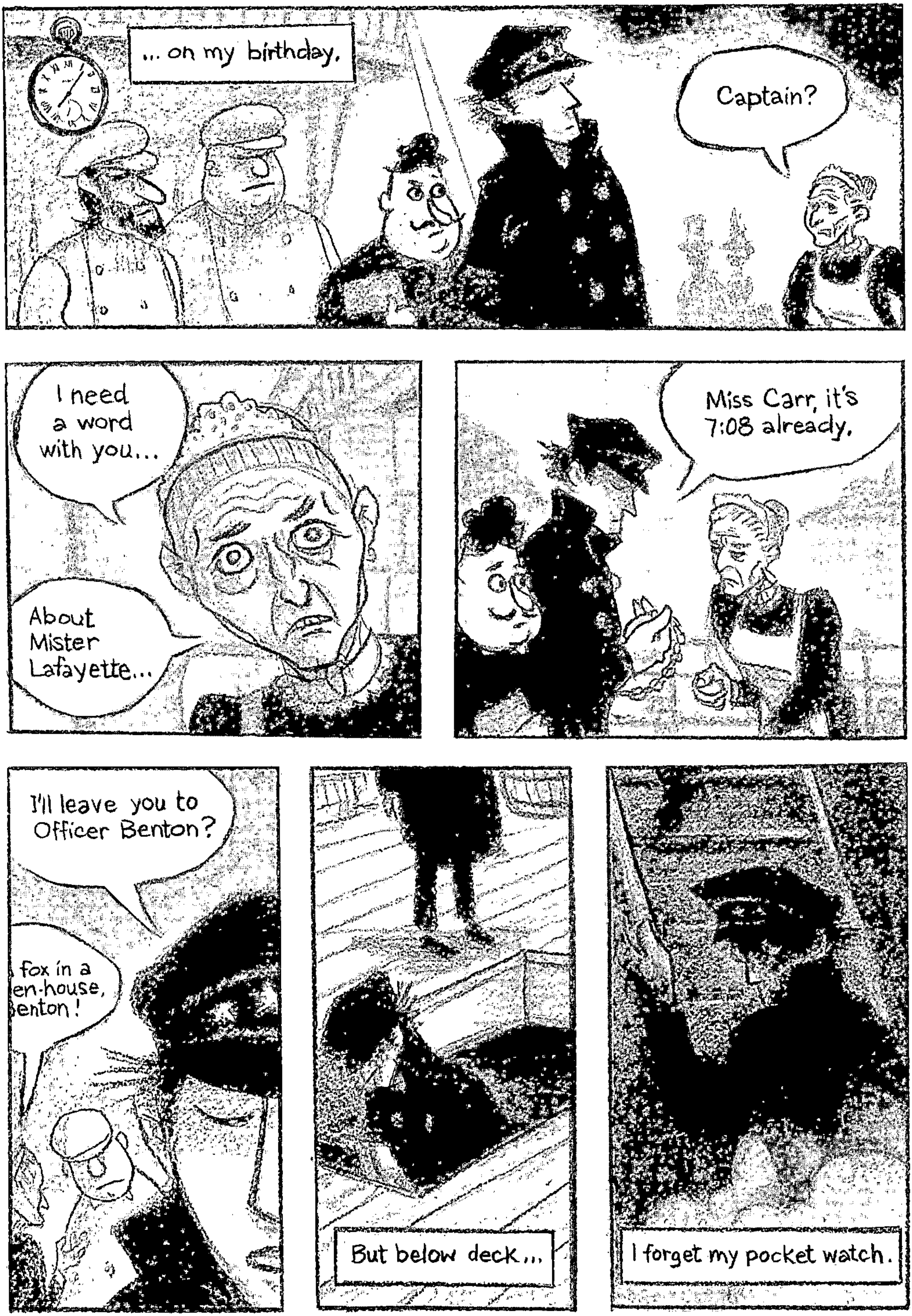
... on my birthday.
Captain?
I need a word with you...
About Mister Lafayette...
Miss Carr, it's 7:08 already.
I'll leave you to Officer Benton?
fox in a en-house, enton!
But below deck...
I forget my pocket watch.

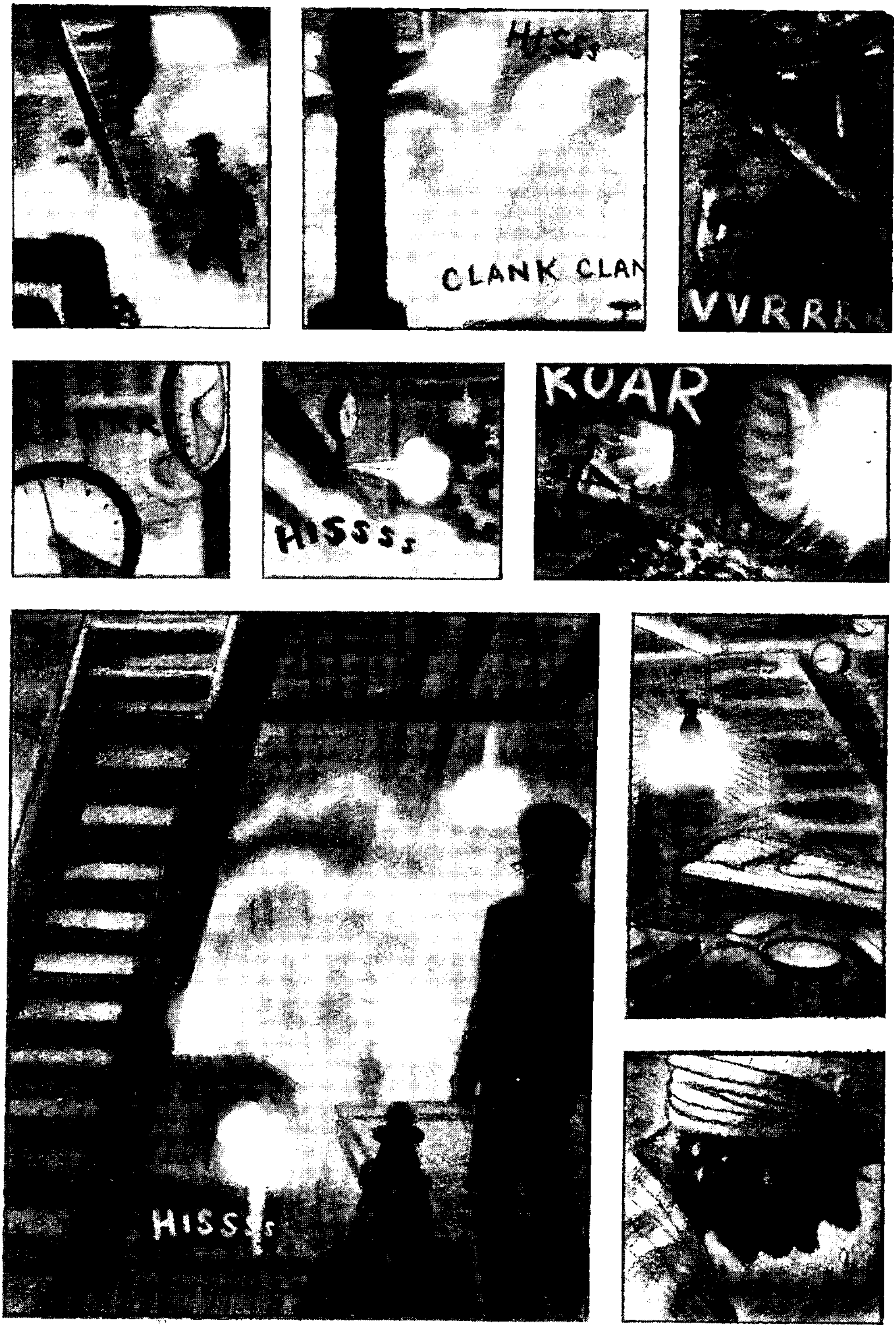
HISSs
CLANK CLAN
VVRRR
HISSSS
KUAR
HISSSs

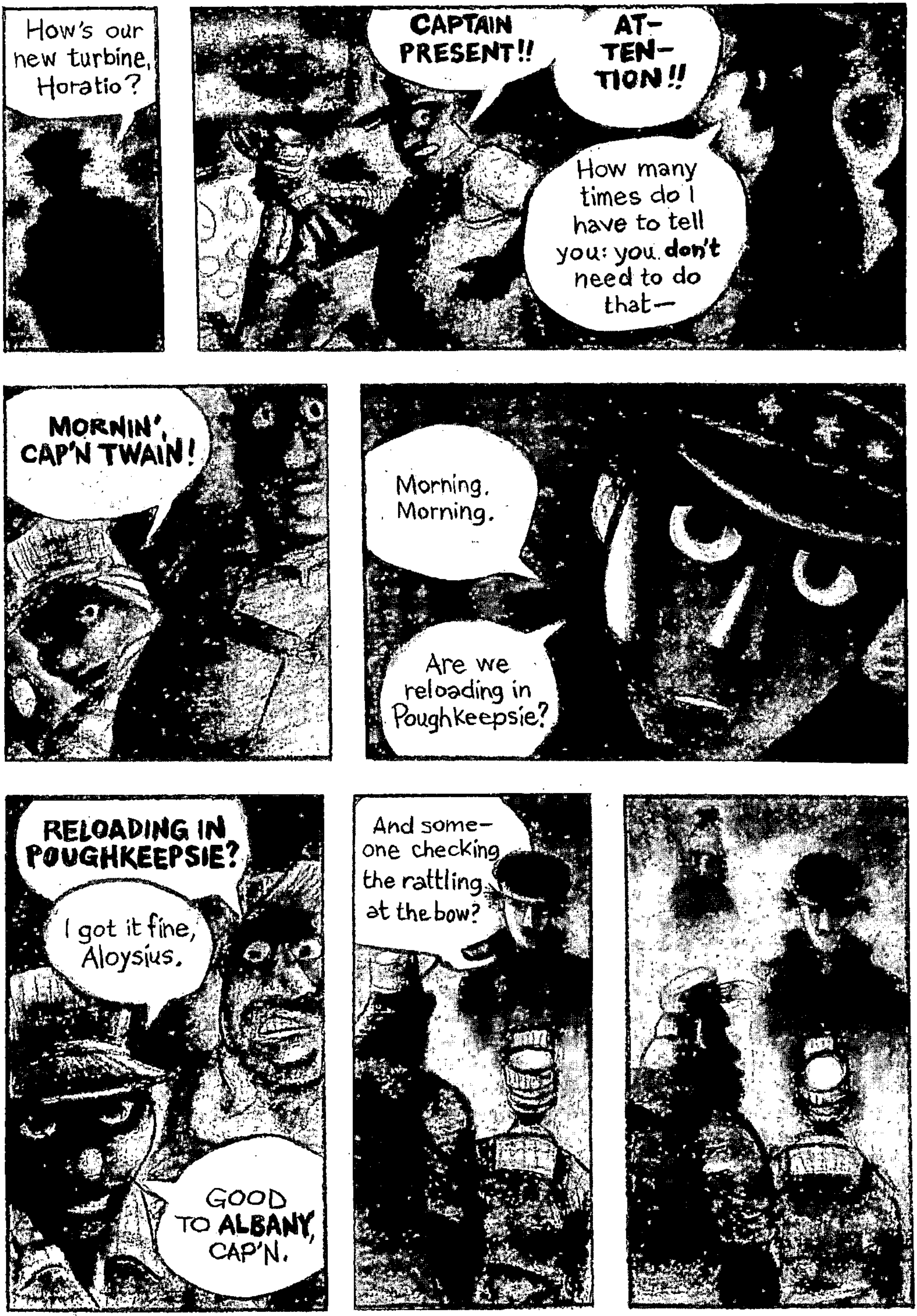
How's our new turbine, Horatio?
CAPTAIN PRESENT!!
AT-TEN-TION!!
How many times do I have to tell you: you **don't** need to do that—
MORNIN', CAP'N TWAIN!
Morning. Morning.
Are we reloading in Poughkeepsie?
RELOADING IN POUGHKEEPSIE?
I got it fine, Aloysius.
GOOD TO **ALBANY**, CAP'N.
And some-one checking the rattling at the bow?

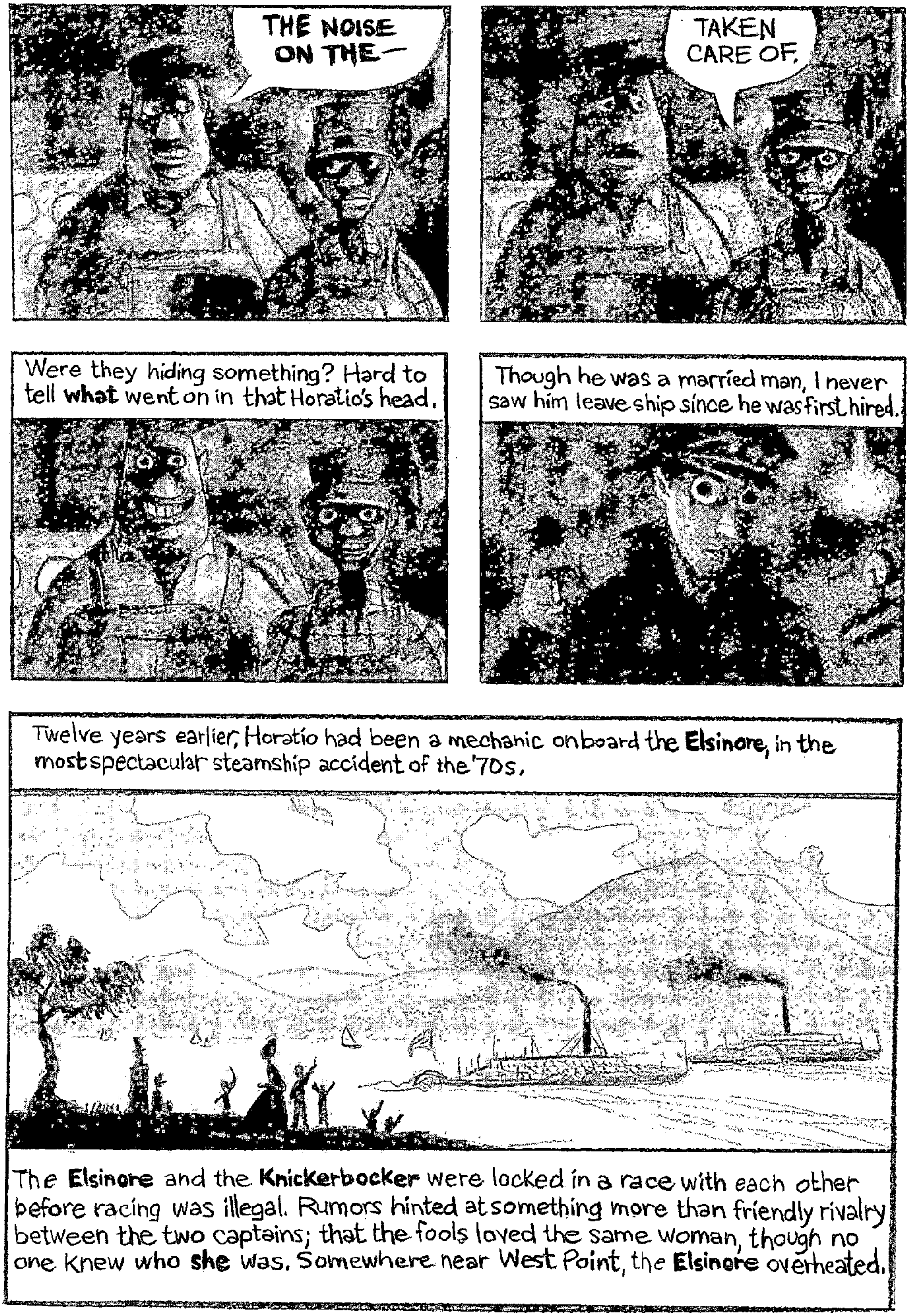
THE NOISE ON THE—
TAKEN CARE OF.
Were they hiding something? Hard to tell **what** went on in that Horatio's head.
Though he was a married man, I never saw him leave ship since he was first hired.
Twelve years earlier, Horatio had been a mechanic onboard the **Elsinore**, in the most spectacular steamship accident of the '70s.
The **Elsinore** and the **Knickerbocker** were locked in a race with each other before racing was illegal. Rumors hinted at something more than friendly rivalry between the two captains; that the fools loved the same woman, though no one knew who **she** was. Somewhere near West Point, the **Elsinore** overheated.

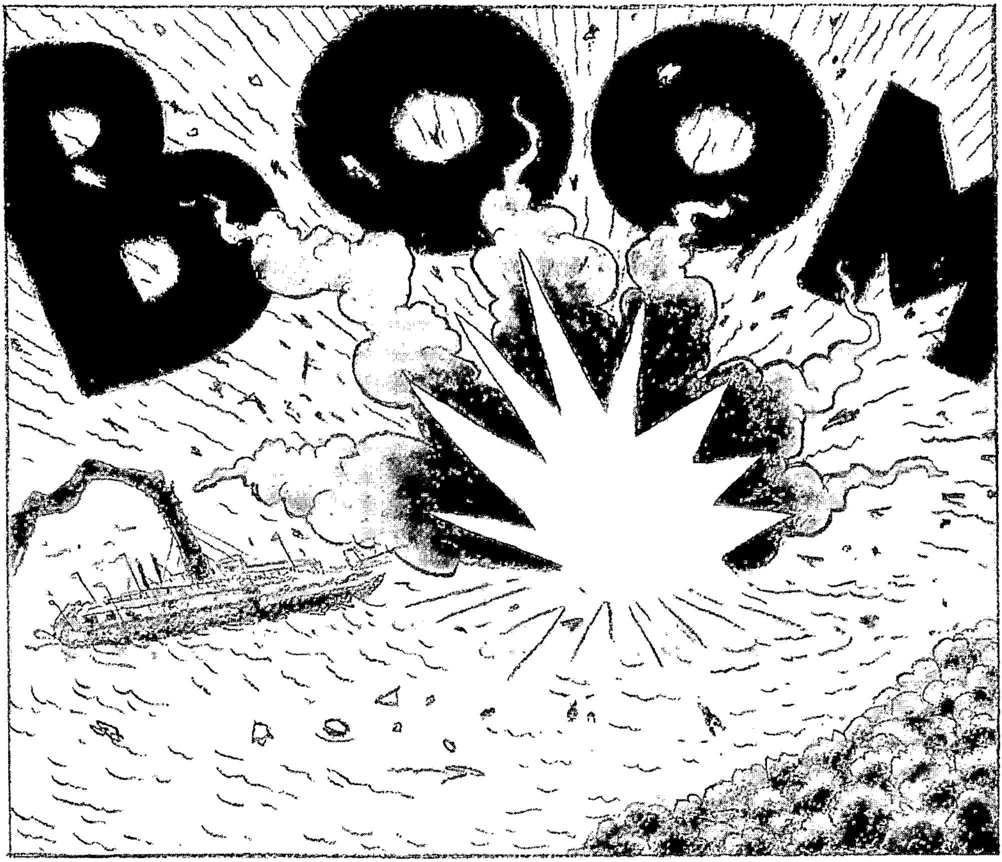
BOOM

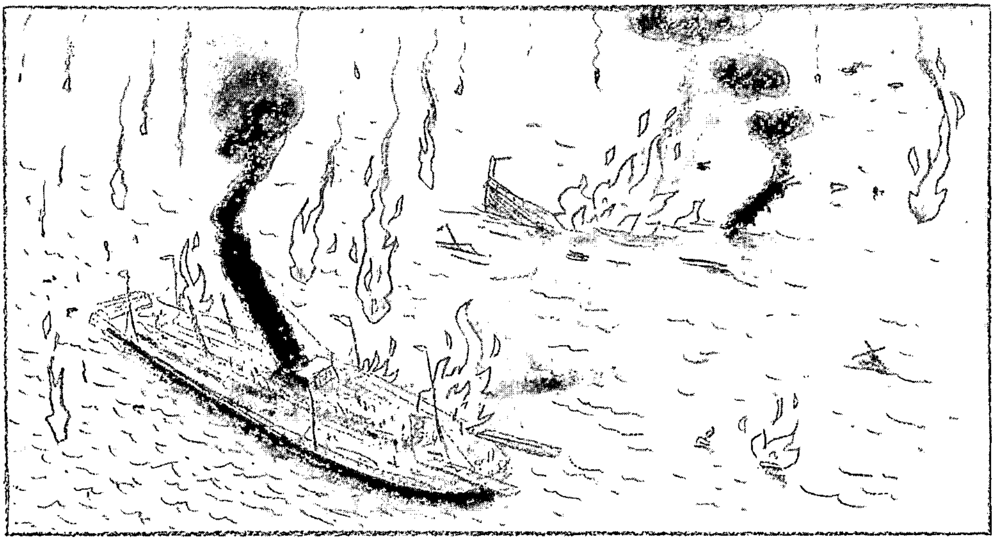

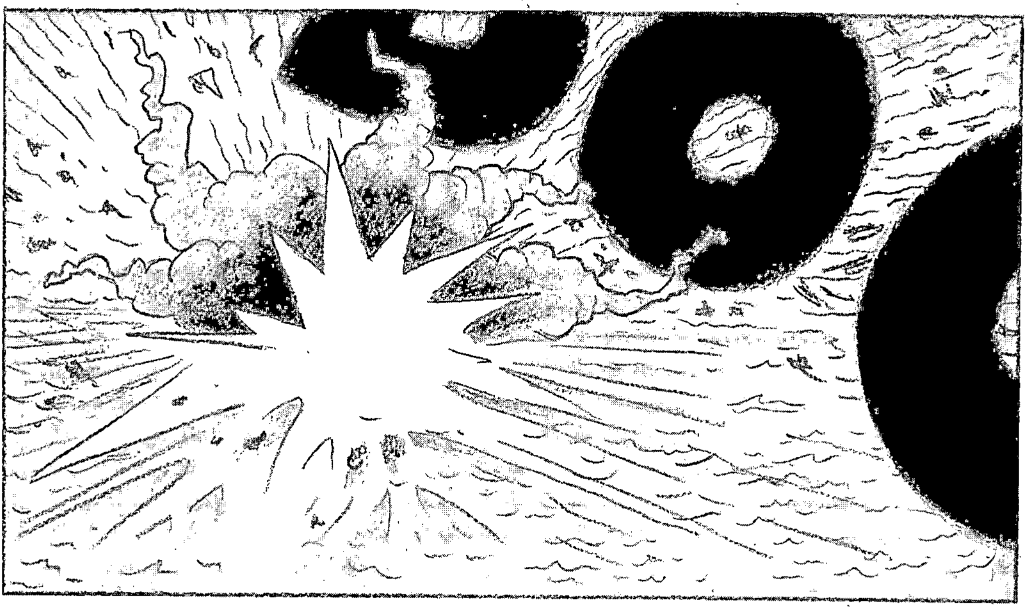

The twin explosions were heard as far south as Croton. Fortunately, the ships were light and had few passengers. **Unfortunately** everyone died—except for one crewman: **Horatio Clover**.

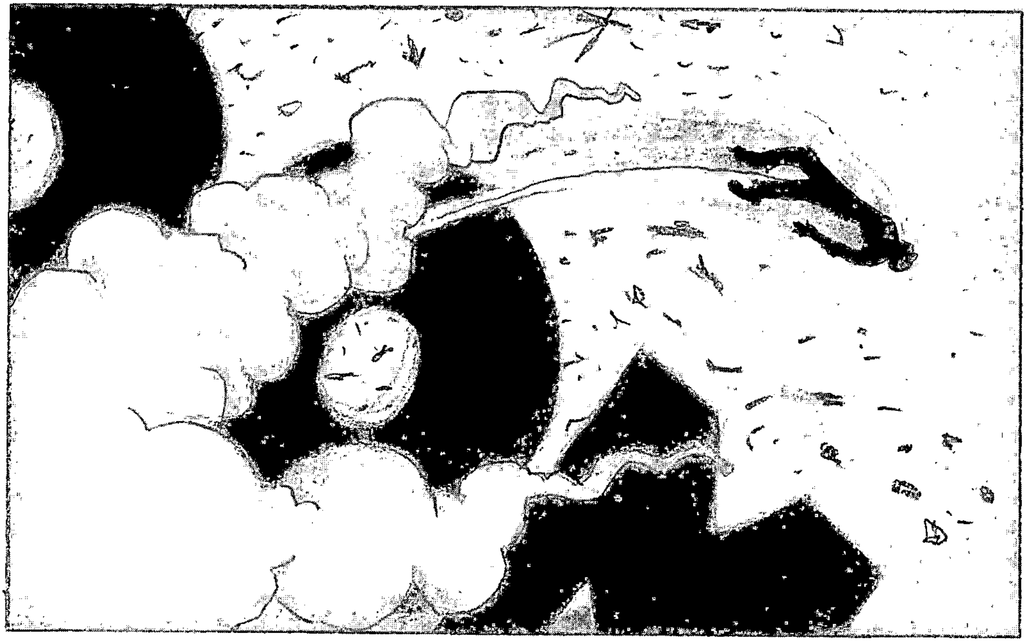

He was thrown an impossible 96 yards over the train tracks and into a tree.

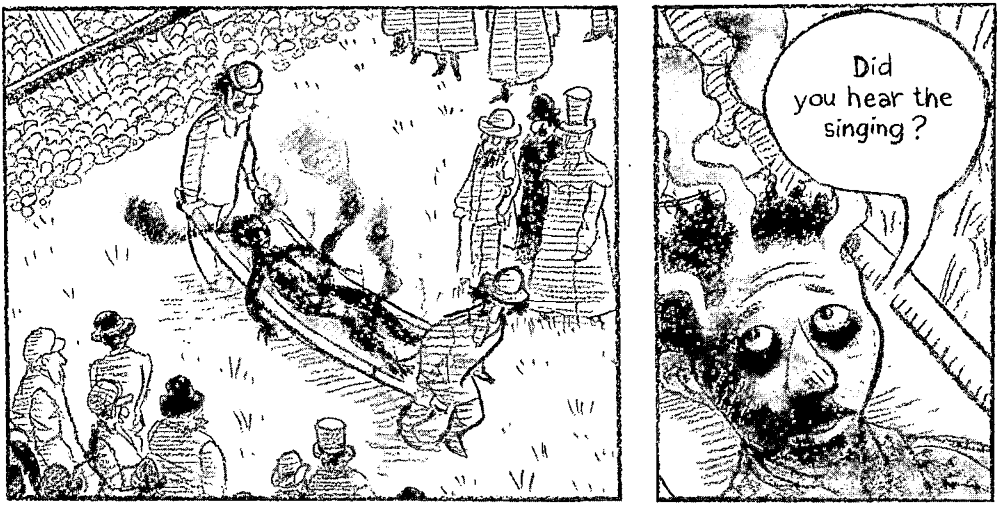
Did you hear the singing?

It did something to his head.
But he came out of it a mechanical genius. No man knew steam engines like he did. When Jacques-Henri called on me for the LORELEI, I drafted Horatio, in spite of some protest on account of his being colored.

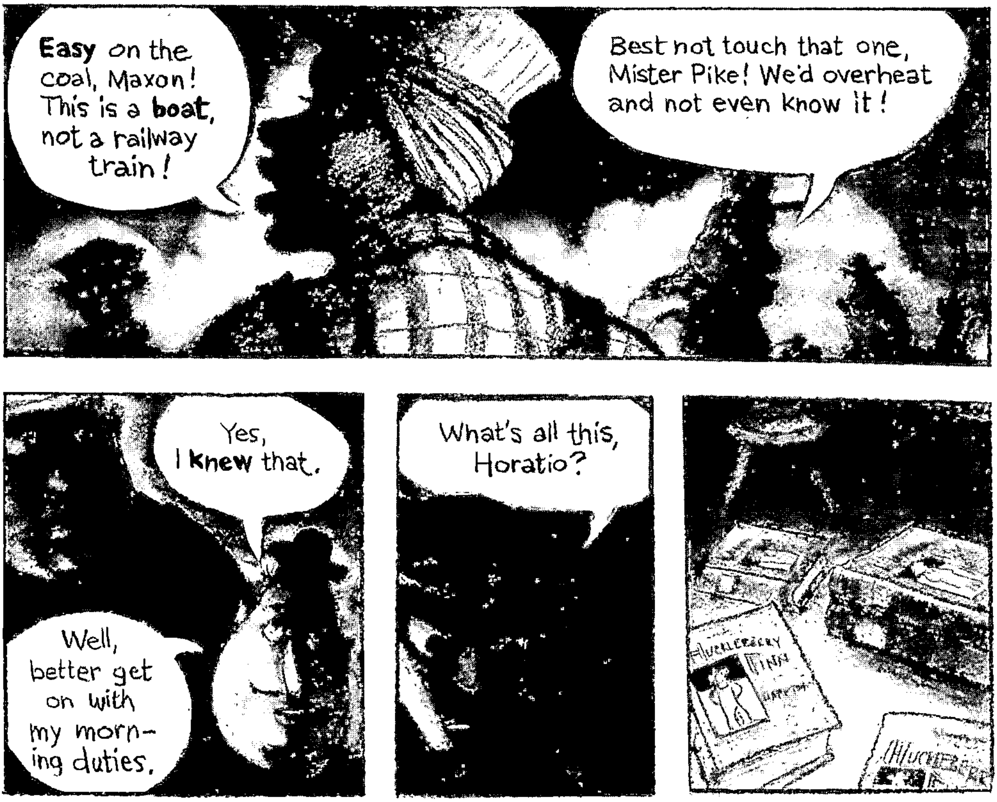
Easy on the coal, Maxon! This is a **boat**, not a railway train!
Best not touch that one, Mister Pike! We'd overheat and not even know it!
Yes, I **knew** that.
Well, better get on with my morning duties.
What's all this, Horatio?

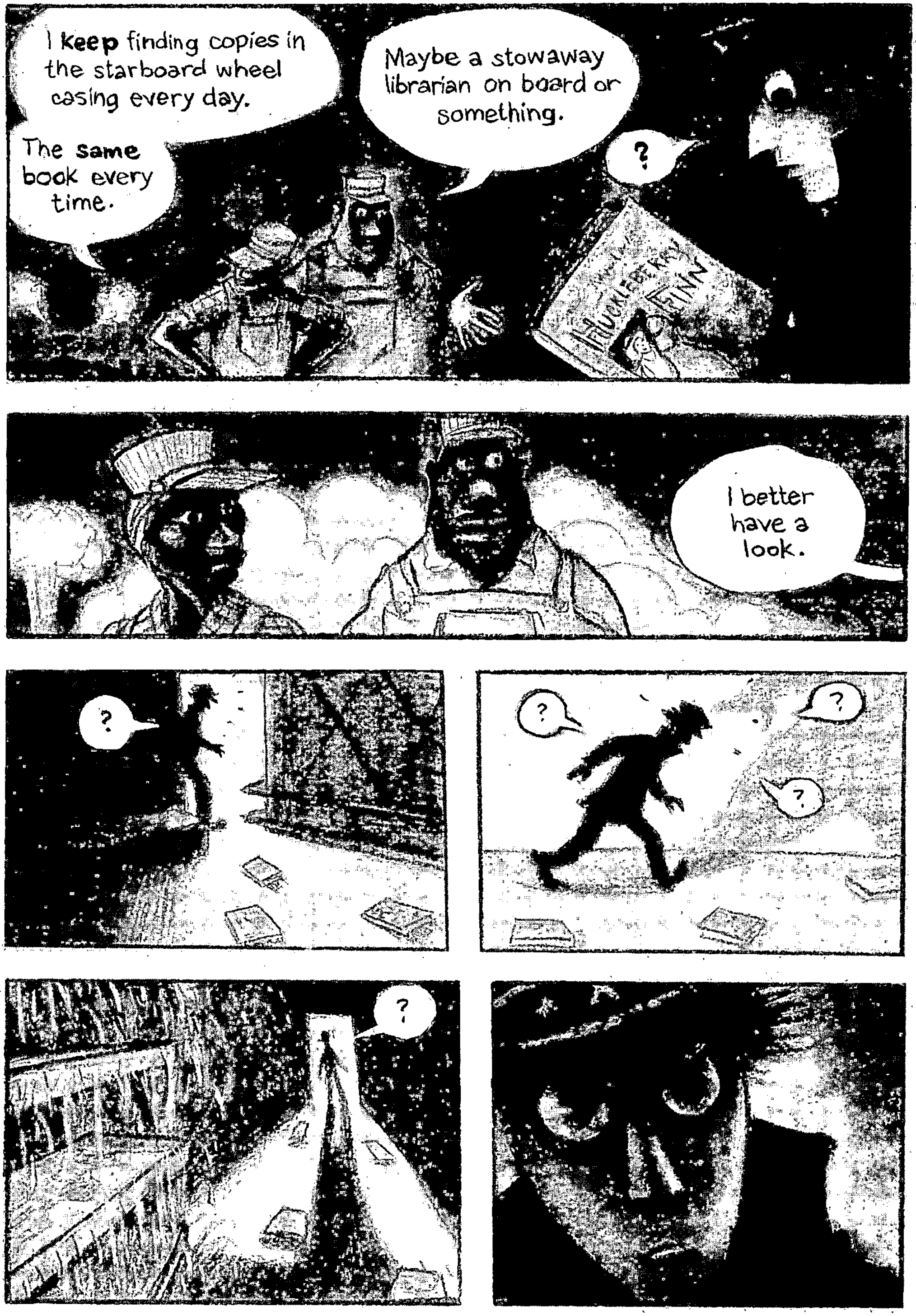
I keep finding copies in the starboard wheel casing every day.
The same book every time.
Maybe a stowaway librarian on board or something.
?
HUCKLEBERRY FINN
I better have a look.
?
?
?
?
?

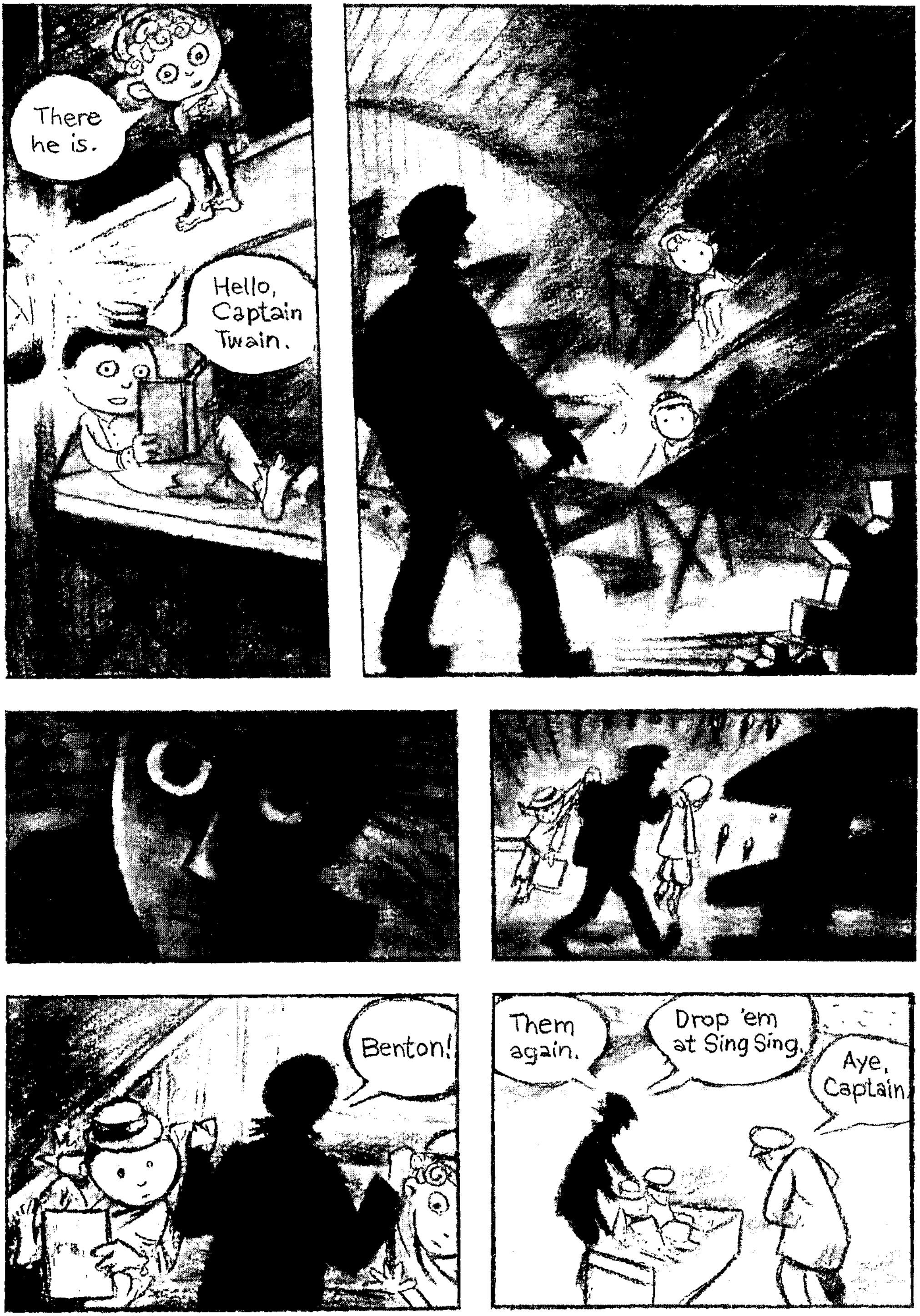
There he is.
Hello, Captain Twain.
Benton!
Them again.
Drop 'em at Sing Sing.
Aye, Captain.

This time I'm watching you, little scoundrels.

Bye, Cap'n Twain!

Read it again, Salty!

"PERSONS attempting to find a motive in this narrative will be prosecuted; persons attempting to find a moral in it will be banished; persons attempting to find a plot in it will be shot."

HA HA HA HA HA

HAHAHA HAHA HAHA

HAHA

Now listen up, ya picaroons, this better be the last—

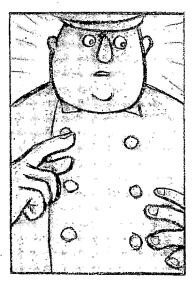

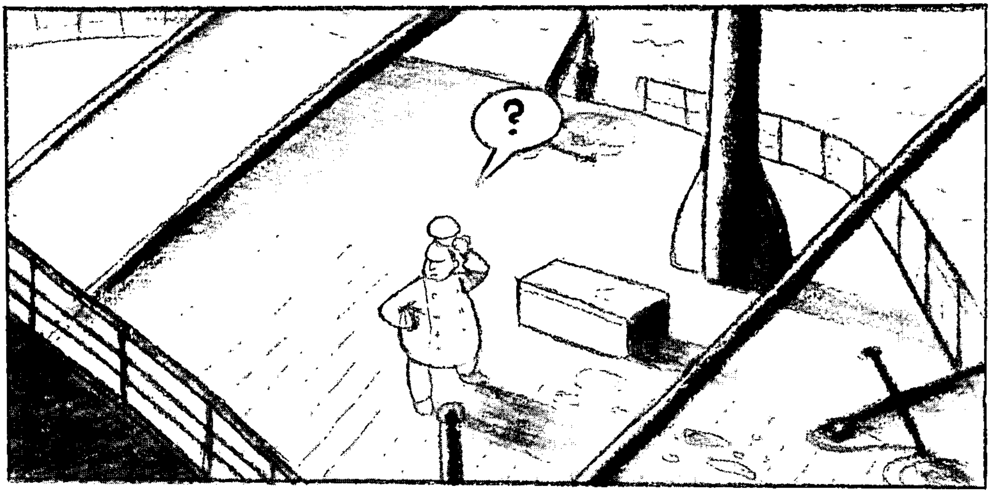
?

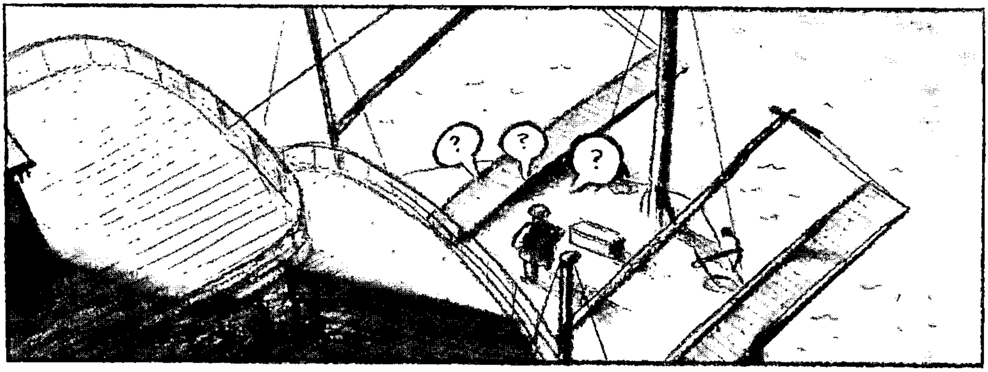
?
?
?

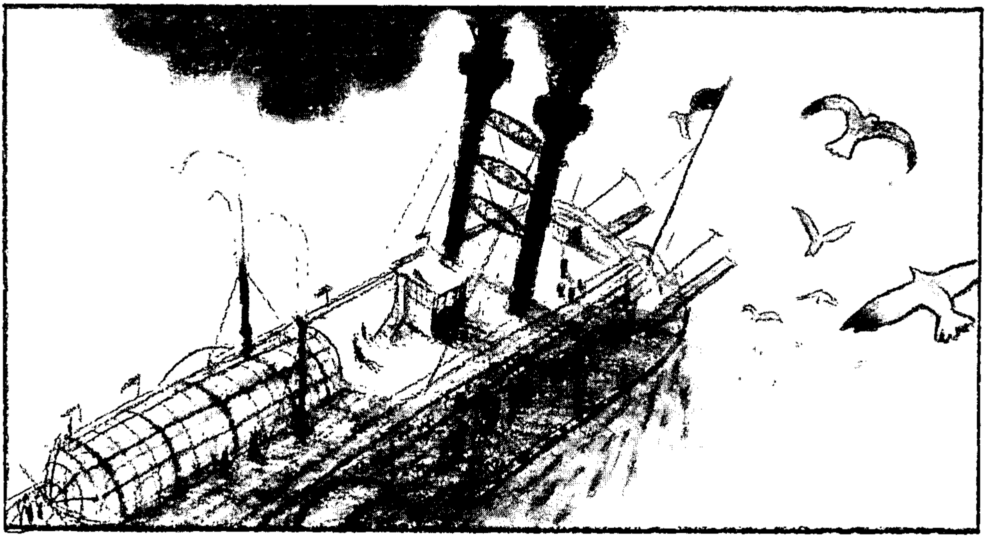

"A PRAYER DOWN BELOW"

Pt I, Chap.3

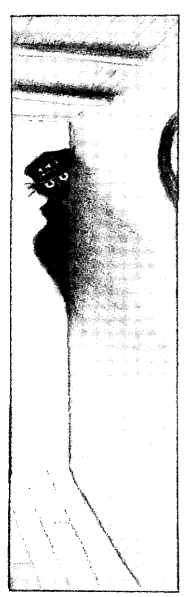

Women didn't find him handsome, did they?

Then again, all Tarrytown knew that old Saunders had two wives, and **he** was no Apollo.

Whatever it was that had troubled Lafayette earlier that morning, I saw no sign of now.

47

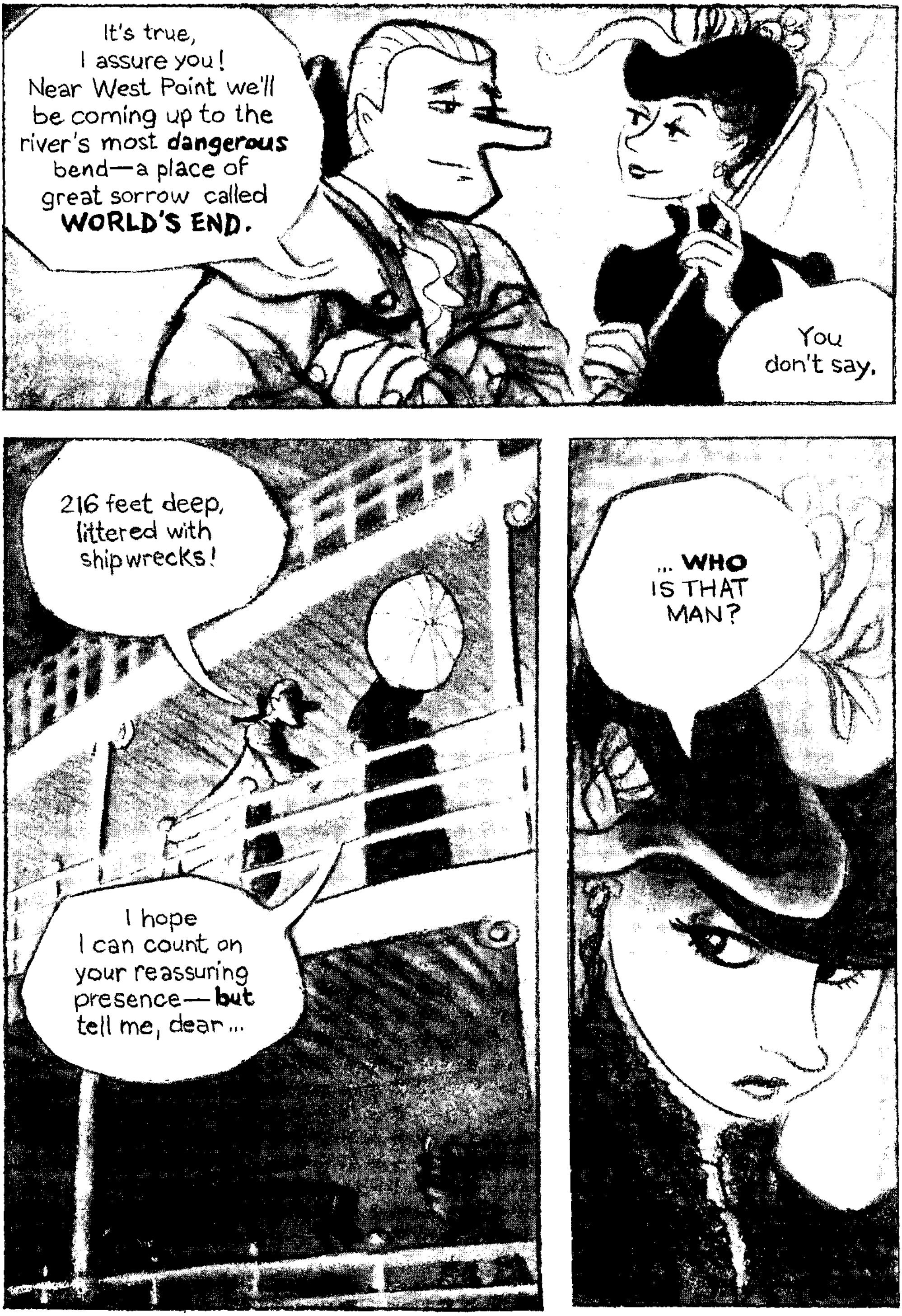
It's true, I assure you! Near West Point we'll be coming up to the river's most **dangerous** bend—a place of great sorrow called **WORLD'S END.**
You don't say.
216 feet deep, littered with shipwrecks!
I hope I can count on your reassuring presence—**but** tell me, dear...
... **WHO** IS THAT MAN?

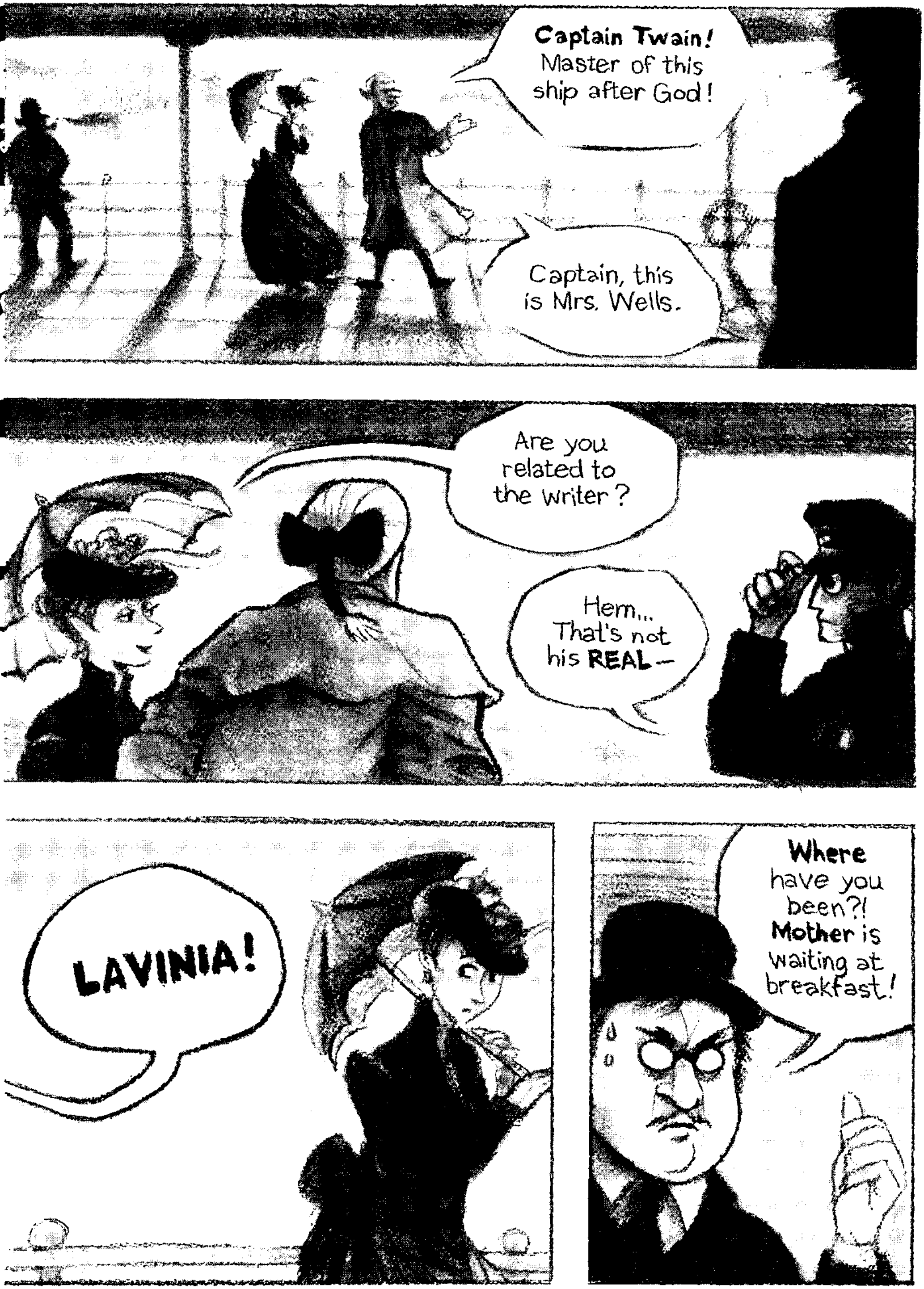

Captain Twain! Master of this ship after God!
Captain, this is Mrs. Wells.
Are you related to the writer?
Hem... That's not his REAL—
LAVINIA!
Where have you been?! Mother is waiting at breakfast!

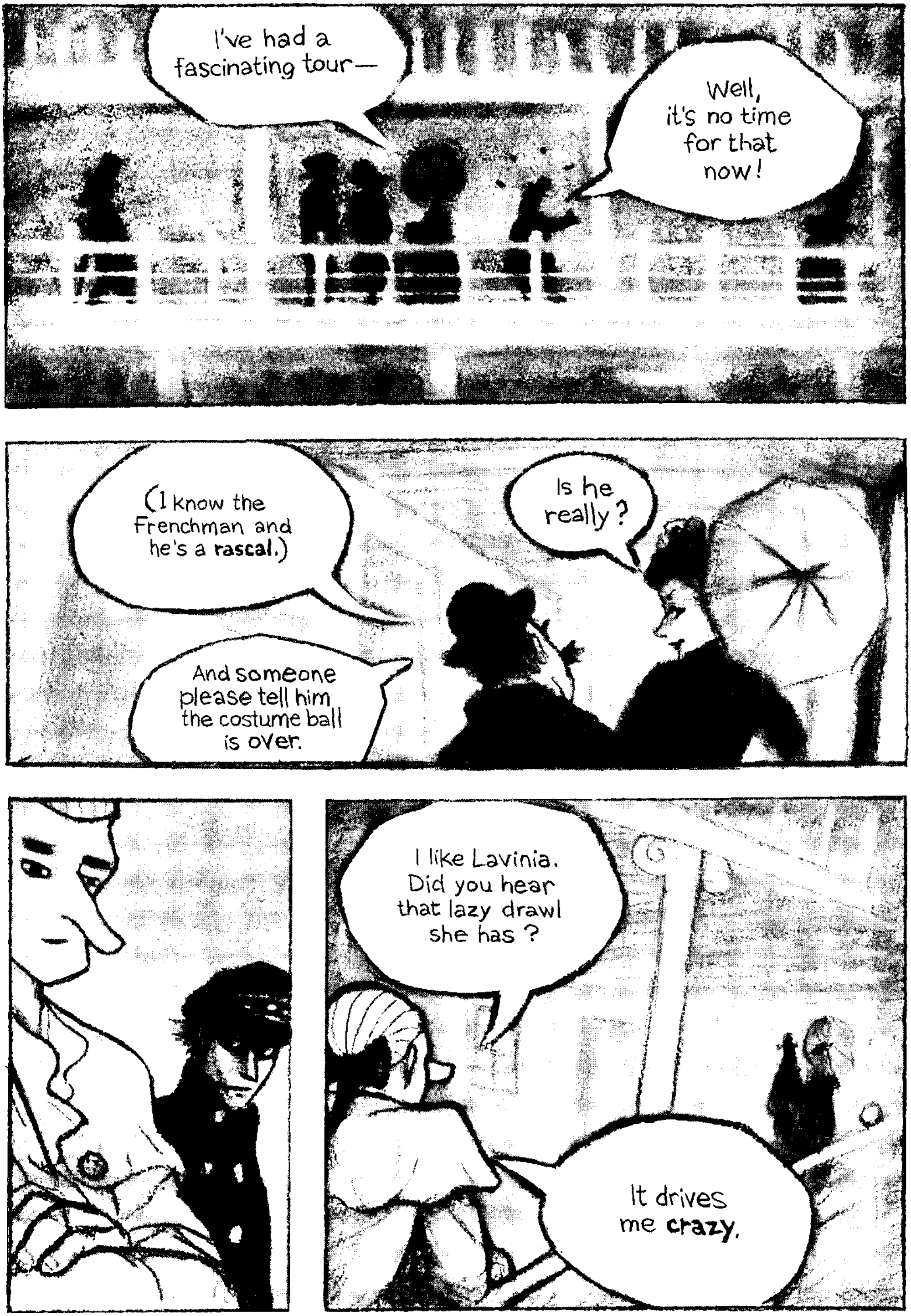
I've had a fascinating tour—
Well, it's no time for that now!
(I know the Frenchman and he's a **rascal**.)
Is he really?
And someone please tell him the costume ball is over.
I like Lavinia. Did you hear that lazy drawl she has?
It drives me **crazy**.

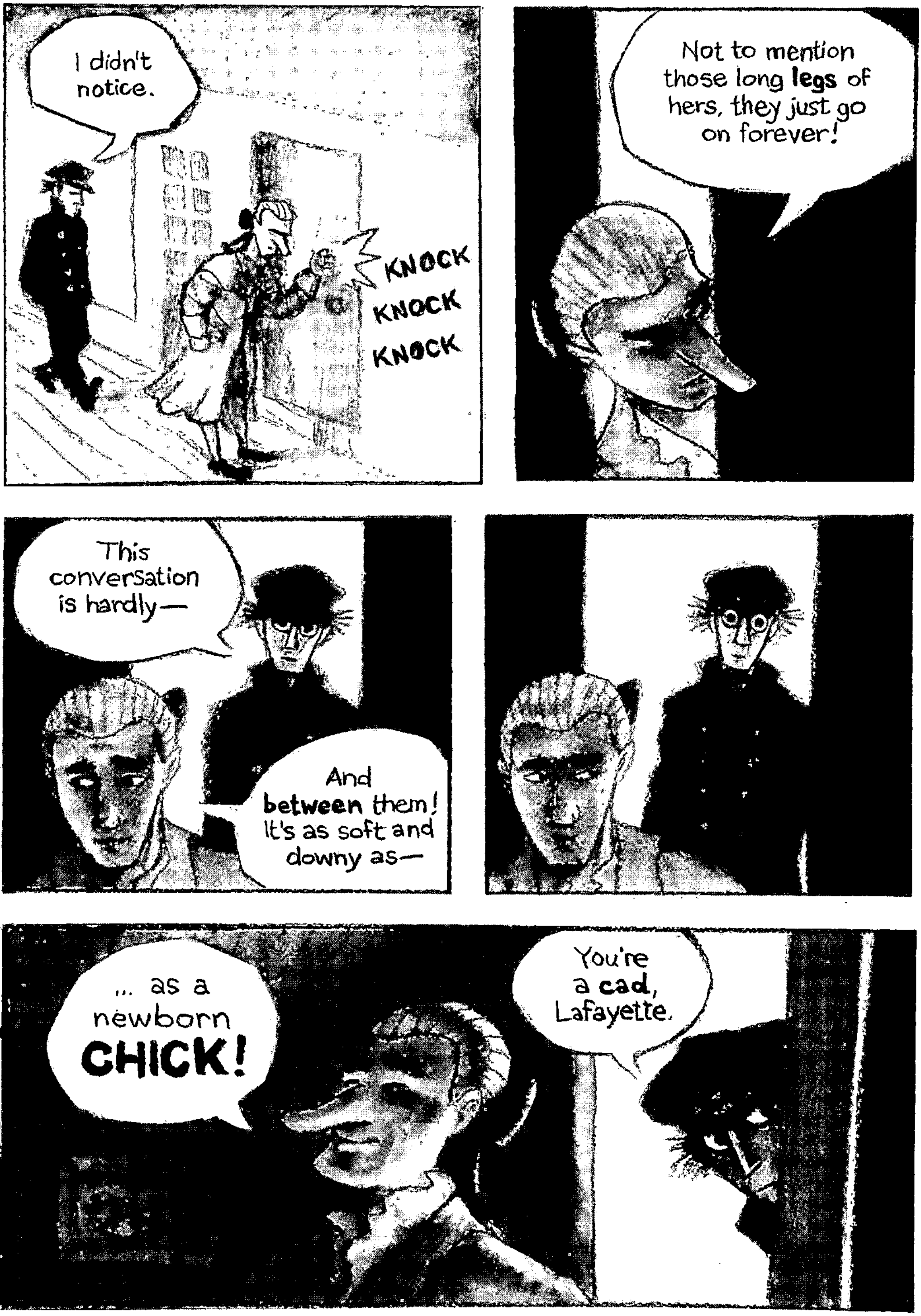
I didn't notice.
KNOCK KNOCK KNOCK
Not to mention those long **legs** of hers, they just go on forever!
This conversation is hardly—
And **between** them! It's as soft and downy as—
... as a newborn **CHICK!**
You're a **cad**, Lafayette.

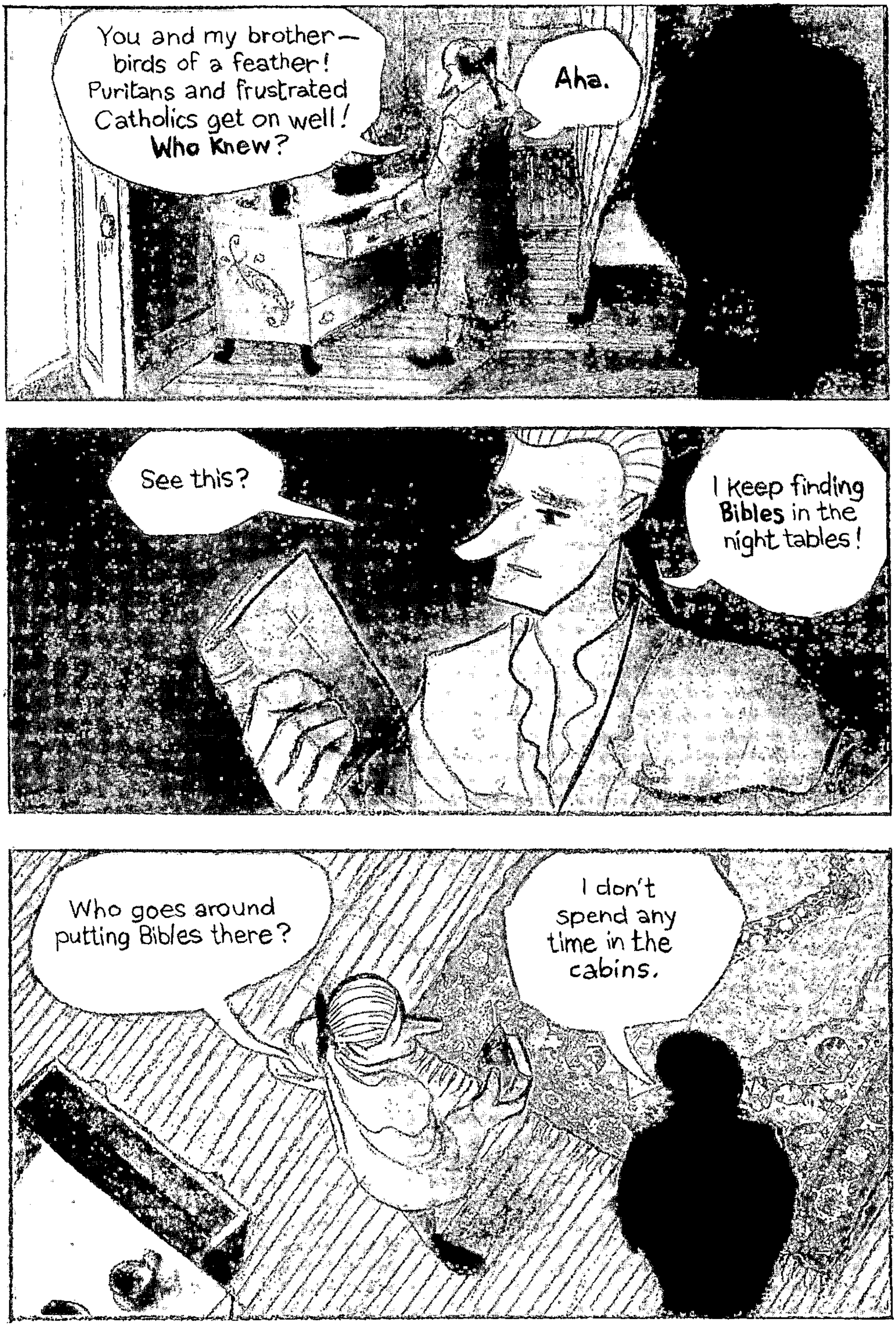
You and my brother—birds of a feather! Puritans and frustrated Catholics get on well! **Who Knew?**
Aha.
See this?
I keep finding **Bibles** in the night tables!
Who goes around putting Bibles there?
I don't spend any time in the cabins.

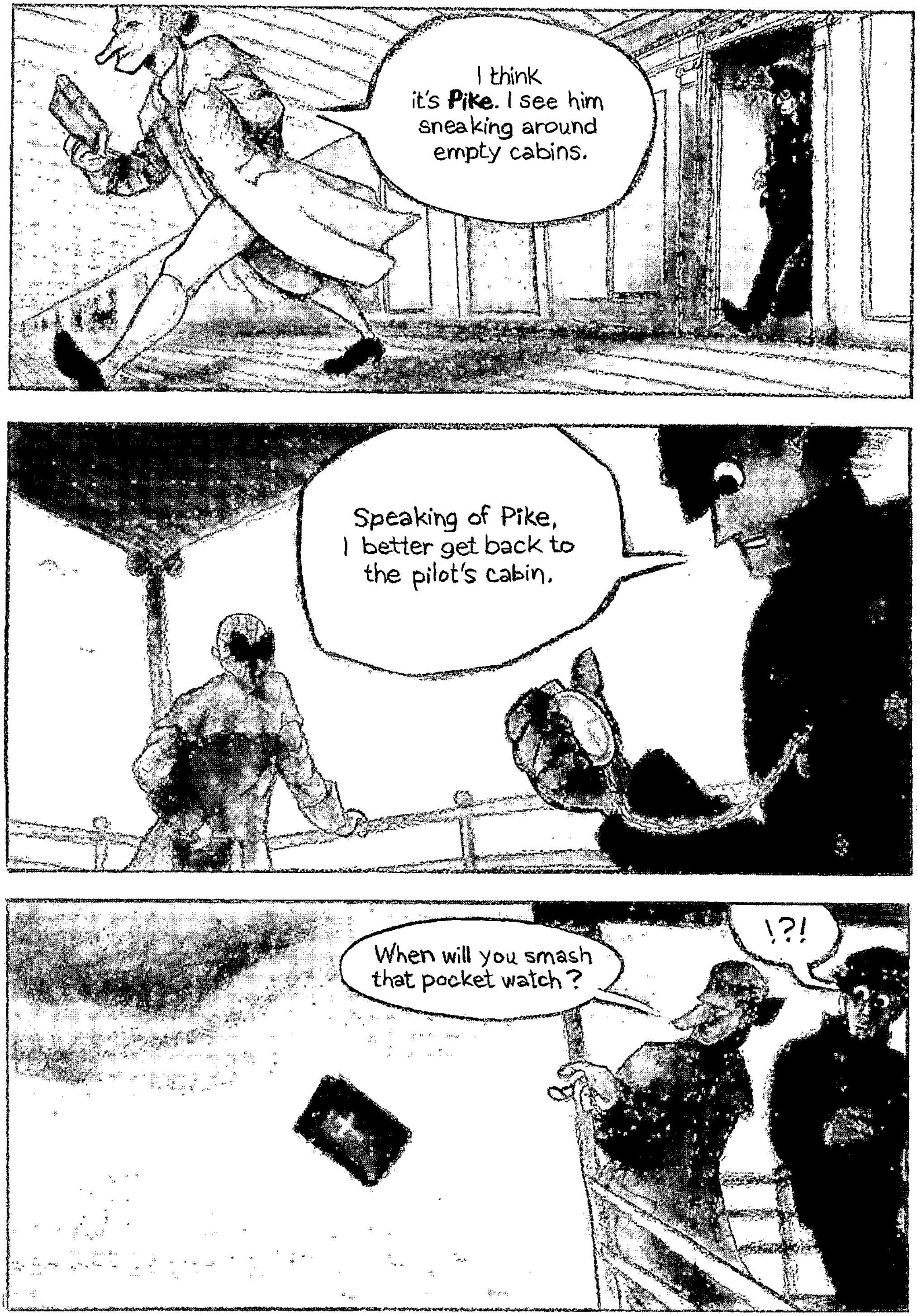
I think it's **Pike**. I see him sneaking around empty cabins.
Speaking of Pike, I better get back to the pilot's cabin.
When will you smash that pocket watch?
!?!

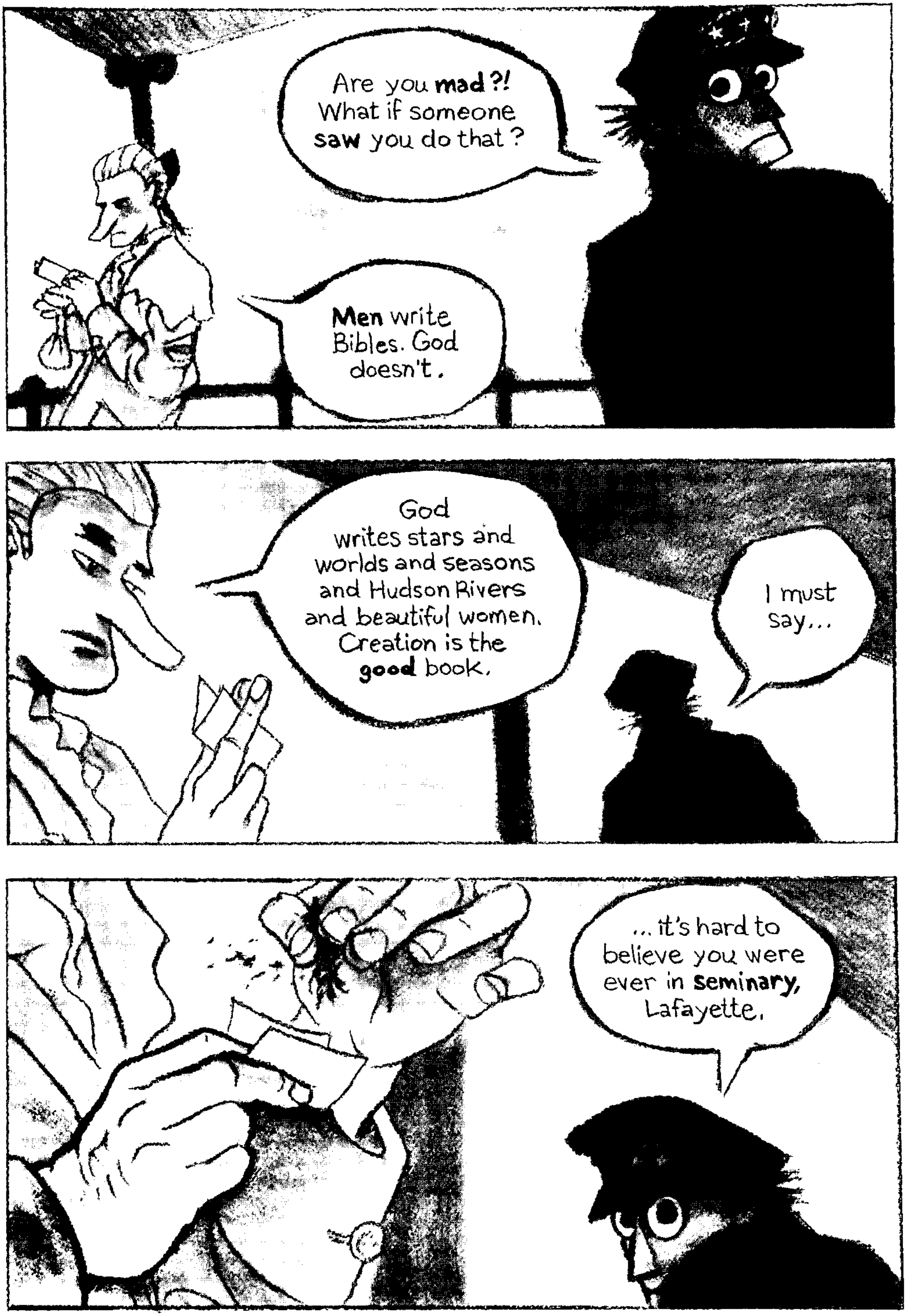
Are you mad?! What if someone saw you do that?
Men write Bibles. God doesn't.
God writes stars and worlds and seasons and Hudson Rivers and beautiful women. Creation is the good book.
I must say...
...it's hard to believe you were ever in seminary, Lafayette.

Bah. Who knows. Maybe someone needs a prayer down below.

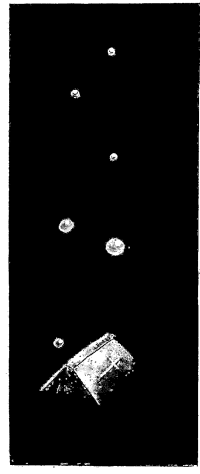

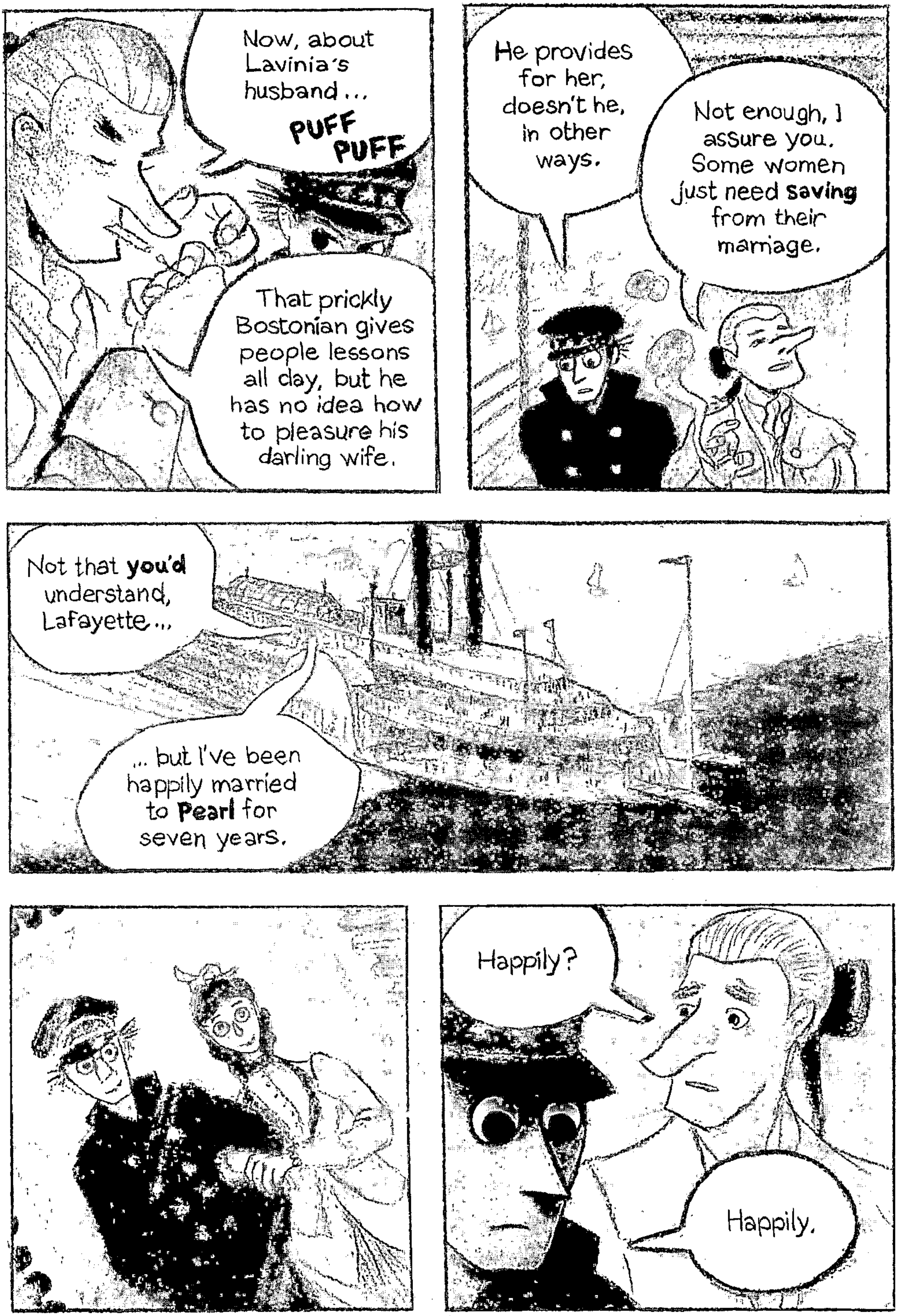
Now, about Lavinia's husband...
PUFF PUFF
That prickly Bostonian gives people lessons all day, but he has no *idea* how to pleasure his darling wife.
He provides for her, doesn't he, in other ways.
Not enough, I assure you. Some women just need **saving** from their marriage.
Not that **you'd** understand, Lafayette...
... but I've been happily married to **Pearl** for seven years.
Happily?
Happily.

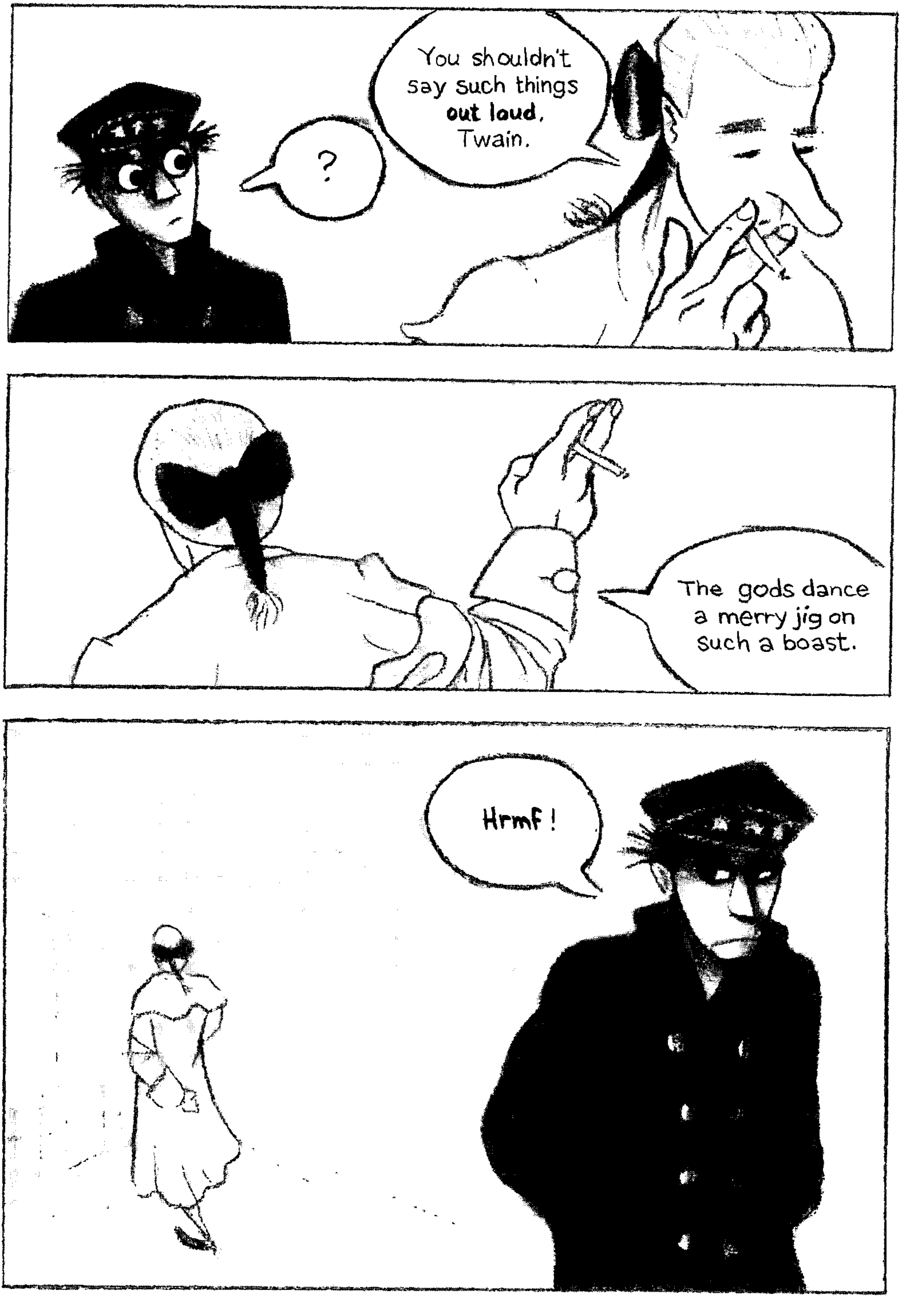
?
You shouldn't say such things **out loud**, Twain.
The gods dance a merry jig on such a boast.
Hrmf!

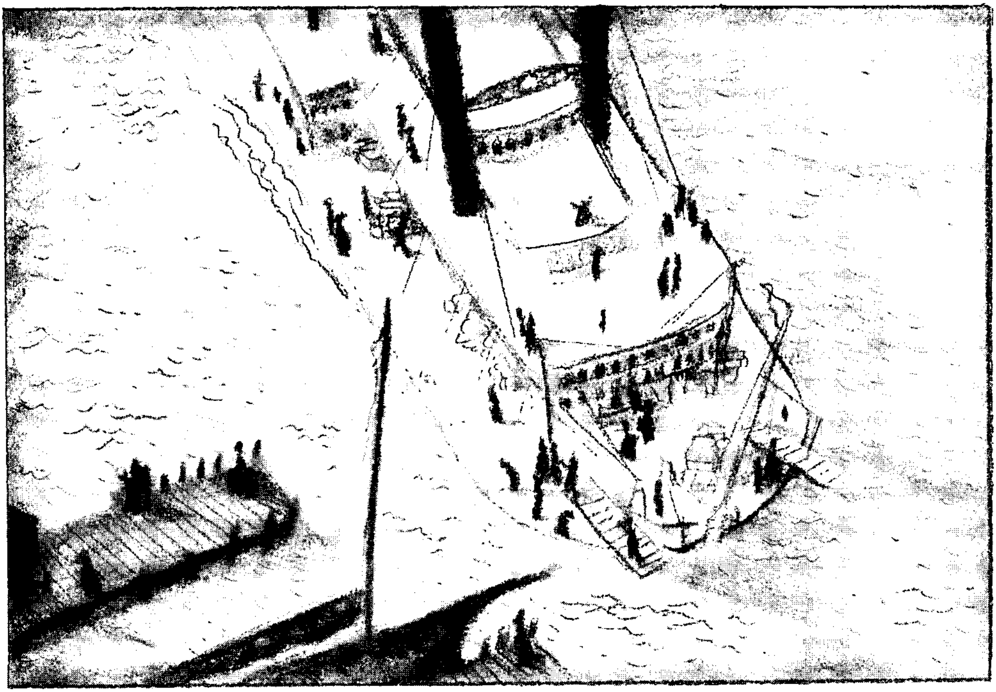

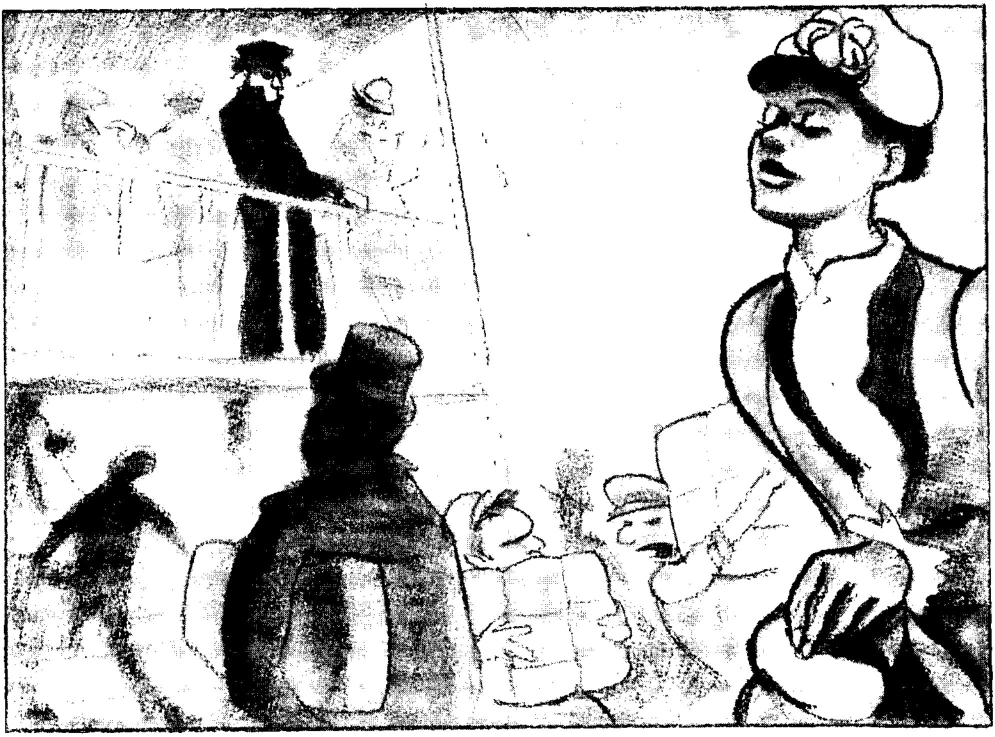

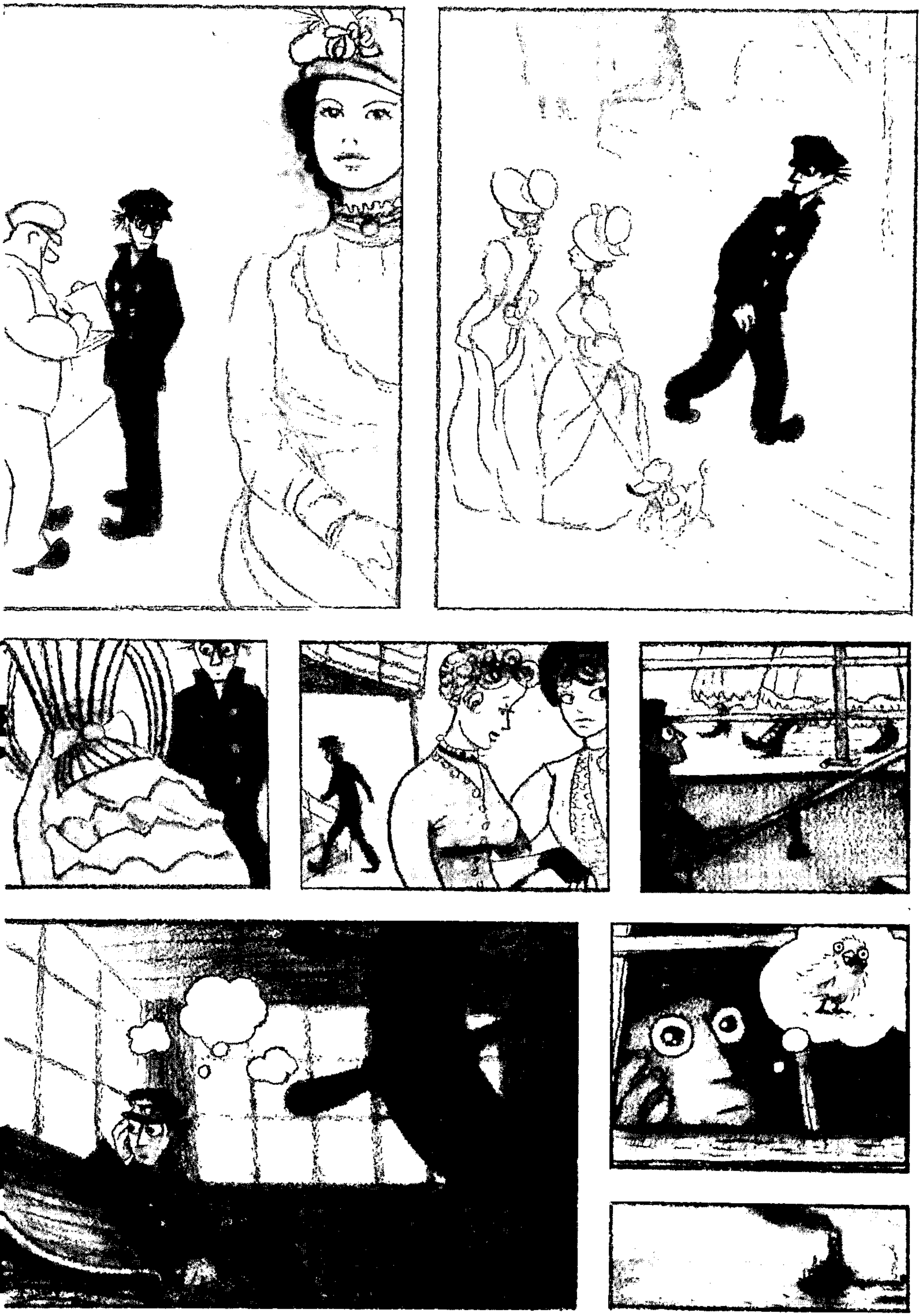

Pt 1, Chap.4

"THE MERMAID IN THE HUDSON"

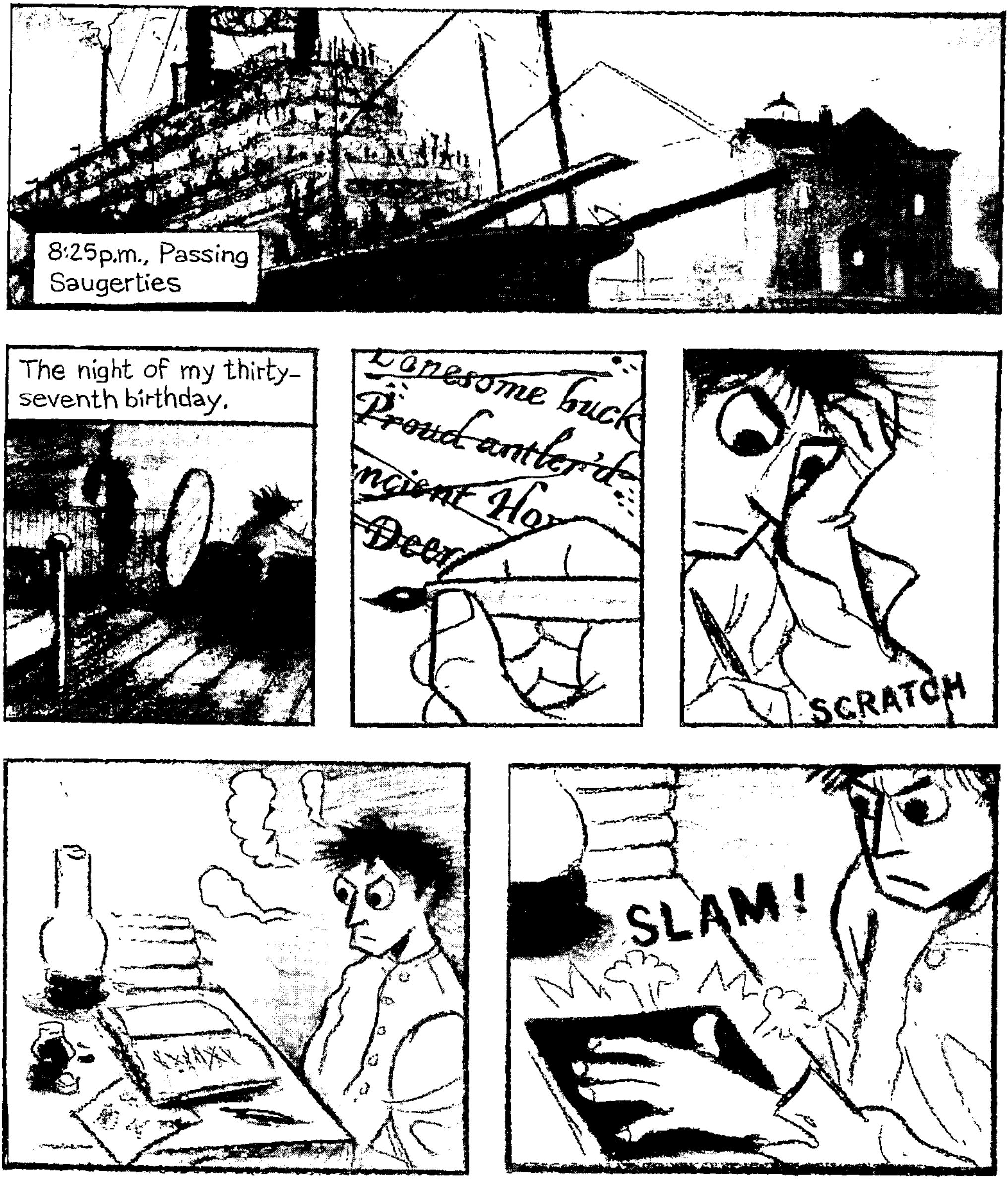
8:25p.m., Passing Saugerties
The night of my thirty-seventh birthday.
Lonesome buck
Proud antler'd
SCRATCH
SLAM!

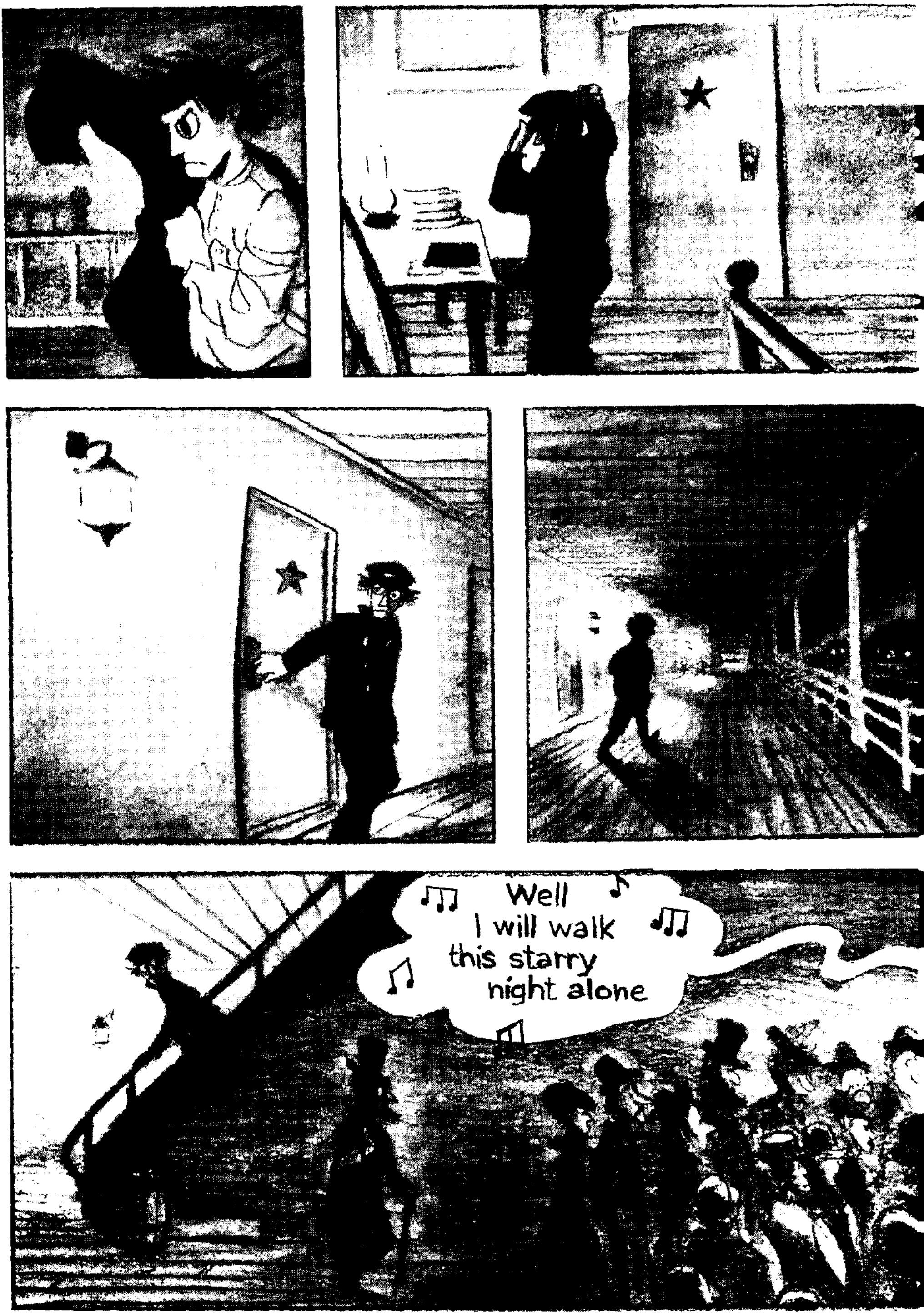
Well I will walk this starry night alone

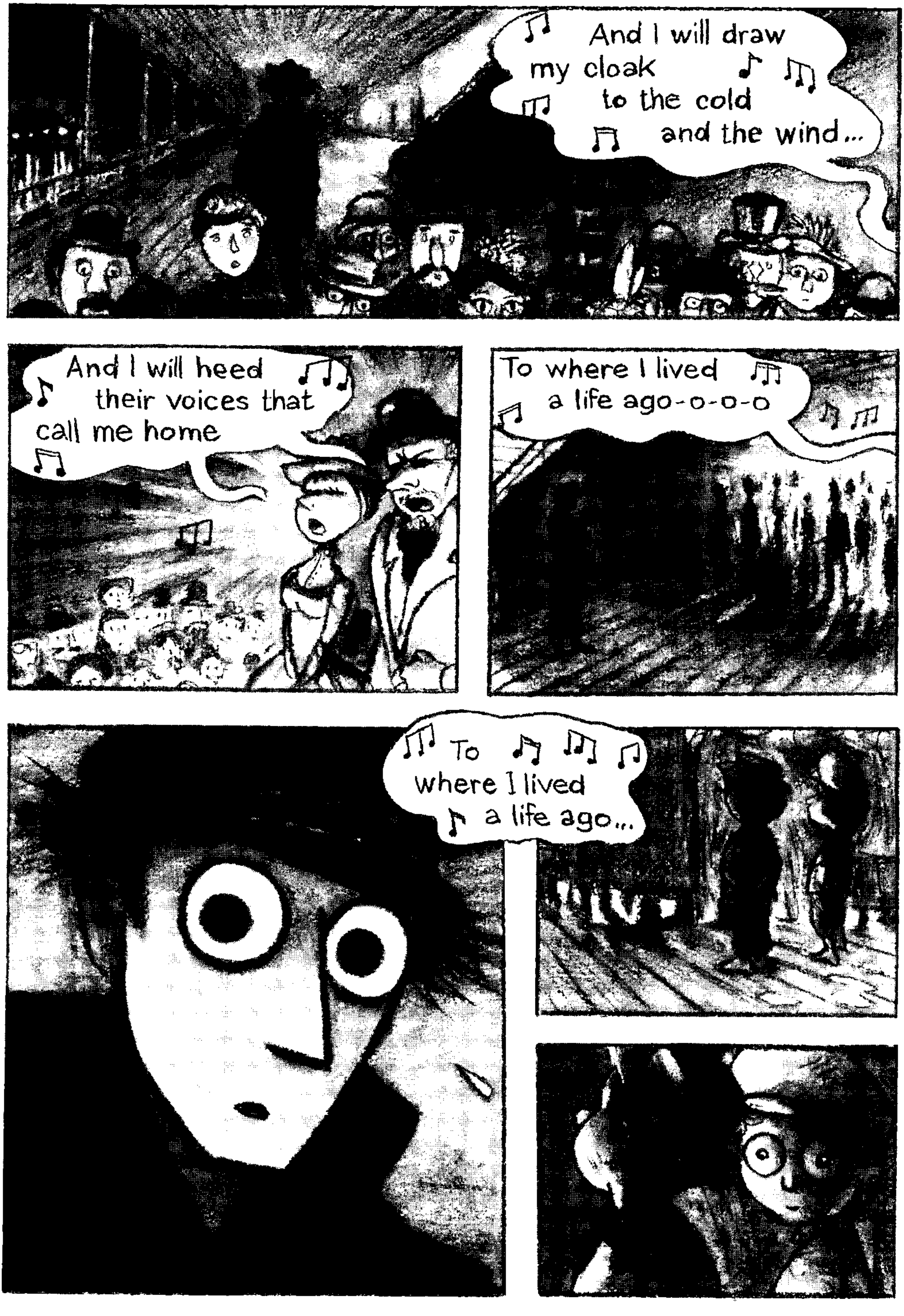
And I will draw my cloak to the cold and the wind...
And I will heed their voices that call me home
To where I lived a life ago-o-o-o
To where I lived a life ago...

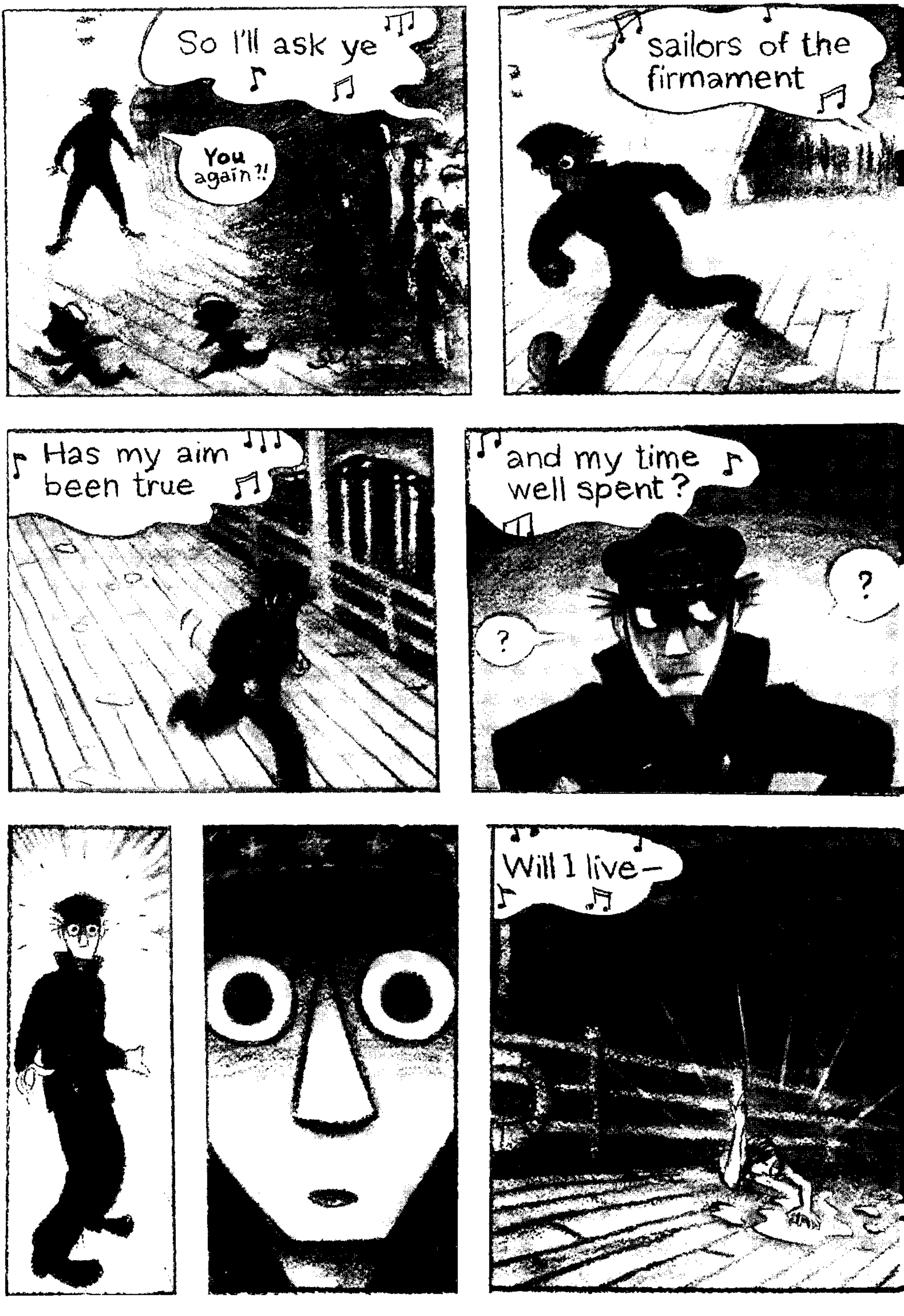
So I'll ask ye
You again?!
sailors of the firmament
Has my aim been true
and my time well spent?
?
?
Will I live—

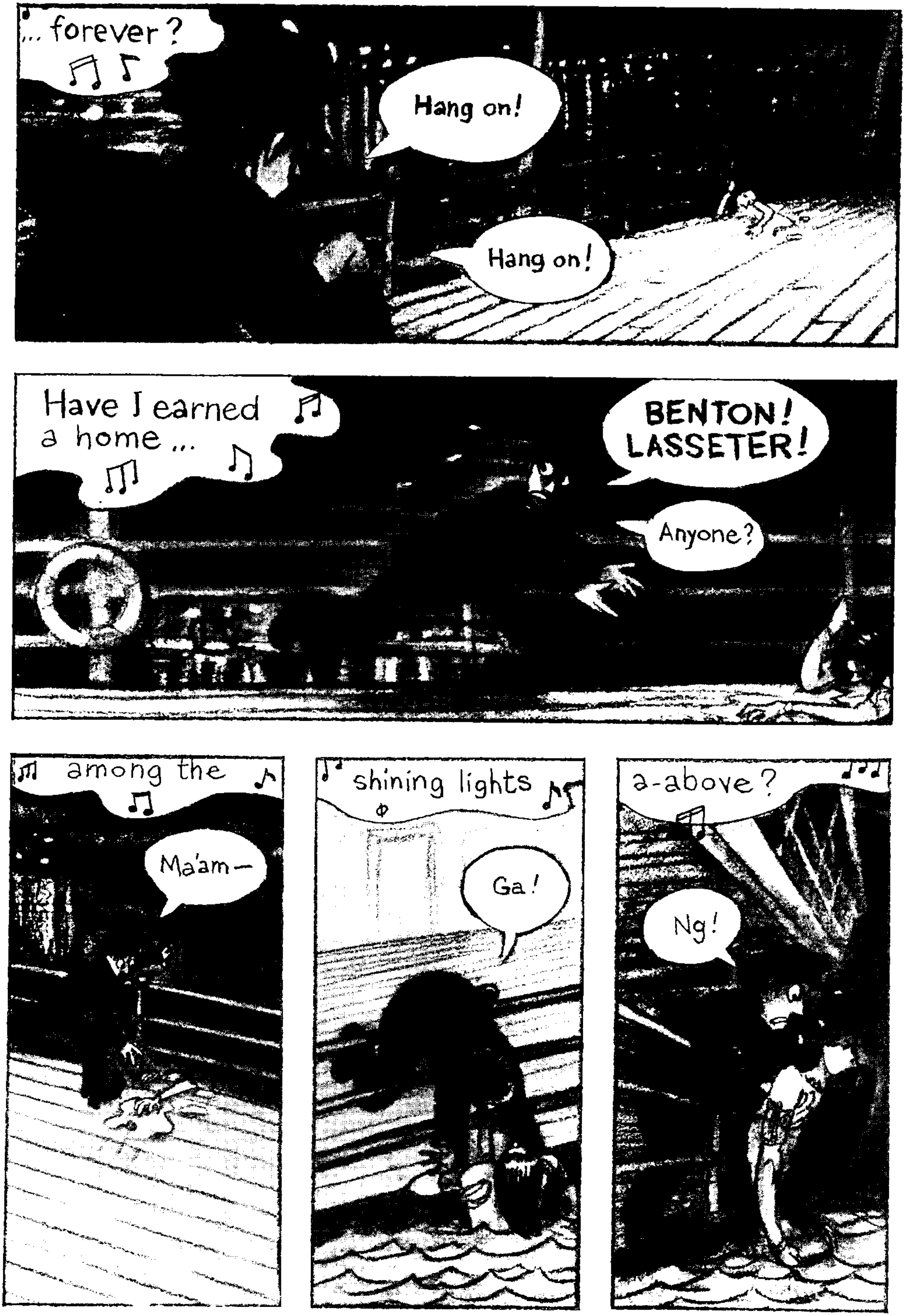
... forever?
Hang on!
Hang on!
Have I earned a home ...
BENTON! LASSETER!
Anyone?
among the
Ma'am—
shining lights
Ga!
a-above?
Ng!

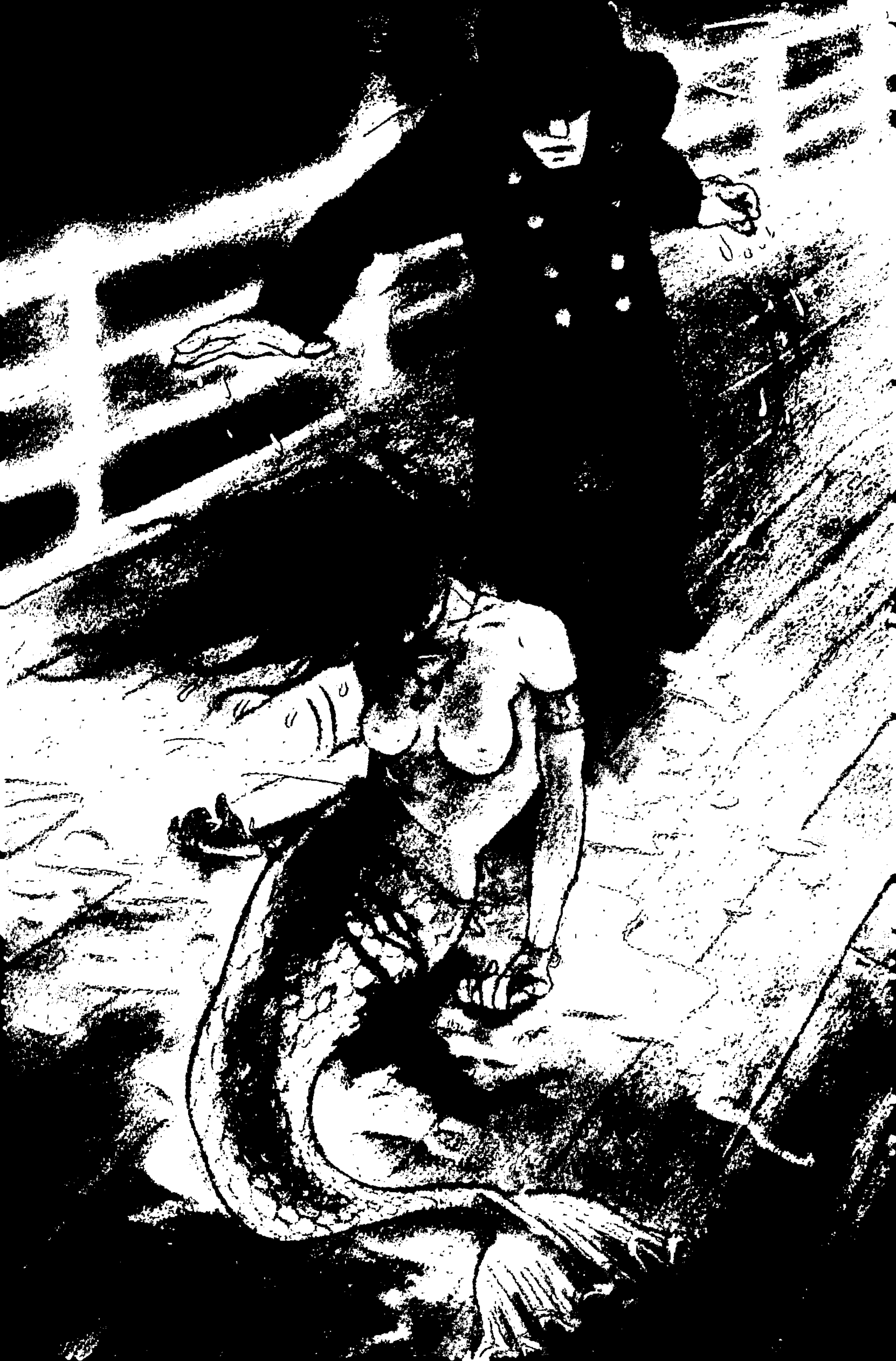

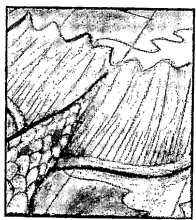

That pungent **smell**! And strange, grayish, oily skin ... She wasn't anything like the P.T. Barnum mummy-thing ...

Imagine how much he would pay for this ... this **creature**! I could quit the river. Our old dream ...

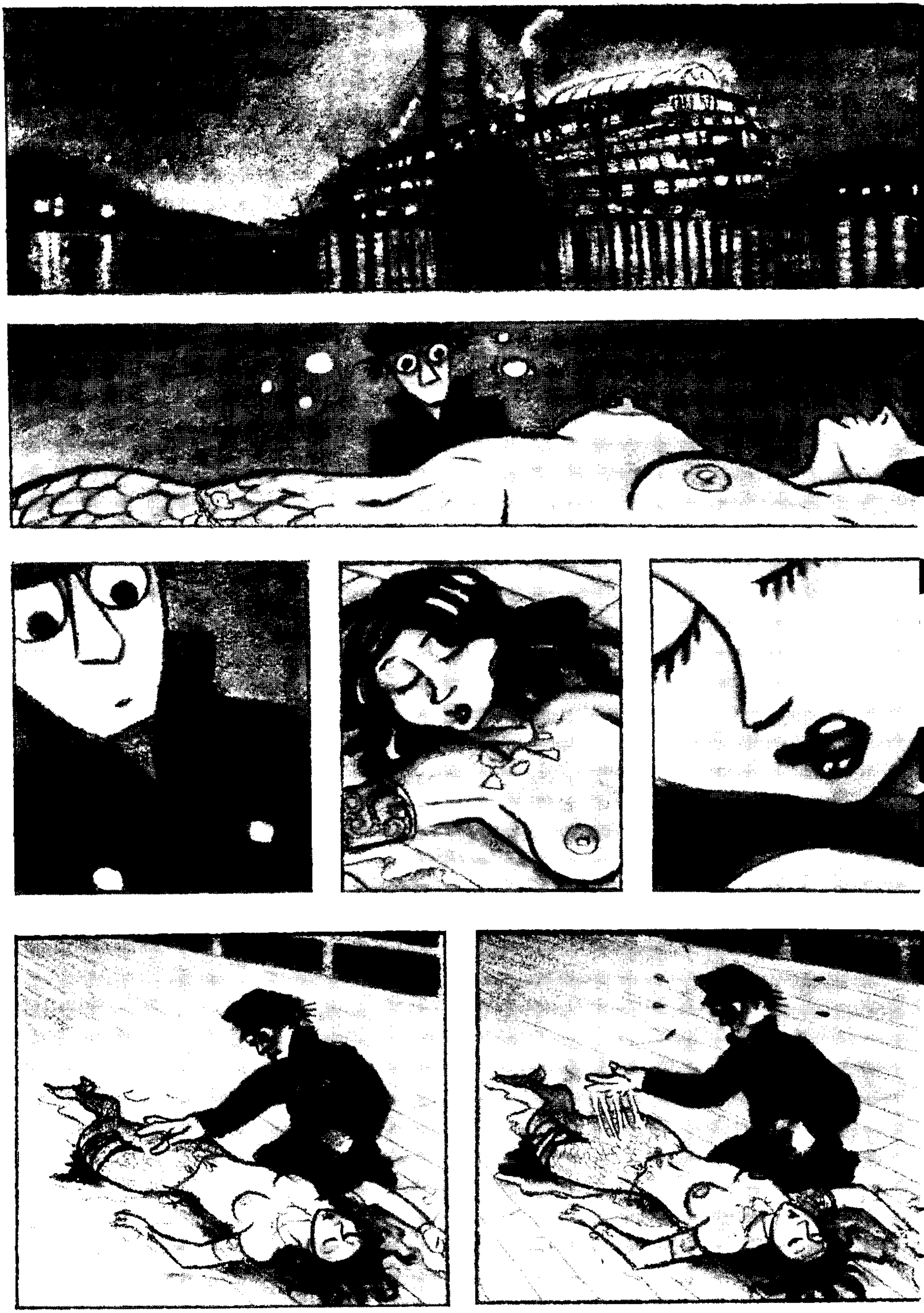

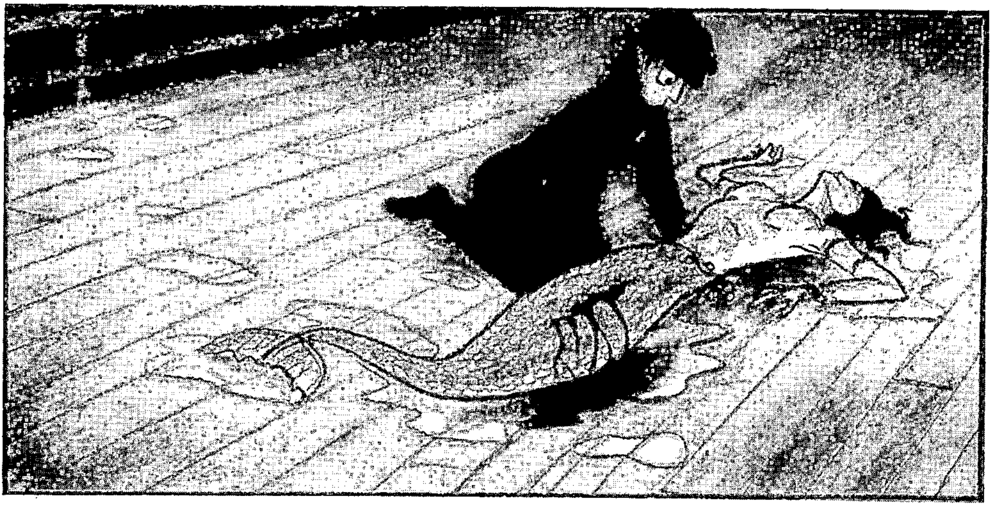

It was hurt. Maybe dying. Get the officers. Lafayette. And Doc Sycamore.

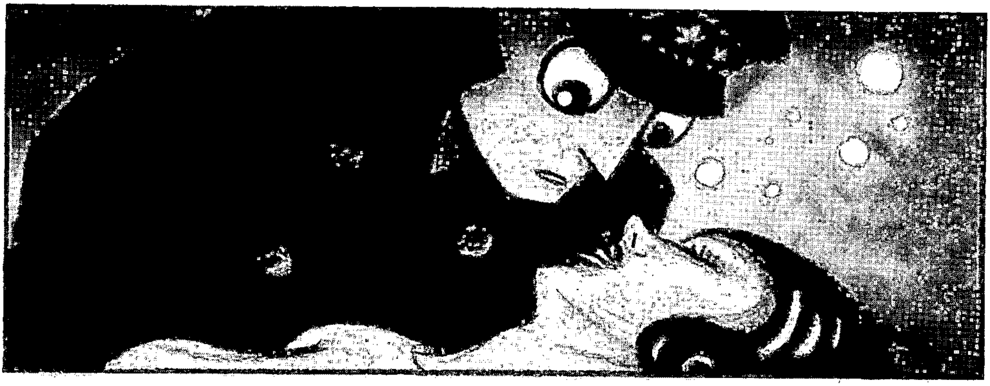

I felt dizzy and strange and a little sick. I wanted to throw the wounded thing back in the water, when suddenly—

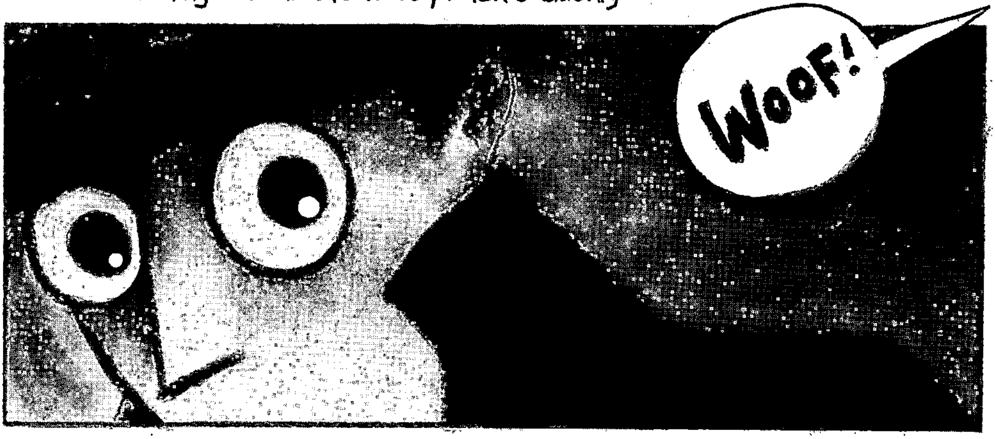
WOOF!

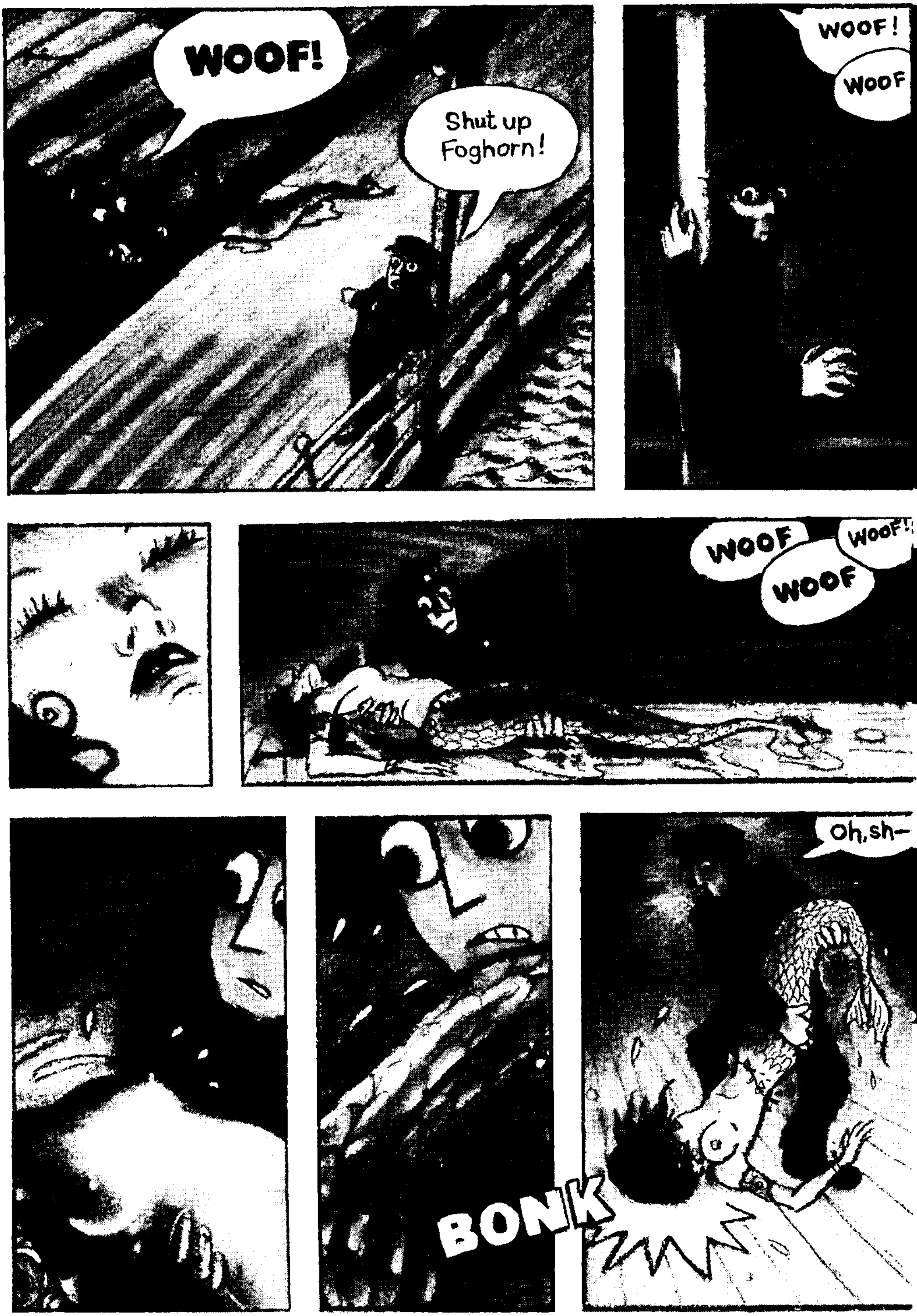
WOOF!
Shut up Foghorn!
WOOF!
WOOF
WOOF
WOOF
WOOF!
Oh, sh–
BONK

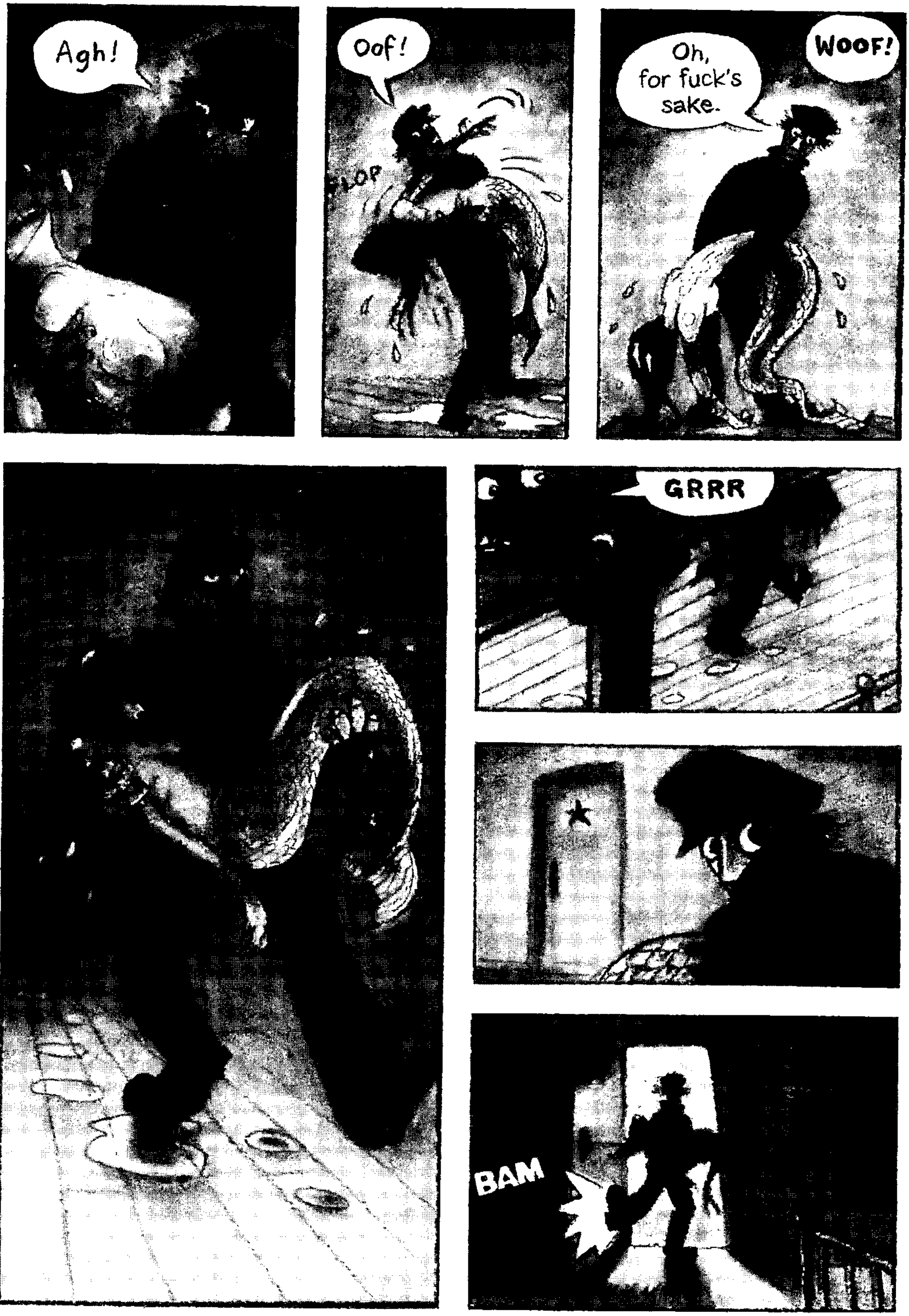
Agh!
Oof!
PLOP
Oh, for fuck's sake.
WOOF!
GRRR
BAM

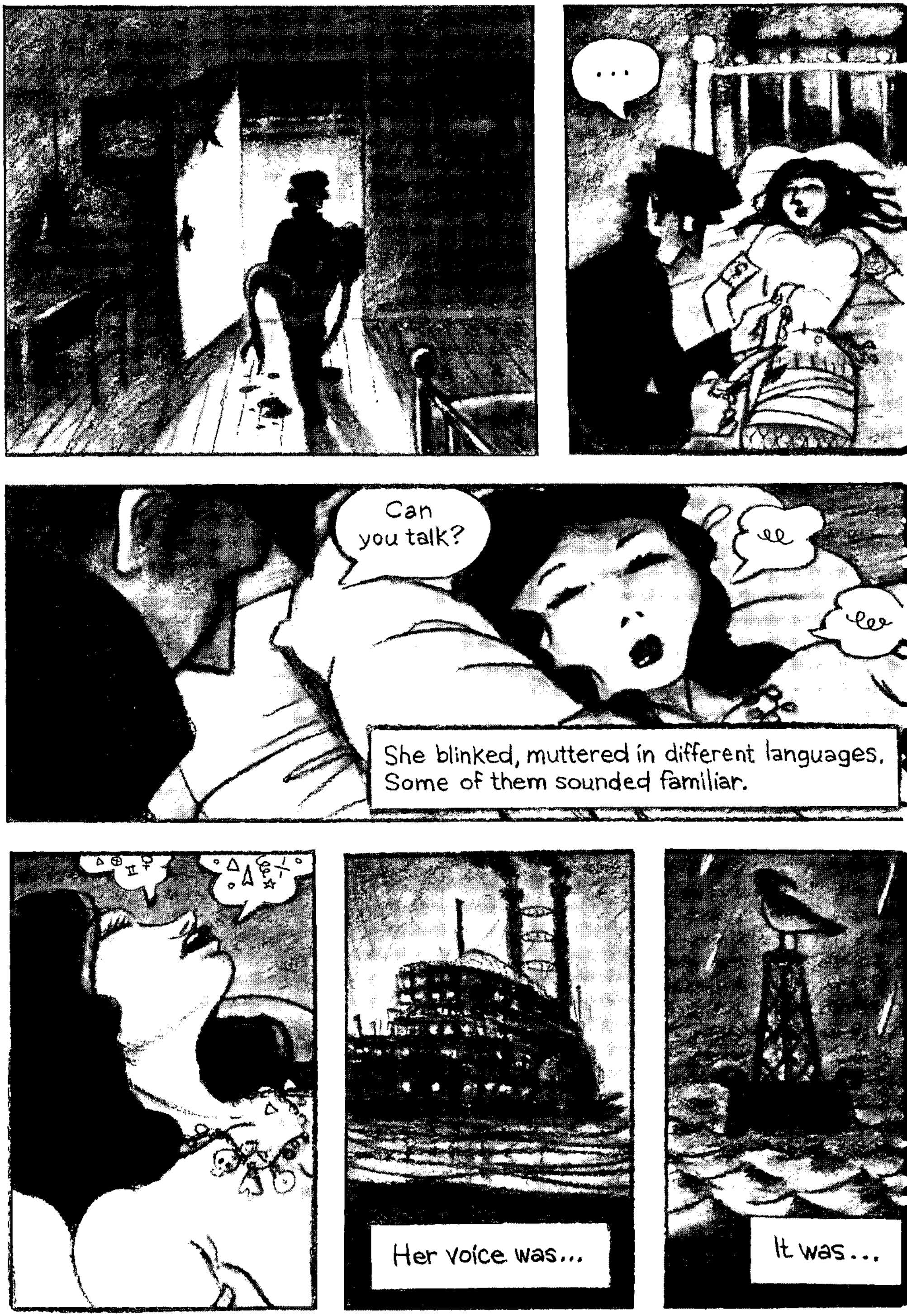
...
Can you talk?
She blinked, muttered in different languages. Some of them sounded familiar.
Her voice was...
It was...

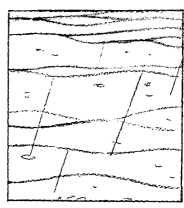

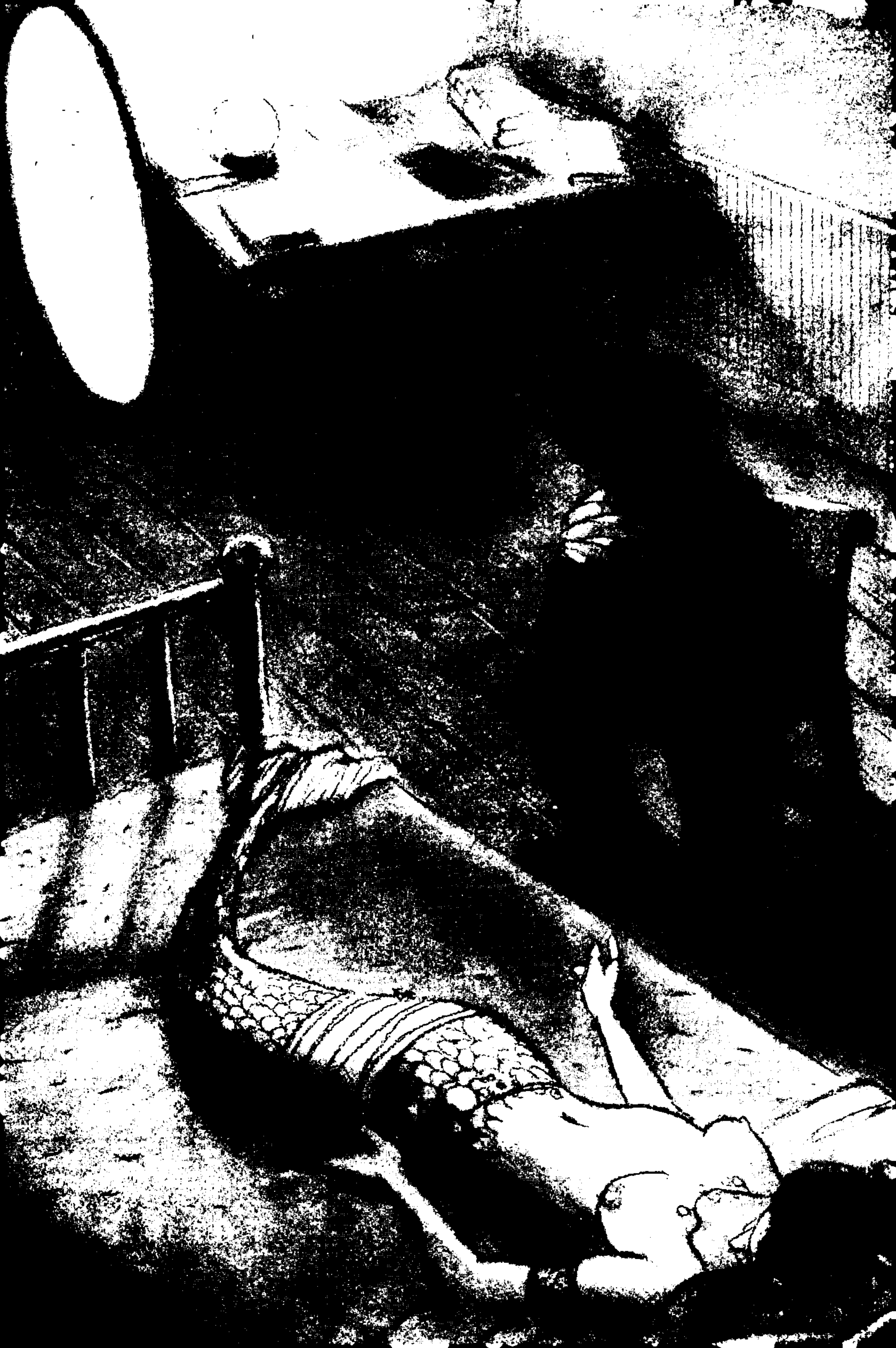

Pt 1, Chap.5

"BEAVERTON'S NEW BOOK"

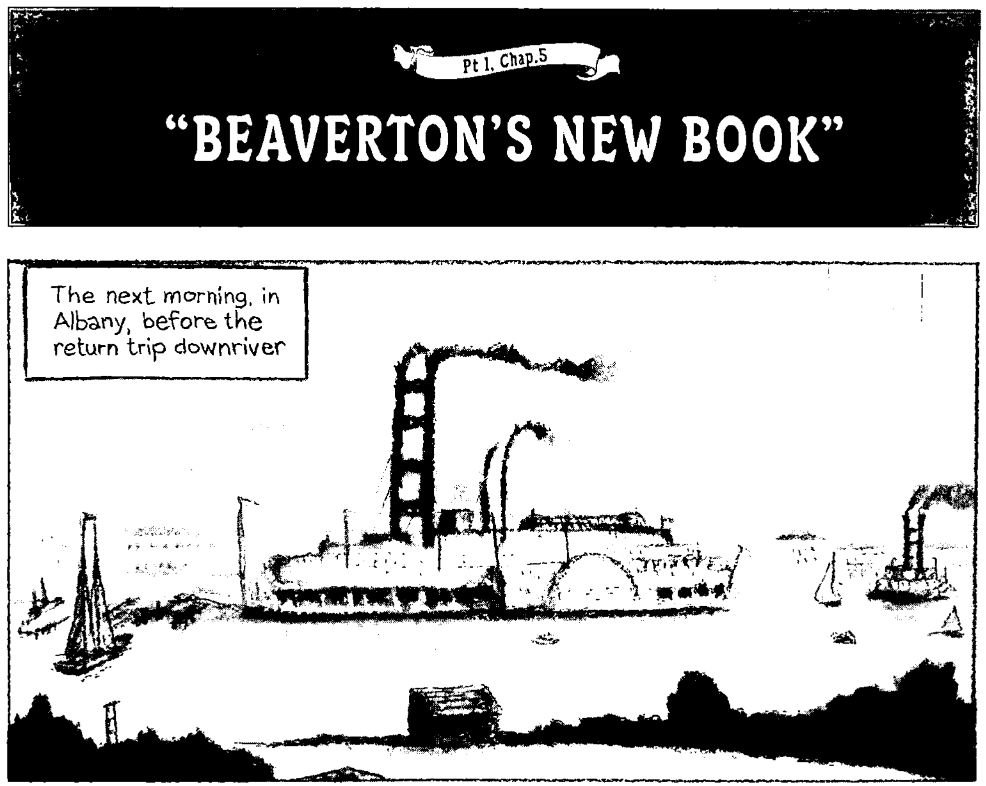
The next morning, in Albany, before the return trip downriver

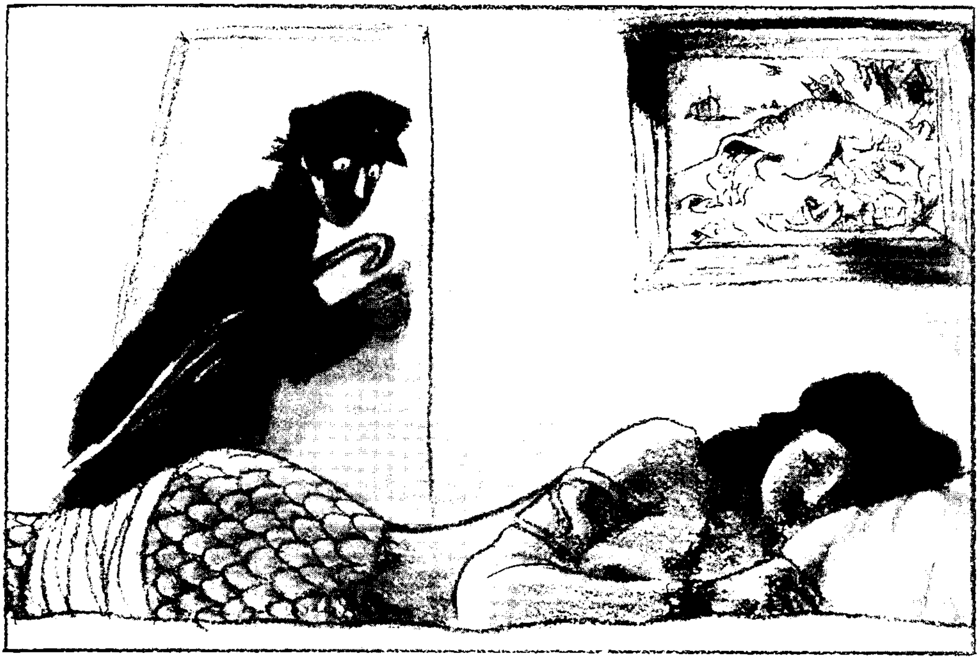

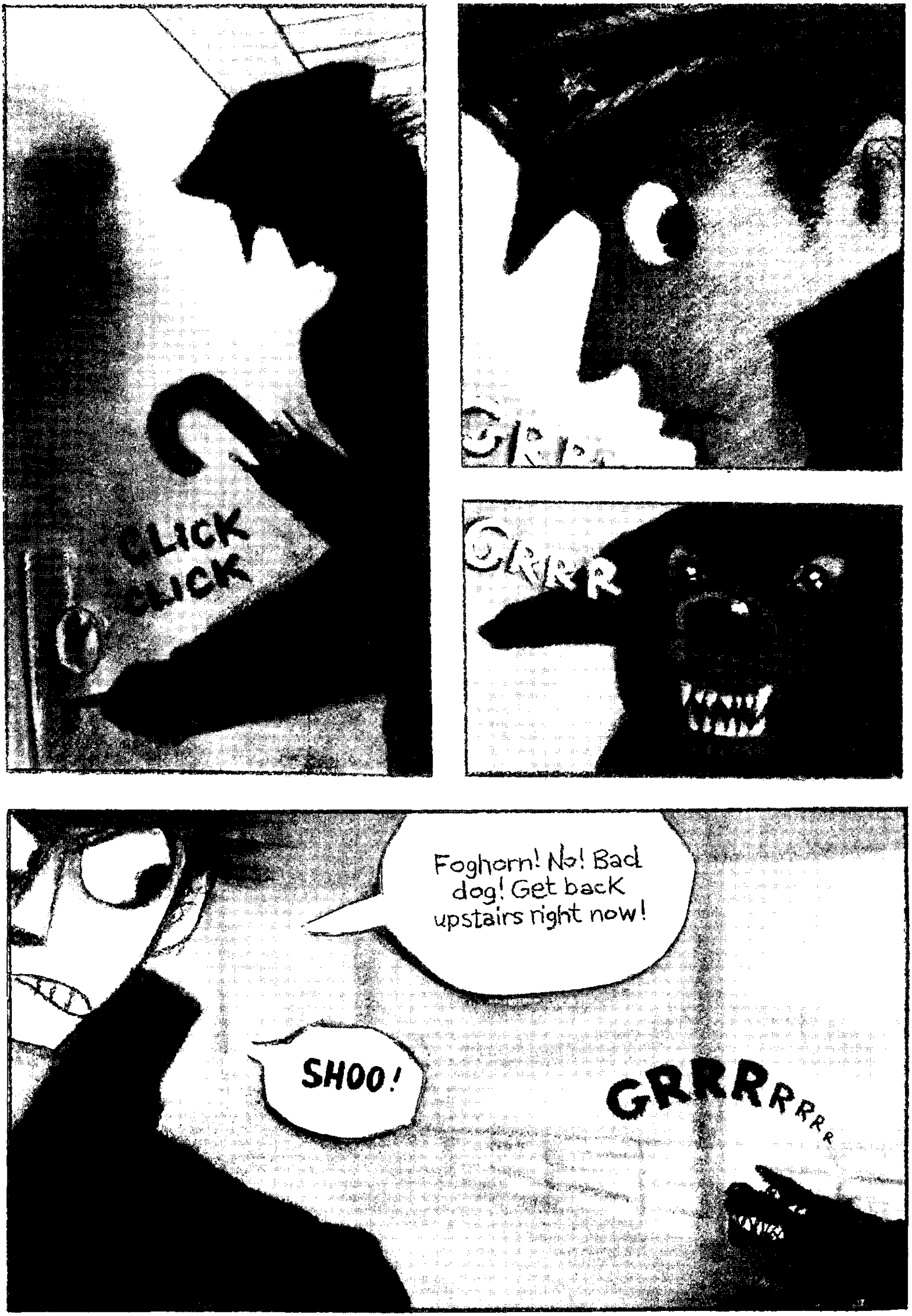
CLICK
CLICK
GRRR
GRRR
Foghorn! No! Bad dog! Get back upstairs right now!
SHOO!
GRRRRRRR

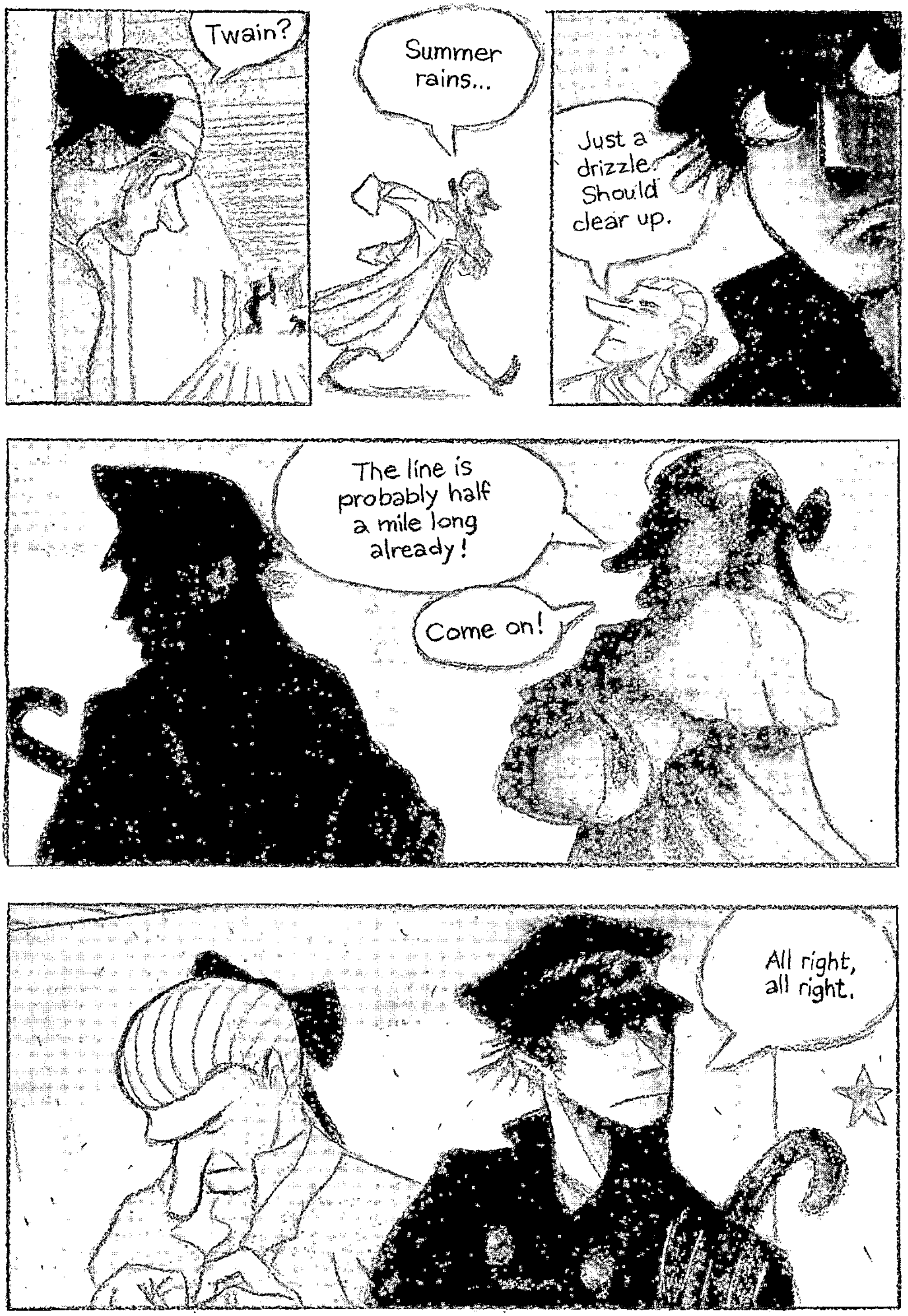
Twain?
Summer rains...
Just a drizzle. Should clear up.
The line is probably half a mile long already!
Come on!
All right, all right.

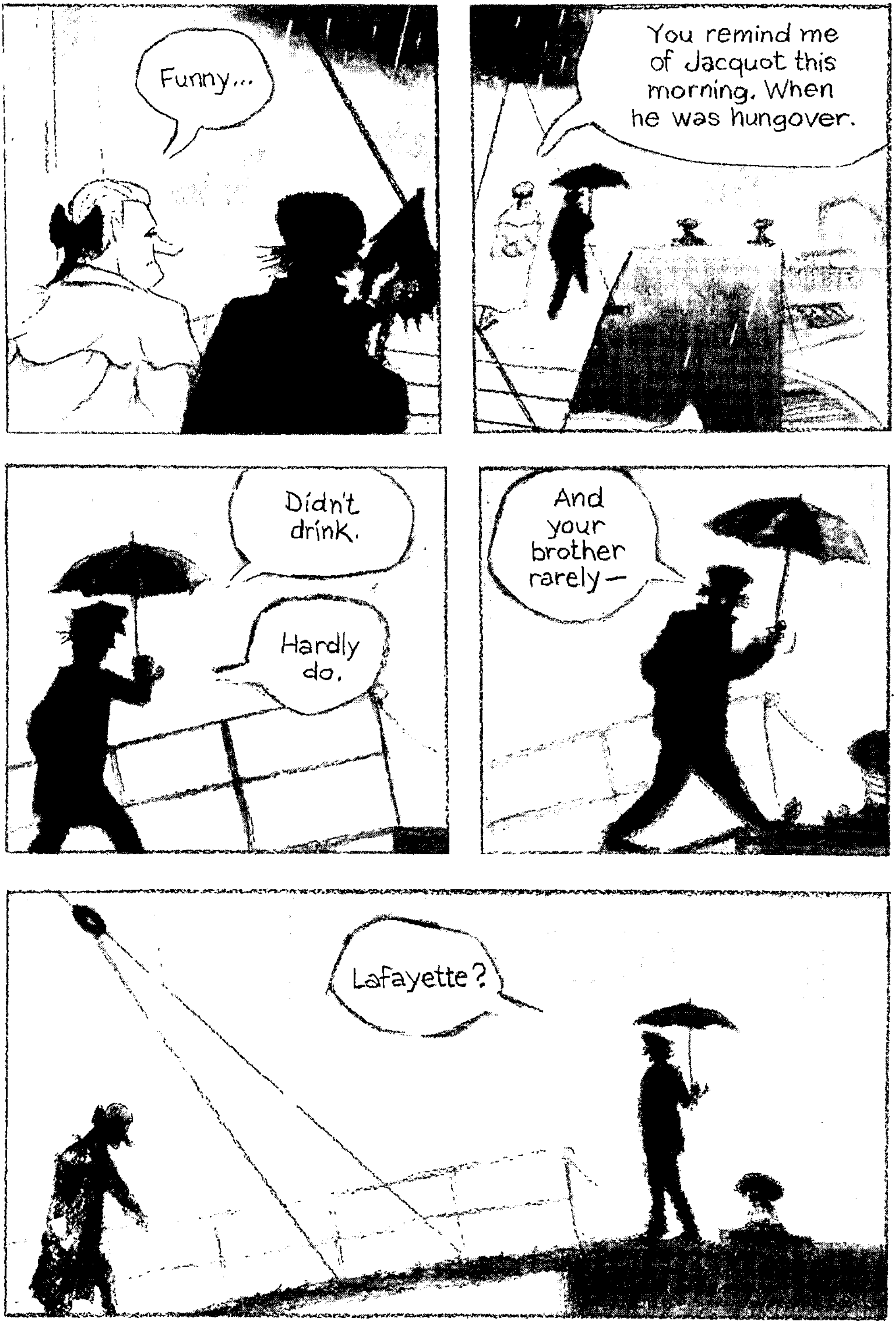
Funny...
You remind me of Jacquot this morning. When he was hungover.
Didn't drink.
Hardly do.
And your brother rarely—
Lafayette?

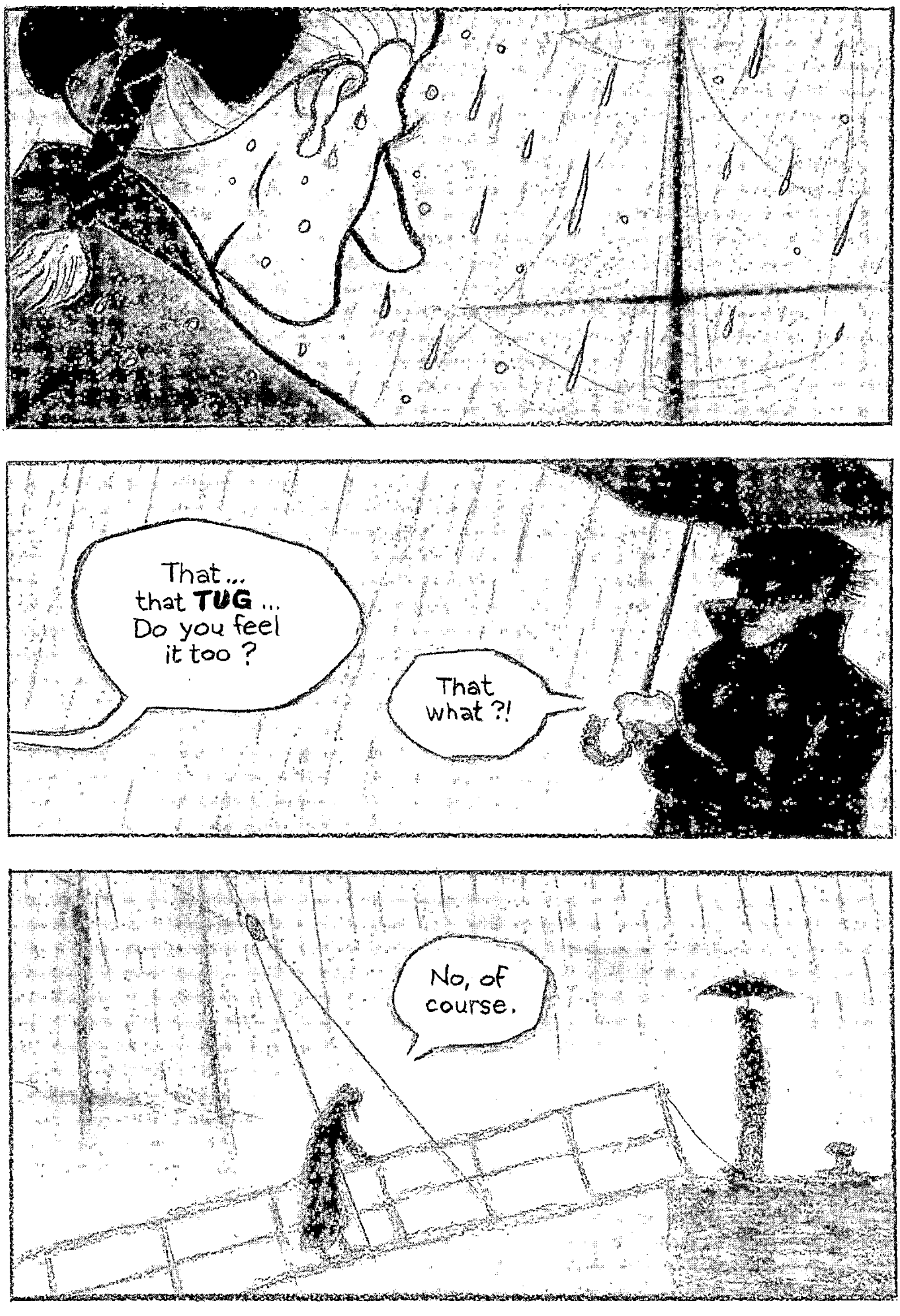
That ... that **TUG** ... Do you feel it too ?
That what ?!
No, of course.

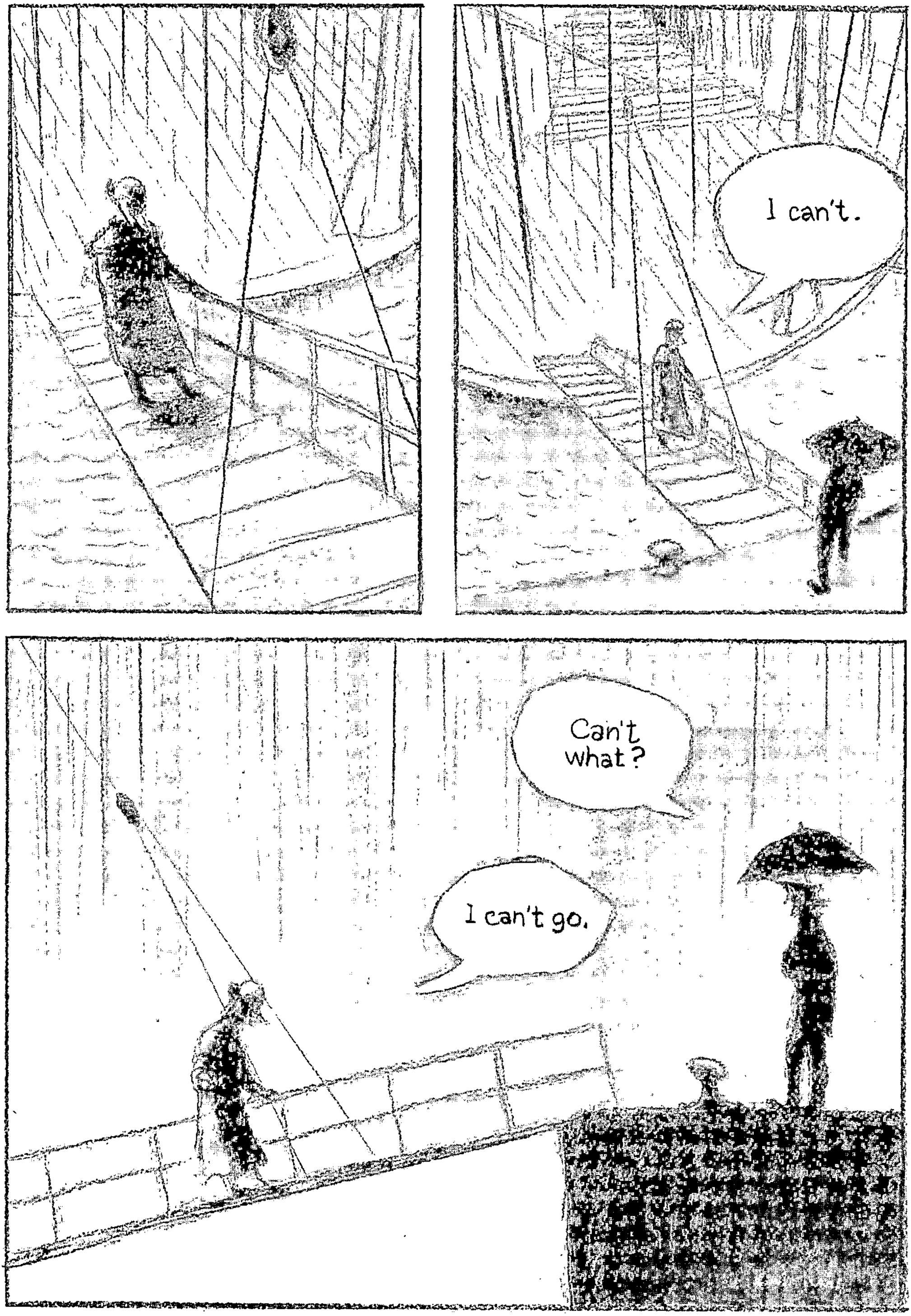
I can't.
Can't what?
I can't go.

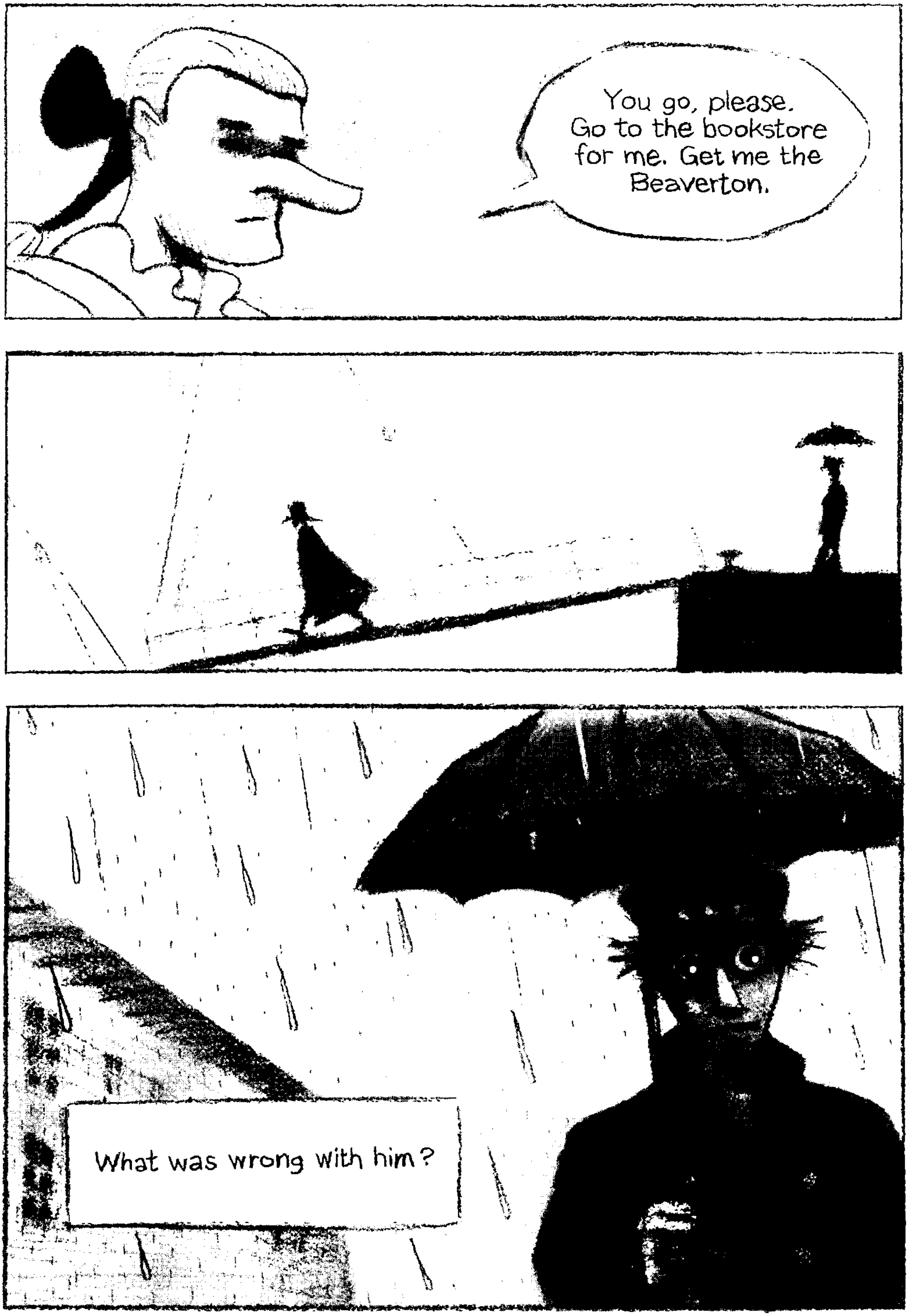
You go, please. Go to the bookstore for me. Get me the Beaverton.
What was wrong with him?

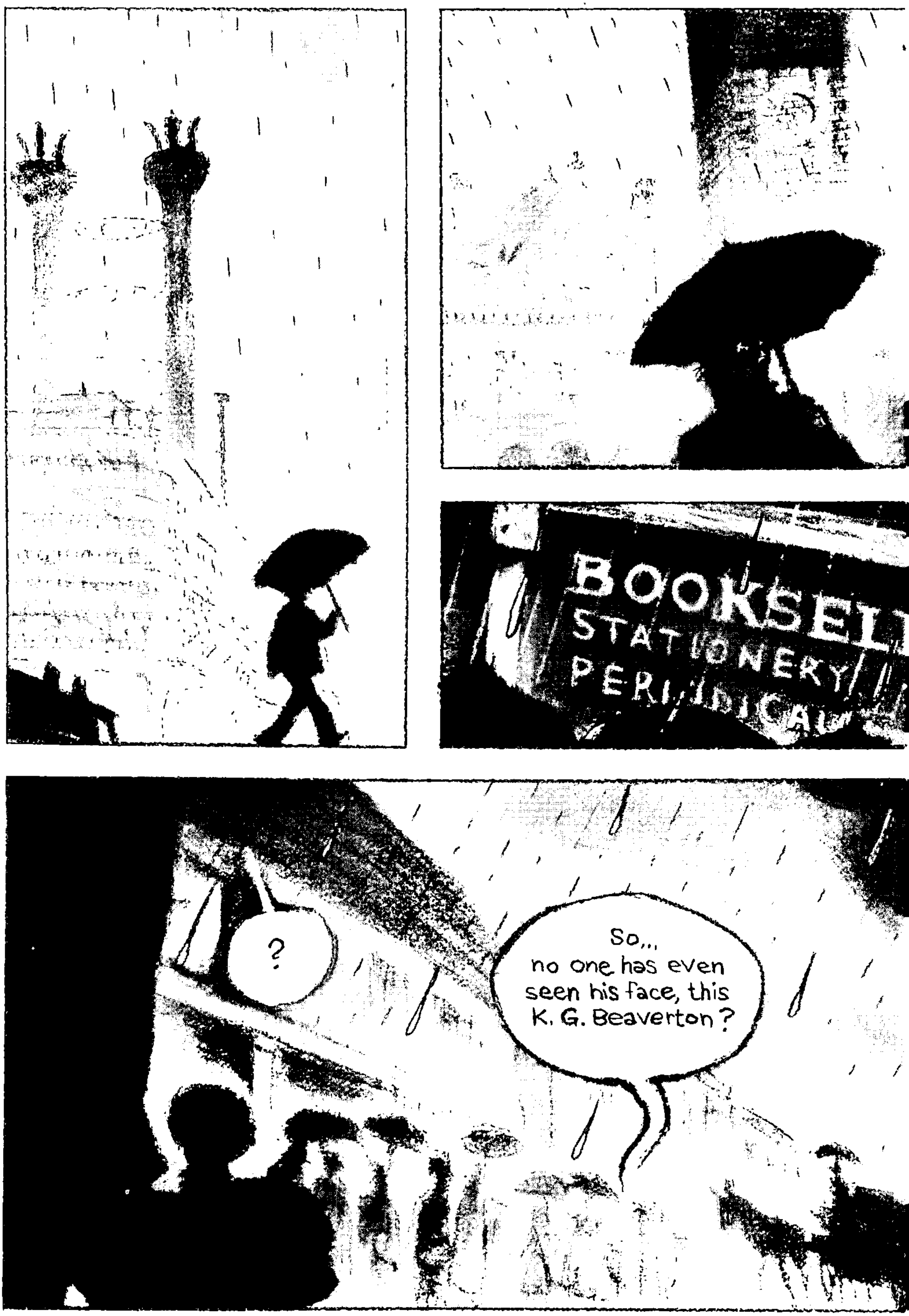
BOOKSEL
STATIONERY
PERI DICAL
?
So...
no one has even
seen his face, this
K. G. Beaverton?

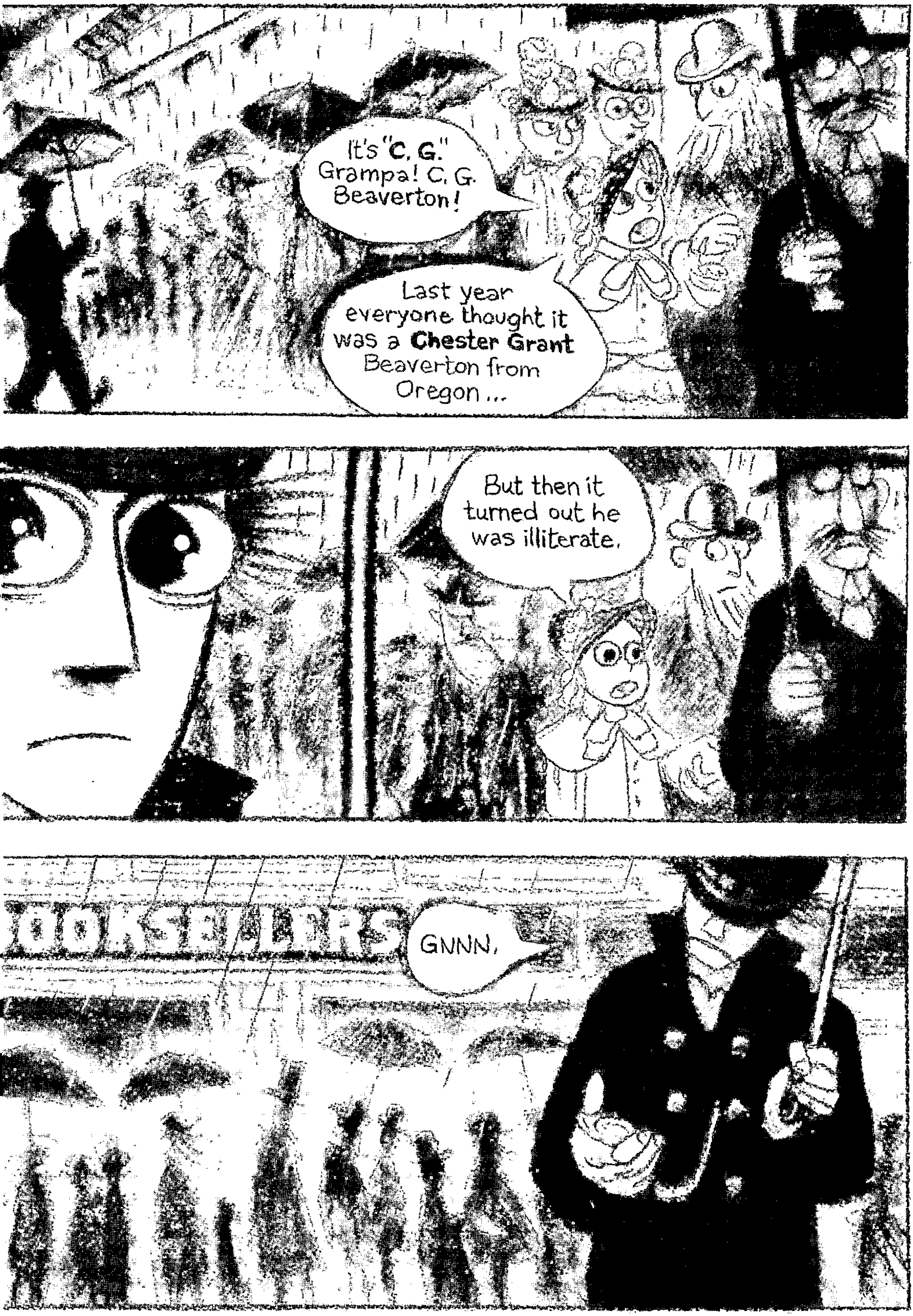
It's "C. G." Grampa! C. G. Beaverton!
Last year everyone thought it was a Chester Grant Beaverton from Oregon ...
But then it turned out he was illiterate.
GNNN.

I don't have time for this!
No, I don't care for the whale story.
I'm American now, I like happy endings.
SCRIBNER
SCRIBNER
Lafayette, you'll have to get it yourself.
You got it? You got it?

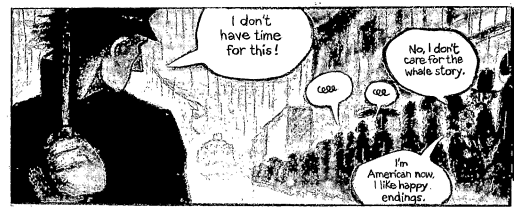

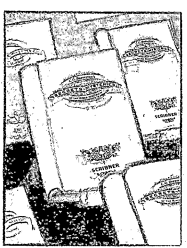

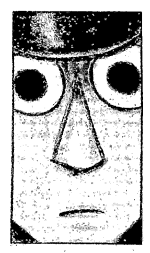

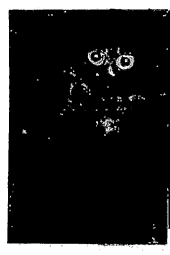

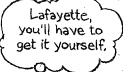

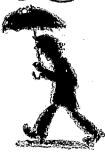

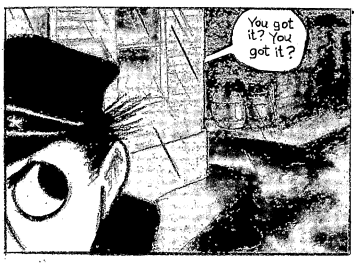

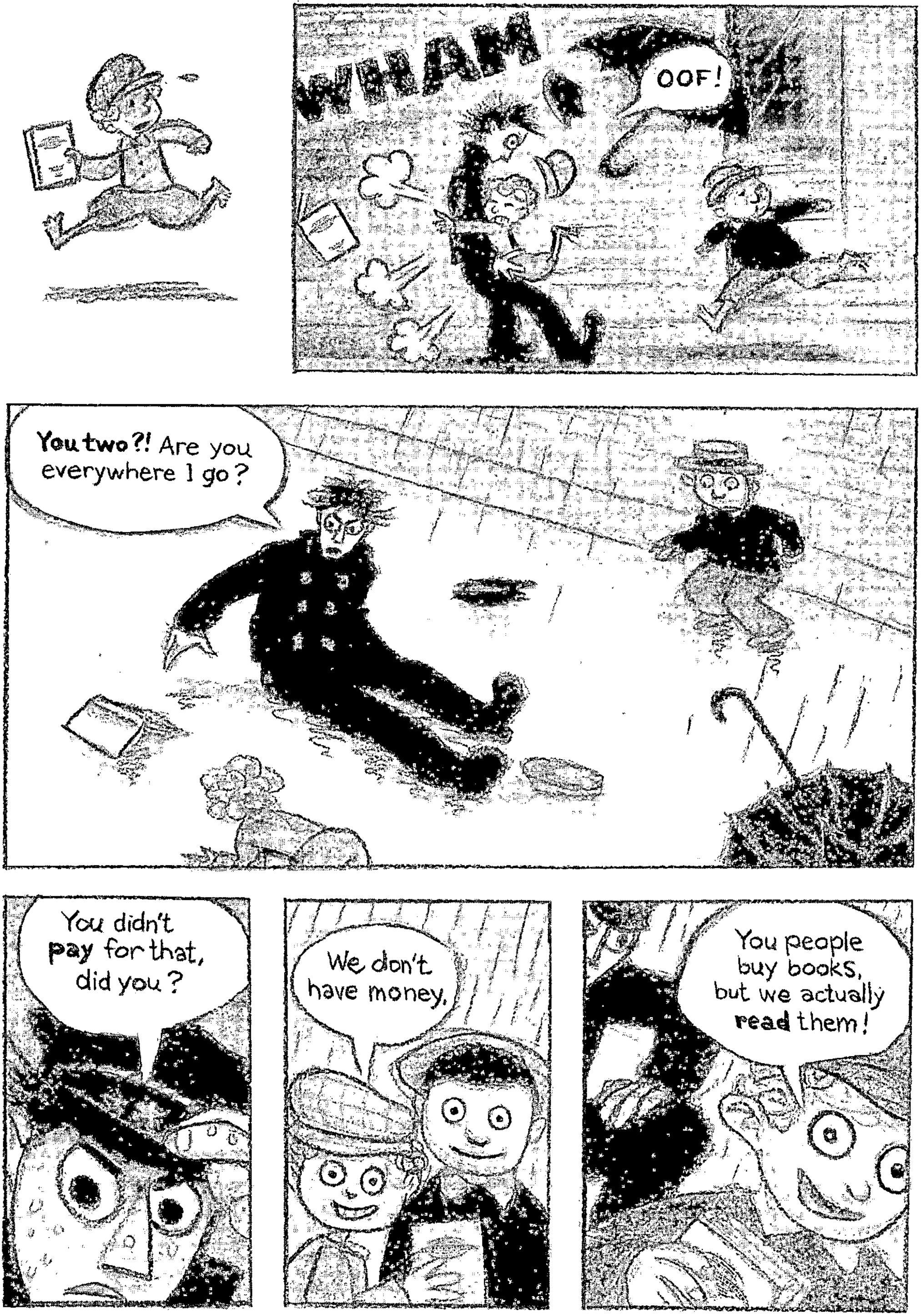
WHAM
OOF!
You two?! Are you everywhere I go?
You didn't pay for that, did you?
We don't have money.
You people buy books, but we actually read them!

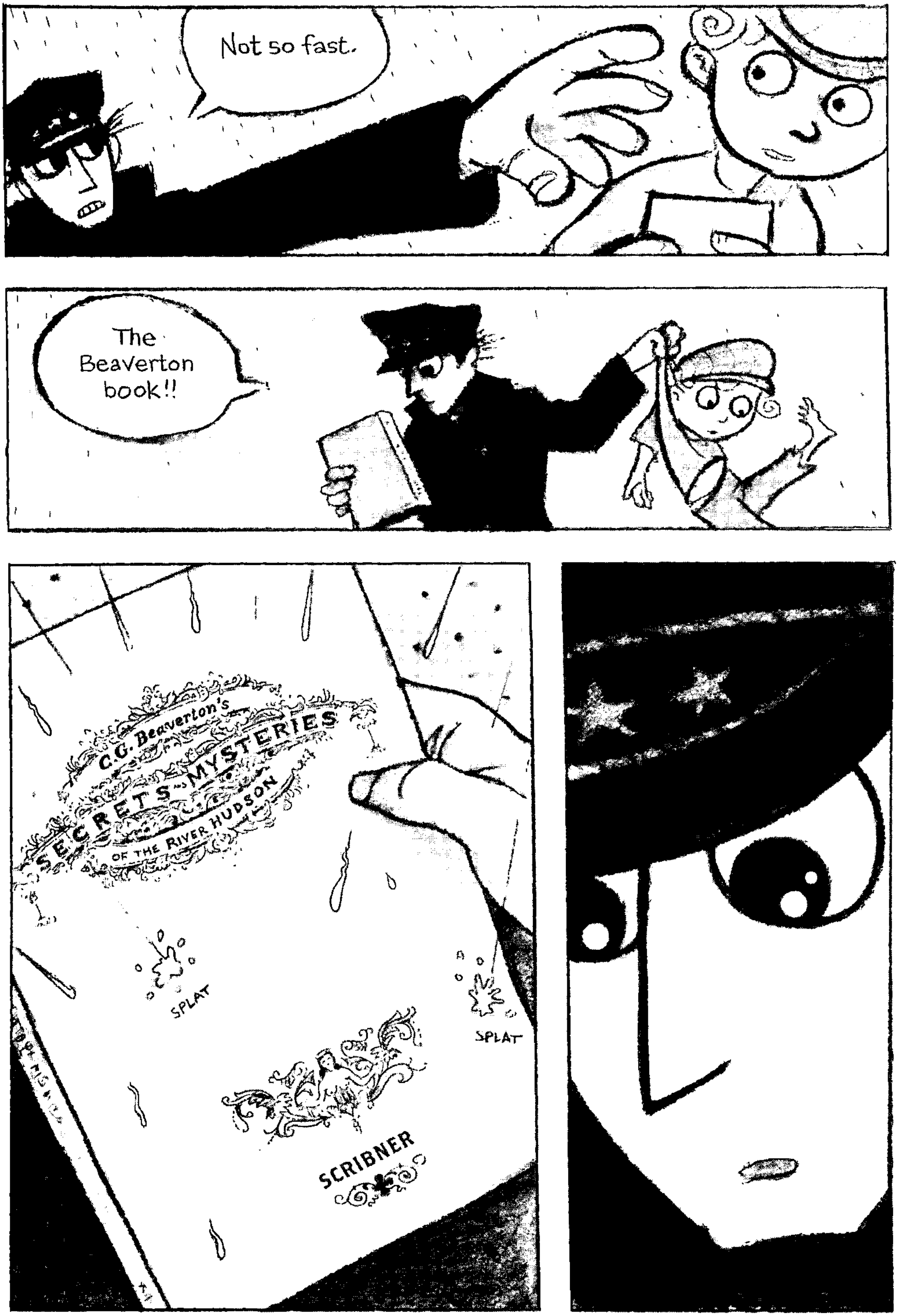
Not so fast.
The Beaverton book!!
C.G. Beaverton's
SECRETS AND MYSTERIES
OF THE RIVER HUDSON
SPLAT
SPLAT
SCRIBNER

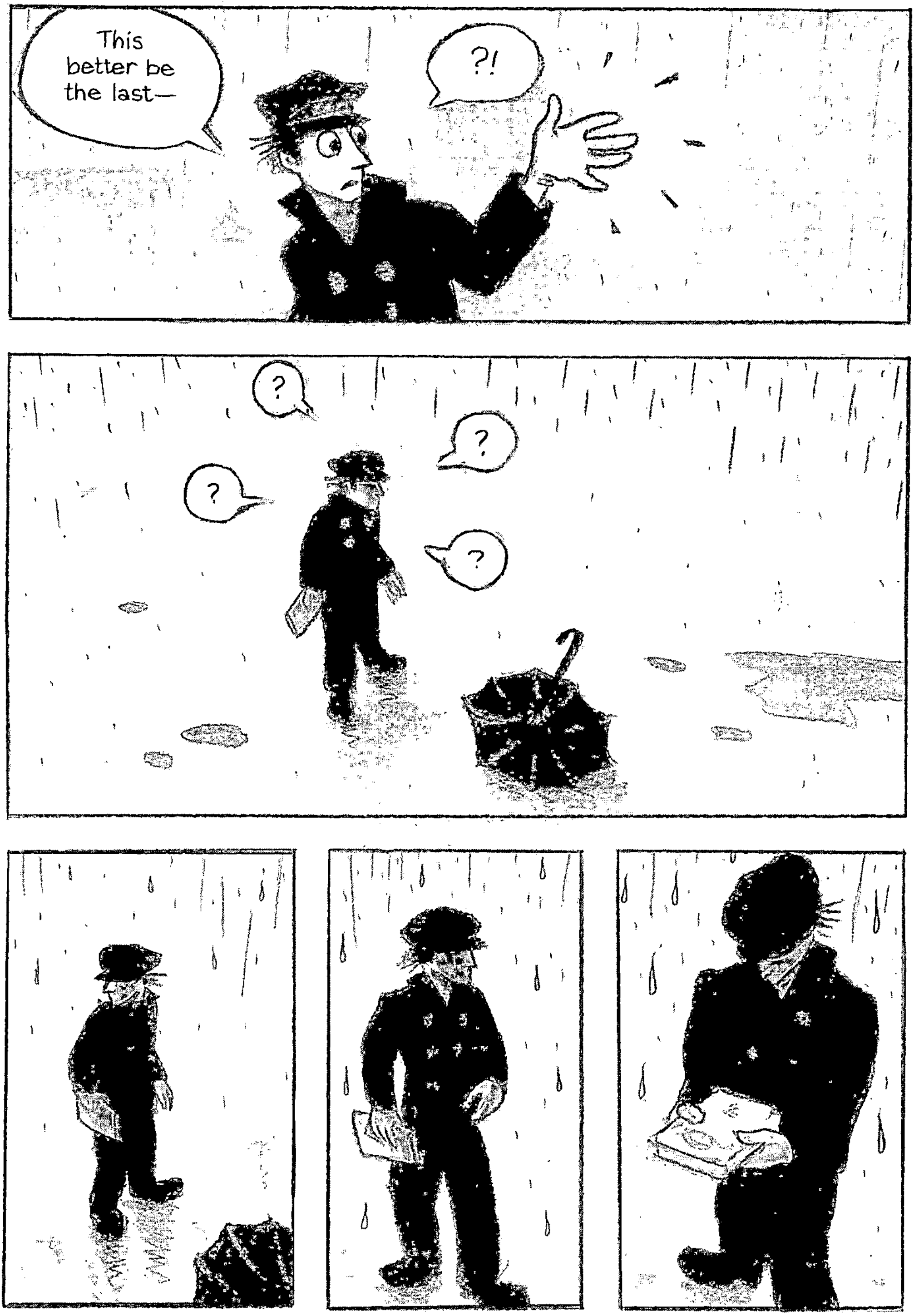
This better be the last—
?!
?
?
?
?

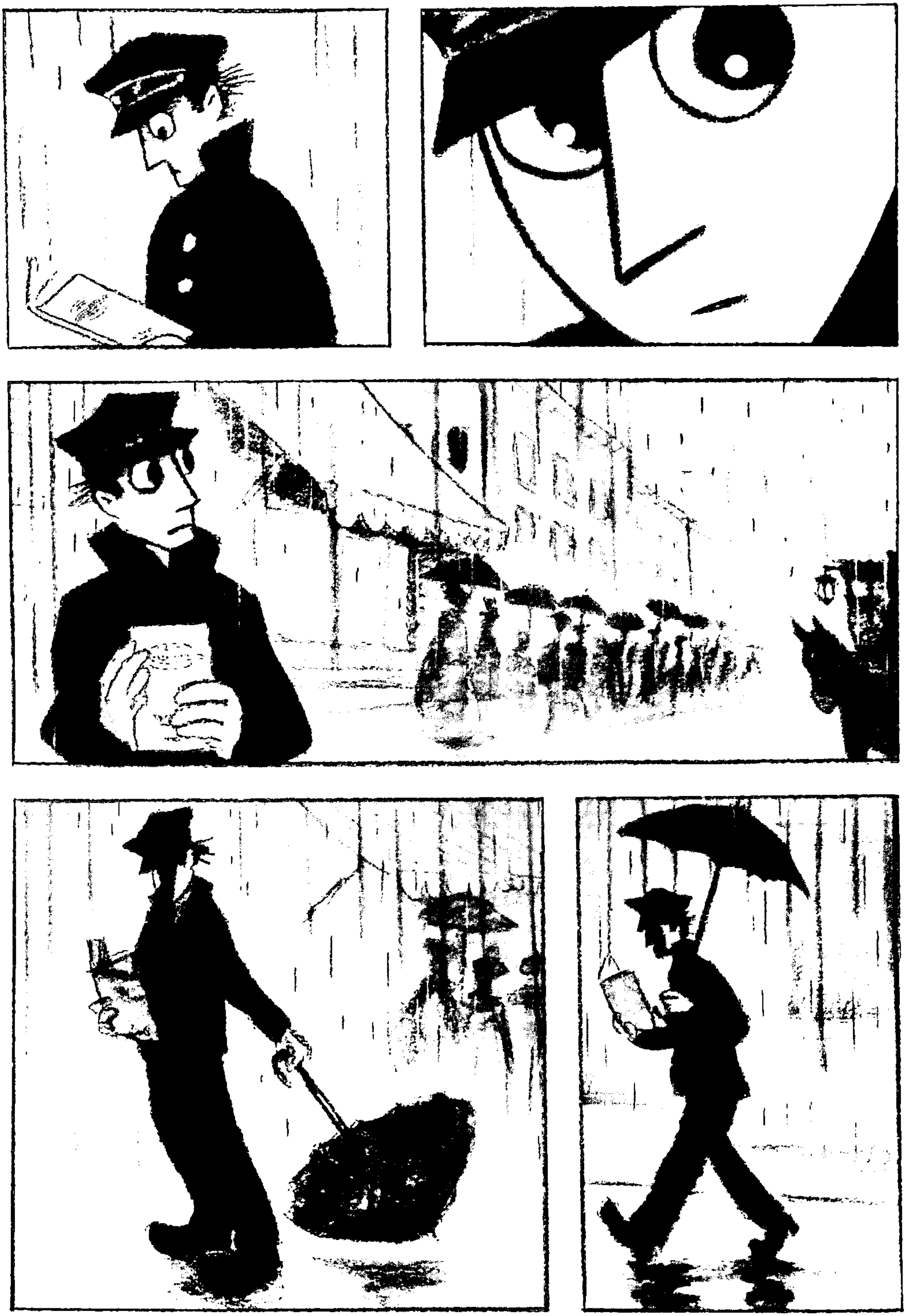

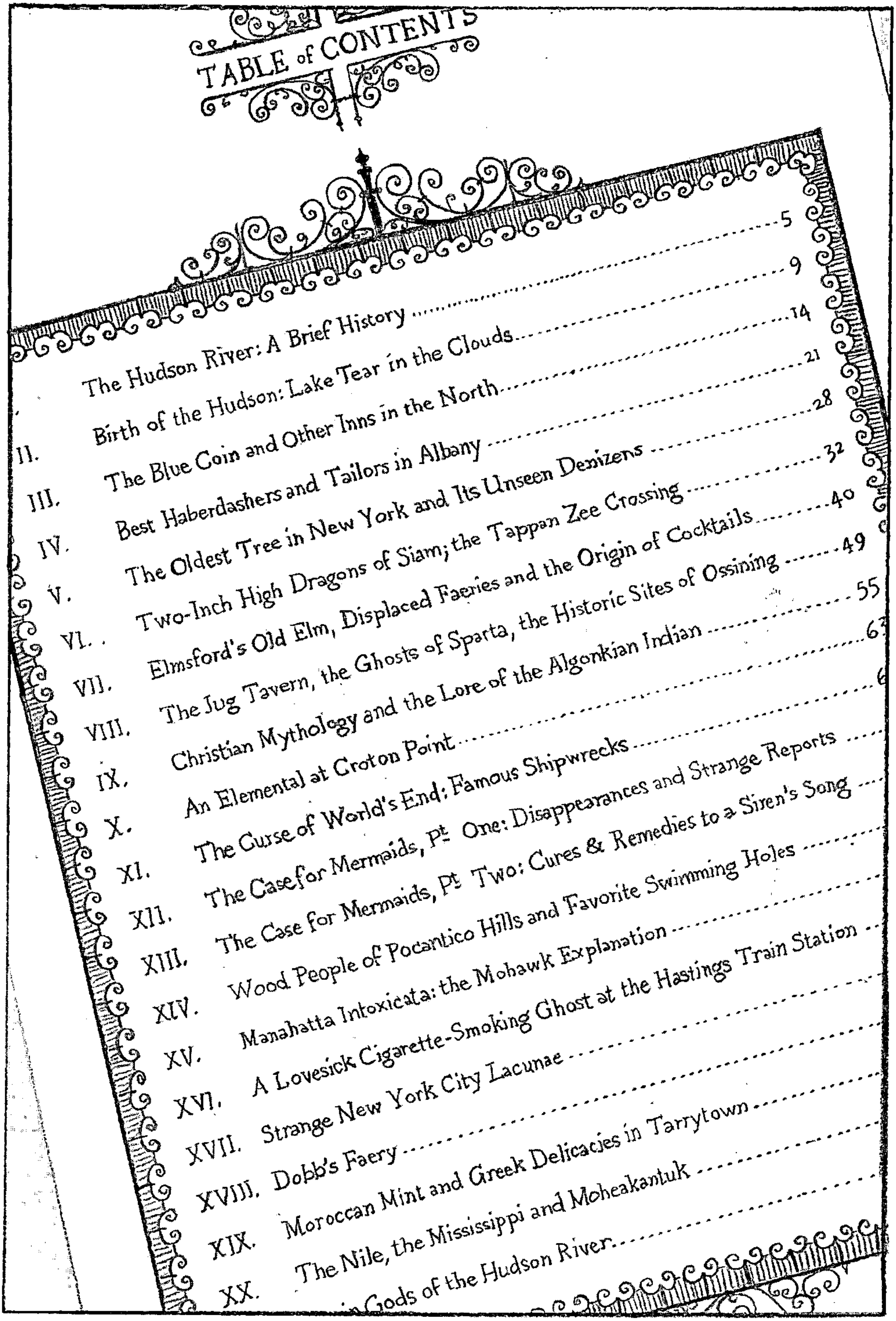
TABLE of CONTENTS
The Hudson River: A Brief History
II. Birth of the Hudson: Lake Tear in the Clouds
III. The Blue Coin and Other Inns in the North
IV. Best Haberdashers and Tailors in Albany
V. The Oldest Tree in New York and Its Unseen Denizens
VI. Two-Inch High Dragons of Siam; the Tappan Zee Crossing
VII. Elmsford's Old Elm, Displaced Faeries and the Origin of Cocktails
VIII. The Jug Tavern, the Ghosts of Sparta, the Historic Sites of Ossining
IX. Christian Mythology and the Lore of the Algonkian Indian
X. An Elemental at Croton Point
XI. The Curse of World's End: Famous Shipwrecks
XII. The Case for Mermaids, Pt One: Disappearances and Strange Reports
XIII. The Case for Mermaids, Pt Two: Cures & Remedies to a Siren's Song
XIV. Wood People of Pocantico Hills and Favorite Swimming Holes
XV. Manahatta Intoxicata: the Mohawk Explanation
XVI. A Lovesick Cigarette-Smoking Ghost at the Hastings Train Station
XVII. Strange New York City Lacunae
XVIII. Dobb's Faery
XIX. Moroccan Mint and Greek Delicacies in Tarrytown
XX. The Nile, the Mississippi and Moheakantuk
Gods of the Hudson River
5
9
14
21
28
32
40
49
55

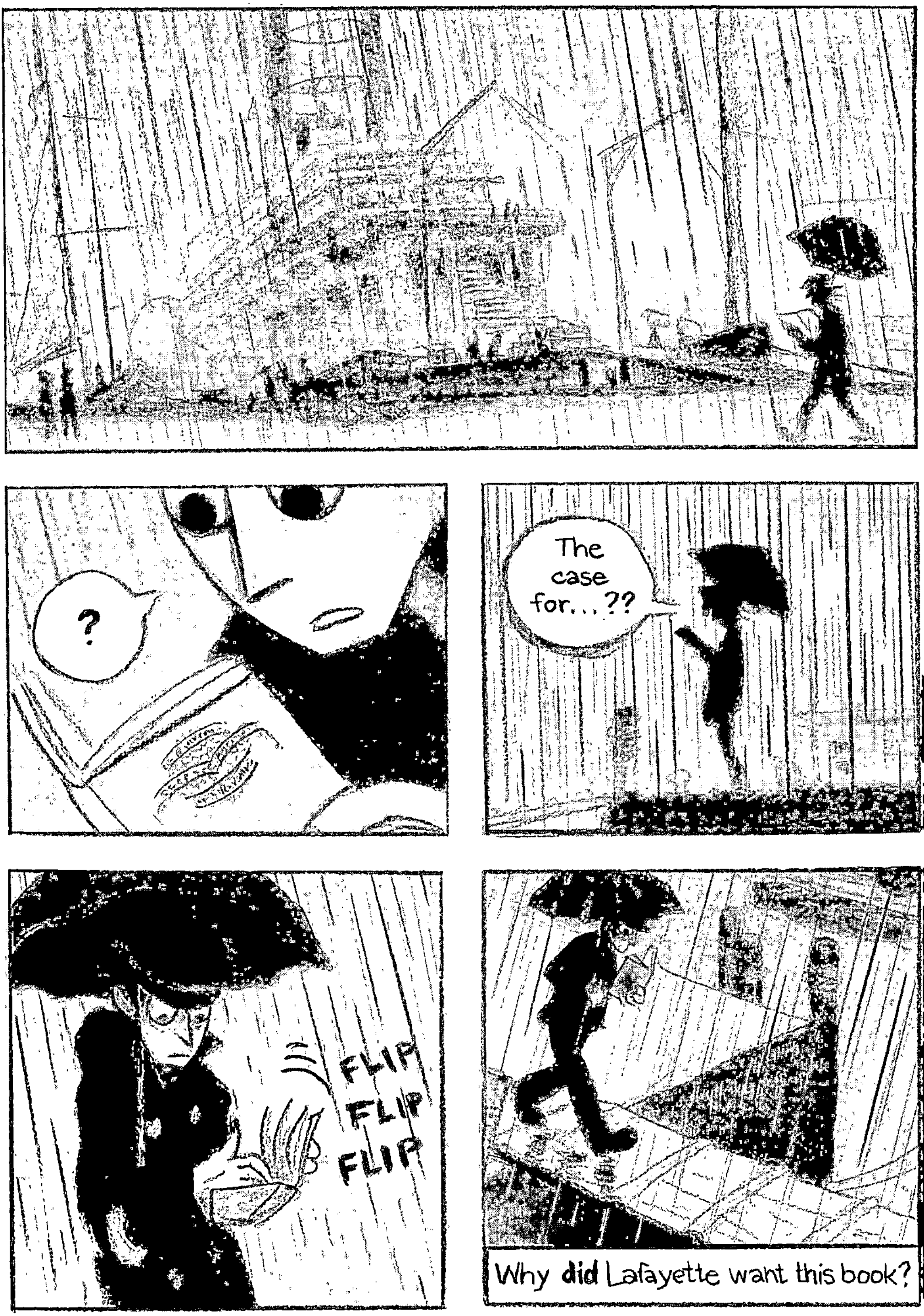
?
The case for...??
FLIP
FLIP
FLIP
Why did Lafayette want this book?

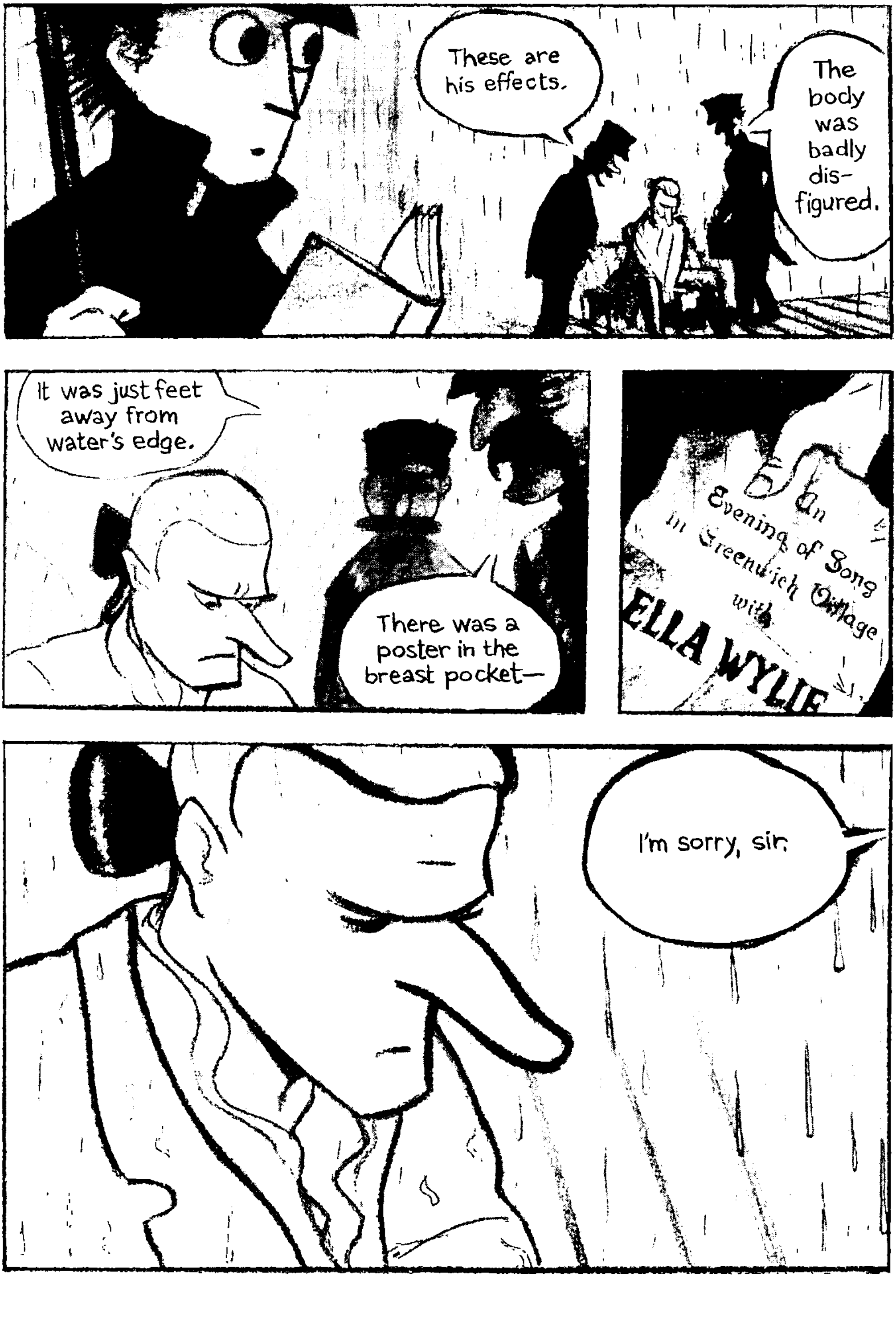
These are his effects.
The body was badly dis-figured.
It was just feet away from water's edge.
There was a poster in the breast pocket—
An Evening of Song in Greenwich Village with
ELLA WYLIE
I'm sorry, sir.

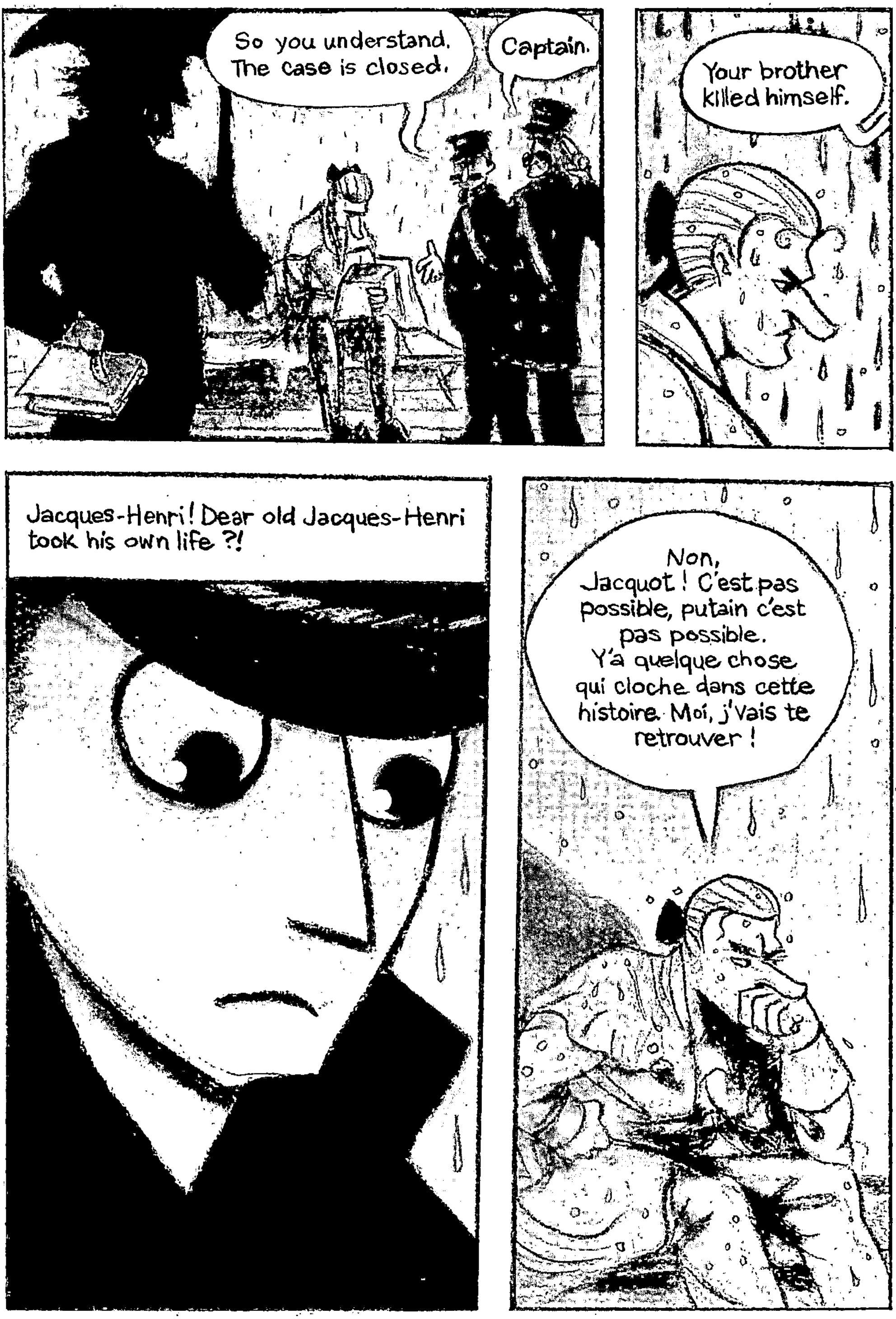
So you understand. The case is closed.
Captain.
Your brother killed himself.
Jacques-Henri! Dear old Jacques-Henri took his own life ?!
Non, Jacquot ! C'est pas possible, putain c'est pas possible. Y'a quelque chose qui cloche dans cette histoire. Moi, j'vais te retrouver !

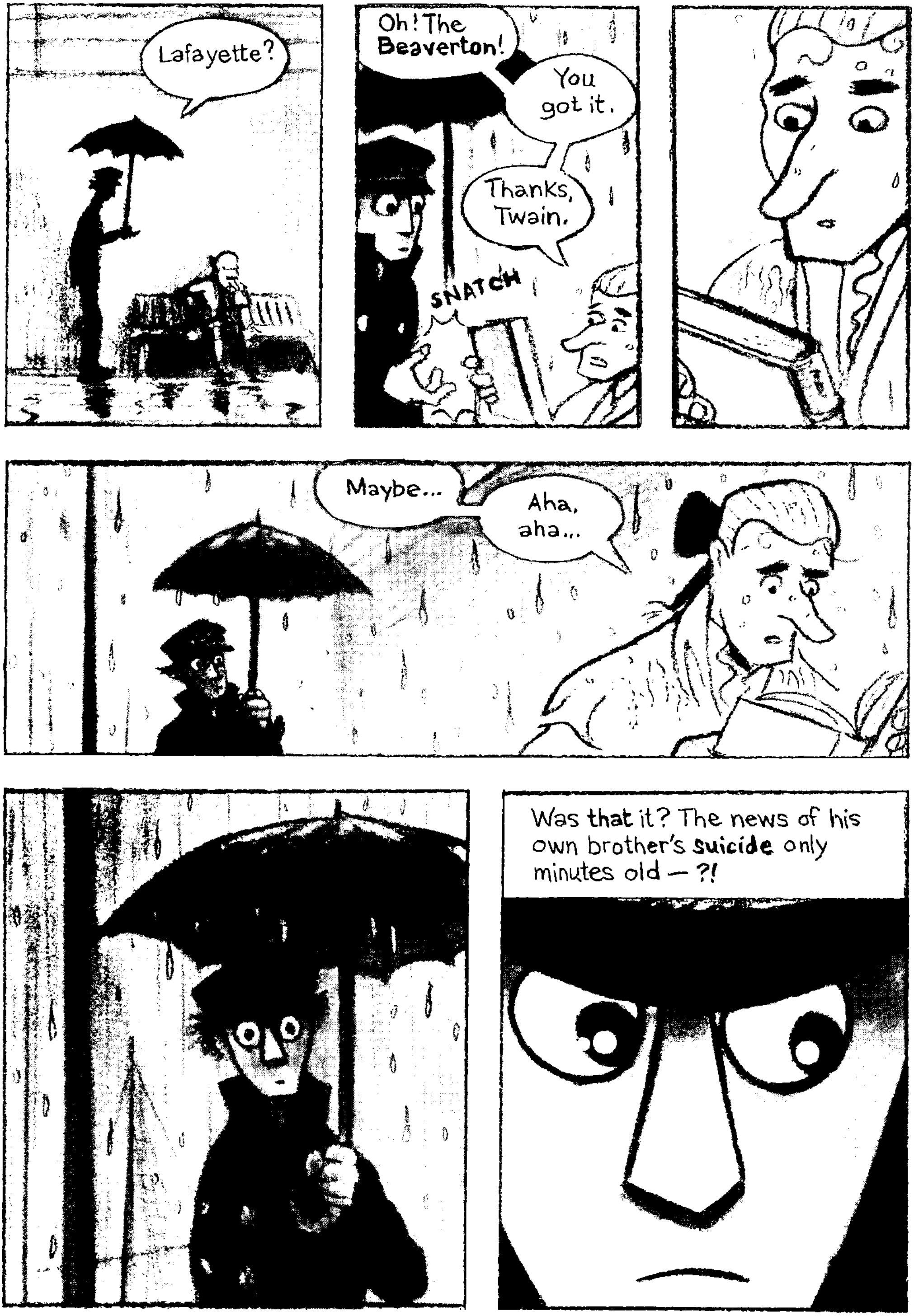
Lafayette?
Oh! The **Beaverton**!
You got it.
Thanks, Twain.
SNATCH
Maybe...
Aha, aha...
Was **that** it? The news of his own brother's **suicide** only minutes old — ?!

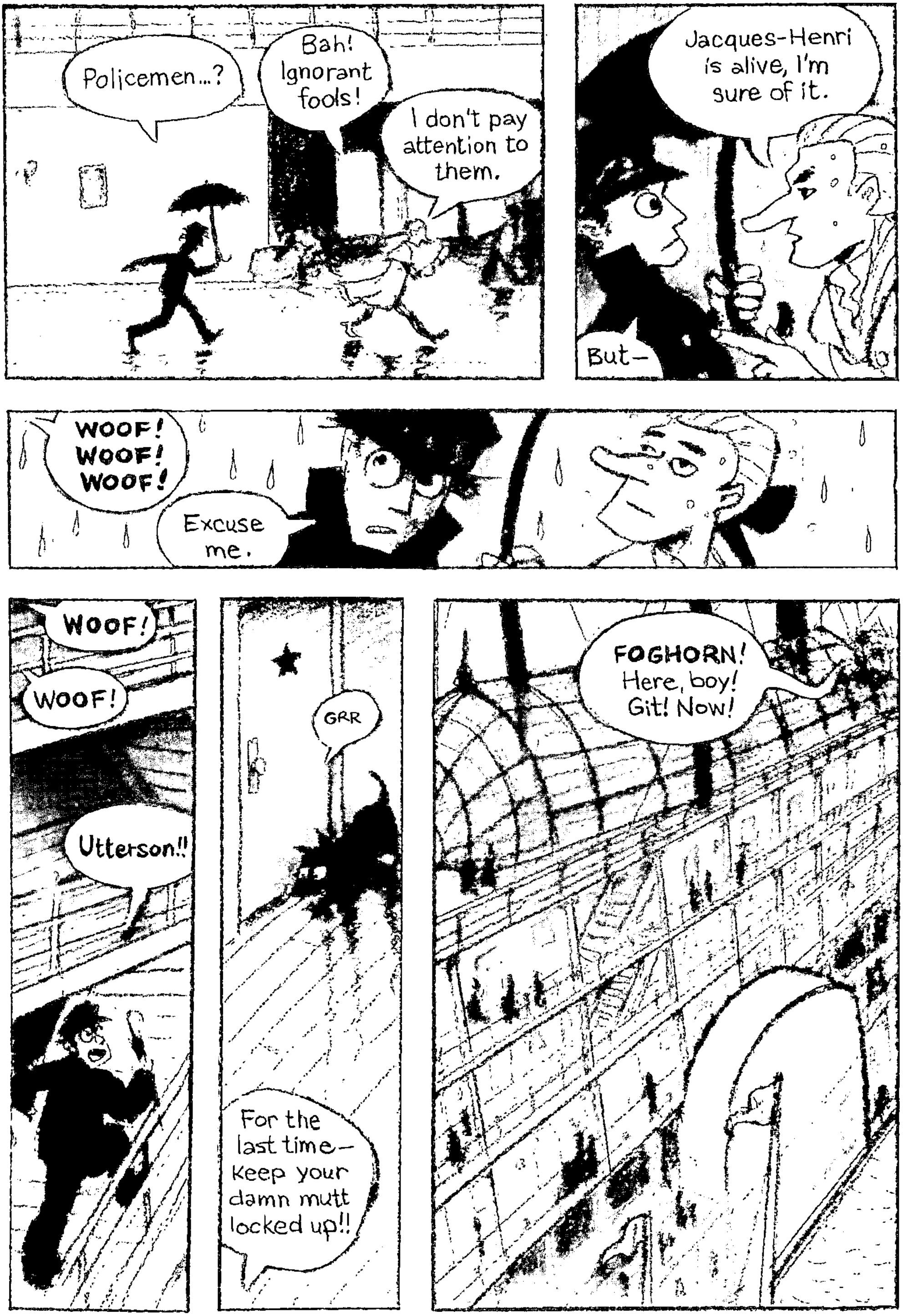
Policemen...?
Bah! Ignorant fools!
I don't pay attention to them.
Jacques-Henri is alive, I'm sure of it.
But—
WOOF! WOOF! WOOF!
Excuse me.
WOOF!
WOOF!
Utterson!!
GRR
For the last time— Keep your damn mutt locked up!!
FOGHORN! Here, boy! Git! Now!

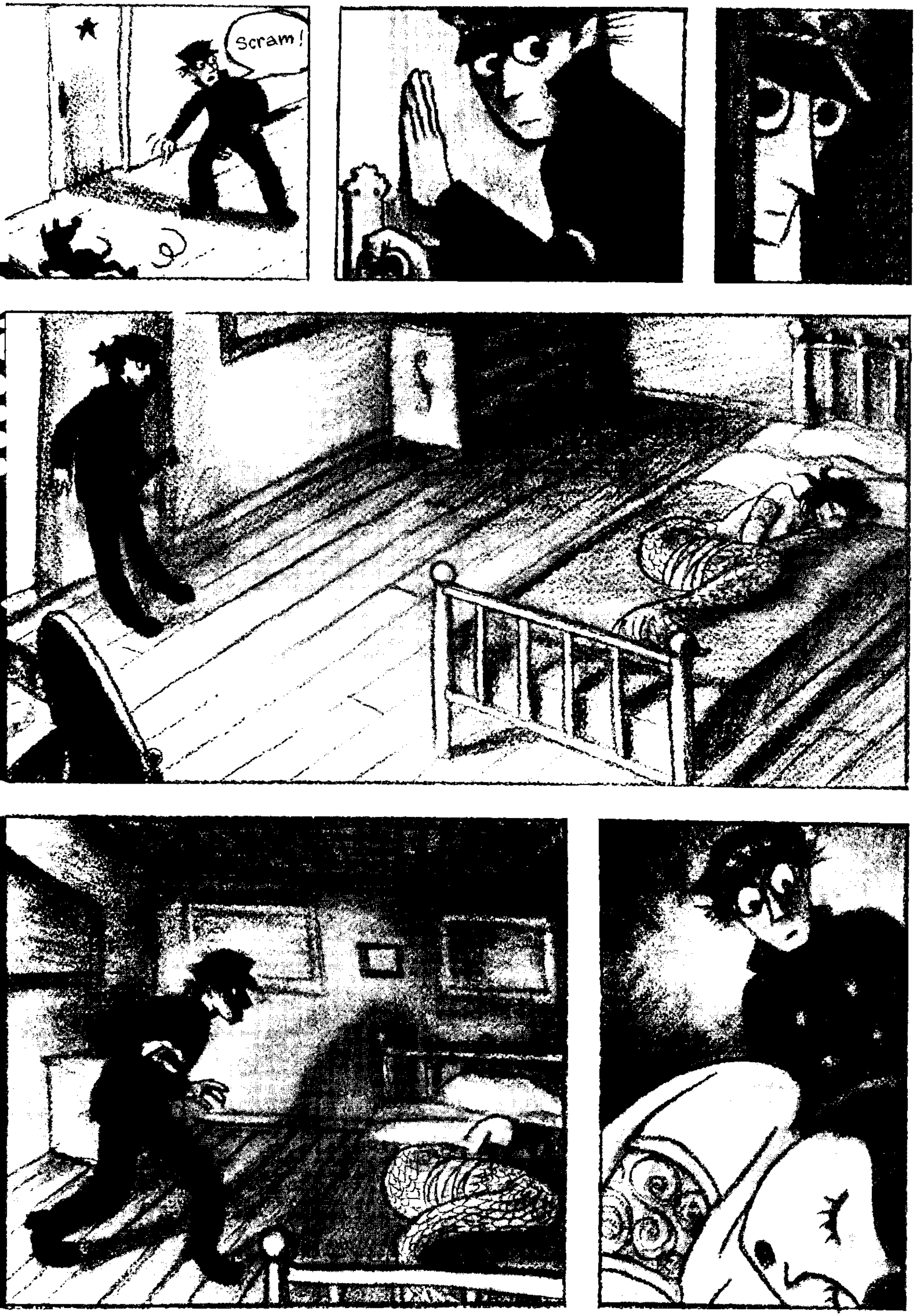
Scram!

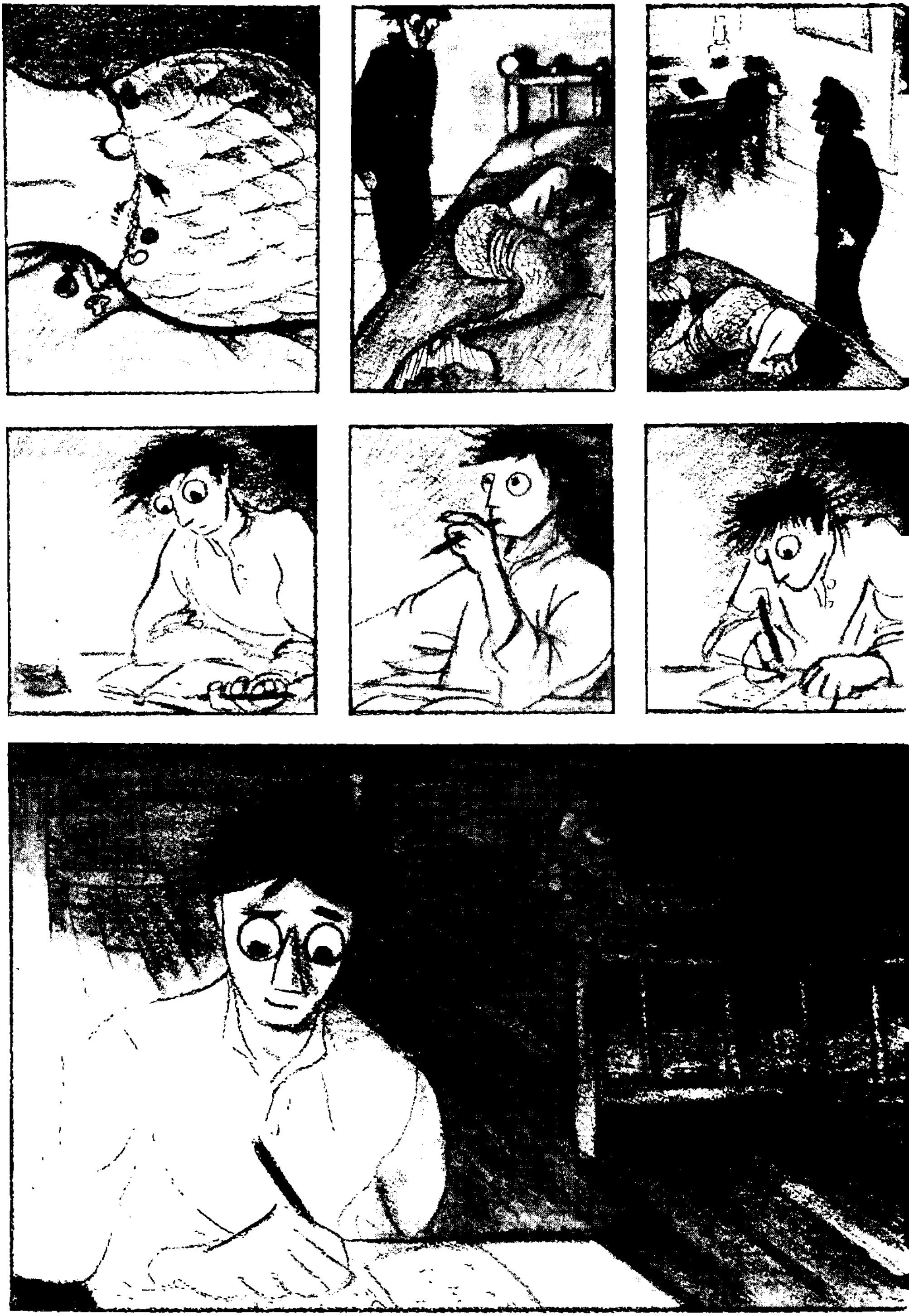

Pt 1, Chap.6

"LAFAYETTE'S LETTER"

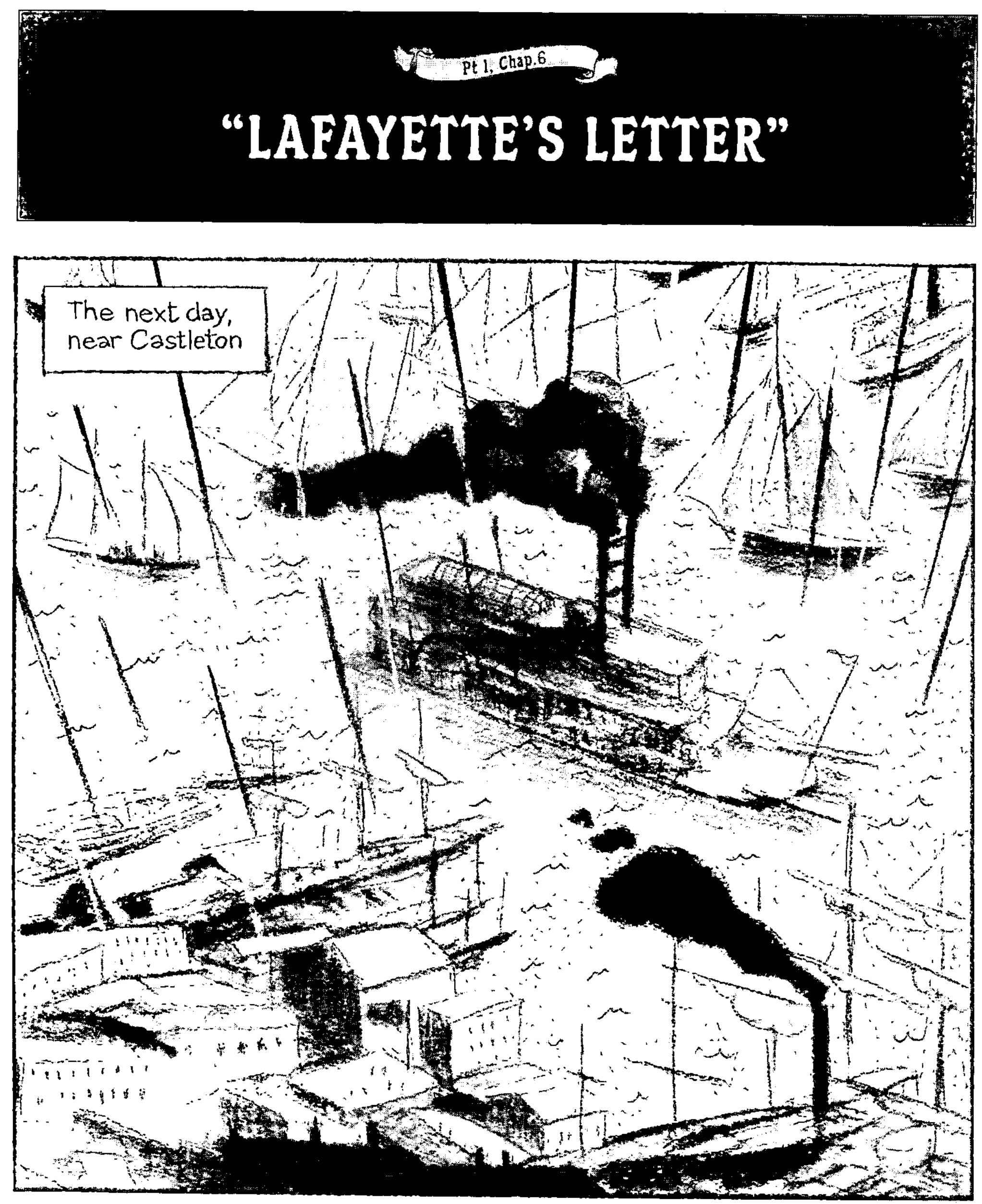
The next day, near Castleton

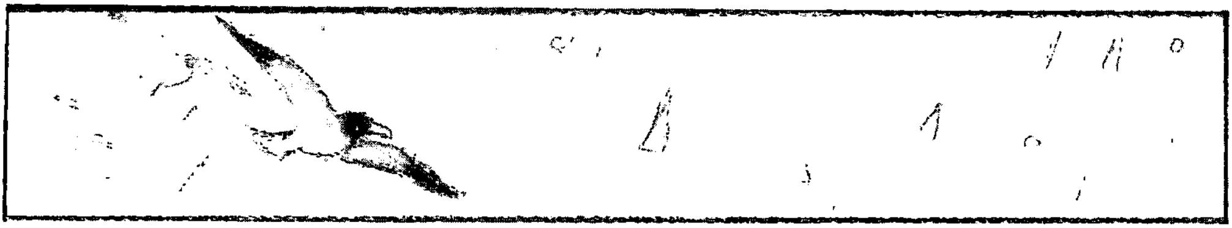

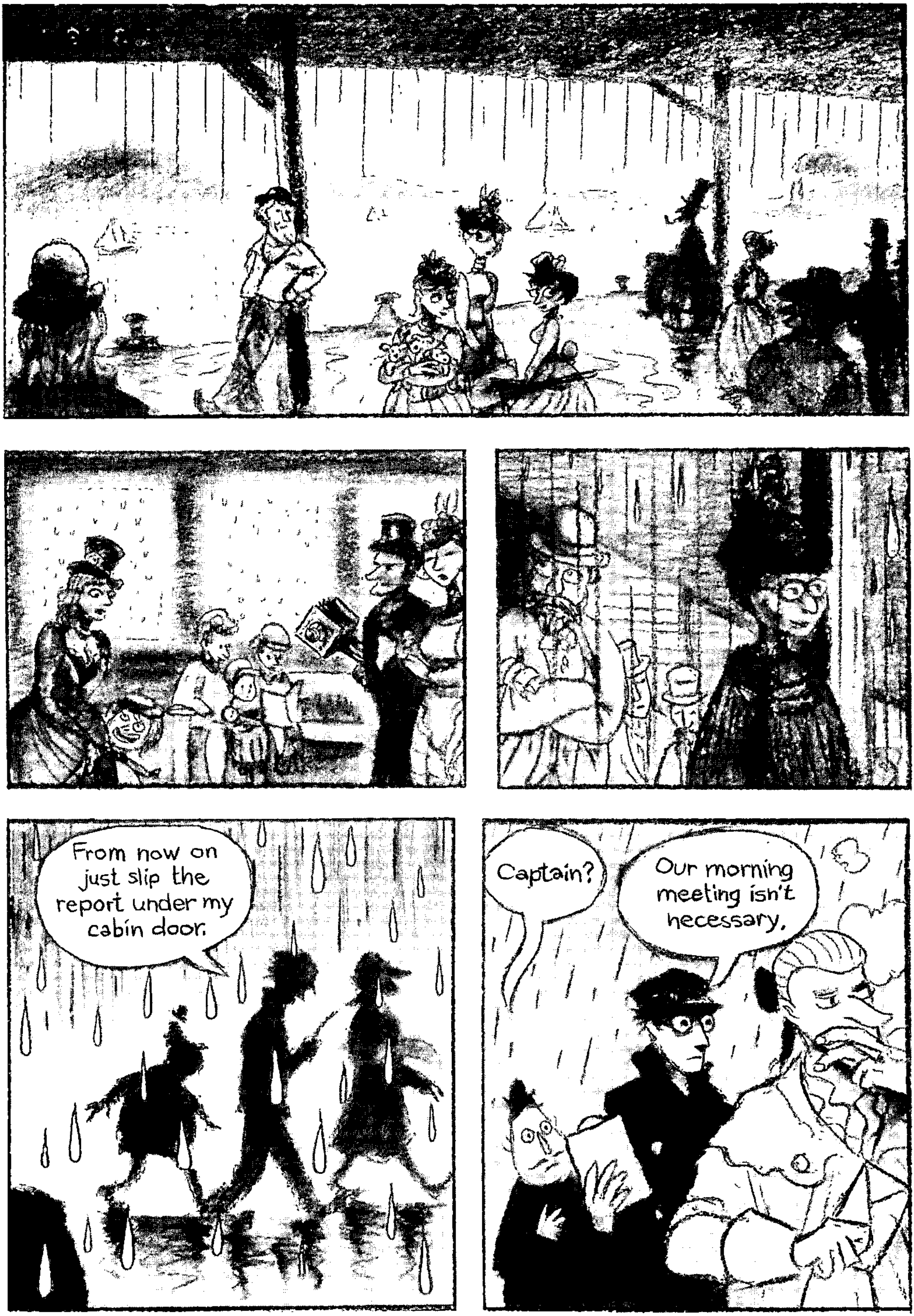
From now on just slip the report under my cabin door.
Captain?
Our morning meeting isn't necessary.

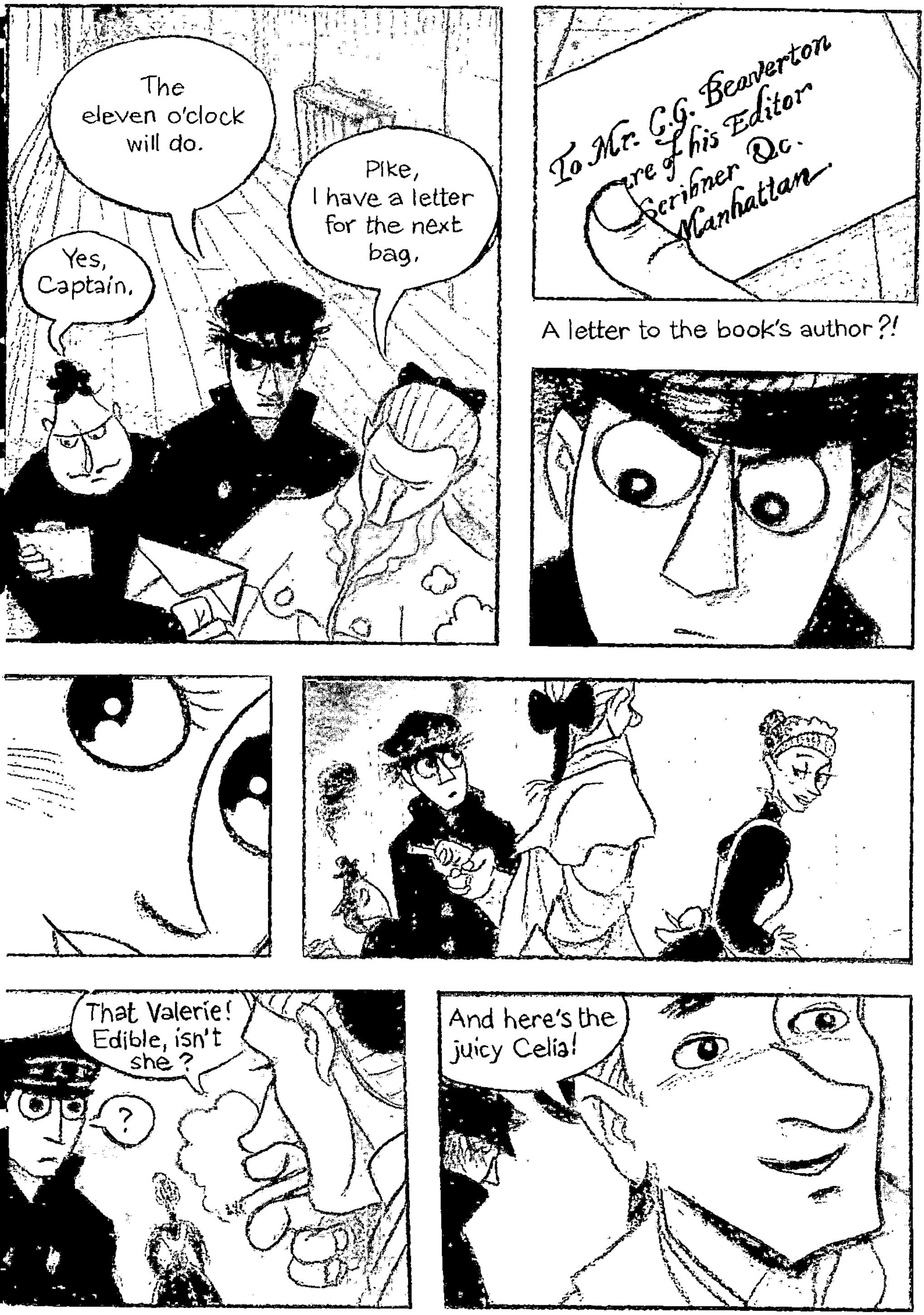
The eleven o'clock will do.
Yes, Captain.
Pike, I have a letter for the next bag.
To Mr. C.G. Beaverton
Care of his Editor
Scribner Co.
Manhattan
A letter to the book's author?!
That Valerie! Edible, isn't she?
?
And here's the juicy Celia!

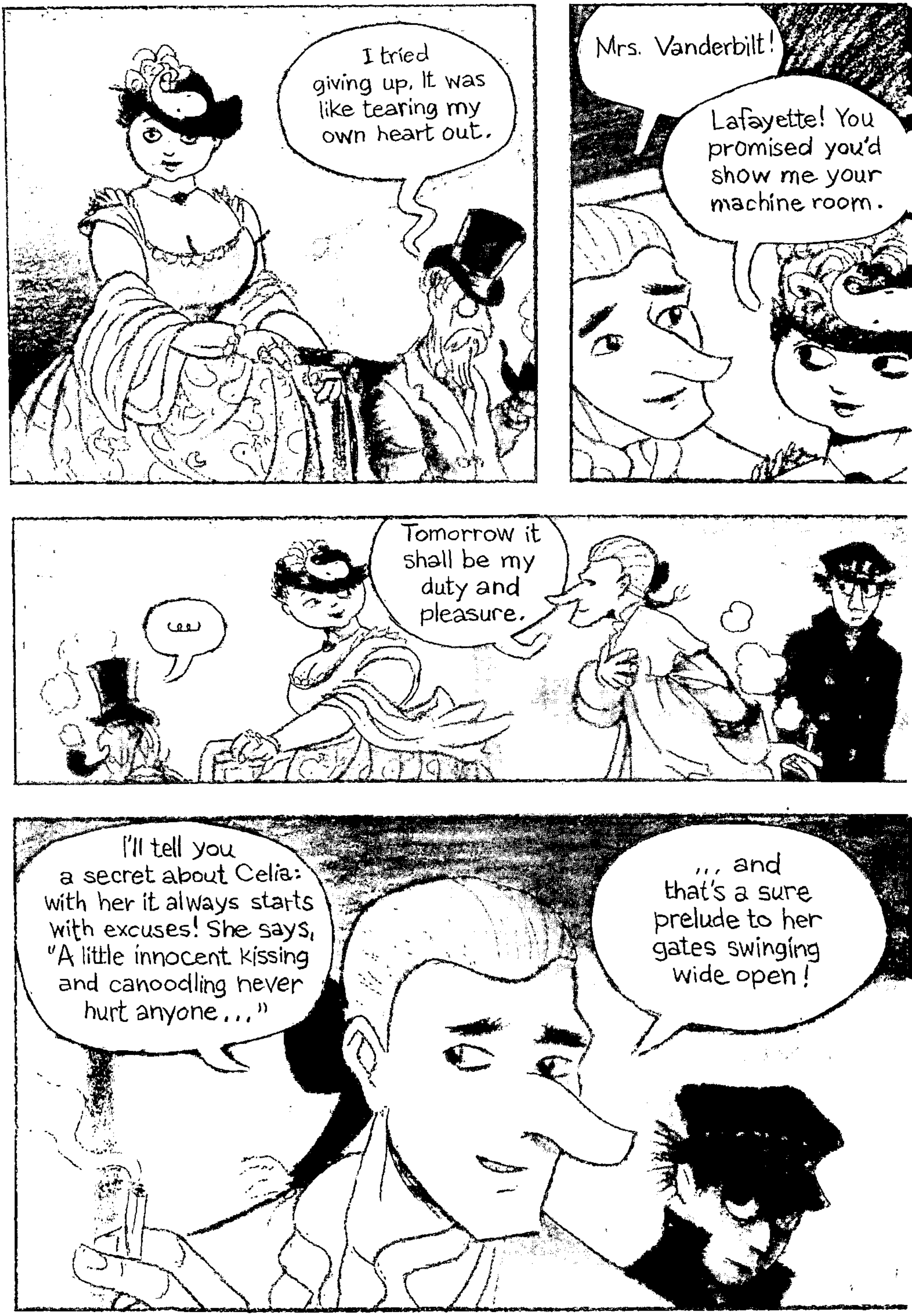
I tried giving up. It was like tearing my own heart out.
Mrs. Vanderbilt!
Lafayette! You promised you'd show me your machine room.
Tomorrow it shall be my duty and pleasure.
I'll tell you a secret about Celia: with her it always starts with excuses! She says, "A little innocent kissing and canoodling never hurt anyone..."
... and that's a sure prelude to her gates swinging wide open!

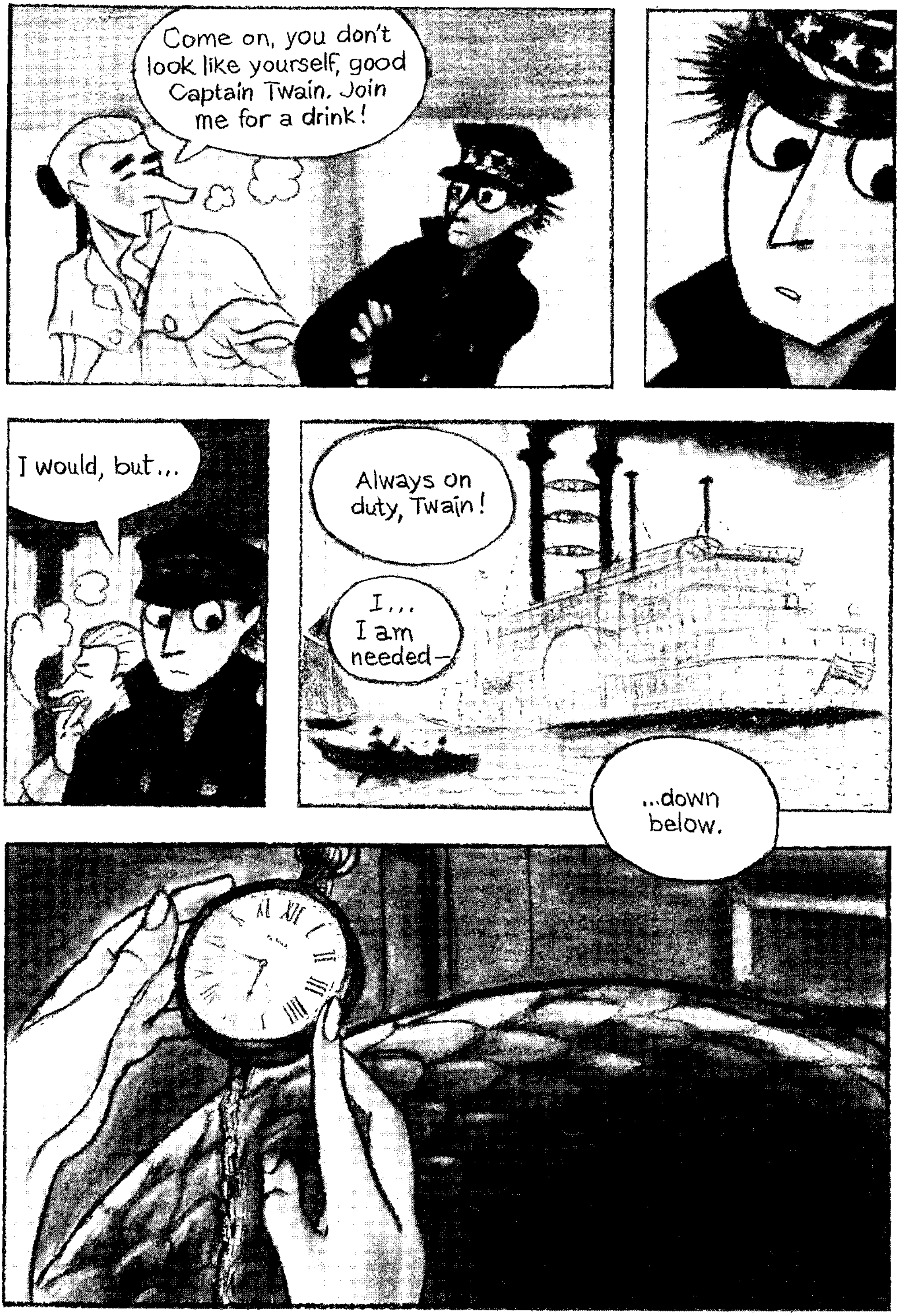
Come on, you don't look like yourself, good Captain Twain. Join me for a drink!
I would, but...
Always on duty, Twain!
I... I am needed—
...down below.

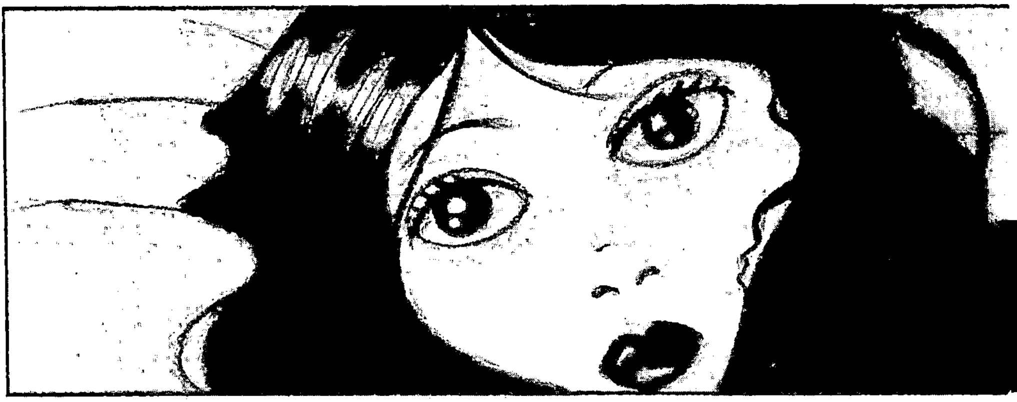

I continued to change her bandage daily. She would wake up for short spells and then fall back asleep.

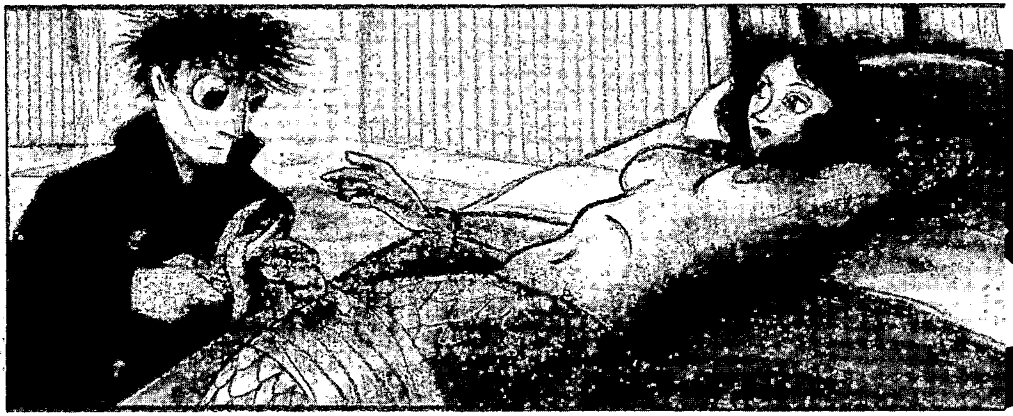

She and I told each other things.

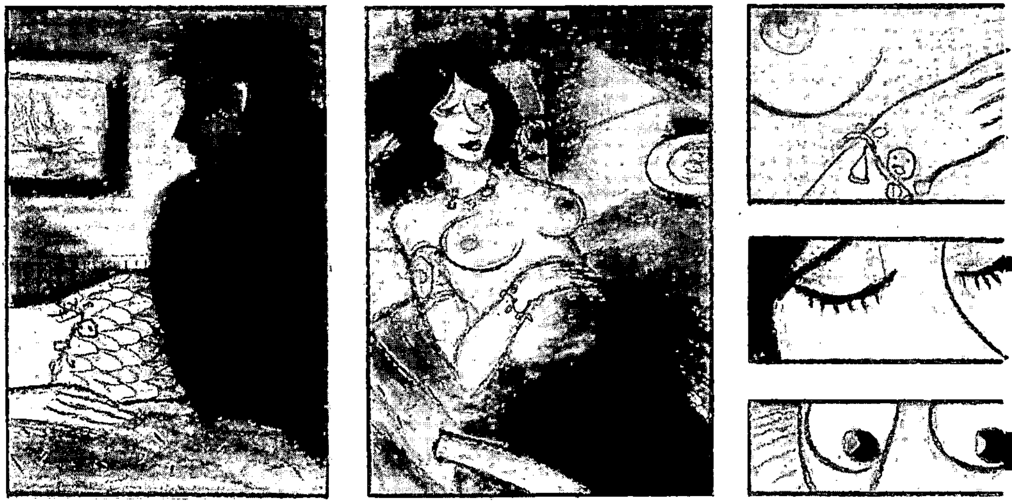

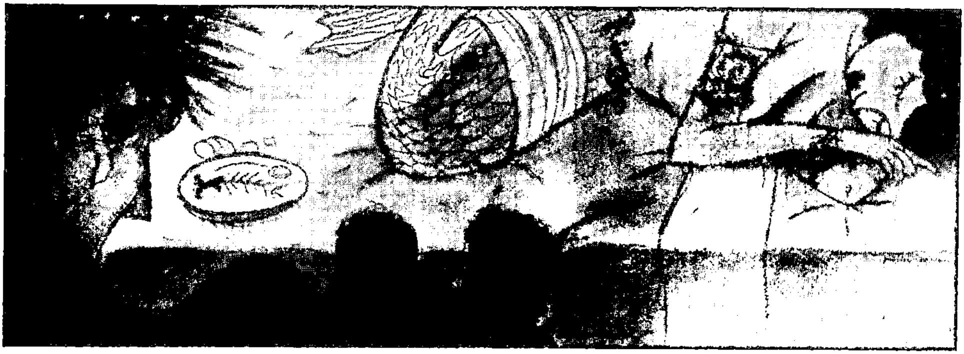

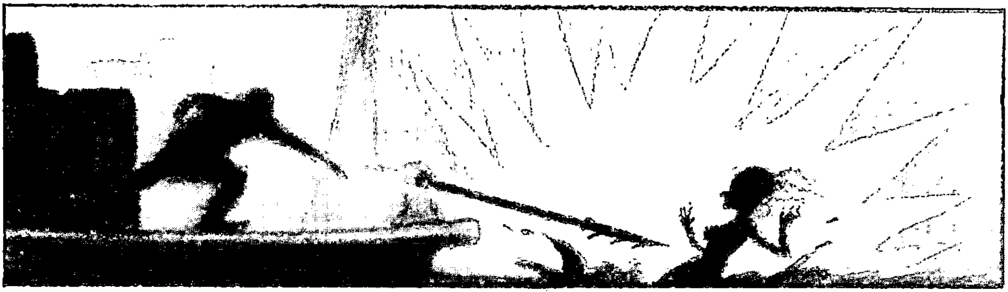

She told me she had been **harpooned.**

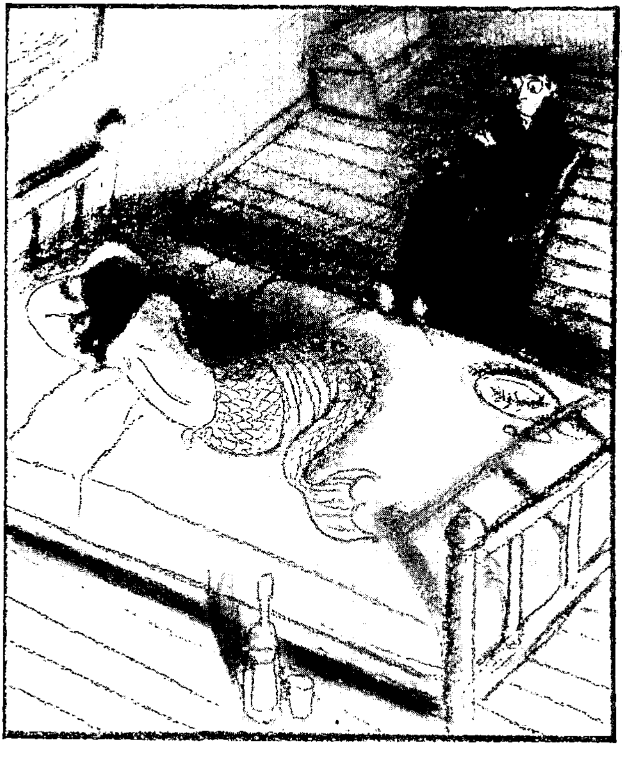

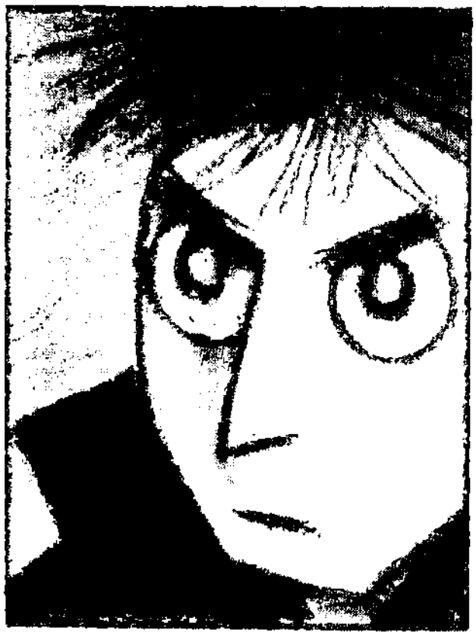

Who would do such a thing?

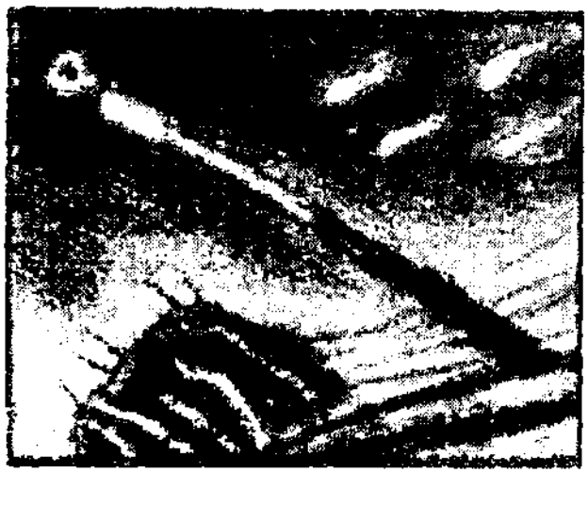

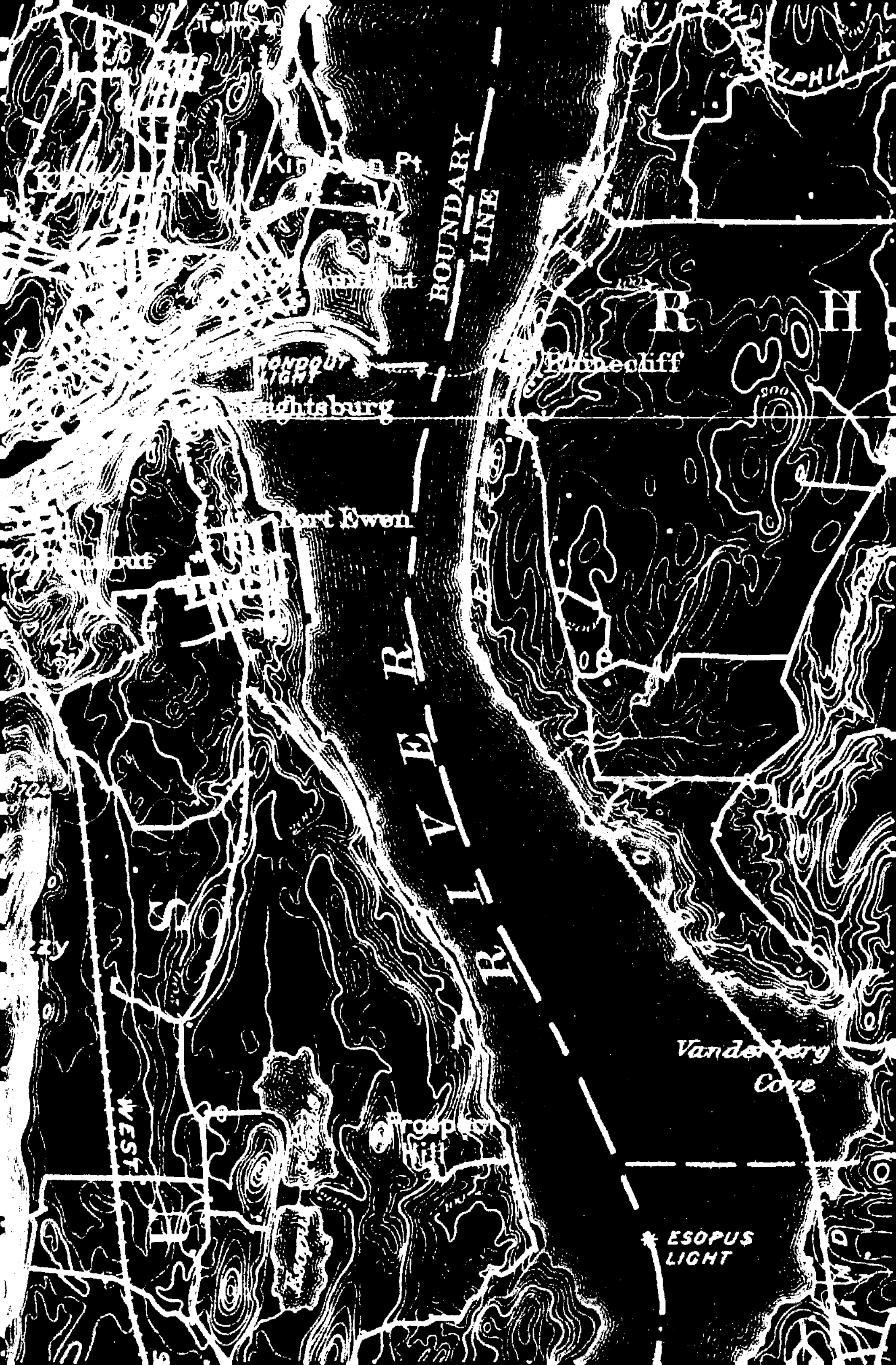
BOUNDARY LINE
Rhinecliff
Port Ewen
RIVER
WEST
ESOPUS LIGHT

Pt 1, Chap.7

"SOUTH'S PROMISE"

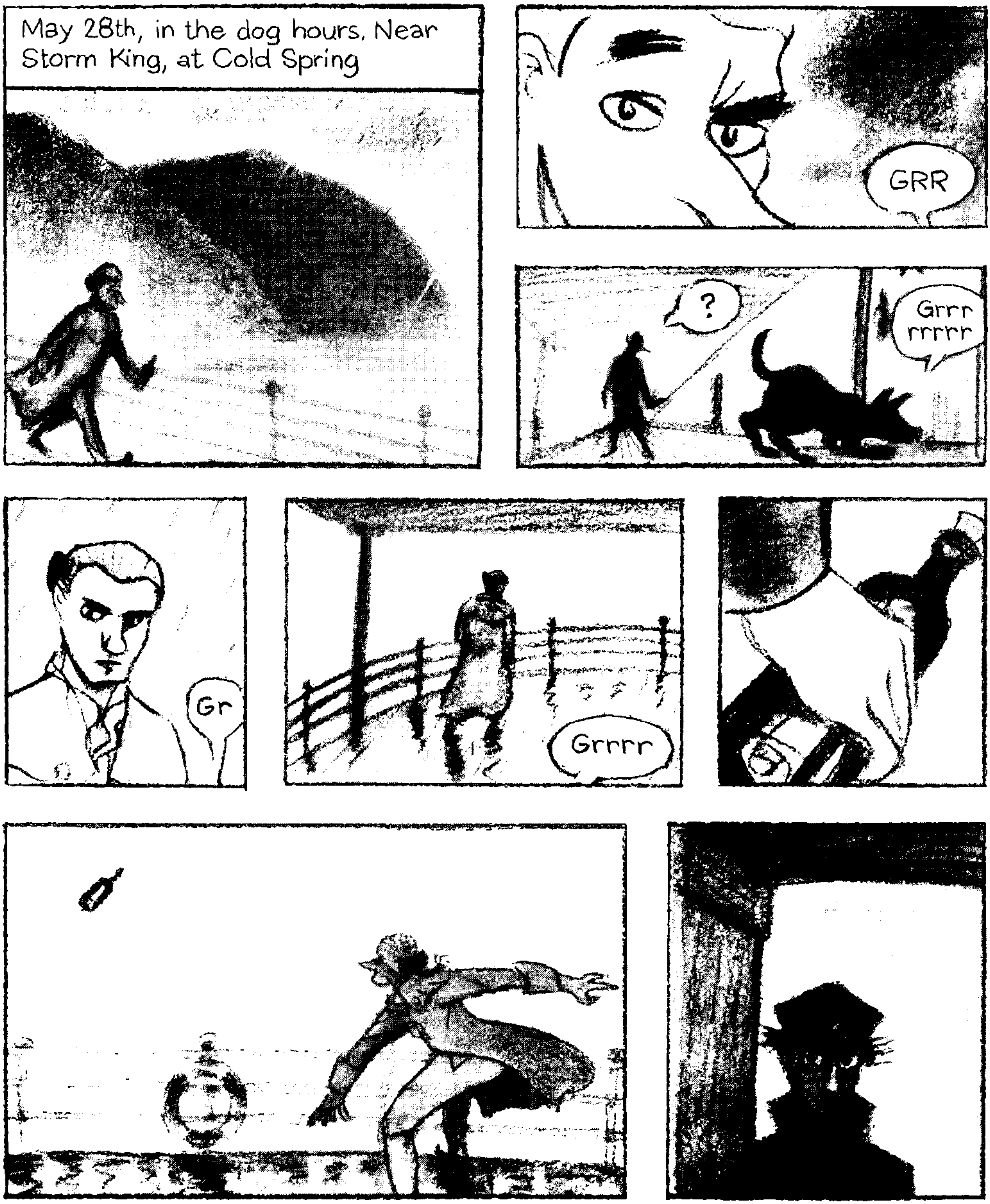
May 28th, in the dog hours, Near Storm King, at Cold Spring
GRR
?
Grrr rrrrr
Gr
Grrrr

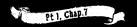

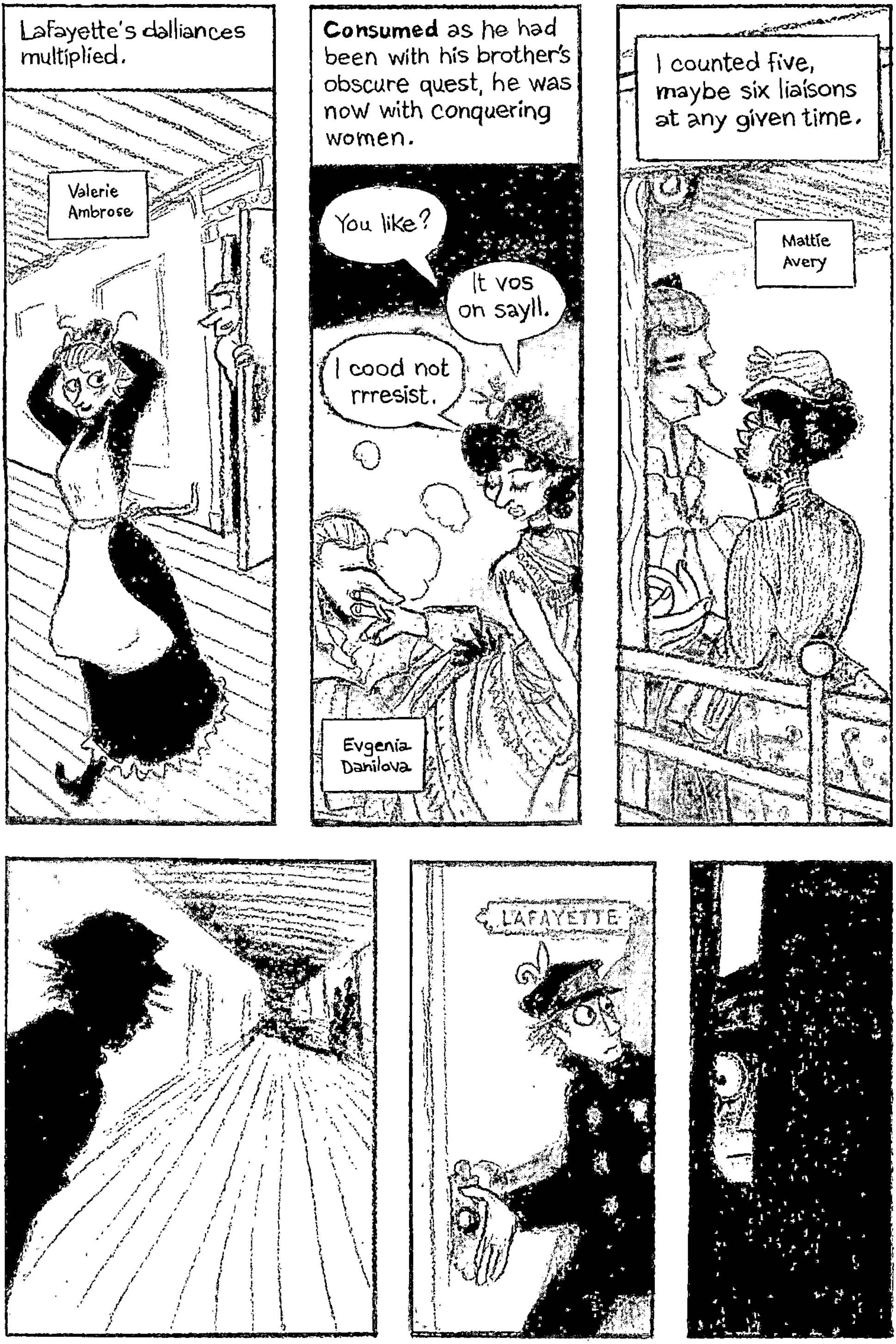
Lafayette's dalliances multiplied.
Valerie Ambrose
Consumed as he had been with his brother's obscure quest, he was now with conquering women.
You like?
It vos on sayll.
I cood not rrresist.
Evgenia Danilova
I counted five, maybe six liaisons at any given time.
Mattie Avery
LAFAYETTE

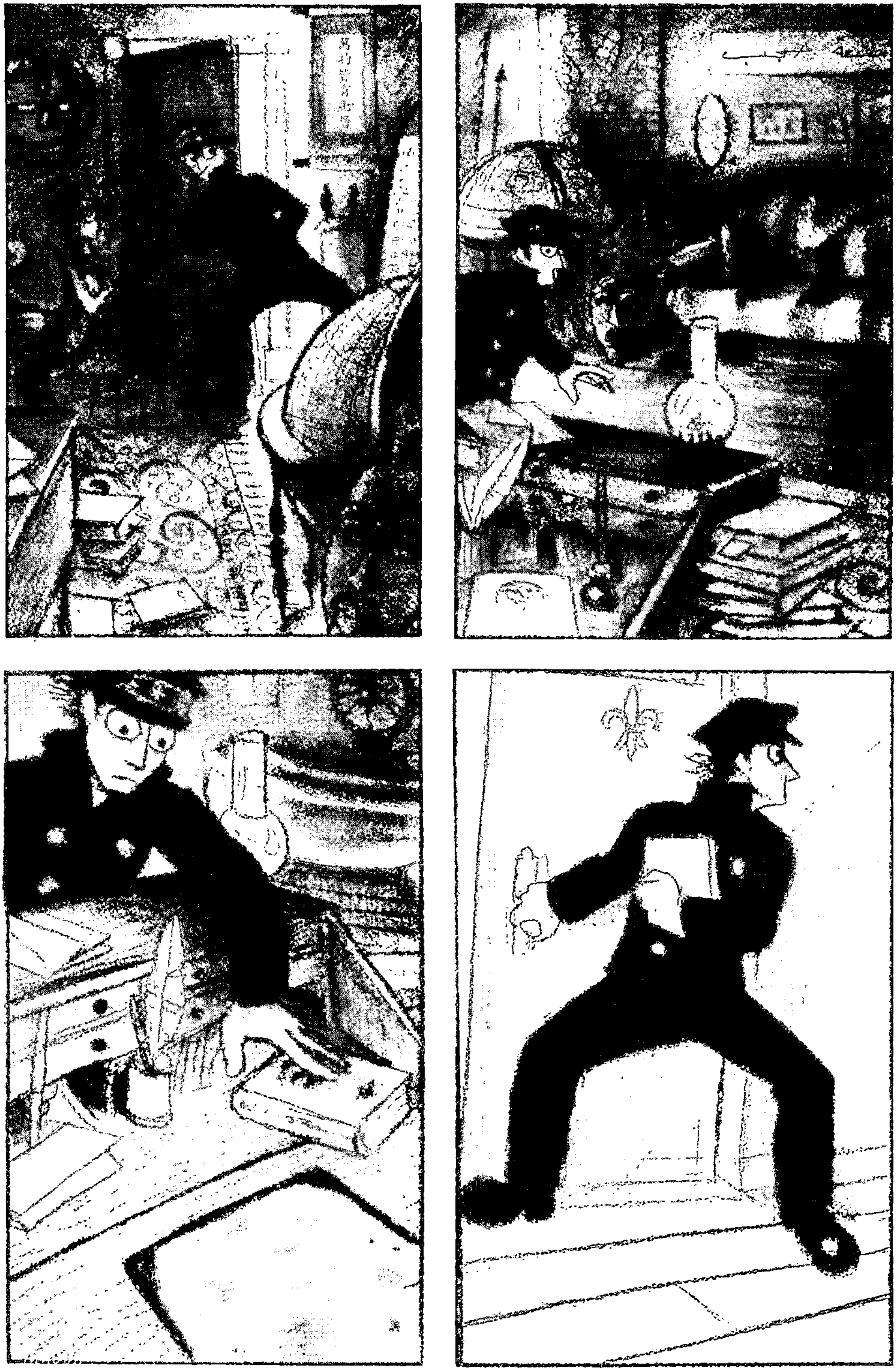

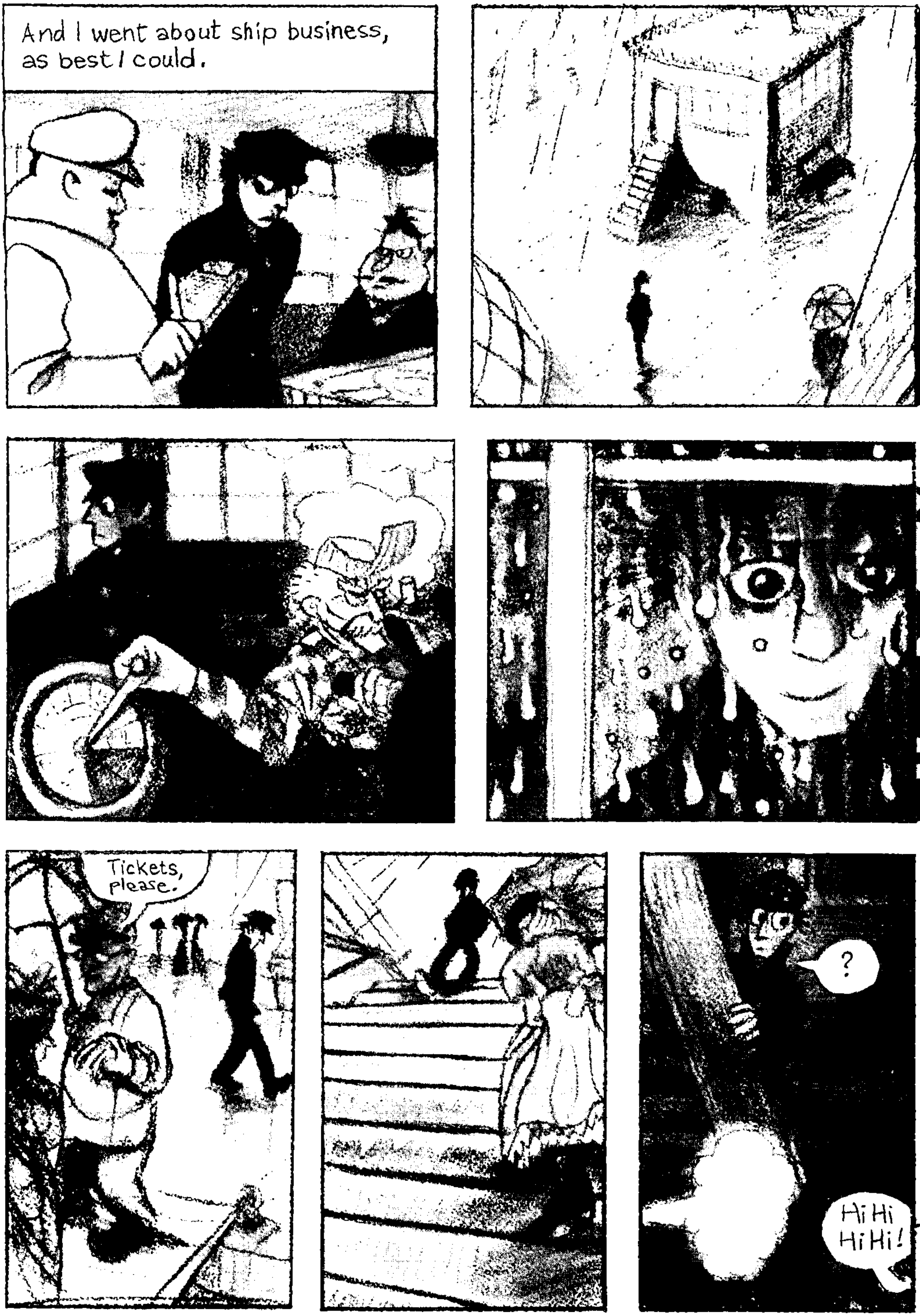
And I went about ship business, as best I could.
Tickets, please.
?
Hi Hi Hi Hi!

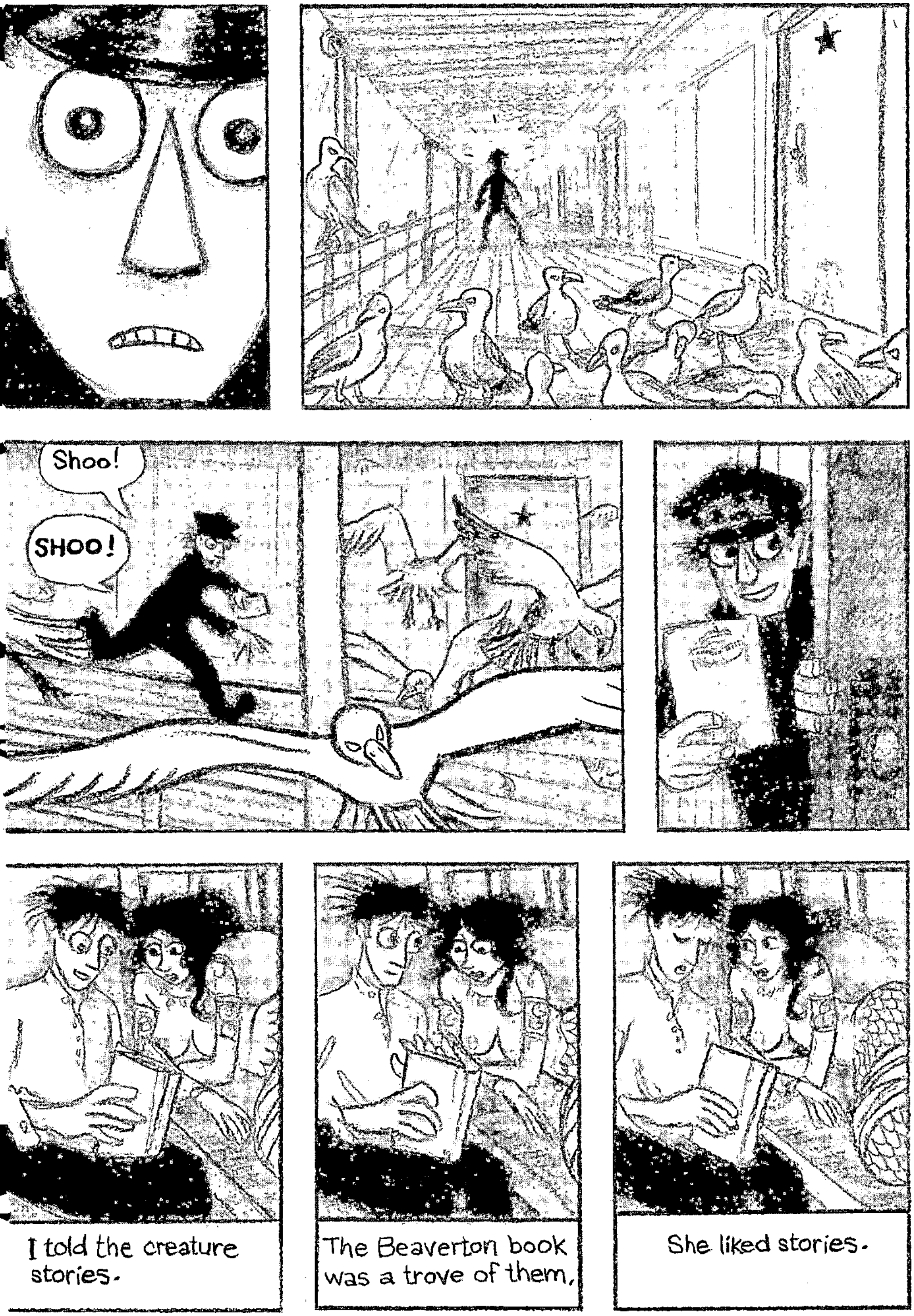
Shoo!
SHOO!
I told the creature stories.
The Beaverton book was a trove of them,
She liked stories.

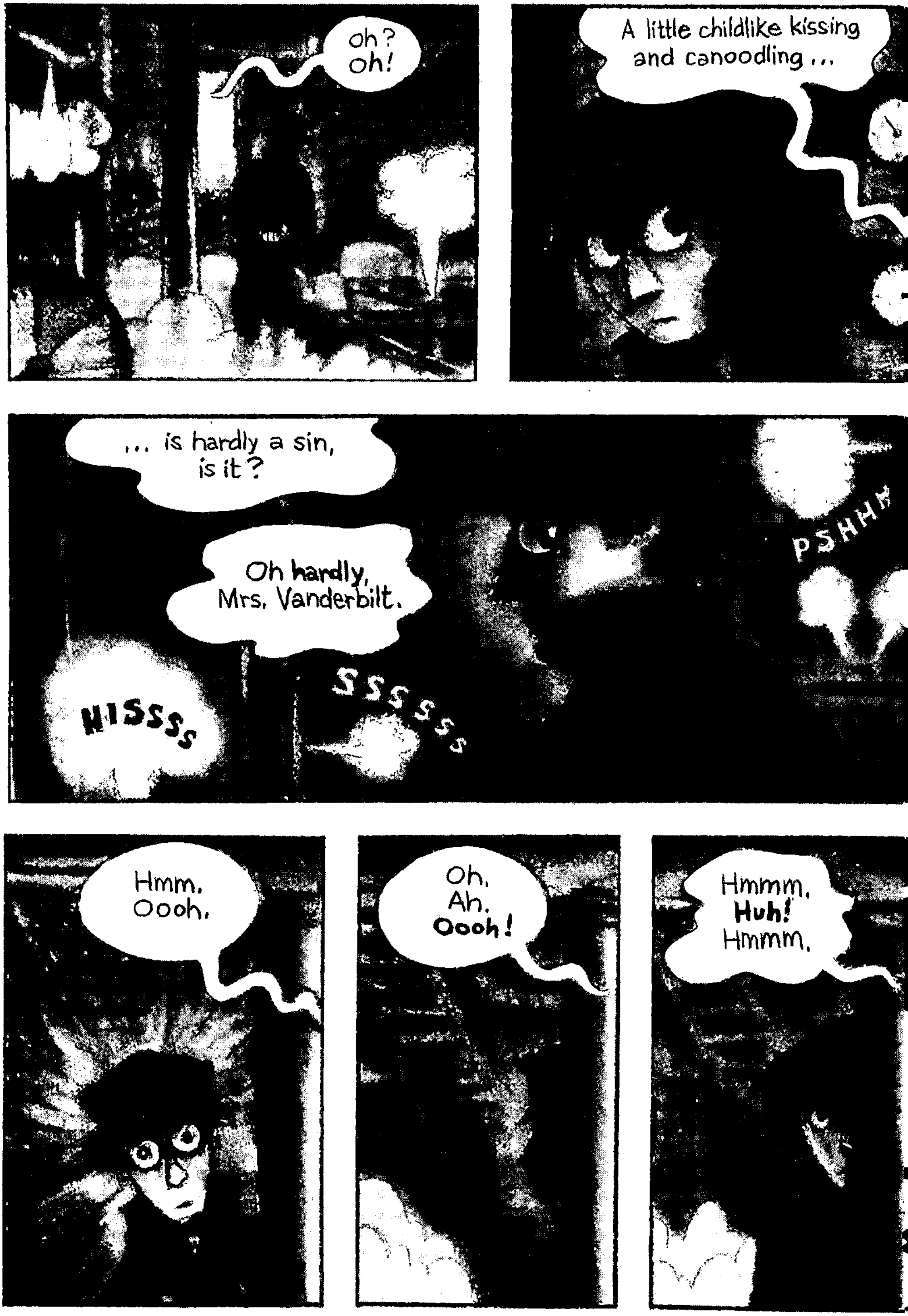
oh? oh!
A little childlike kissing and canoodling ...
... is hardly a sin, is it?
Oh hardly, Mrs. Vanderbilt.
PSHHH
HISSSS
SSSSSS
Hmm. Oooh.
Oh. Ah. Oooh!
Hmmm. Huh! Hmmm.

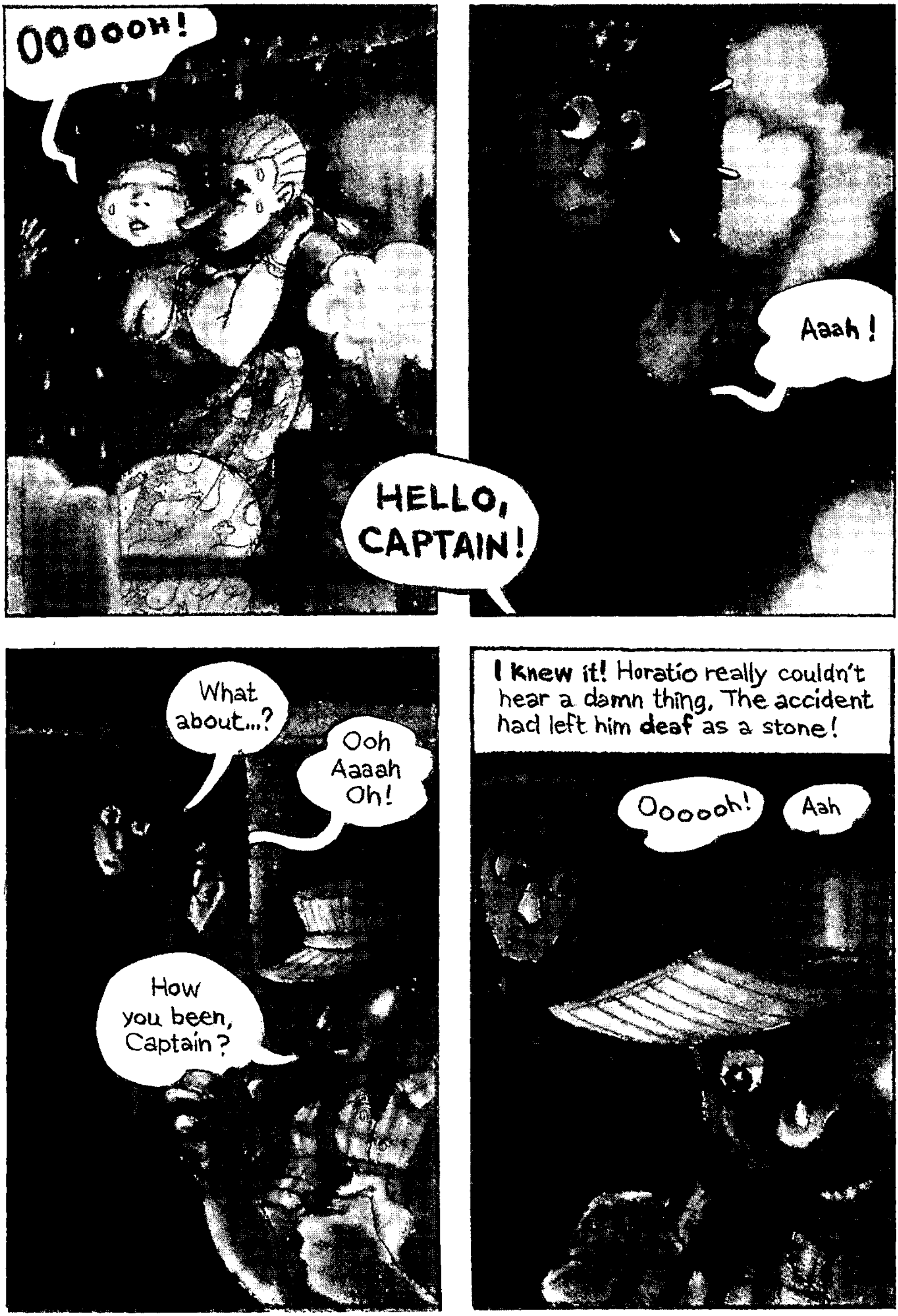
OOOOOH!
HELLO, CAPTAIN!
Aaah!
What about...?
Ooh Aaaah Oh!
How you been, Captain?
I knew it! Horatio really couldn't hear a damn thing. The accident had left him deaf as a stone!
Oooooh!
Aah

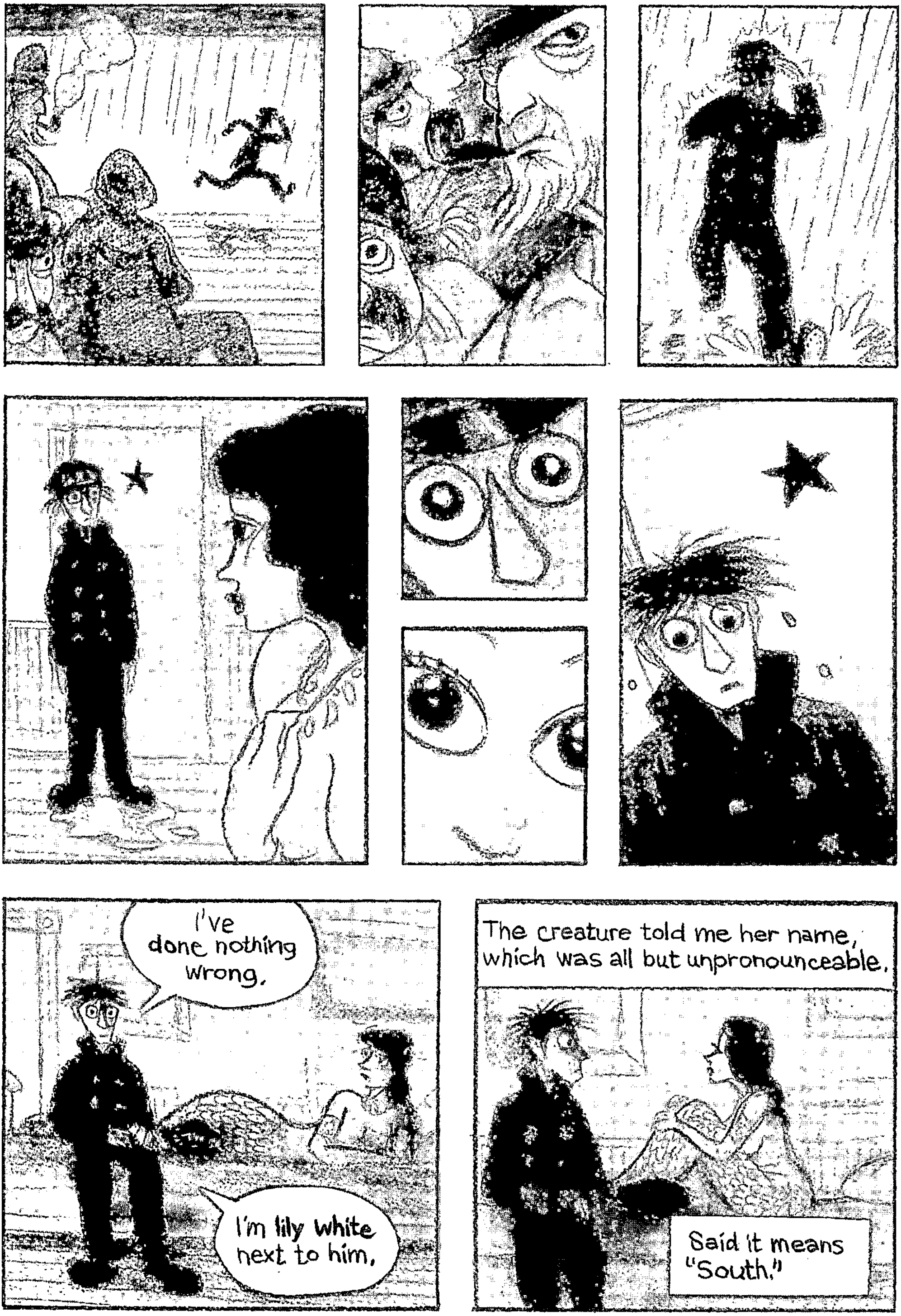
I've done nothing wrong.
I'm lily white next to him.
The creature told me her name, which was all but unpronounceable.
Said it means "South."

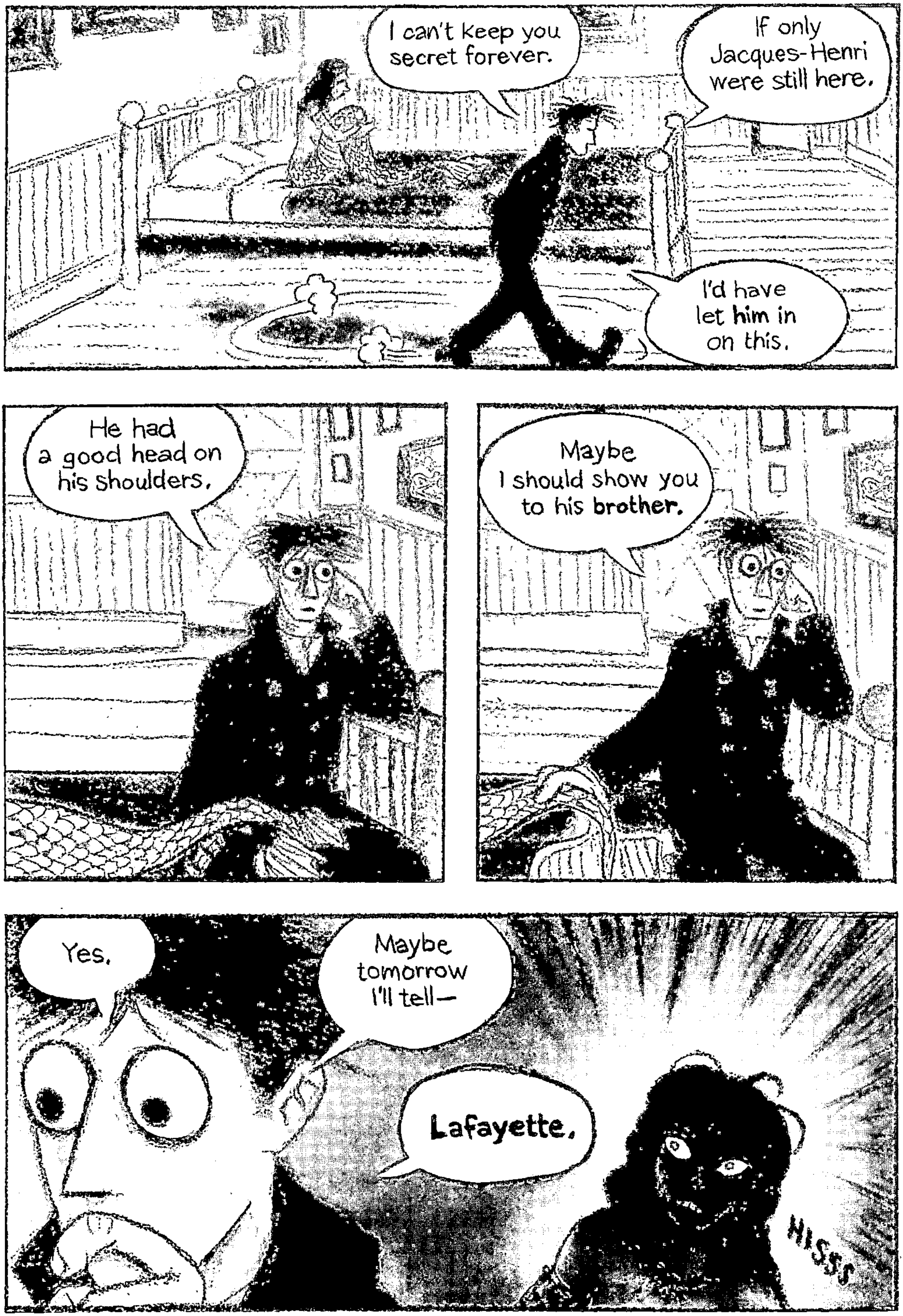
I can't keep you secret forever.
If only Jacques-Henri were still here.
I'd have let **him** in on this.
He had a good head on his shoulders.
Maybe I should show you to his **brother.**
Yes.
Maybe tomorrow I'll tell—
Lafayette.
HISSS

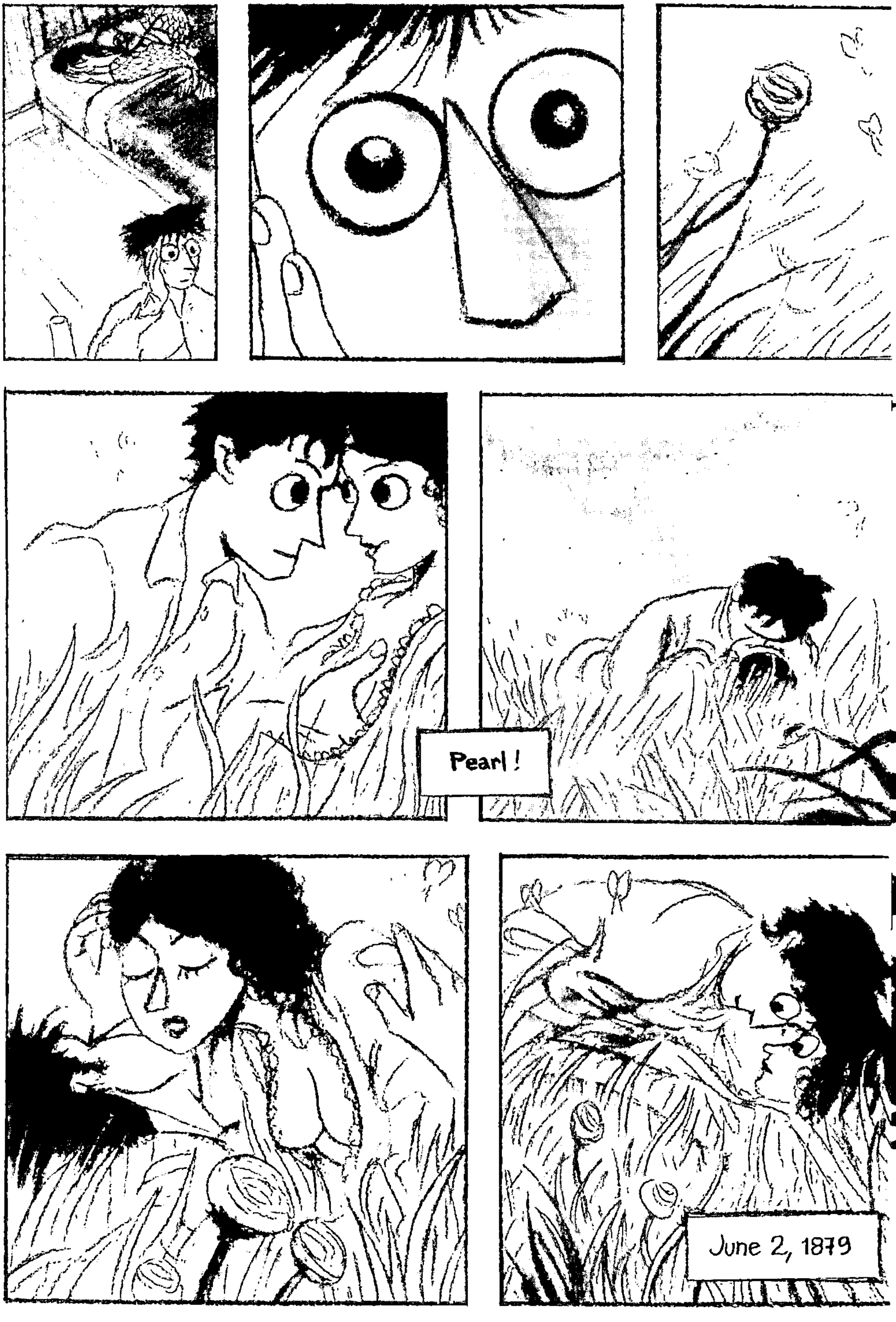
Pearl!
June 2, 1879

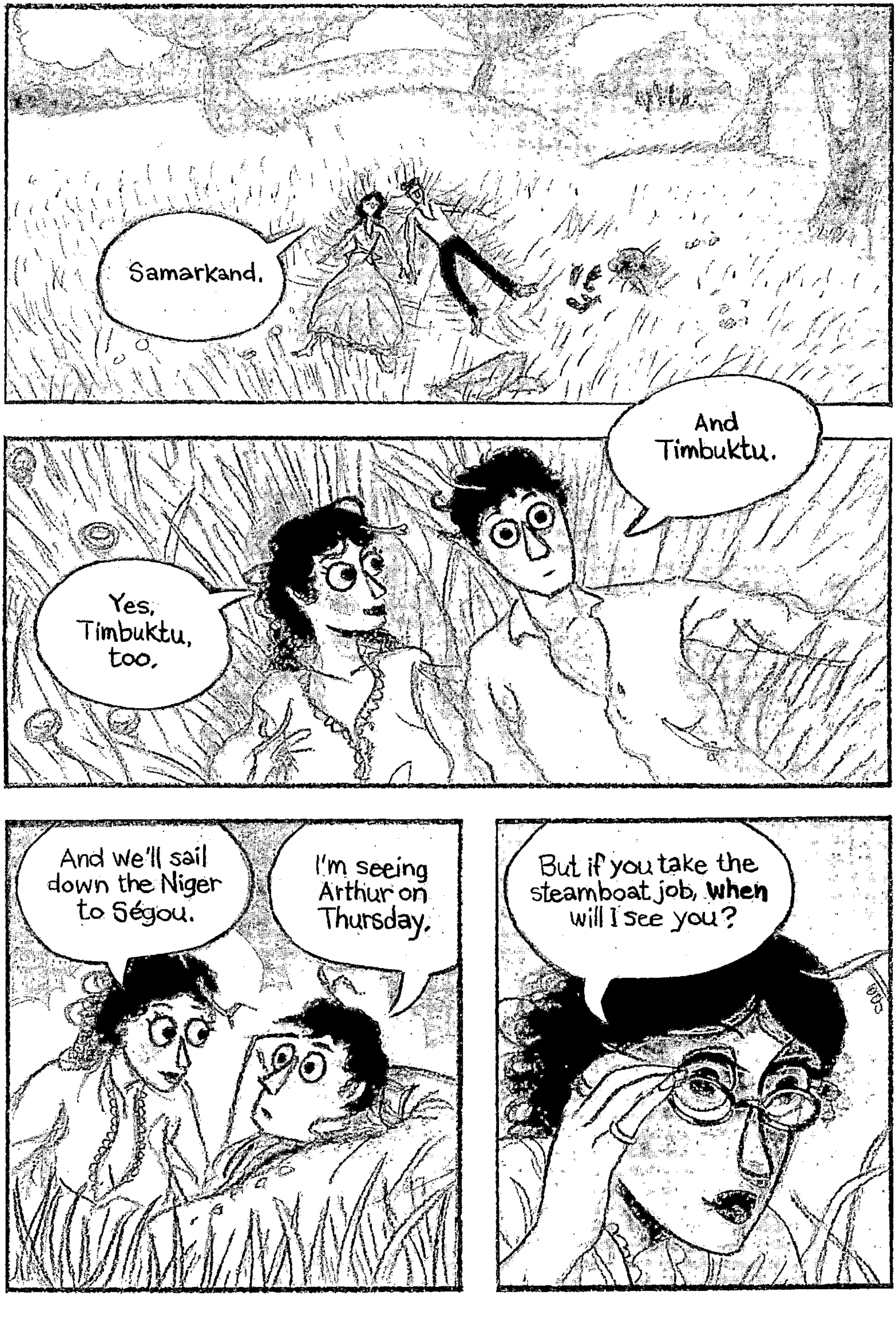
Samarkand.
And Timbuktu.
Yes, Timbuktu, too.
And we'll sail down the Niger to Ségou.
I'm seeing Arthur on Thursday.
But if you take the steamboat job, **when** will I see you?

On Sundays, mostly. In a couple years, I'll have saved up enough.

With my singing classes, you'll escape from the river even sooner, Elijah.

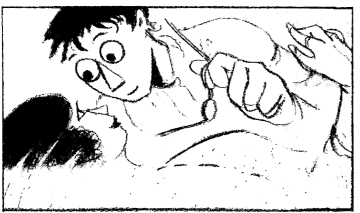

You need to promise me something.

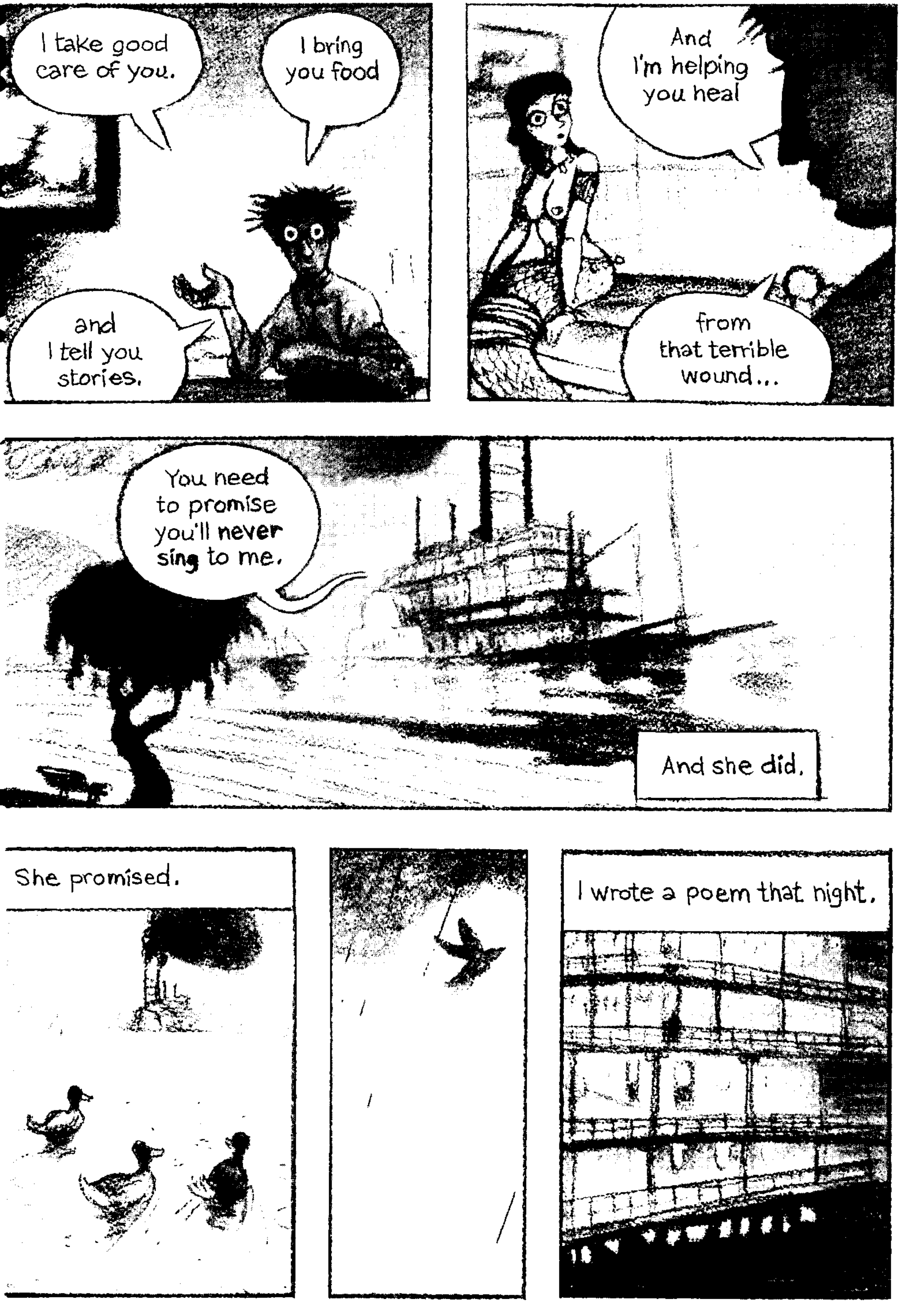
I take good care of you.
I bring you food
and I tell you stories.
And I'm helping you heal
from that terrible wound...
You need to promise you'll **never sing** to me.
And she did.
She promised.
I wrote a poem that night.

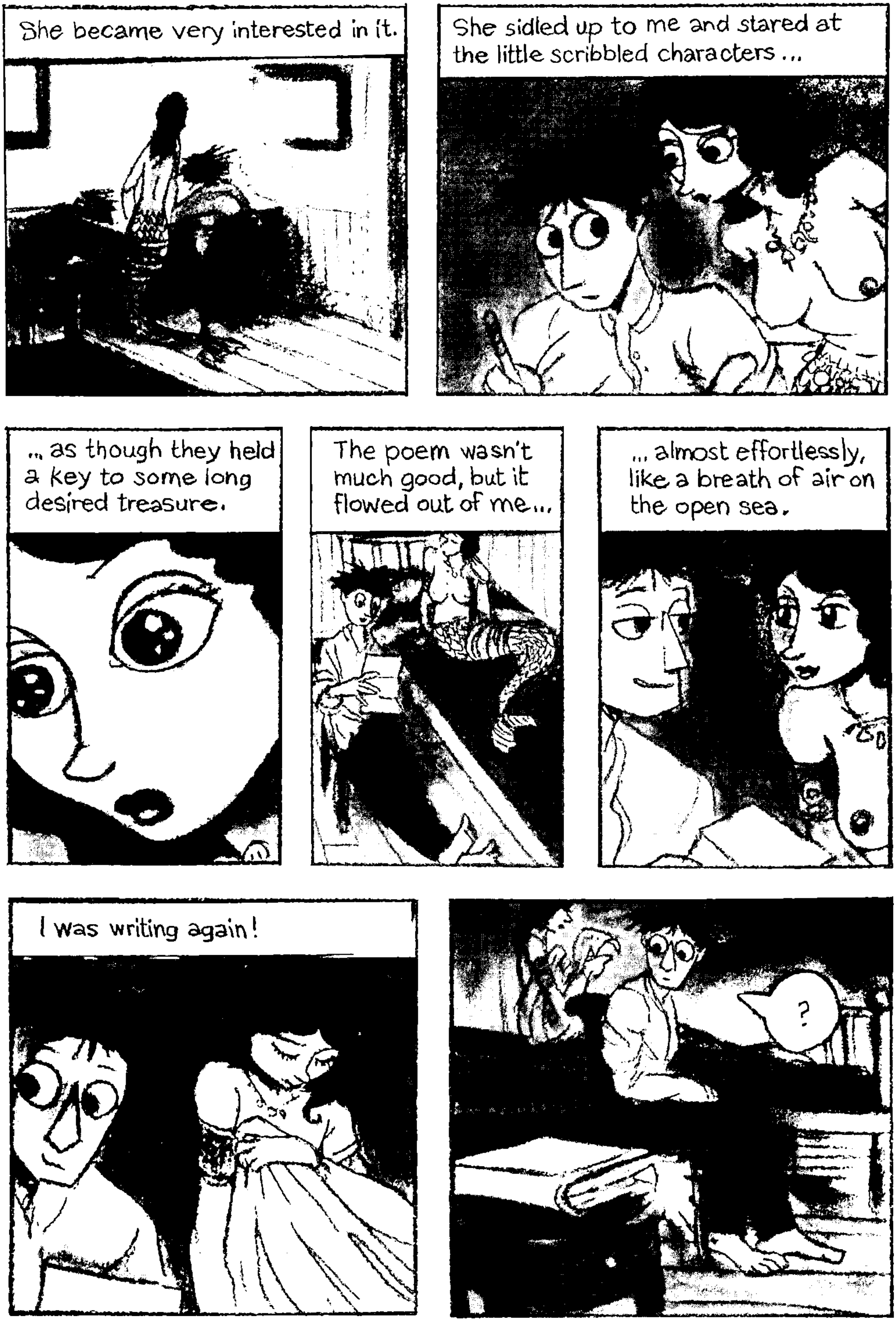
She became very interested in it.
She sidled up to me and stared at the little scribbled characters ...
... as though they held a key to some long desired treasure.
The poem wasn't much good, but it flowed out of me...
... almost effortlessly, like a breath of air on the open sea.
I was writing again!
?

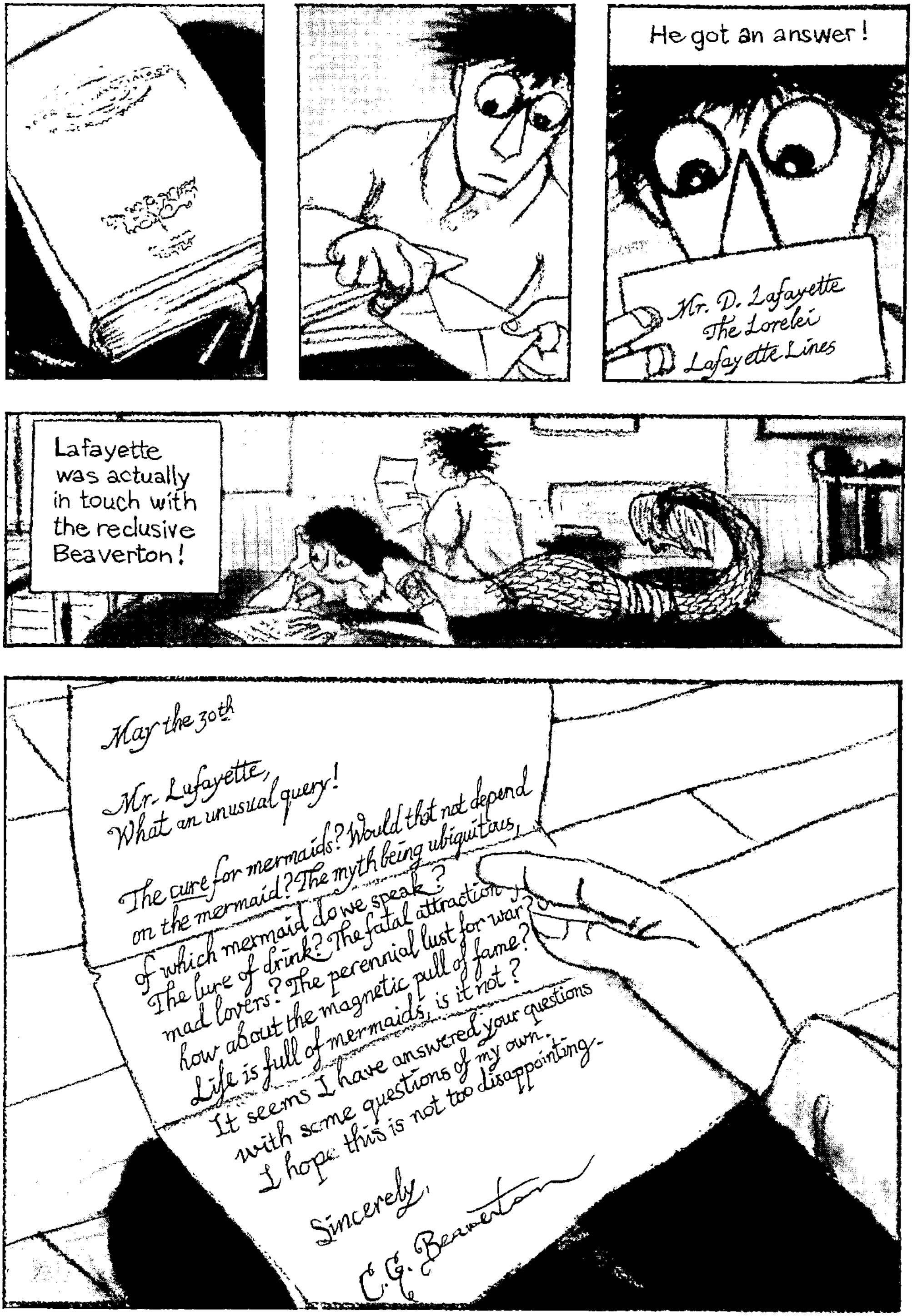
He got an answer!
Mr. D. Lafayette
The Lorelei
Lafayette Lines
Lafayette was actually in touch with the reclusive Beaverton!
May the 30th
Mr. Lafayette,
What an unusual query!
The cure for mermaids? Would that not depend
on the mermaid? The myth being ubiquitous,
of which mermaid do we speak?
The lure of drink? The fatal attraction
mad lovers? The perennial lust for war?
how about the magnetic pull of fame?
Life is full of mermaids, is it not?
It seems I have answered your questions
with some questions of my own.
I hope this is not too disappointing.
Sincerely,
C.G. Beaverton

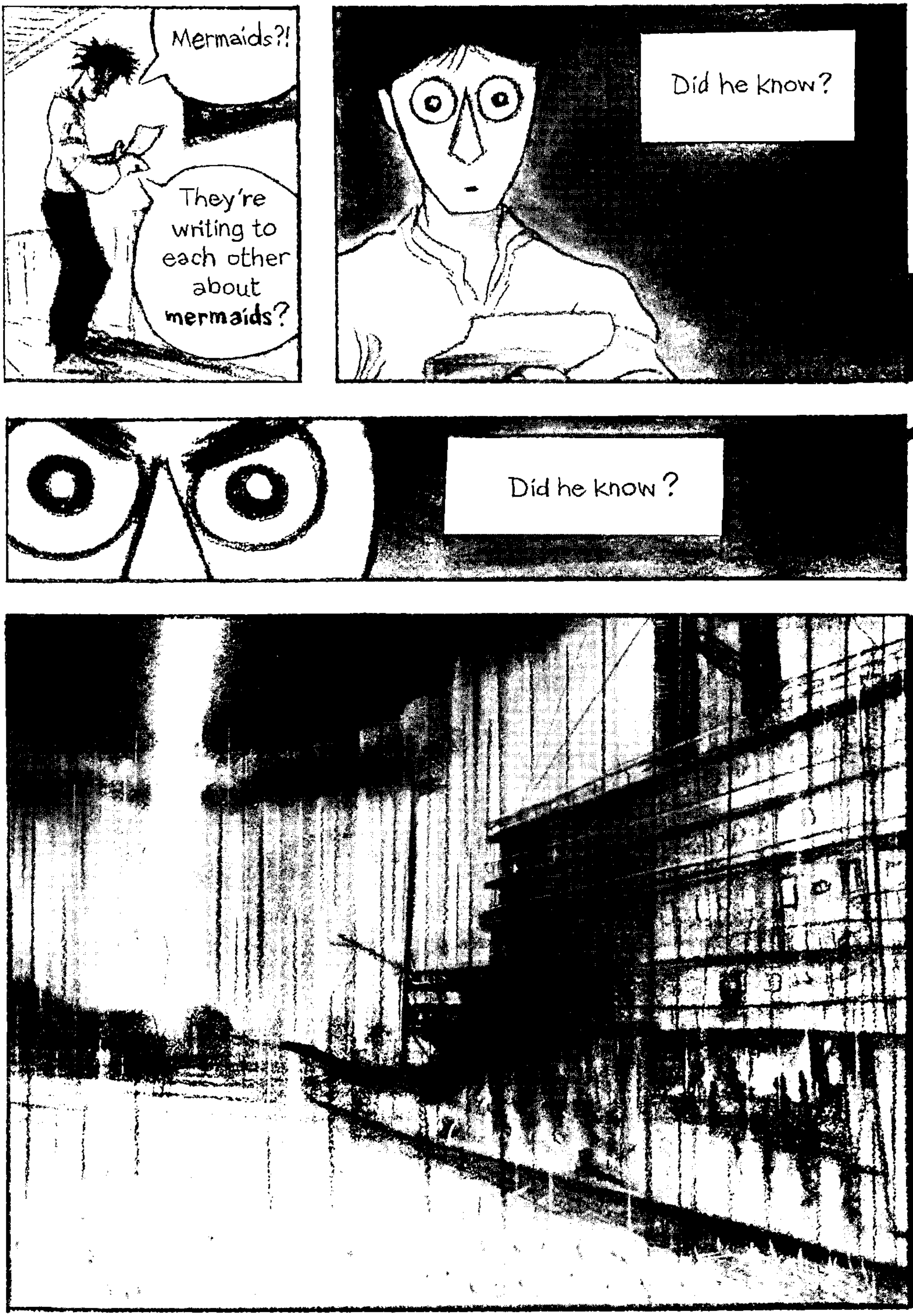
Mermaids?!
They're writing to each other about **mermaids**?
Did he know?
Did he know?

Pt 1. Chap.8

"PEARL'S SONG"

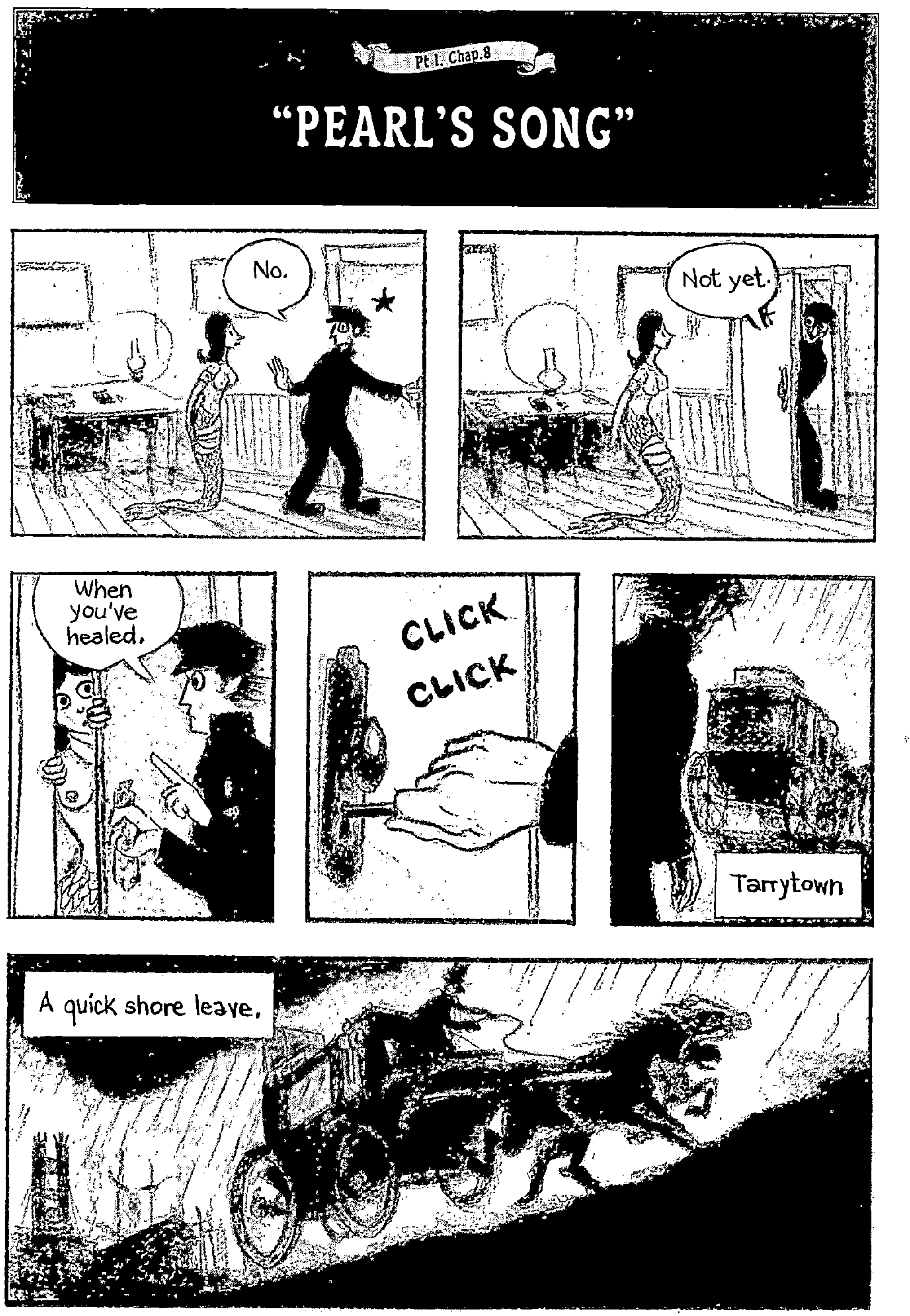
No.
Not yet.
When you've healed.
CLICK
CLICK
Tarrytown
A quick shore leave.

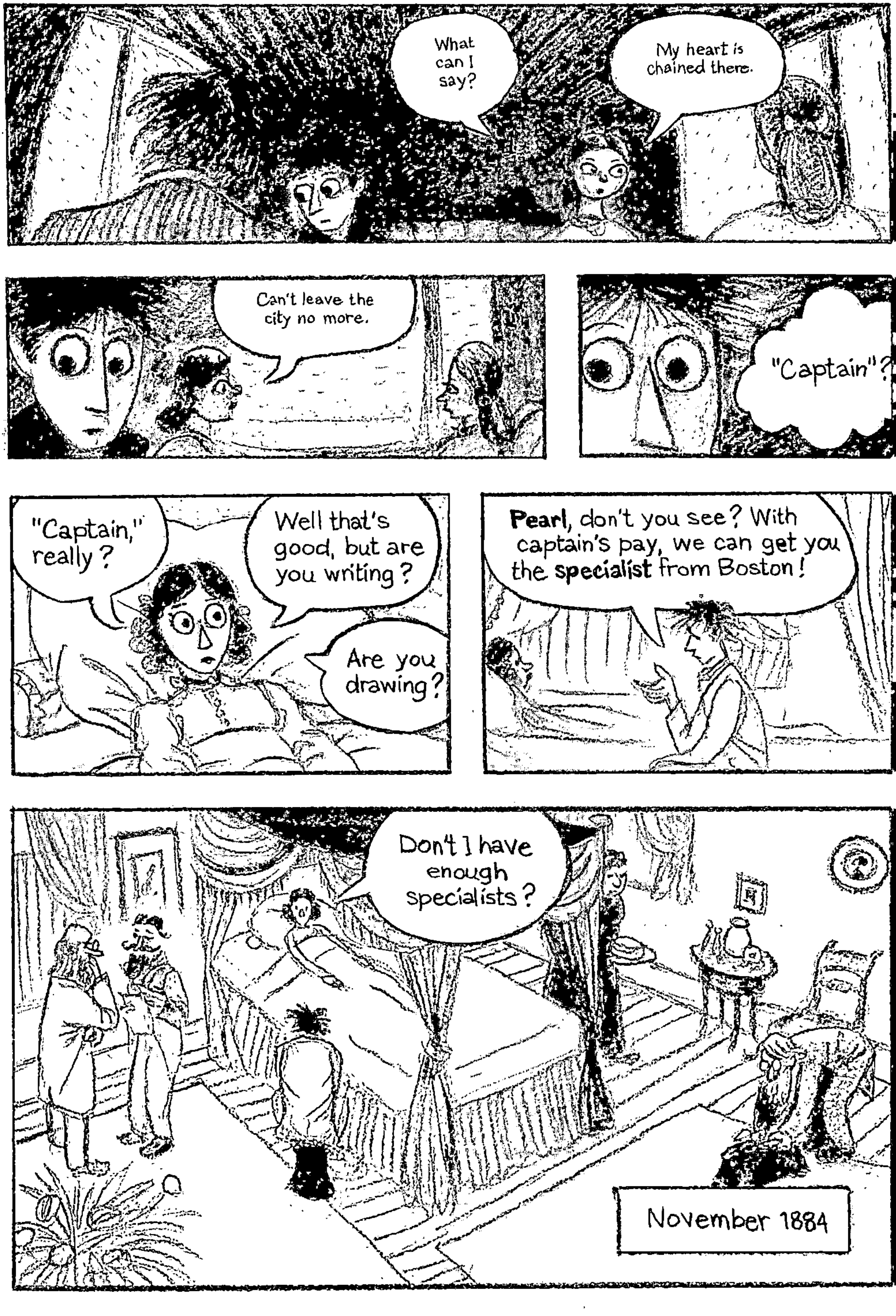
What can I say?
My heart is chained there.
Can't leave the city no more.
"Captain"?
"Captain," really?
Well that's good, but are you writing?
Are you drawing?
Pearl, don't you see? With captain's pay, we can get you the specialist from Boston!
Don't I have enough specialists?
November 1884

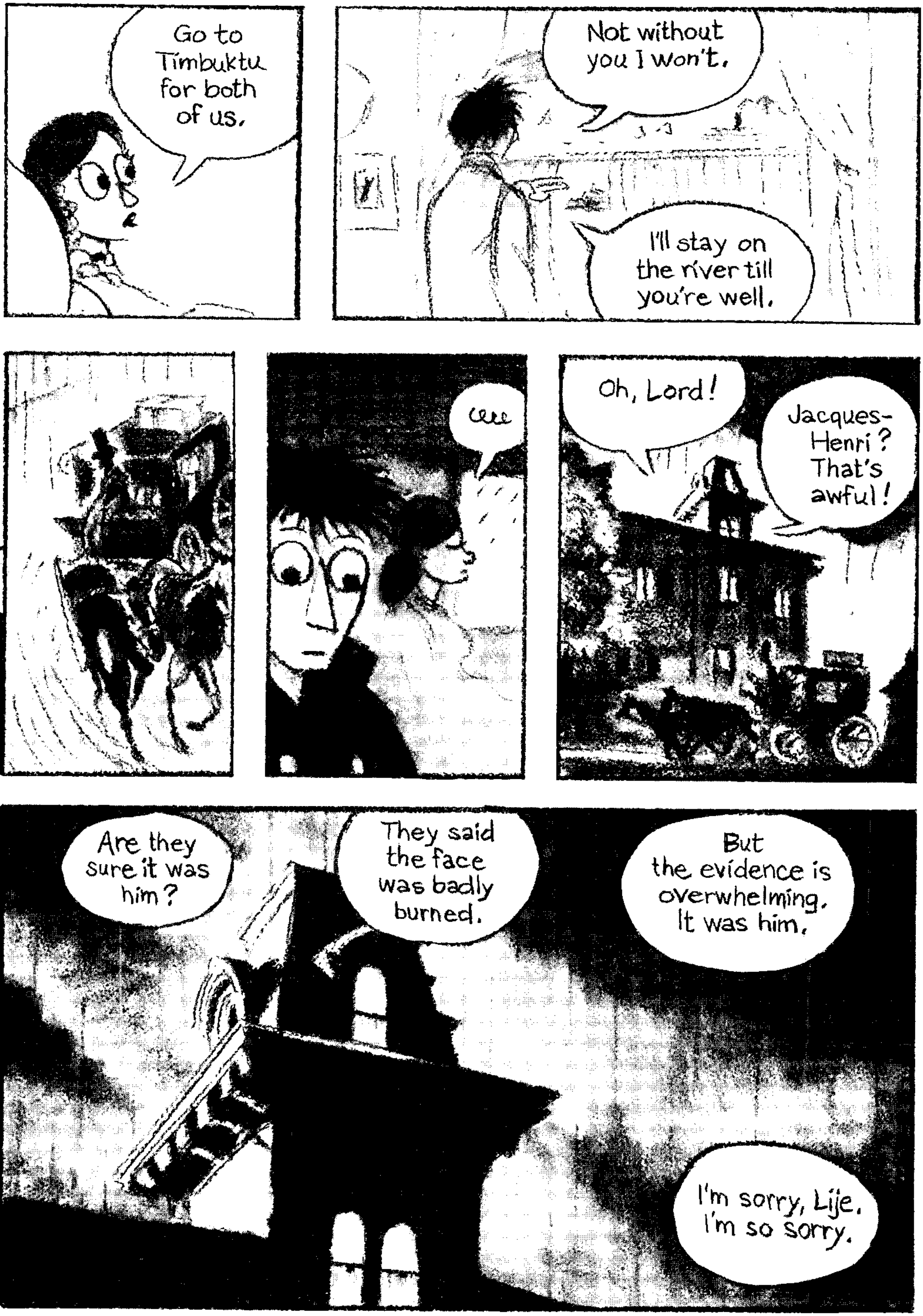

Go to Timbuktu for both of us.
Not without you I won't.
I'll stay on the river till you're well.
Oh, Lord!
Jacques-Henri? That's awful!
Are they sure it was him?
They said the face was badly burned.
But the evidence is overwhelming. It was him.
I'm sorry, Lije. I'm so sorry.

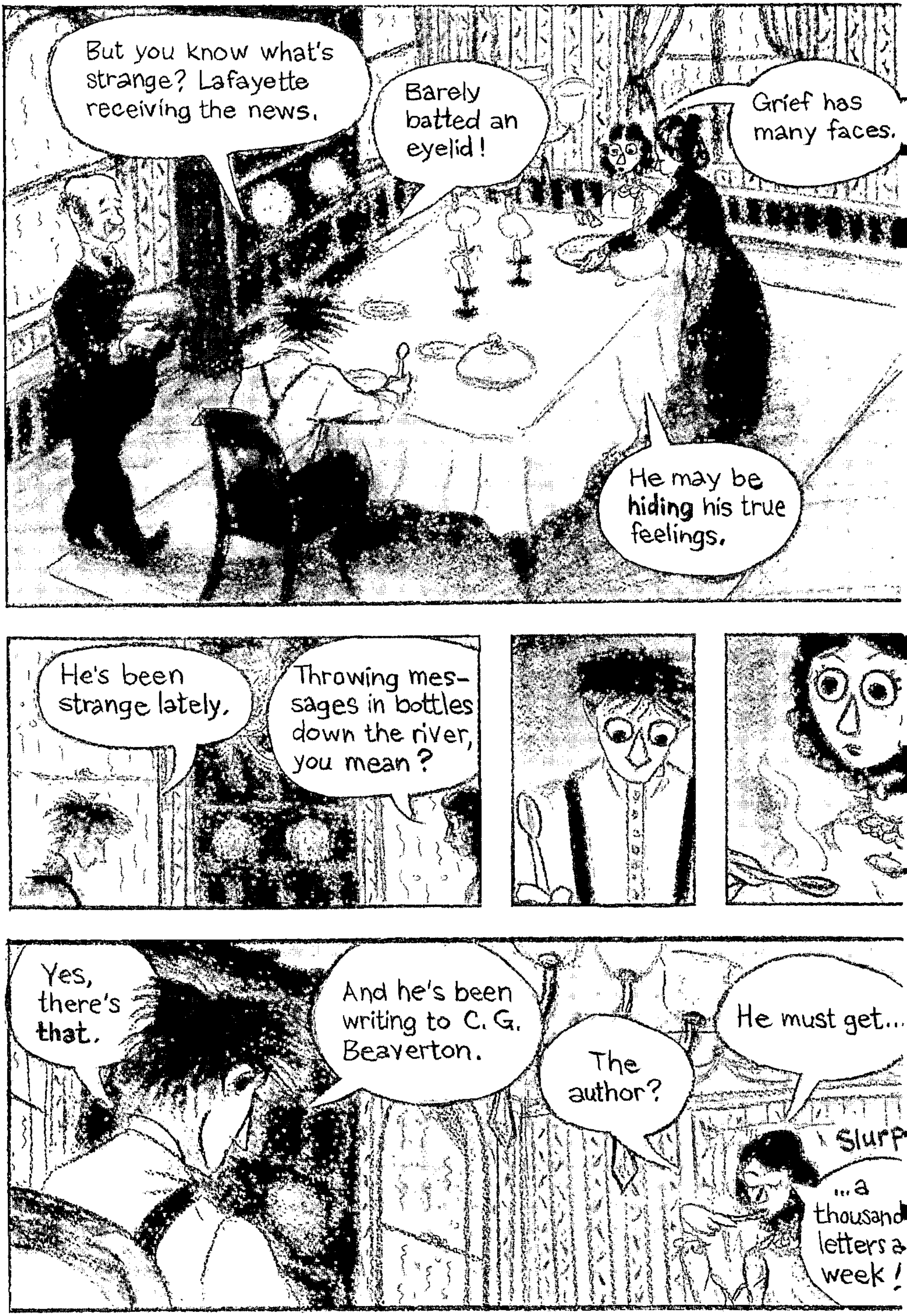
But you know what's strange? Lafayette receiving the news.
Barely batted an eyelid!
Grief has many faces.
He may be **hiding** his true feelings.
He's been strange lately.
Throwing messages in bottles down the river, you mean?
Yes, there's **that**.
And he's been writing to C. G. Beaverton.
The author?
He must get...
Slurp
...a thousand letters a week!

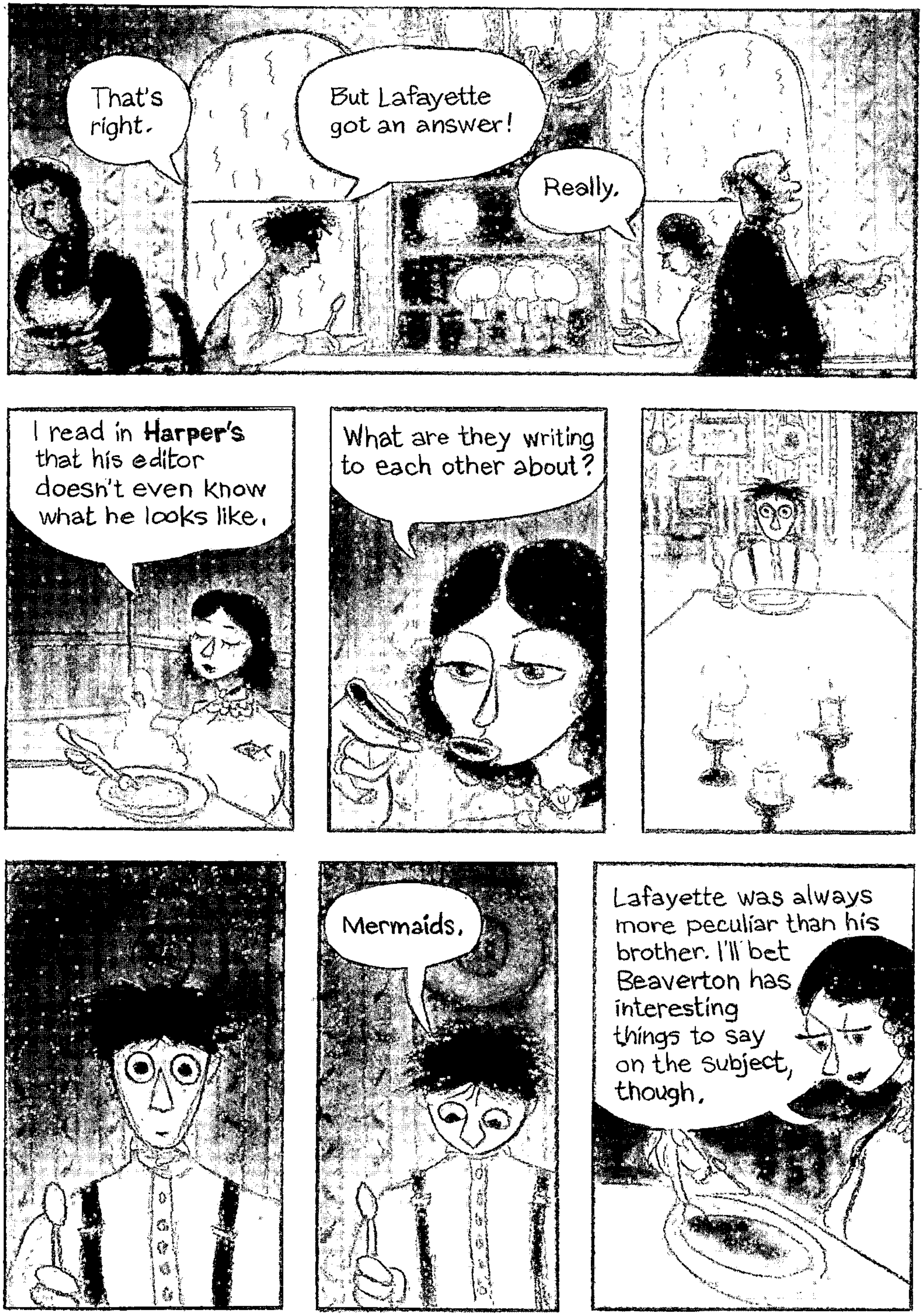
That's right.
But Lafayette got an answer!
Really.
I read in **Harper's** that his editor doesn't even know what he looks like.
What are they writing to each other about?
Mermaids.
Lafayette was always more peculiar than his brother. I'll bet Beaverton has interesting things to say on the subject, though.

Arthur wrote me.

In California there's a new kind of **cure** he thinks I should try.

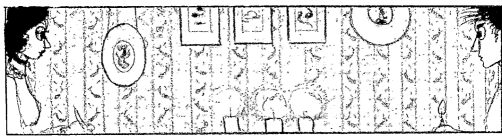

You're not eating your—

Pearl.

Are we a couple of cold fish?

Why do you say that?

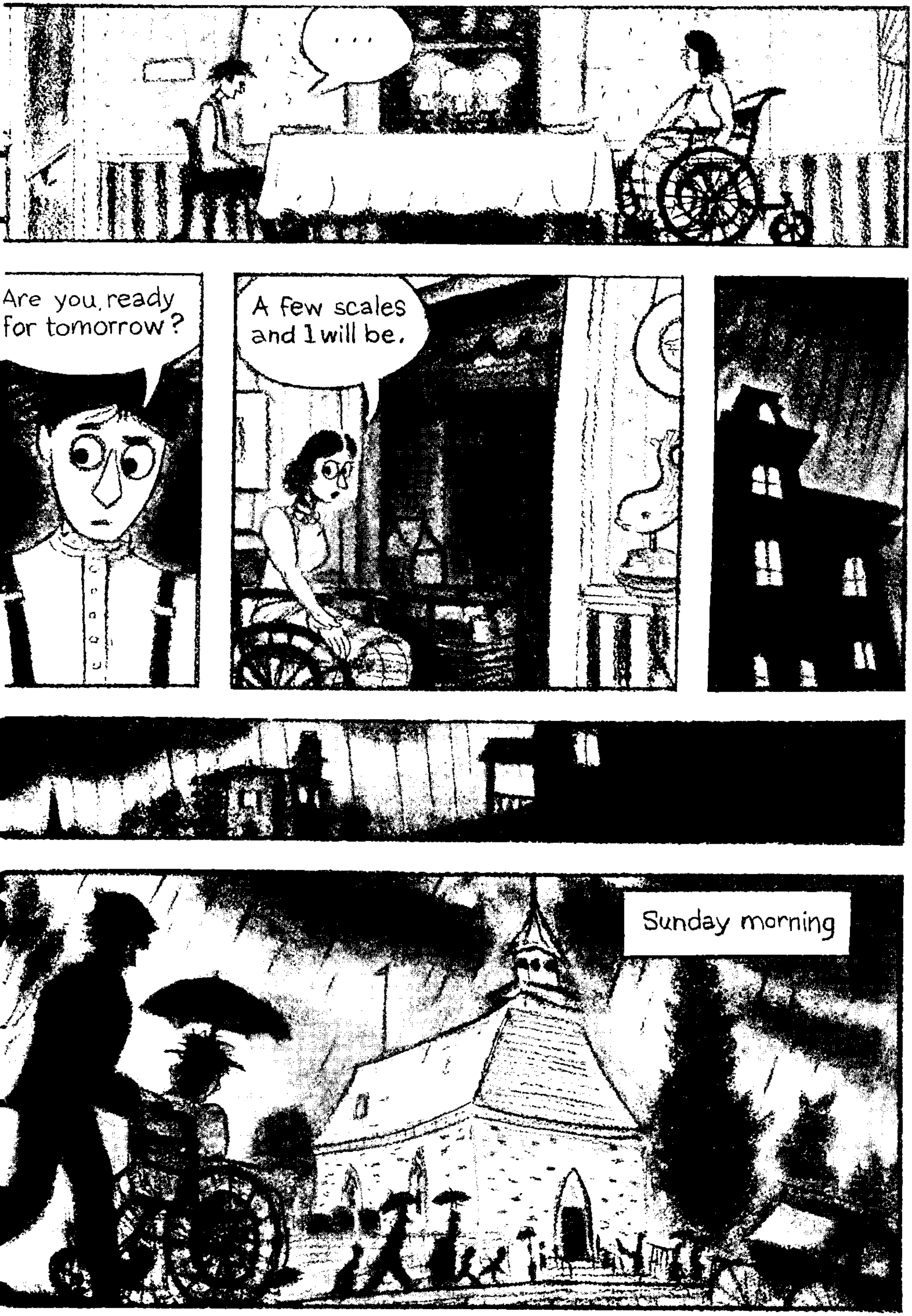
...
Are you ready for tomorrow?
A few scales and I will be.
Sunday morning

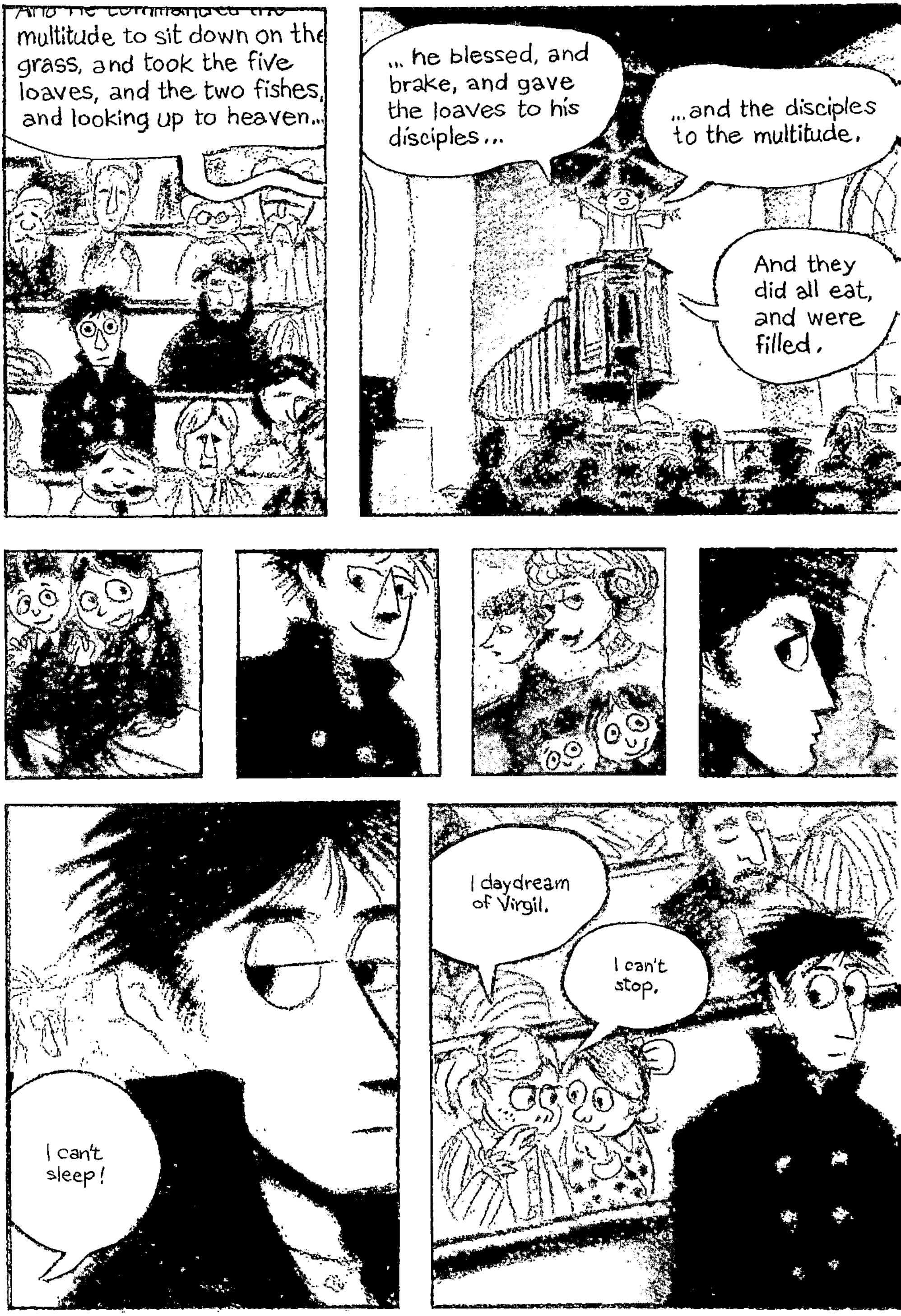
multitude to sit down on the grass, and took the five loaves, and the two fishes, and looking up to heaven...
... he blessed, and brake, and gave the loaves to his disciples...
...and the disciples to the multitude.
And they did all eat, and were filled.
I can't sleep!
I daydream of Virgil.
I can't stop.

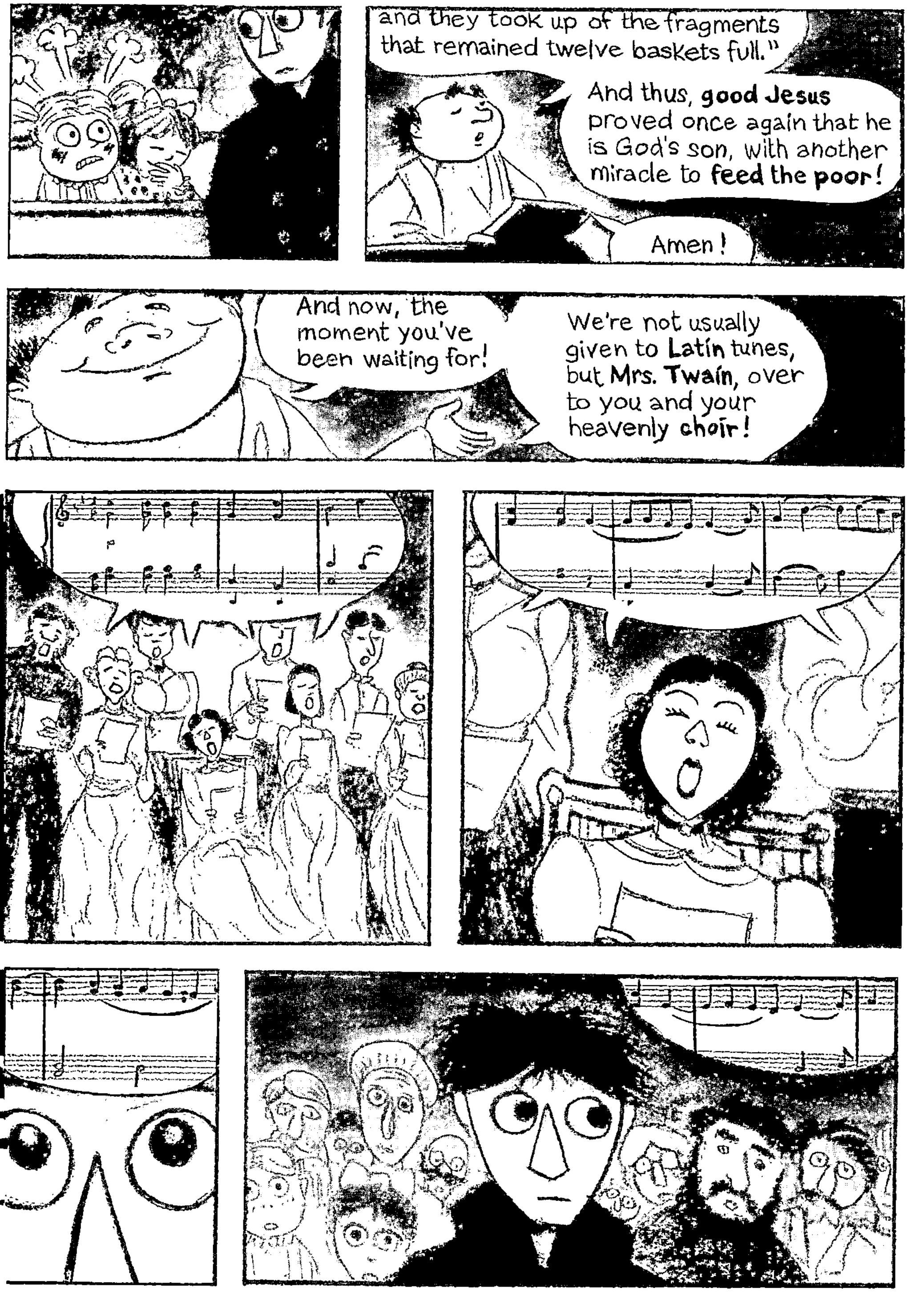
and they took up of the fragments that remained twelve baskets full."
And thus, good Jesus proved once again that he is God's son, with another miracle to feed the poor!
Amen!
And now, the moment you've been waiting for!
We're not usually given to Latin tunes, but Mrs. Twain, over to you and your heavenly choir!

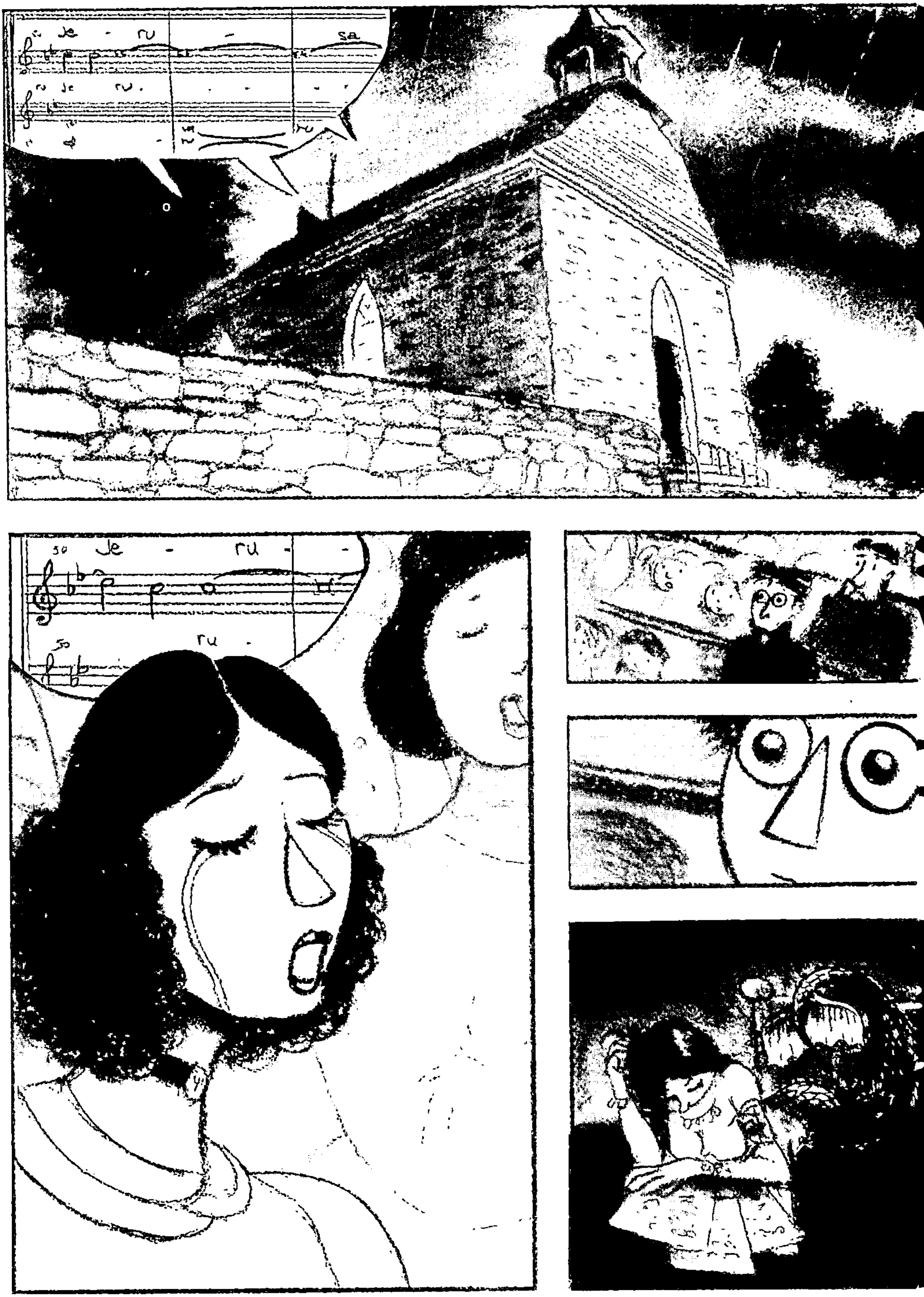
Je - ru - sa
Je ru.
Je - ru -
ru -

She had been
alone all night...

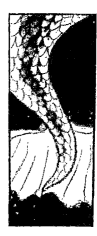

... and **Lafayette** still aboard!

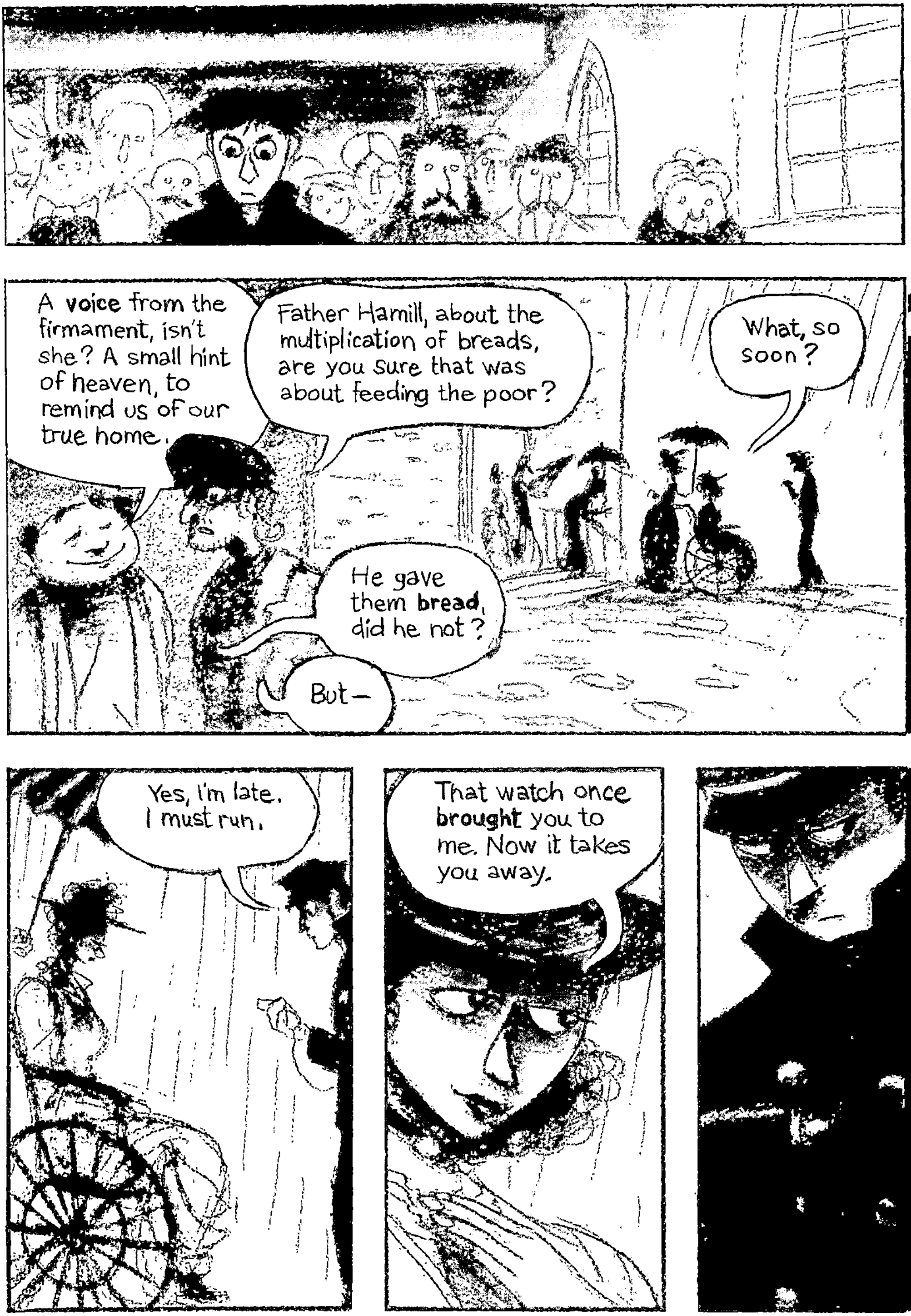
A voice from the firmament, isn't she? A small hint of heaven, to remind us of our true home.
Father Hamill, about the multiplication of breads, are you sure that was about feeding the poor?
What, so soon?
He gave them bread, did he not?
But—
Yes, I'm late. I must run.
That watch once brought you to me. Now it takes you away.

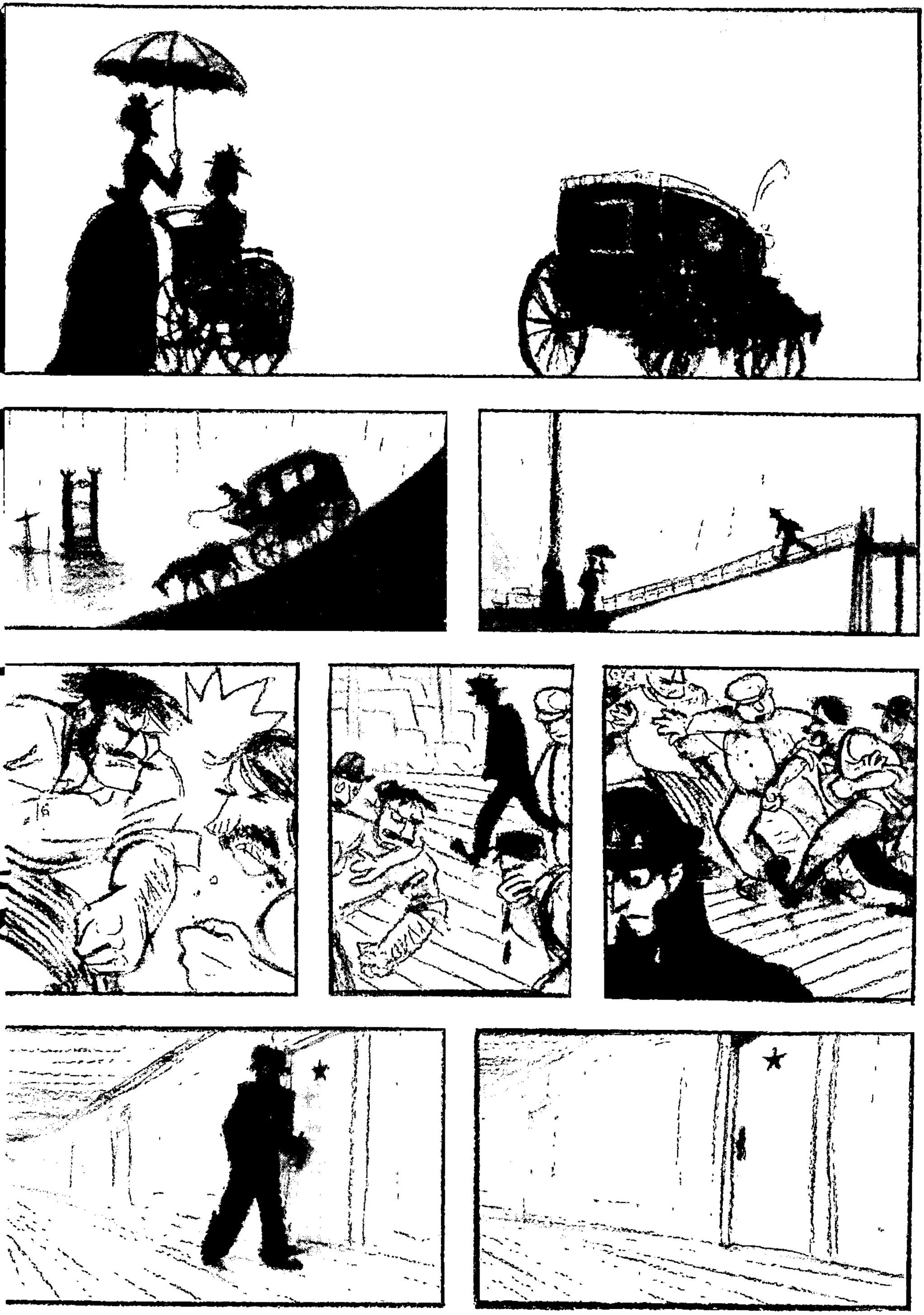

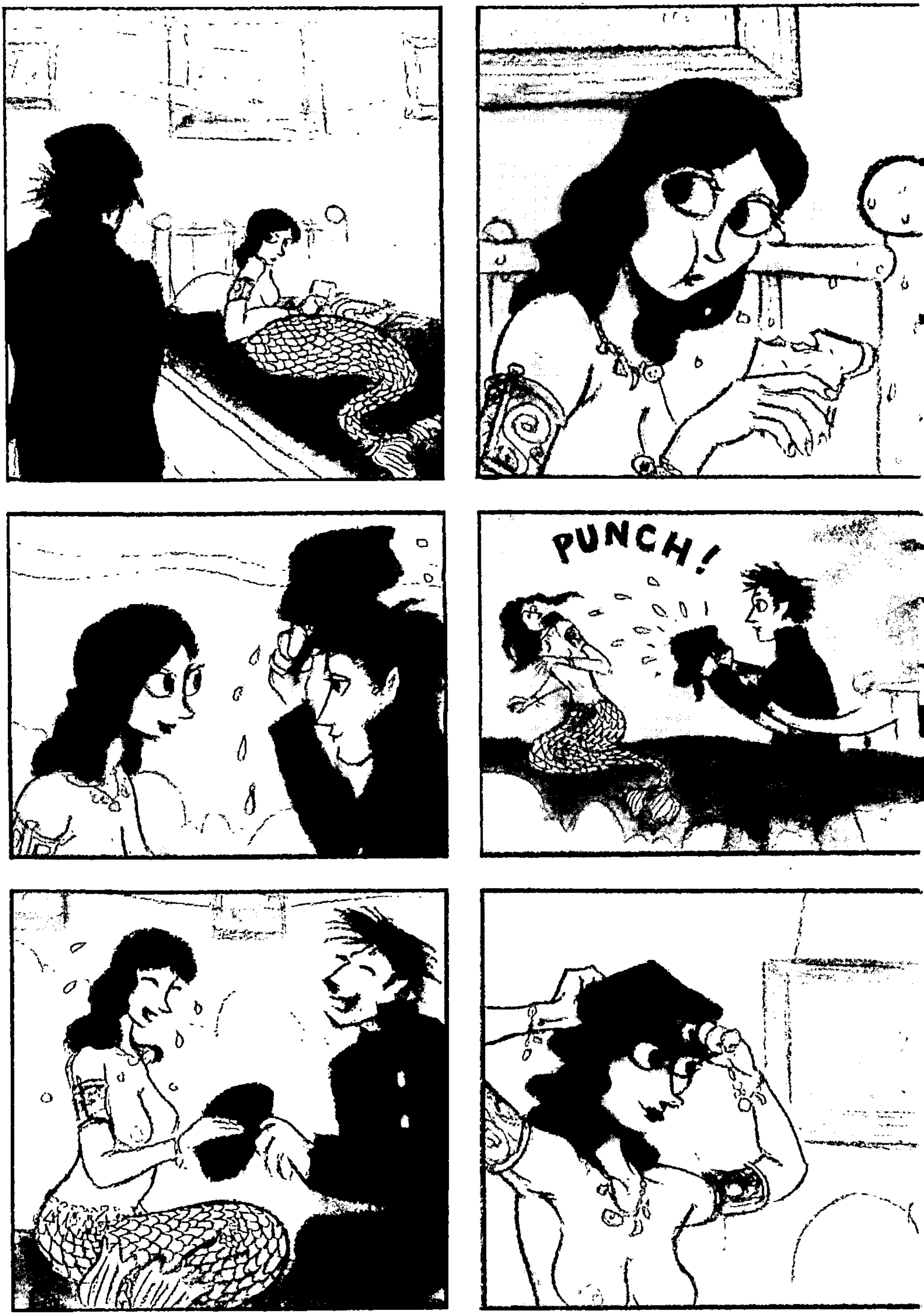
PUNCH!

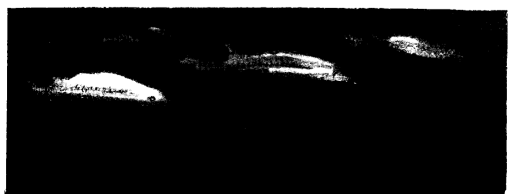

"THREE PRISONERS"

Early morning

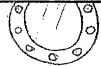

There he was again with his bottles.

Was he writing to Jacques-Henri?

The Frenchman and his secrets were no concern of mine.

137

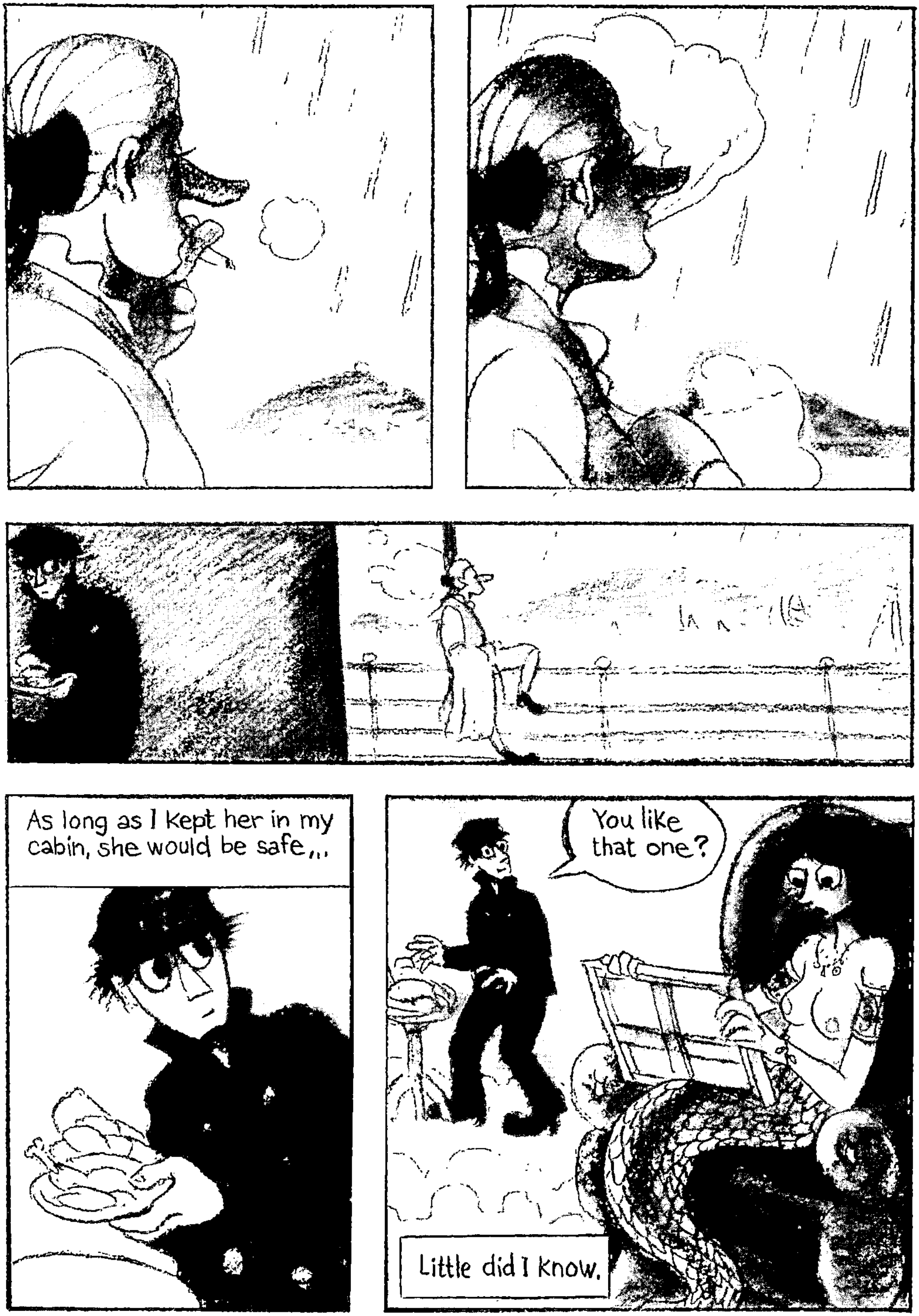
As long as I kept her in my cabin, she would be safe,,.
You like that one?
Little did I know.

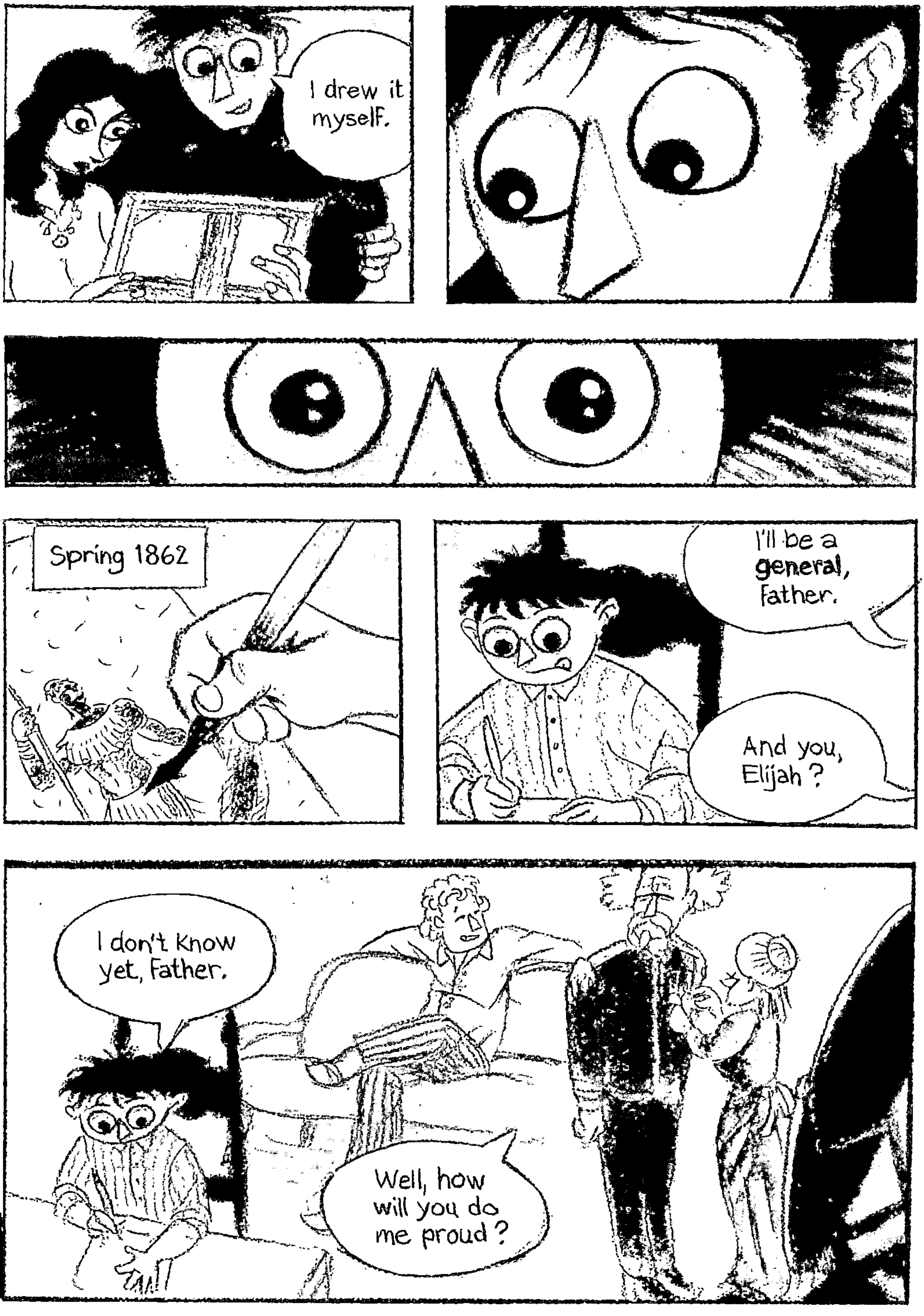
I drew it myself.
Spring 1862
I'll be a **general**, Father.
And you, Elijah?
I don't know yet, Father.
Well, how will you do me proud?

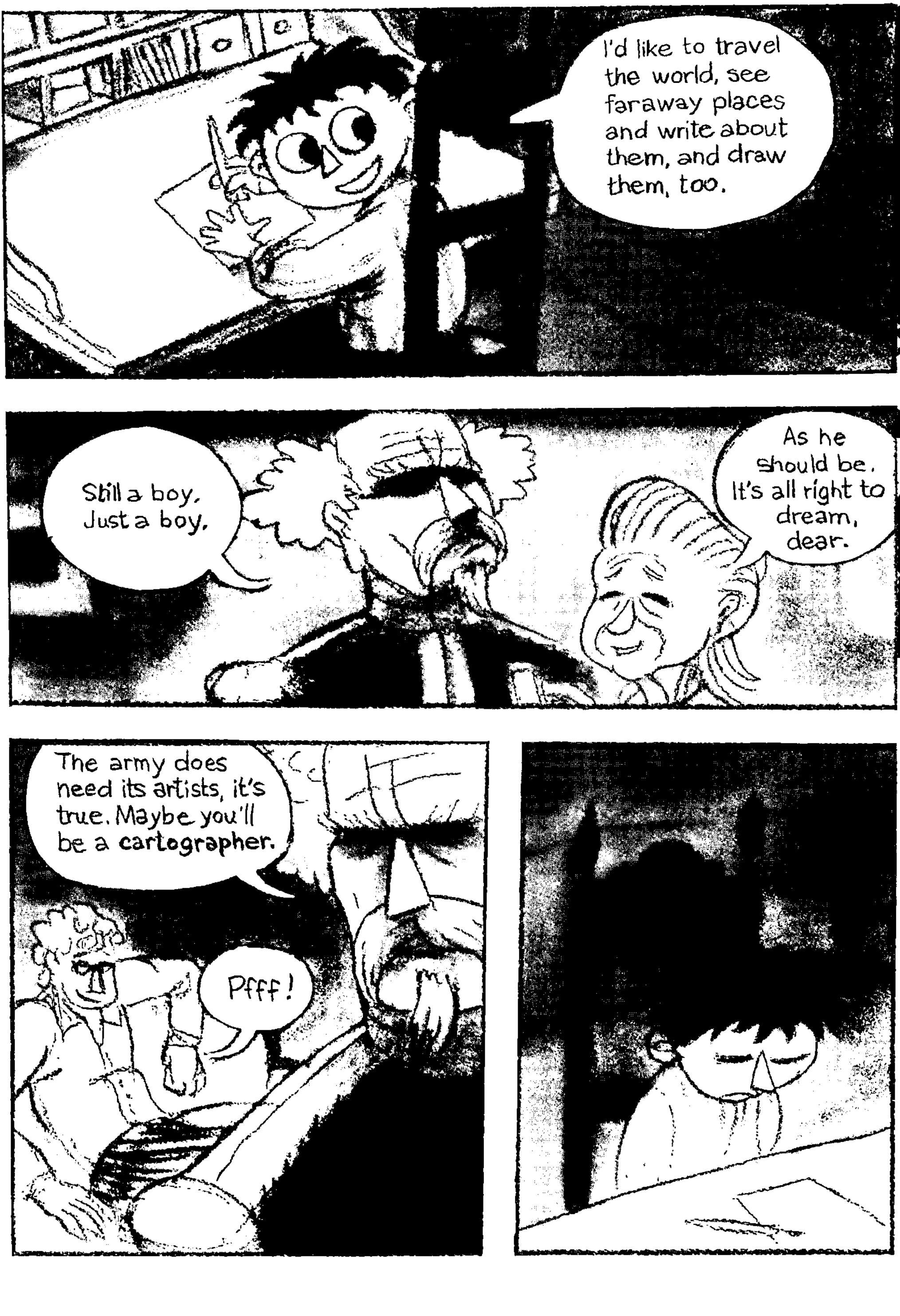
I'd like to travel the world, see faraway places and write about them, and draw them, too.
Still a boy. Just a boy.
As he should be. It's all right to dream, dear.
The army does need its artists, it's true. Maybe you'll be a **cartographer.**
Pfff!

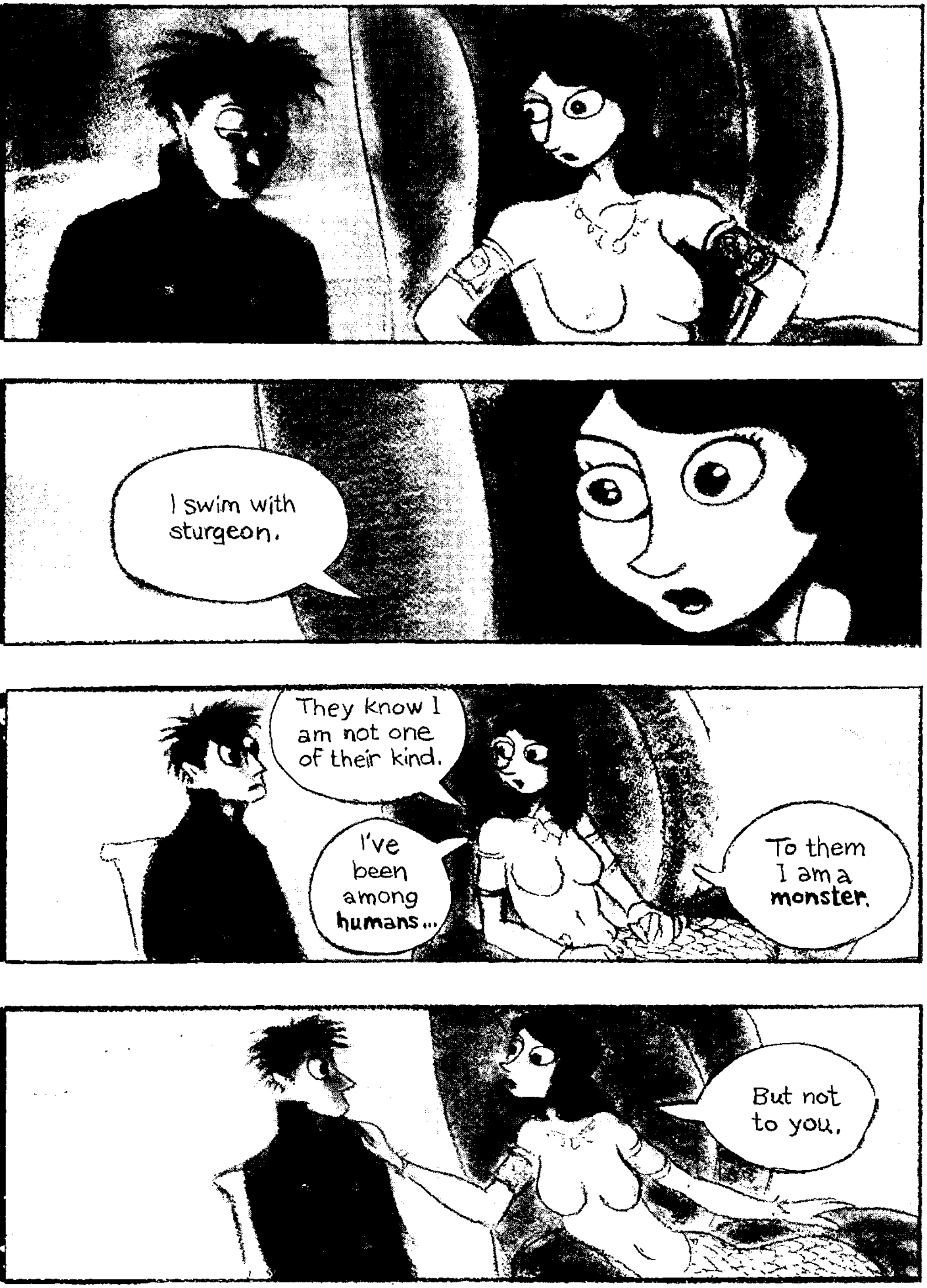
I swim with sturgeon.
They know I am not one of their kind.
I've been among **humans**...
To them I am a **monster**.
But not to you.

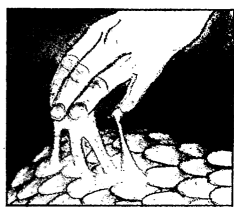

142

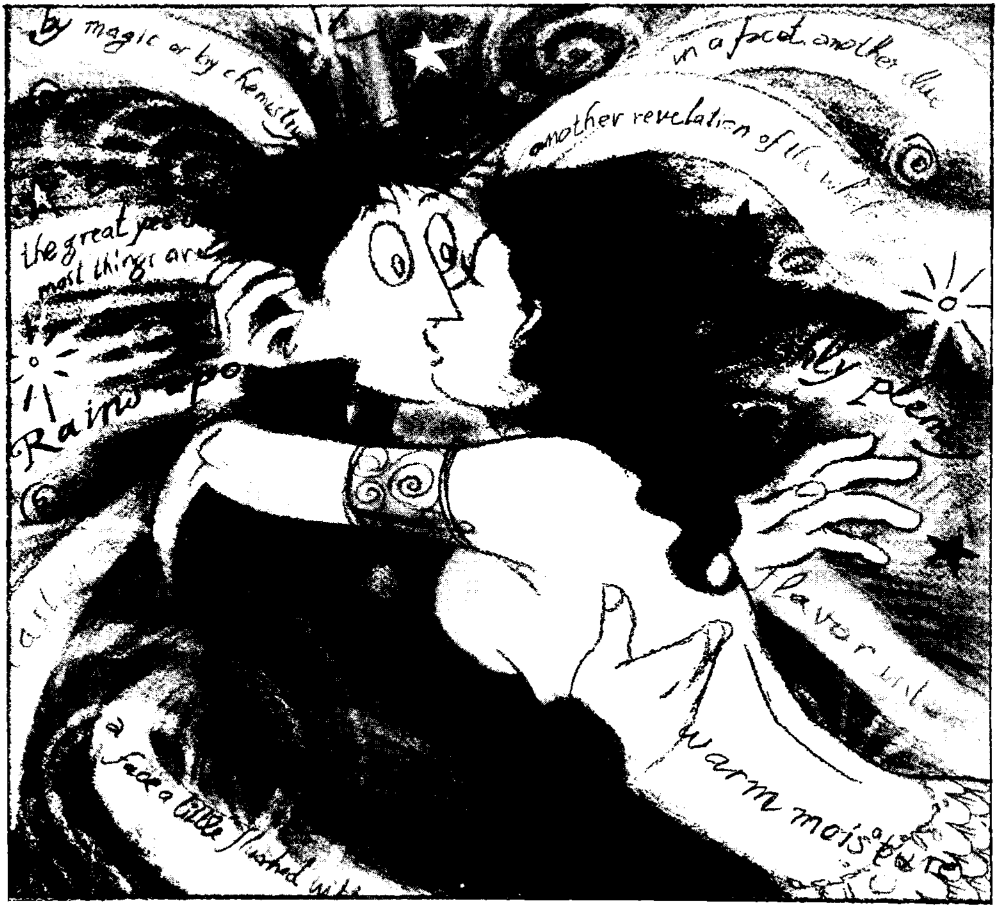
by magic or by chemistry
another revelation of
warm moisture

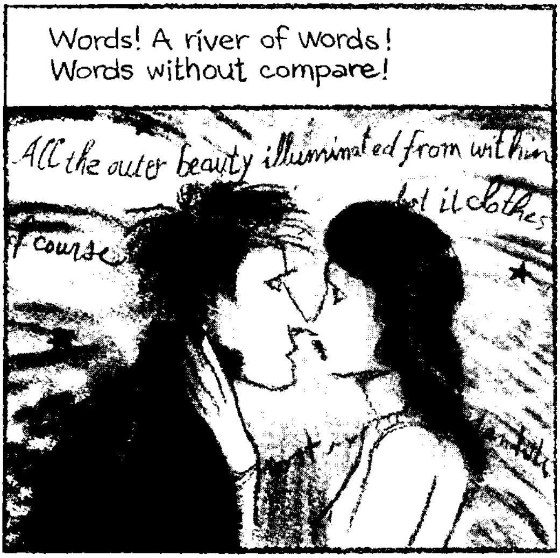
Words! A river of words!
Words without compare!
All the outer beauty illuminated from within

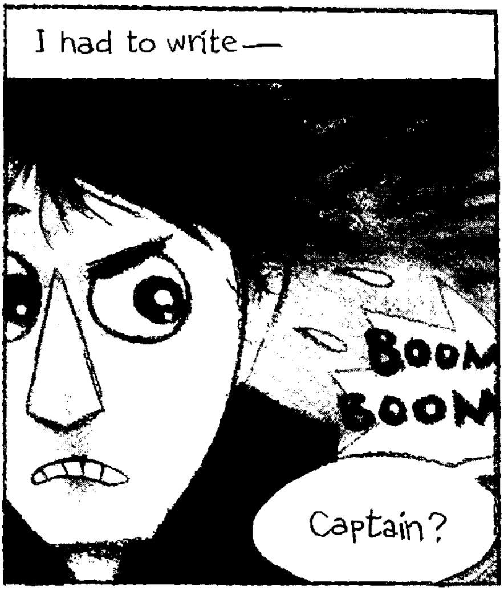
I had to write—
BOOM
BOOM
Captain?

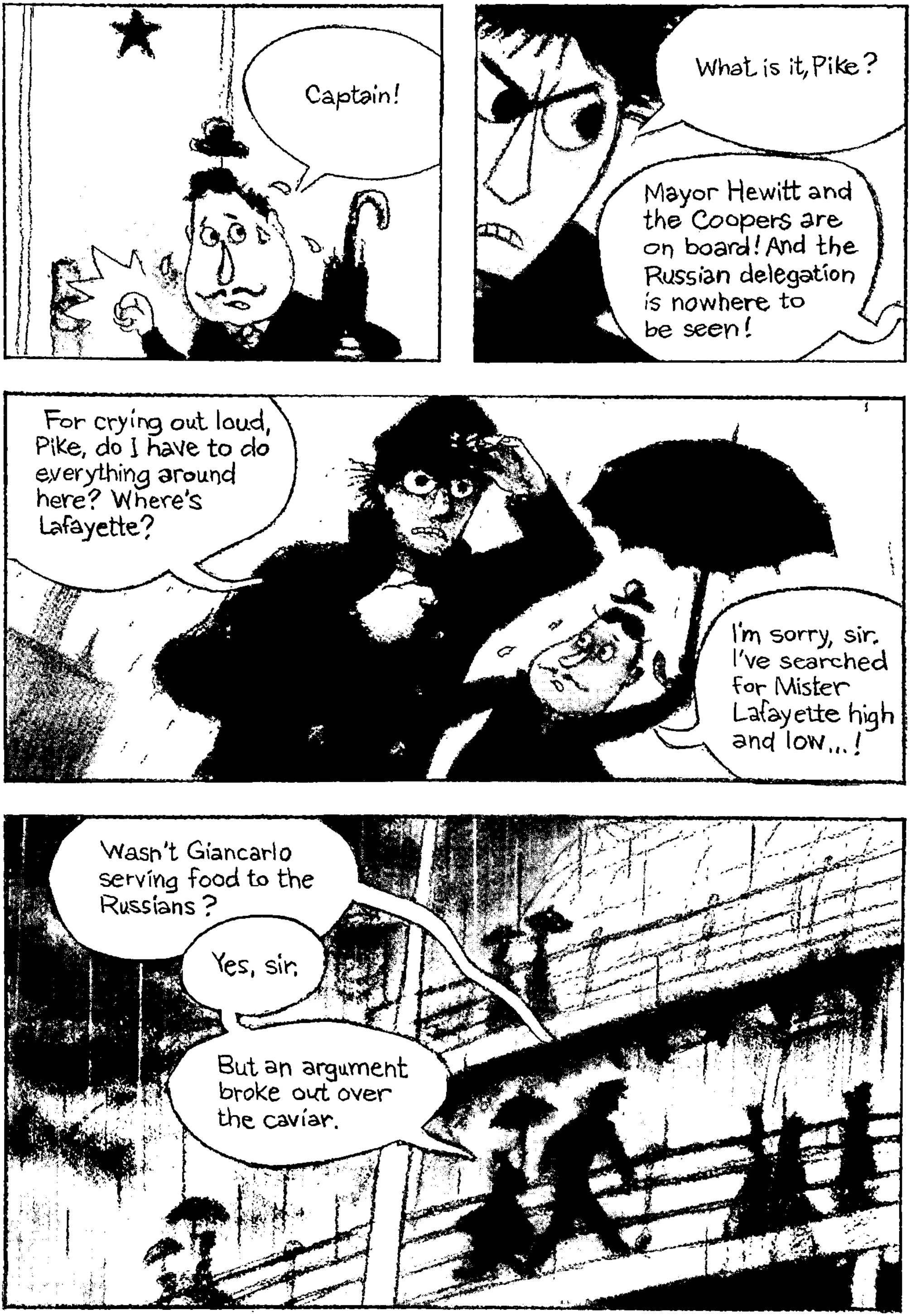
Captain!
What is it, Pike?
Mayor Hewitt and the Coopers are on board! And the Russian delegation is nowhere to be seen!
For crying out loud, Pike, do I have to do everything around here? Where's Lafayette?
I'm sorry, sir. I've searched for Mister Lafayette high and low...!
Wasn't Giancarlo serving food to the Russians?
Yes, sir.
But an argument broke out over the caviar.

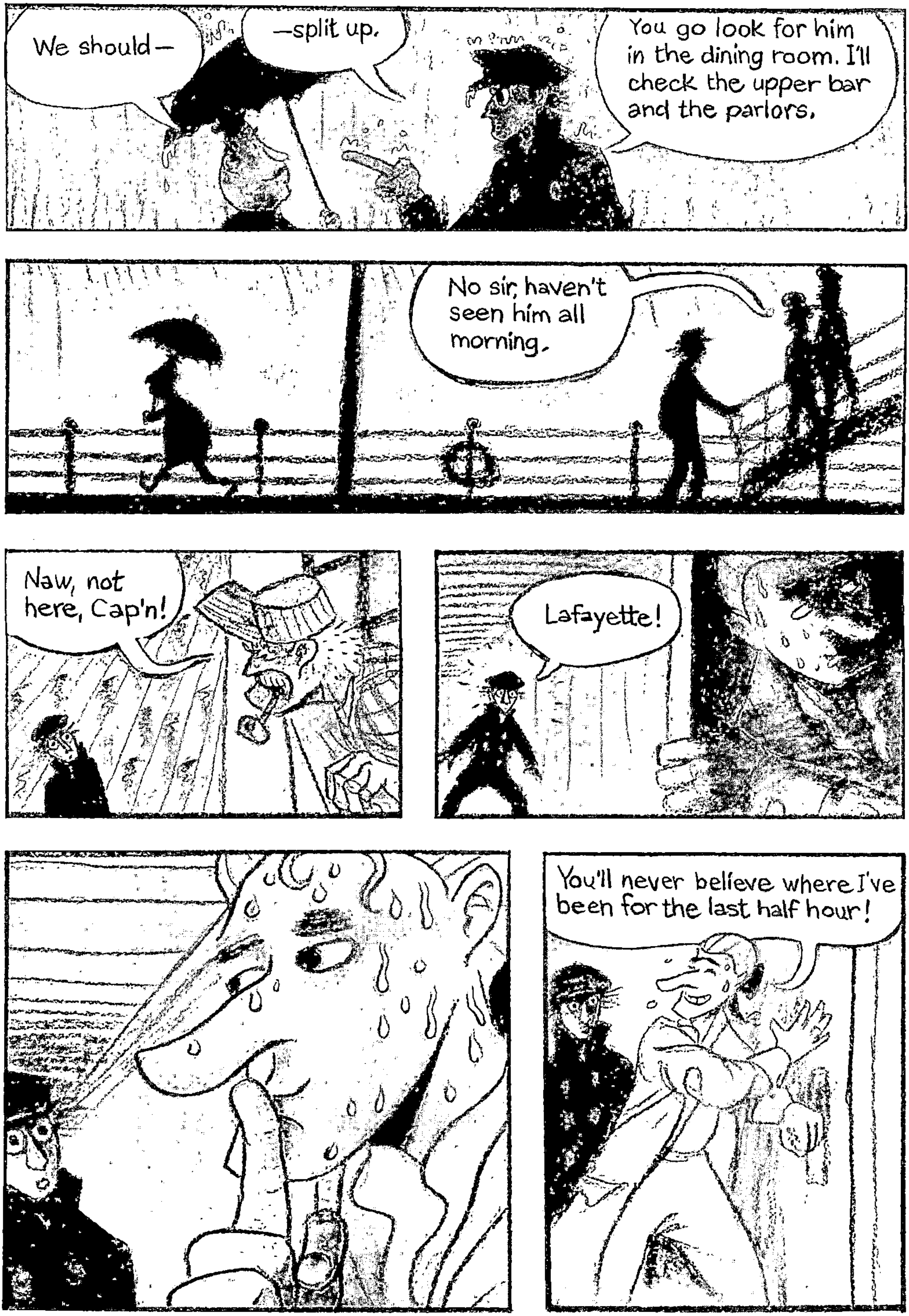
We should—
—split up.
You go look for him in the dining room. I'll check the upper bar and the parlors.
No sir, haven't seen him all morning.
Naw, not here, Cap'n!
Lafayette!
You'll never believe where I've been for the last half hour!

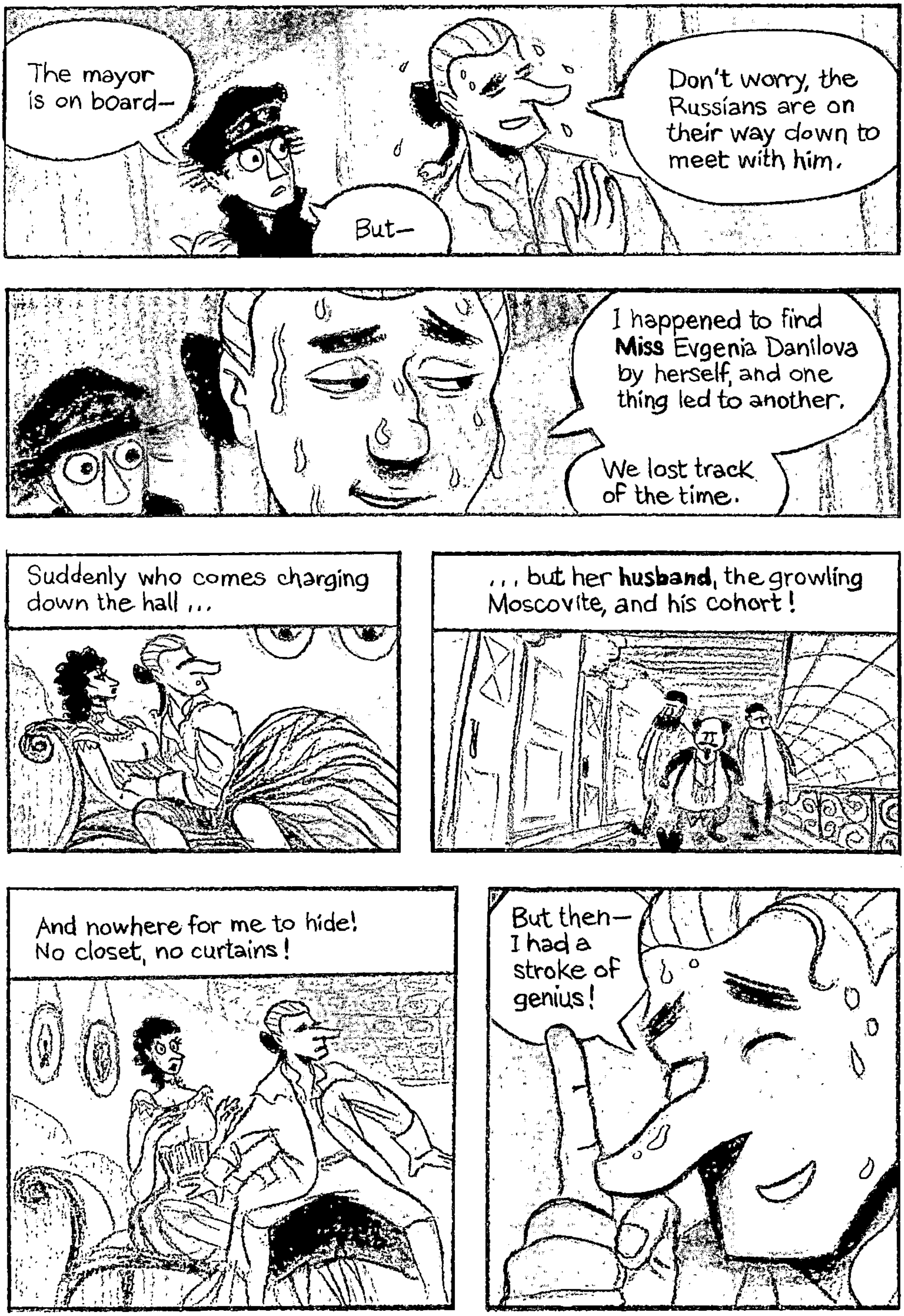
The mayor is on board–
But–
Don't worry, the Russians are on their way down to meet with him.
I happened to find **Miss** Evgenia Danilova by herself, and one thing led to another.
We lost track of the time.
Suddenly who comes charging down the hall ...
... but her **husband**, the growling Moscovite, and his cohort!
And nowhere for me to hide! No closet, no curtains!
But then– I had a stroke of genius!

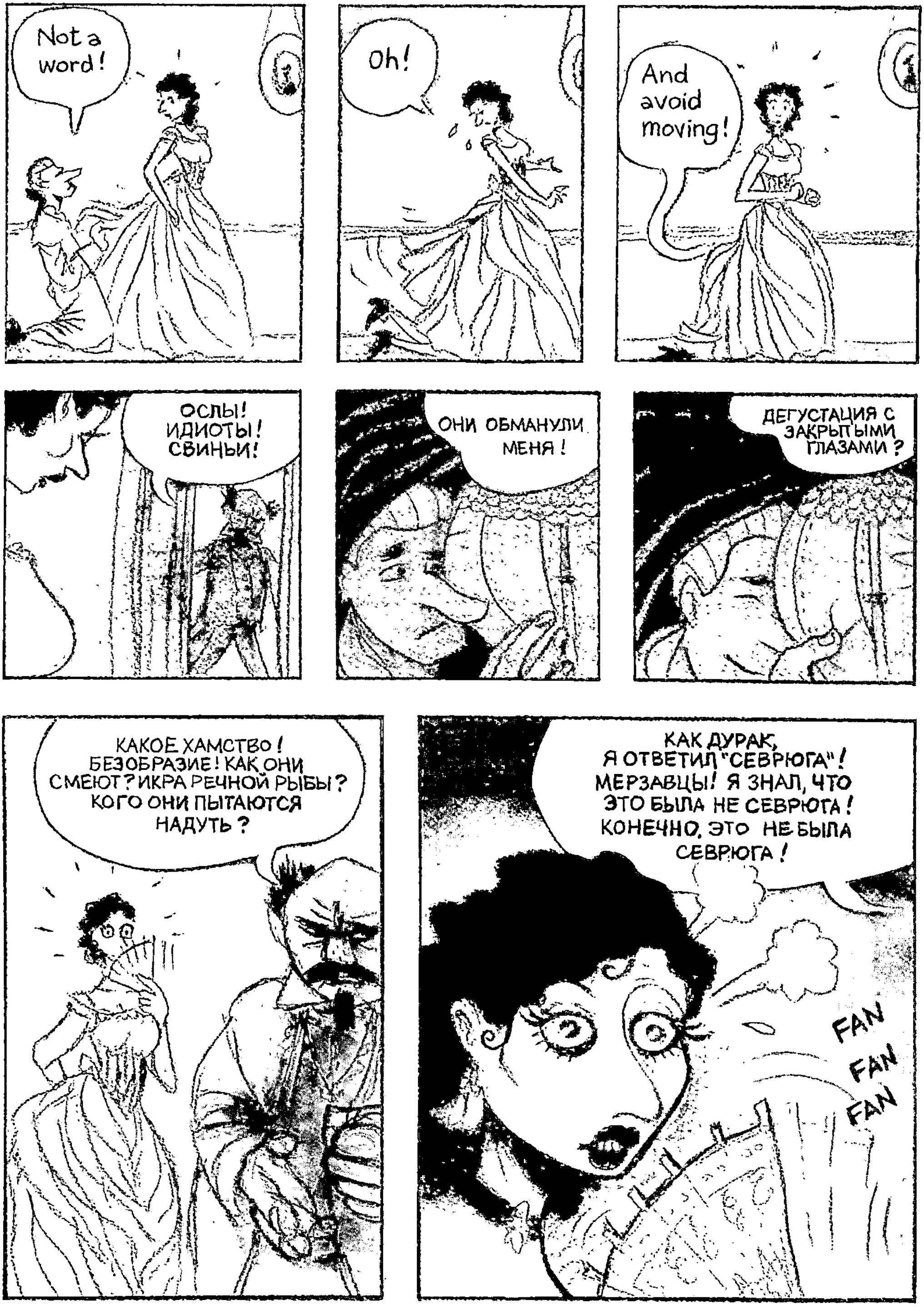
Not a word!
Oh!
And avoid moving!
ОСЛЫ! ИДИОТЫ! СВИНЬИ!
ОНИ ОБМАНУЛИ МЕНЯ!
ДЕГУСТАЦИЯ С ЗАКРЫТЫМИ ГЛАЗАМИ?
КАКОЕ ХАМСТВО! БЕЗОБРАЗИЕ! КАК ОНИ СМЕЮТ? ИКРА РЕЧНОЙ РЫБЫ? КОГО ОНИ ПЫТАЮТСЯ НАДУТЬ?
КАК ДУРАК, Я ОТВЕТИЛ "СЕВРЮГА"! МЕРЗАВЦЫ! Я ЗНАЛ, ЧТО ЭТО БЫЛА НЕ СЕВРЮГА! КОНЕЧНО, ЭТО НЕ БЫЛА СЕВРЮГА!
FAN
FAN
FAN

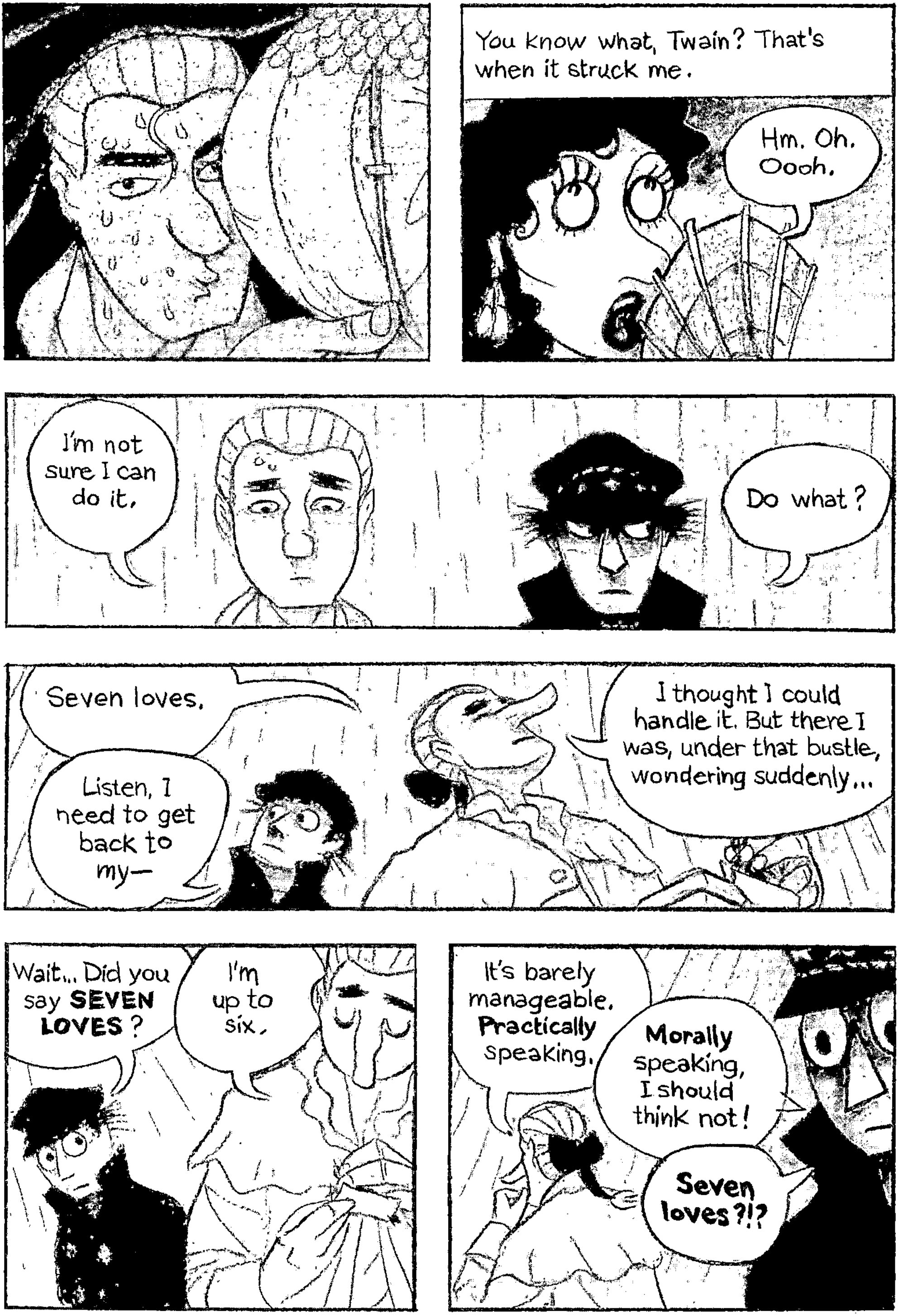

You know what, Twain? That's when it struck me.
Hm. Oh. Oooh.
I'm not sure I can do it.
Do what?
Seven loves.
Listen, I need to get back to my—
I thought I could handle it. But there I was, under that bustle, wondering suddenly...
Wait... Did you say **SEVEN LOVES**?
I'm up to six.
It's barely manageable. **Practically** speaking.
Morally speaking, I should think not!
Seven loves?!?

Long story.

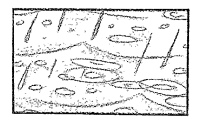

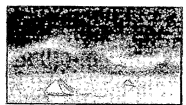

My sky needs more than one star. I'm a man of constellations, me.

And what of your loves, do many stars fill **their** sky?

They're **day-time** beings who crave a singular sun!

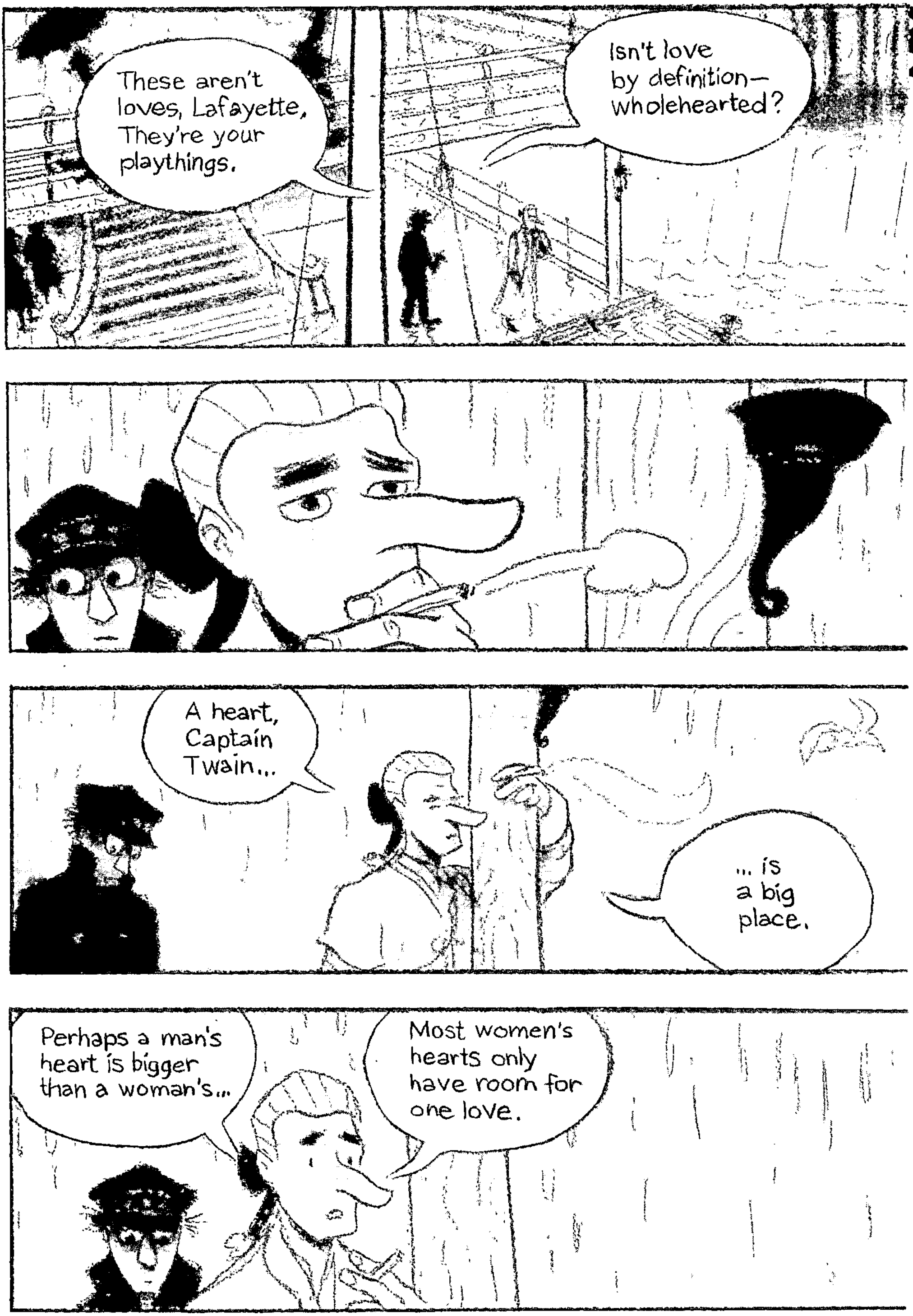
These aren't loves, Lafayette, They're your playthings.
Isn't love by definition— wholehearted?
A heart, Captain Twain...
... is a big place.
Perhaps a man's heart is bigger than a woman's...
Most women's hearts only have room for one love.

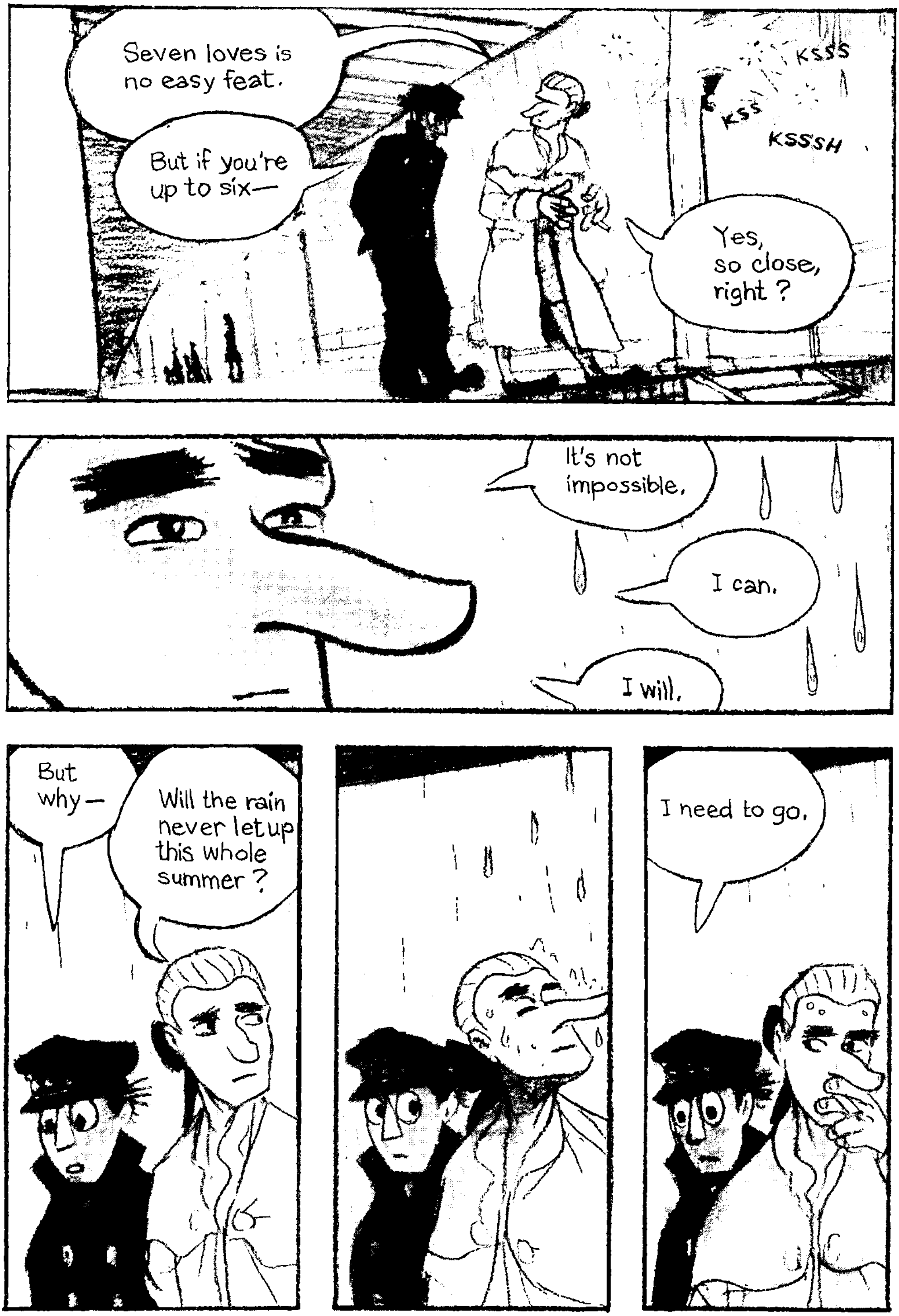
Seven loves is no easy feat.
But if you're up to six—
KSSS
KSS
KSSSH
Yes, so close, right ?
It's not impossible.
I can.
I will.
But why—
Will the rain never let up this whole summer ?
I need to go.

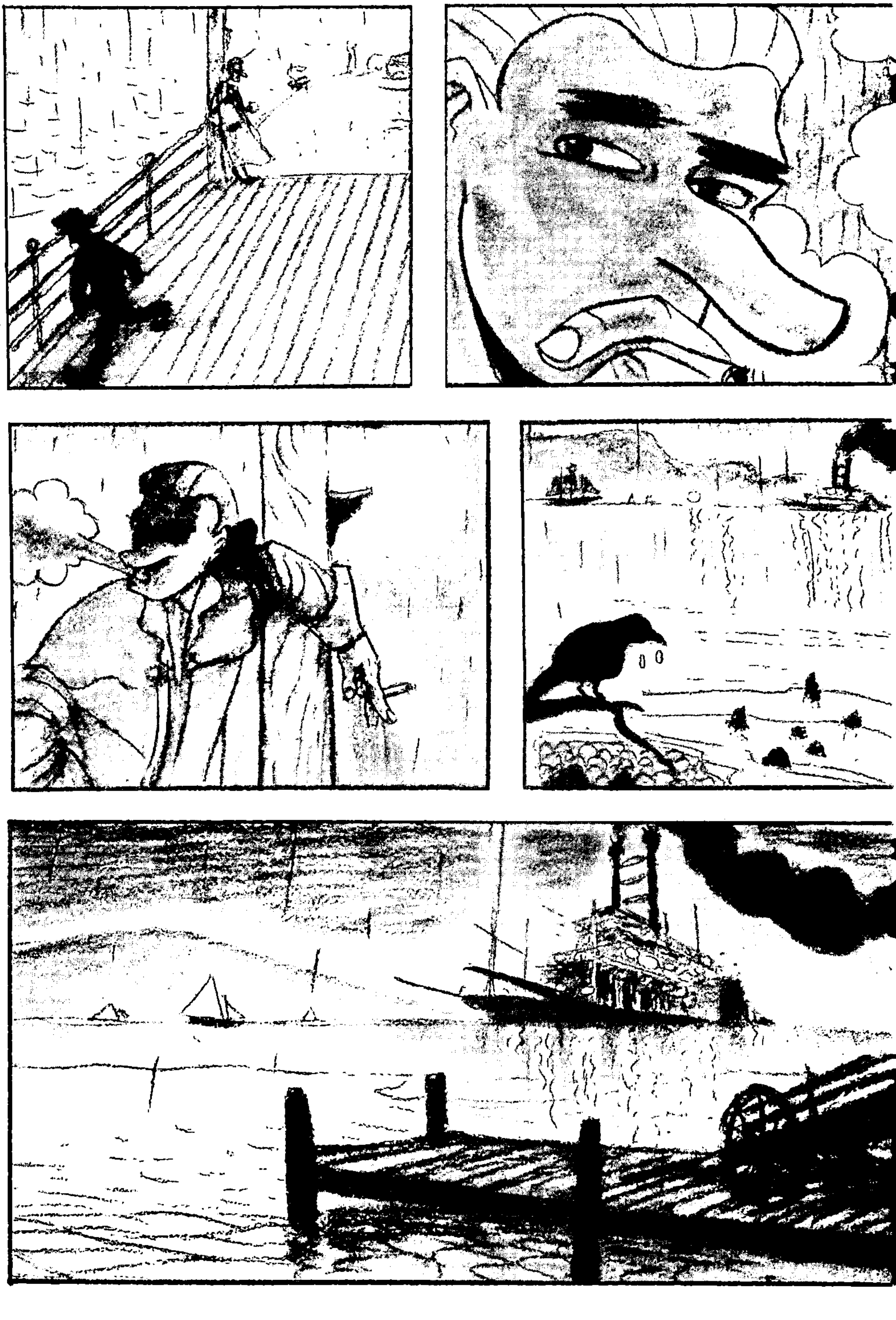

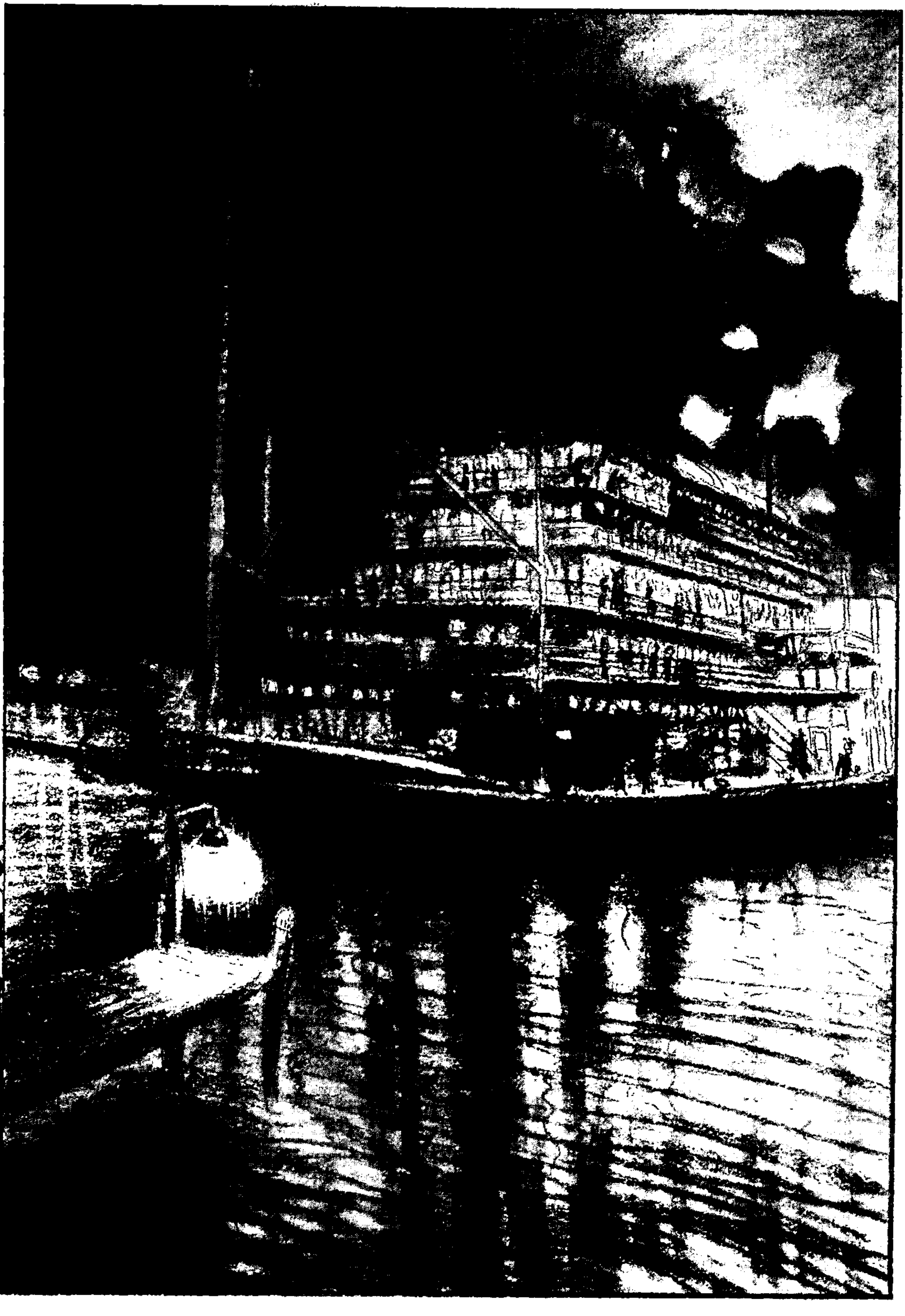

Pt 1, Chap.10

"THE CURE FOR MERMAIDS"

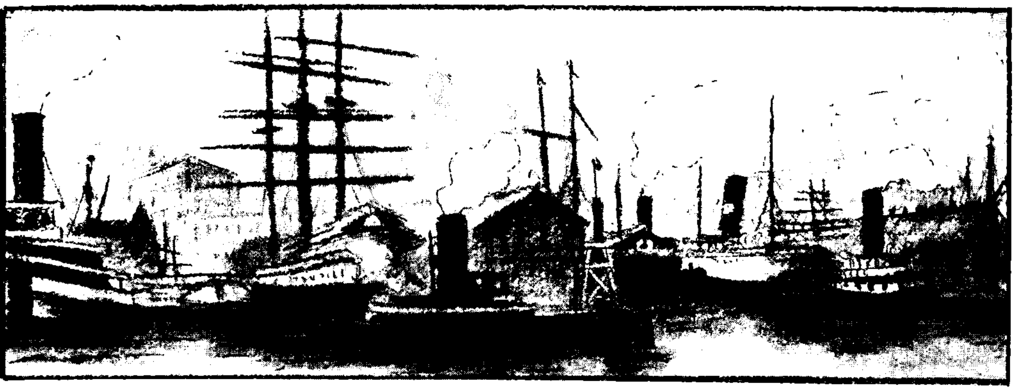

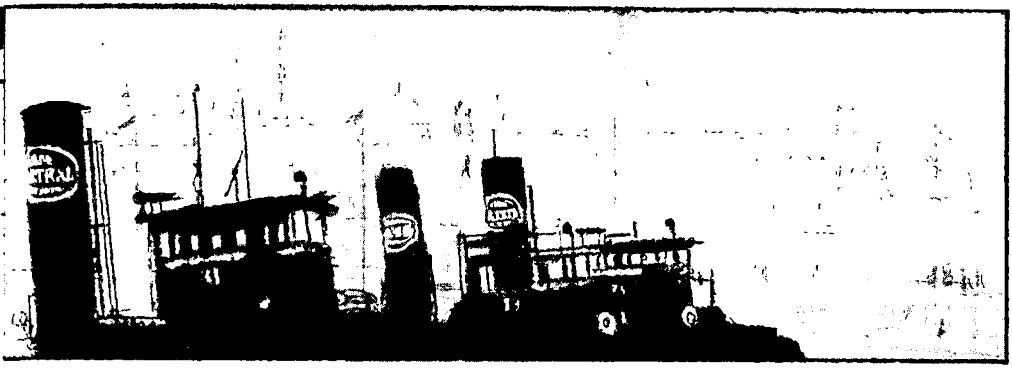

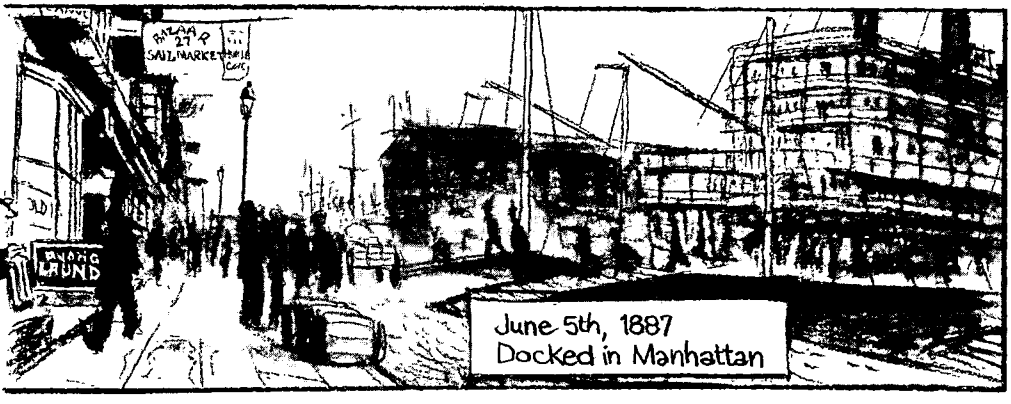
June 5th, 1887
Docked in Manhattan

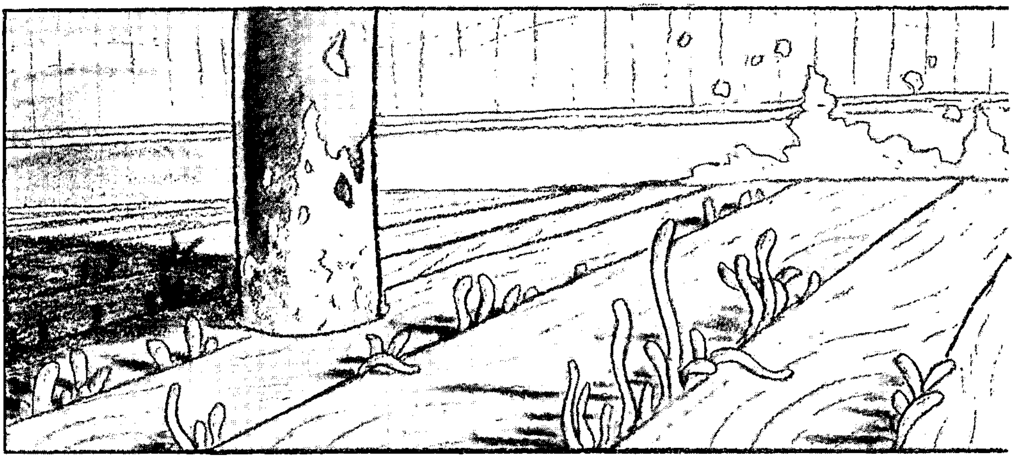

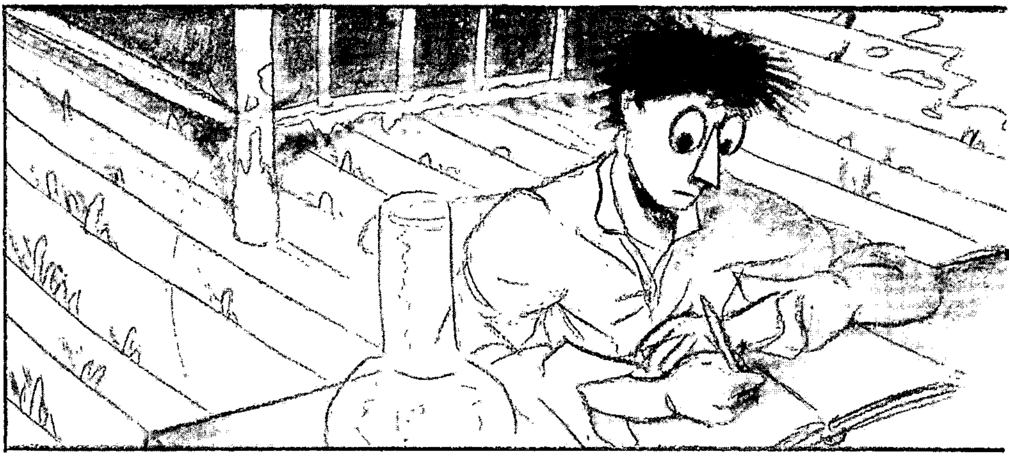

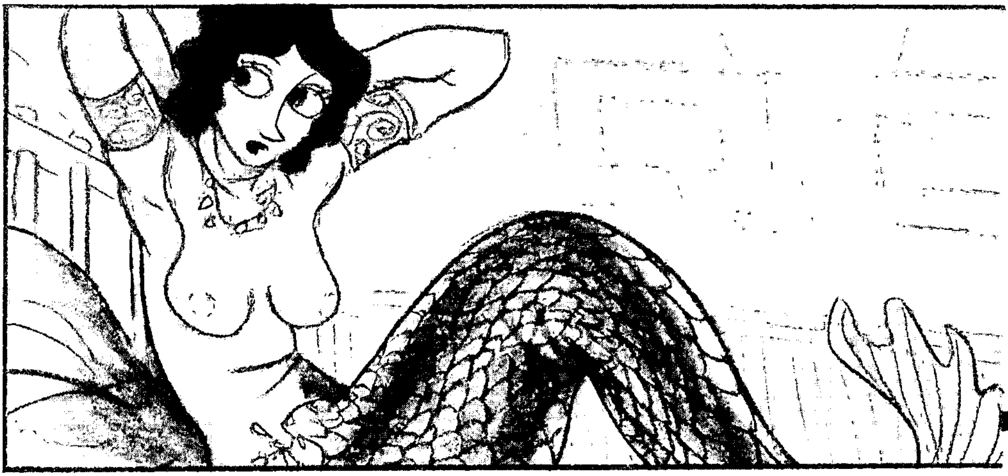

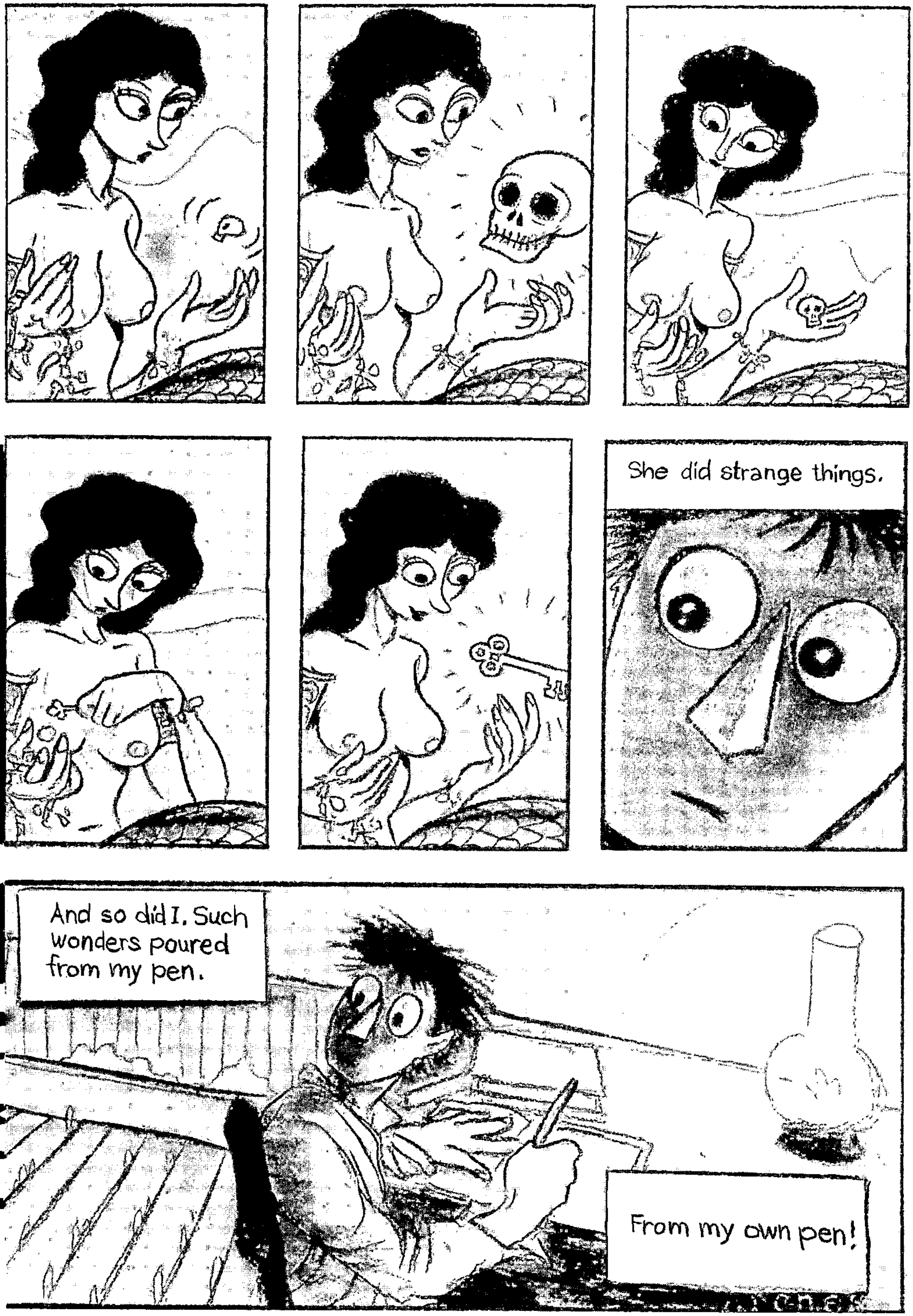
She did strange things.
And so did I. Such wonders poured from my pen.
From my own pen!

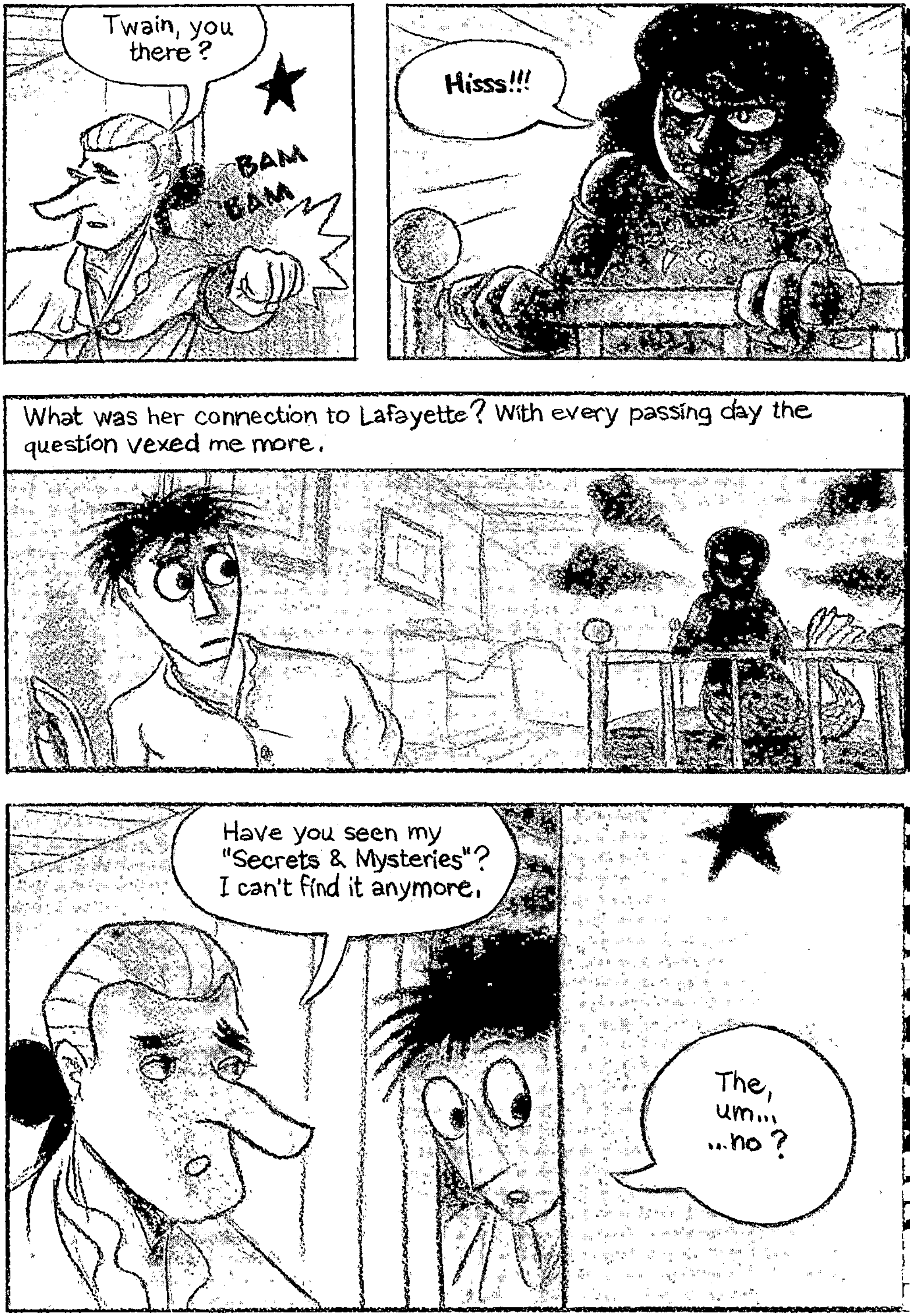
Twain, you there?
BAM
BAM
Hisss!!!
What was her connection to Lafayette? With every passing day the question vexed me more.
Have you seen my "Secrets & Mysteries"? I can't find it anymore.
The, um... ...no?

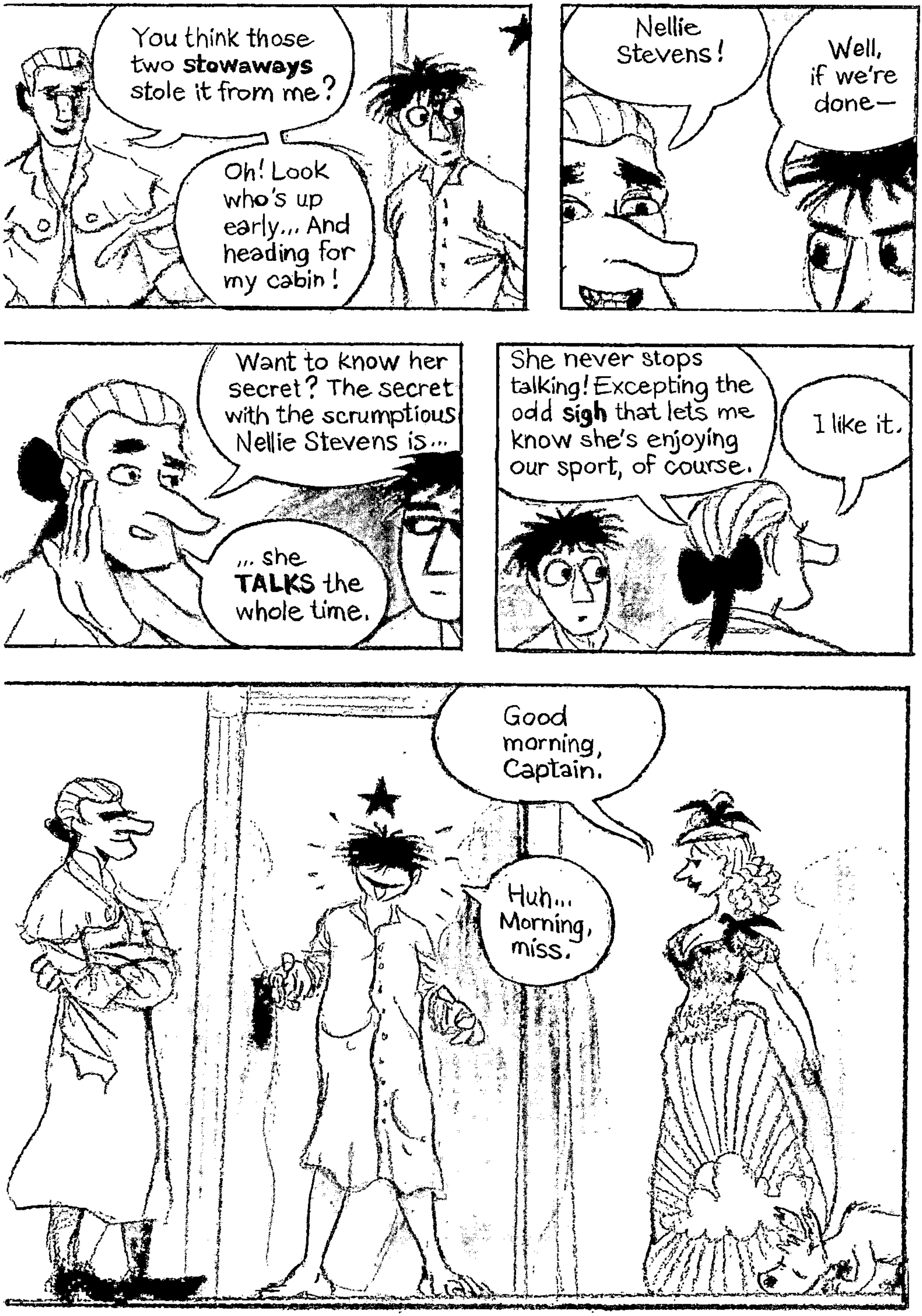
You think those two **stowaways** stole it from me?
Oh! Look who's up early... And heading for my cabin!
Nellie Stevens!
Well, if we're done—
Want to know her secret? The secret with the scrumptious Nellie Stevens is...
... she **TALKS** the whole time.
She never stops talking! Excepting the odd **sigh** that lets me know she's enjoying our sport, of course.
I like it.
Good morning, Captain.
Huh... Morning, miss.

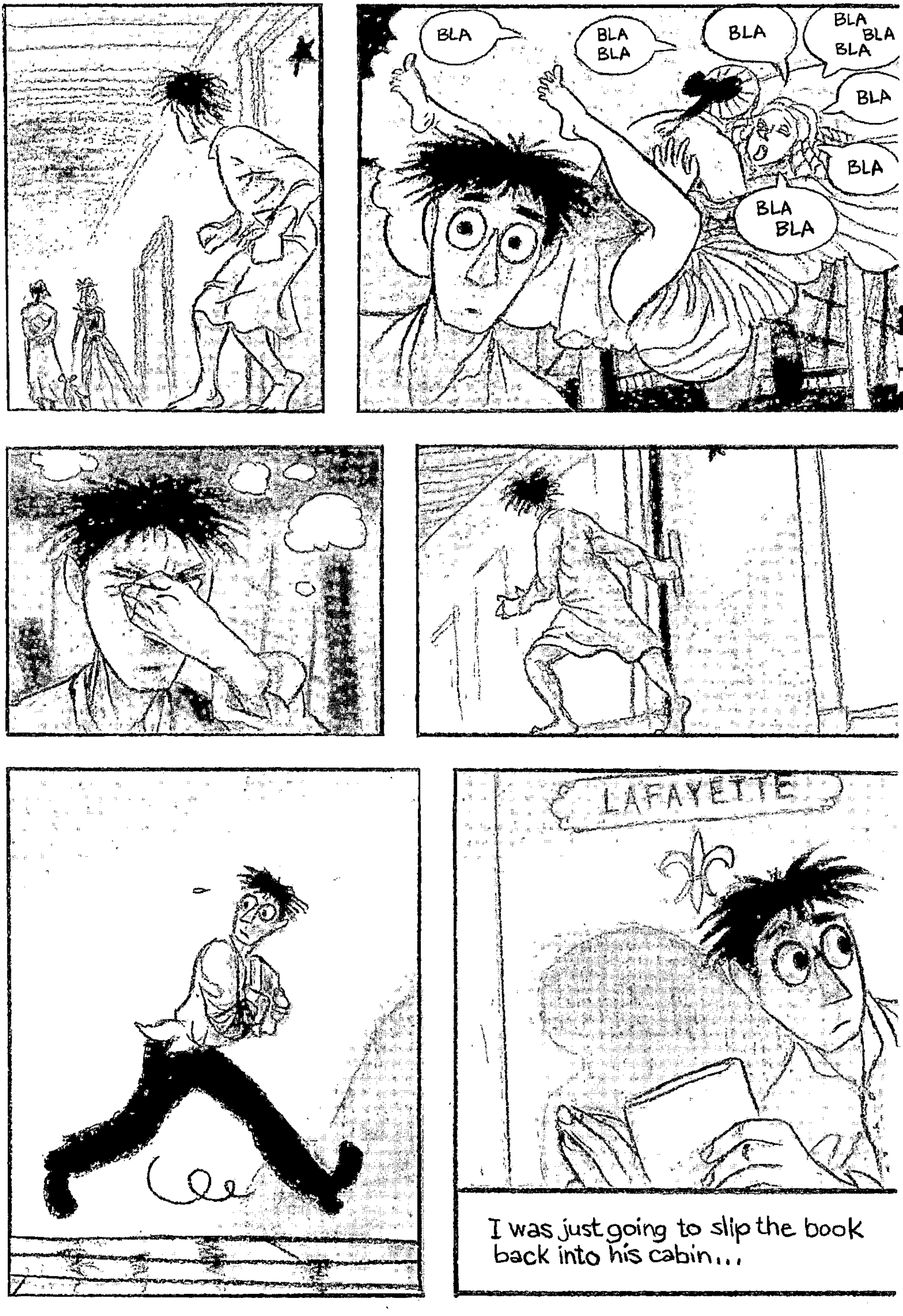
BLA
BLA
BLA
BLA
BLA
BLA
BLA
BLA
BLA
BLA
BLA
LAFAYETTE
I was just going to slip the book back into his cabin...

... when I accidentally glimpsed another letter from Beaverton himself...

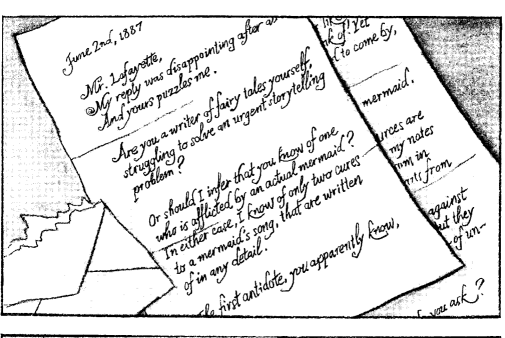

June 2nd, 1887

Mr. Lafayette,

My reply was disappointing after a... [...] Yet [...] to come by,

And yours puzzles me.

Are you a writer of fairy tales yourself, struggling to solve an urgent storytelling problem?

mermaid.

Or should I infer that you know of one who is afflicted by an actual mermaid? ...urces are

In either case, I know of only two cures — my notes
to a mermaid's song, that are written ...m in
of in any detail. ...ts from

...against
...t they

...le first antidote, you apparently know, ...of un-

... you ask?

What ?!

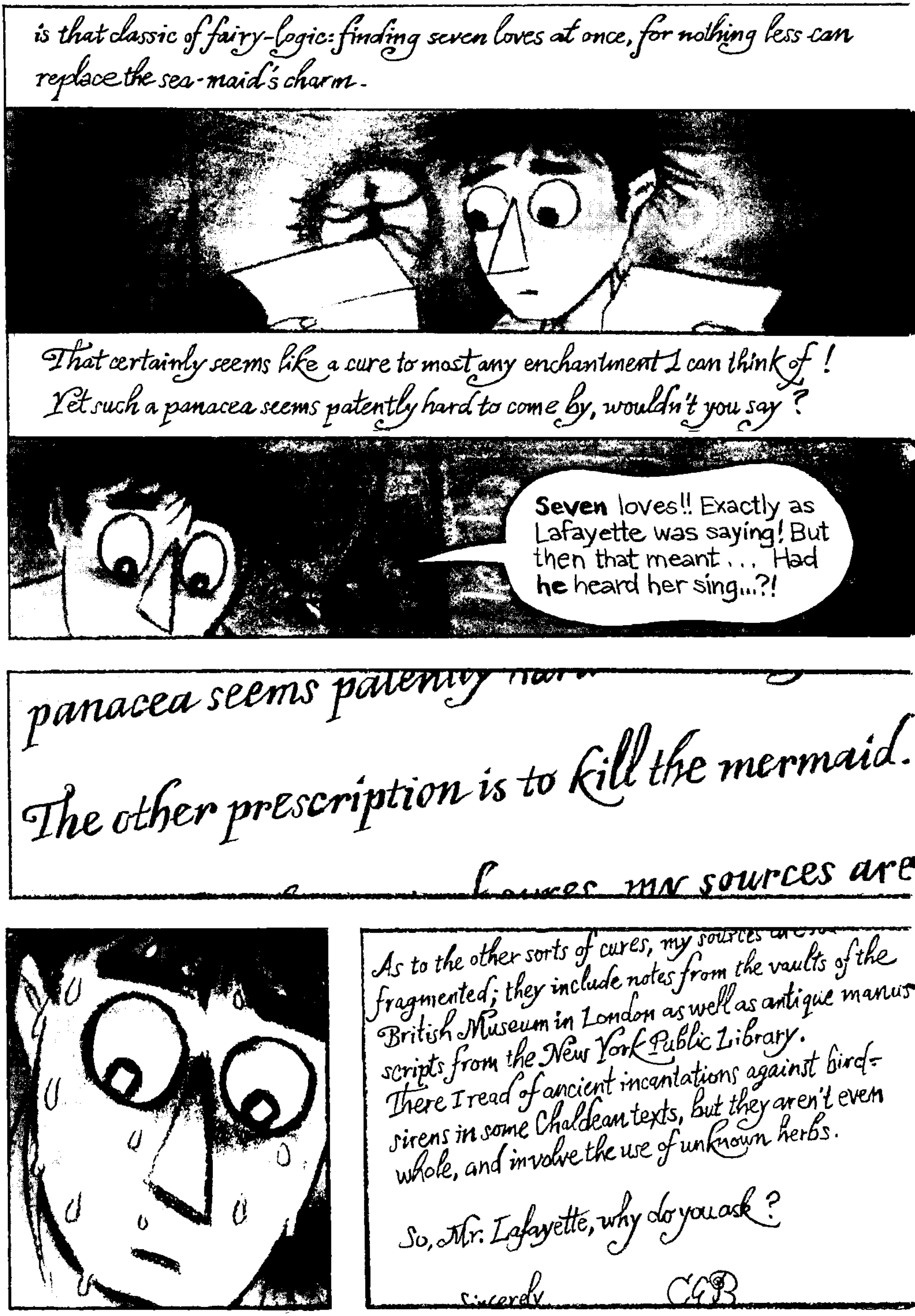
is that classic of fairy-logic: finding seven loves at once, for nothing less can replace the sea-maid's charm -
That certainly seems like a cure to most any enchantment I can think of! Yet such a panacea seems patently hard to come by, wouldn't you say?
Seven loves!! Exactly as Lafayette was saying! But then that meant... Had he heard her sing...?!
panacea seems patently
The other prescription is to kill the mermaid.
sources are
As to the other sorts of cures, my sources
fragmented; they include notes from the vaults of the British Museum in London as well as antique manus-
scripts from the New York Public Library.
There I read of ancient incantations against bird-sirens in some Chaldean texts, but they aren't even whole, and involve the use of unknown herbs.
So, Mr. Lafayette, why do you ask?
Sincerely
CGB

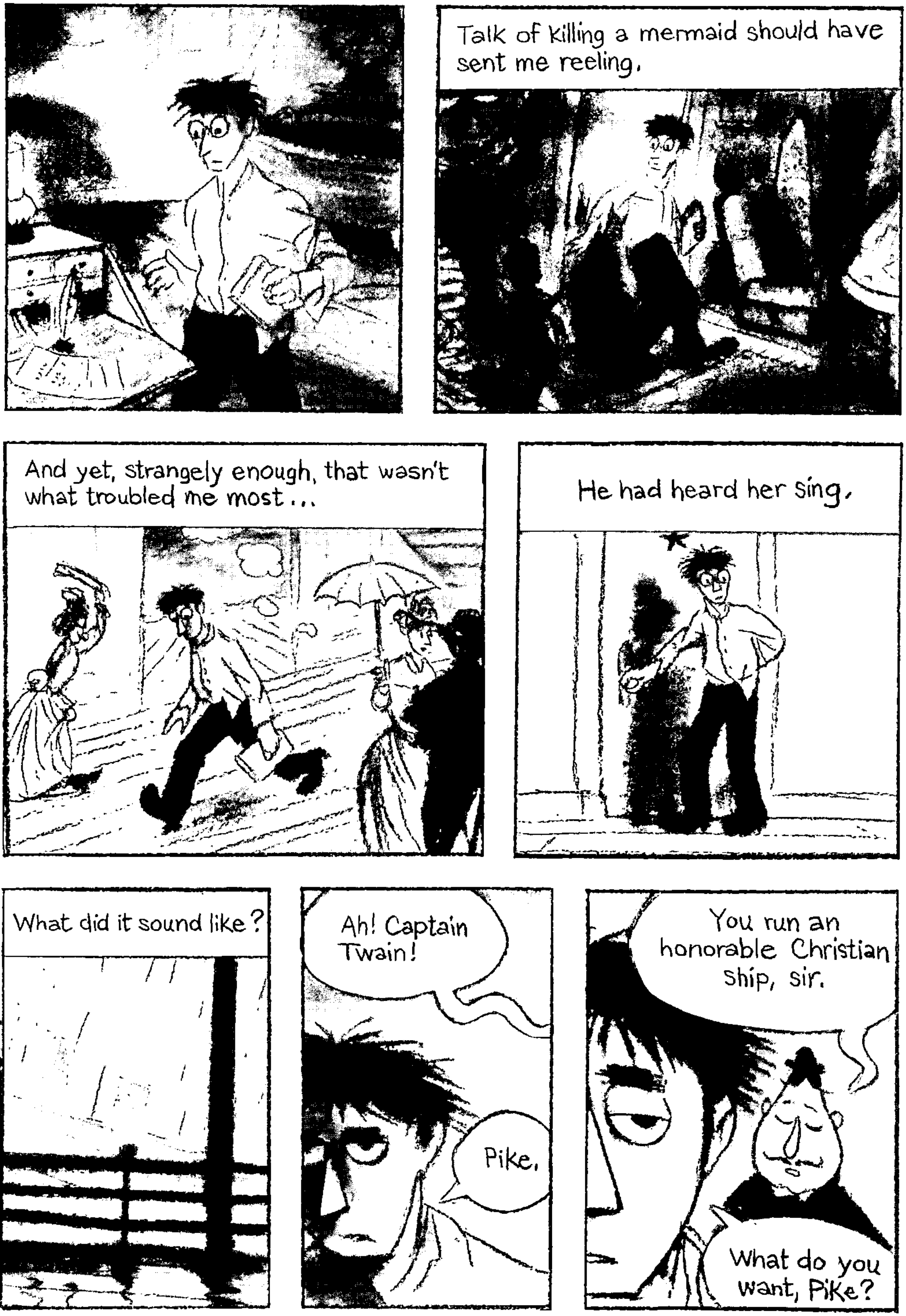
Talk of killing a mermaid should have sent me reeling.
And yet, strangely enough, that wasn't what troubled me most...
He had heard her sing.
What did it sound like?
Ah! Captain Twain!
Pike.
You run an honorable Christian ship, sir.
What do you want, Pike?

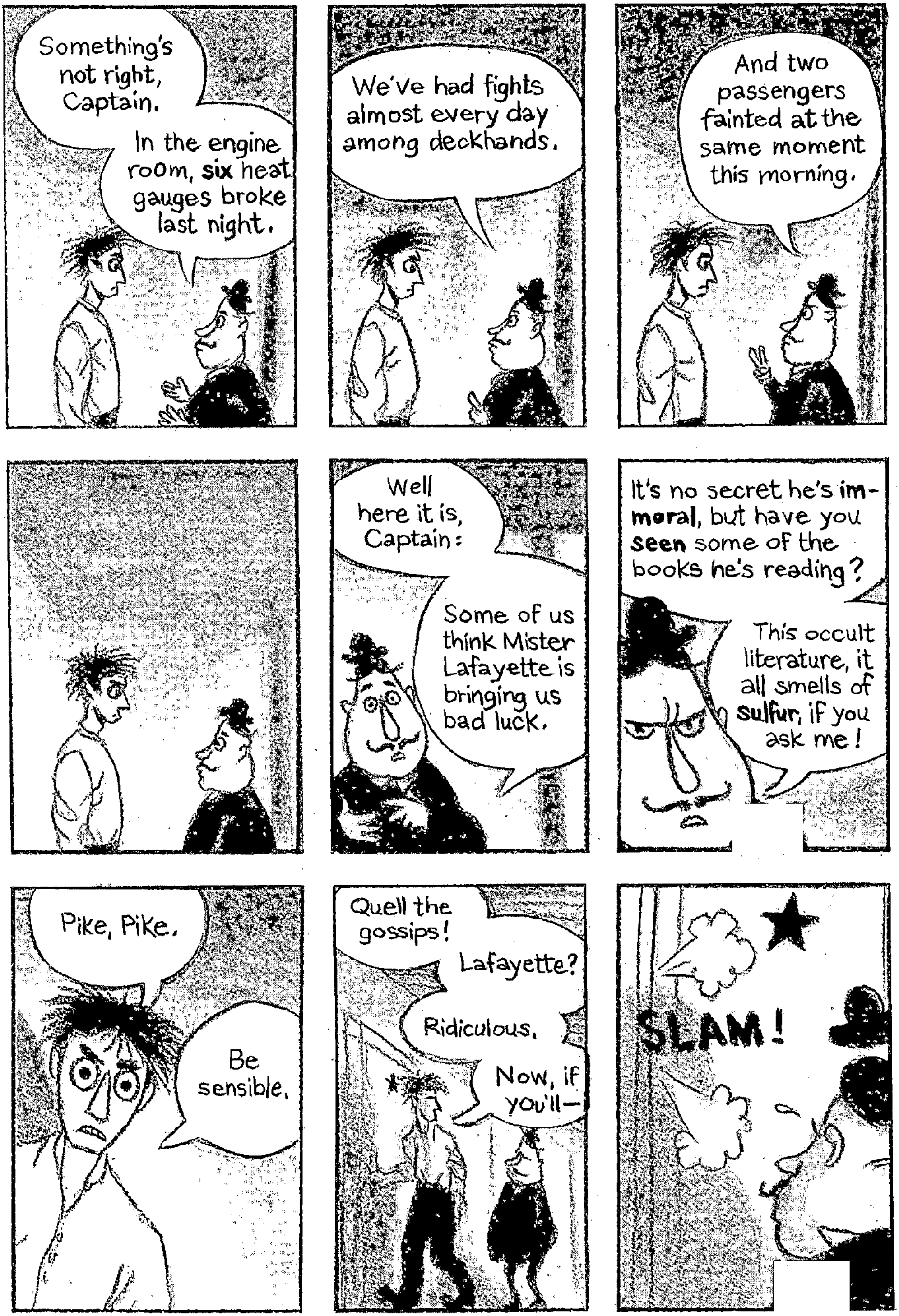
Something's not right, Captain.
In the engine room, **six** heat gauges broke last night.
We've had fights almost every day among deckhands.
And two passengers fainted at the same moment this morning.
Well here it is, Captain:
Some of us think Mister Lafayette is bringing us bad luck.
It's no secret he's **immoral**, but have you **seen** some of the books he's reading?
This occult literature, it all smells of **sulfur**, if you ask me!
Pike, Pike.
Be sensible.
Quell the gossips!
Lafayette?
Ridiculous.
Now, if you'll—
SLAM!

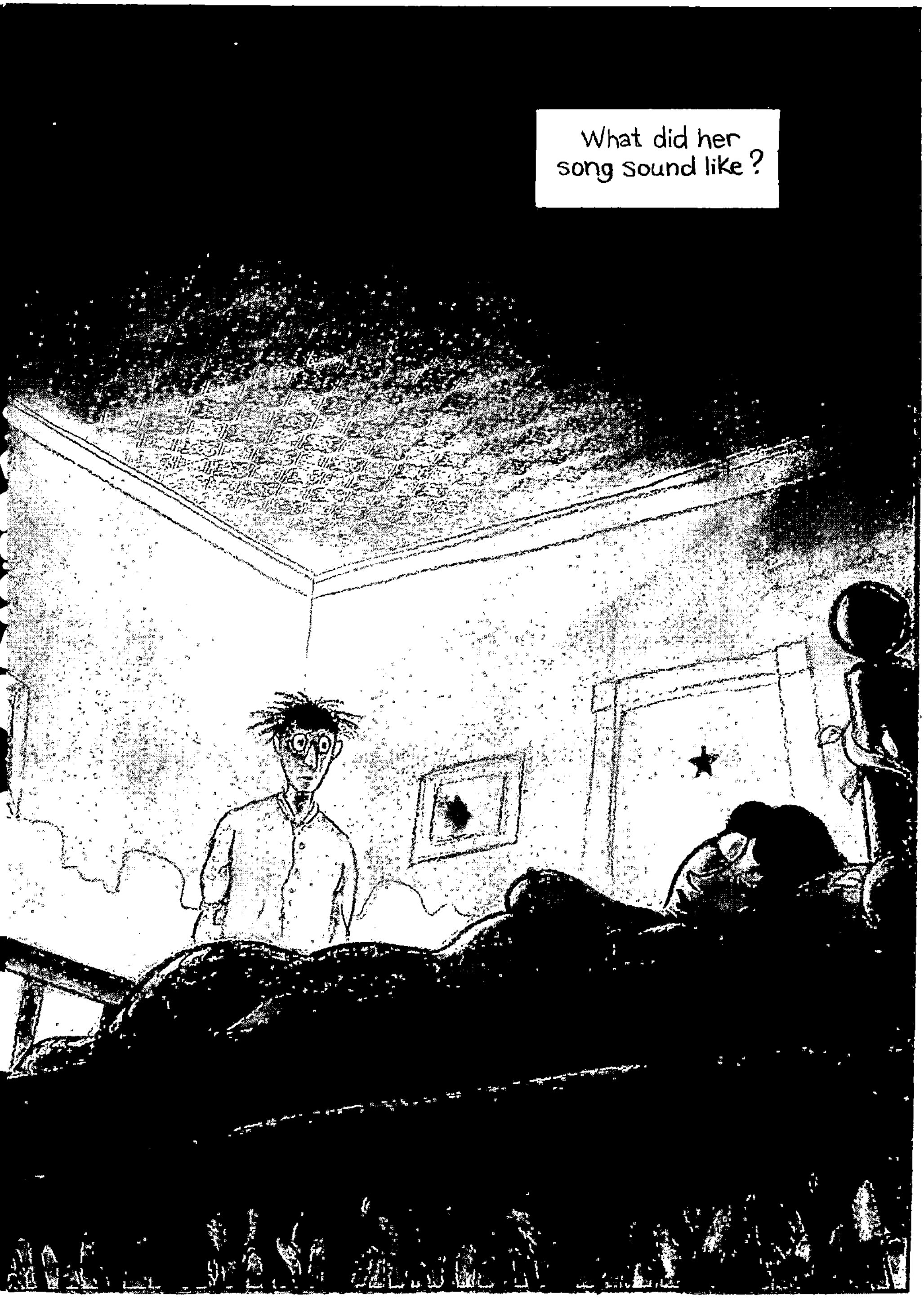
What did her song sound like?

Pt 1, Chap.11

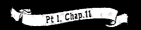

"SOUTH OF THE NORTH RIVER"

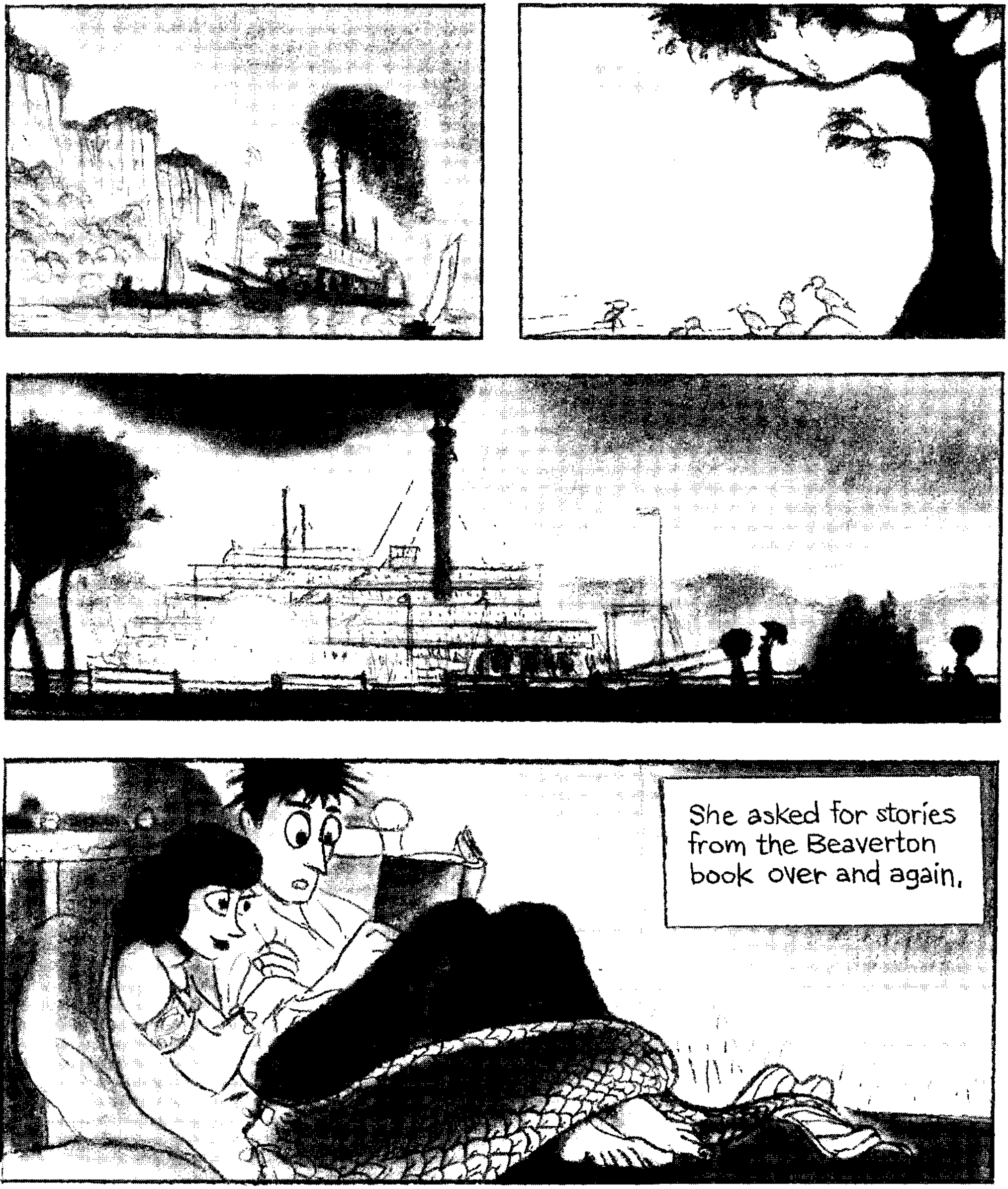
She asked for stories from the Beaverton book over and again.

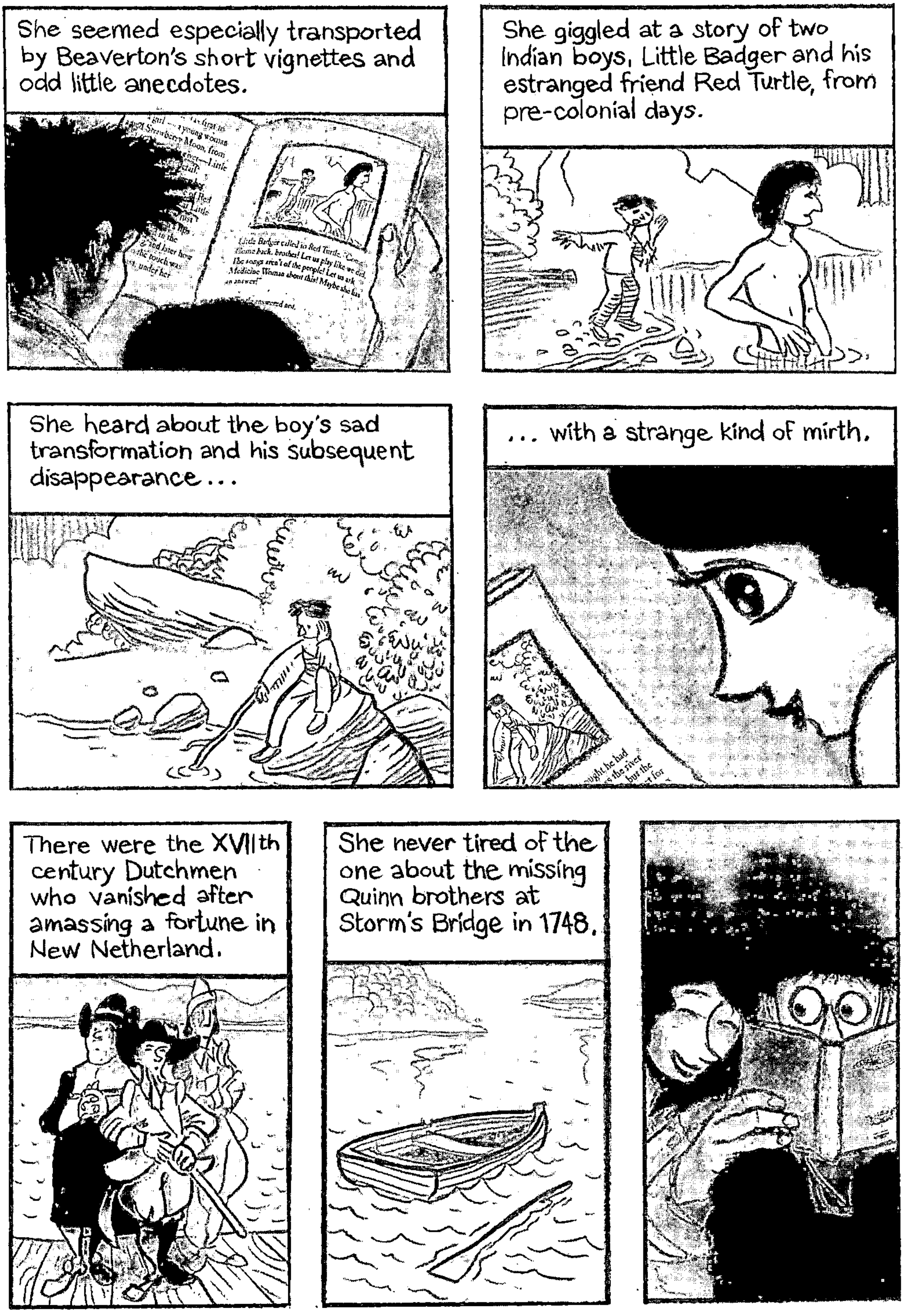

She seemed especially transported by Beaverton's short vignettes and odd little anecdotes.
She giggled at a story of two Indian boys, Little Badger and his estranged friend Red Turtle, from pre-colonial days.
She heard about the boy's sad transformation and his subsequent disappearance...
... with a strange kind of mirth.
There were the XVIIth century Dutchmen who vanished after amassing a fortune in New Netherland.
She never tired of the one about the missing Quinn brothers at Storm's Bridge in 1748.

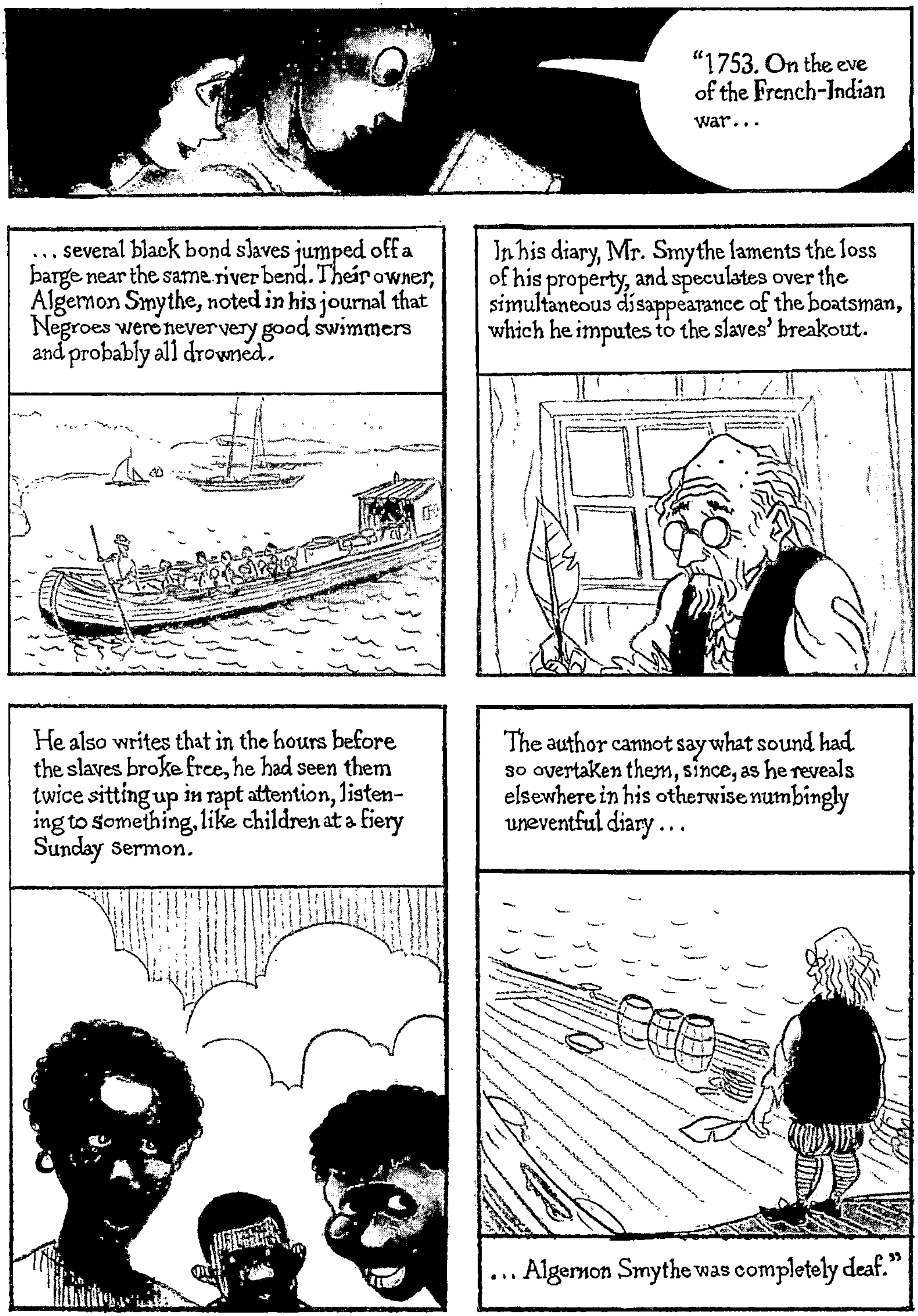
"1753. On the eve of the French-Indian war...
... several black bond slaves jumped off a barge near the same river bend. Their owner, Algernon Smythe, noted in his journal that Negroes were never very good swimmers and probably all drowned.
In his diary, Mr. Smythe laments the loss of his property, and speculates over the simultaneous disappearance of the boatsman, which he imputes to the slaves' breakout.
He also writes that in the hours before the slaves broke free, he had seen them twice sitting up in rapt attention, listening to something, like children at a fiery Sunday sermon.
The author cannot say what sound had so overtaken them, since, as he reveals elsewhere in his otherwise numbingly uneventful diary...
... Algernon Smythe was completely deaf."

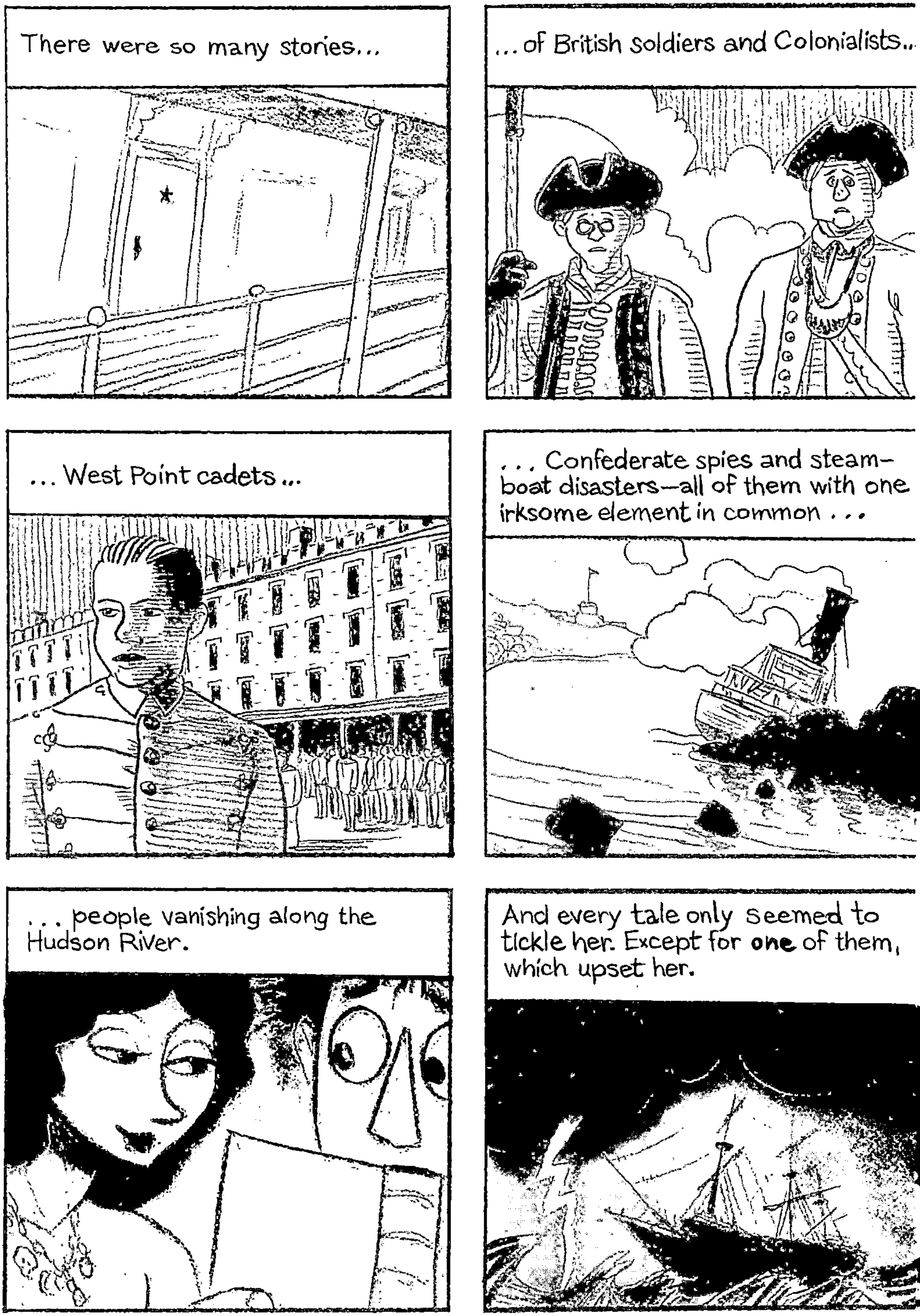
There were so many stories...
...of British soldiers and Colonialists...
...West Point cadets...
...Confederate spies and steam-boat disasters—all of them with one irksome element in common...
...people vanishing along the Hudson River.
And every tale only seemed to tickle her. Except for one of them, which upset her.

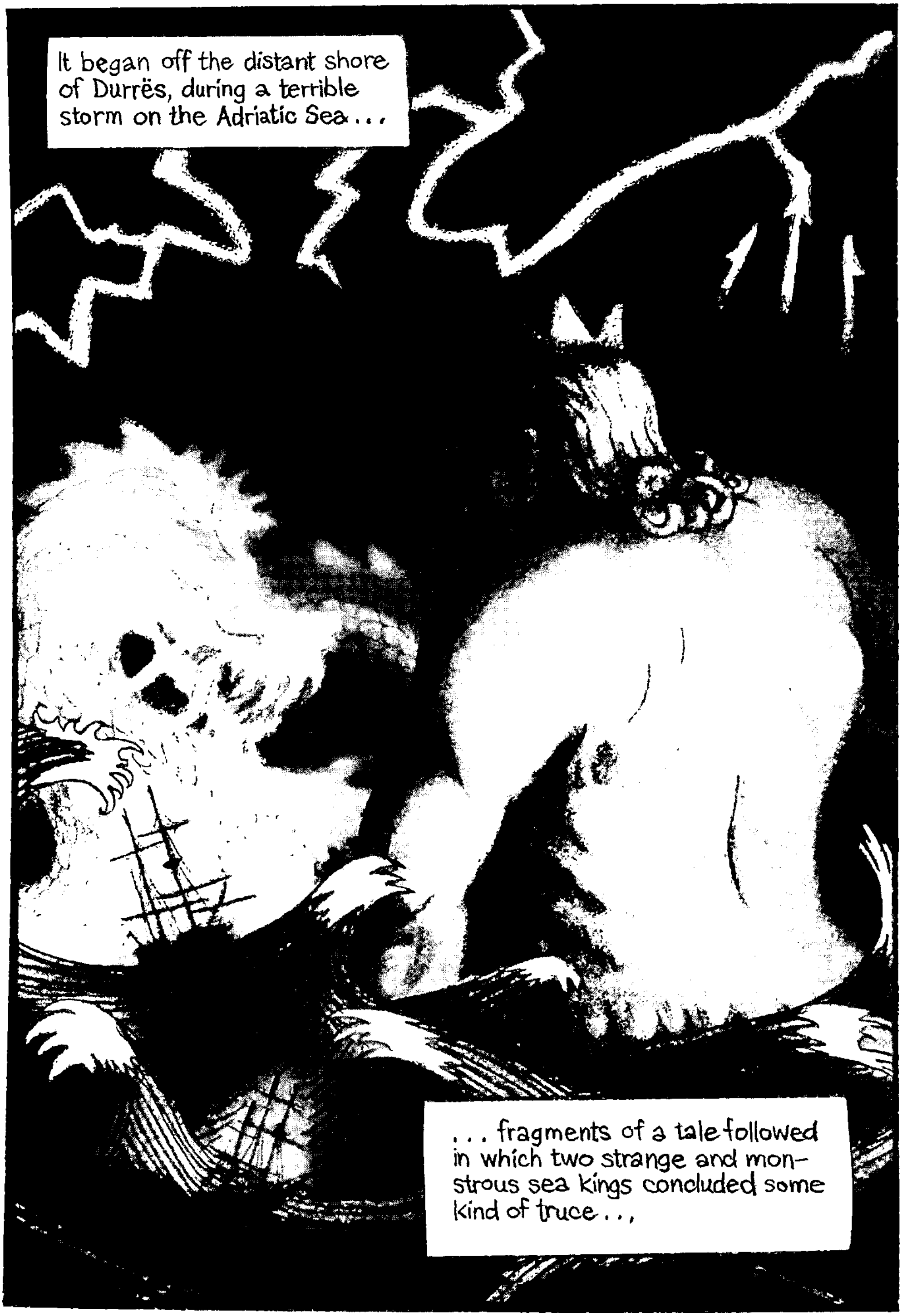
It began off the distant shore of Durrës, during a terrible storm on the Adriatic Sea . . .
. . . fragments of a tale followed in which two strange and monstrous sea kings concluded some kind of truce . . .

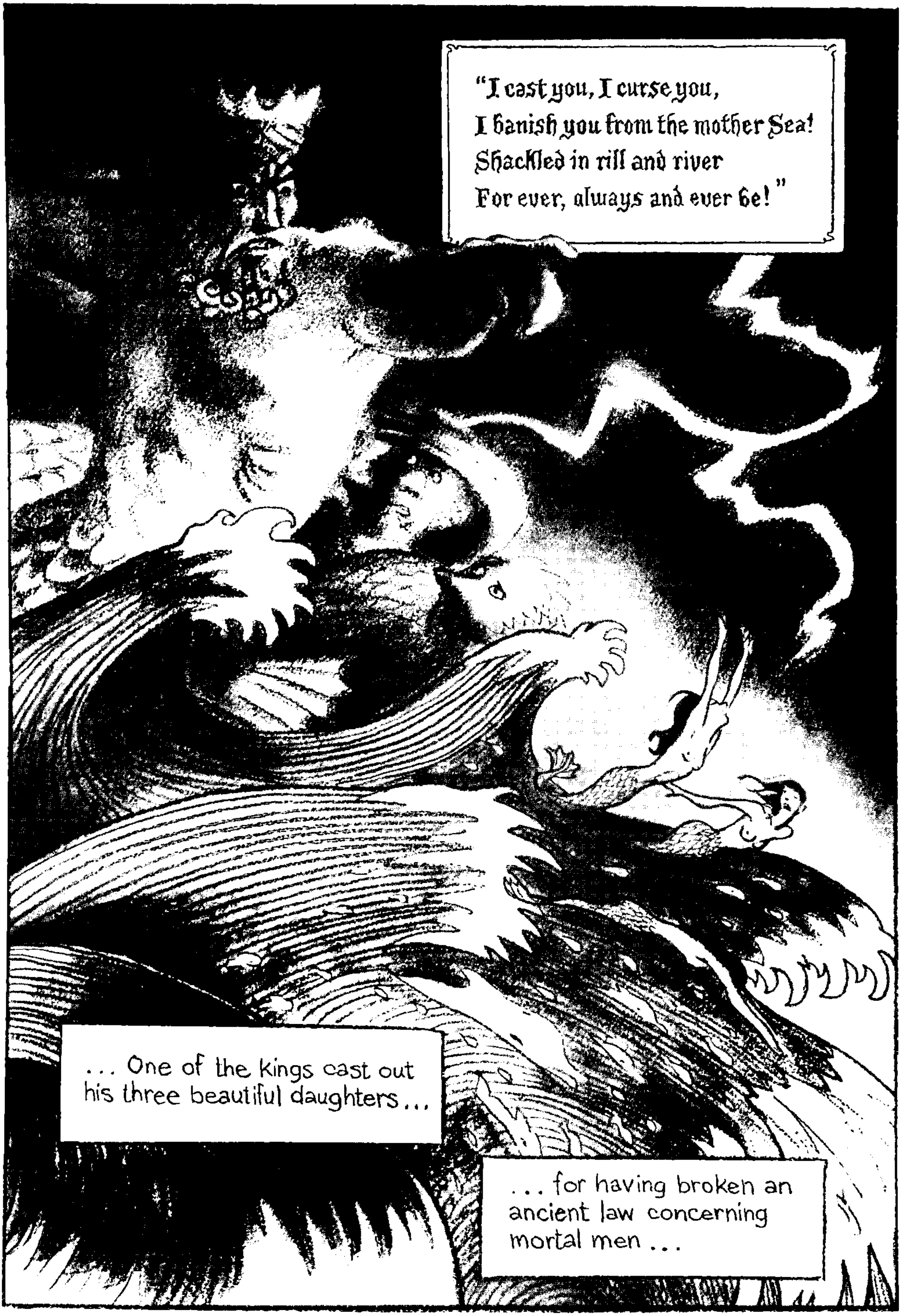
"I cast you, I curse you,
I banish you from the mother Sea!
Shackled in rill and river
For ever, always and ever be!"
... One of the kings cast out his three beautiful daughters...
... for having broken an ancient law concerning mortal men ...

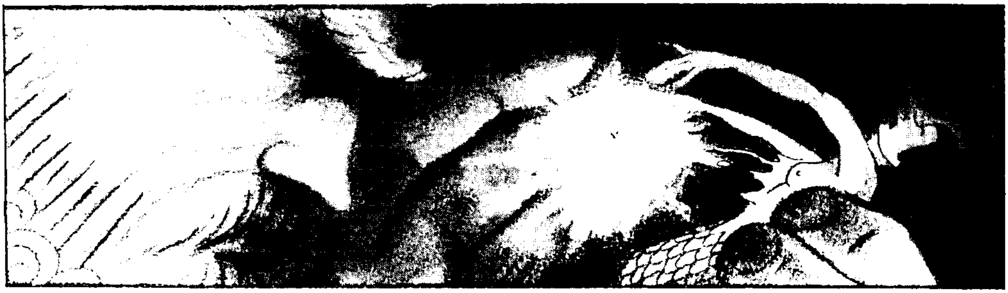

But before that, he tore their hearts away.

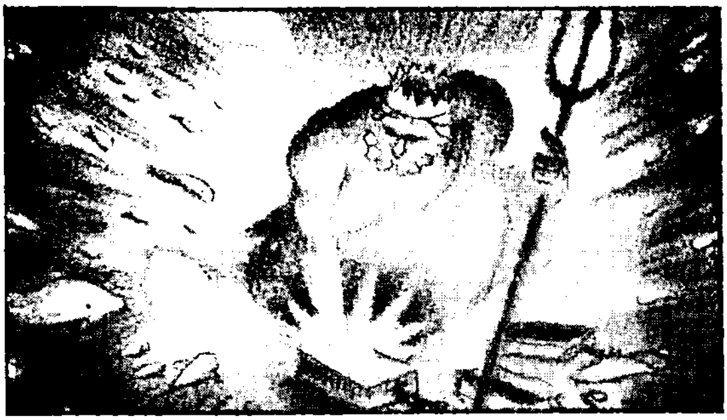

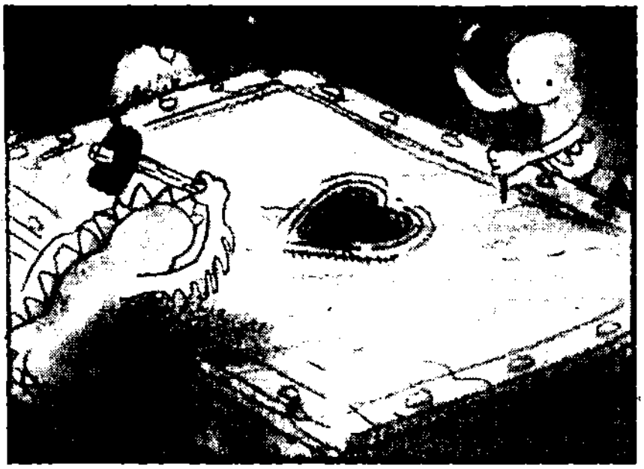

He locked each heart in a granite chest sealed with seven curses
and cast each chest into the deepest part of three

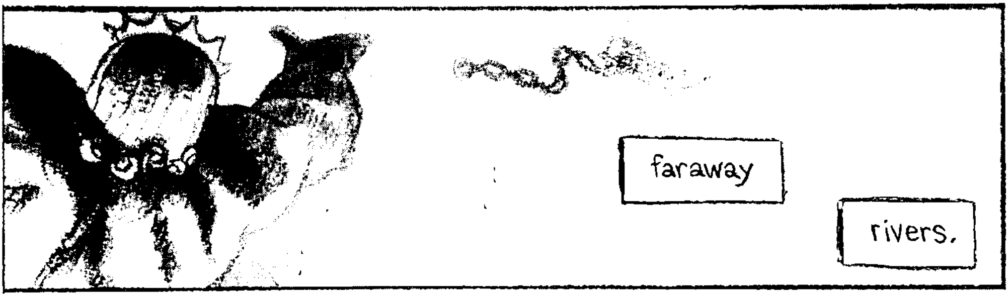
faraway
rivers.

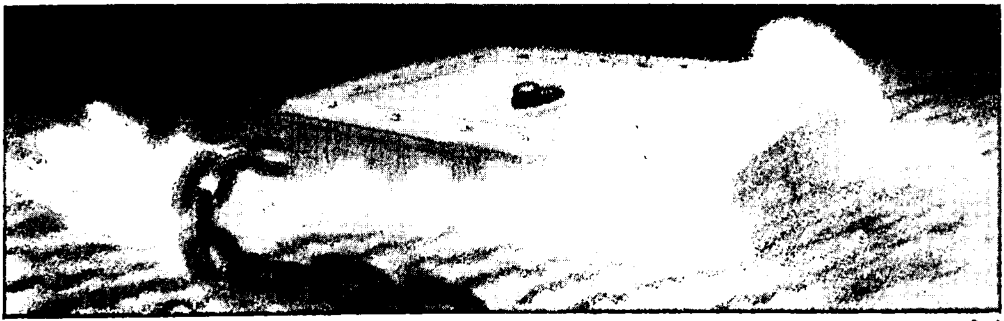

As punishment for their mysterious trespass, each heart was bound by powerful spells in seven ancient tongues, then sealed by twenty-one sacred images...

... One of the sisters was confined in the Rhine ...

... one in the Danube...

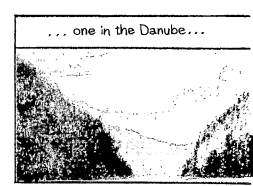

... and the guiltiest of them, who had led her sisters astray,

was sent to a distant land in a mighty river that flows in two directions,

in water sometimes fresh, sometimes salty — to forever remind her of the ocean

from whence she had been driven ...

She wailed and sobbed as I read that passage. I stopped before it was over.

But it wasn't over. I read on to myself. The blood chilled in my vein:

"And nothing shall unbind thee
Save the love of a mortal lover,
Given, given free, whole and sound!
With nary a trick nor a chant!
With neither song nor spell!
No less shall sever the thrall!

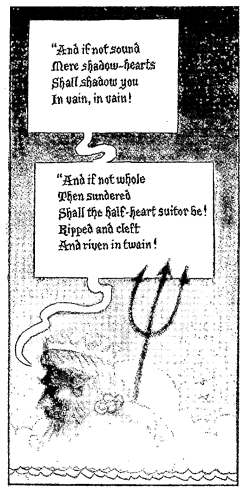

"And if not sound
Mere shadow-hearts
Shall shadow you
In vain, in vain!

"And if not whole
Then sundered
Shall the half-heart suitor be!
Ripped and cleft
And riven in twain!

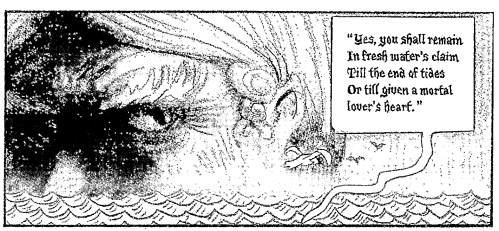

"Yes, you shall remain
In fresh water's claim
Till the end of tides
Or till given a mortal
lover's heart."

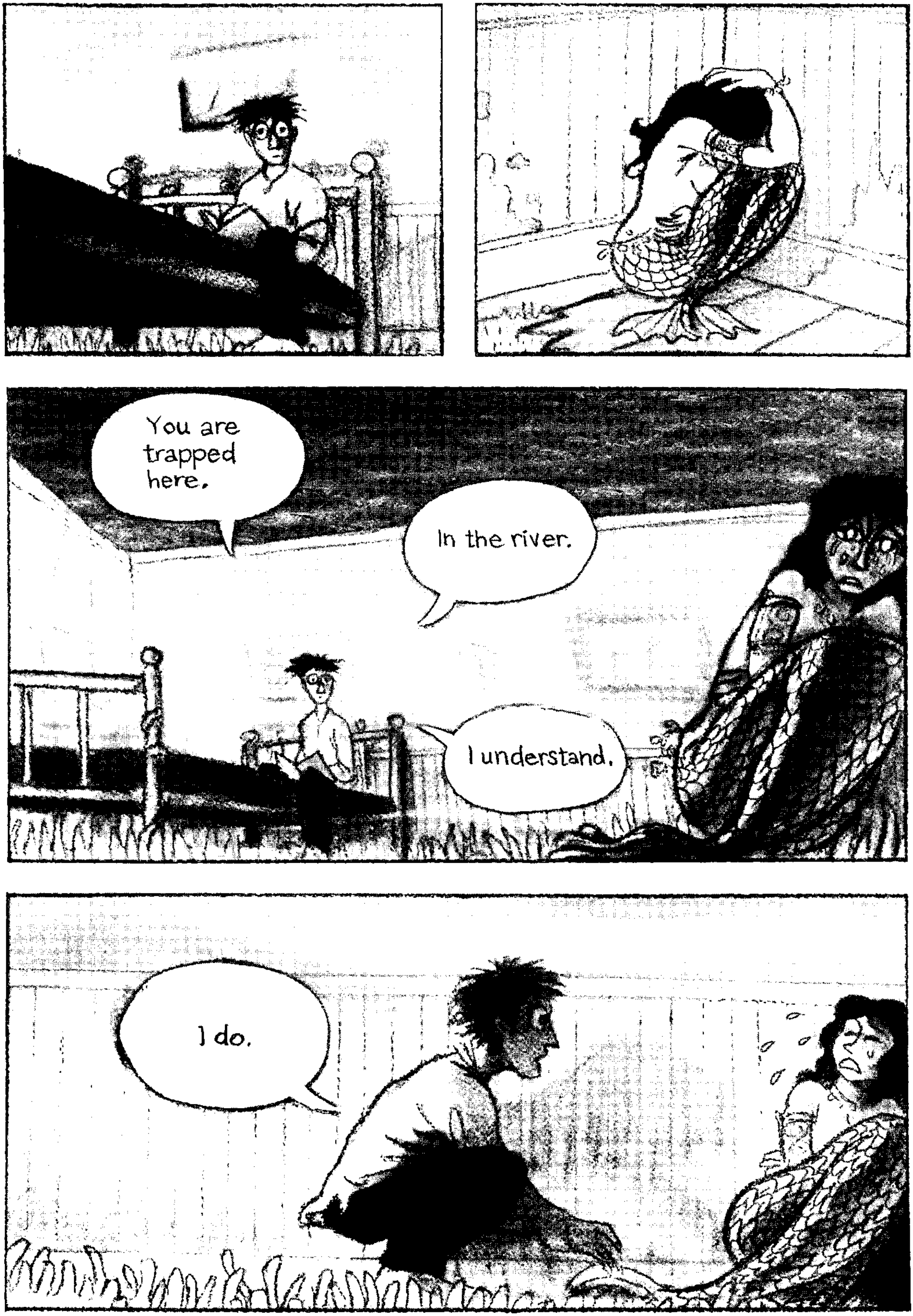
You are trapped here.
In the river.
I understand.
I do.

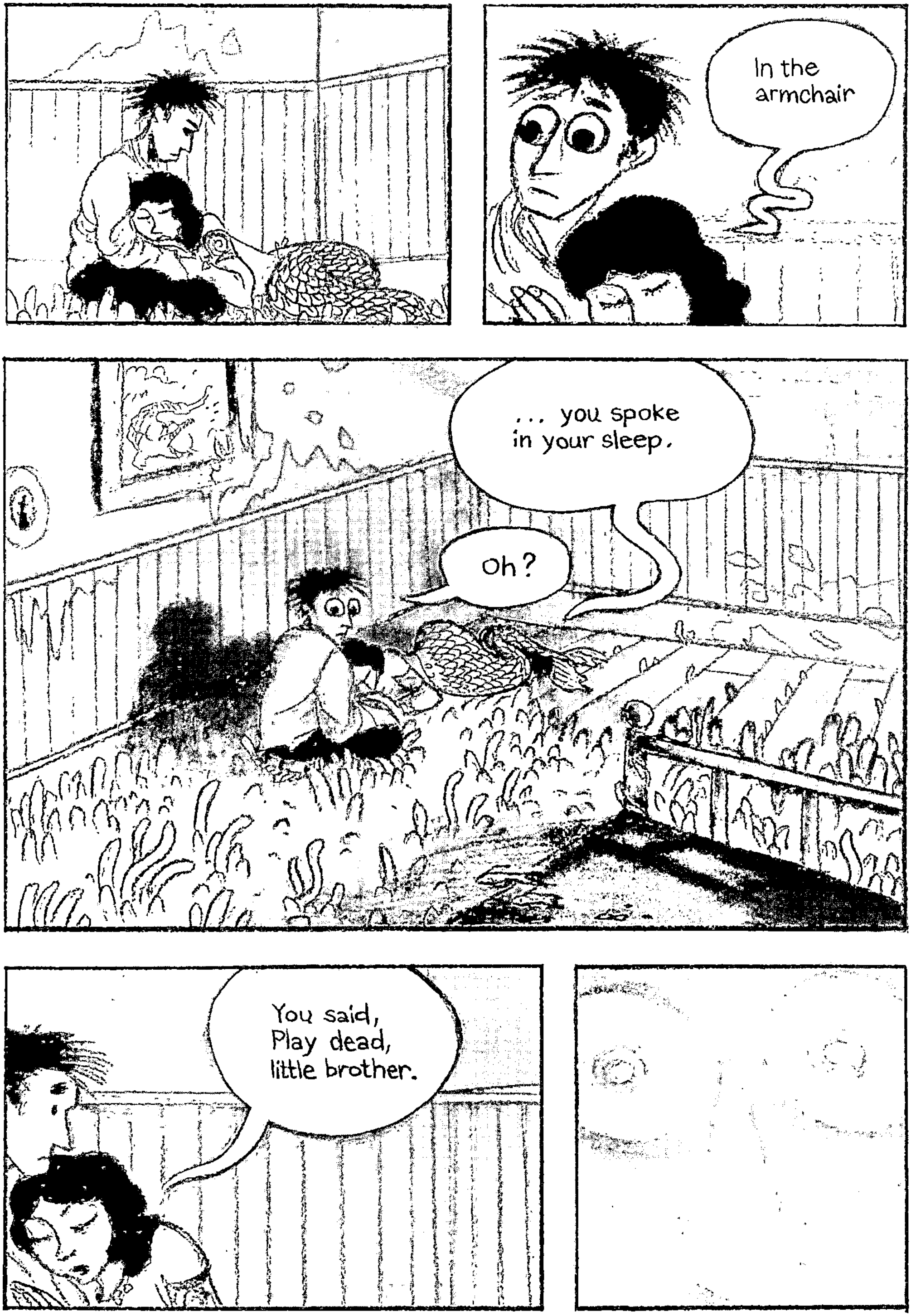
In the armchair
... you spoke in your sleep.
Oh?
You said, Play dead, little brother.

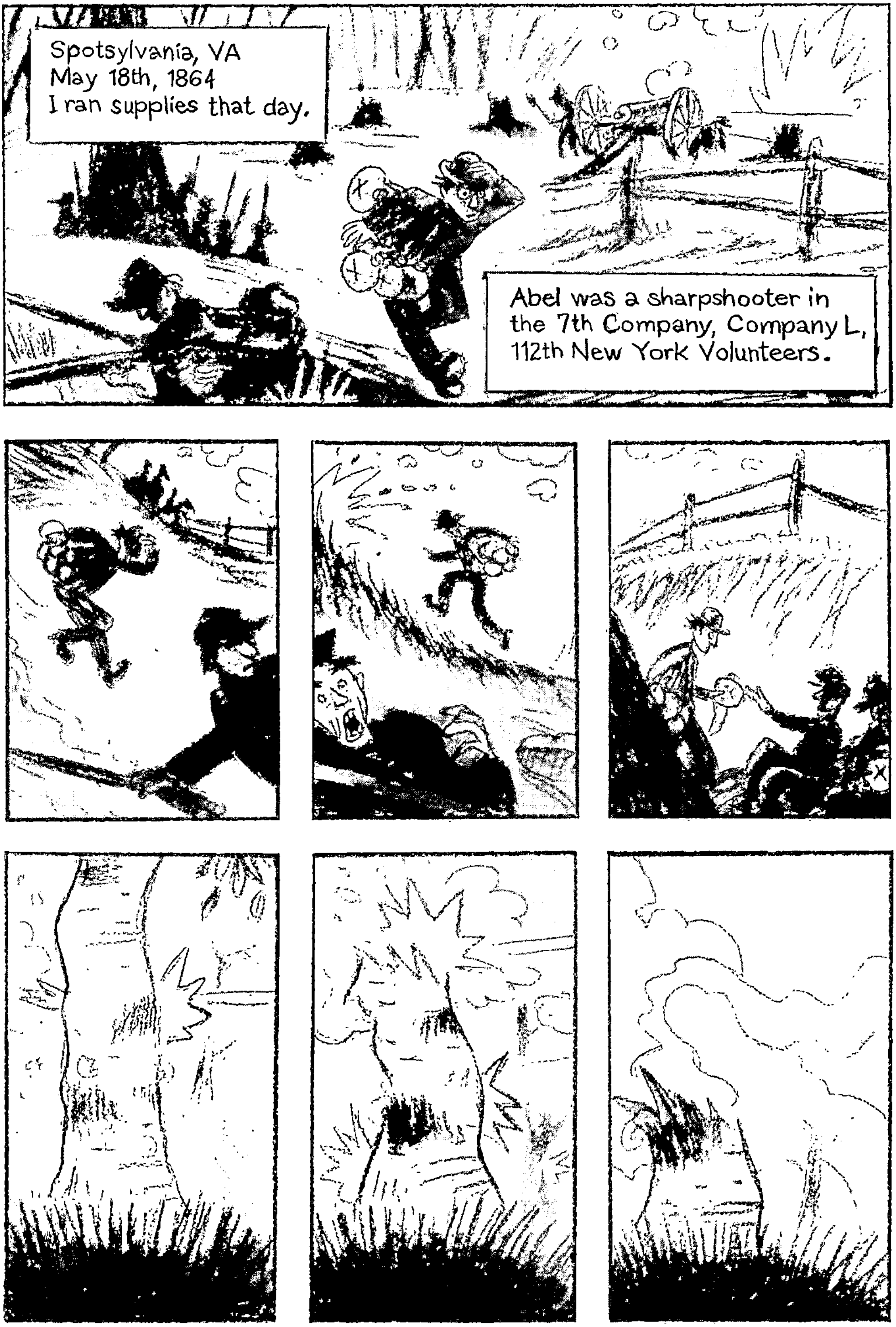
Spotsylvania, VA
May 18th, 1864
I ran supplies that day.
Abel was a sharpshooter in the 7th Company, Company L, 112th New York Volunteers.

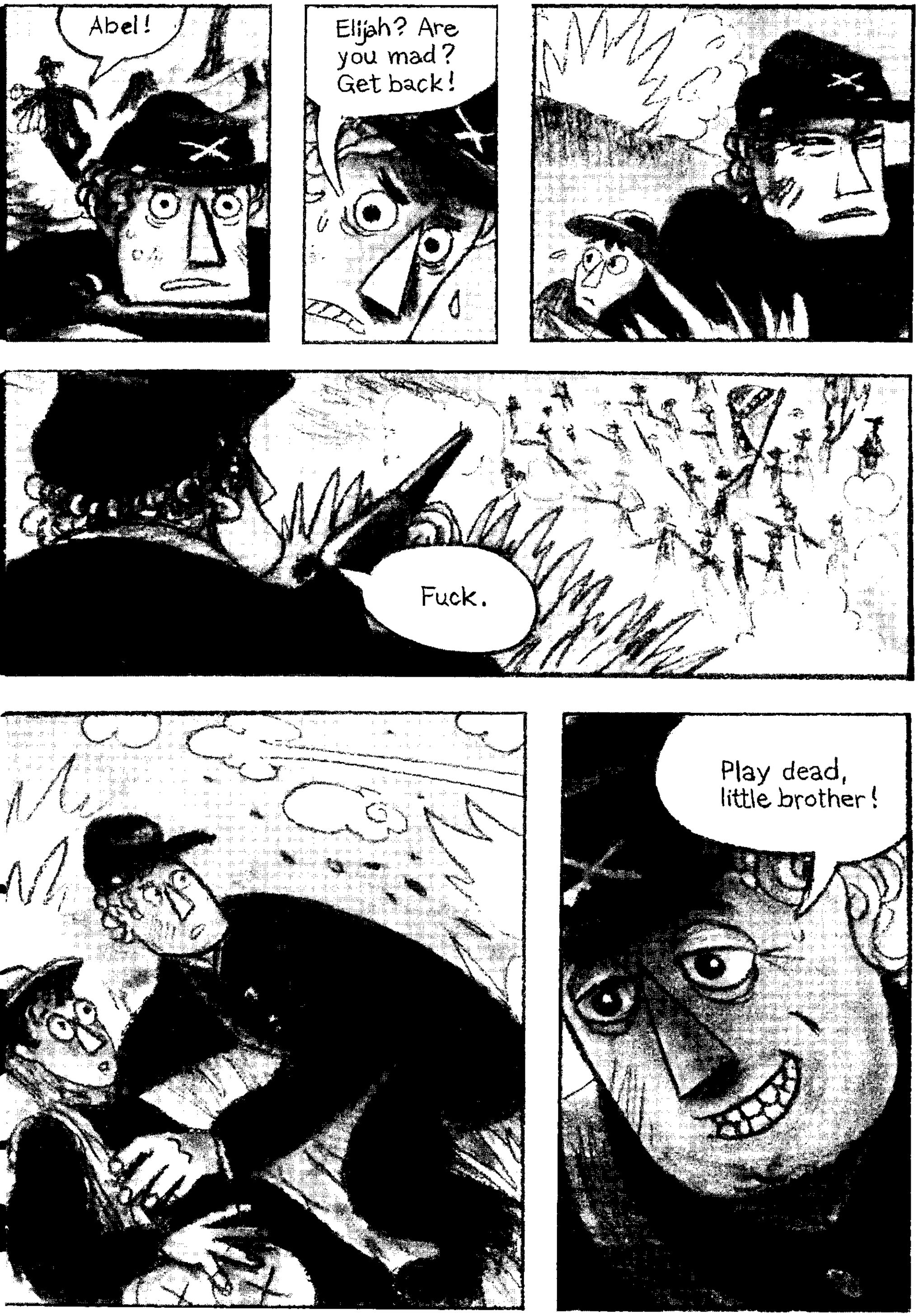
Abel!
Elijah? Are you mad? Get back!
Fuck.
Play dead, little brother!

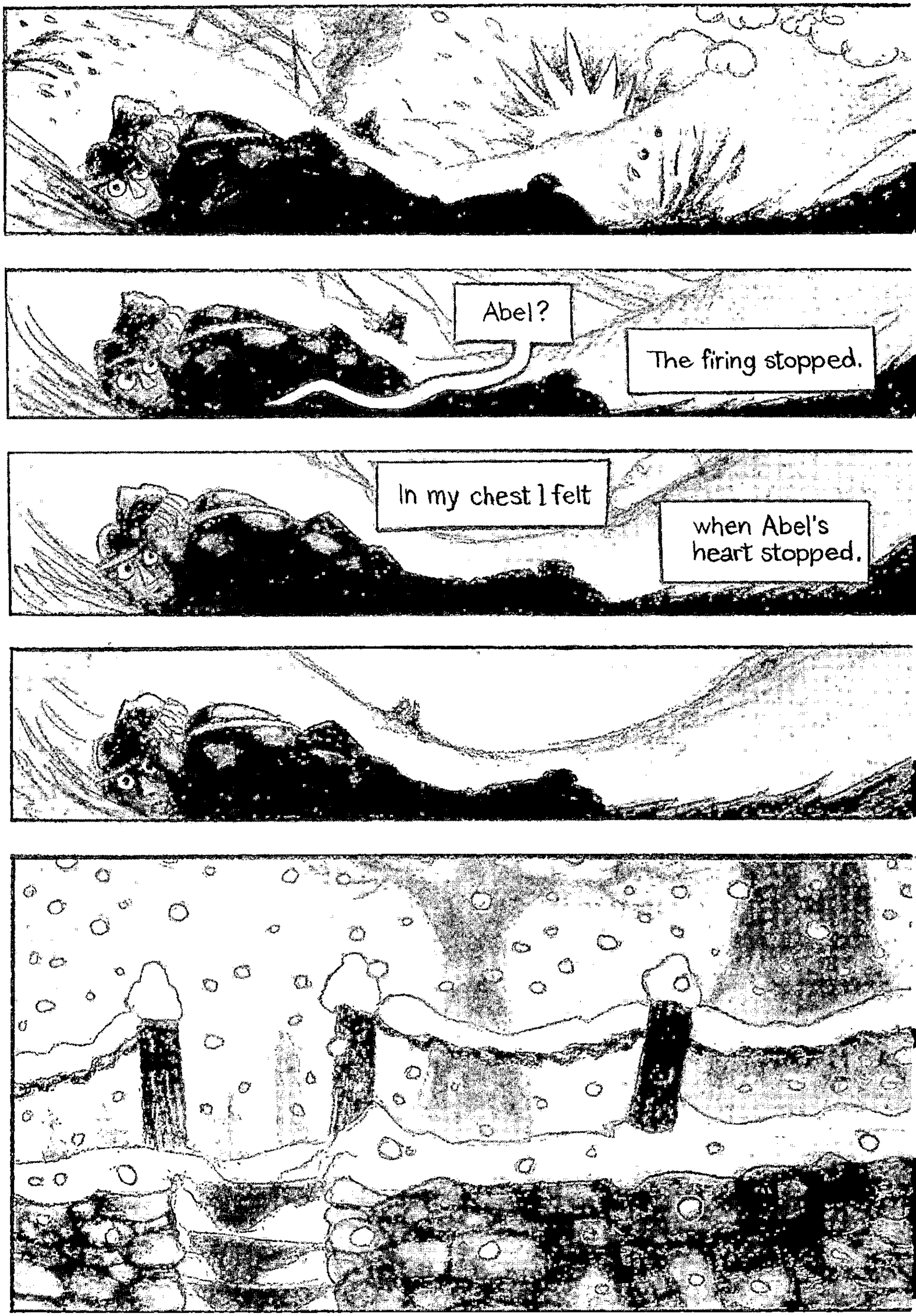
Abel?
The firing stopped.
In my chest I felt
when Abel's heart stopped.

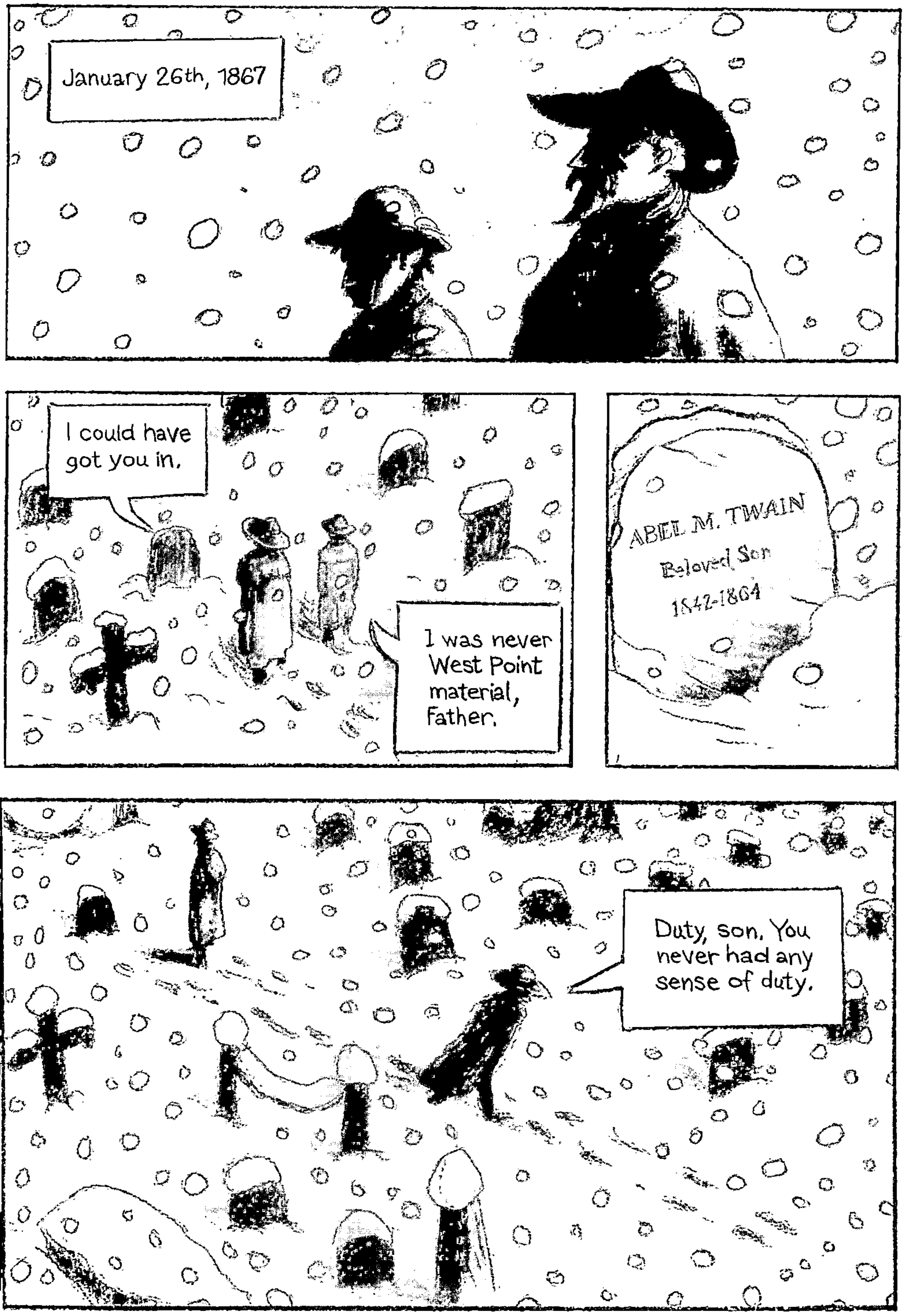
January 26th, 1867
I could have got you in.
I was never West Point material, father.
ABEL M. TWAIN
Beloved Son
1842-1864
Duty, son. You never had any sense of duty.

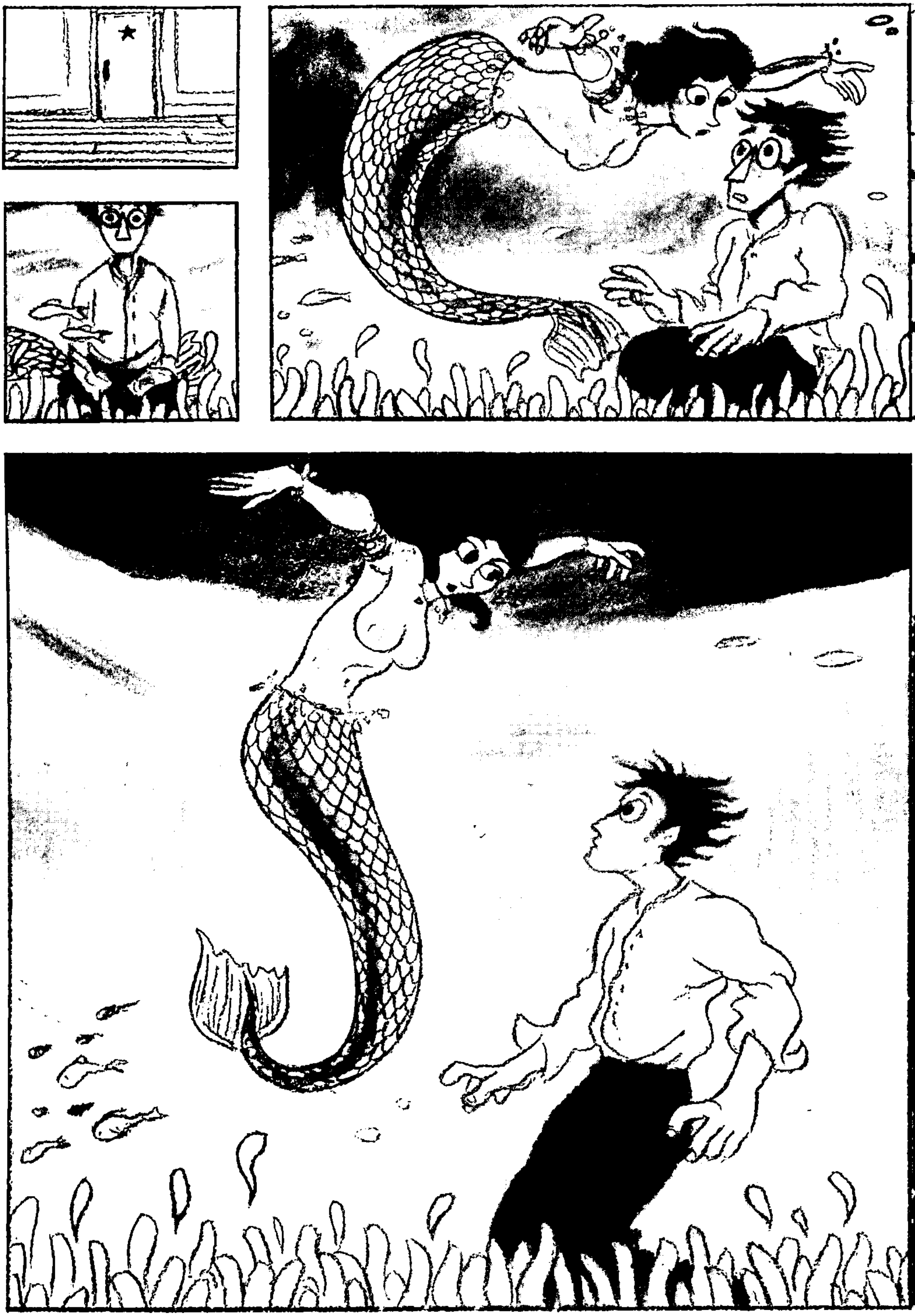

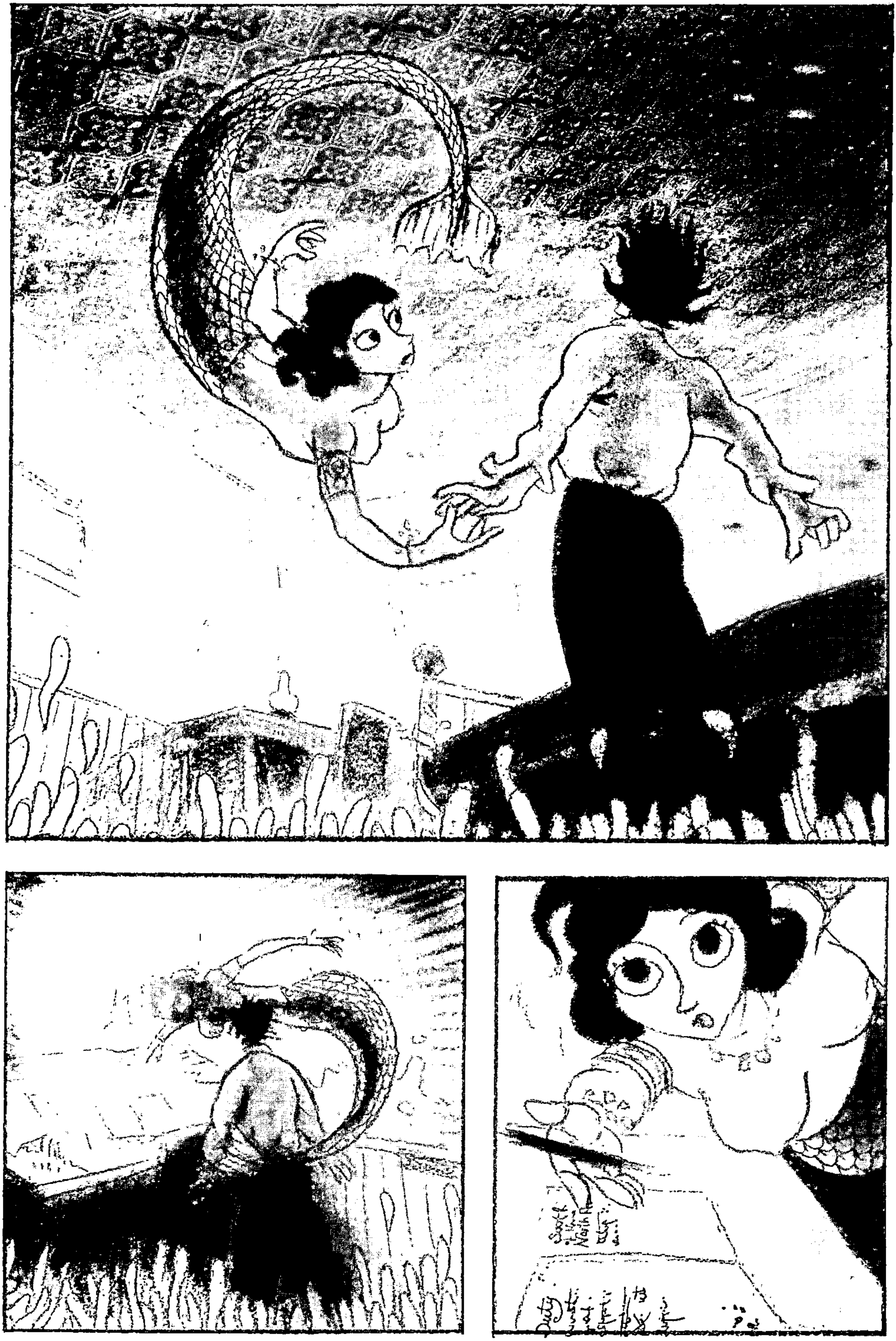

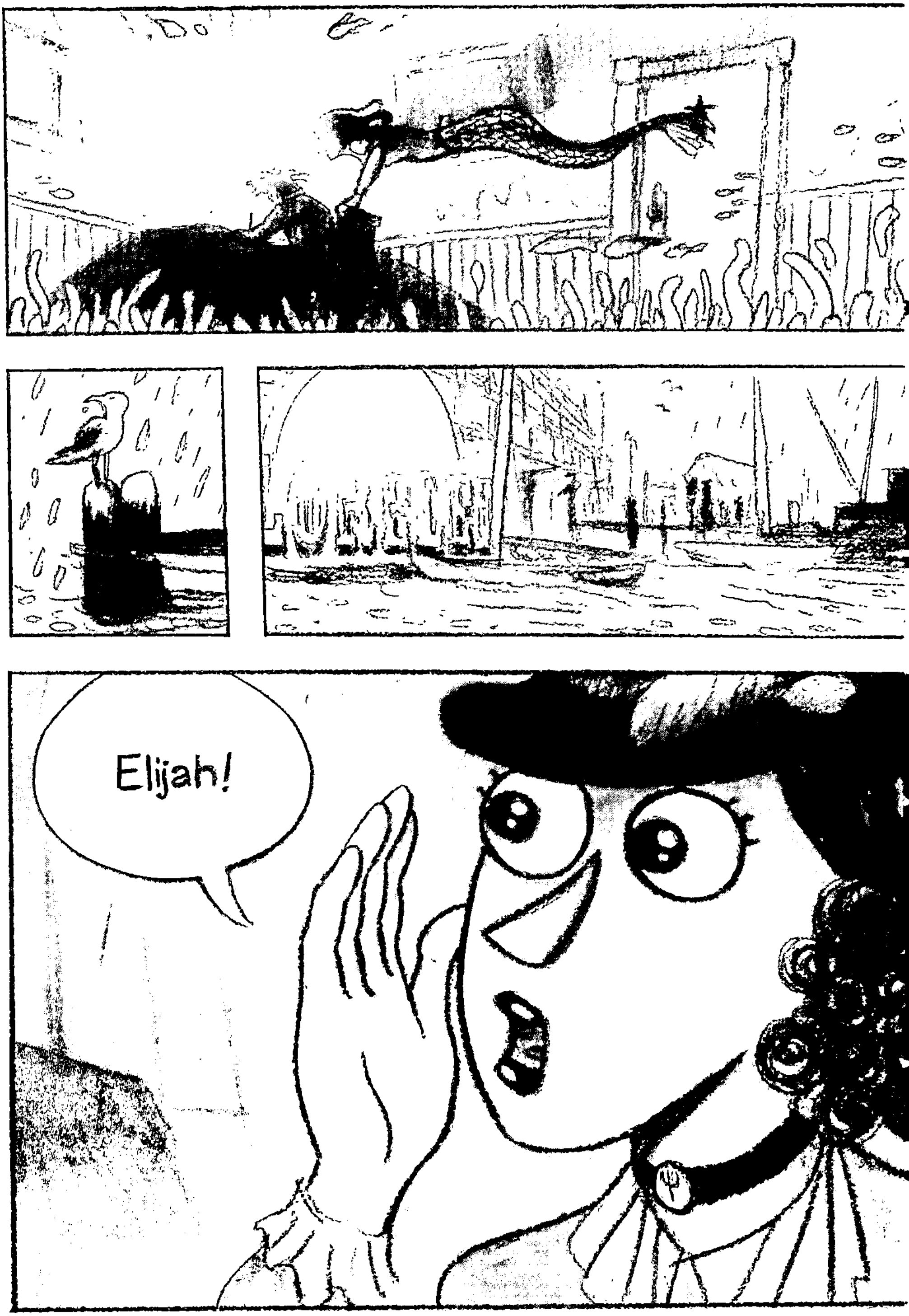
Elijah!

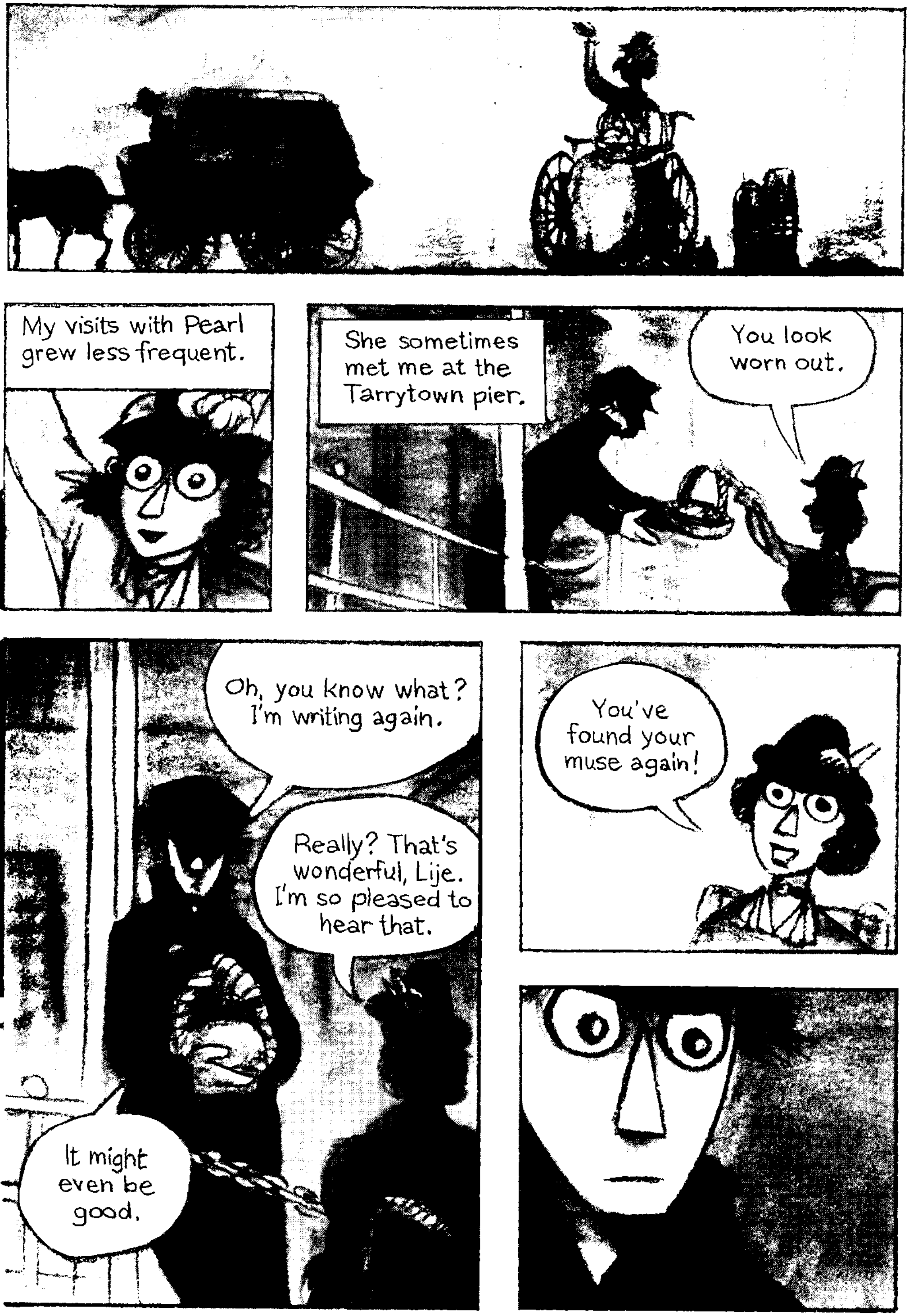

My visits with Pearl grew less frequent.
She sometimes met me at the Tarrytown pier.
You look worn out.
Oh, you know what? I'm writing again.
Really? That's wonderful, Lije. I'm so pleased to hear that.
It might even be good.
You've found your muse again!

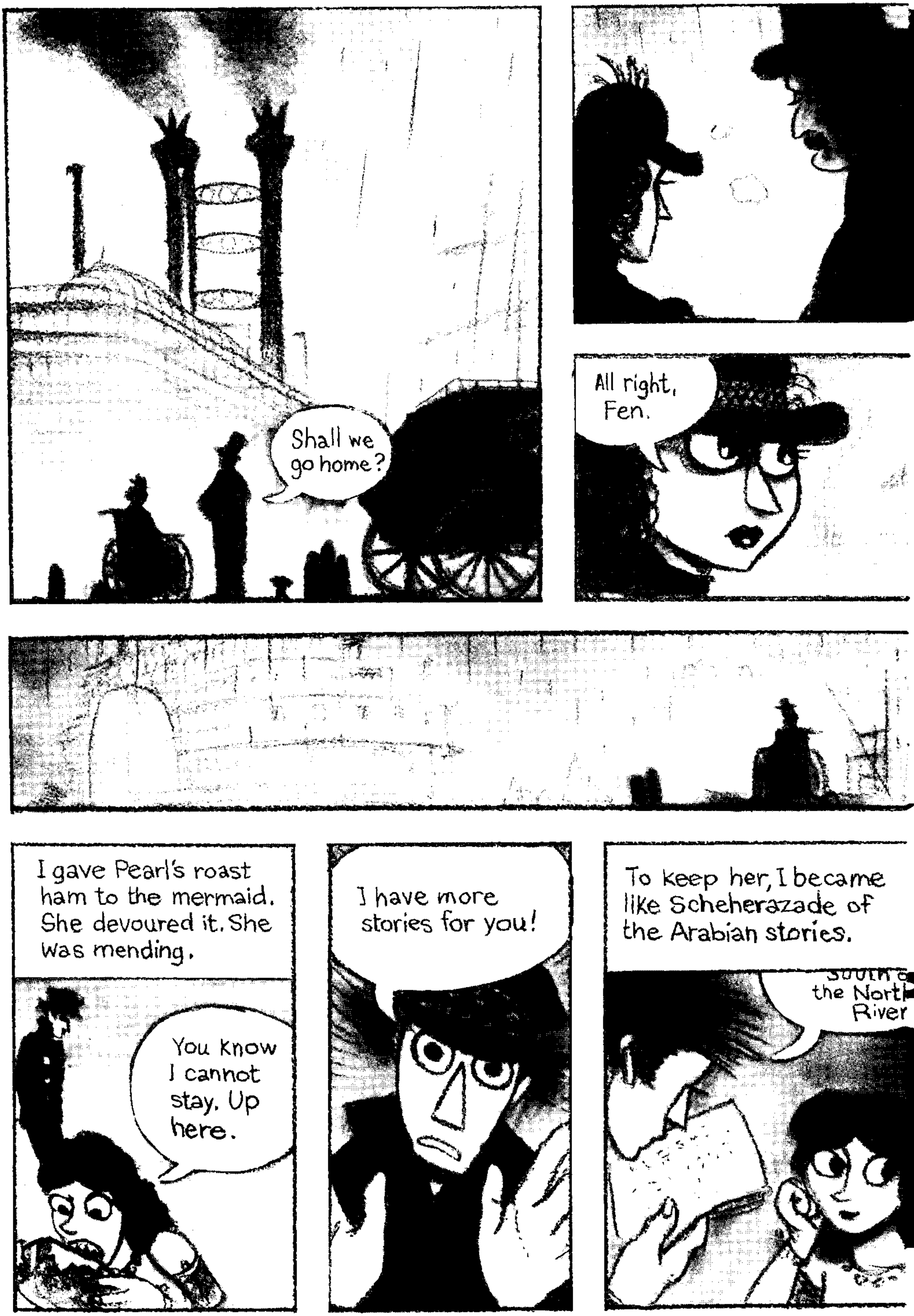

Shall we go home?
All right, Fen.
I gave Pearl's roast ham to the mermaid. She devoured it. She was mending.
You know I cannot stay. Up here.
I have more stories for you!
To keep her, I became like Scheherazade of the Arabian stories.
the North River

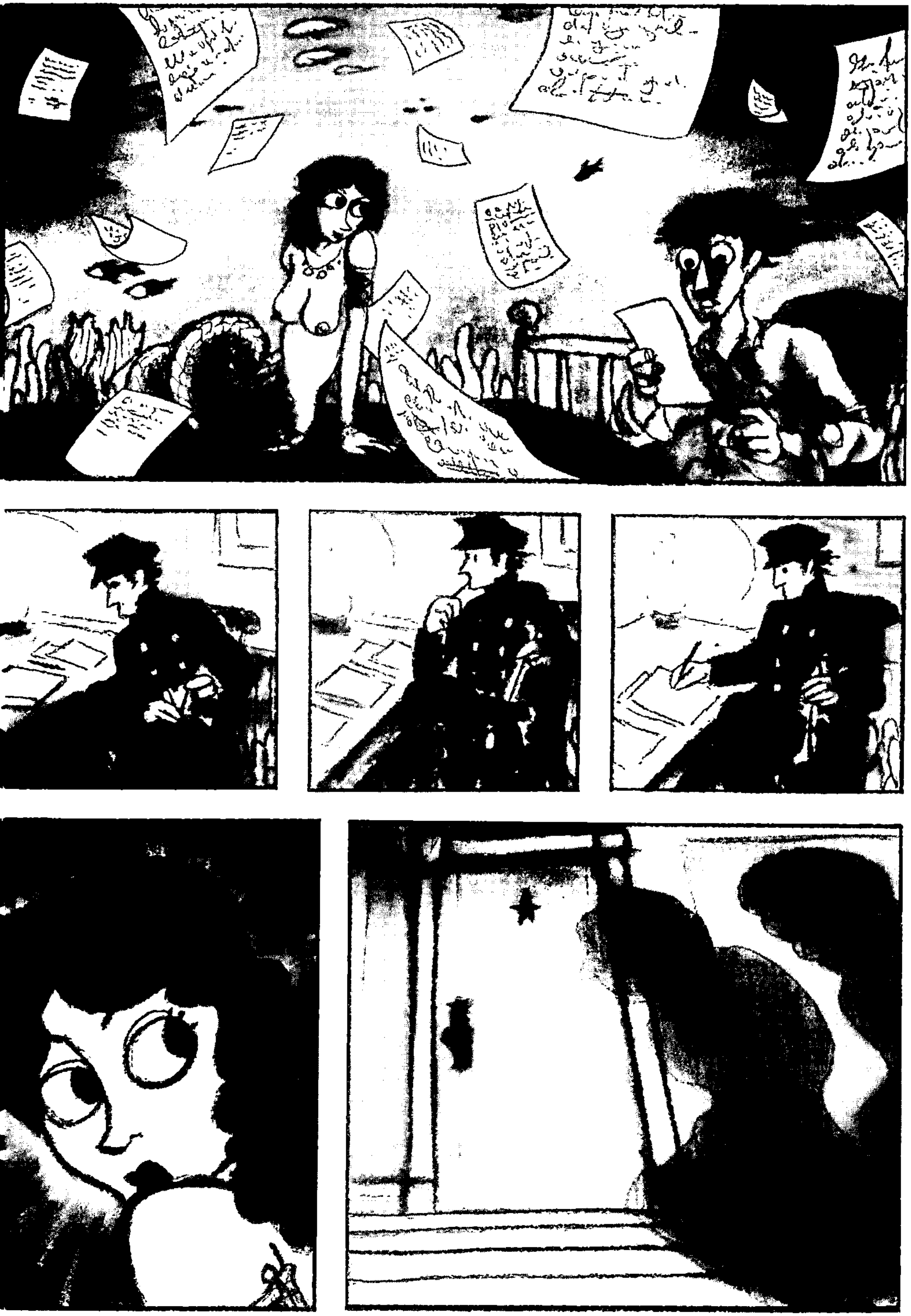

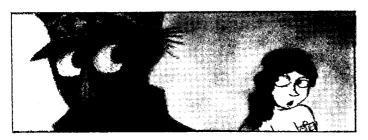

is þes he?

þonne læde hine tó þære heortan

ábric þín fæderes galdorléoð

ábric þa galdorléoð

188

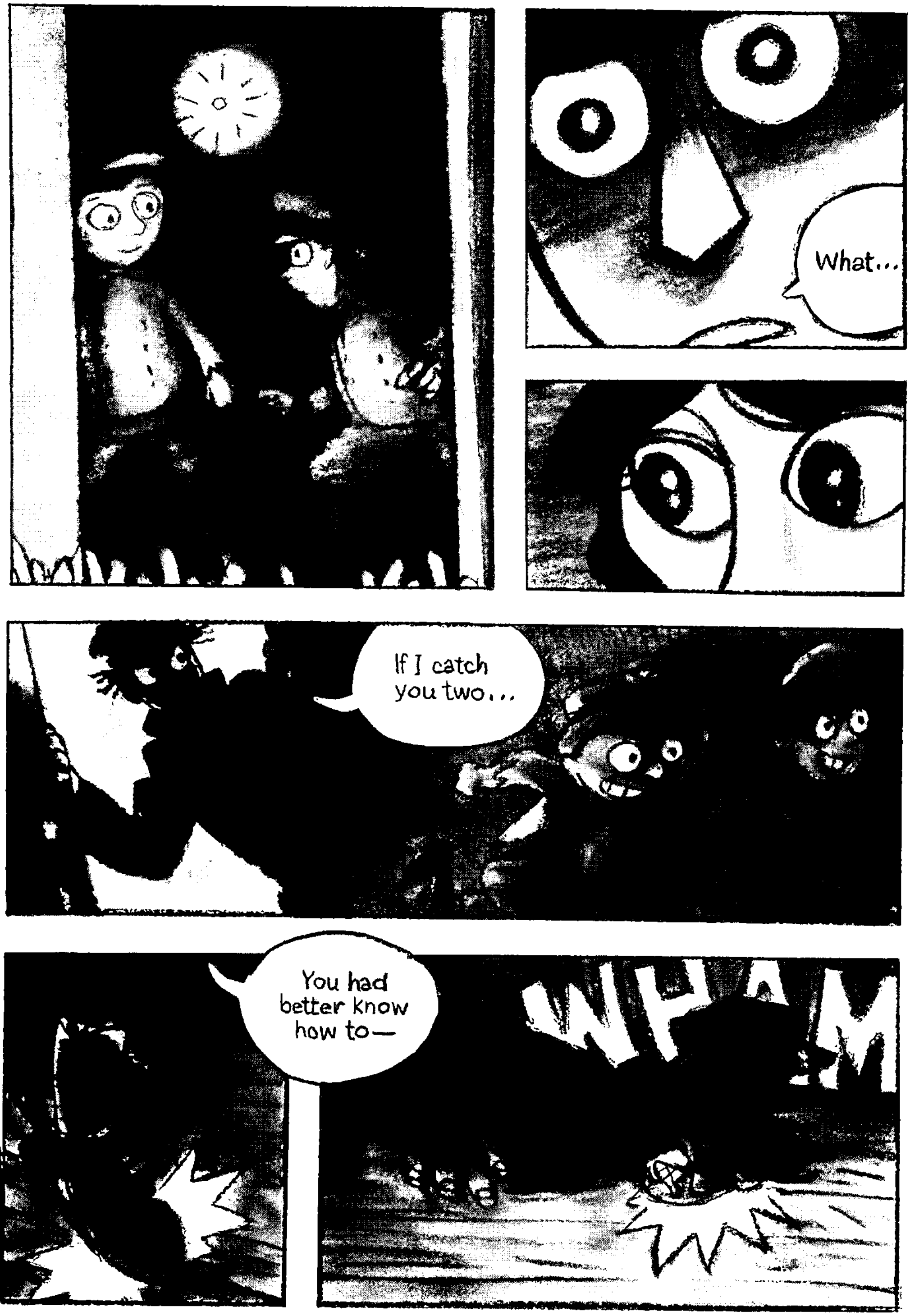
What...
If I catch you two...
You had better know how to—
WHAM

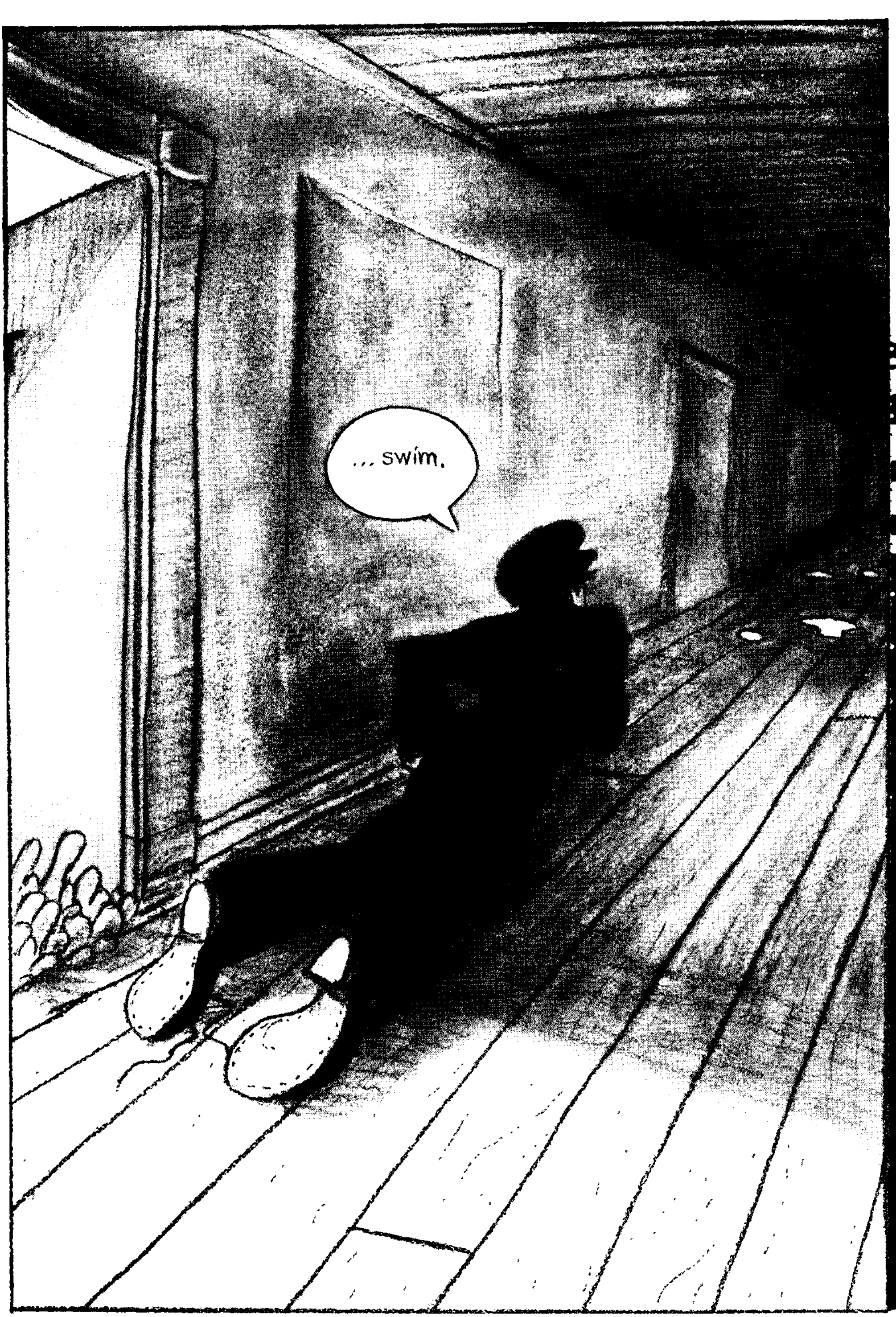
... swim.

Pt 1, Chap.12

"THE MISSING MUSE"

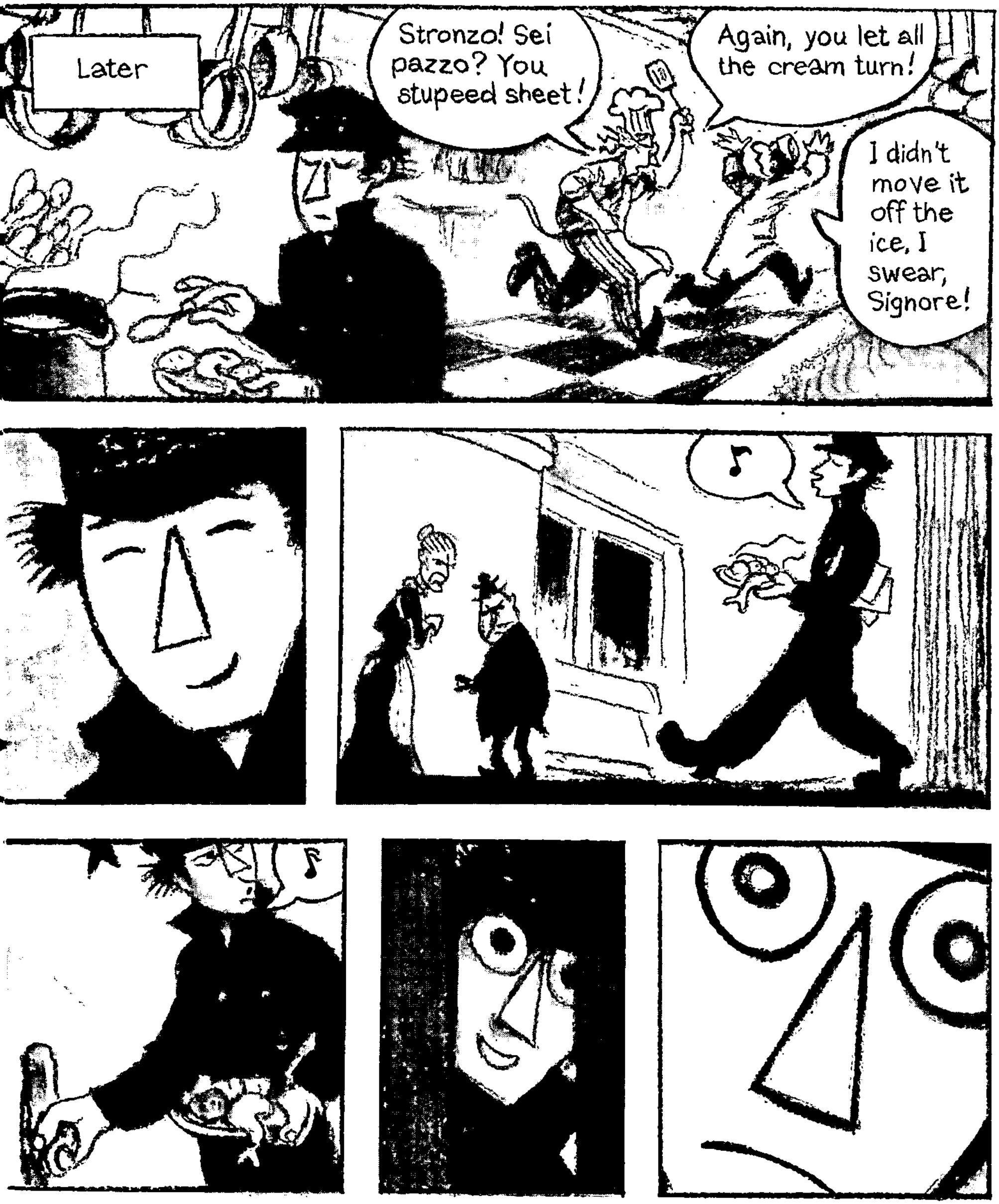

Later
Stronzo! Sei pazzo? You stupeed sheet!
Again, you let all the cream turn!
I didn't move it off the ice, I swear, Signore!

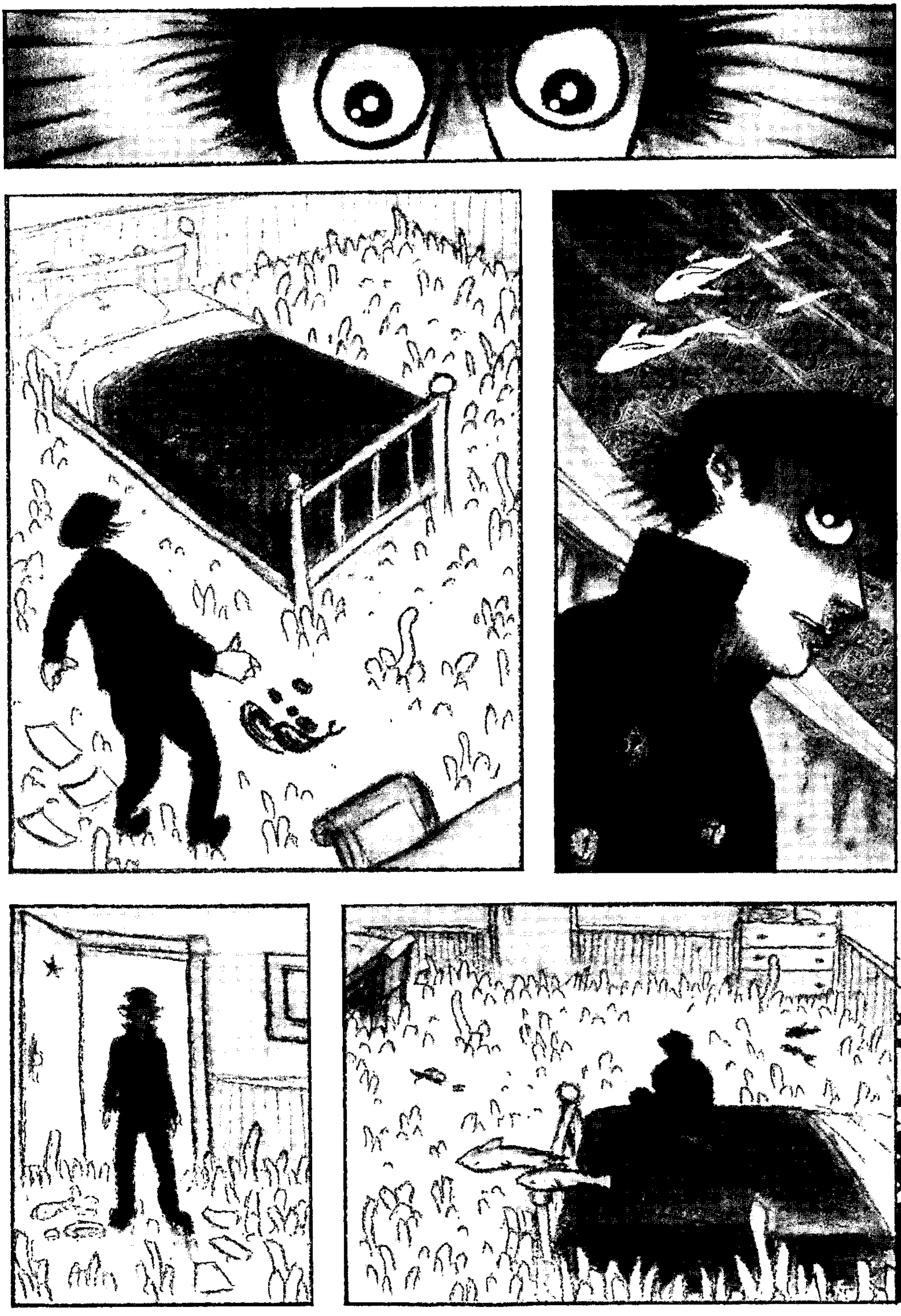

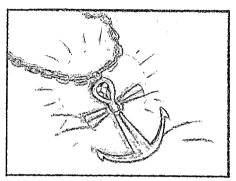

I'm tellin' you true, Aloysius! I can't leave, even if I try.

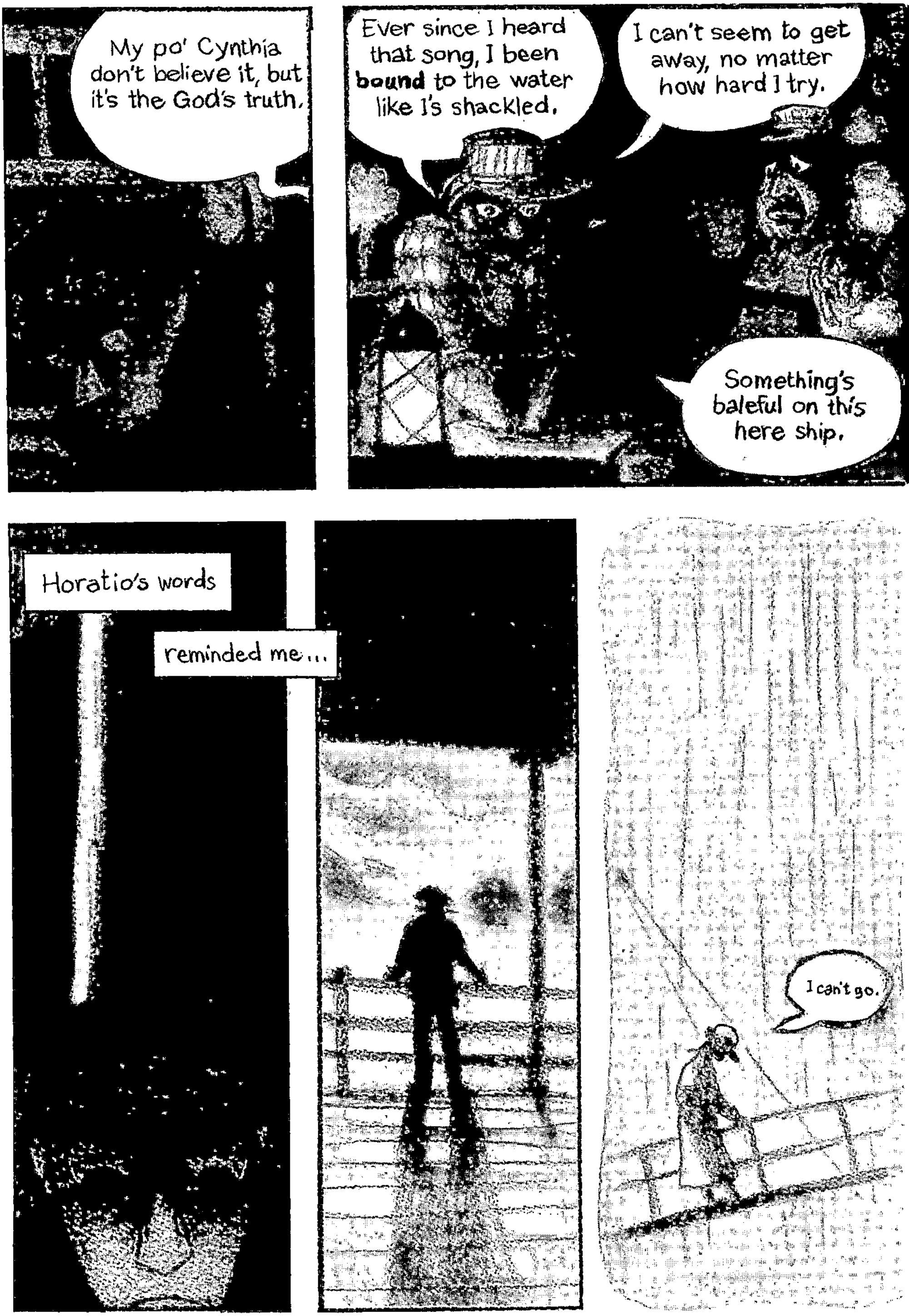
My po' Cynthia don't believe it, but it's the God's truth.
Ever since I heard that song, I been **bound** to the water like I's shackled.
I can't seem to get away, no matter how hard I try.
Something's baleful on this here ship.
Horatio's words
reminded me...
I can't go.

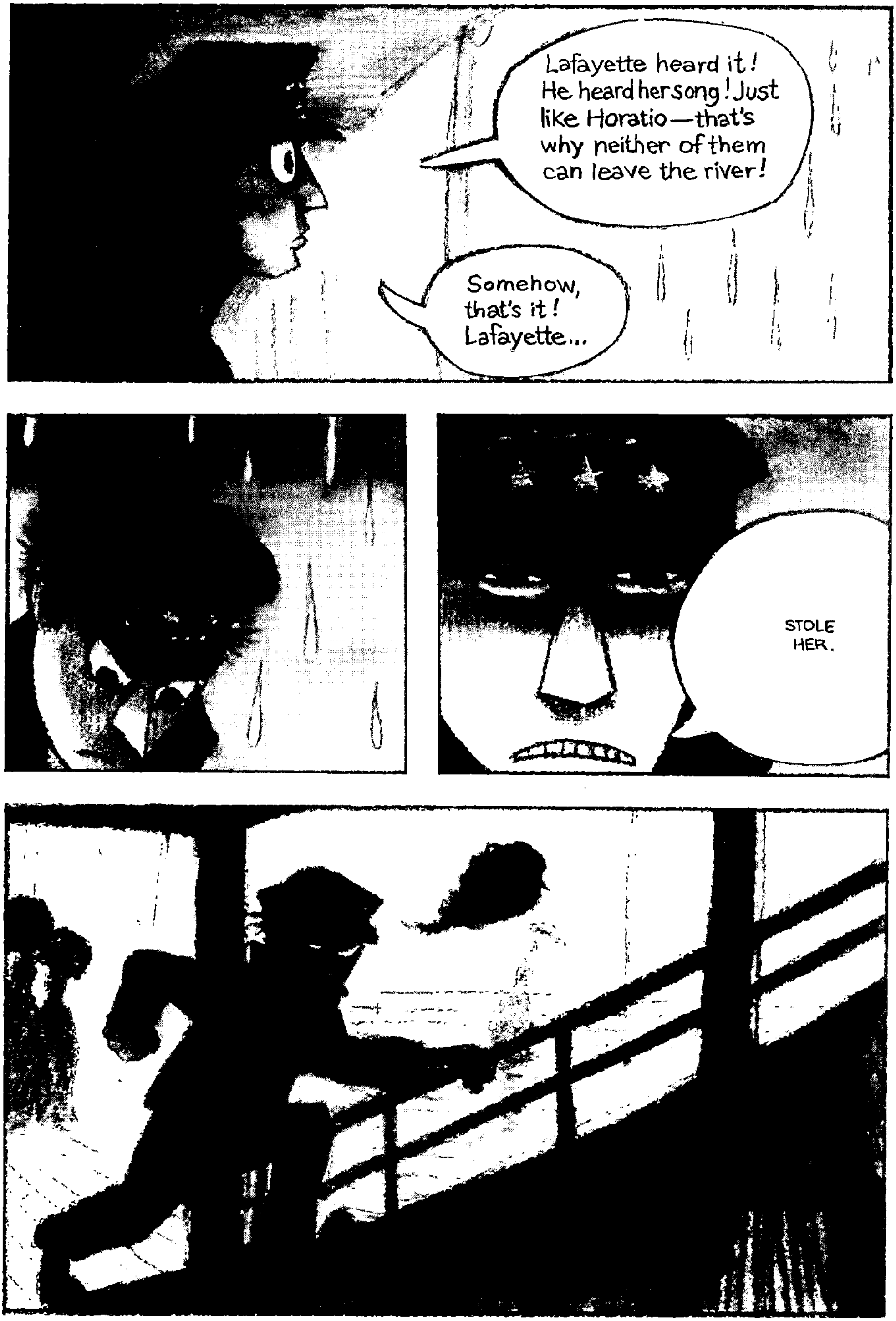
Lafayette heard it! He heard her song! Just like Horatio—that's why neither of them can leave the river!
Somehow, that's it! Lafayette...
STOLE HER.

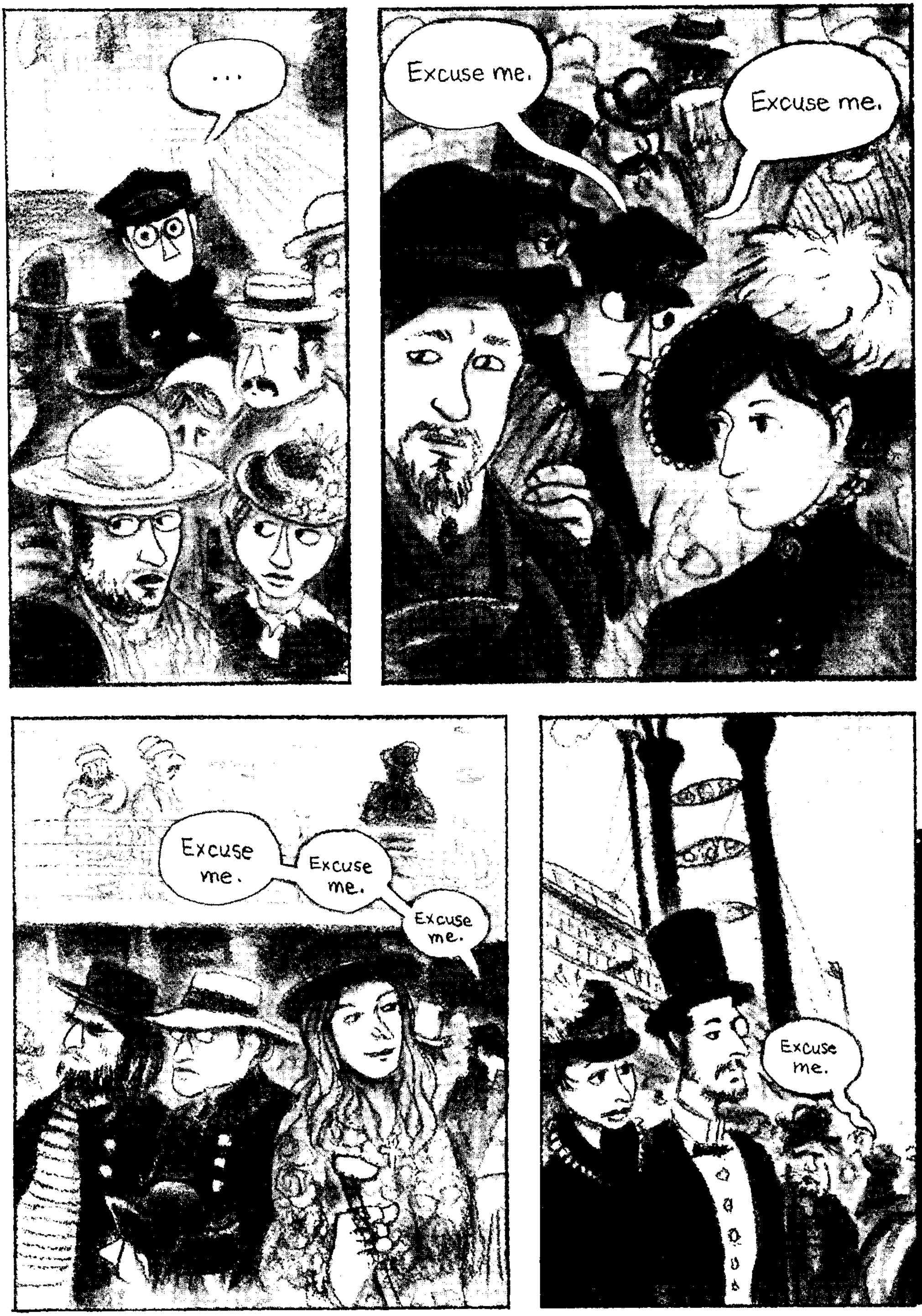
...
Excuse me.
Excuse me.
Excuse me.
Excuse me.
Excuse me.
Excuse me.

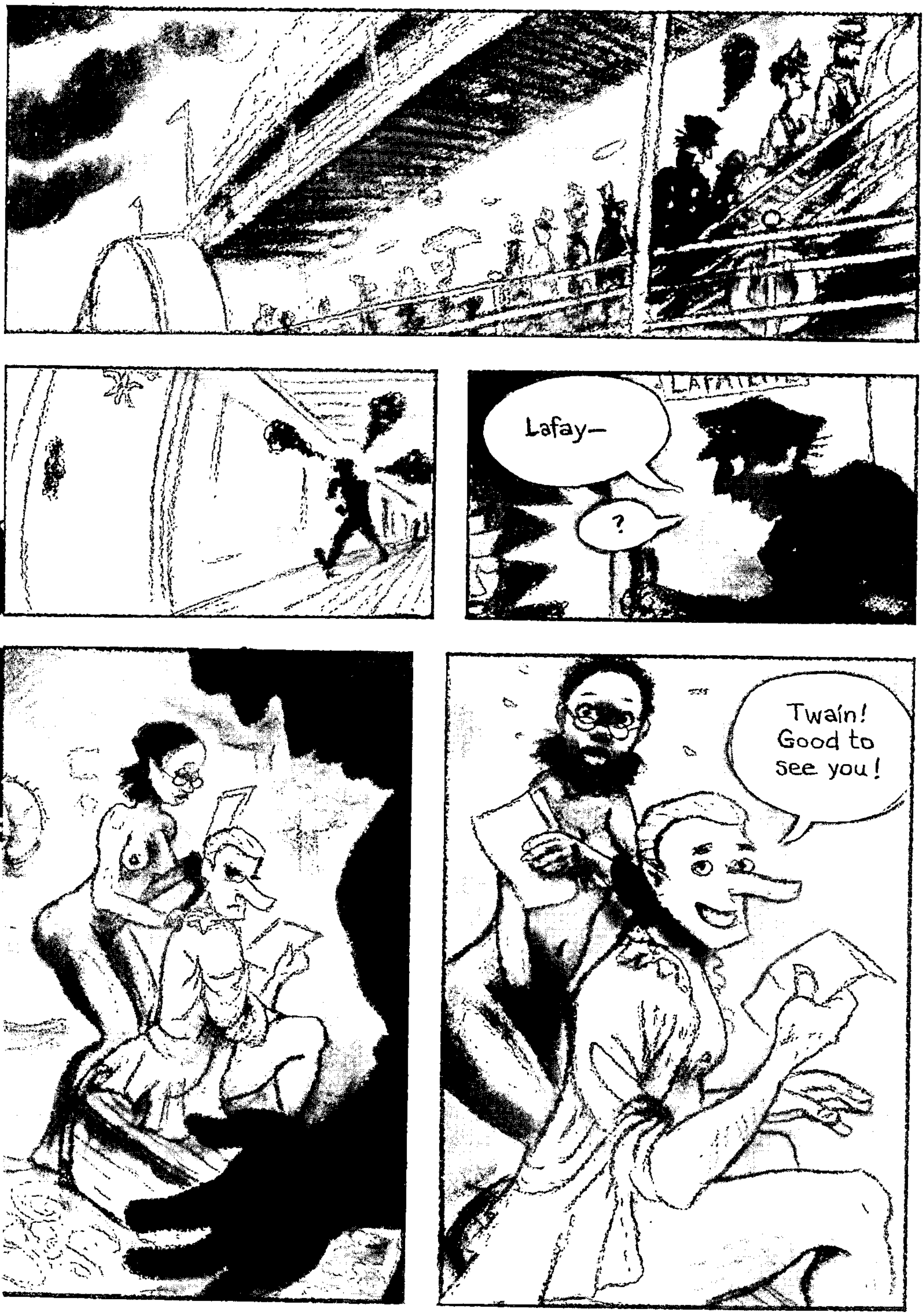
Lafay—
?
Twain!
Good to
see you!

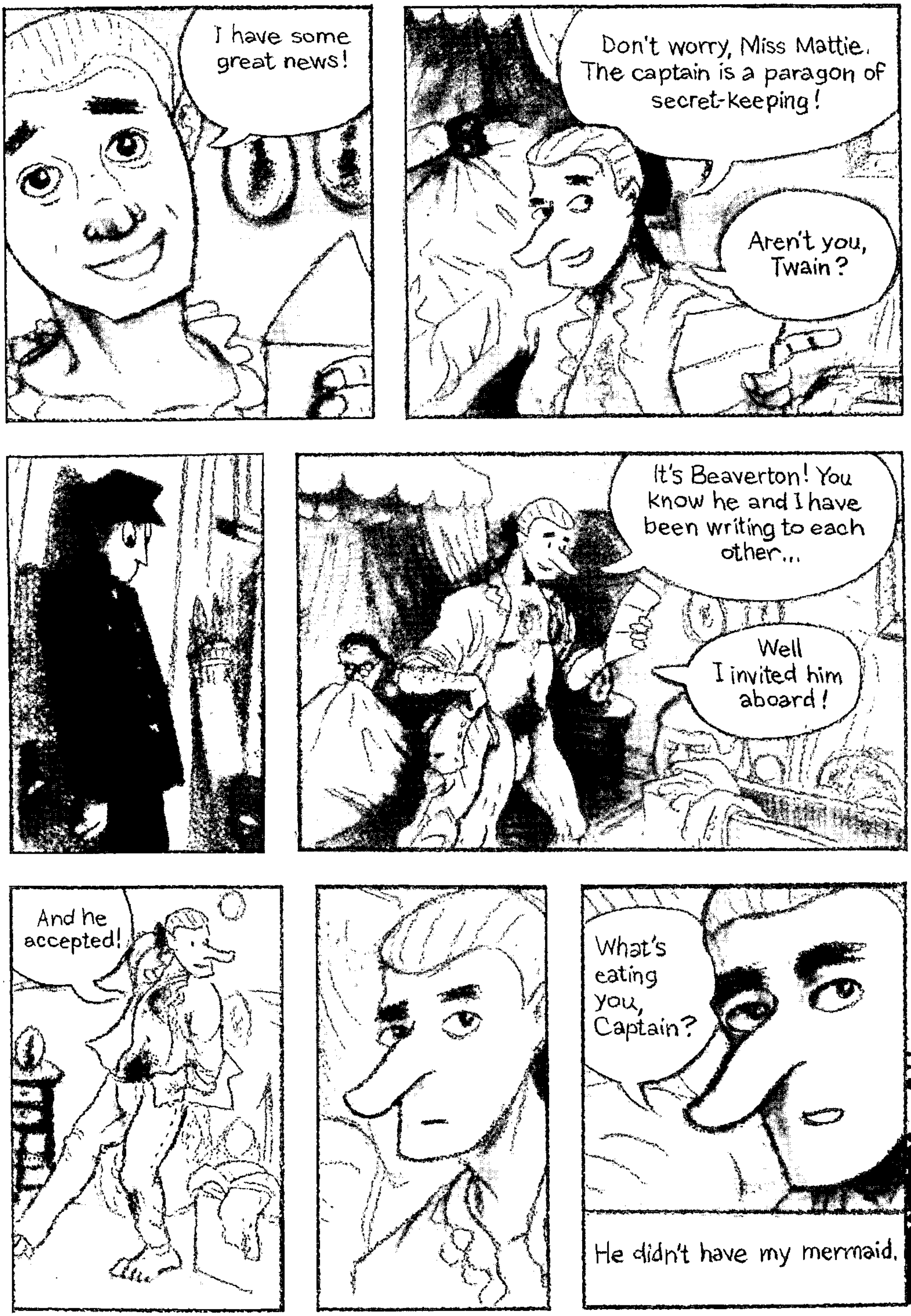
I have some great news!
Don't worry, Miss Mattie. The captain is a paragon of secret-keeping!
Aren't you, Twain?
It's Beaverton! You know he and I have been writing to each other...
Well I invited him aboard!
And he accepted!
What's eating you, Captain?
He didn't have my mermaid.

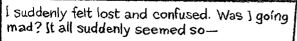

I suddenly felt lost and confused. Was I going mad? It all suddenly seemed so—

My apologies, Miss Avery.

I'll go now.

Jacques—Henri...

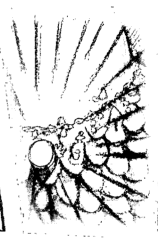

Where did I put

my

pocket

watch?

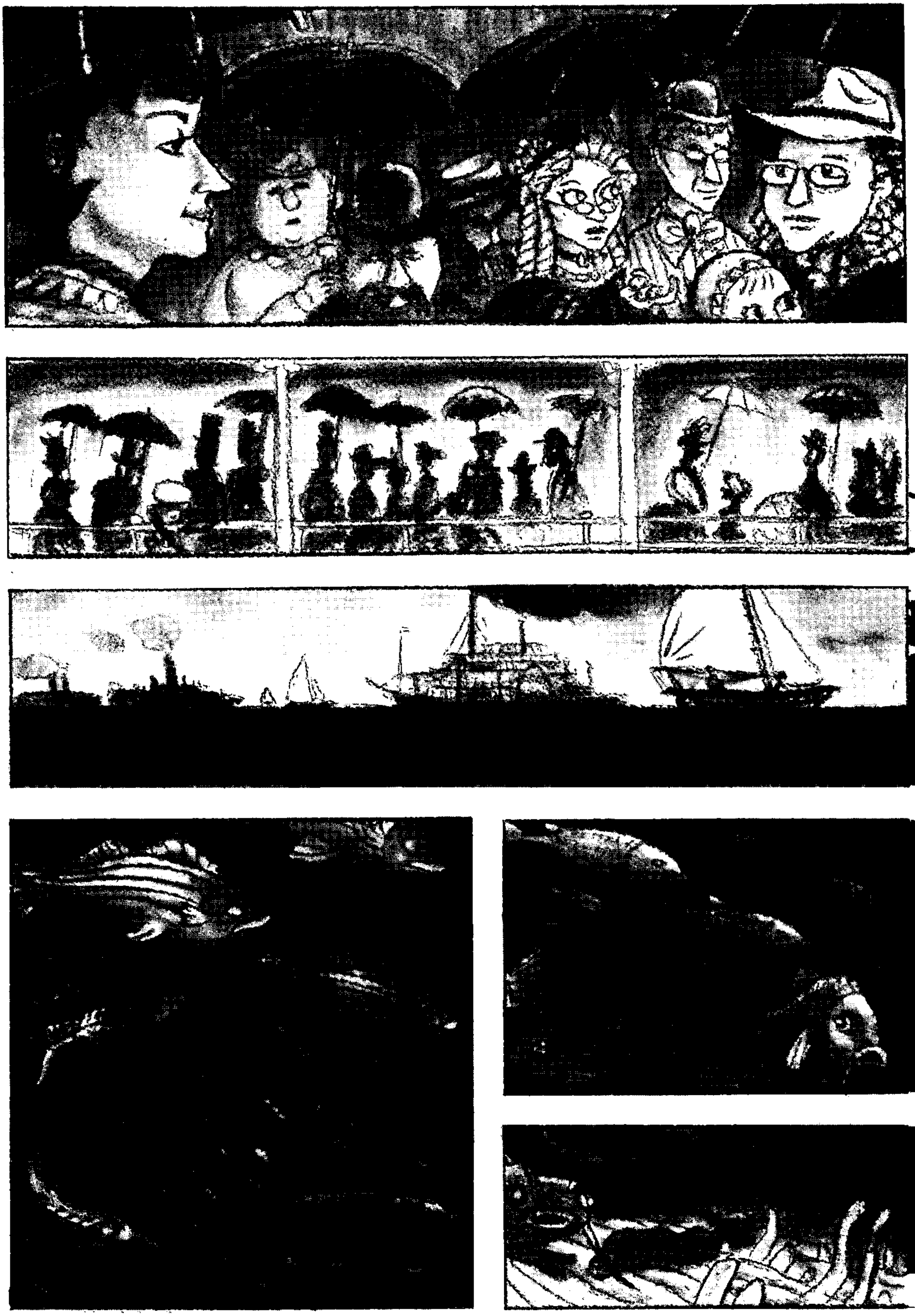

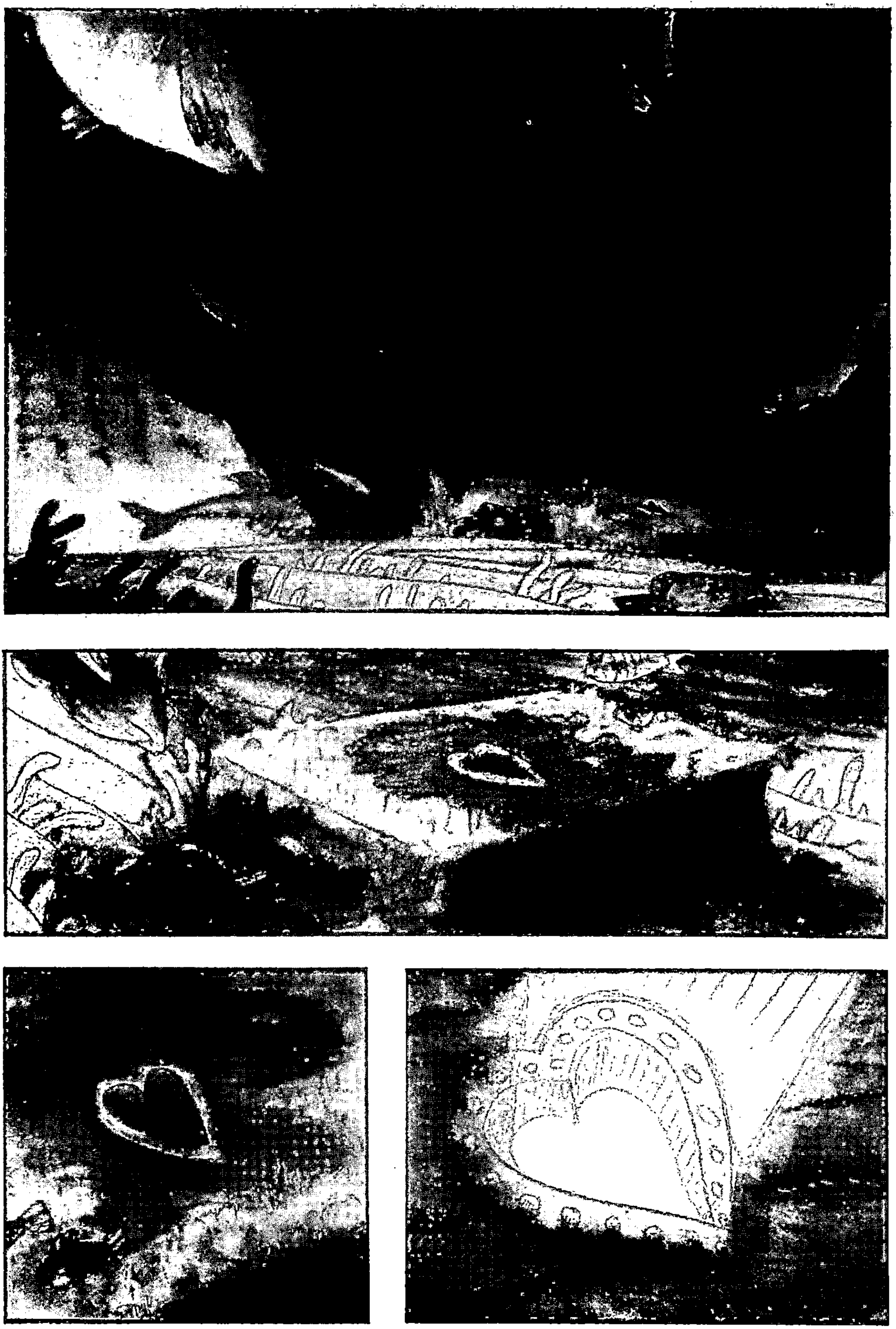

June 30th, 1887

Dear Mister Lafayette,

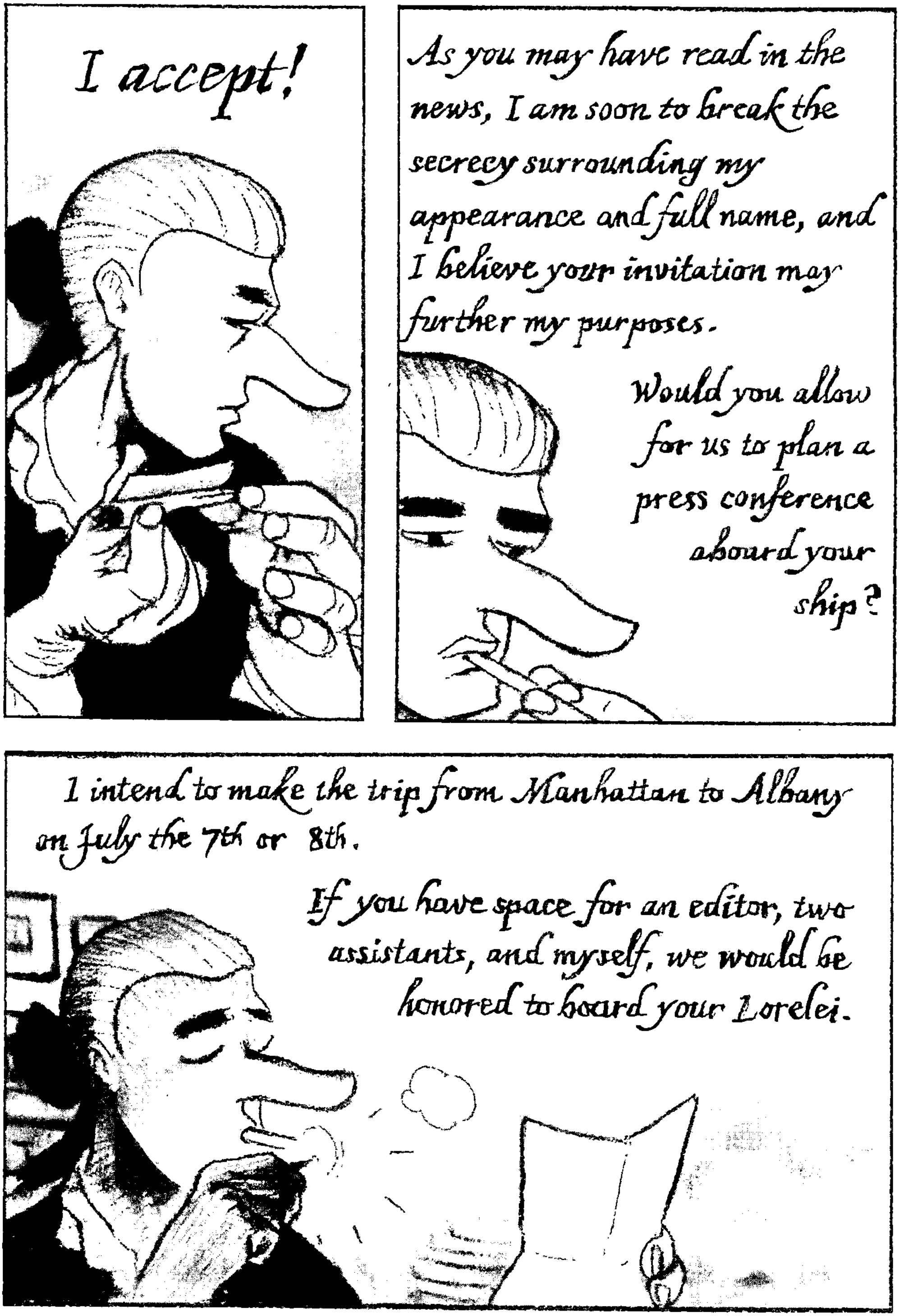
I accept!
As you may have read in the news, I am soon to break the secrecy surrounding my appearance and full name, and I believe your invitation may further my purposes.
Would you allow for us to plan a press conference aboard your ship?
I intend to make the trip from Manhattan to Albany on July the 7th or 8th.
If you have space for an editor, two assistants, and myself, we would be honored to board your Lorelei.

If you would kindly confirm I should be most obliged. I shall bring my papers

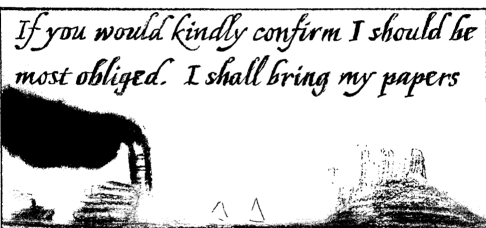

concerning the lore of mermaids and repairing from their deleterious effects; perhaps my notes will be of use to you.

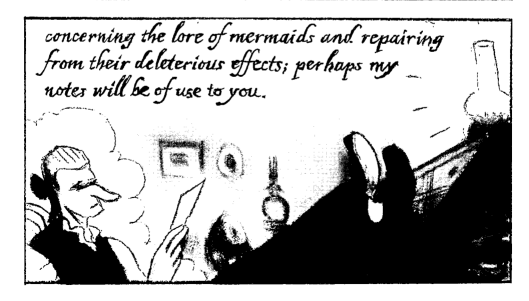

As for speaking "eye to eye, man to man," as you wrote, please hold no high hopes, for I am no match to anyone's great expectations, nor am I the man most people would like to think.

Yours Sincerely,

CGB

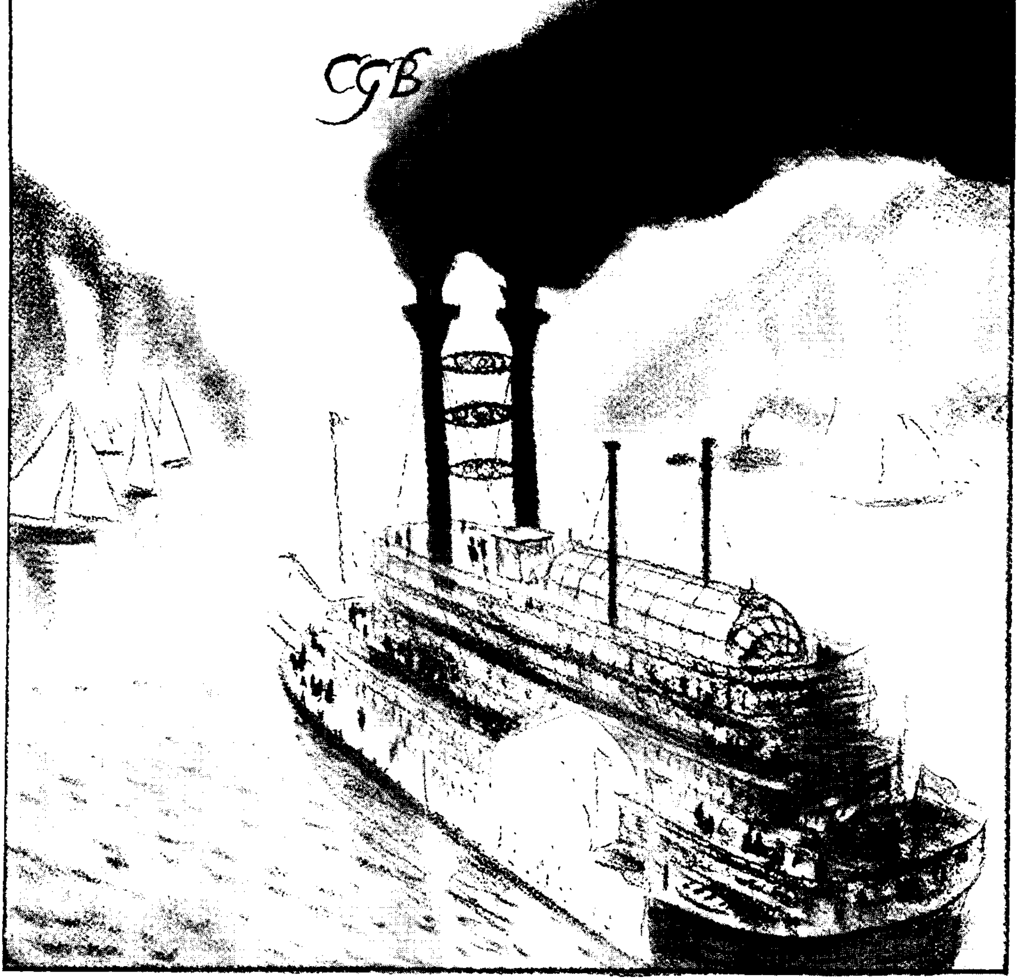

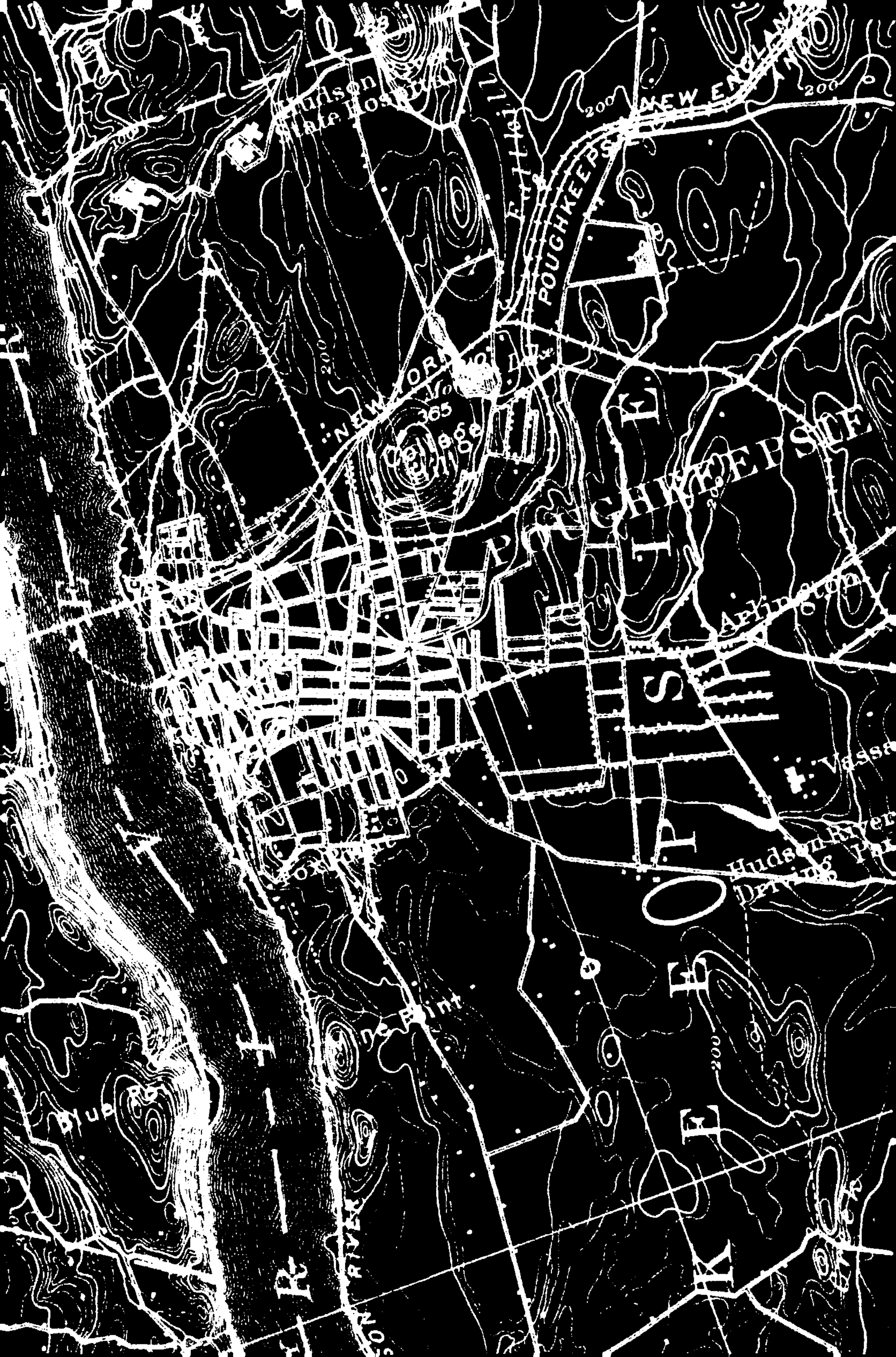
NEW ENGLAND
POUGHKEEPSIE
NEW YORK
College
365
200
POUGHKEEPSIE
Arlington
Hudson River
Driving Park
RIVER

Part Two
CAMOMILLE

C WINE
intage

bathed in dramatic
a miles of pipes large
valves, faucets, dials
e is the glowing furn
:WMEN is shoveli
at other smaller lan
as the capstan wit
or a small corner
couple of stools a
rsonal belongings
iss out here and
and vertically fi
on the ground; s
different areas a
ngine room like
ustrial age fro

MR HY

TEVENSON

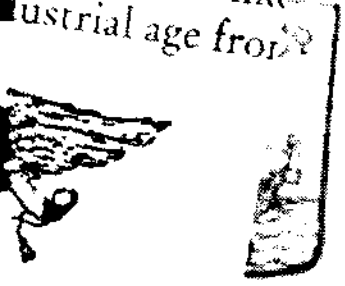

HOR TO

At last, some readers of C G Beaverton will have a chance to see the author in person. A press conference is to be held onboard a ship in Manhattan on July 7th, to be followed by a series of speaking engagements around the nation. The latest offering from Beaverton will not disappoint; this new supernatural travelogue doesn't whisk the reader to North Africa, Mesopotamia, the Hindu Kush, nor to the steppes of Russia; no, it is our own backyard Beaverton investigates. We are to be acquainted with the unexplained Hudson River Valley. With characteristic humor, the author punctuates h ... of inns and taverns ... historic curiosities from ...hattan to Albany, and eve... 300 year old tree in Elmsf... ...r which it is pleasant to n... ...a matter-of-fact expositic... among others, faery-life to... spotted in Sleepy-Hollow, gh... in Ossining, a healing presen... Croton Point, and even com... ling evidence of a mermaid i...

A FAST STEAMBOAT
...GHKEEPSIE, N. Y., July 18
...oat New-York, with a thousan...
...rd, made her first regular trip up
and was enthusiastically rec...
by shouts and cheers, bell ringin...
ving. She left New-York at 9:...
...inutes behind at Yonkers, twel...
...of time at Stony Point, and made
...s from New-York, at 11:40 A. M.

...Y POWELL IN COLLISION.
..., N. Y., May 19.—The steam...
...tin, of the Newburg and Alba...
...ine, left here on time at 7 o'clock
... usual run up north. At
... ...ondout on

THE MARY POWELL IN COLLI...
... N. Y., May 19.—The
... and ...

...PRINGFIELD REPUBLICAN
JUNE 29TH, 1887

...VERSION MORE POPULAR THAN EVER

...ourageous libraries have done us the service of resisting the current popularity of ...verton and upholding the ban on his works. Citing the "moral mudslide under ...s foundation" and the brazenly pagan nature of these so-called imaginary travel- ...ommittee formed under the Reverend C.C. Gladwell has submitted a petition to ...y of Congress . . . (CONTINUED ON PAGE 7)

...ly
...r

...ly
...gued
...ng all
...nvita-

...is large...
...curred Lawson ...
...on a thick bank of fog. Briggs say...
...vas standing still, and Capt. Ander-
...engineer concur in this statement.

...two minutes be...
...ahead of time at Stony Point

Pt II, Chap.1

"THE BEAVERTON REVELATION"

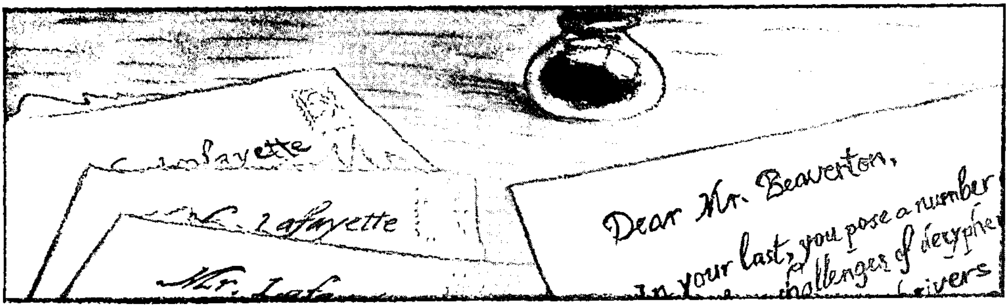
Lafayette
Lafayette
Dear Mr. Beaverton,
In your last, you pose a number of challenges of decypher

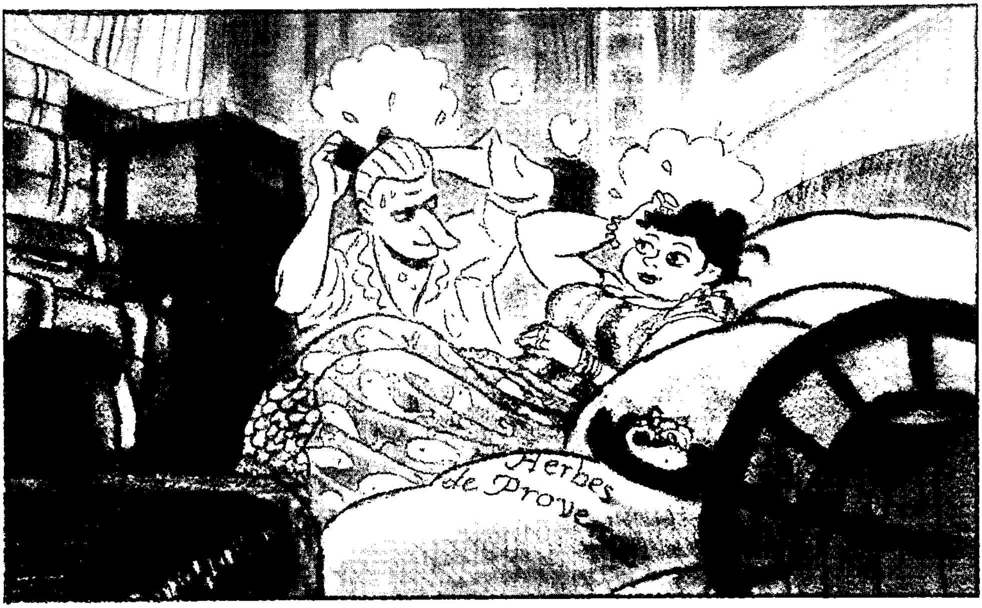
Herbes de Prove

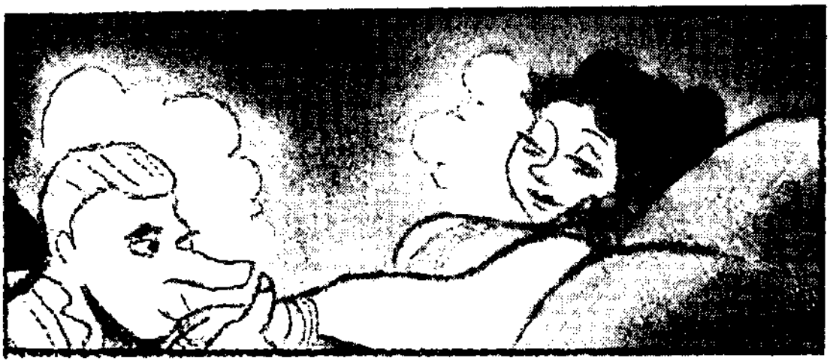

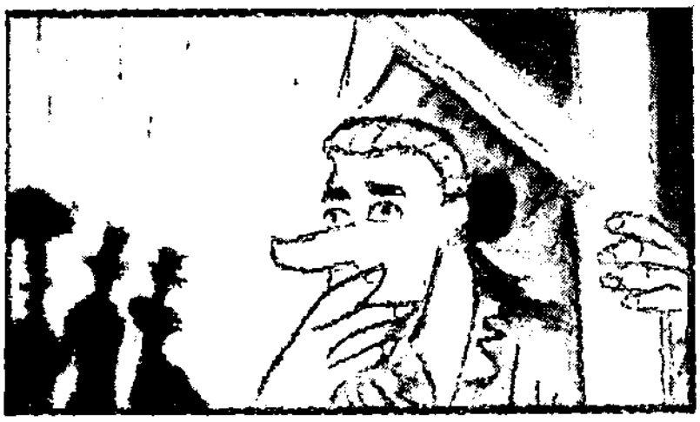

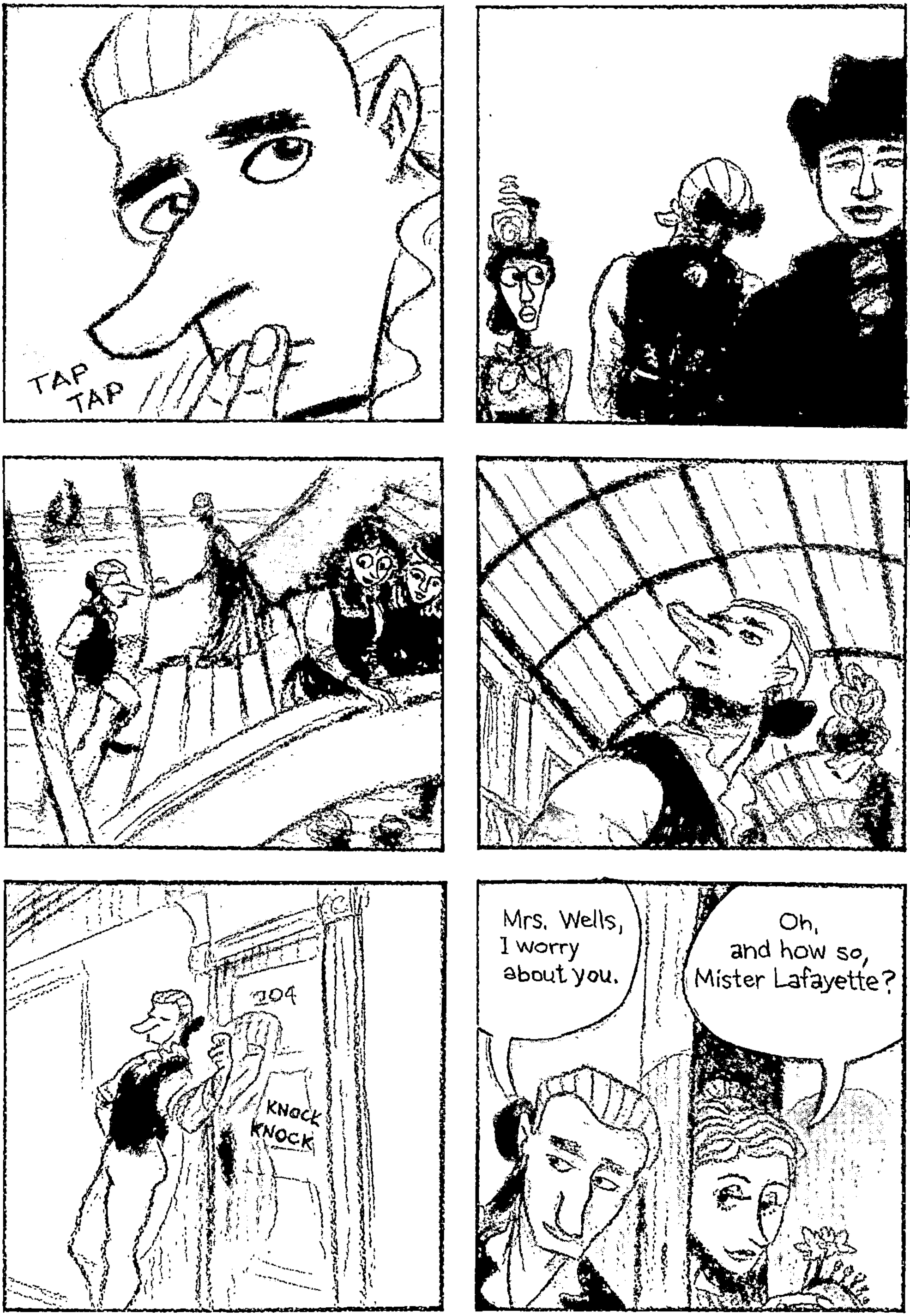
TAP
TAP
204
KNOCK
KNOCK
Mrs. Wells, I worry about you.
Oh, and how so, Mister Lafayette?

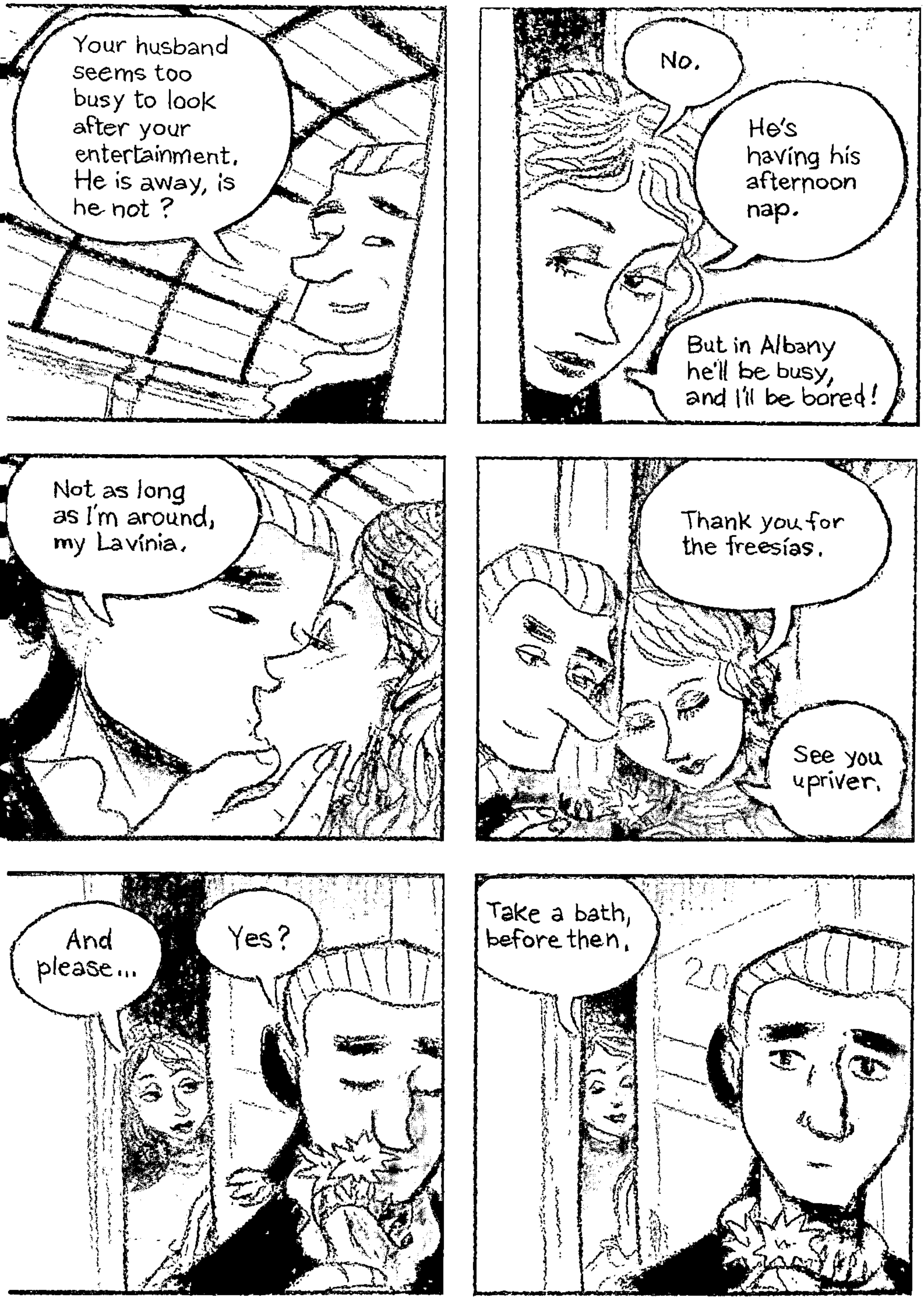
Your husband seems too busy to look after your entertainment. He is away, is he not ?
No.
He's having his afternoon nap.
But in Albany he'll be busy, and I'll be bored!
Not as long as I'm around, my Lavínia.
Thank you for the freesías.
See you upriver.
And please...
Yes?
Take a bath, before then.

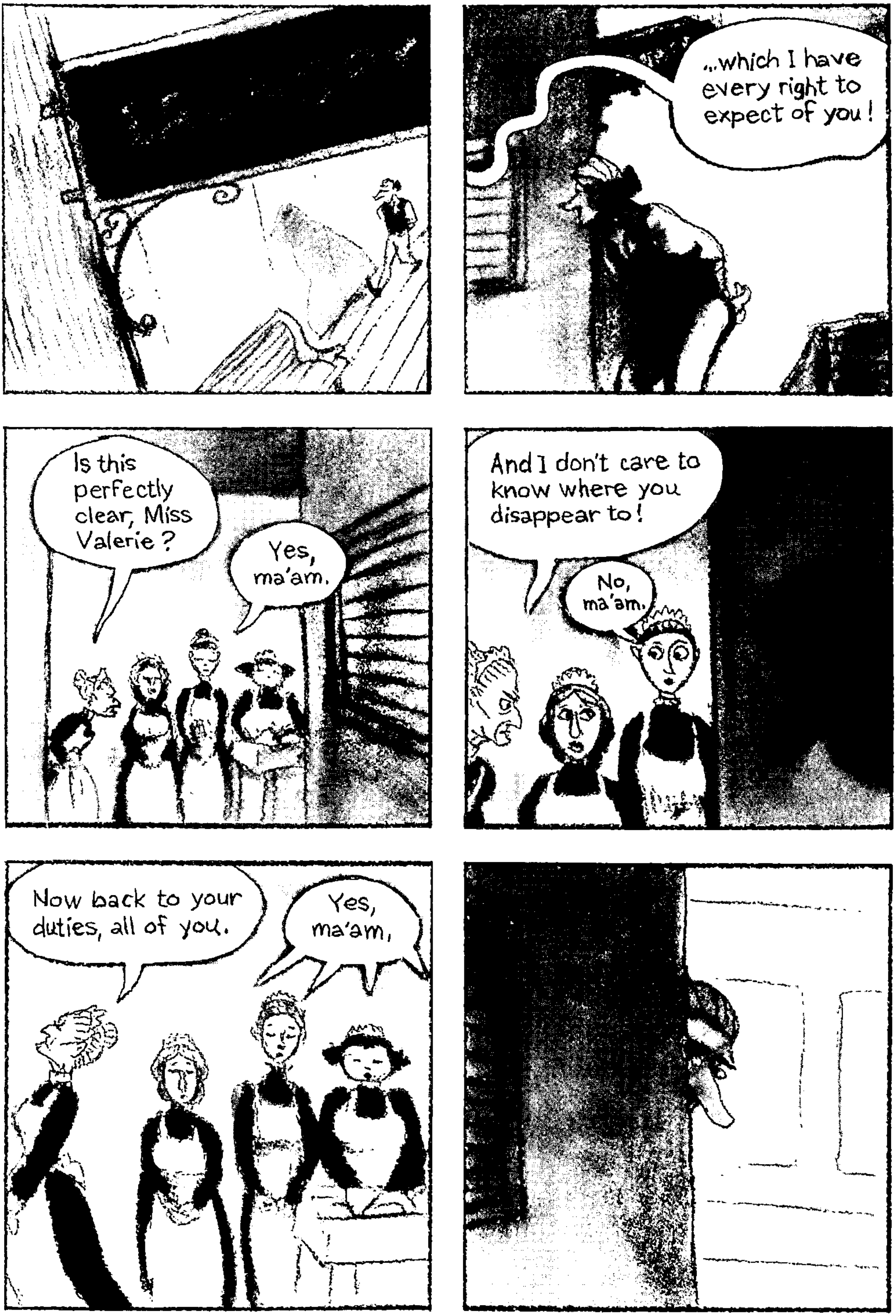

...which I have every right to expect of you!
Is this perfectly clear, Miss Valerie?
Yes, ma'am.
And I don't care to know where you disappear to!
No, ma'am.
Now back to your duties, all of you.
Yes, ma'am,

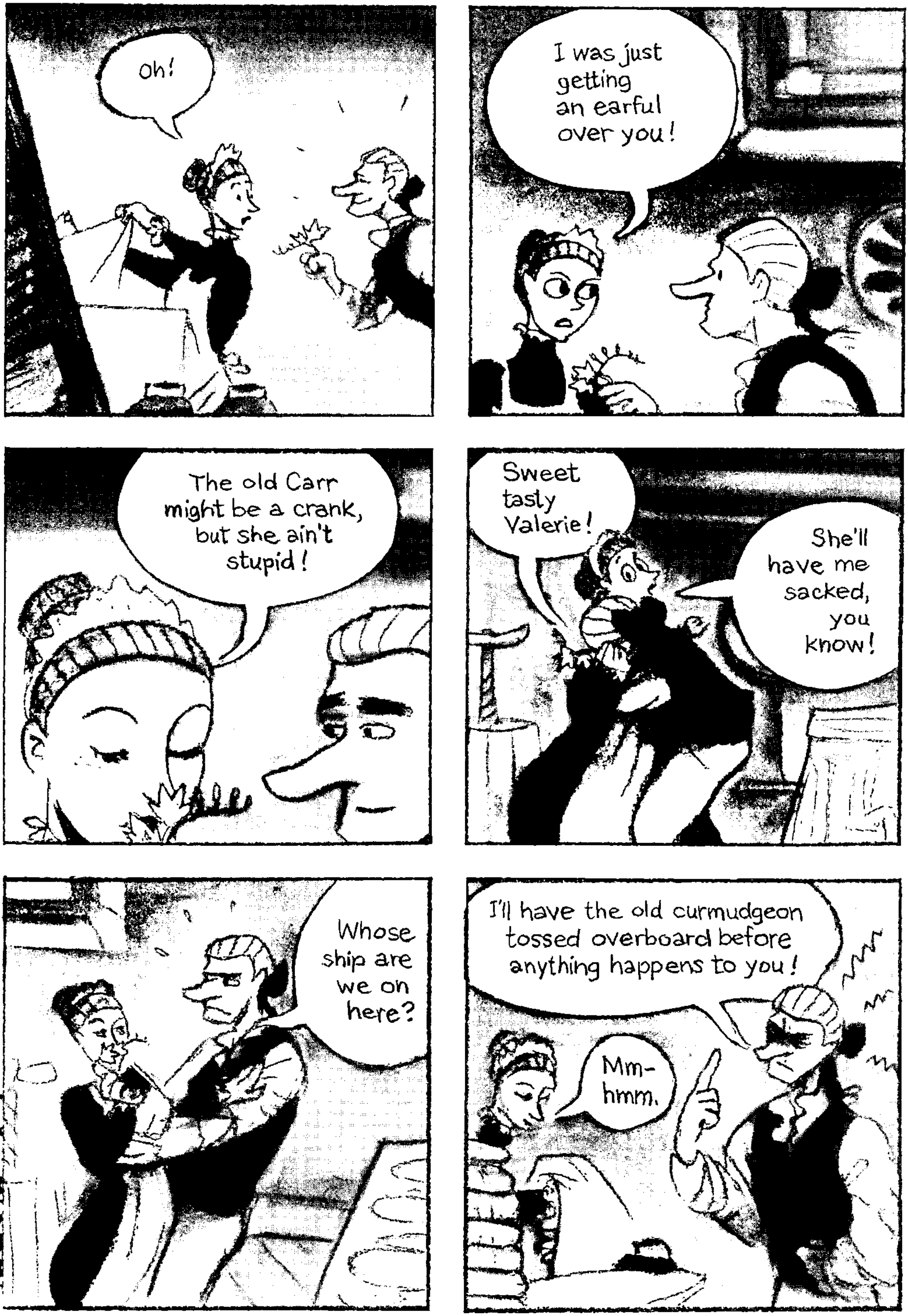
Oh!
I was just getting an earful over you!
The old Carr might be a crank, but she ain't stupid!
Sweet tasty Valerie!
She'll have me sacked, you know!
Whose ship are we on here?
I'll have the old curmudgeon tossed overboard before anything happens to you!
Mm-hmm.

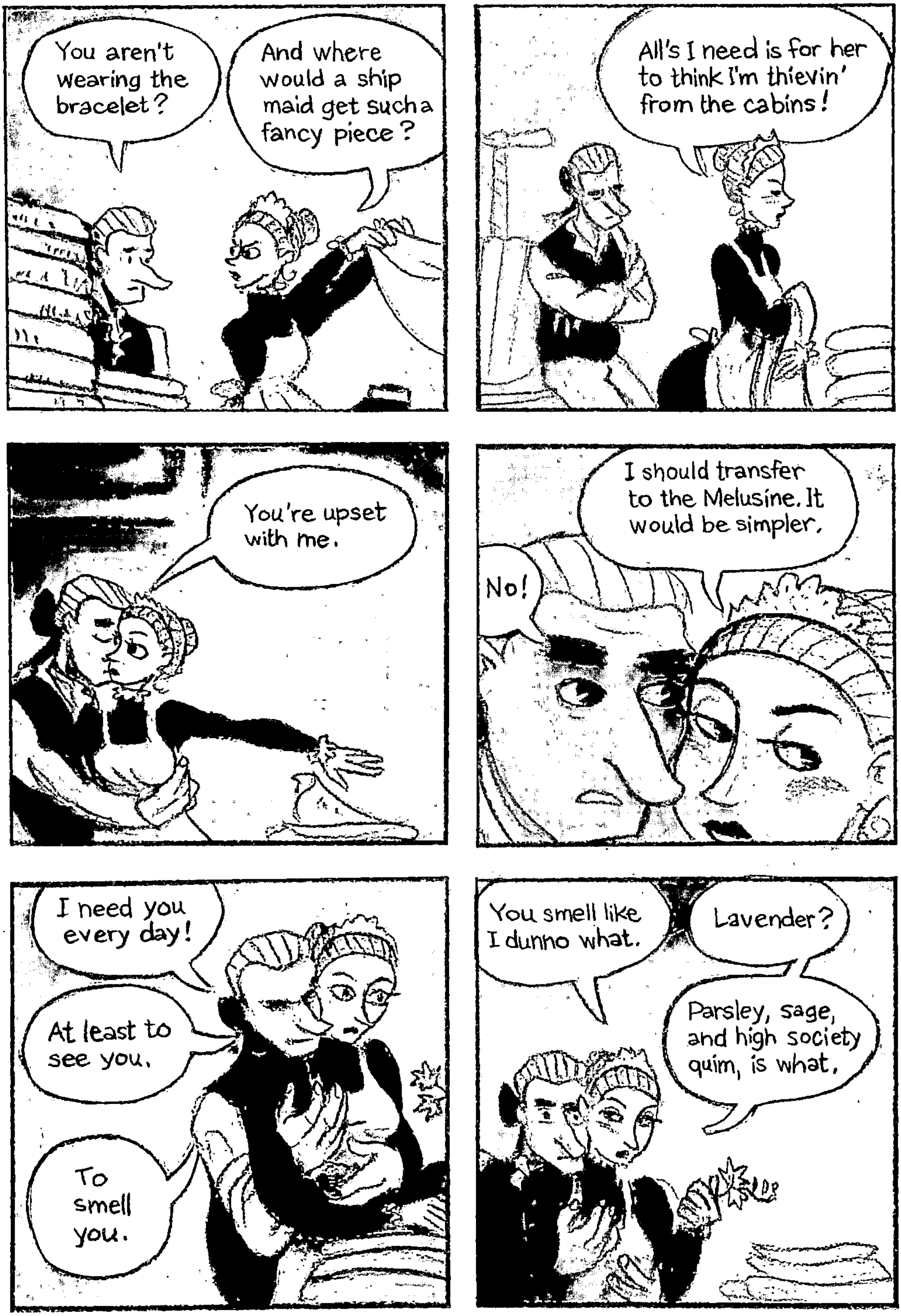
You aren't wearing the bracelet?
And where would a ship maid get such a fancy piece?
All's I need is for her to think I'm thievin' from the cabins!
You're upset with me.
I should transfer to the Melusine. It would be simpler.
No!
I need you every day!
At least to see you.
To smell you.
You smell like I dunno what.
Lavender?
Parsley, sage, and high society quim, is what.

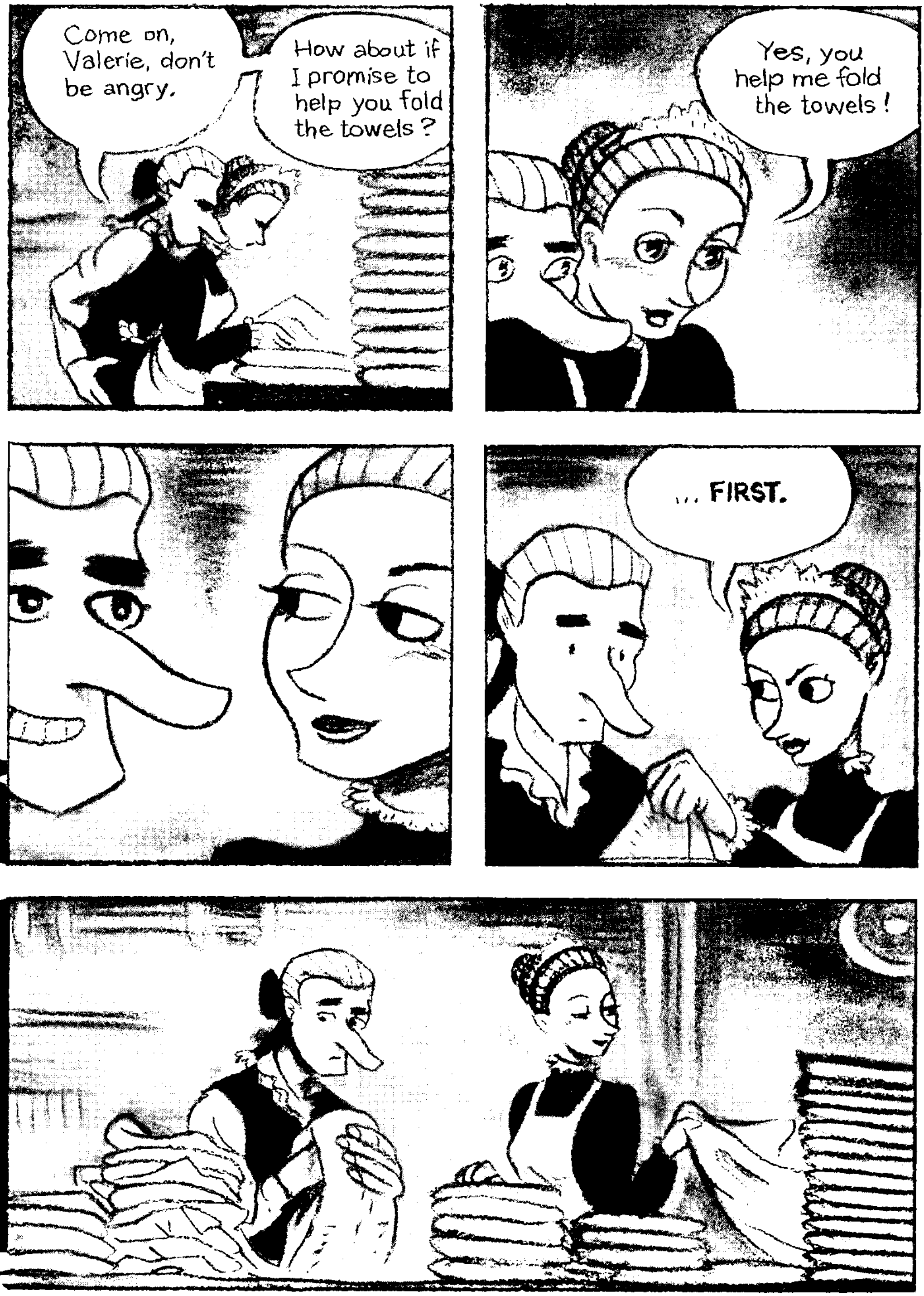
Come on, Valerie, don't be angry.
How about if I promise to help you fold the towels?
Yes, you help me fold the towels!
... FIRST.

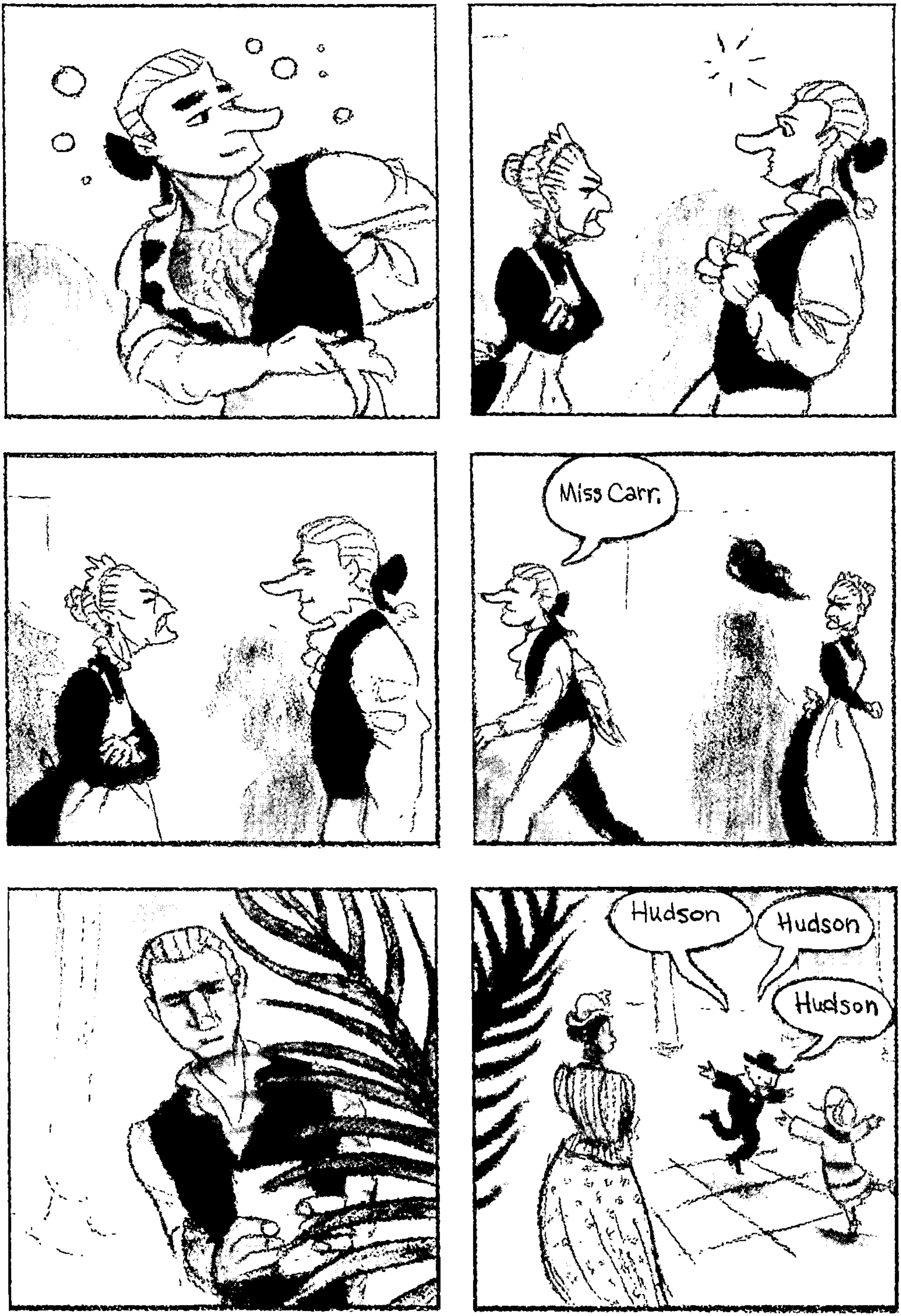
Miss Carr.
Hudson
Hudson
Hudson

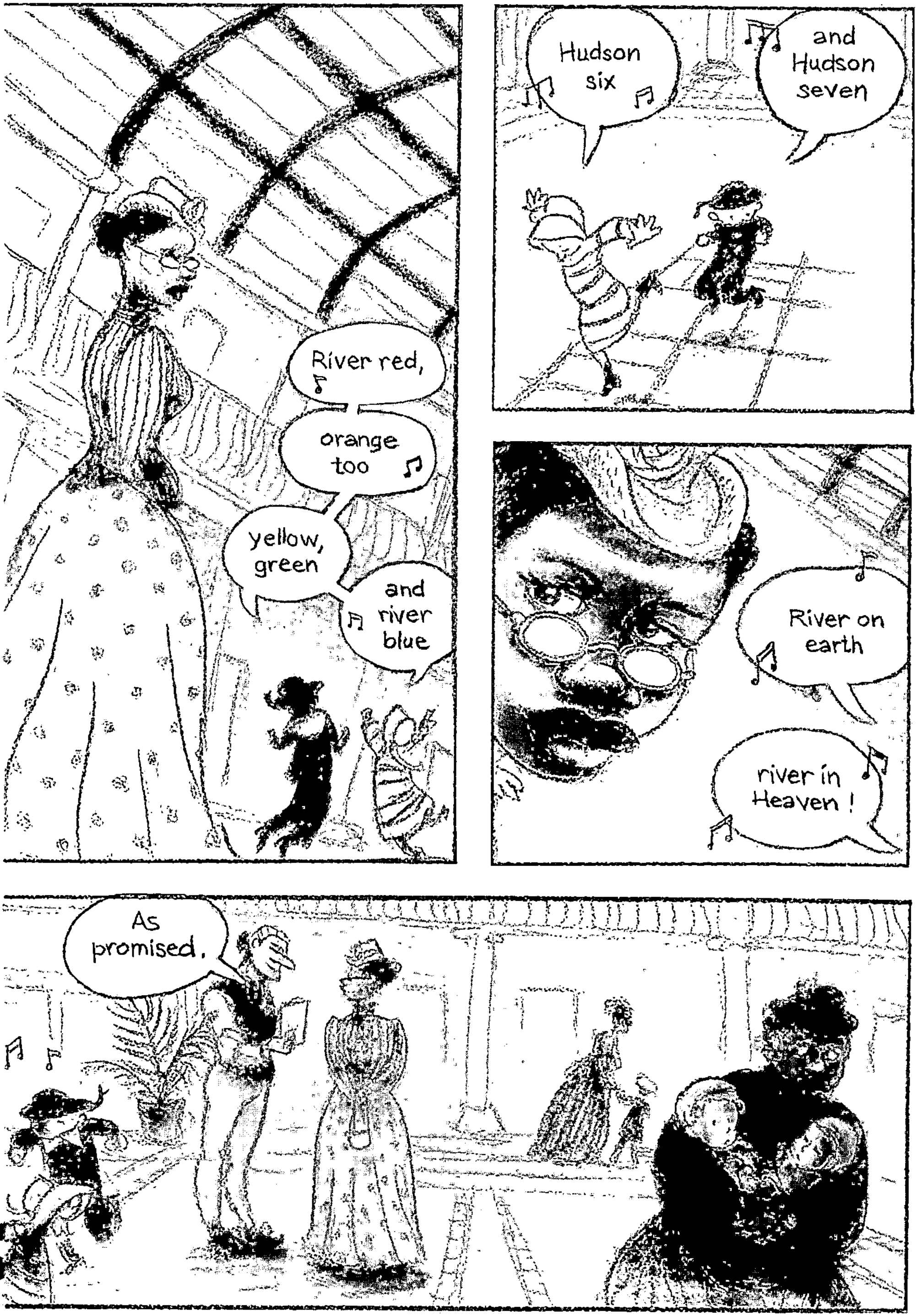
River red,
orange too
yellow, green
and river blue
Hudson six
and Hudson seven
River on earth
river in Heaven!
As promised.

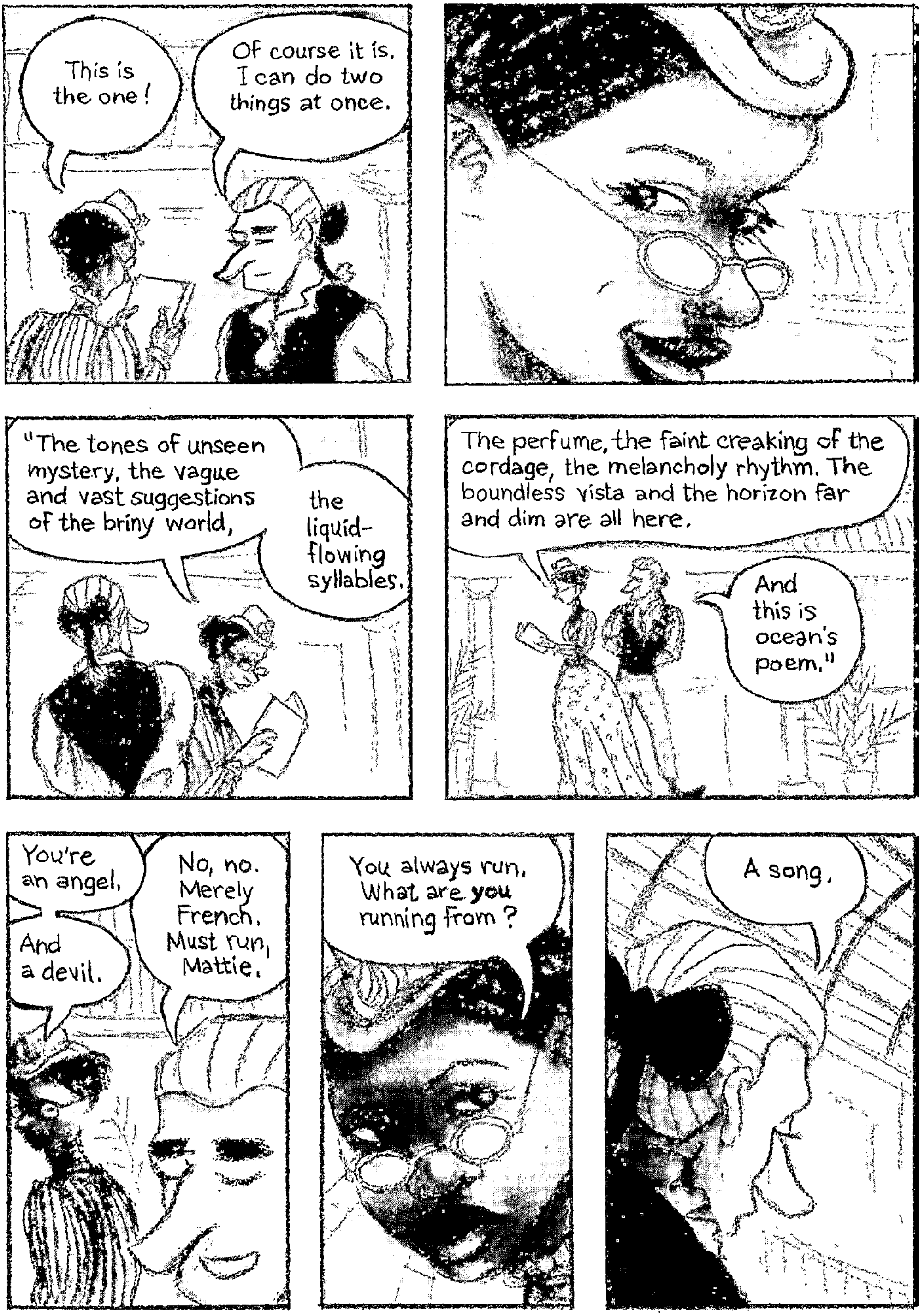

This is the one!
Of course it is. I can do two things at once.
"The tones of unseen mystery, the vague and vast suggestions of the briny world,
the liquid-flowing syllables.
The perfume, the faint creaking of the cordage, the melancholy rhythm. The boundless vista and the horizon far and dim are all here.
And this is ocean's poem."
You're an angel,
And a devil.
No, no. Merely French. Must run, Mattie.
You always run. What are **you** running from?
A song.

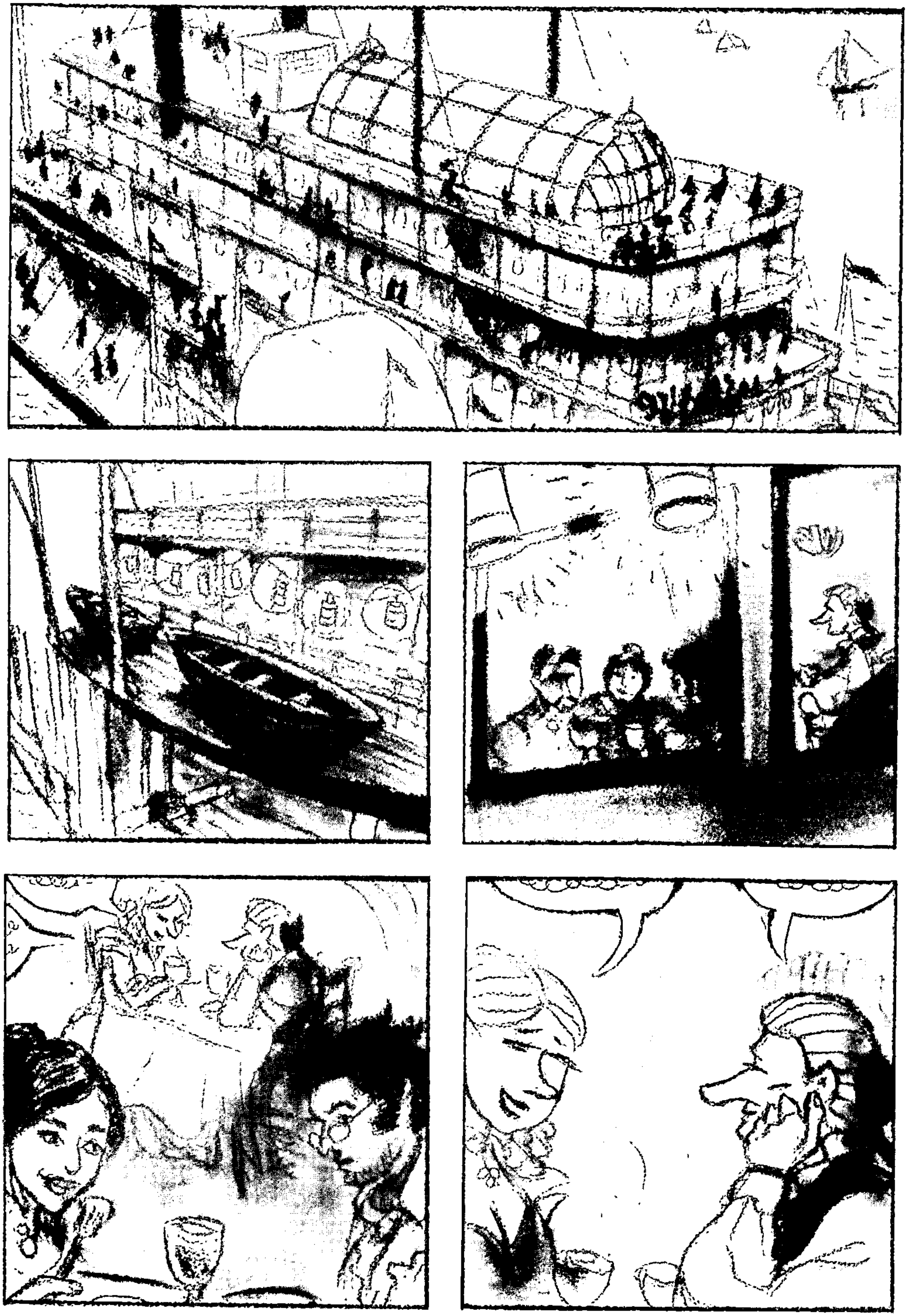

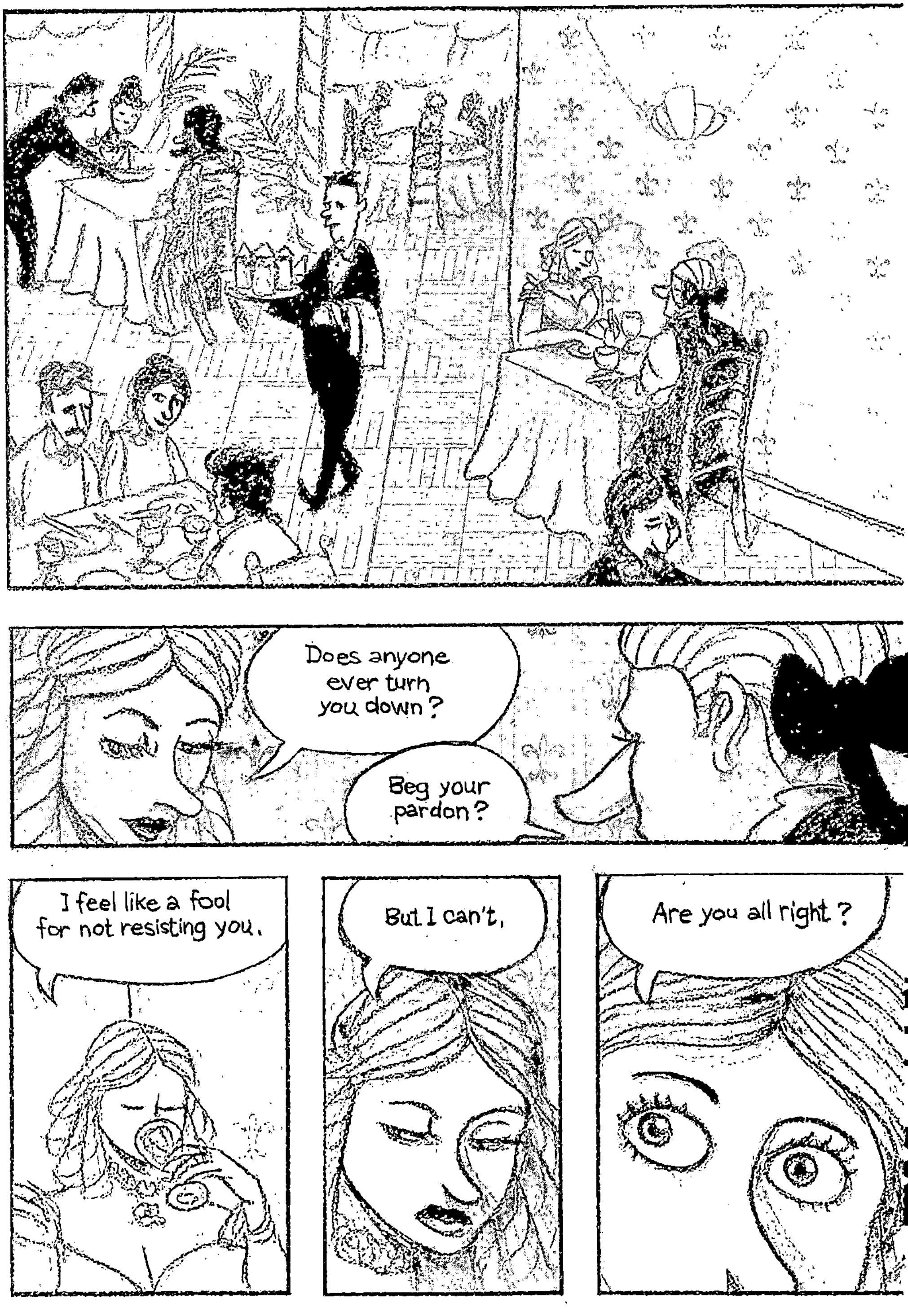
Does anyone ever turn you down?
Beg your pardon?
I feel like a fool for not resisting you.
But I can't.
Are you all right?

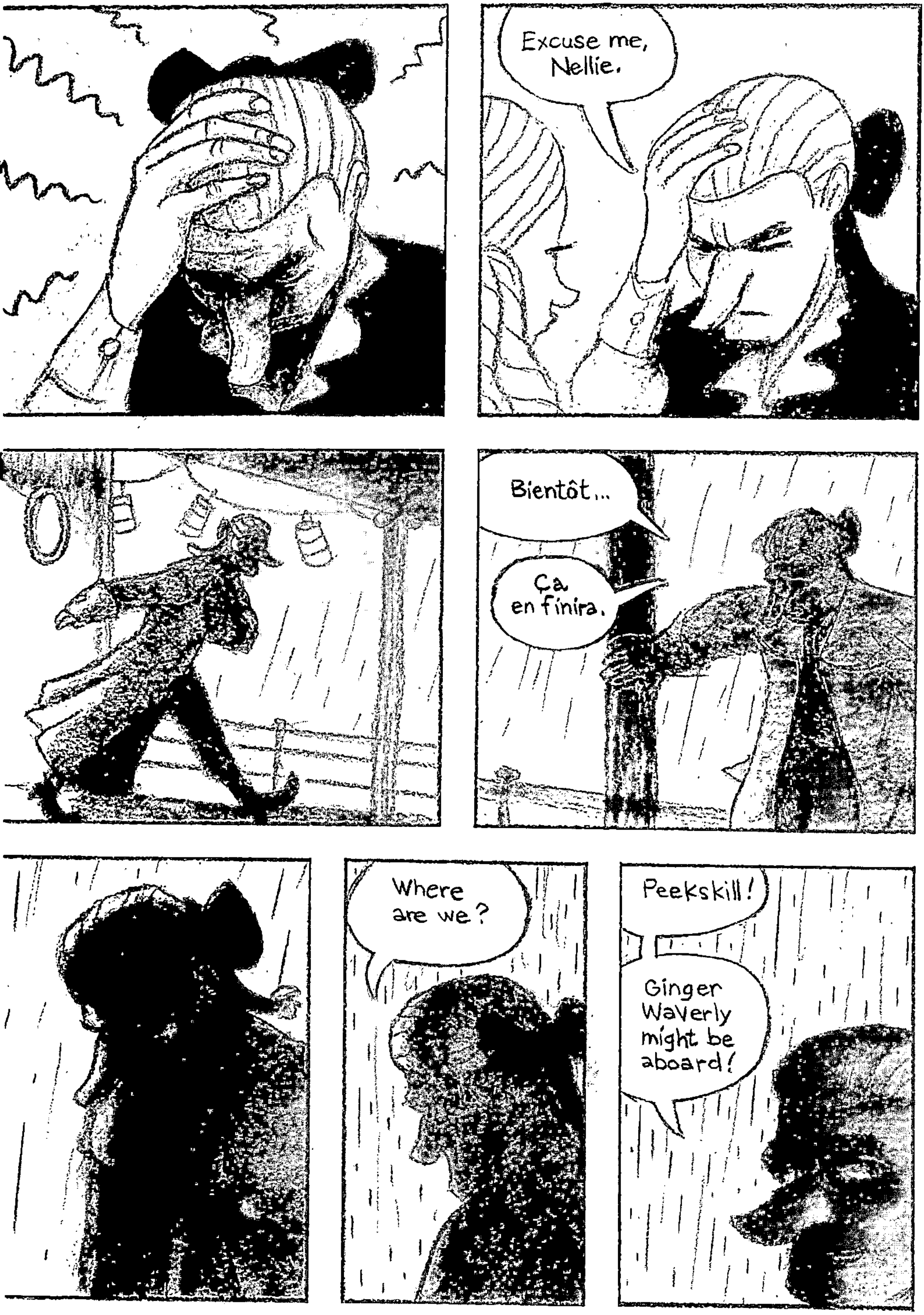
Excuse me, Nellie.
Bientôt...
Ça en finira.
Where are we?
Peekskill!
Ginger Waverly might be aboard!

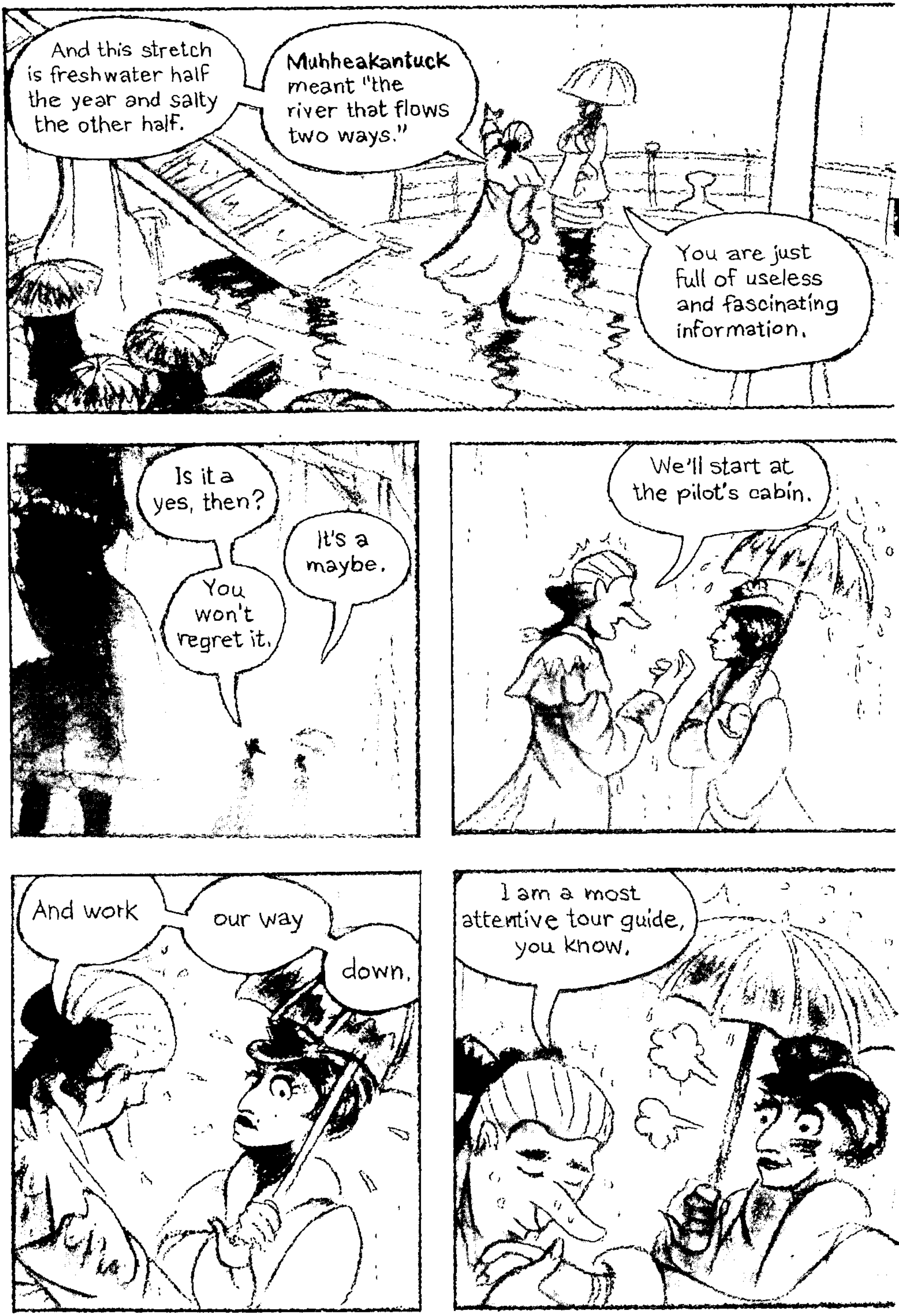
And this stretch is freshwater half the year and salty the other half.
Muhheakantuck meant "the river that flows two ways."
You are just full of useless and fascinating information.
Is it a yes, then?
You won't regret it.
It's a maybe.
We'll start at the pilot's cabin.
And work
our way
down.
I am a most attentive tour guide, you know.

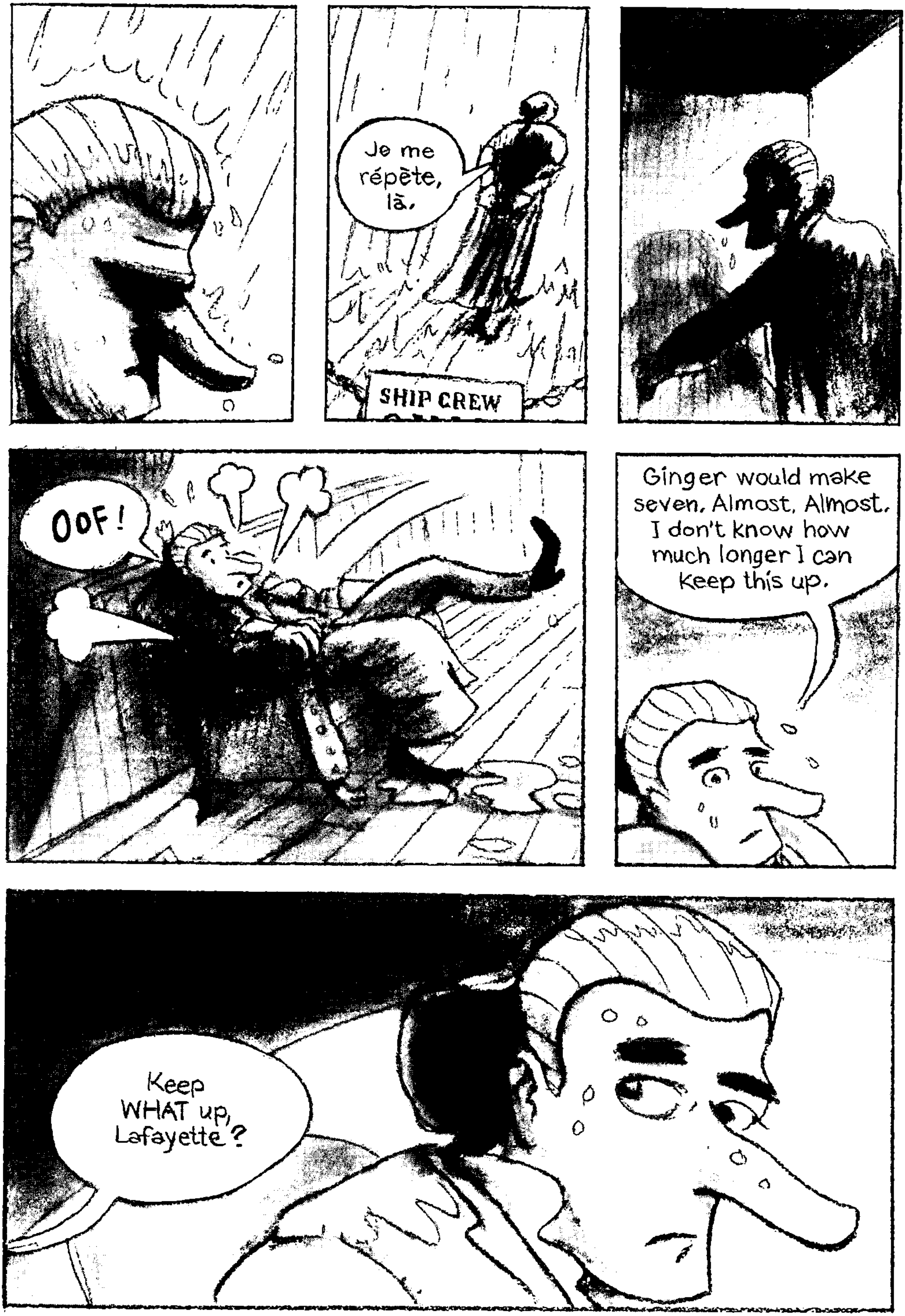
Je me répête, là.
SHIP CREW
OOF!
Ginger would make seven. Almost. Almost. I don't know how much longer I can keep this up.
Keep WHAT up, Lafayette?

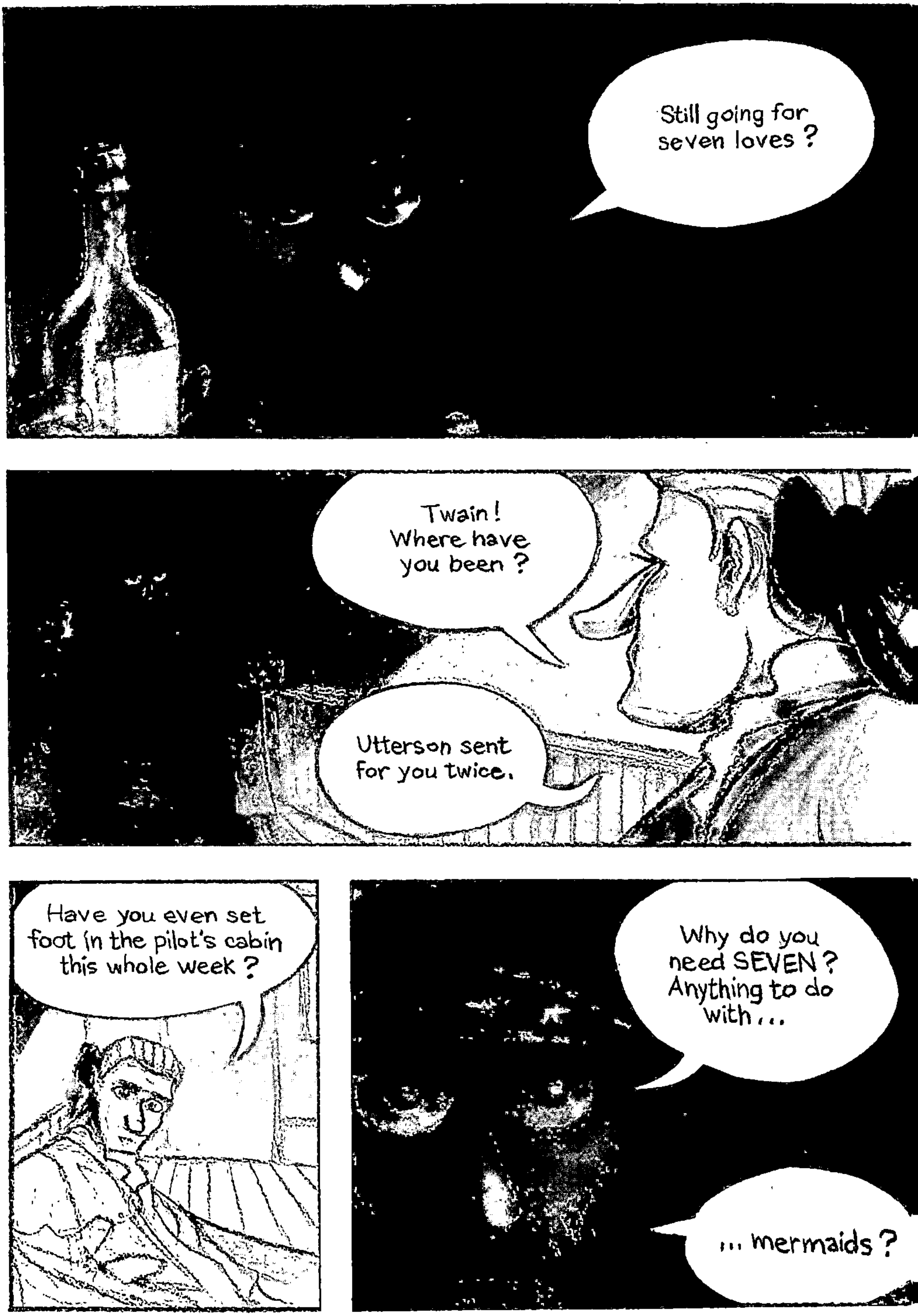
Still going for seven loves?
Twain! Where have you been?
Utterson sent for you twice.
Have you even set foot in the pilot's cabin this whole week?
Why do you need SEVEN? Anything to do with...
... mermaids?

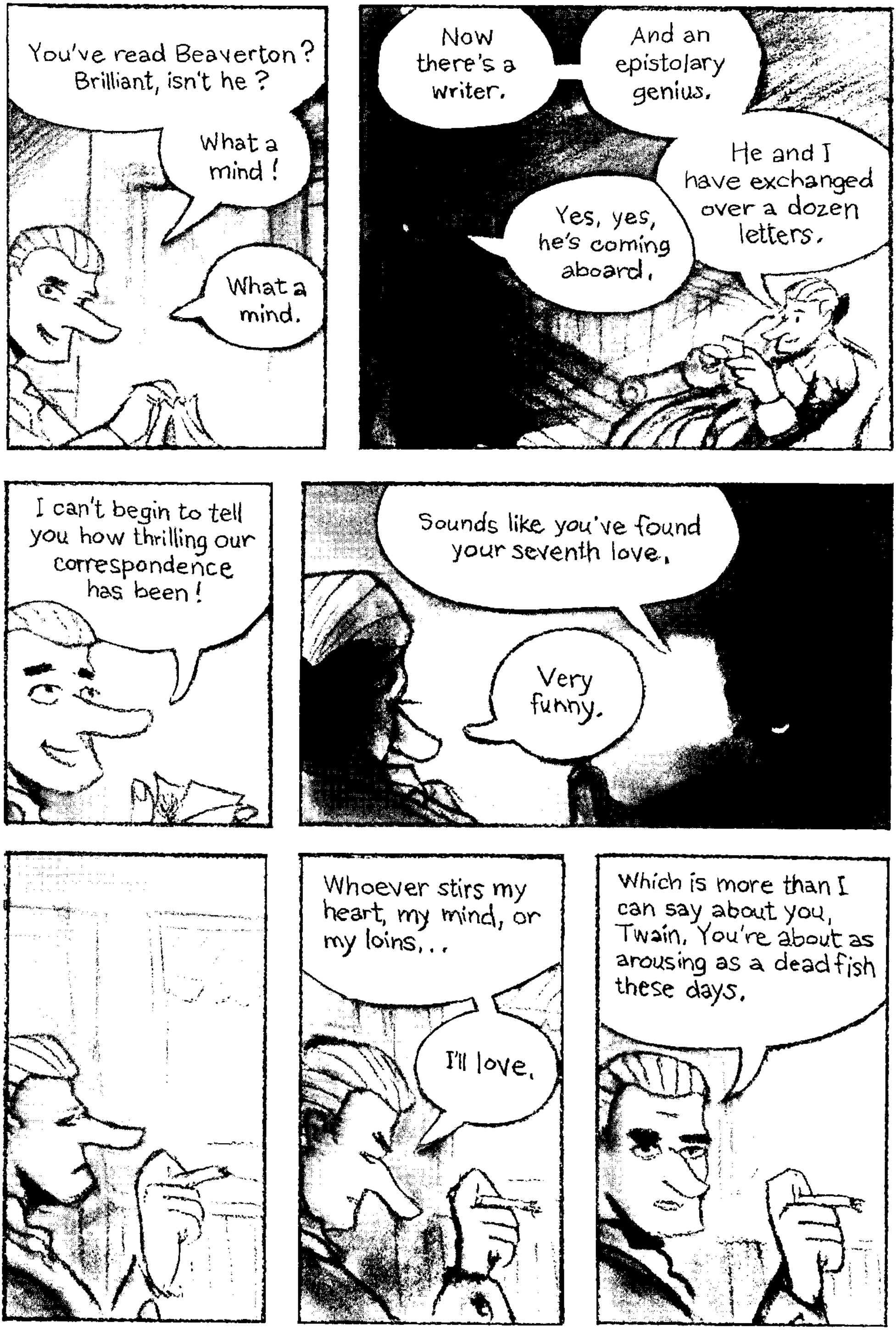
You've read Beaverton? Brilliant, isn't he?
What a mind!
What a mind.
Now there's a writer.
And an epistolary genius.
He and I have exchanged over a dozen letters.
Yes, yes, he's coming aboard.
I can't begin to tell you how thrilling our correspondence has been!
Sounds like you've found your seventh love.
Very funny.
Whoever stirs my heart, my mind, or my loins...
I'll love.
Which is more than I can say about you, Twain. You're about as arousing as a dead fish these days.

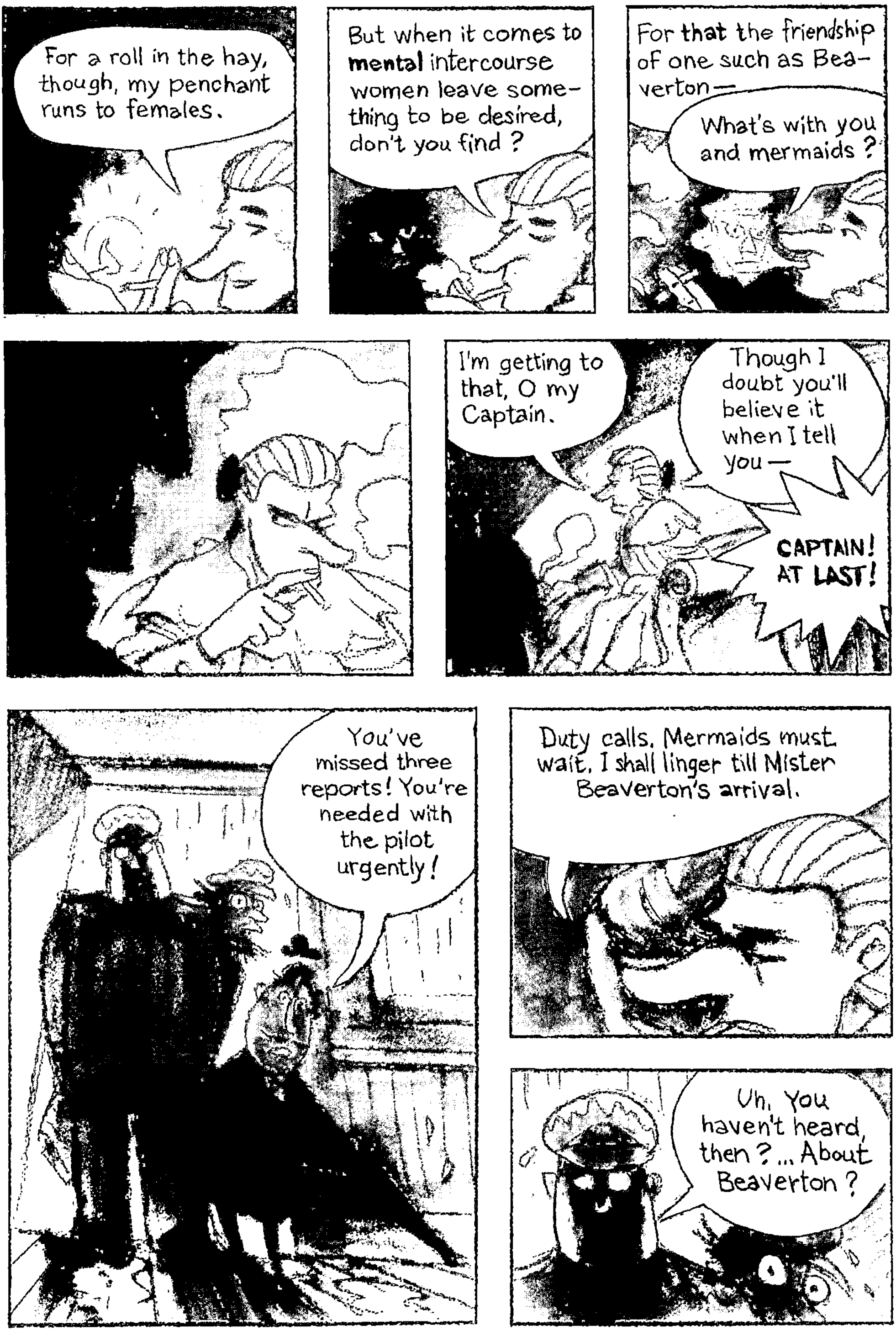
For a roll in the hay, though, my penchant runs to females.
But when it comes to **mental** intercourse women leave something to be desired, don't you find?
For **that** the friendship of one such as Beaverton —
What's with you and mermaids?
I'm getting to that, O my Captain.
Though I doubt you'll believe it when I tell you —
CAPTAIN! AT LAST!
You've missed three reports! You're needed with the pilot urgently!
Duty calls. Mermaids must wait. I shall linger till Mister Beaverton's arrival.
Uh, You haven't heard, then? ... About Beaverton?

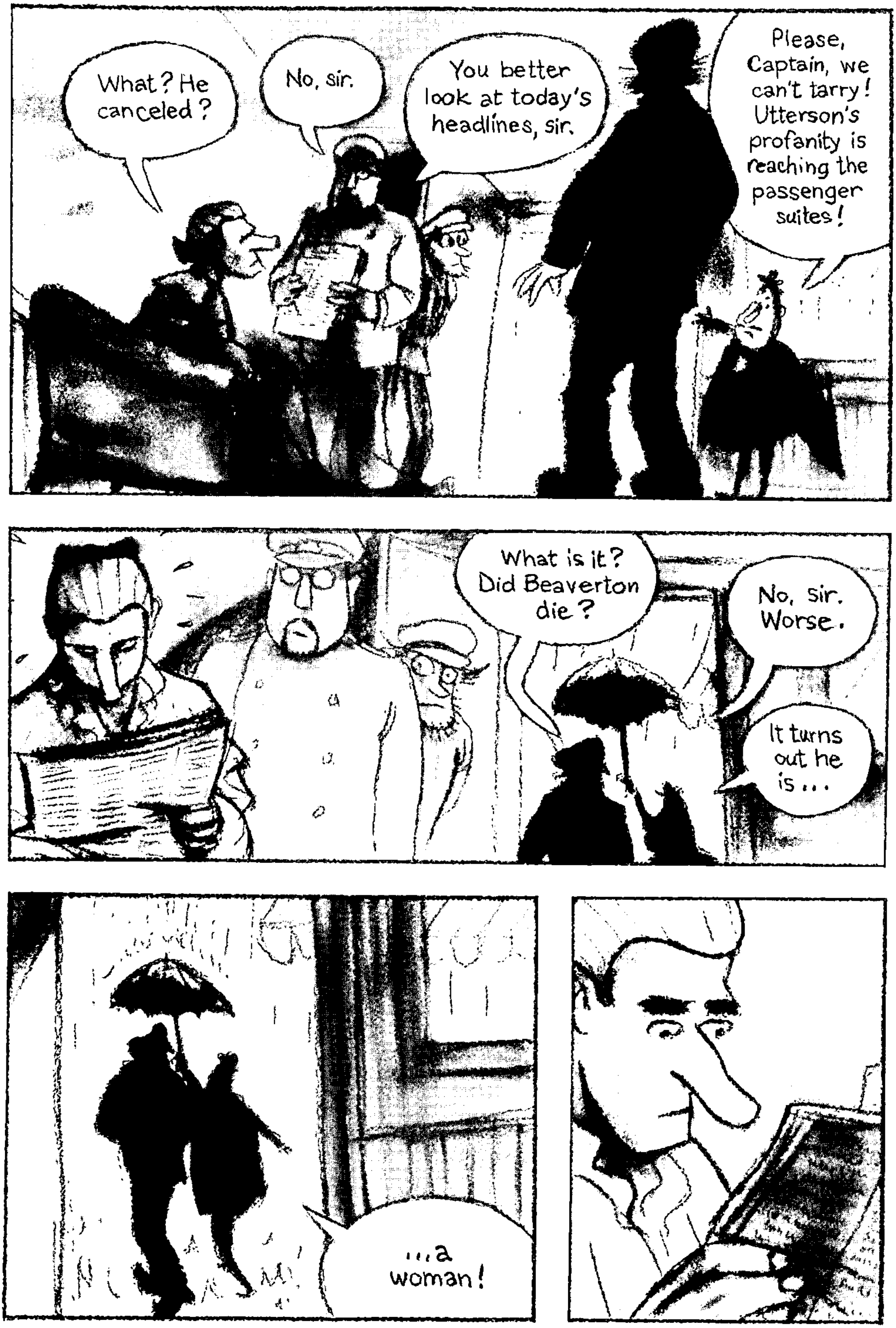
What? He canceled?
No, sir.
You better look at today's headlines, sir.
Please, Captain, we can't tarry! Utterson's profanity is reaching the passenger suites!
What is it? Did Beaverton die?
No, sir. Worse.
It turns out he is...
...a woman!

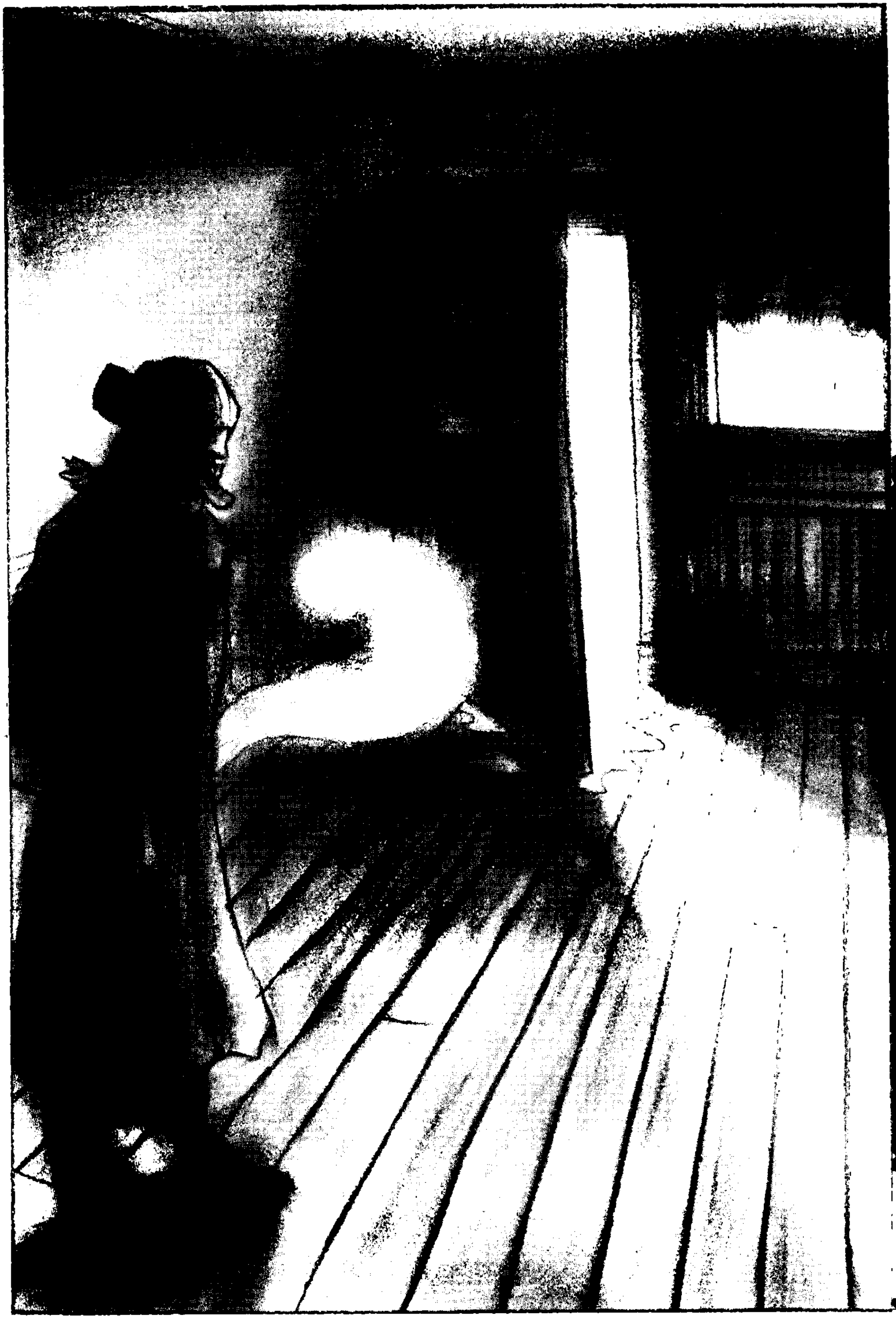

Pt II, Chap.2

"INK STAINS"

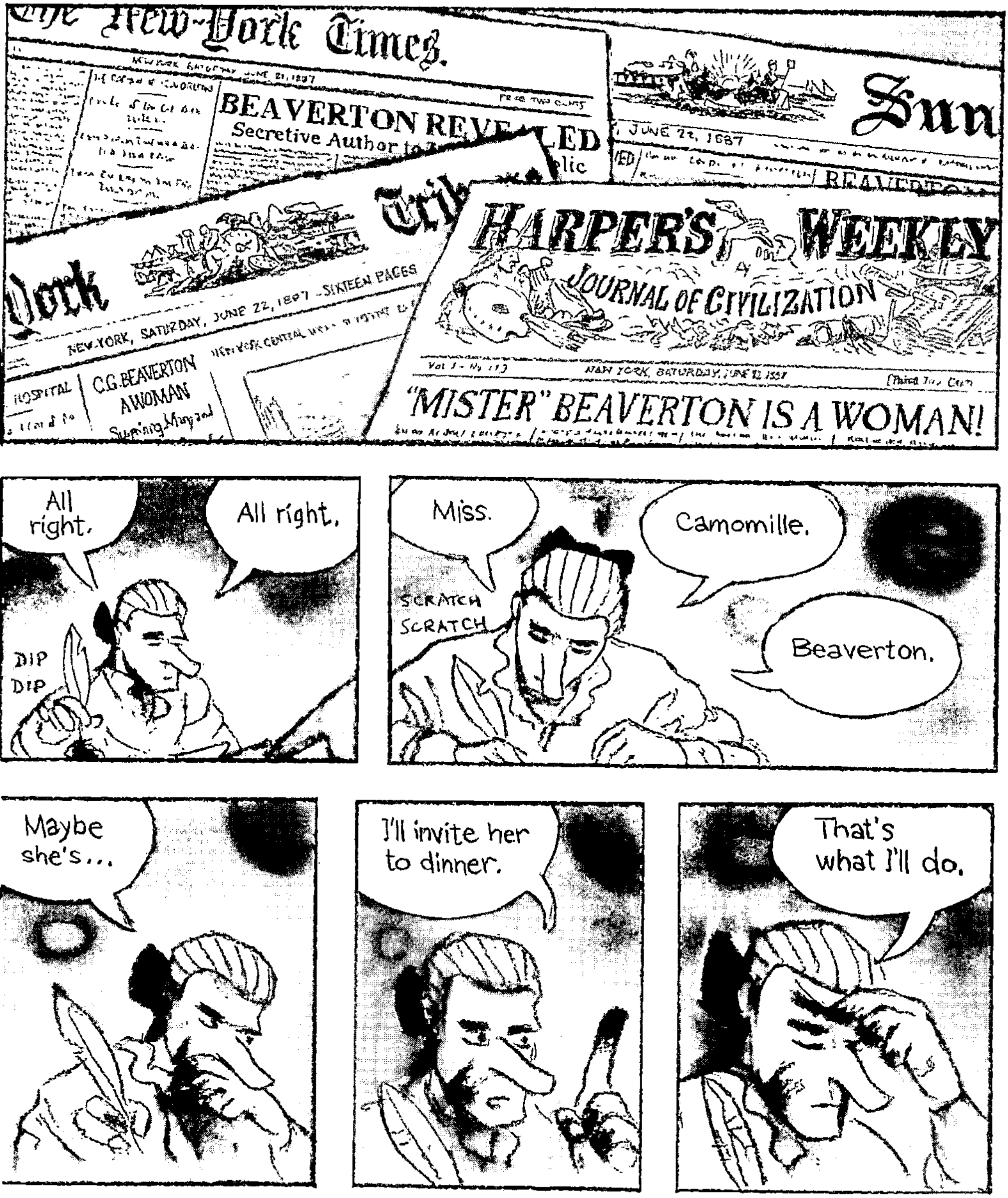
The New-York Times.
BEAVERTON REVEALED
Secretive Author
Sun
JUNE 22, 1887
York
NEW-YORK, SATURDAY, JUNE 22, 1887 - SIXTEEN PAGES
C.G. BEAVERTON A WOMAN
HOSPITAL
HARPER'S WEEKLY
JOURNAL OF CIVILIZATION
"MISTER" BEAVERTON IS A WOMAN!
All right.
All right.
DIP
DIP
Miss.
SCRATCH
SCRATCH
Camomille.
Beaverton.
Maybe she's...
I'll invite her to dinner.
That's what I'll do.

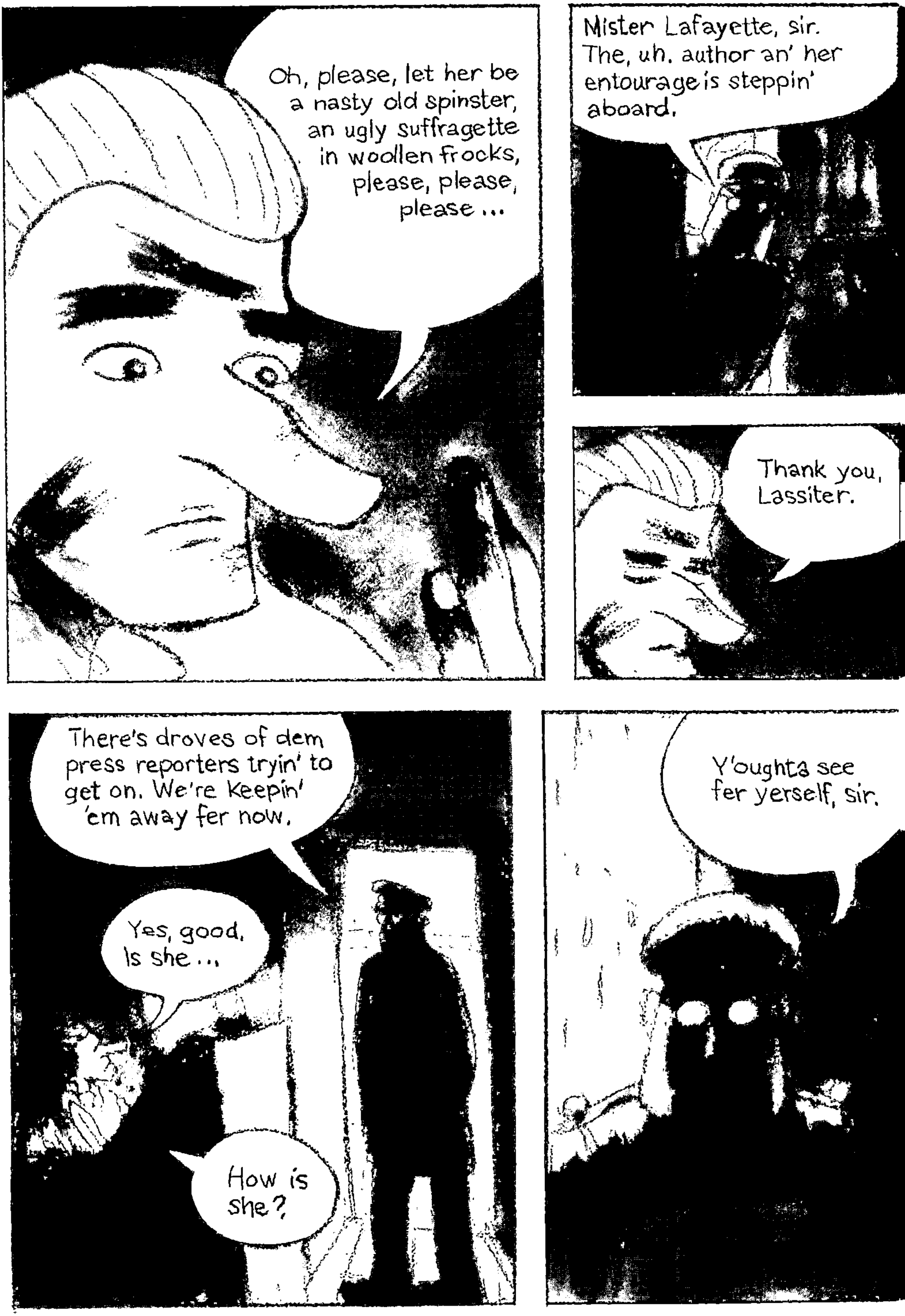
Oh, please, let her be a nasty old spinster, an ugly suffragette in woollen frocks, please, please, please ...
Mister Lafayette, sir. The, uh. author an' her entourage is steppin' aboard.
Thank you, Lassiter.
There's droves of dem press reporters tryin' to get on. We're keepin' 'em away fer now.
Yes, good. Is she ...
How is she?
Y'oughta see fer yerself, sir.

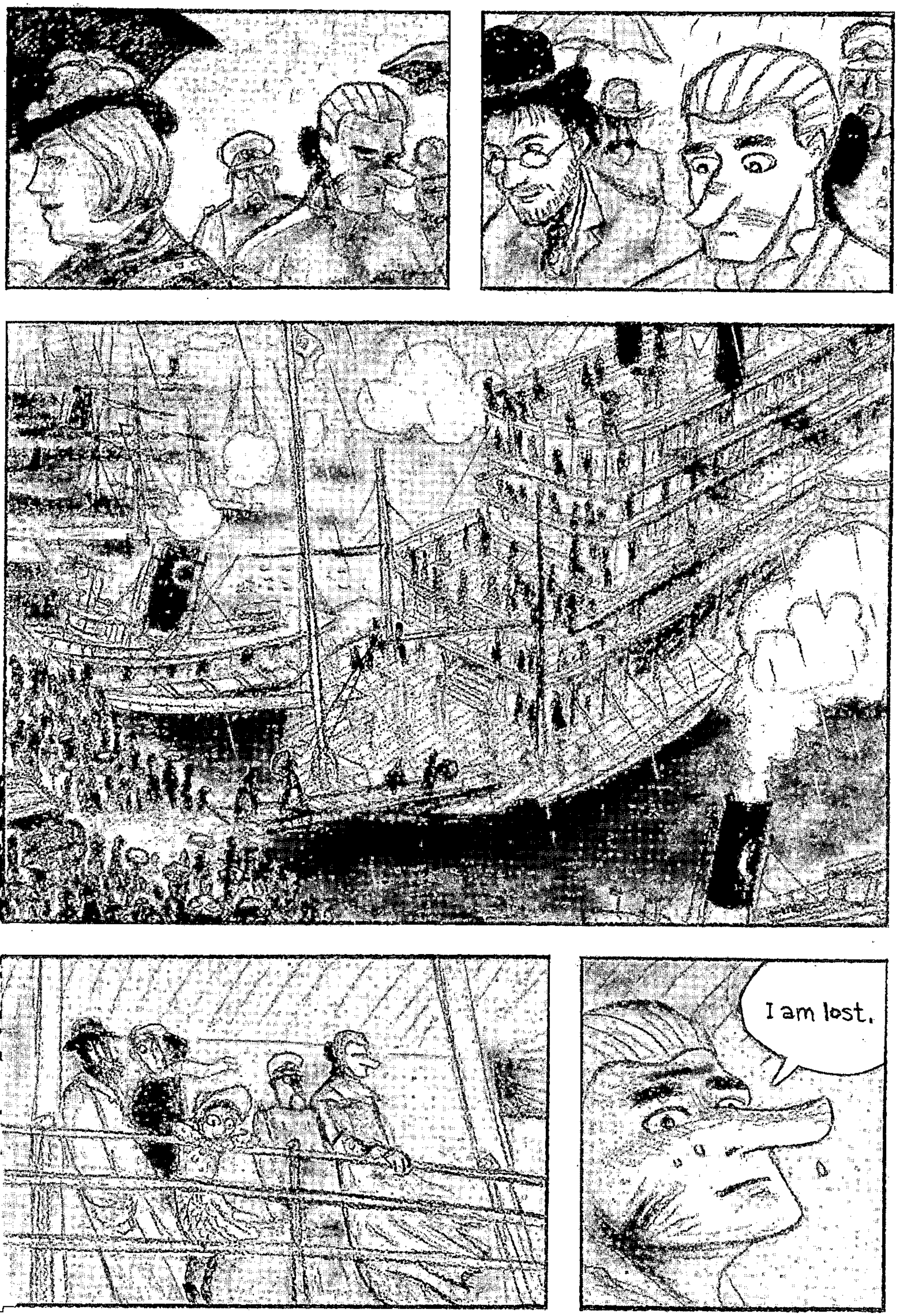
I am lost.

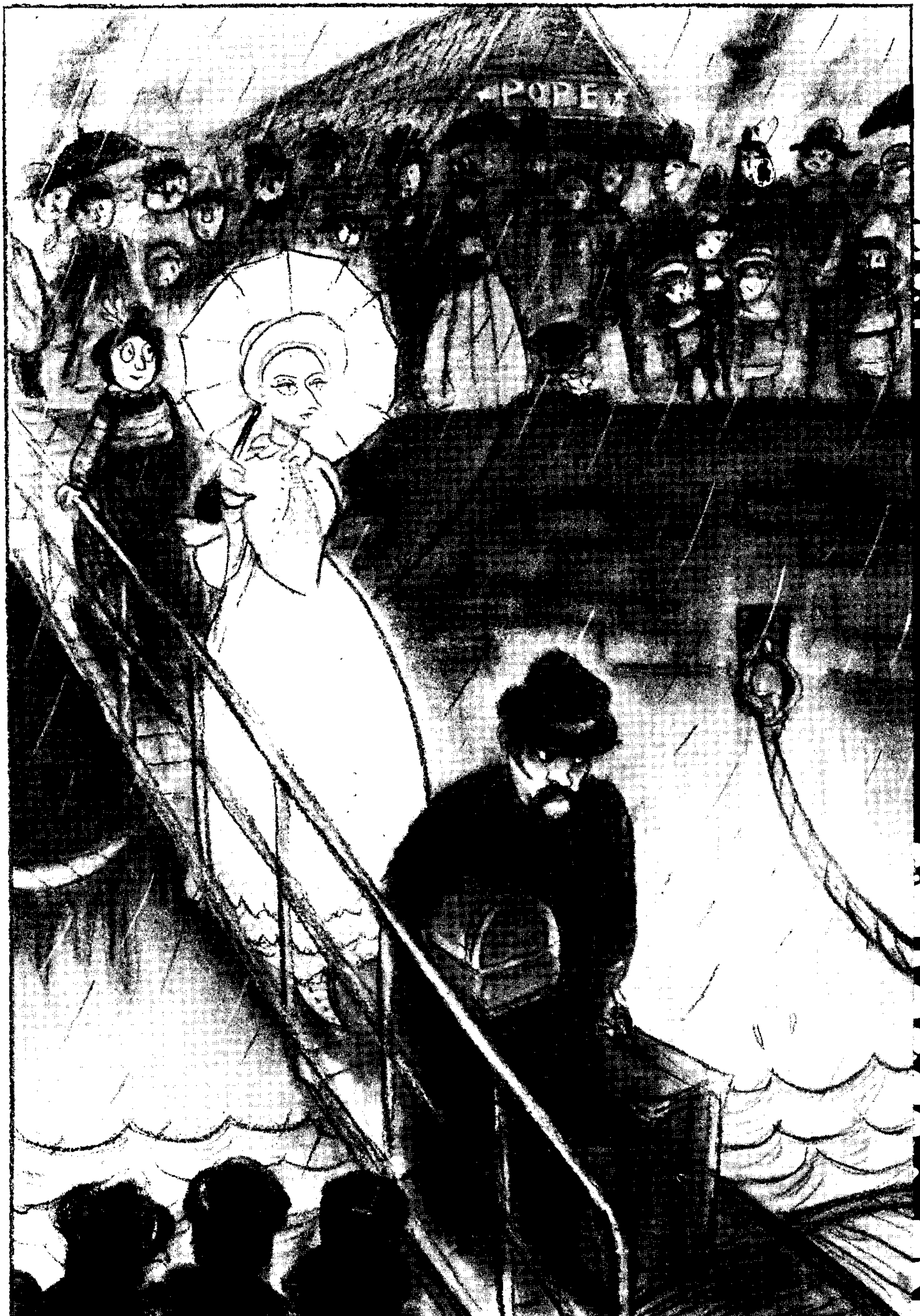
POPE

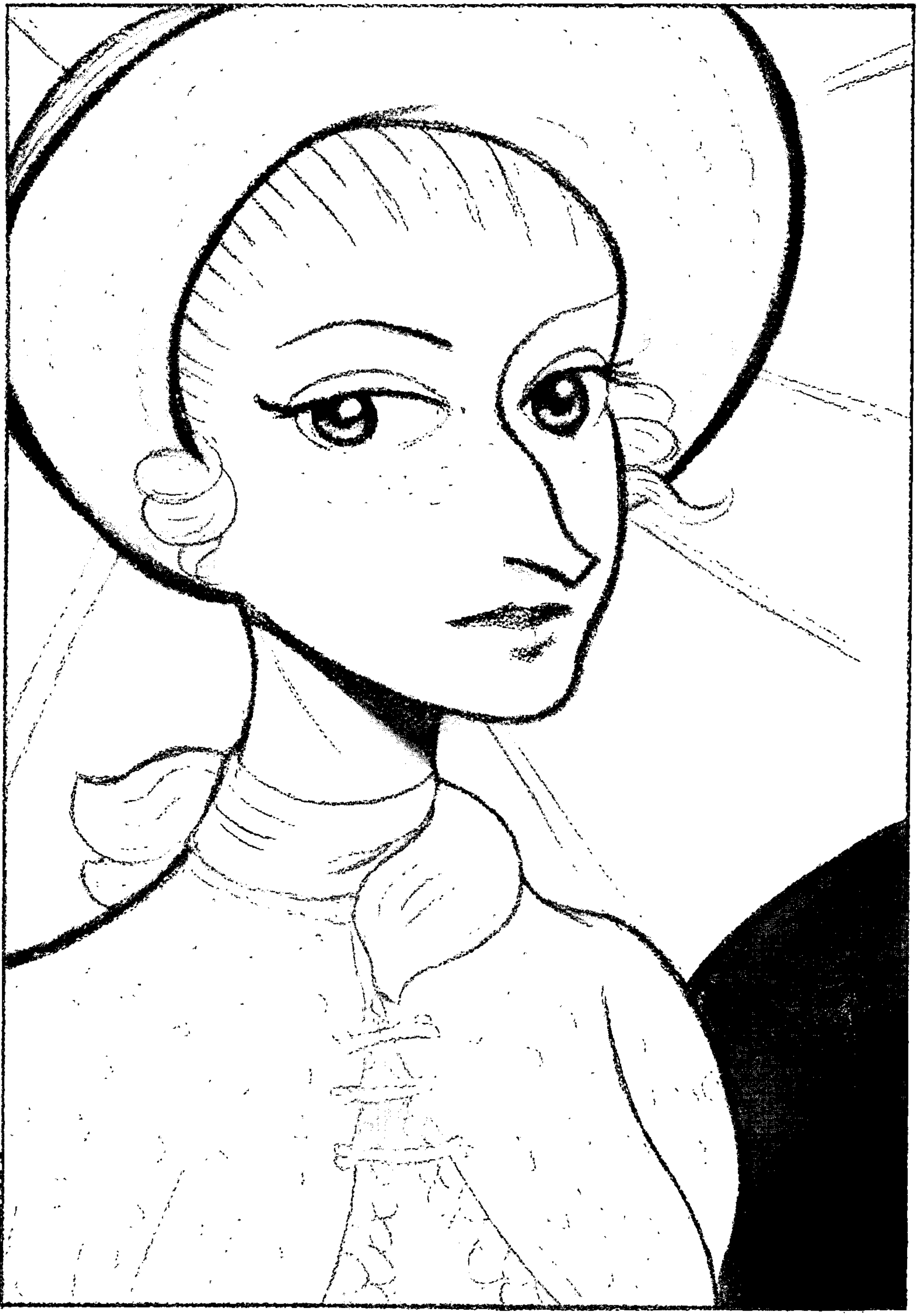

Pt II, Chap.3

"THE DAME'S AUDACIOUS"

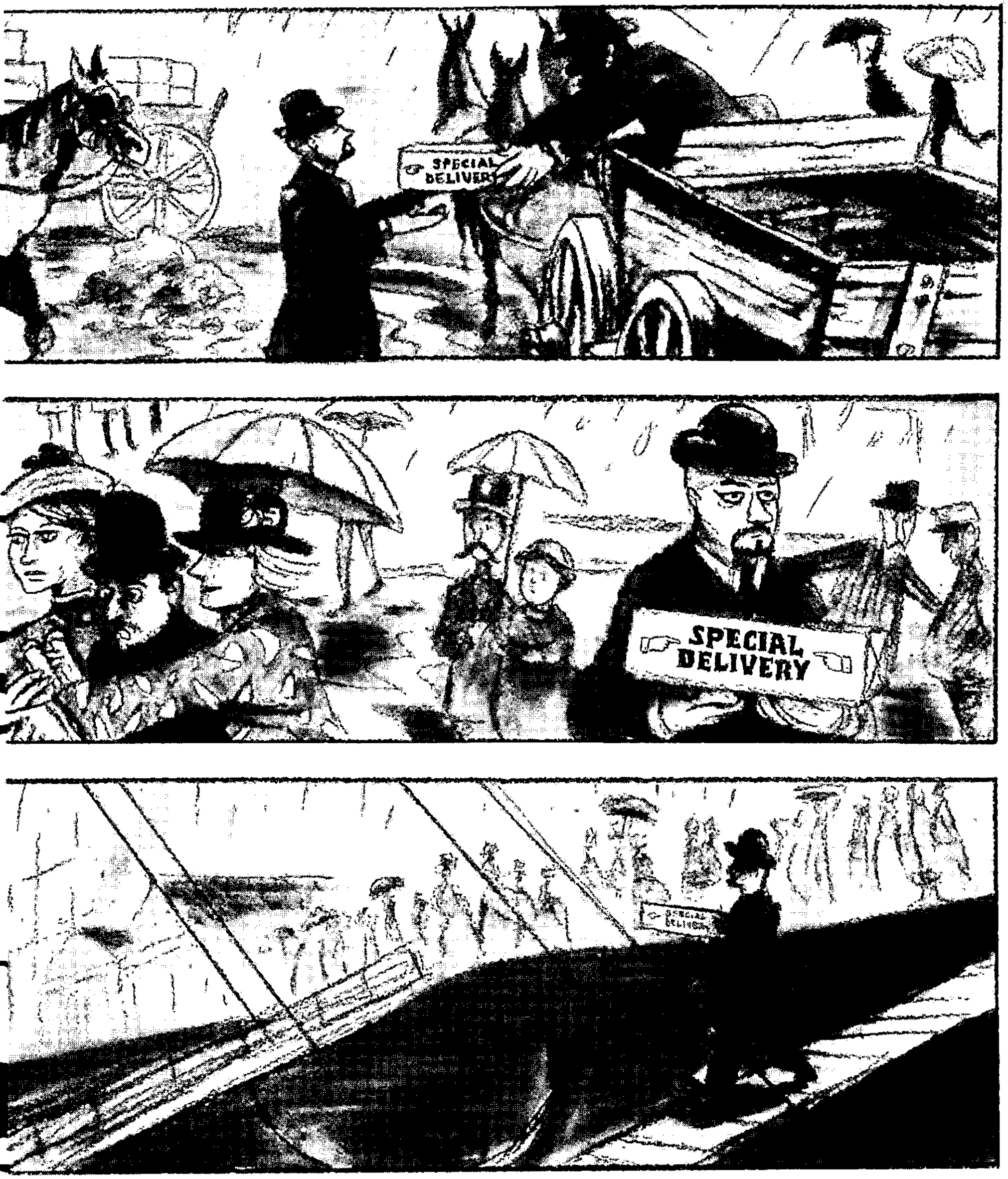
SPECIAL DELIVERY
SPECIAL DELIVERY

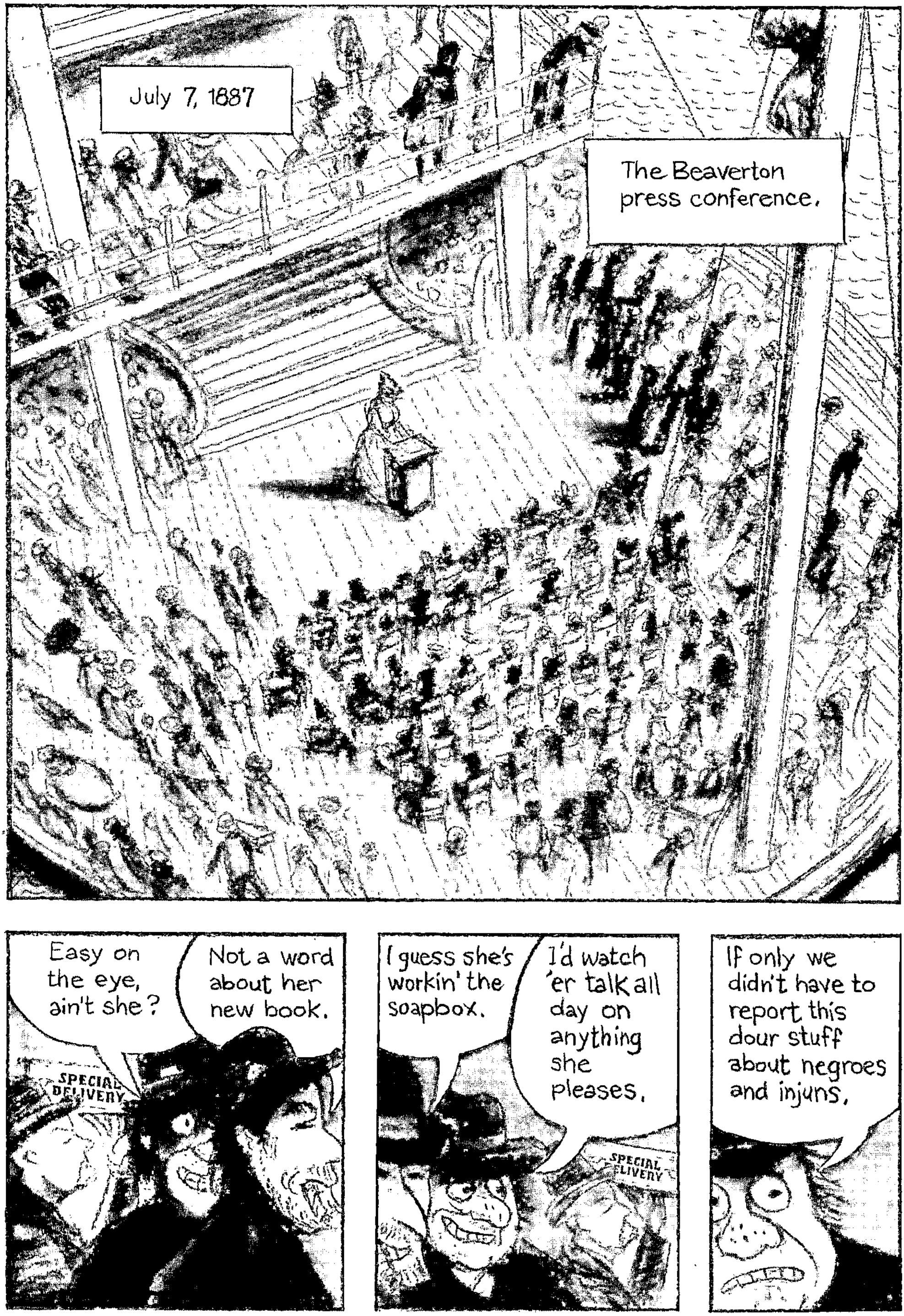
July 7, 1887
The Beaverton press conference.
Easy on the eye, ain't she?
Not a word about her new book.
SPECIAL DELIVERY
I guess she's workin' the soapbox.
I'd watch 'er talk all day on anything she pleases.
SPECIAL DELIVERY
If only we didn't have to report this dour stuff about negroes and injuns.

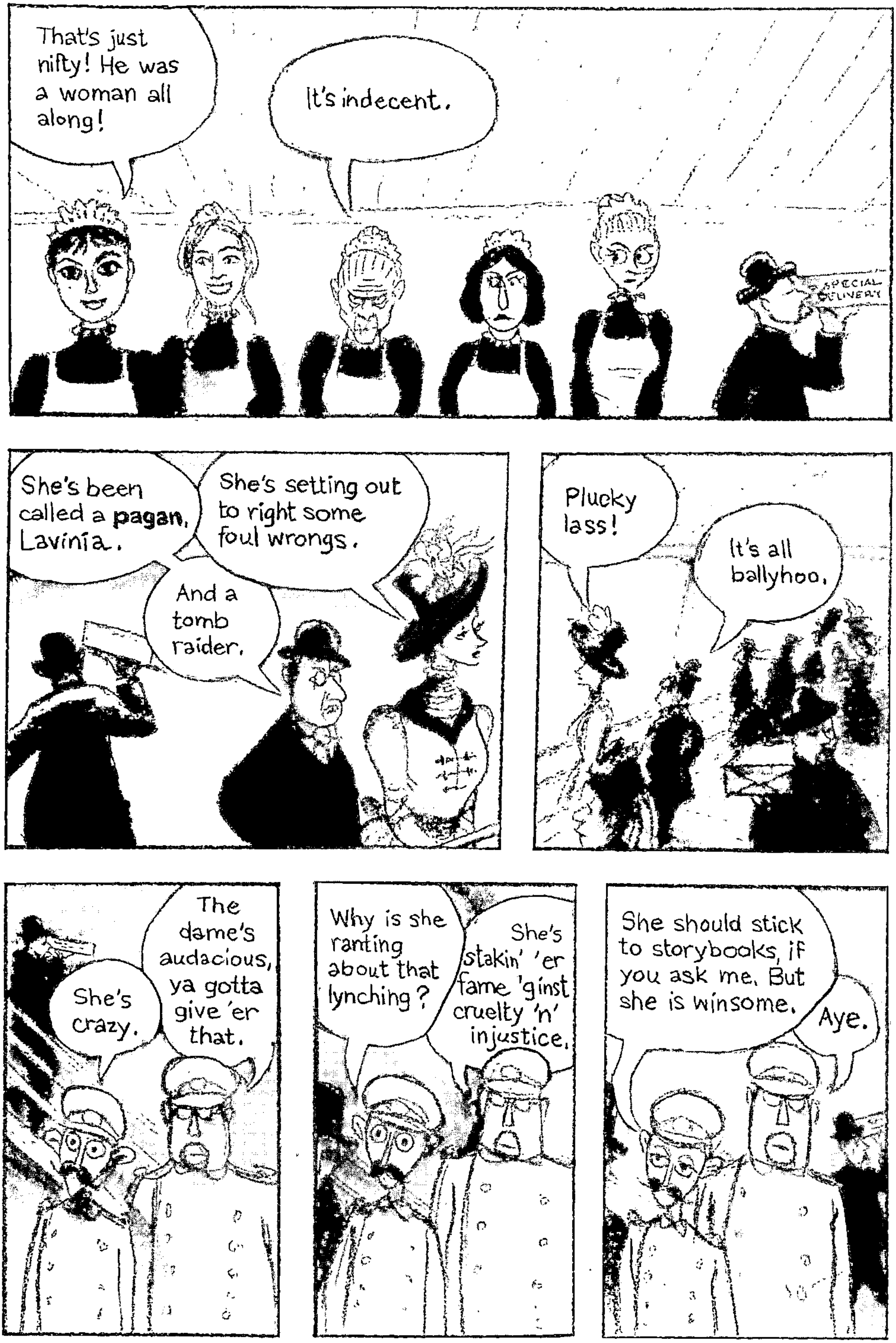
That's just nifty! He was a woman all along!
It's indecent.
SPECIAL DELIVERY
She's been called a **pagan**, Lavinia.
She's setting out to right some foul wrongs.
And a tomb raider.
Plucky lass!
It's all ballyhoo.
The dame's audacious, ya gotta give 'er that.
She's crazy.
Why is she ranting about that lynching?
She's stakin' 'er fame 'ginst cruelty 'n' injustice.
She should stick to storybooks, if you ask me. But she is winsome.
Aye.

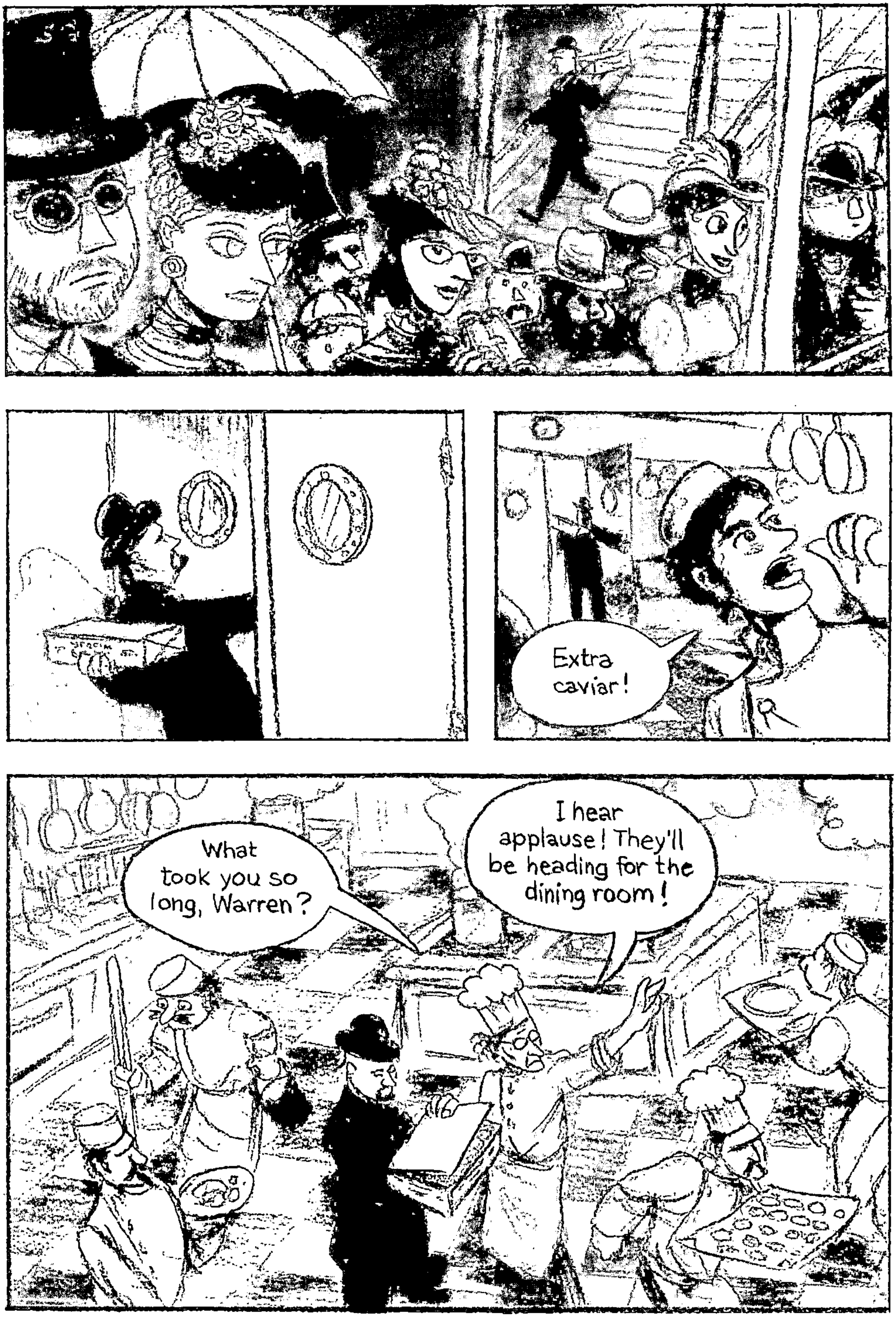
Extra caviar!
What took you so long, Warren?
I hear applause! They'll be heading for the dining room!

Pt II, Chap.4

"ECLIPSE"

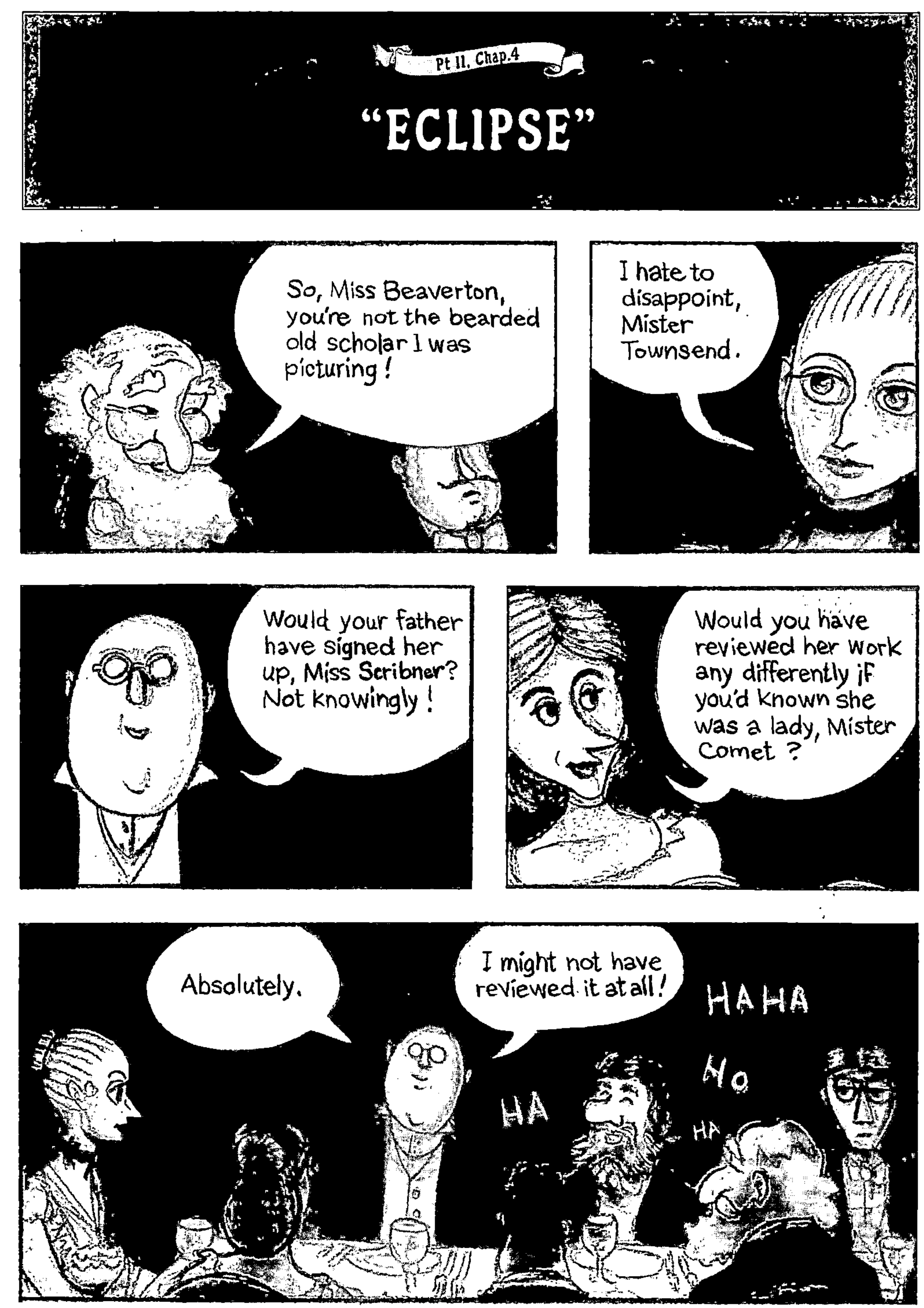

So, Miss Beaverton, you're not the bearded old scholar I was picturing!
I hate to disappoint, Mister Townsend.
Would your father have signed her up, Miss Scribner? Not knowingly!
Would you have reviewed her work any differently if you'd known she was a lady, Mister Comet?
Absolutely.
I might not have reviewed it at all!
HAHA
HA
HO
HA

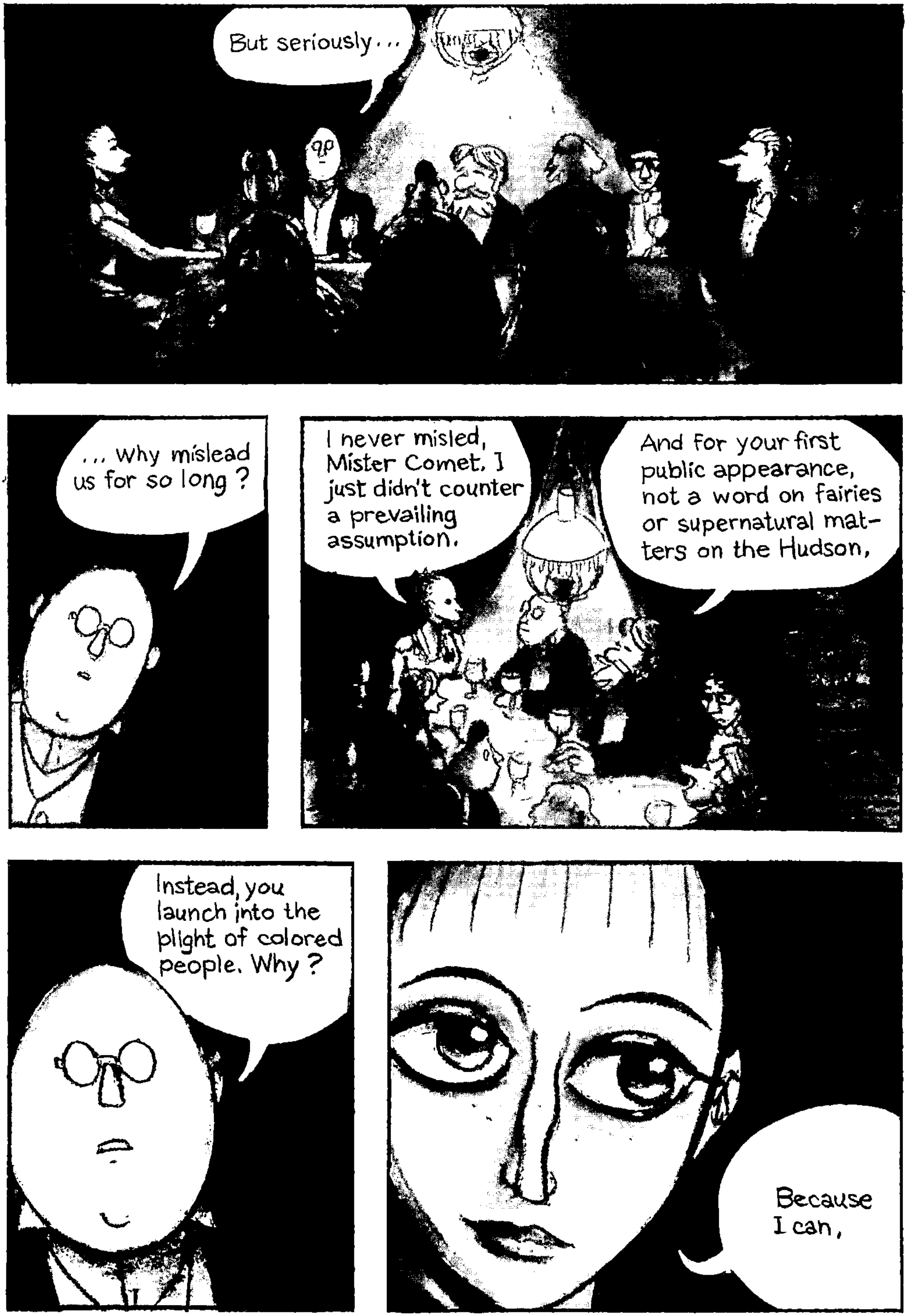
But seriously...
... Why mislead us for so long?
I never misled, Mister Comet. I just didn't counter a prevailing assumption.
And for your first public appearance, not a word on fairies or supernatural matters on the Hudson,
Instead, you launch into the plight of colored people. Why?
Because I can,

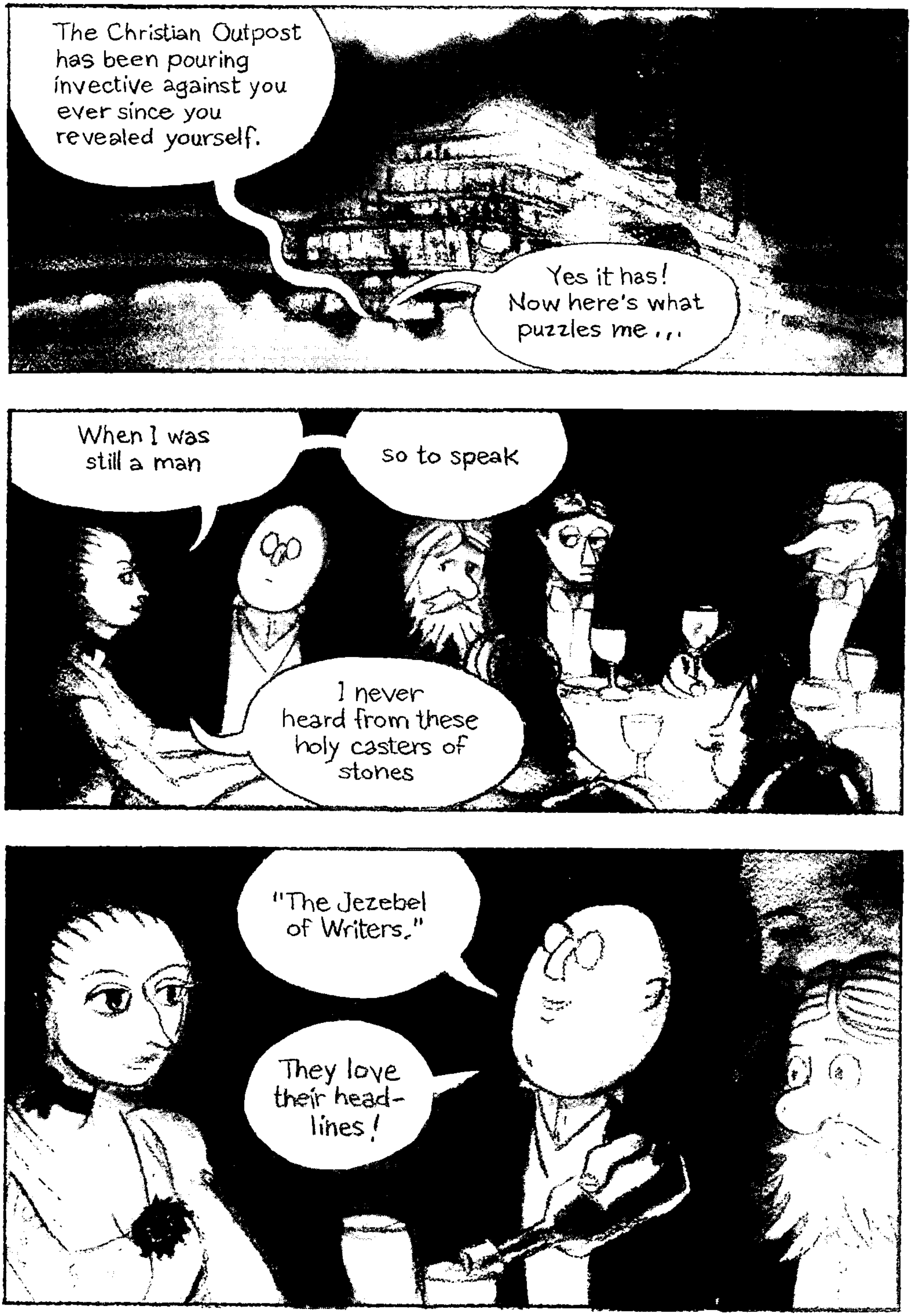
The Christian Outpost has been pouring invective against you ever since you revealed yourself.
Yes it has! Now here's what puzzles me ...
When I was still a man
so to speak
I never heard from these holy casters of stones
"The Jezebel of Writers."
They love their head-lines!

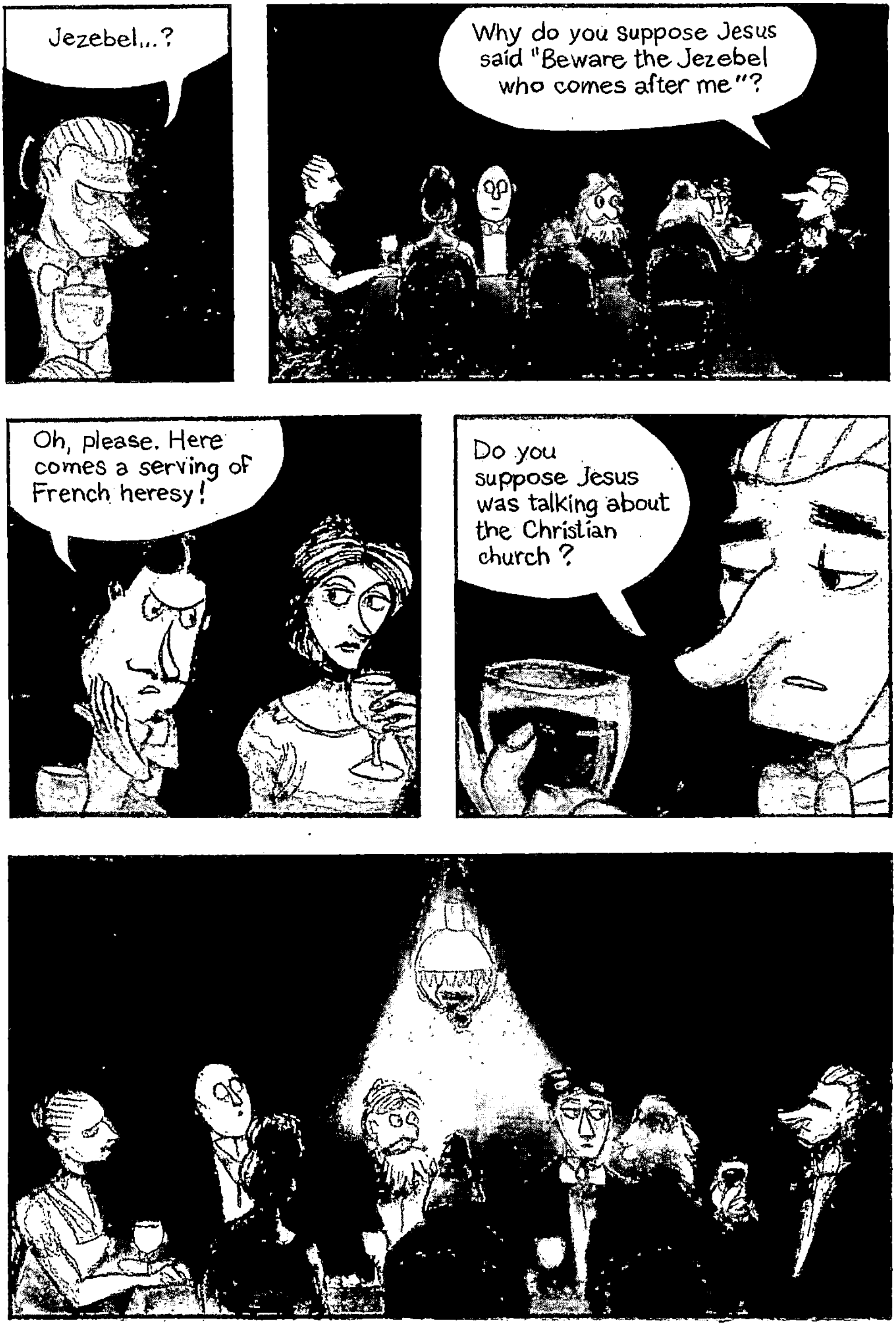
Jezebel...?
Why do you suppose Jesus said "Beware the Jezebel who comes after me"?
Oh, please. Here comes a serving of French heresy!
Do you suppose Jesus was talking about the Christian church?

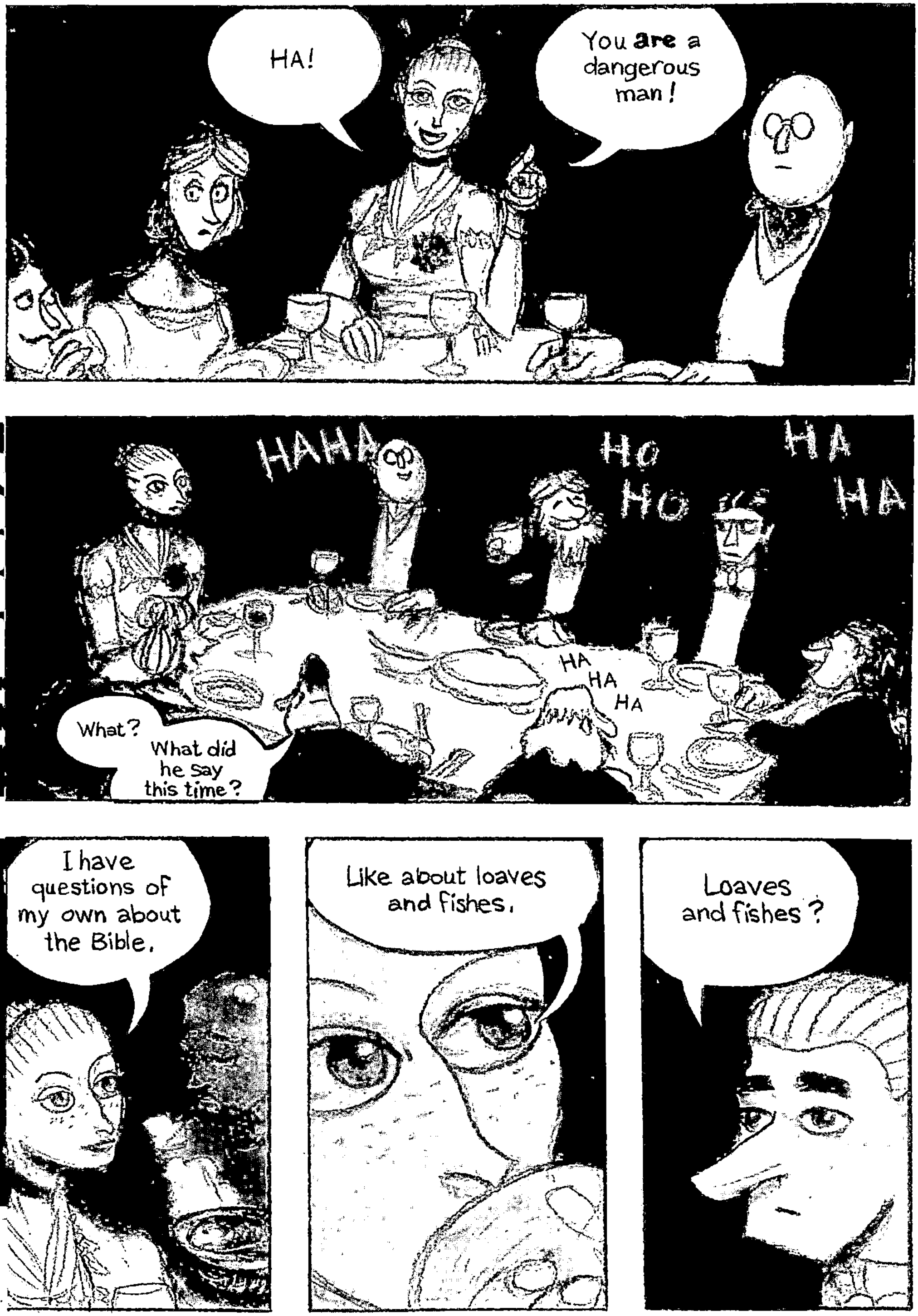
HA!
You are a dangerous man!
HAHA
HO HO
HA HA
HA HA HA
What? What did he say this time?
I have questions of my own about the Bible.
Like about loaves and fishes.
Loaves and fishes?

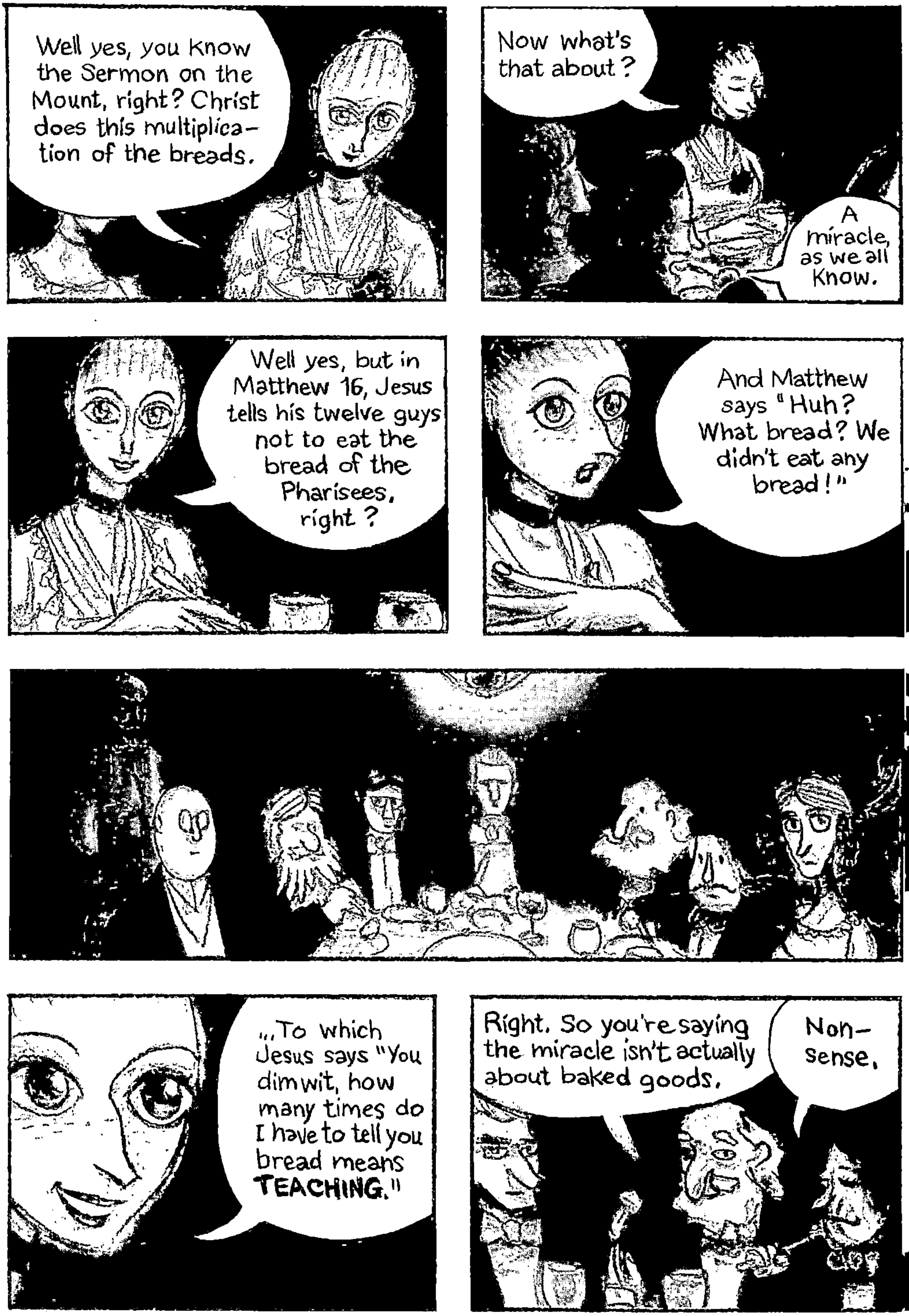
Well yes, you know the Sermon on the Mount, right? Christ does this multiplication of the breads.
Now what's that about?
A miracle, as we all know.
Well yes, but in Matthew 16, Jesus tells his twelve guys not to eat the bread of the Pharisees, right?
And Matthew says "Huh? What bread? We didn't eat any bread!"
...To which Jesus says "You dimwit, how many times do I have to tell you bread means TEACHING."
Right. So you're saying the miracle isn't actually about baked goods.
Nonsense.

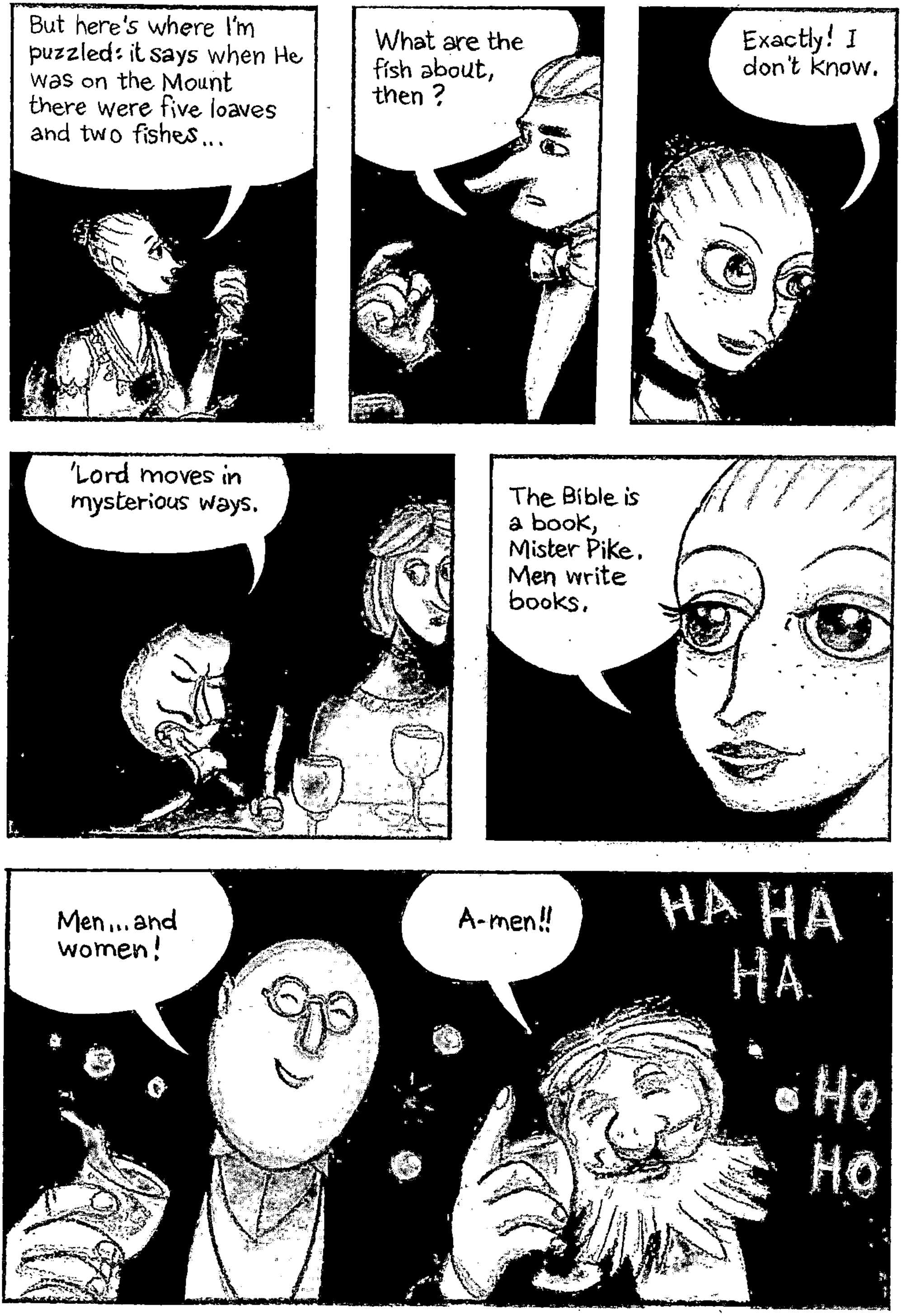
But here's where I'm puzzled: it says when He was on the Mount there were five loaves and two fishes...
What are the fish about, then ?
Exactly! I don't know.
'Lord moves in mysterious ways.
The Bible is a book, Mister Pike. Men write books.
Men... and women!
A-men!!
HA HA HA
HA
HO HO

Fallible men write books.

God writes in sunlight and rivers and planets.

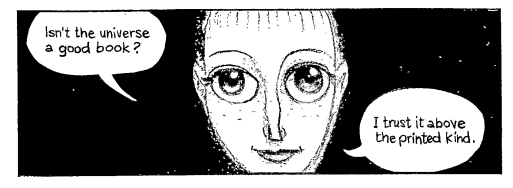

Isn't the universe a good book?

I trust it above the printed kind.

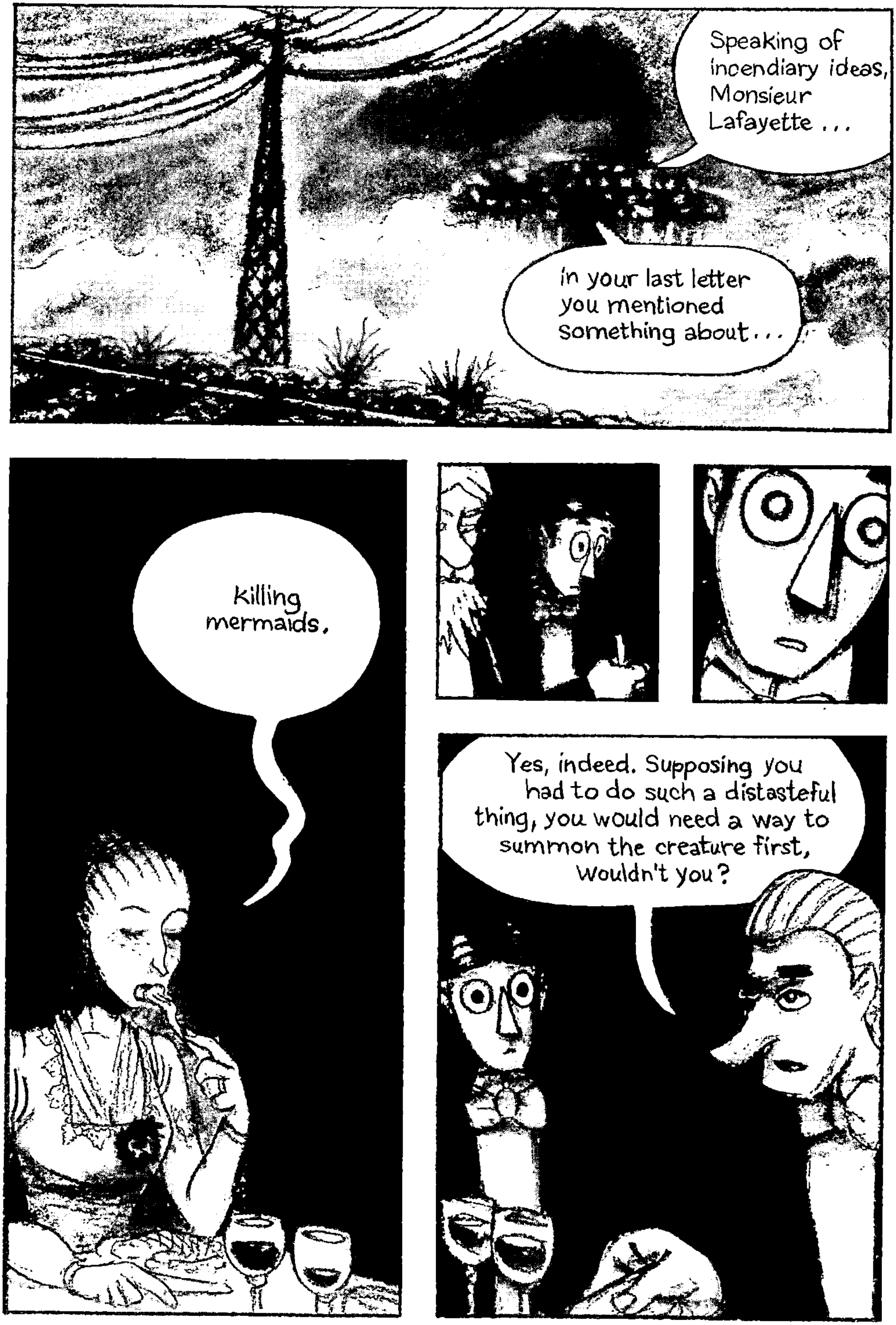
Speaking of incendiary ideas, Monsieur Lafayette . . .
in your last letter you mentioned something about . . .
Killing mermaids.
Yes, indeed. Supposing you had to do such a distasteful thing, you would need a way to summon the creature first, wouldn't you?

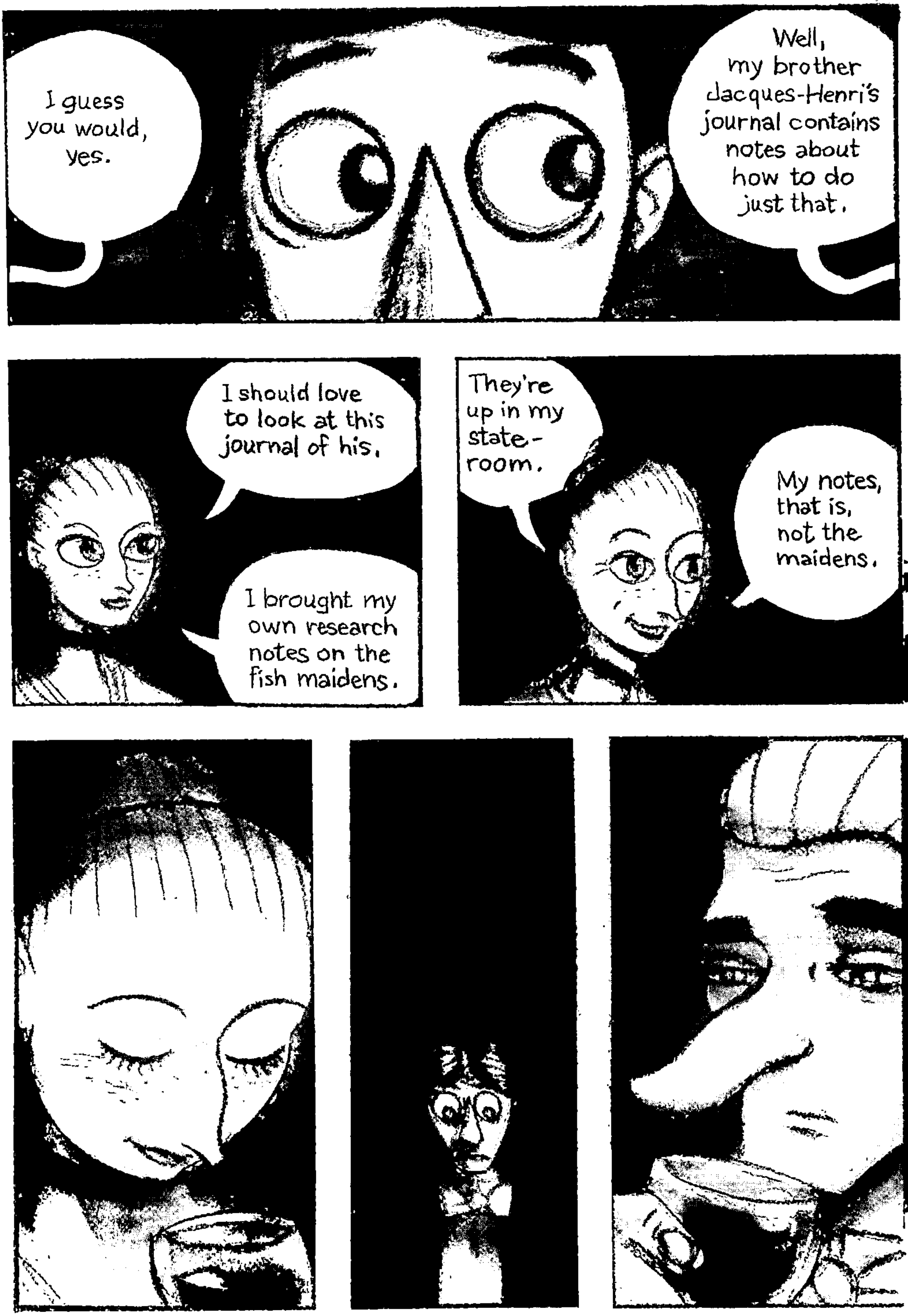
I guess you would, yes.
Well, my brother Jacques-Henri's journal contains notes about how to do just that.
I should love to look at this journal of his.
I brought my own research notes on the fish maidens.
They're up in my state-room.
My notes, that is, not the maidens.

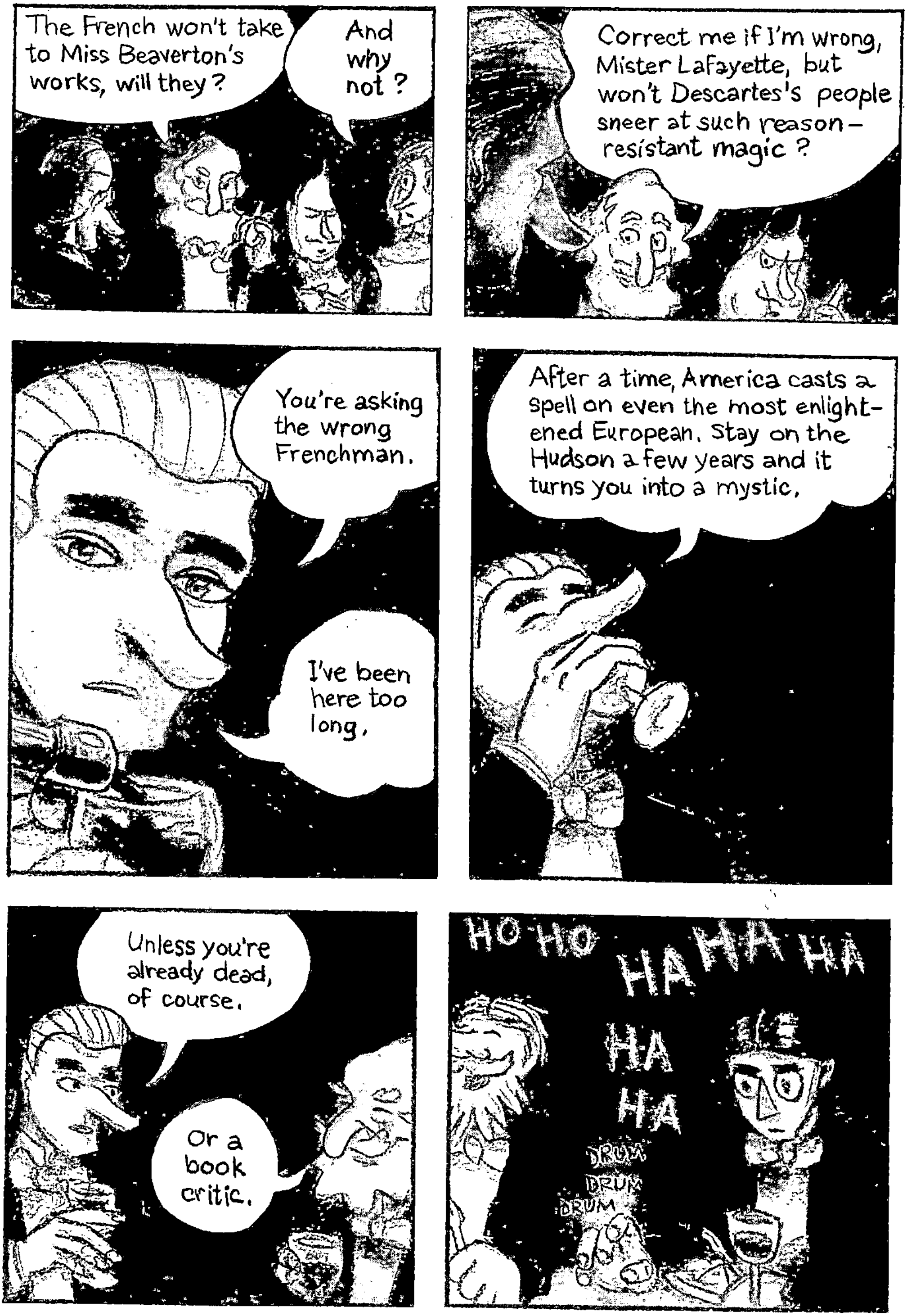
The French won't take to Miss Beaverton's works, will they?
And why not?
Correct me if I'm wrong, Mister Lafayette, but won't Descartes's people sneer at such reason-resistant magic?
You're asking the wrong Frenchman.
I've been here too long.
After a time, America casts a spell on even the most enlightened European. Stay on the Hudson a few years and it turns you into a mystic.
Unless you're already dead, of course.
Or a book critic.
HO HO
HA HA HA HA
HA
HA
DRUM
DRUM
DRUM

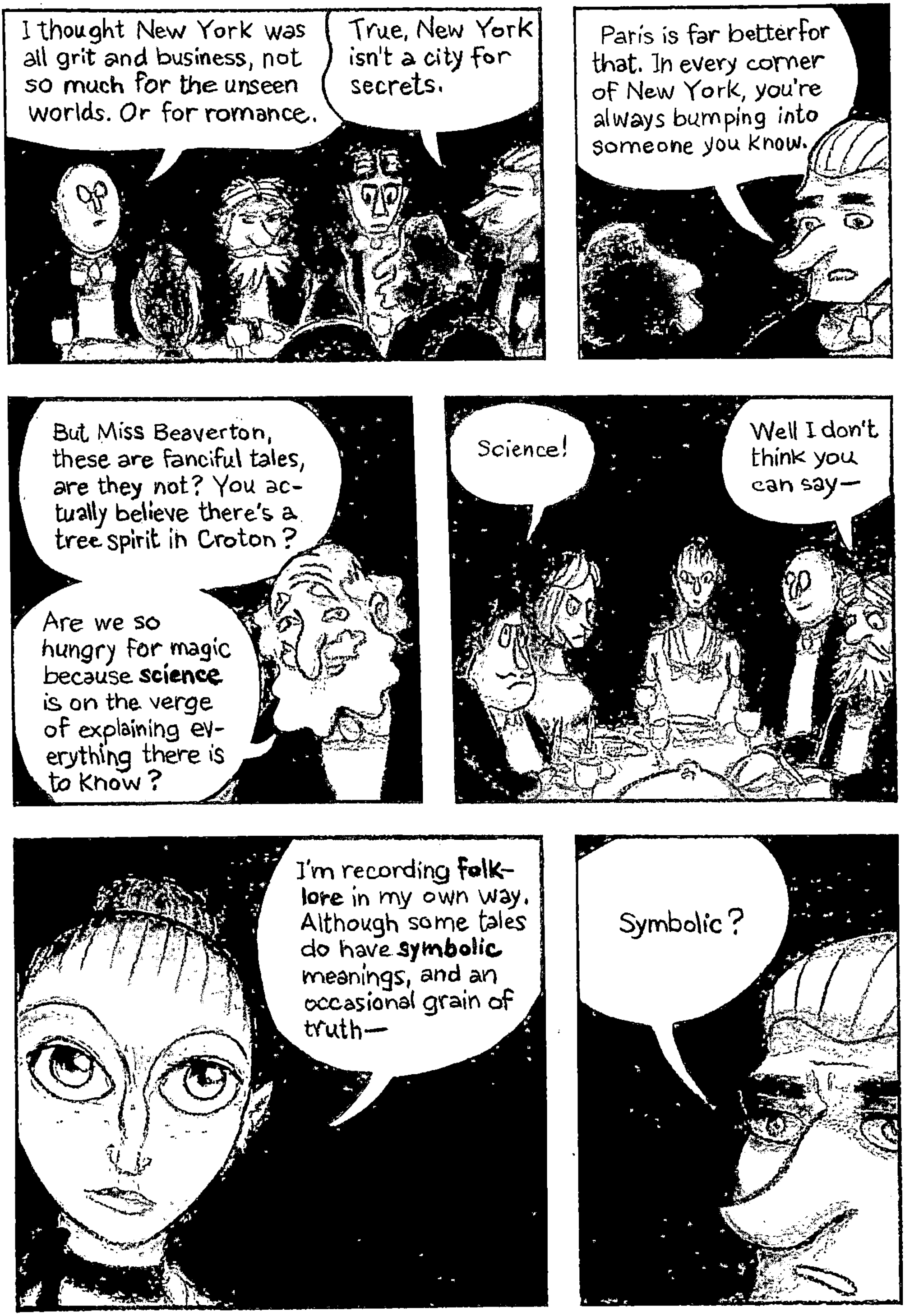
I thought New York was all grit and business, not so much for the unseen worlds. Or for romance.
True, New York isn't a city for secrets.
Paris is far better for that. In every corner of New York, you're always bumping into someone you know.
But Miss Beaverton, these are fanciful tales, are they not? You actually believe there's a tree spirit in Croton?
Are we so hungry for magic because science is on the verge of explaining everything there is to know?
Science!
Well I don't think you can say—
I'm recording folklore in my own way. Although some tales do have symbolic meanings, and an occasional grain of truth—
Symbolic?

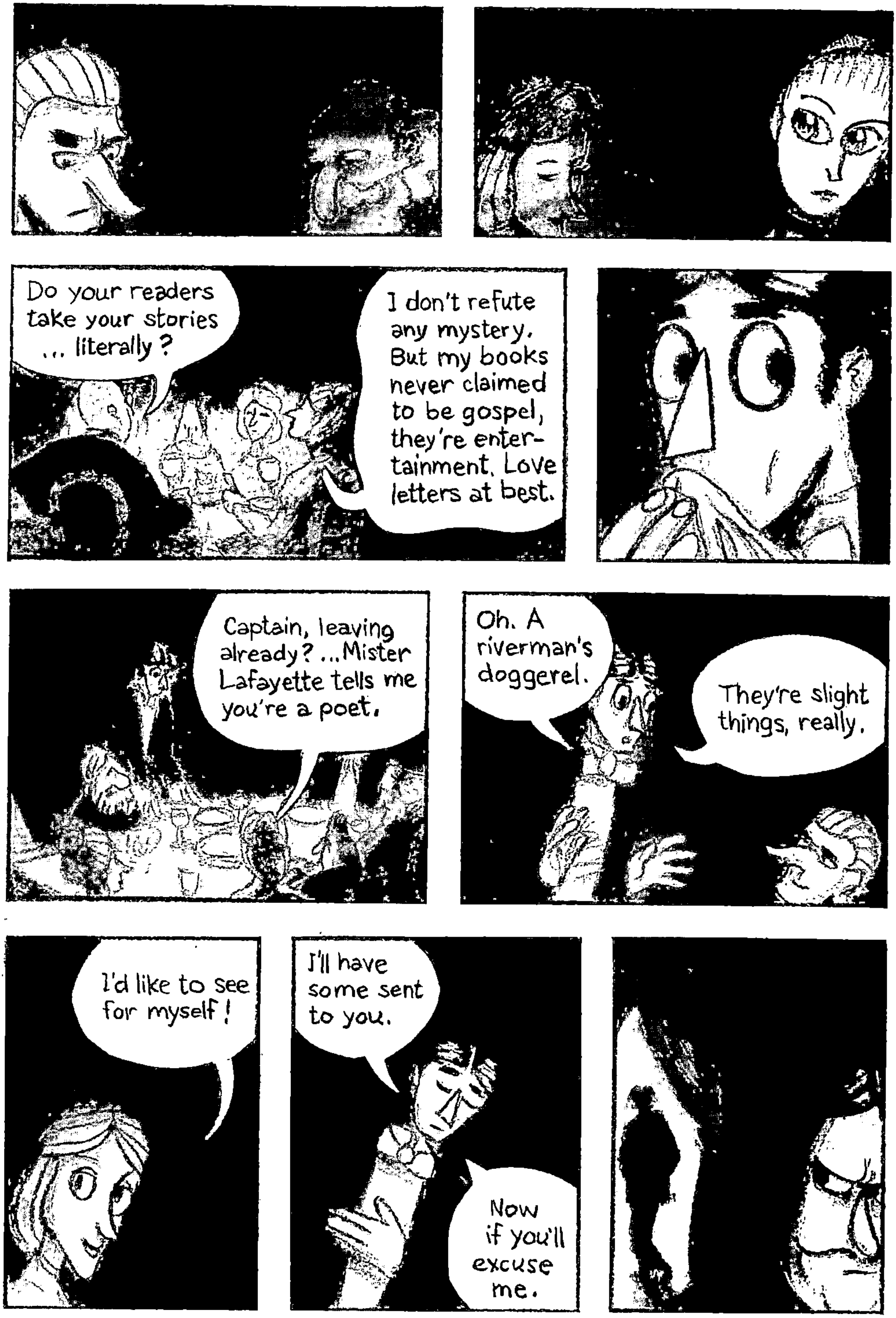

Do your readers take your stories ... literally?
I don't refute any mystery. But my books never claimed to be gospel, they're entertainment. Love letters at best.
Captain, leaving already? ...Mister Lafayette tells me you're a poet.
Oh. A riverman's doggerel.
They're slight things, really.
I'd like to see for myself!
I'll have some sent to you.
Now if you'll excuse me.

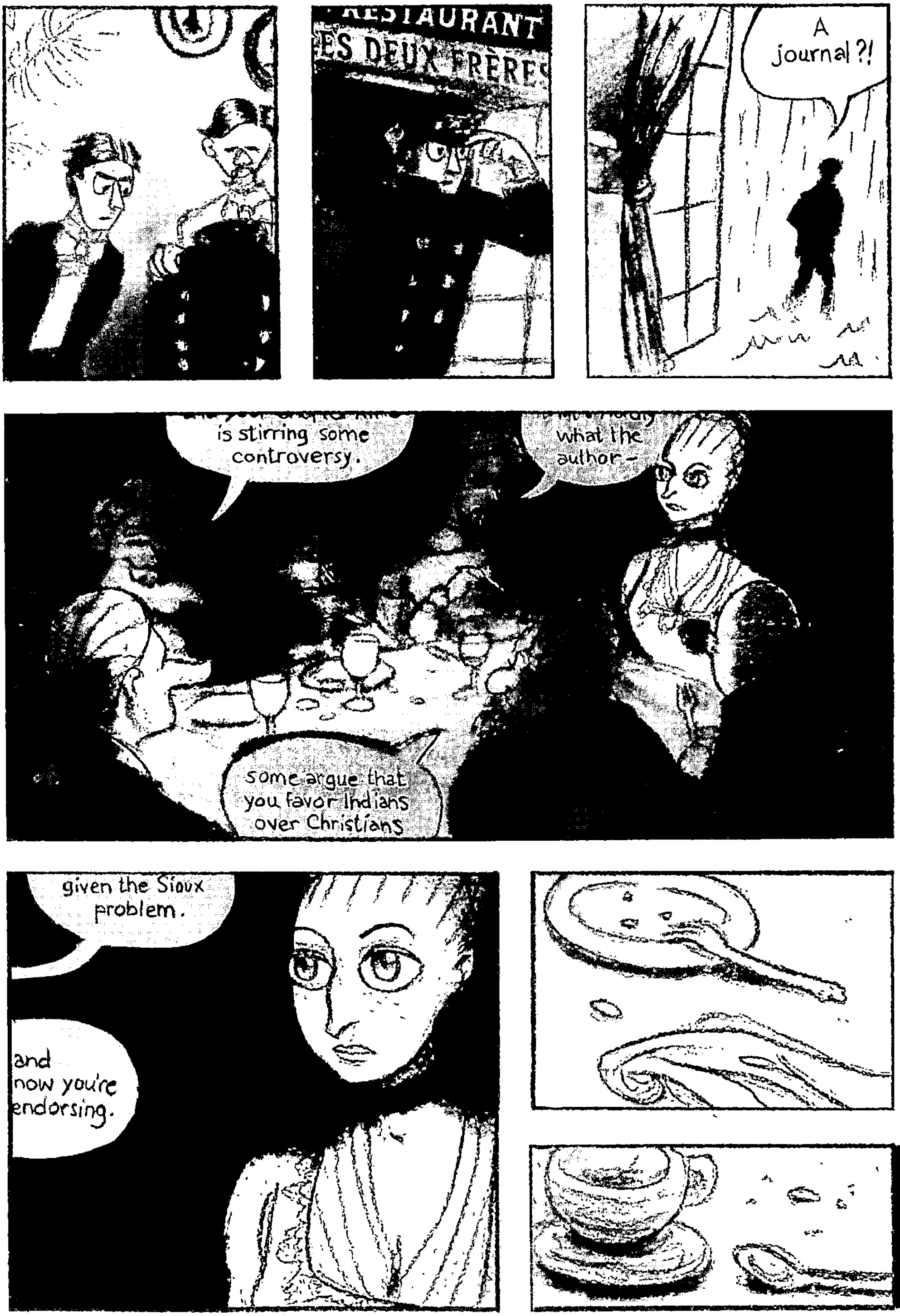
RESTAURANT
ES DEUX FRÈRE
A journal?!
is stirring some controversy.
what the author–
some argue that you favor Indians over Christians
given the Sioux problem.
and now you're endorsing.

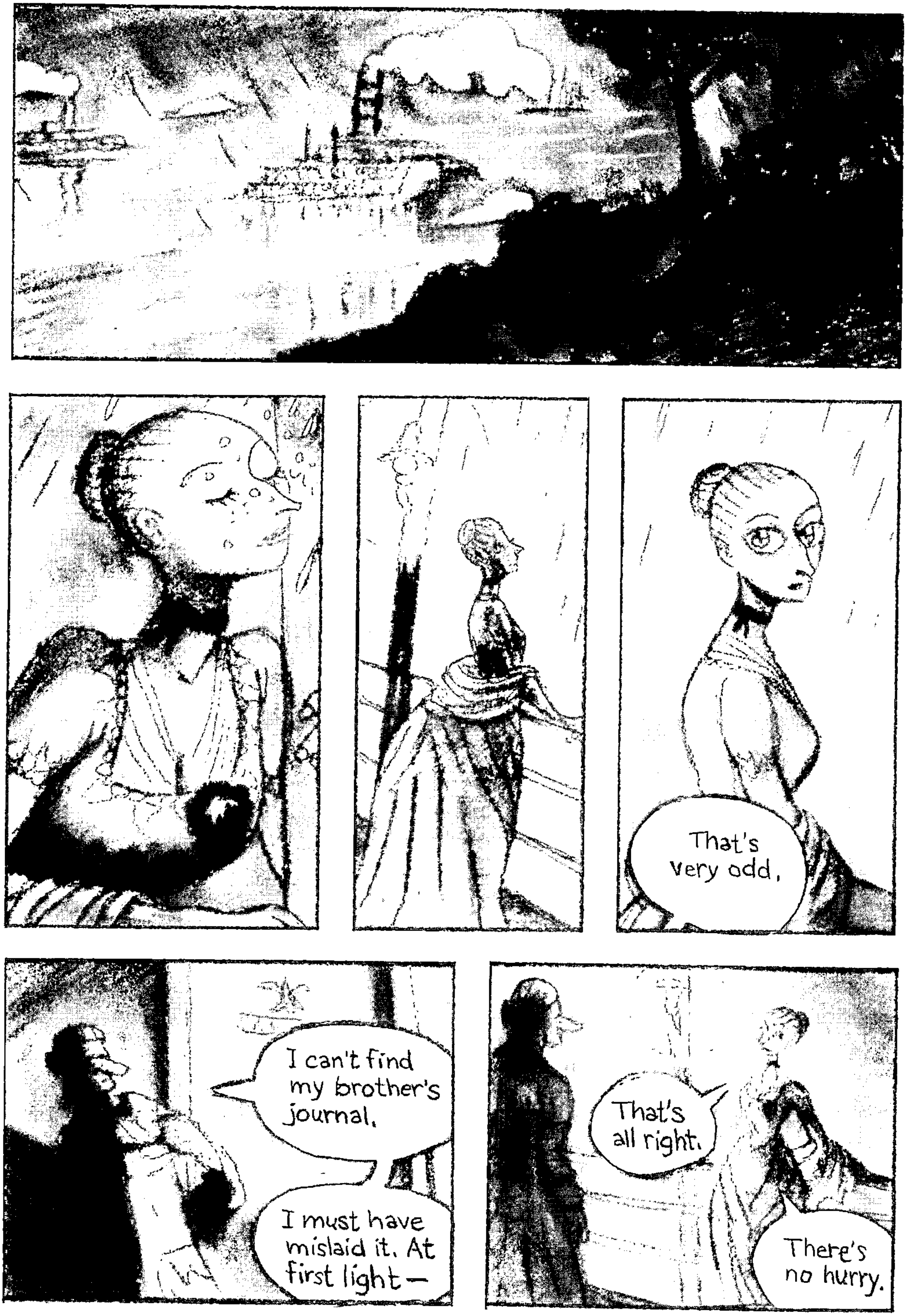
That's very odd.
I can't find my brother's journal.
I must have mislaid it. At first light—
That's all right.
There's no hurry.

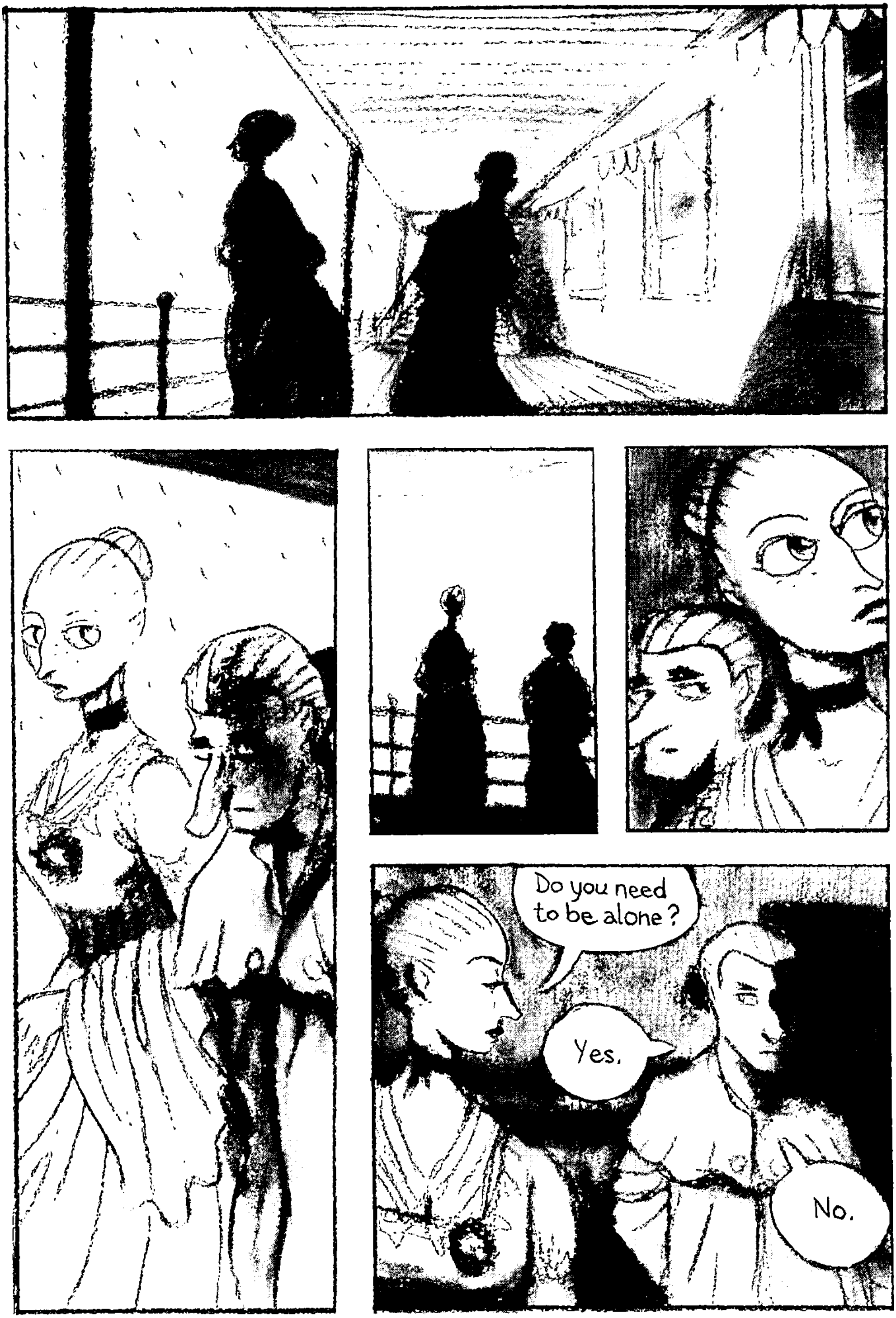
Do you need to be alone?
Yes.
No.

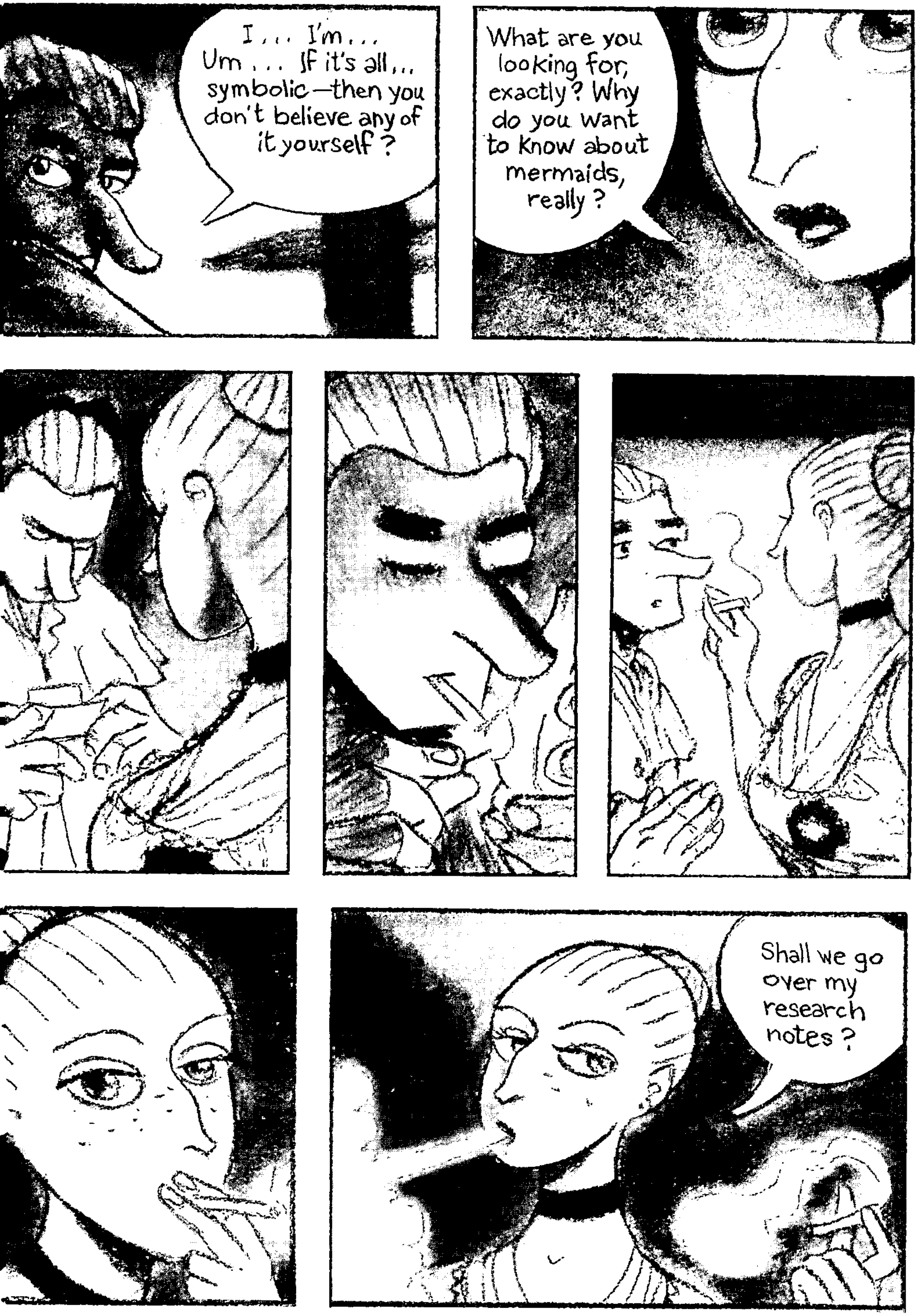

I... I'm... Um... If it's all... symbolic—then you don't believe any of it yourself?
What are you looking for, exactly? Why do you want to know about mermaids, really?
Shall we go over my research notes?

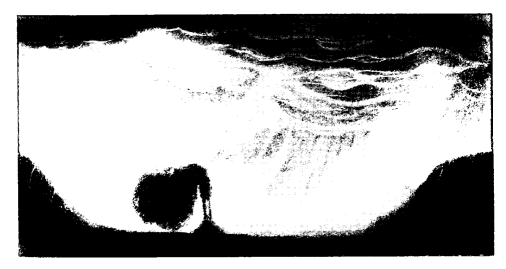

Pt II. Chap.5

"SEVENING"

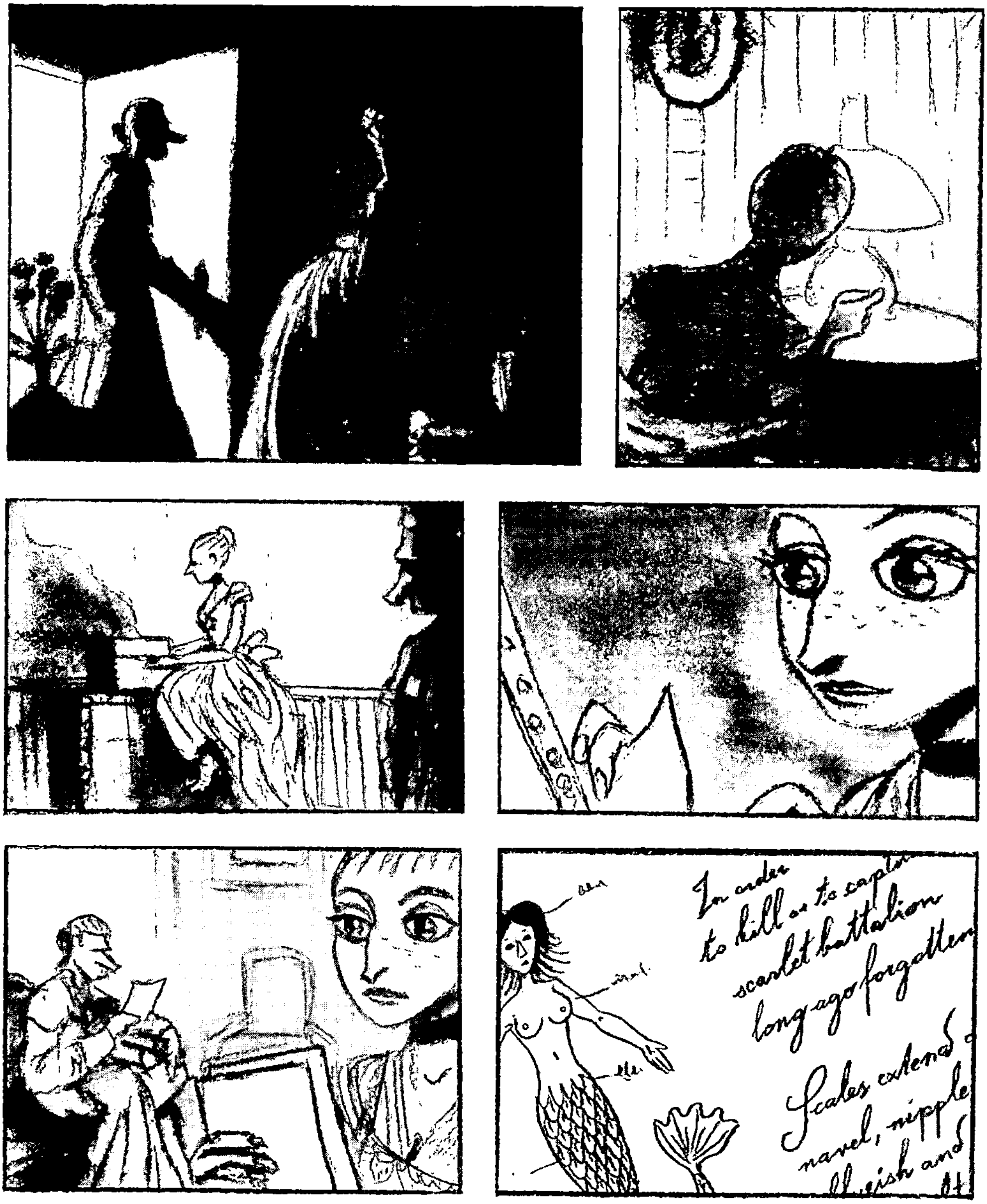
In order
to kill or to
scarlet battalion
long ago forgotten
Scales extend
navel, nipple

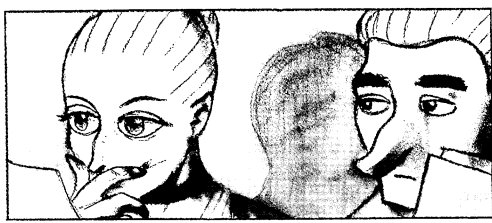

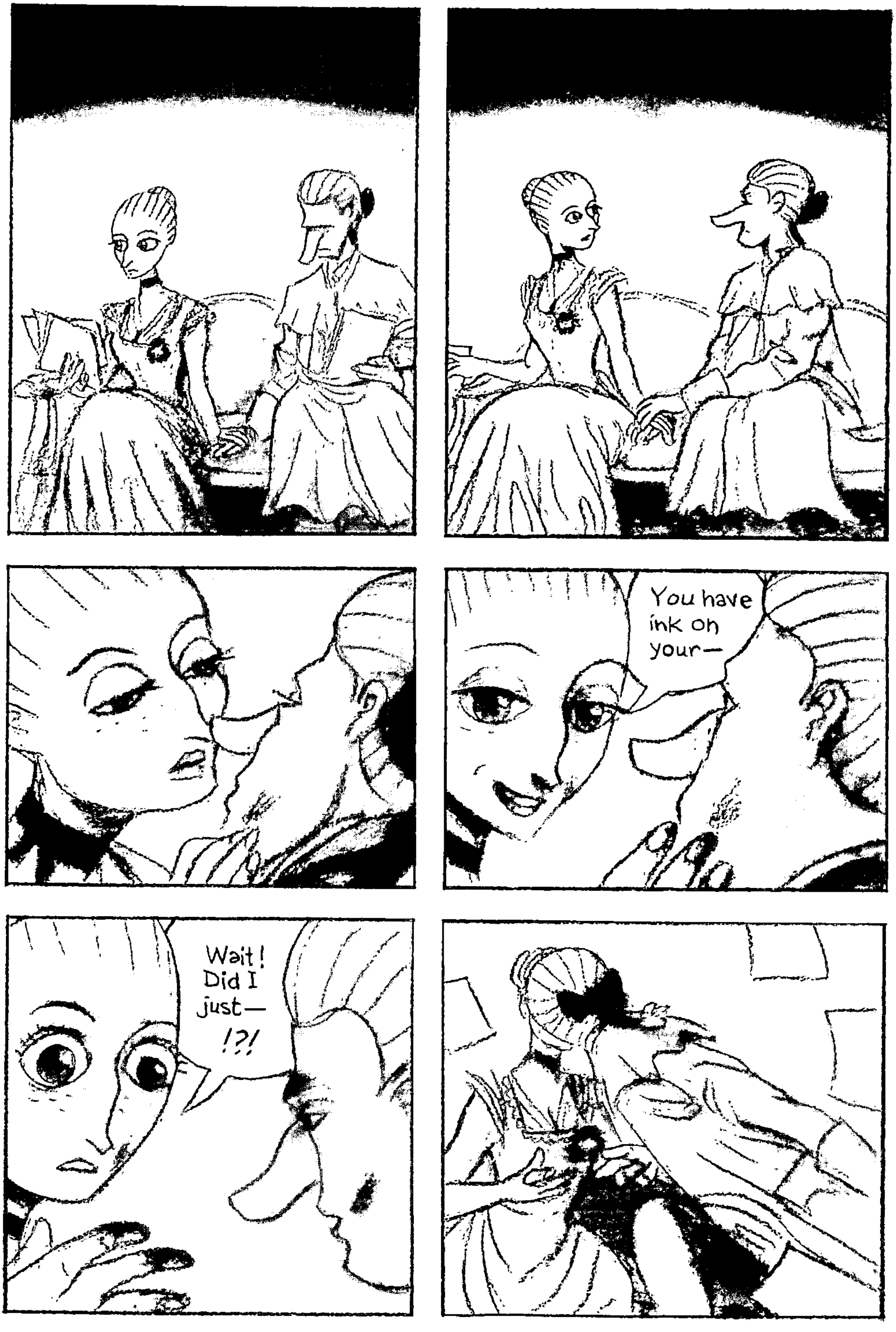
You have ink on your—
Wait! Did I just—
!?!

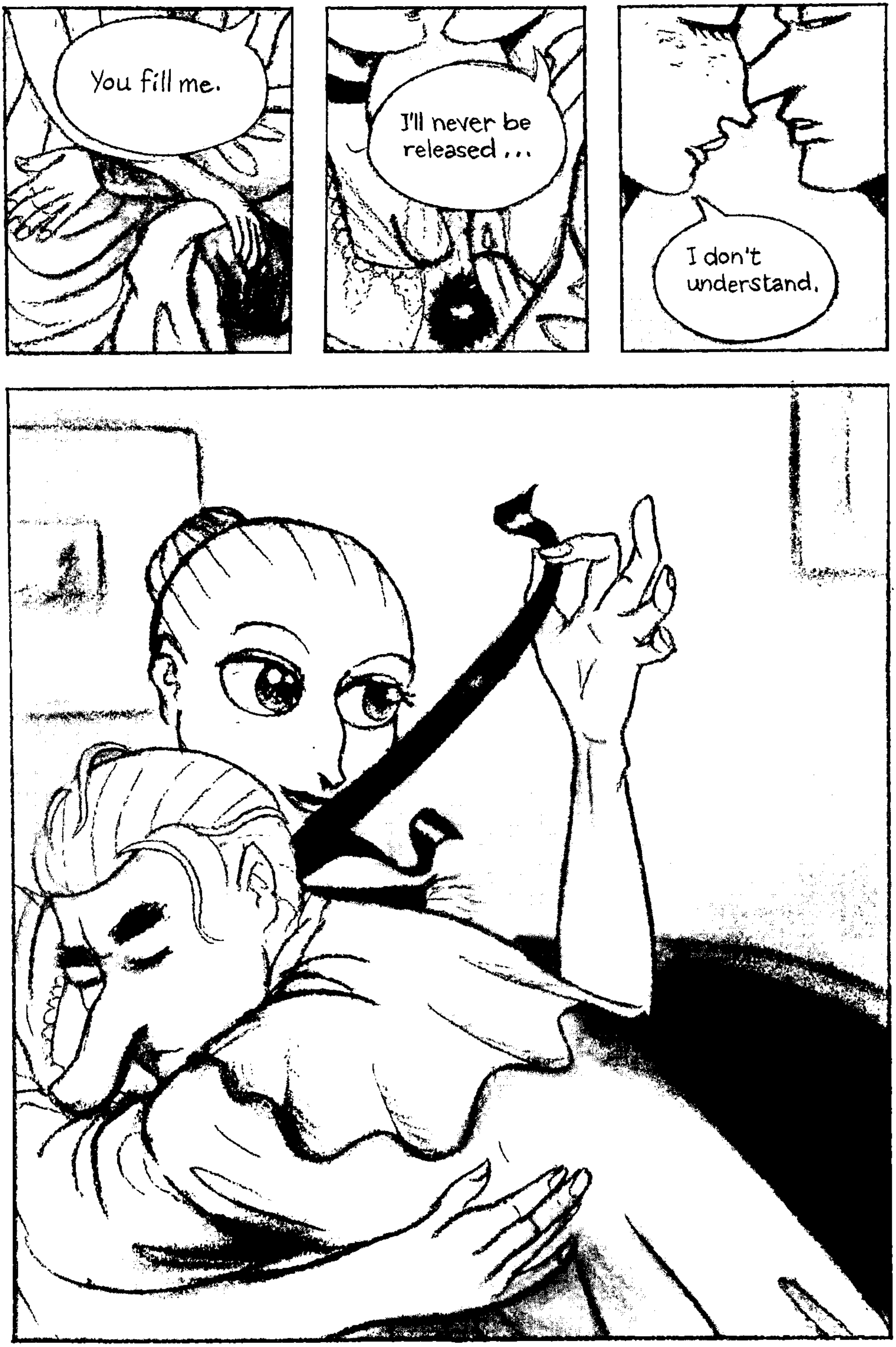
You fill me.
I'll never be released ...
I don't understand.

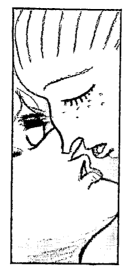

I'm going to return to my cabin.

Yes.

Pt II, Chap.6

"ENTICEMENT"

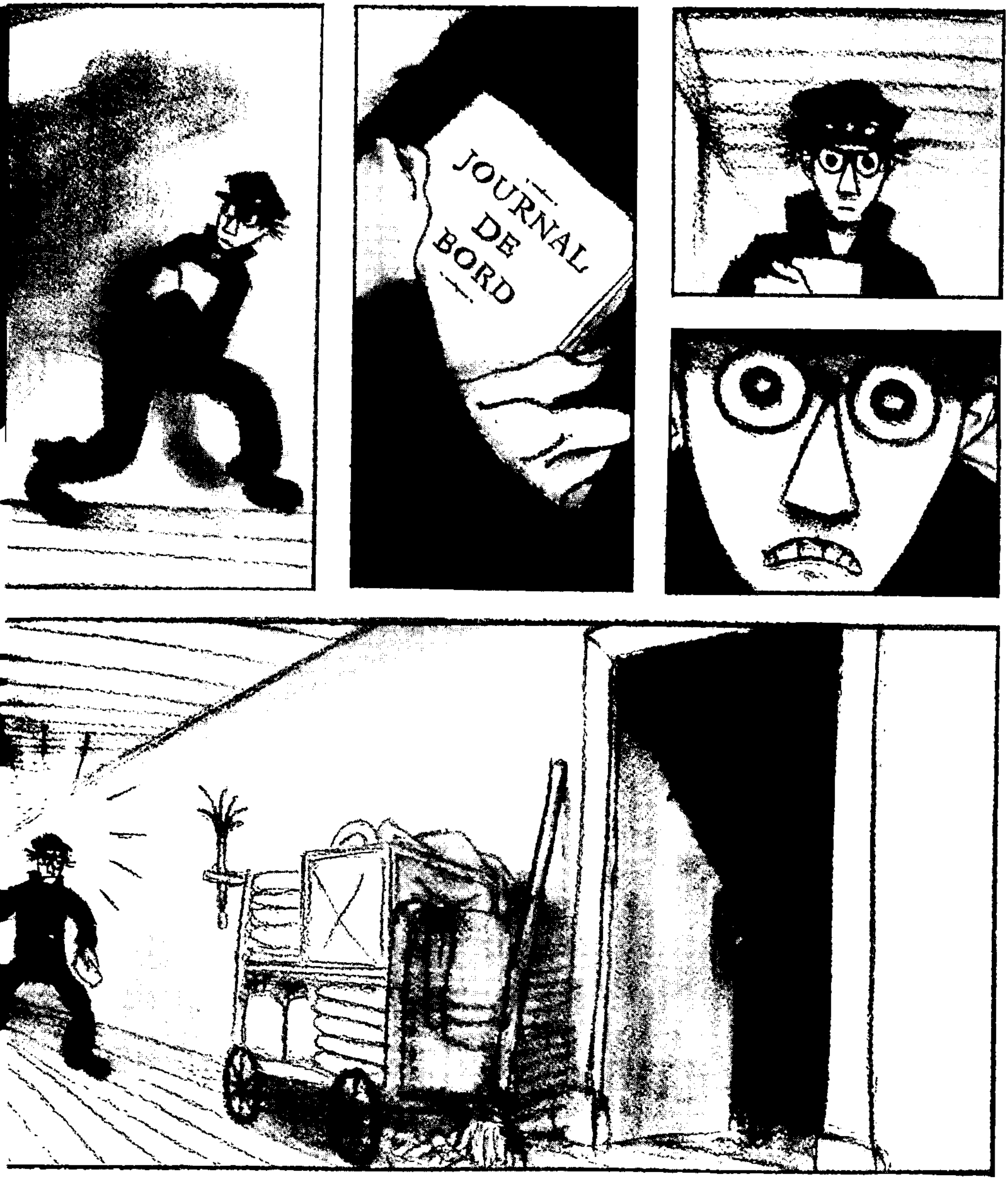
JOURNAL
DE
BORD

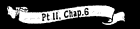

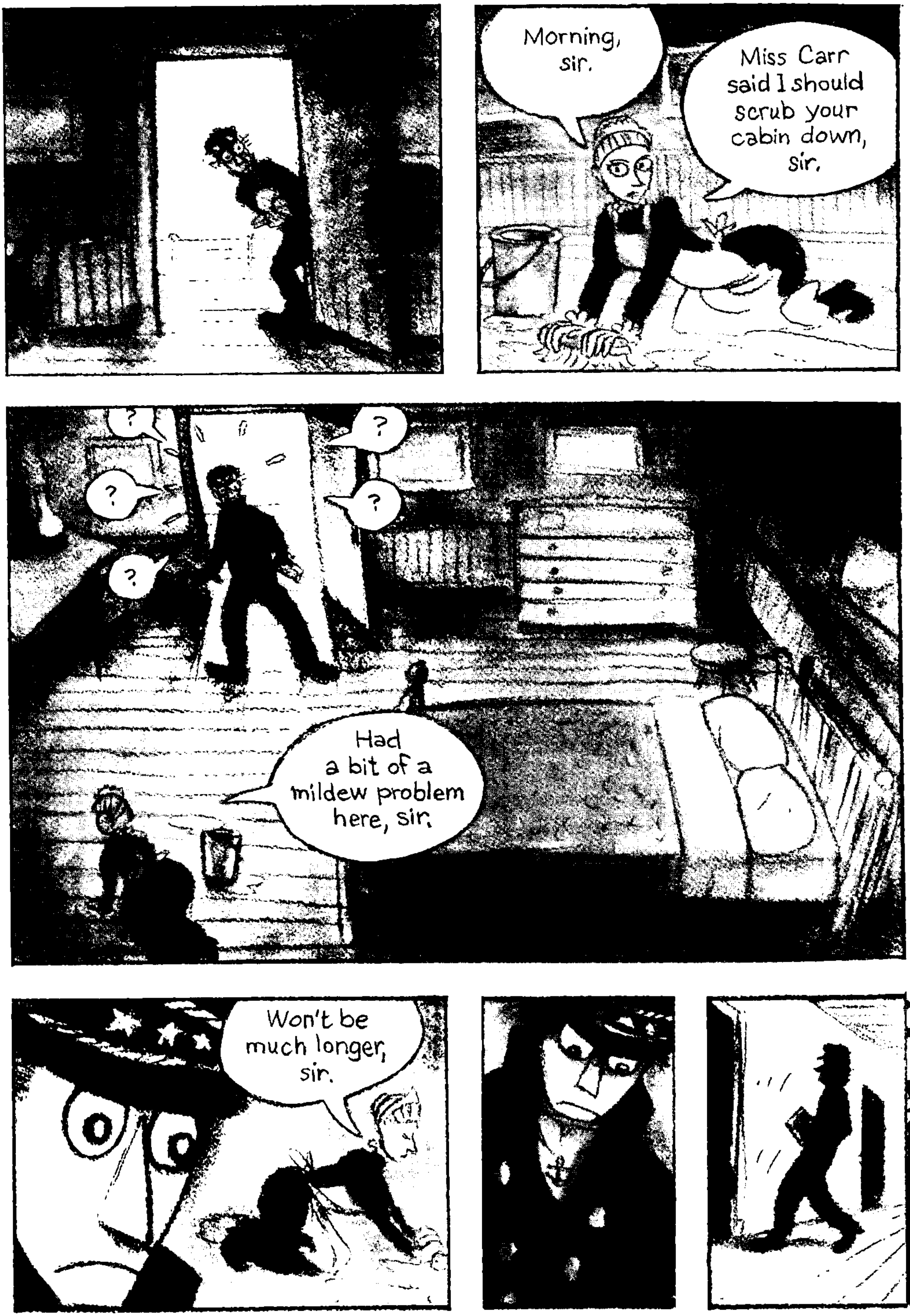
Morning, sir.
Miss Carr said I should scrub your cabin down, sir.
?
?
?
?
?
Had a bit of a mildew problem here, sir.
Won't be much longer, sir.

Did Jacques-Henri's journal hold the answer?

she dwells

There have been others

"The Summoner" aquatic companions with in tendrils

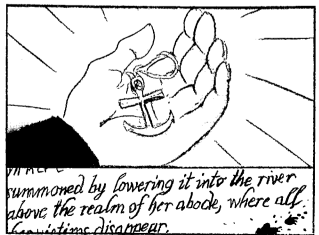

summoned by lowering it into the river above the realm of her abode, where all victims disappear.

265

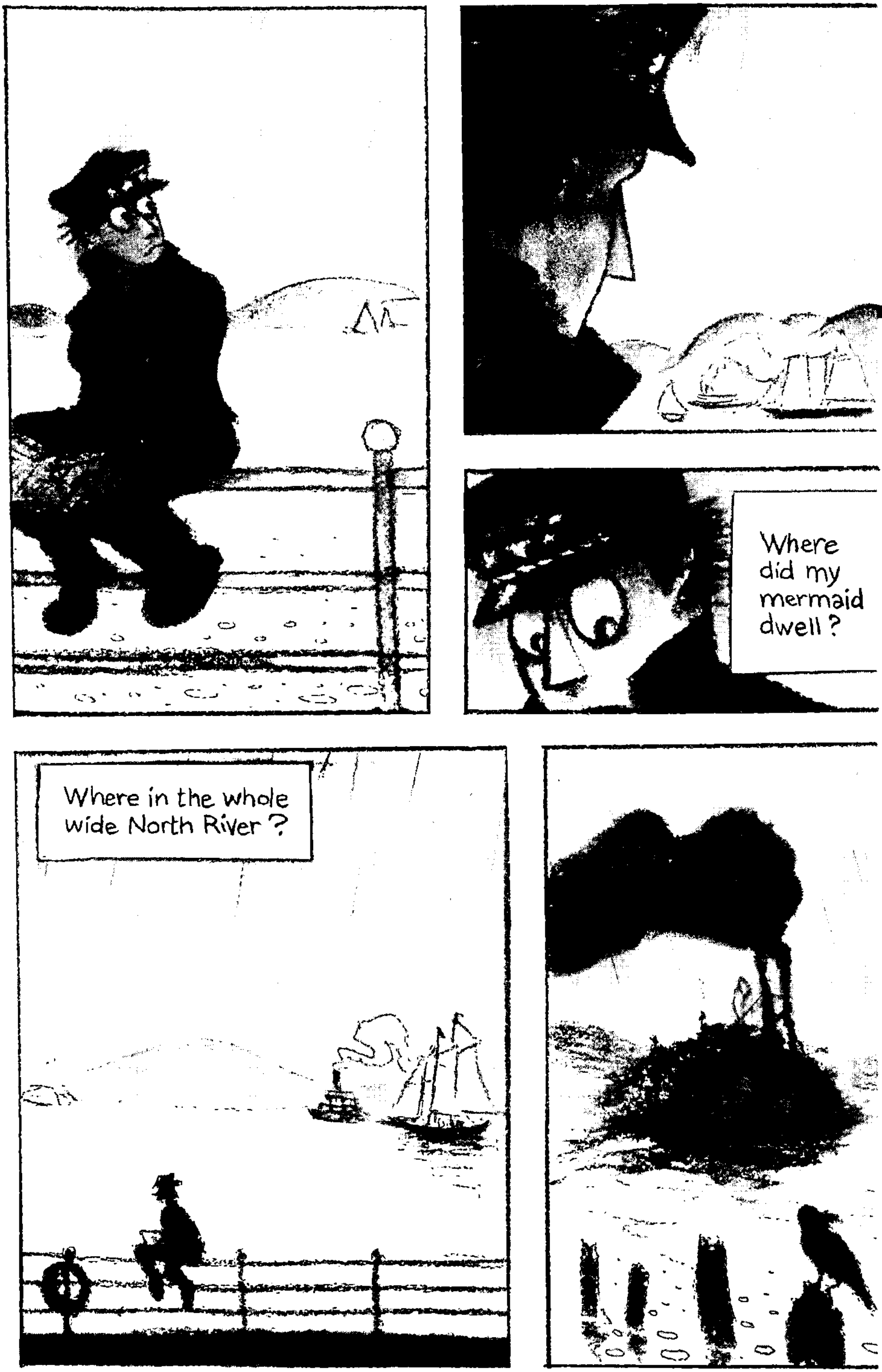
Where did my mermaid dwell?
Where in the whole wide North River?

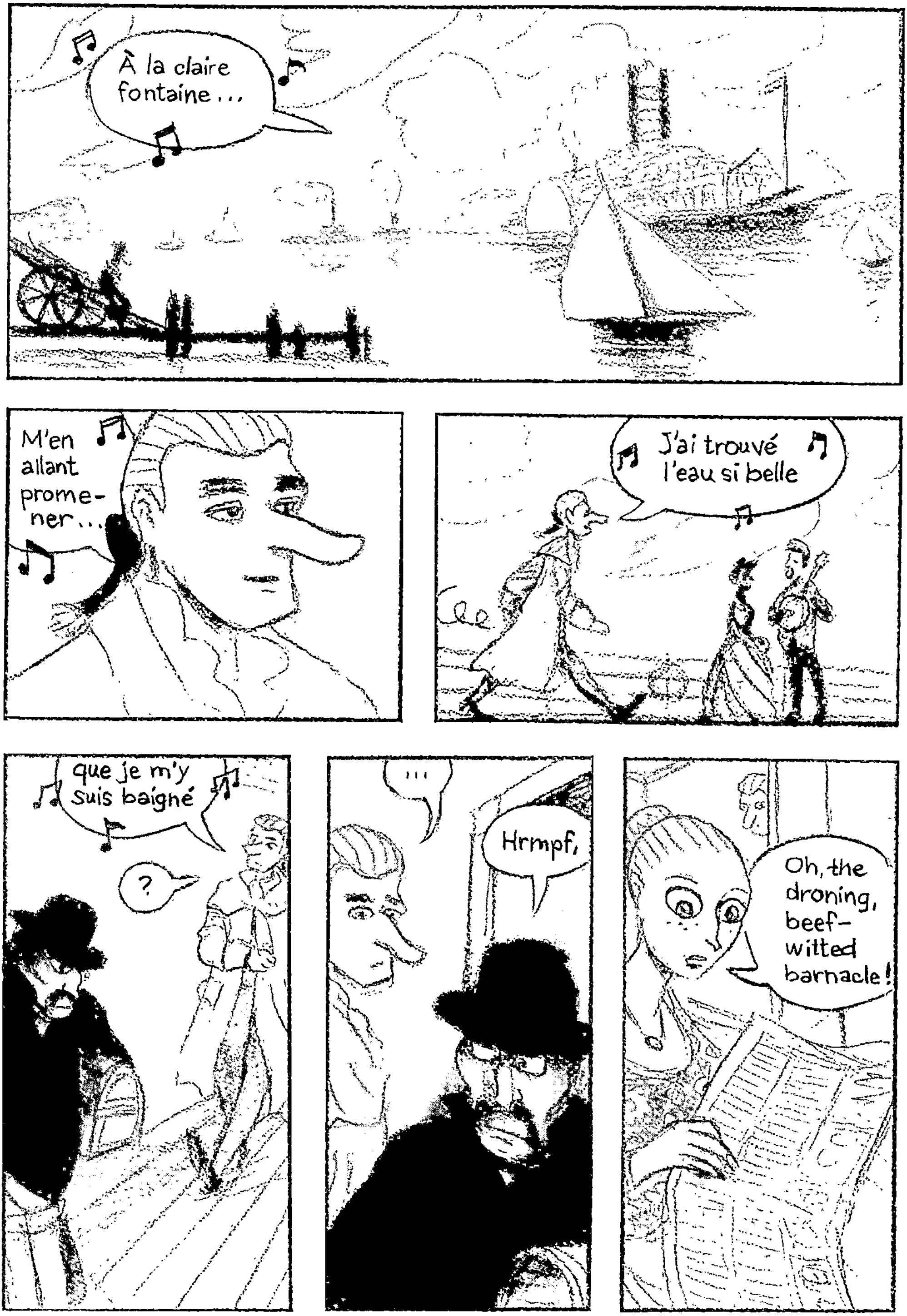
À la claire fontaine...
M'en allant promener...
J'ai trouvé l'eau si belle
que je m'y suis baigné
?
...
Hrmpf,
Oh, the droning, beef-witted barnacle!

Adding deception to the roster of offenses linked to the works of C.G. Beaverton, it was revealed that the source of such feverish drivel as 'Enigmas of the Orient', 'Curios and Puzzles of India' and the recent 'Secrets & Mysteries of the River Hudson is in fact a woman. Her name is Camomille G. Beaverton. How telling that, amidst a table of contents promising fairies, ghosts, dragons and other stuff of superstition she titles a chapter "Christian Mythology". This slap in the face of American decency calls to be noticed, and we can only encourage [...]ns and booksellers [...] aisles free

from works of such devious persuasion. It is indeed a great alarm bell ringing in the decadence of our nation, when the sales of this latest is reportedly in the hundreds of thousands of copies. Ironically, Beaverton devotes several chapters to the creature of the mermaid, not as a figure of myth, but as a real being living in our midst. Here at last, we may concur with the wily woman Beaverton: for the siren's song is none other than the author's seductive appeal to lost souls, obliviously followin[...] the call to their own perditio[...]

[...]NE 1st, 1887

Don't tell me you're surprised. They were bound to take the gloves off.

"... that wily woman Beaverton"?!

It's no way to speak of a lady.

Oh? You think this delicate little lady is *too* dainty to take it on the chin?

Don't get me wrong, Camomille

My idea of a true lady is someone with a mean left hook.

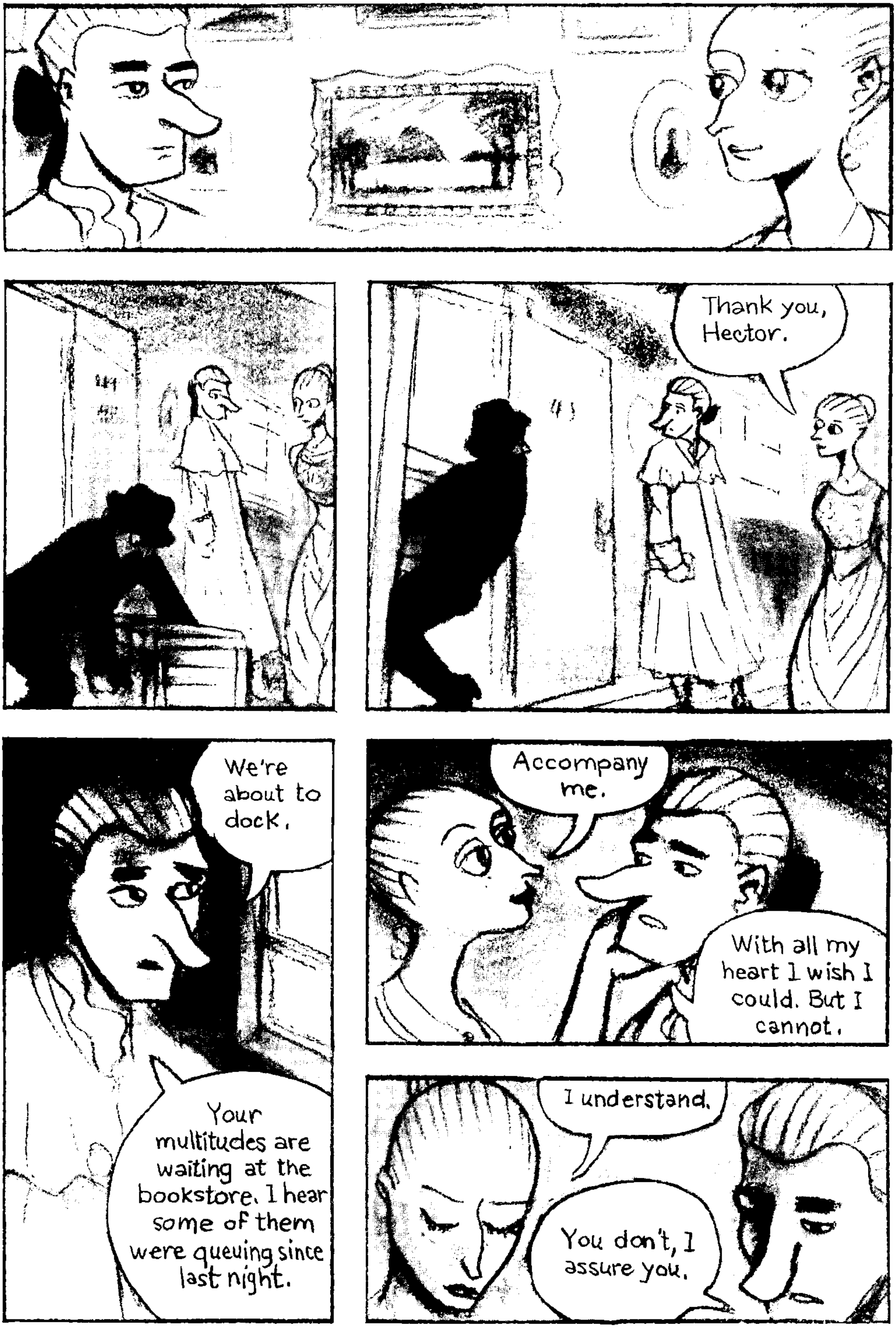
Thank you, Hector.
We're about to dock.
Your multitudes are waiting at the bookstore. I hear some of them were queuing since last night.
Accompany me.
With all my heart I wish I could. But I cannot.
I understand.
You don't, I assure you.

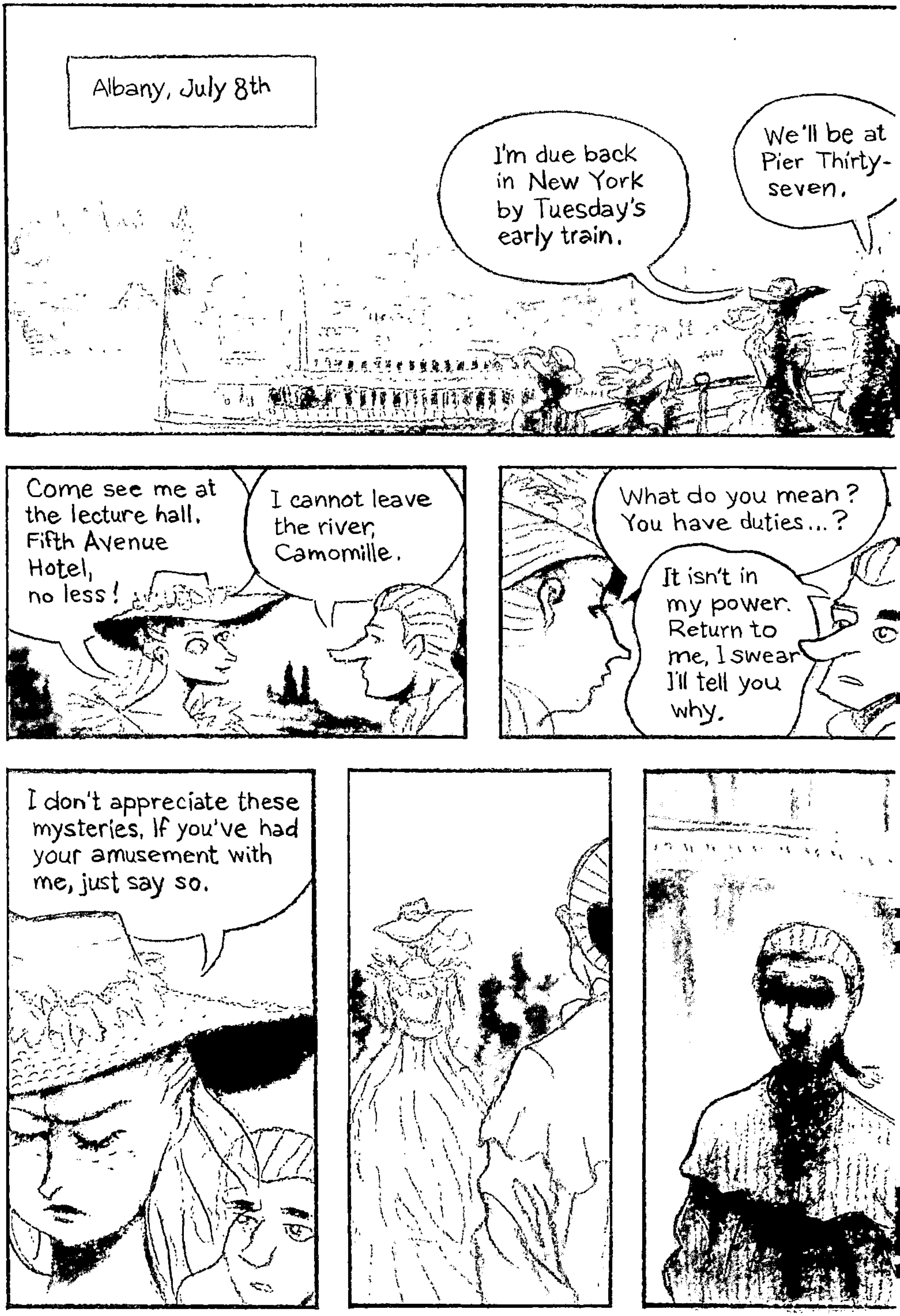

Albany, July 8th
I'm due back in New York by Tuesday's early train.
We'll be at Pier Thirty-seven.
Come see me at the lecture hall. Fifth Avenue Hotel, no less!
I cannot leave the river, Camomille.
What do you mean? You have duties...?
It isn't in my power. Return to me, I swear I'll tell you why.
I don't appreciate these mysteries. If you've had your amusement with me, just say so.

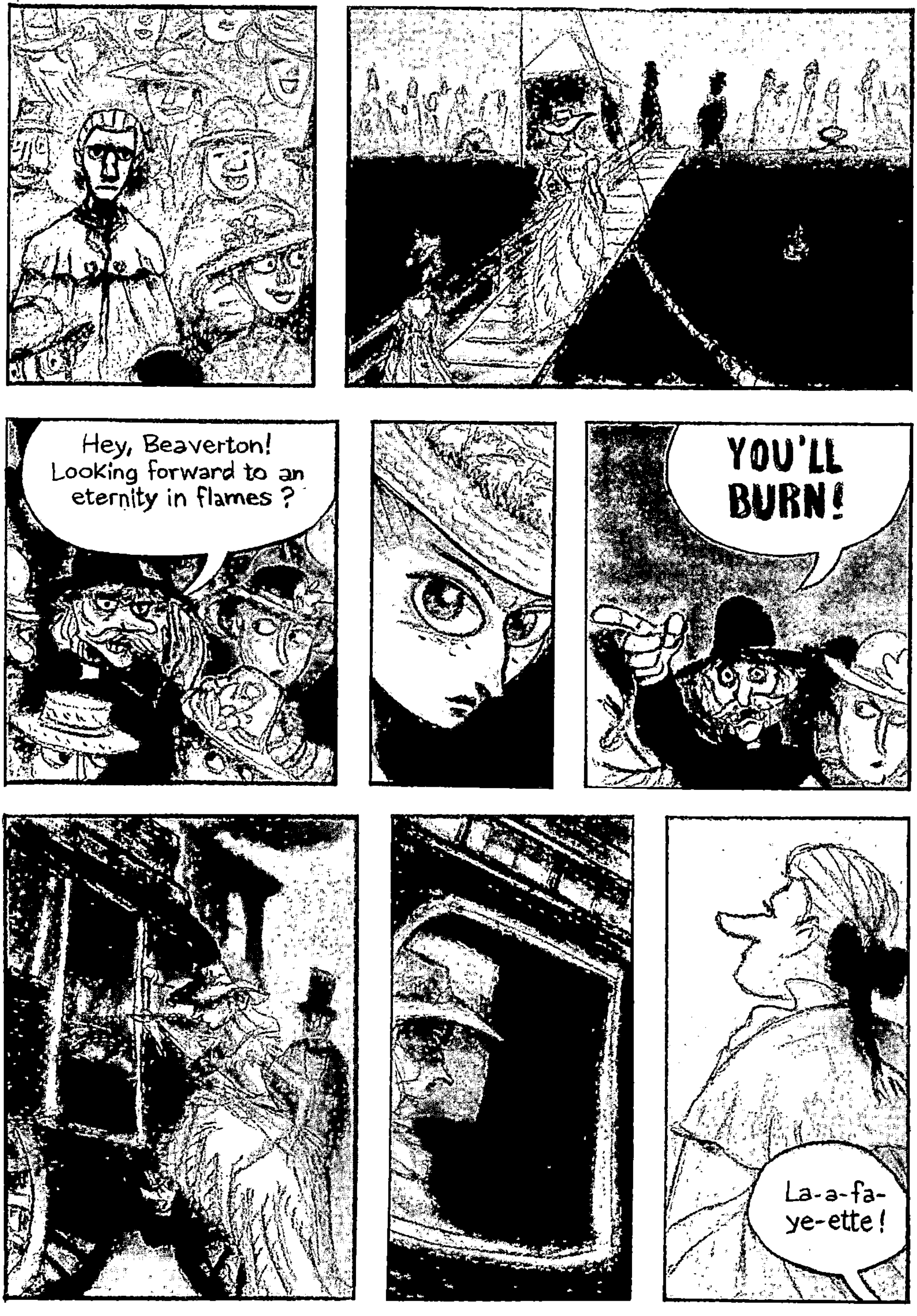
Hey, Beaverton! Looking forward to an eternity in flames?
YOU'LL BURN!
La-a-fa-ye-ette!

Hillo, my A-hab, von't you come harrrpoon me?

What did you say? Why did you say that?

Vat—

You know... Da Moby Vhale—

С меня хватит!

И о чём я только думала?

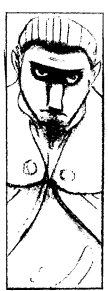

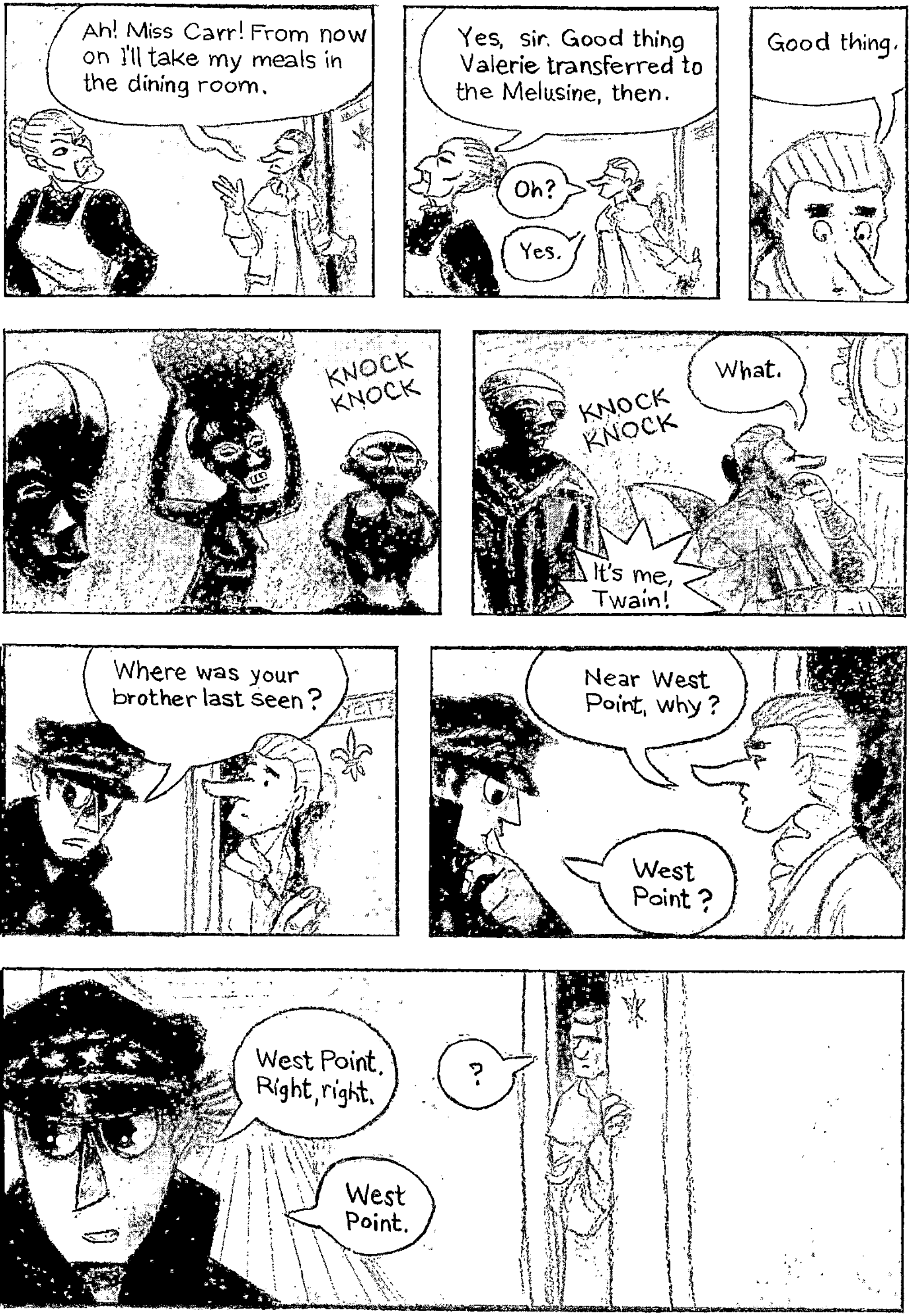
Ah! Miss Carr! From now on I'll take my meals in the dining room.
Yes, sir. Good thing Valerie transferred to the Melusine, then.
Oh?
Yes.
Good thing.
KNOCK KNOCK
KNOCK KNOCK
What.
It's me, Twain!
Where was your brother last seen?
Near West Point, why?
West Point?
West Point. Right, right.
?
West Point.

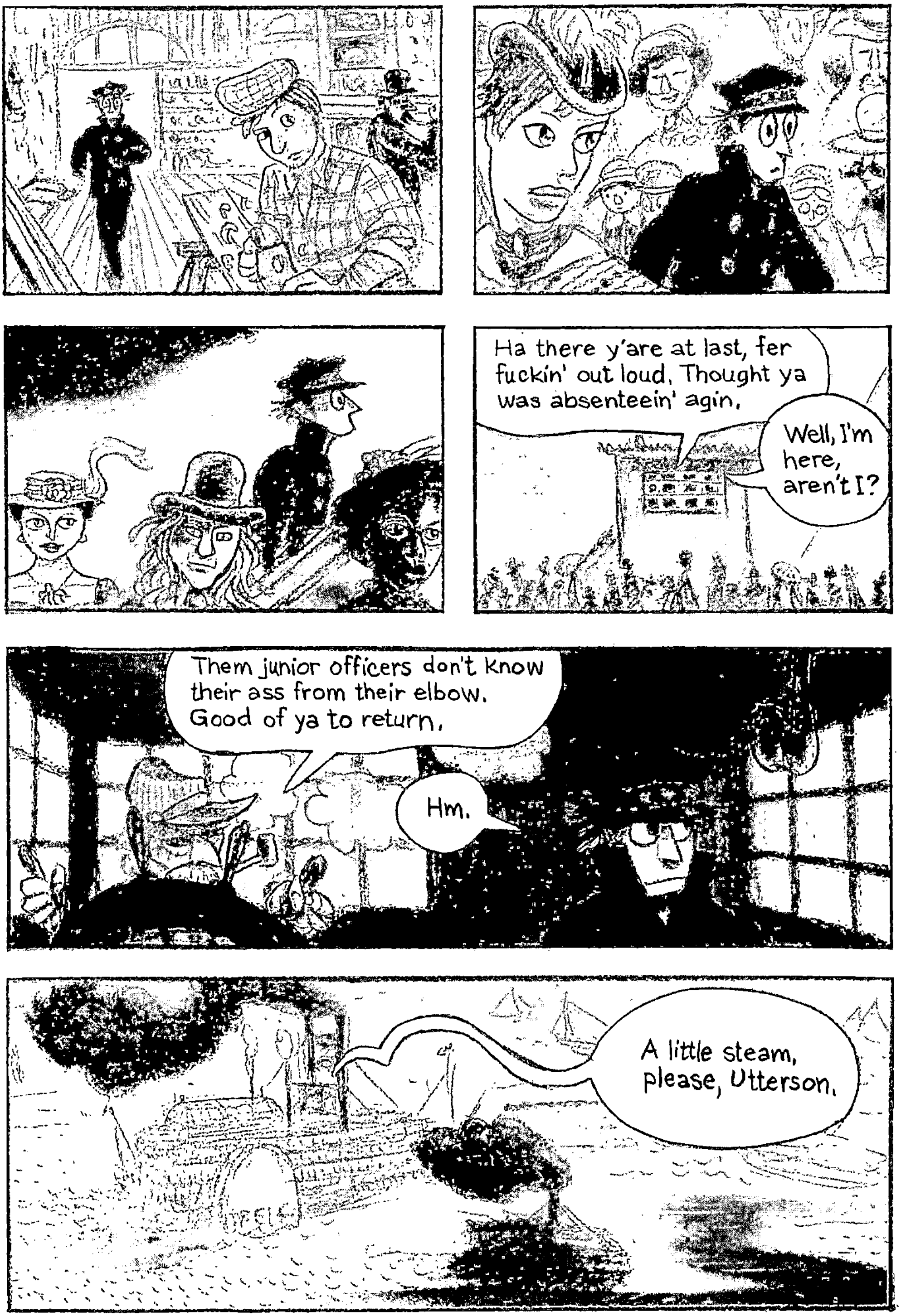
Ha there y'are at last, fer fuckin' out loud. Thought ya was absenteein' agin.
Well, I'm here, aren't I?
Them junior officers don't know their ass from their elbow. Good of ya to return.
Hm.
A little steam, please, Utterson.

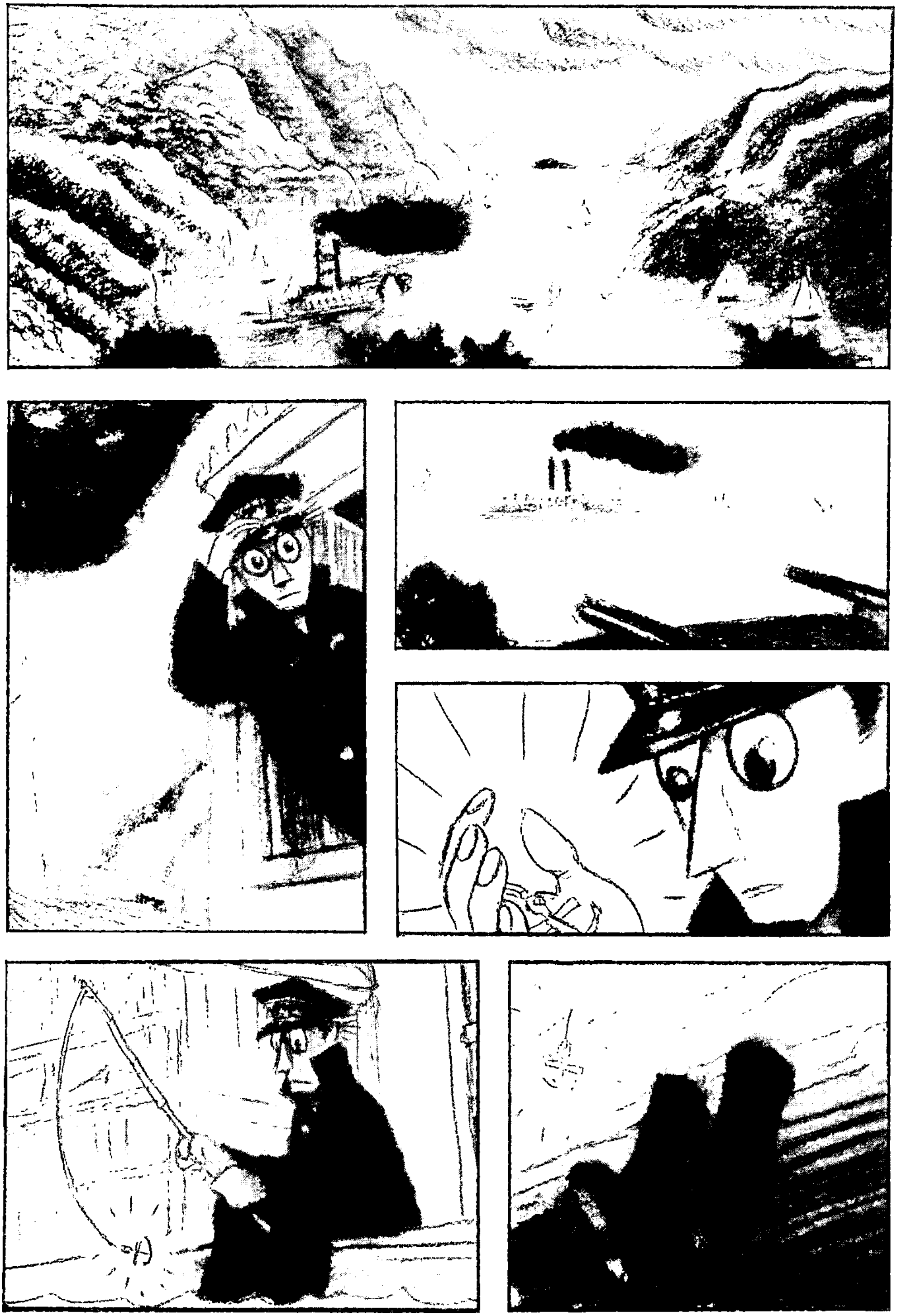

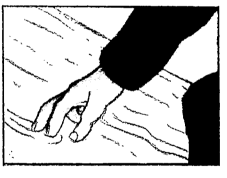

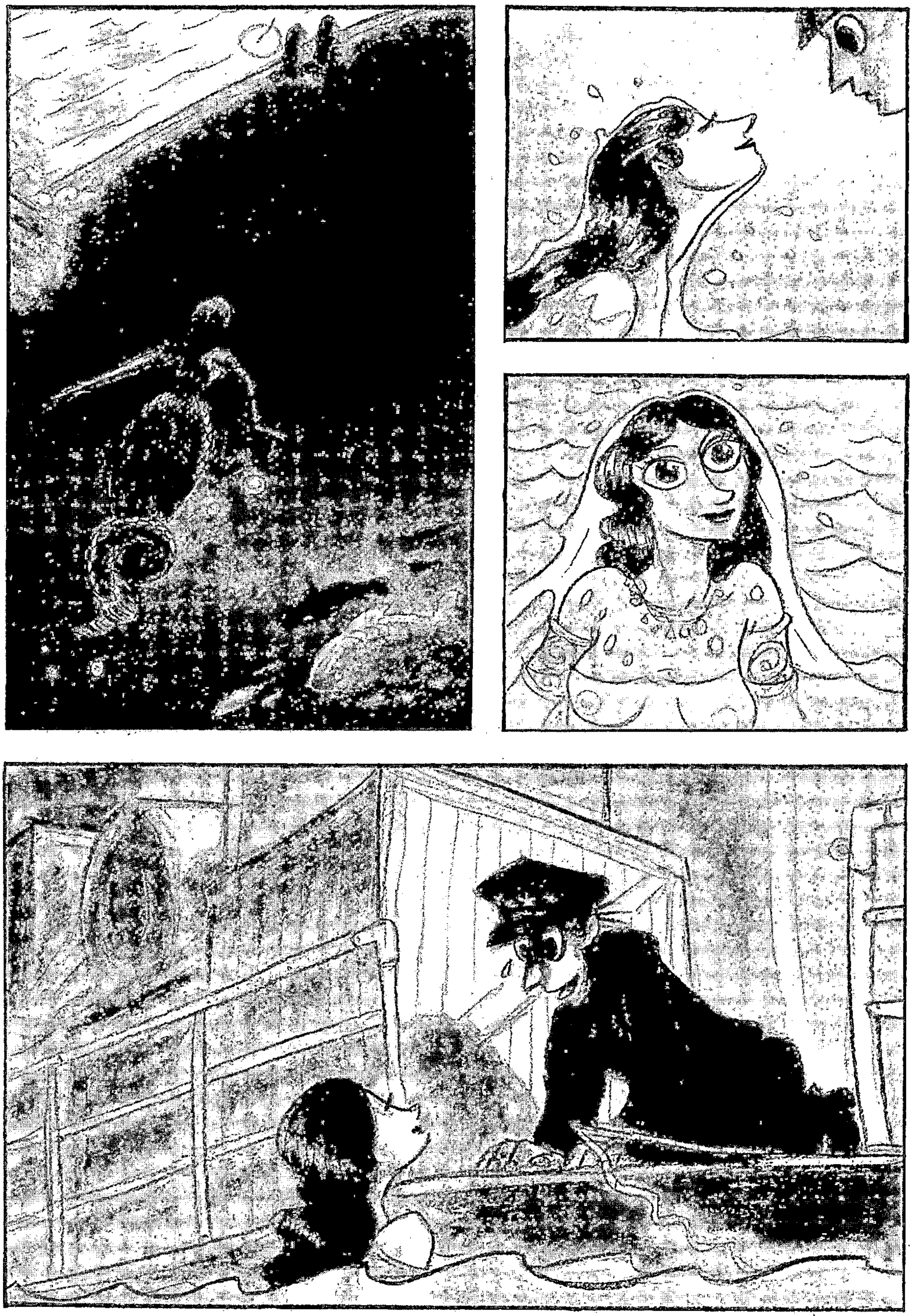

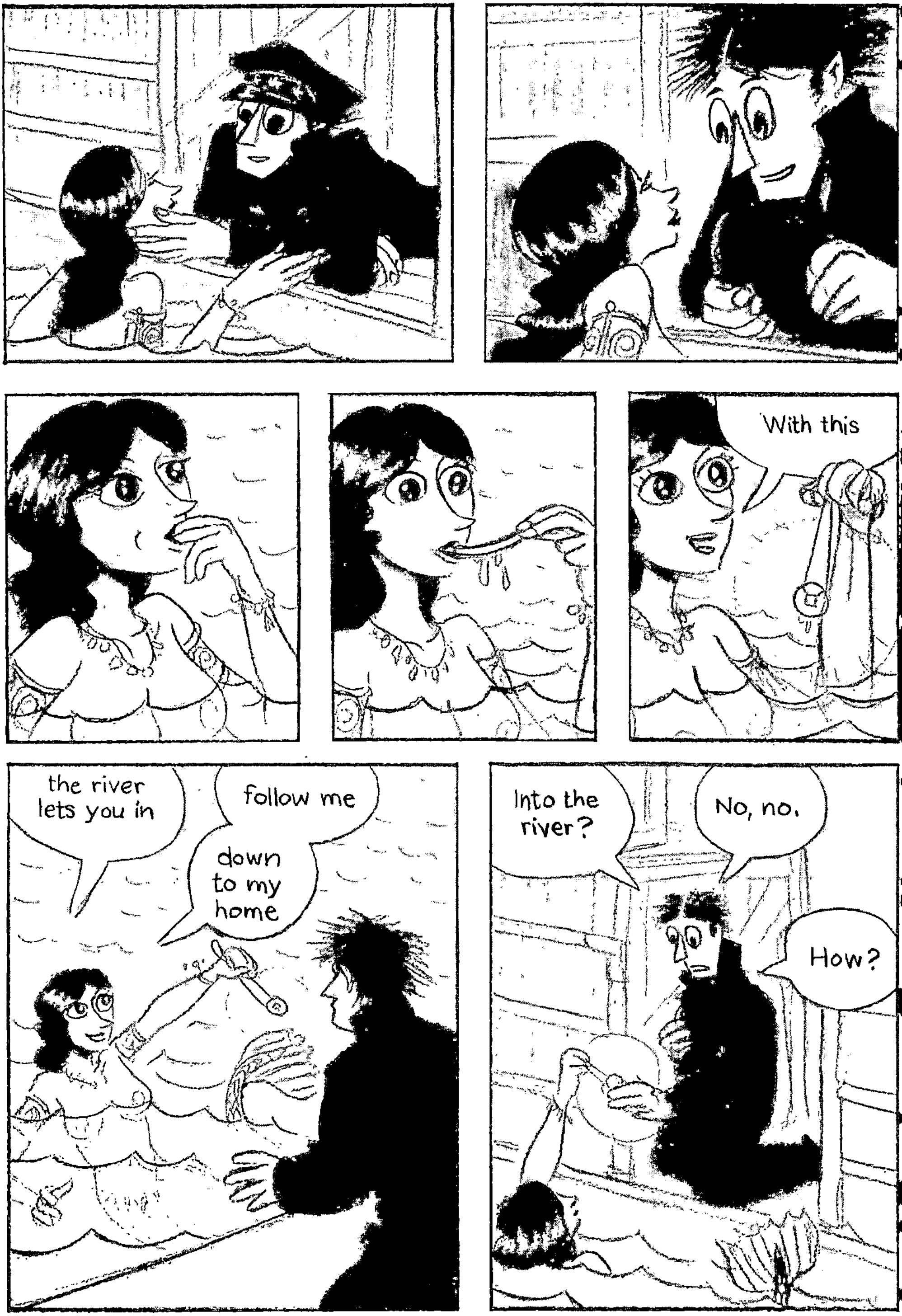
With this
the river lets you in
follow me
down to my home
Into the river?
No, no.
How?

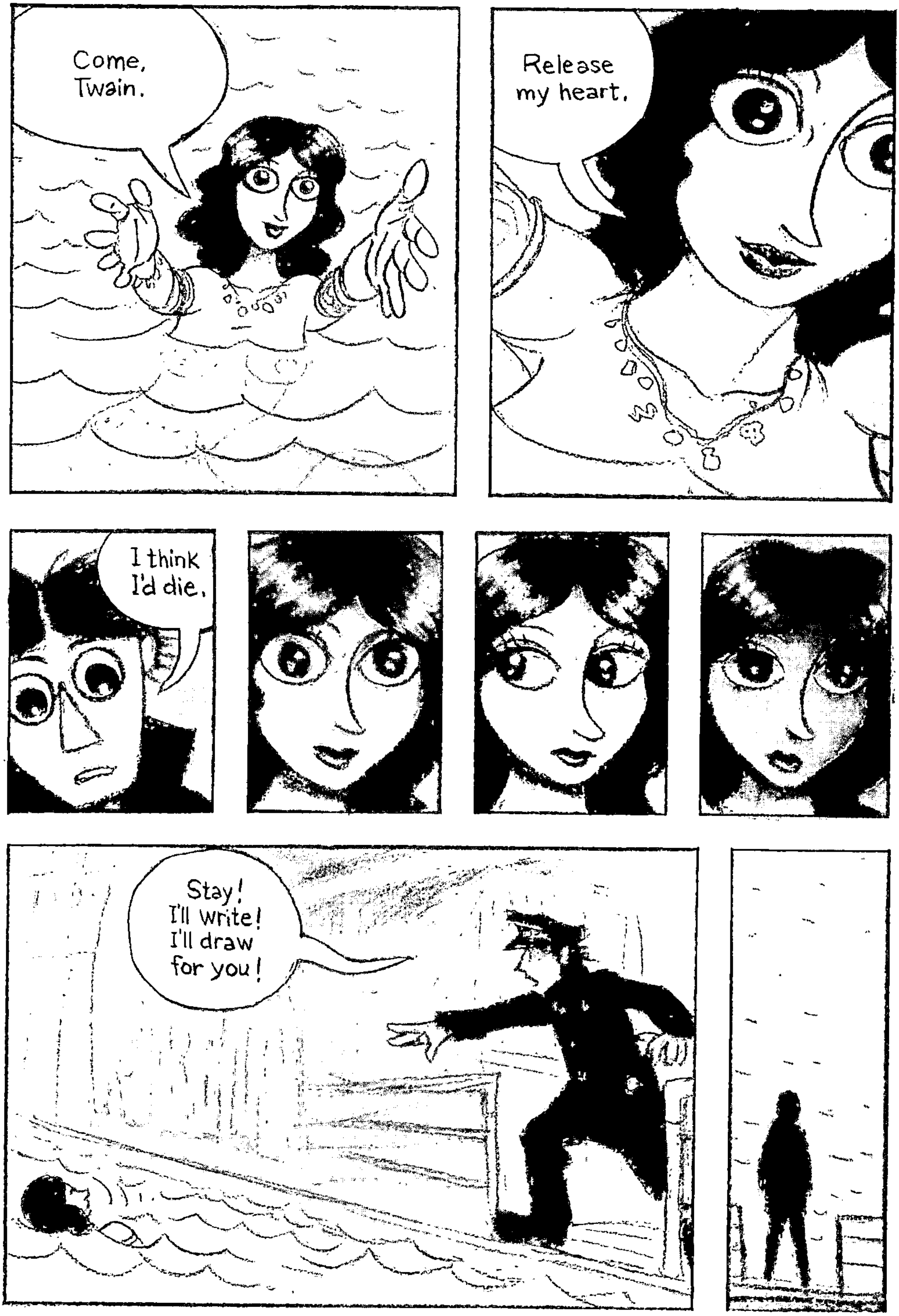
Come, Twain.
Release my heart.
I think I'd die.
Stay! I'll write! I'll draw for you!

Was she gone?

Would she come back?
Was it panic I felt?

Or relief?

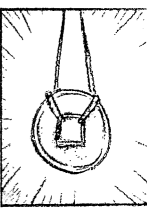

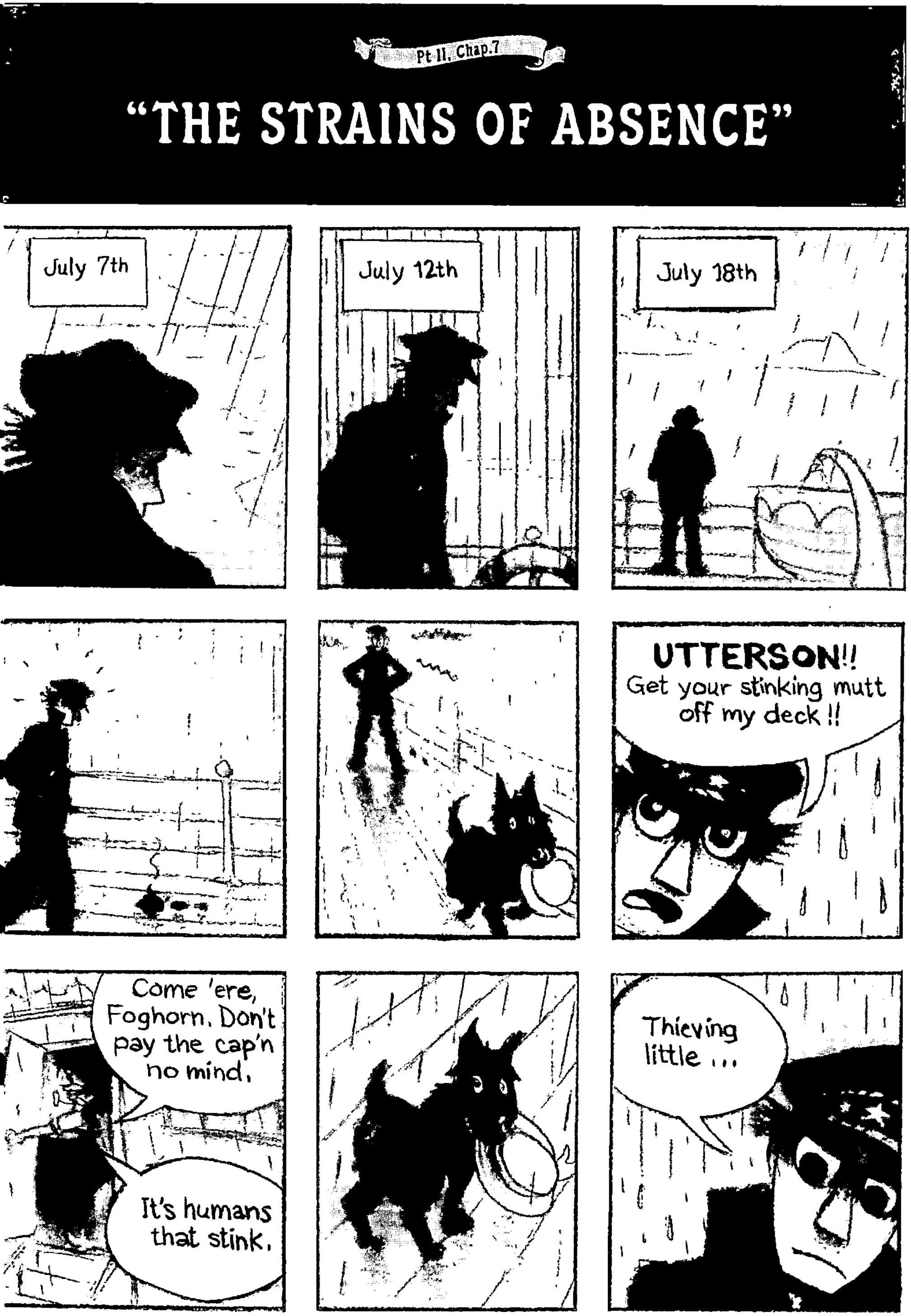

Pt II, Chap.7
"THE STRAINS OF ABSENCE"
July 7th
July 12th
July 18th
UTTERSON!! Get your stinking mutt off my deck!!
Come 'ere, Foghorn. Don't pay the cap'n no mind.
It's humans that stink.
Thieving little ...

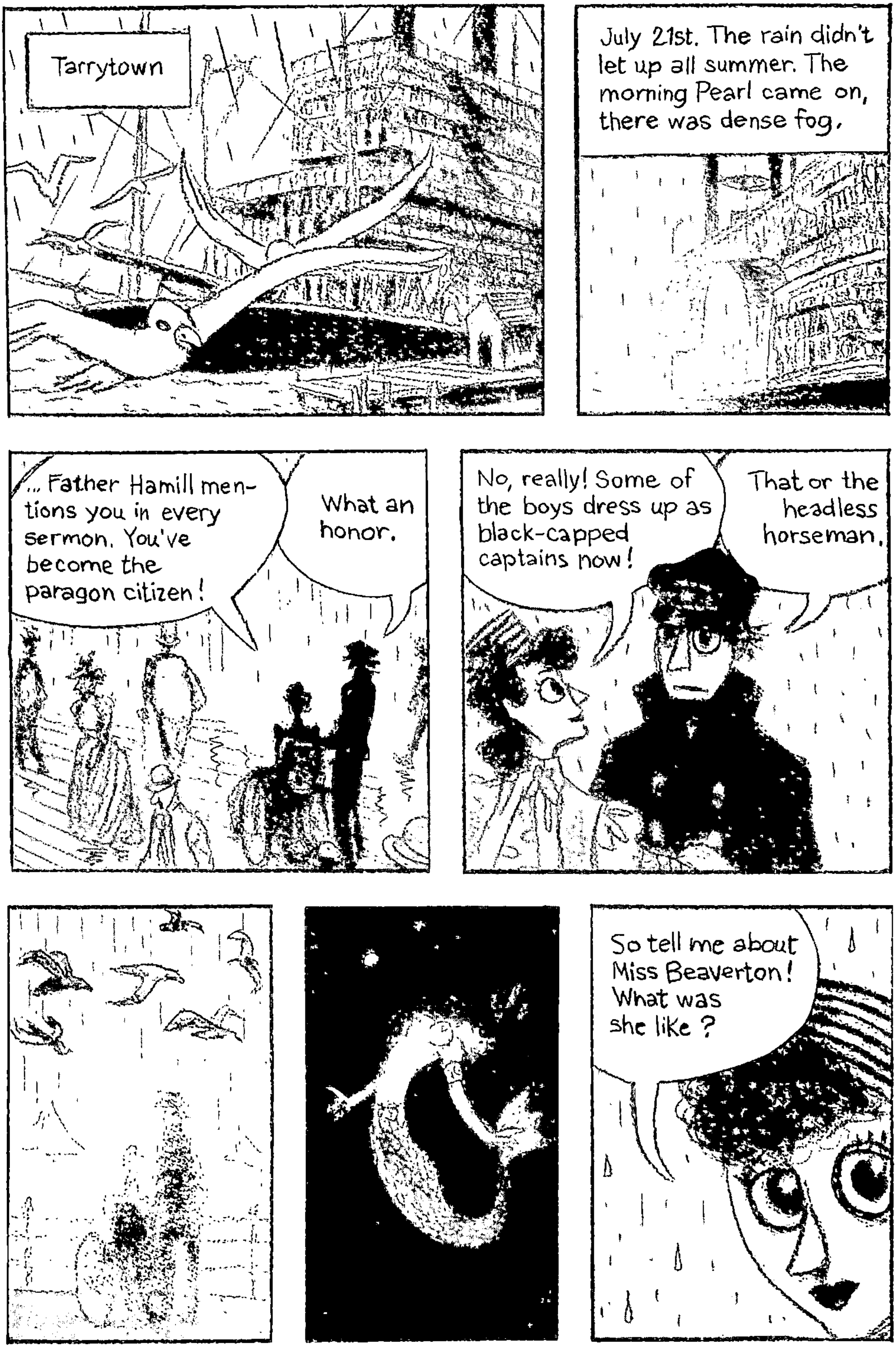
Tarrytown
July 21st. The rain didn't let up all summer. The morning Pearl came on, there was dense fog.
... Father Hamill mentions you in every sermon. You've become the paragon citizen!
What an honor.
No, really! Some of the boys dress up as black-capped captains now!
That or the headless horseman.
So tell me about Miss Beaverton! What was she like?

Hmm? Yes. Yes. She's a real...

...A real beauty, I hear.

I suppose, yes. She's fetching.

You seem sad, Elijah.

Your river is becoming a prison.

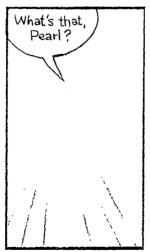

What's that, Pearl?

Nothing, my love.

283

Pt II, Chap.8

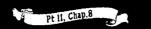

"TWAIN DREAMS"

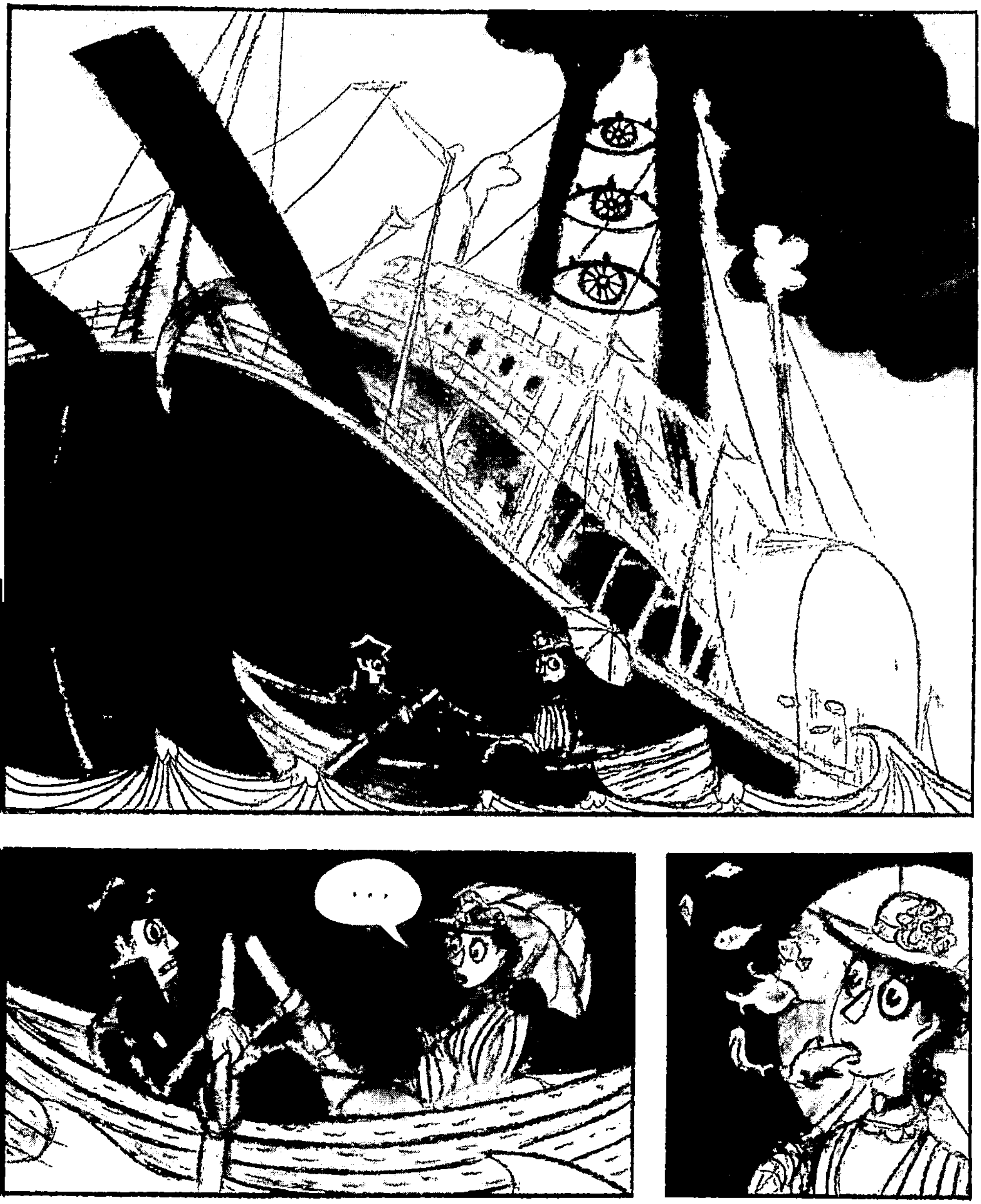
. . .

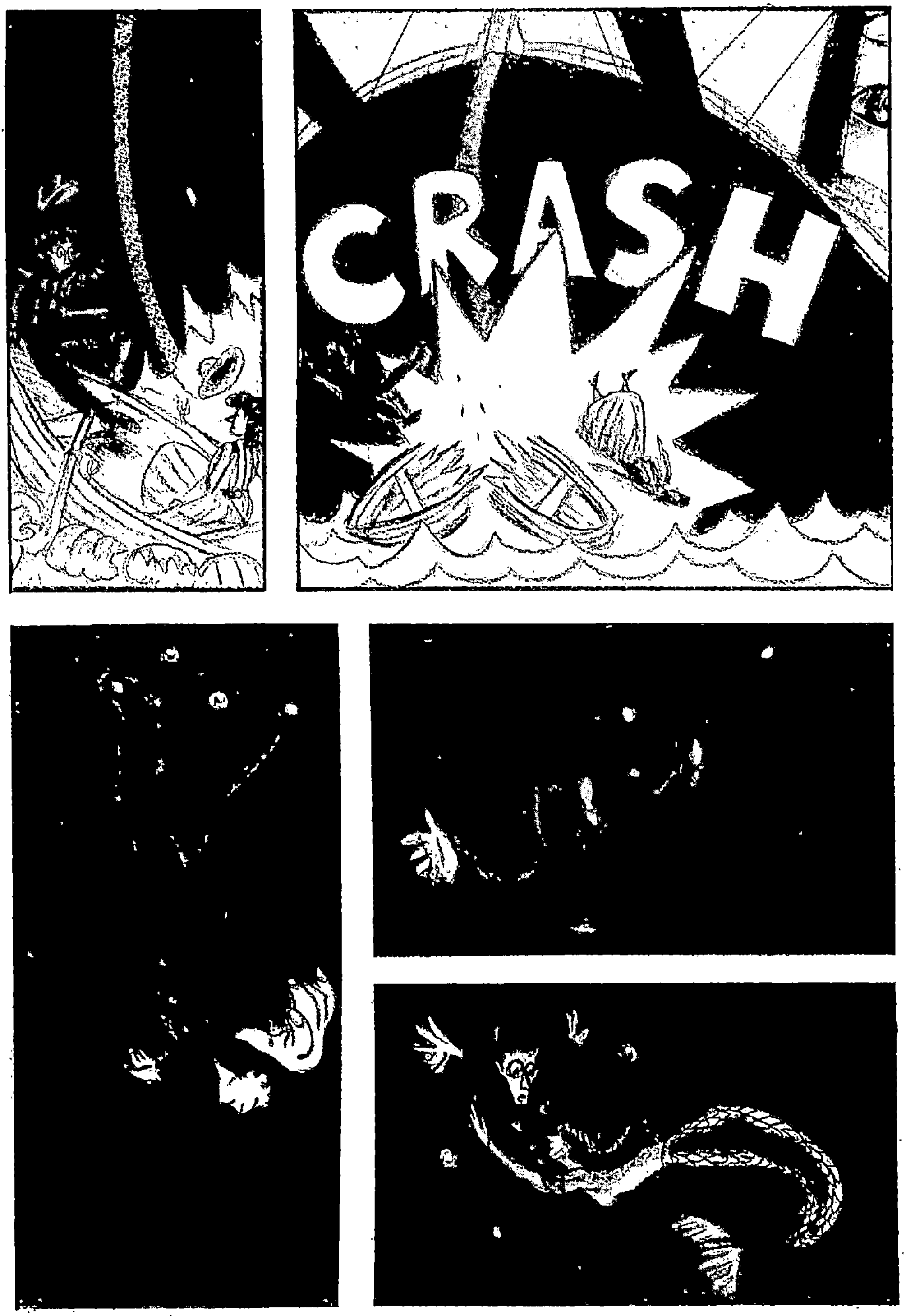
CRASH

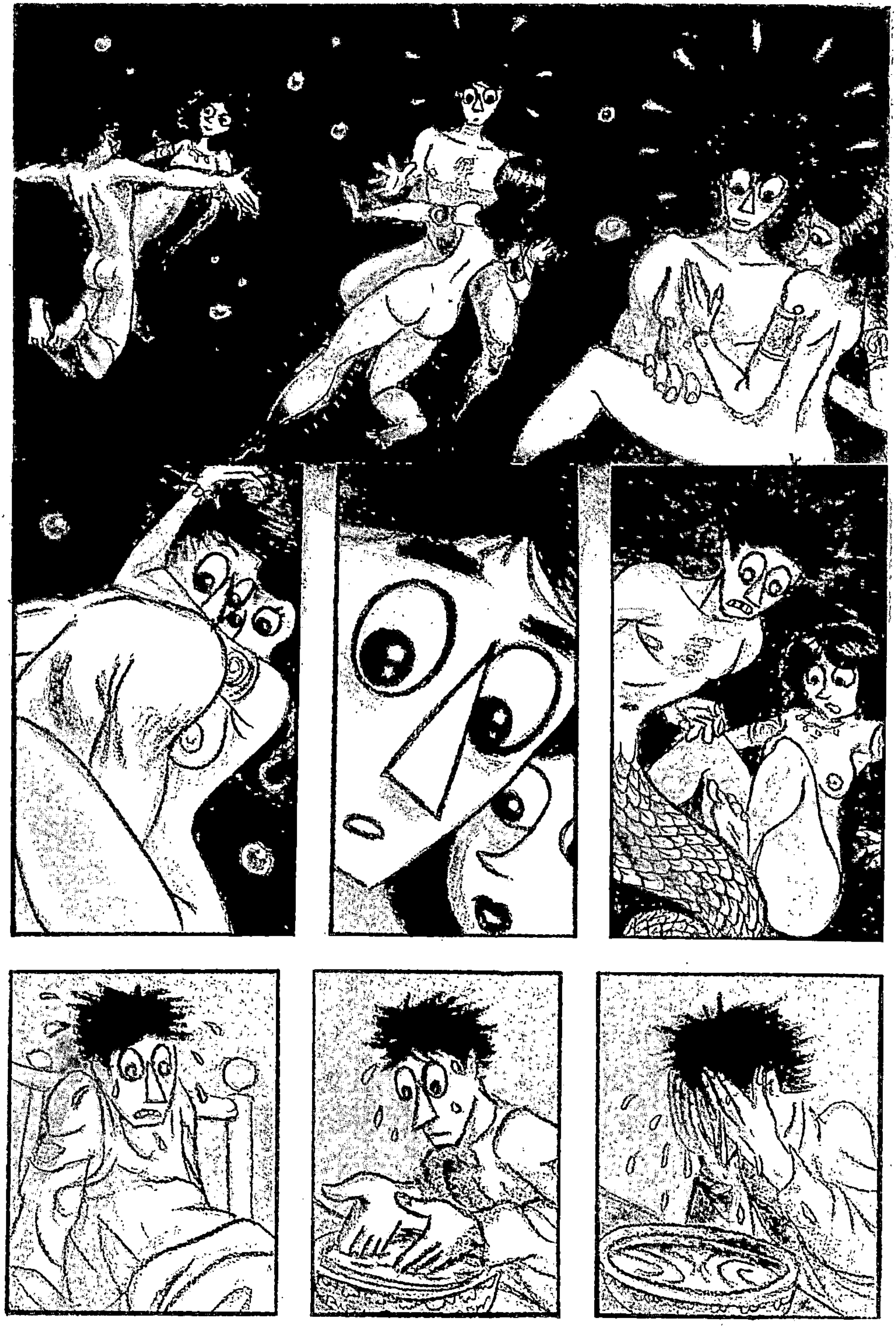

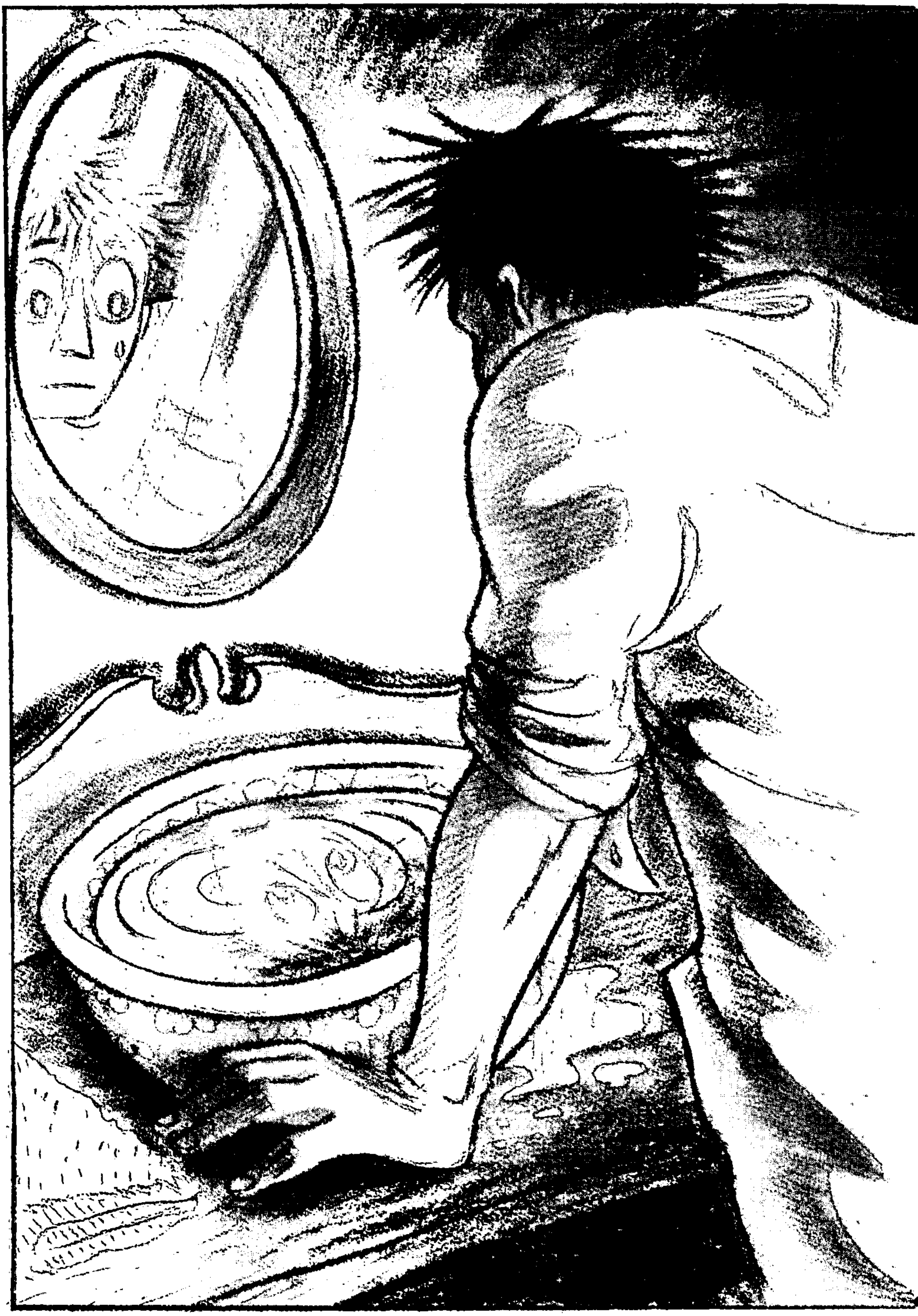

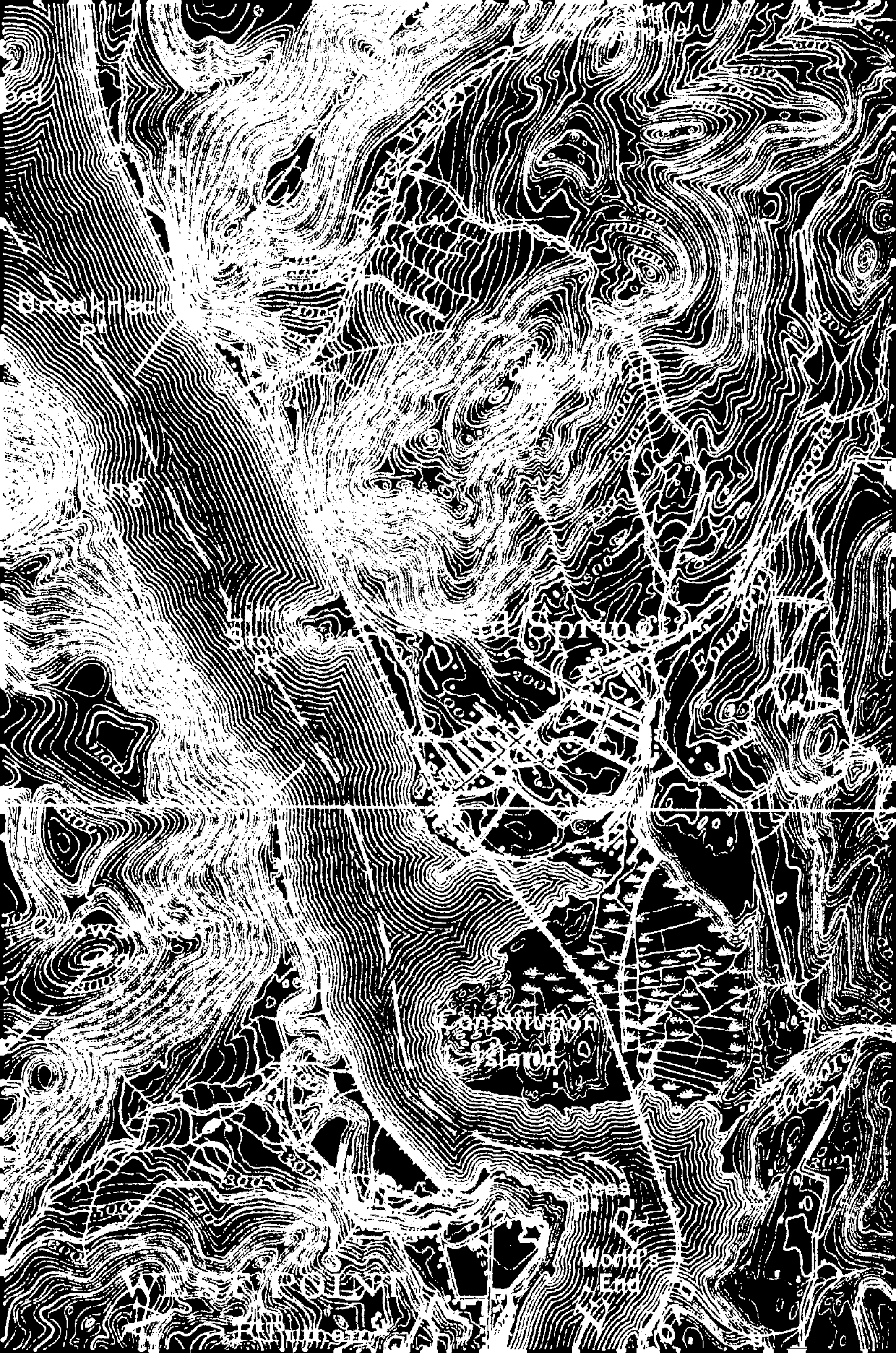
Constitution
Island
World's
End

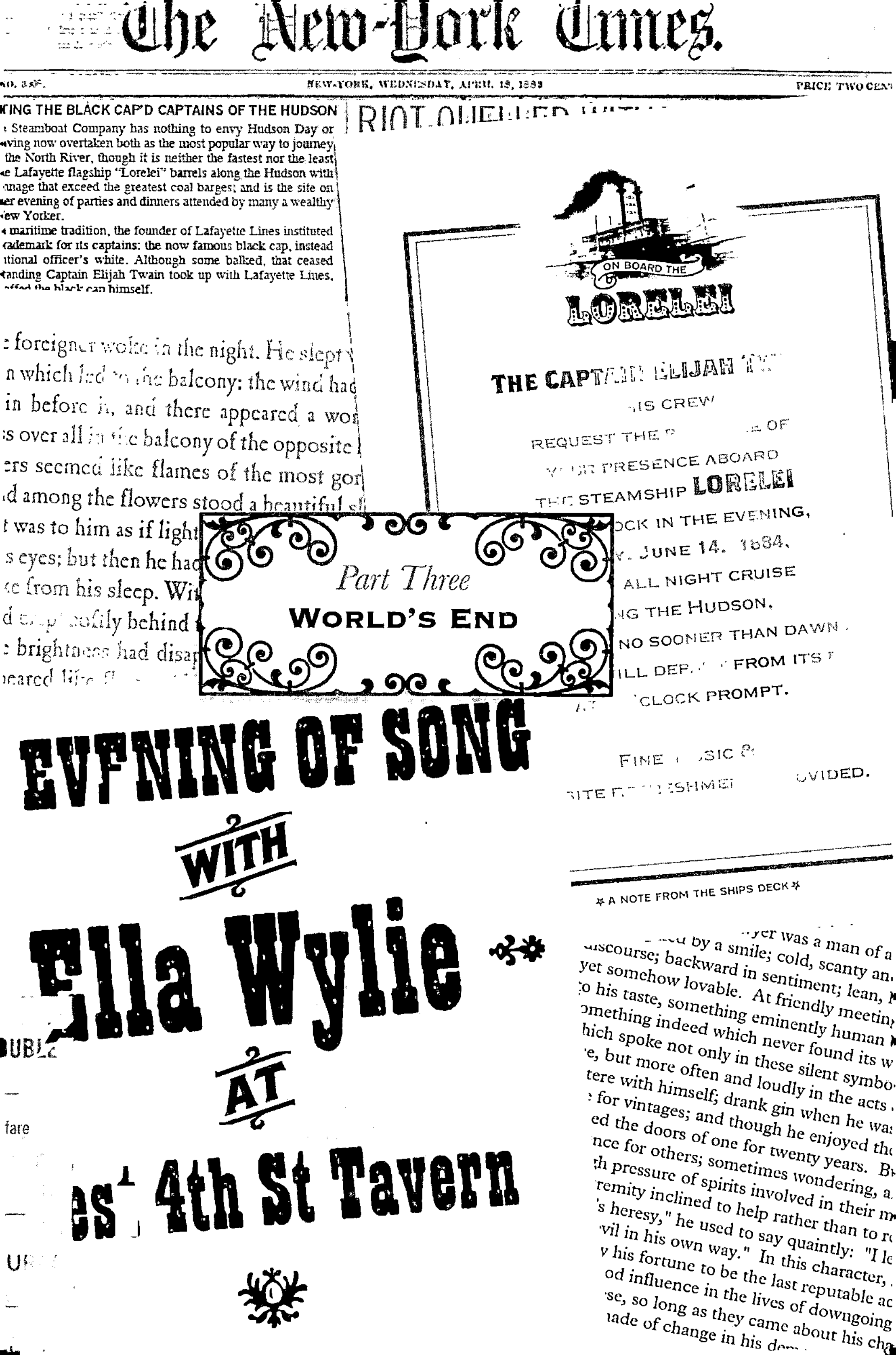

The New-York Times.
NEW-YORK, WEDNESDAY, APRIL 18, 1883
PRICE TWO CENTS
KING THE BLACK CAP'D CAPTAINS OF THE HUDSON
Steamboat Company has nothing to envy Hudson Day or
having now overtaken both as the most popular way to journey
the North River, though it is neither the fastest nor the least
Lafayette flagship "Lorelei" barrels along the Hudson with
tonnage that exceed the greatest coal barges; and is the site on
evening of parties and dinners attended by many a wealthy
New Yorker.
maritime tradition, the founder of Lafayette Lines instituted
trademark for its captains: the now famous black cap, instead
traditional officer's white. Although some balked, that ceased
standing Captain Elijah Twain took up with Lafayette Lines,
doffed the black cap himself.
foreigner woke in the night. He slept
n which led to the balcony: the wind had
in before it, and there appeared a wo
is over all in the balcony of the opposite
ers seemed like flames of the most gor
d among the flowers stood a beautiful
t was to him as if light
s eyes; but then he had
e from his sleep. Wi
d softly behind
brightness had disap
peared
ON BOARD THE
LORELEI
THE CAPTAIN ELIJAH
HIS CREW
REQUEST THE OF
YOUR PRESENCE ABOARD
THE STEAMSHIP LORELEI
OCK IN THE EVENING,
JUNE 14. 1884.
ALL NIGHT CRUISE
NG THE HUDSON.
NO SOONER THAN DAWN
ILL DEP FROM ITS
CLOCK PROMPT.
FINE SIC
ITE ESHME VIDED.
EVENING OF SONG
WITH
Ella Wylie
AT
4th St Tavern
A NOTE FROM THE SHIPS DECK
yer was a man of a
by a smile; cold, scanty an
discourse; backward in sentiment; lean,
yet somehow lovable. At friendly meetin
to his taste, something eminently human
omething indeed which never found its w
hich spoke not only in these silent symbo
e, but more often and loudly in the acts
tere with himself; drank gin when he wa
for vintages; and though he enjoyed th
ed the doors of one for twenty years. B
nce for others; sometimes wondering, a
th pressure of spirits involved in their m
remity inclined to help rather than to r
's heresy," he used to say quaintly: "I le
vil in his own way." In this character,
y his fortune to be the last reputable ac
od influence in the lives of downgoing
se, so long as they came about his ch
made of change in his de

Part Three

World's End

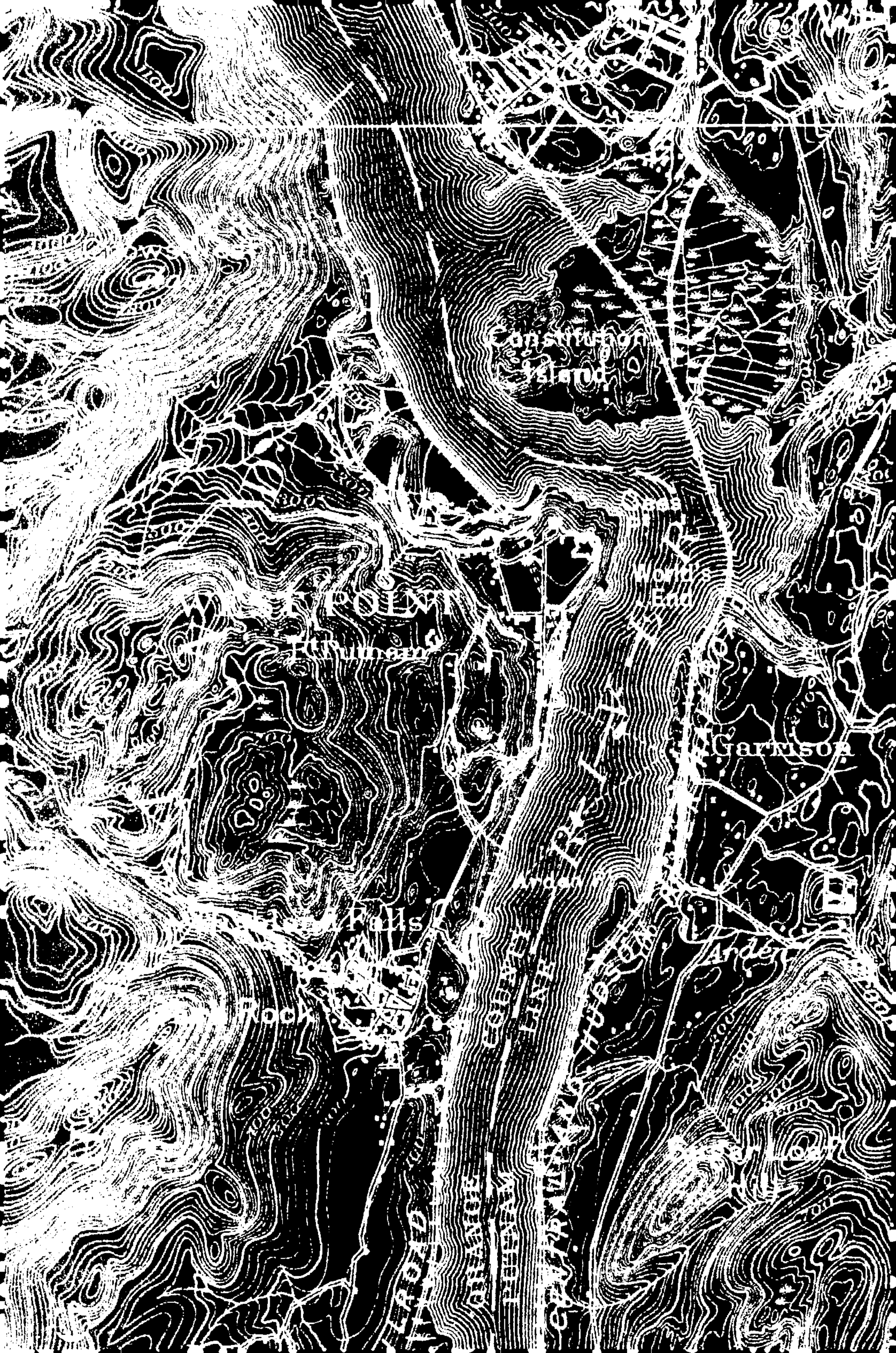

Constitution
Island
World's
End
Garrison
Falls

Pt III, Chap.1

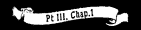

"IN THE OTHER REALM"

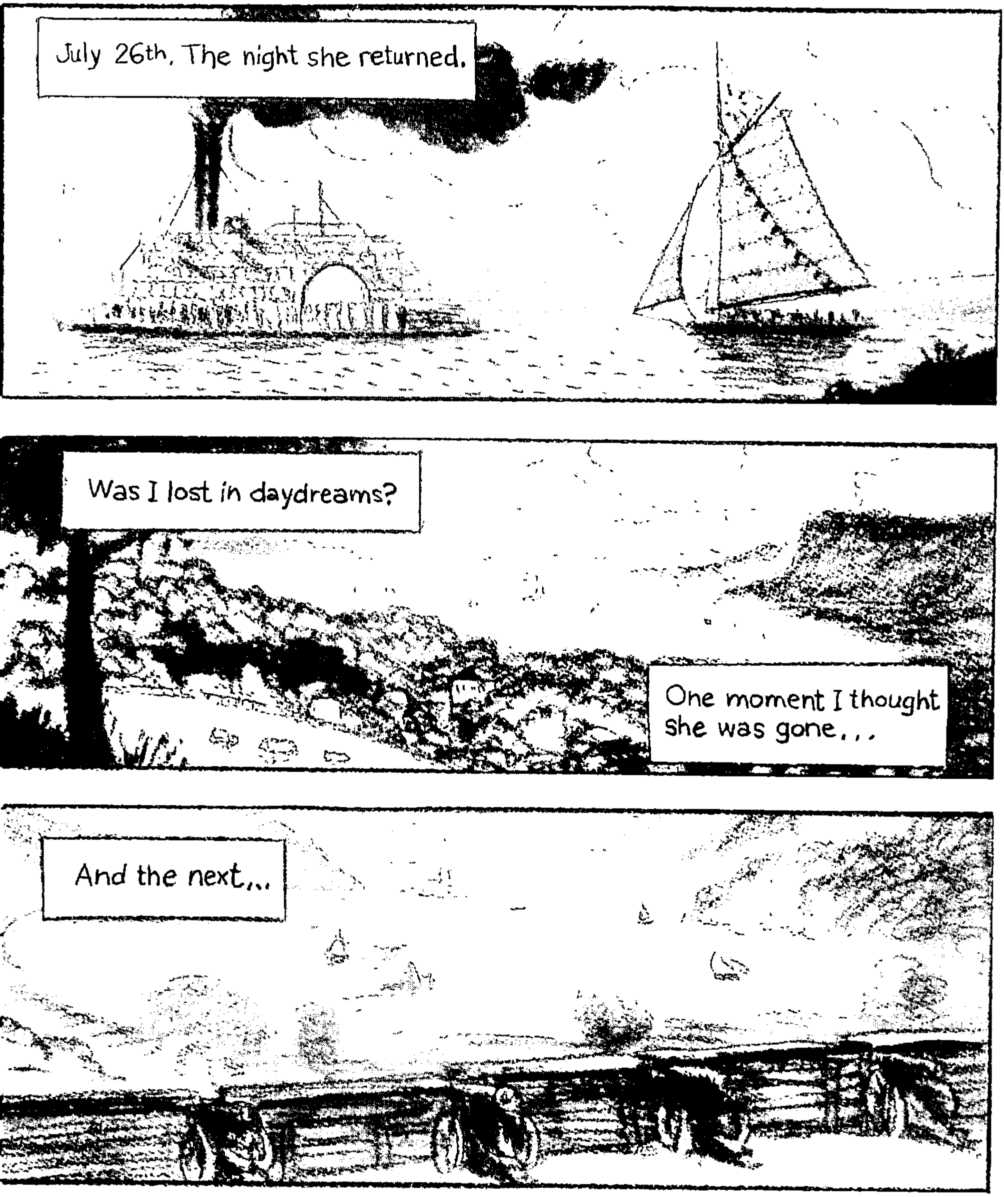
July 26th, The night she returned.
Was I lost in daydreams?
One moment I thought she was gone...
And the next...

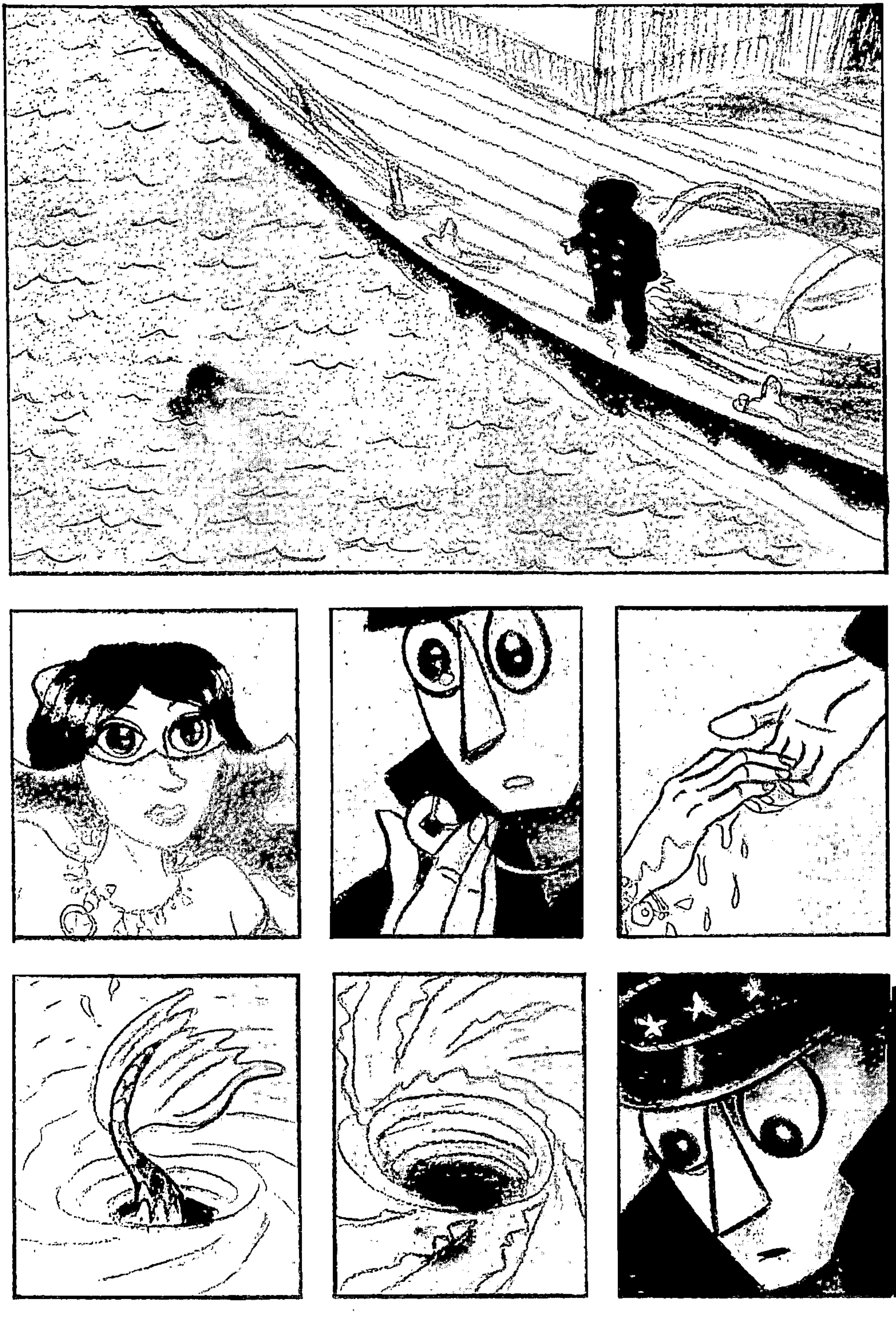

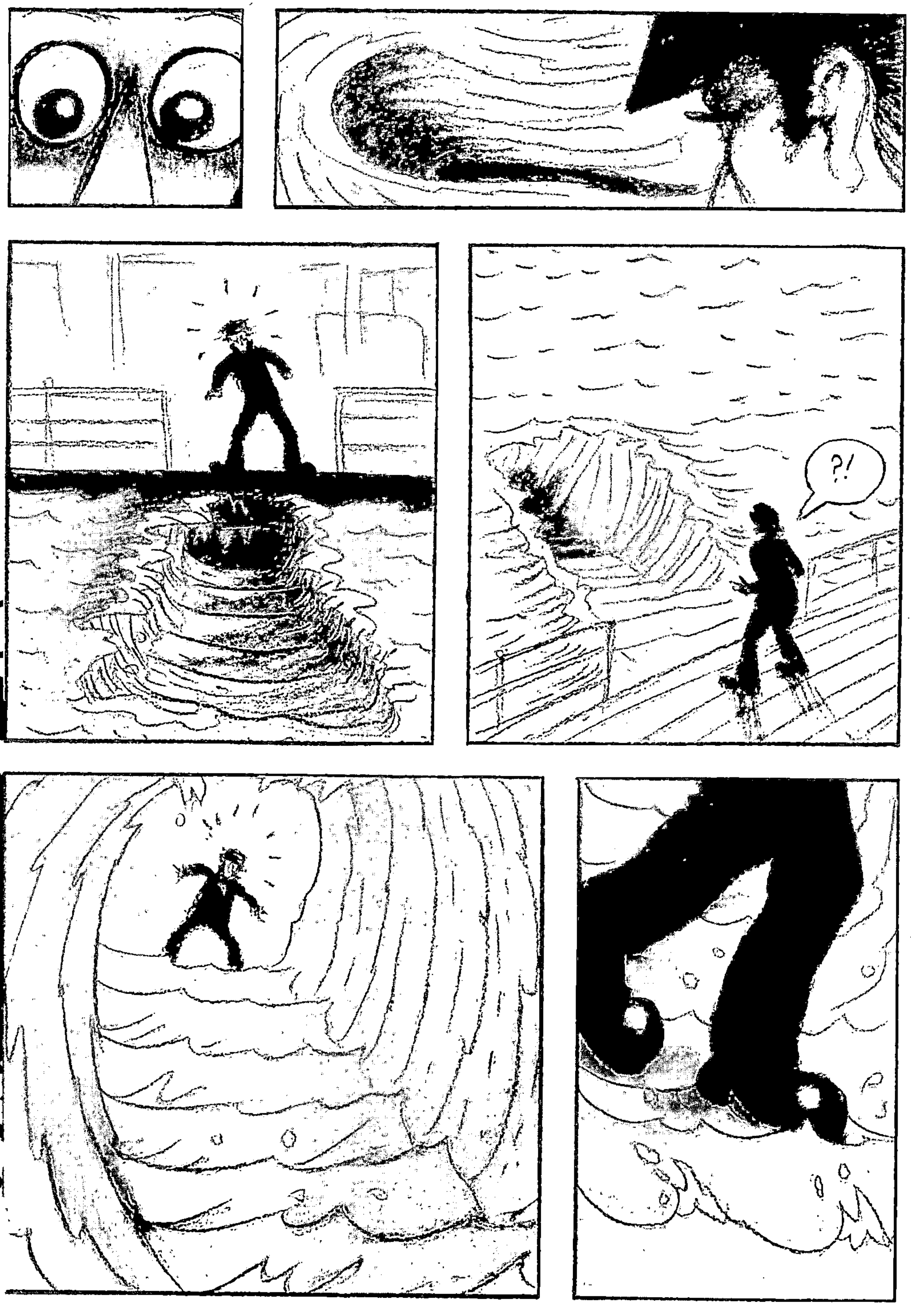
?!

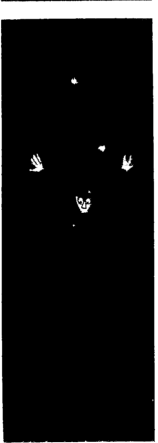

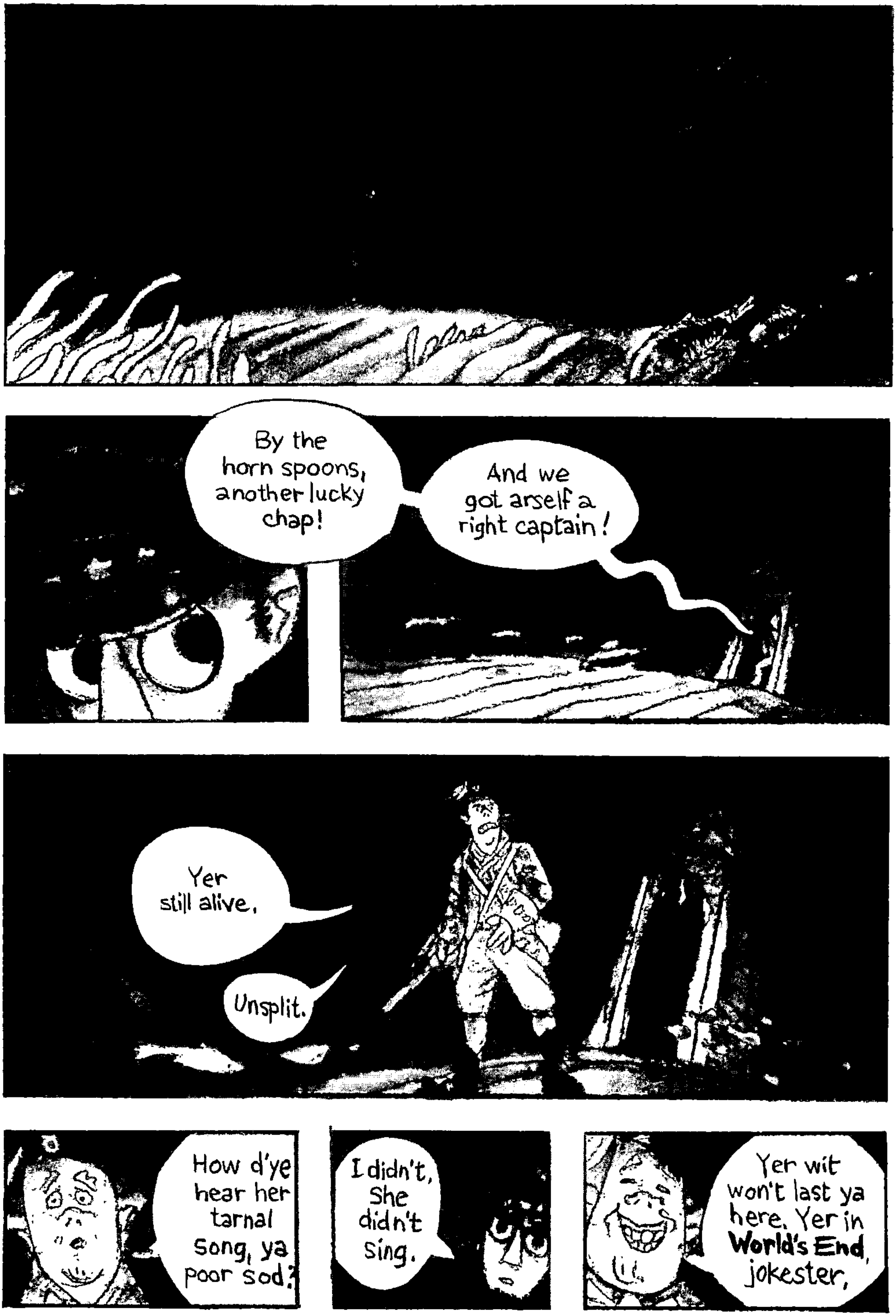
By the horn spoons, another lucky chap!
And we got arself a right captain!
Yer still alive.
Unsplit.
How d'ye hear her tarnal song, ya poor sod?
I didn't. She didn't sing.
Yer wit won't last ya here. Yer in **World's End**, jokester.

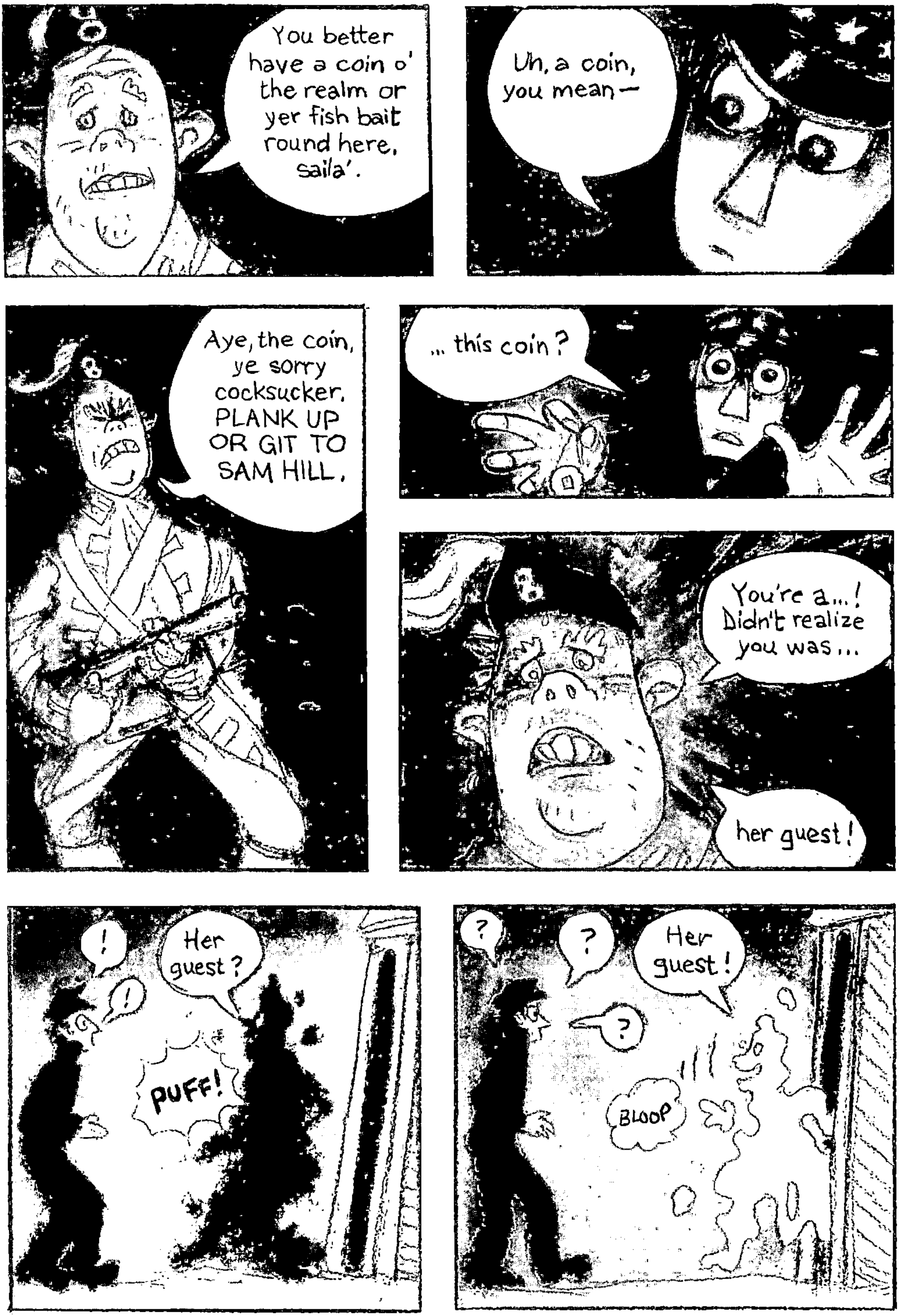
You better have a coin o' the realm or yer fish bait round here, saila'.
Uh, a coin, you mean—
Aye, the coin, ye sorry cocksucker. PLANK UP OR GIT TO SAM HILL.
... this coin?
You're a...! Didn't realize you was...
her guest!
!
!
Her guest?
PUFF!
?
?
Her guest!
?
BLOOP

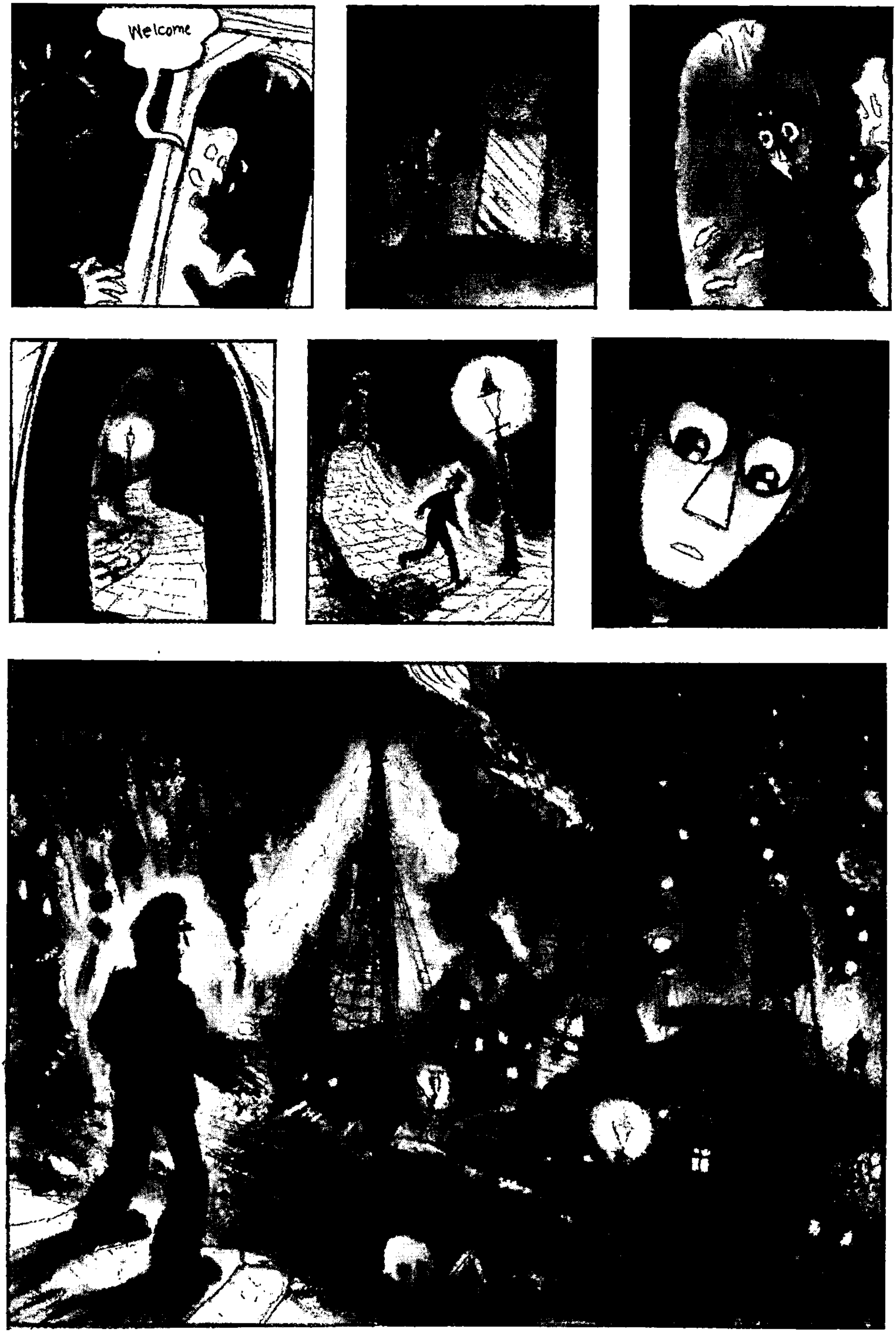
Welcome

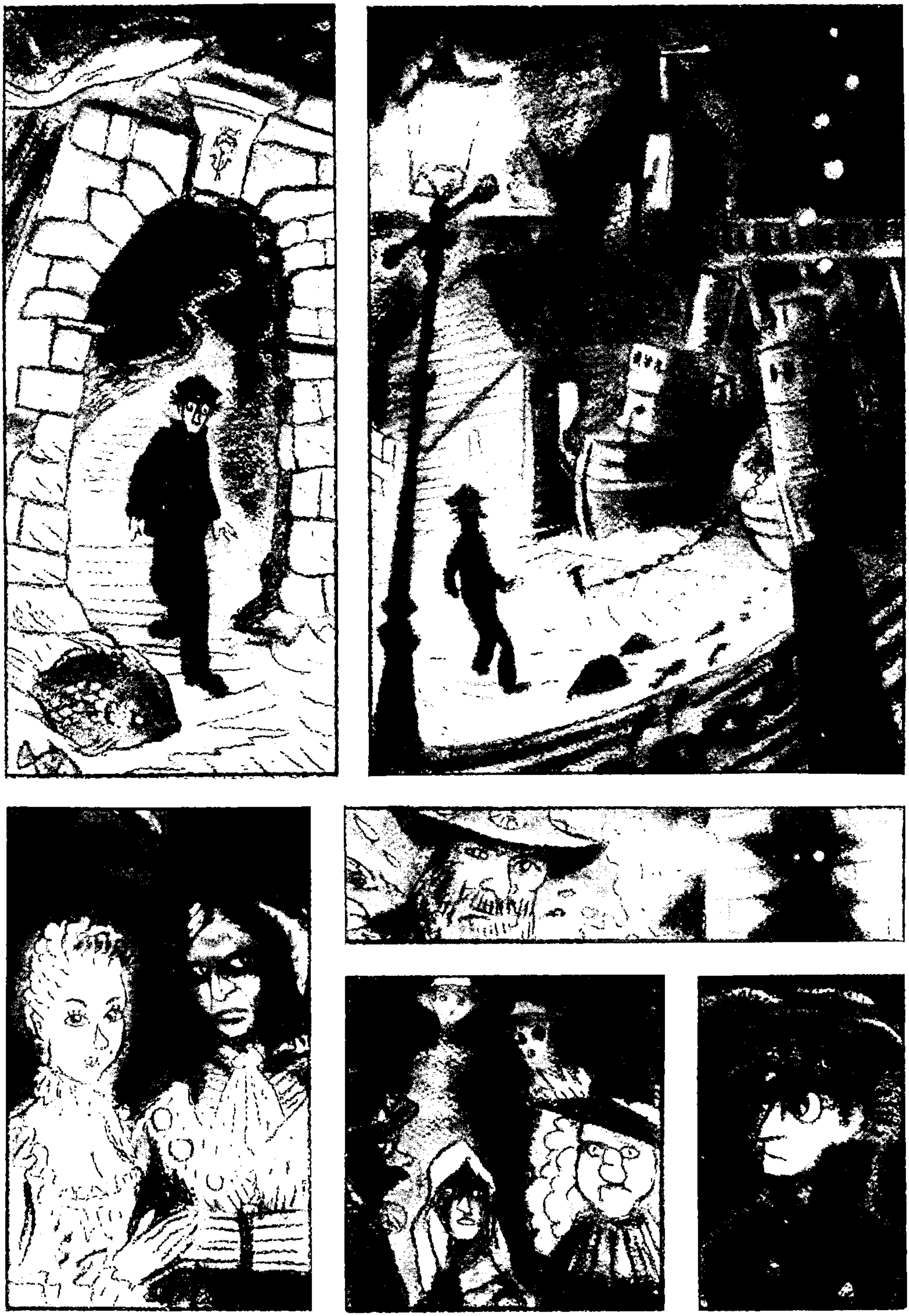

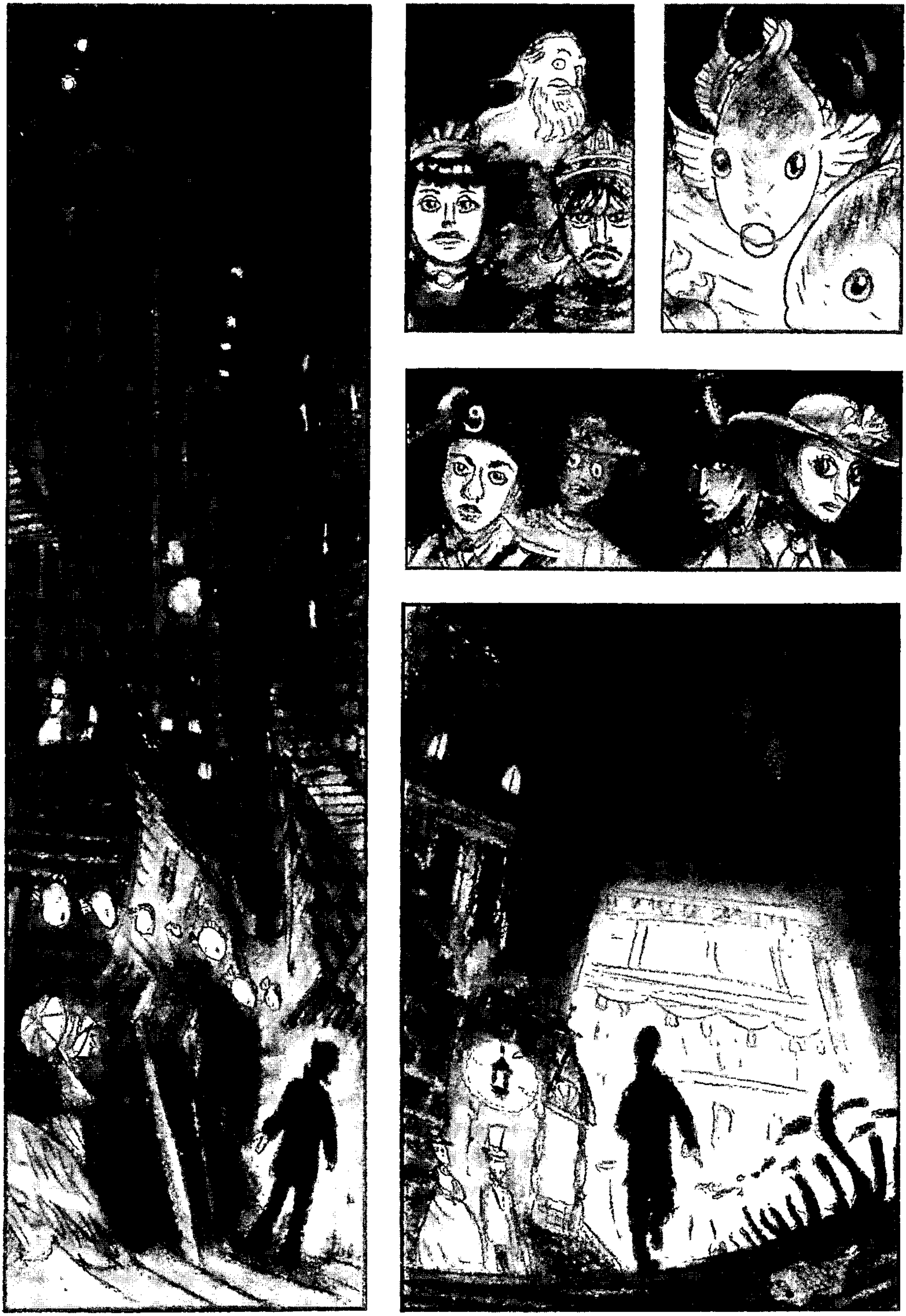

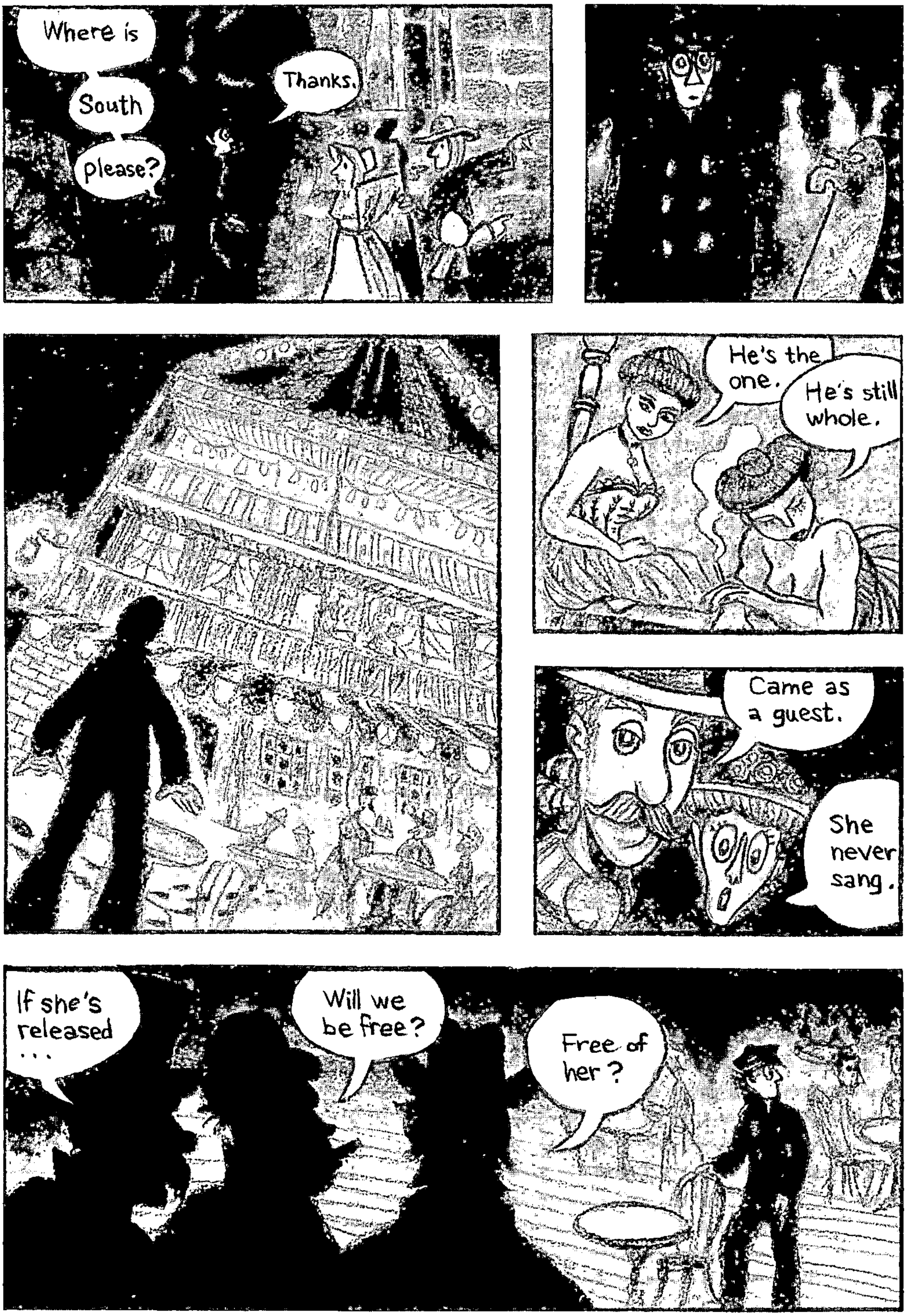
Where is
South
please?
Thanks.
He's the one.
He's still whole.
Came as a guest.
She never sang.
If she's released . . .
Will we be free?
Free of her?

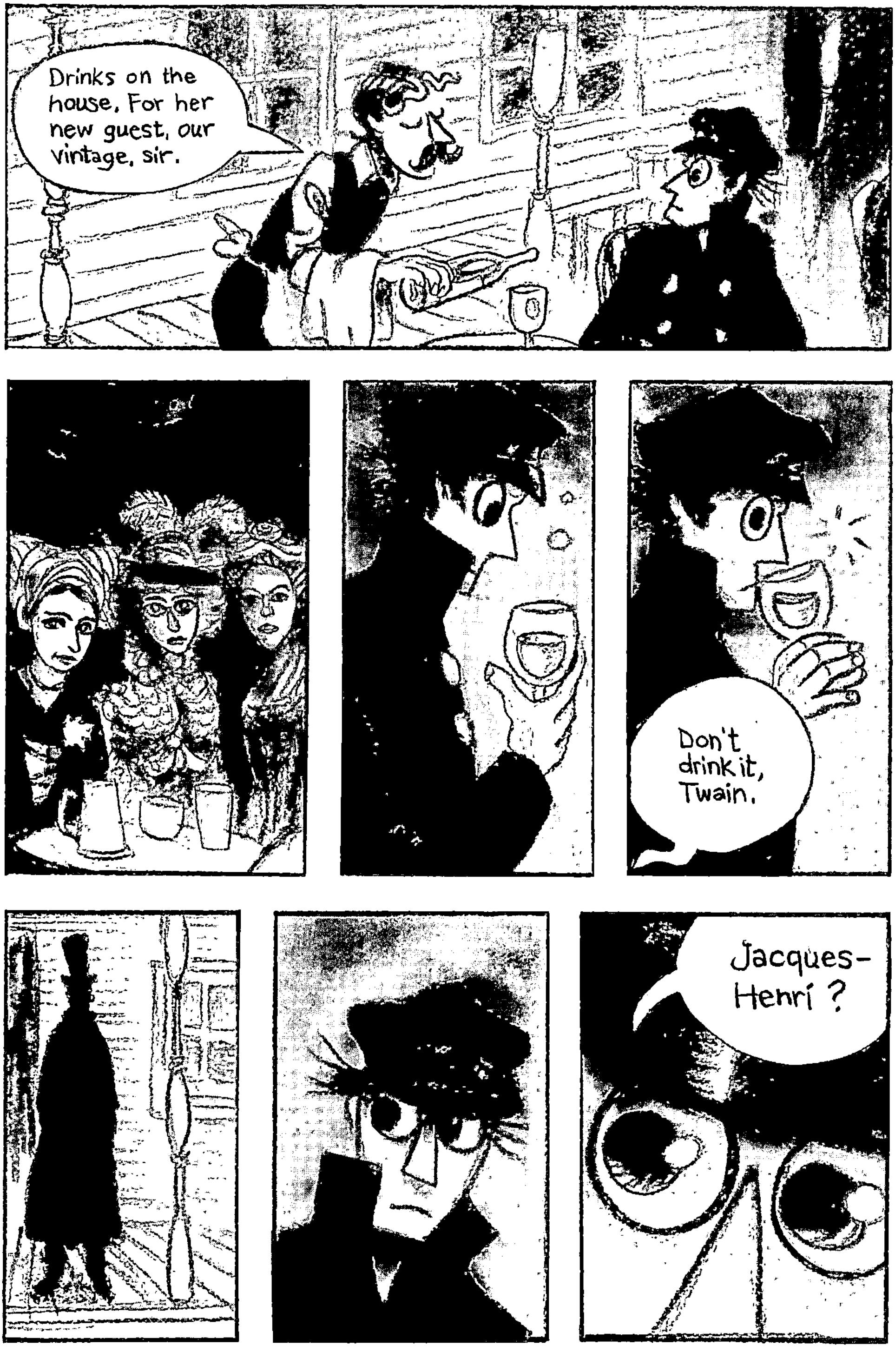
Drinks on the house. For her new guest, our vintage, sir.
Don't drink it, Twain.
Jacques-Henri ?

"THE LOST BROTHER"

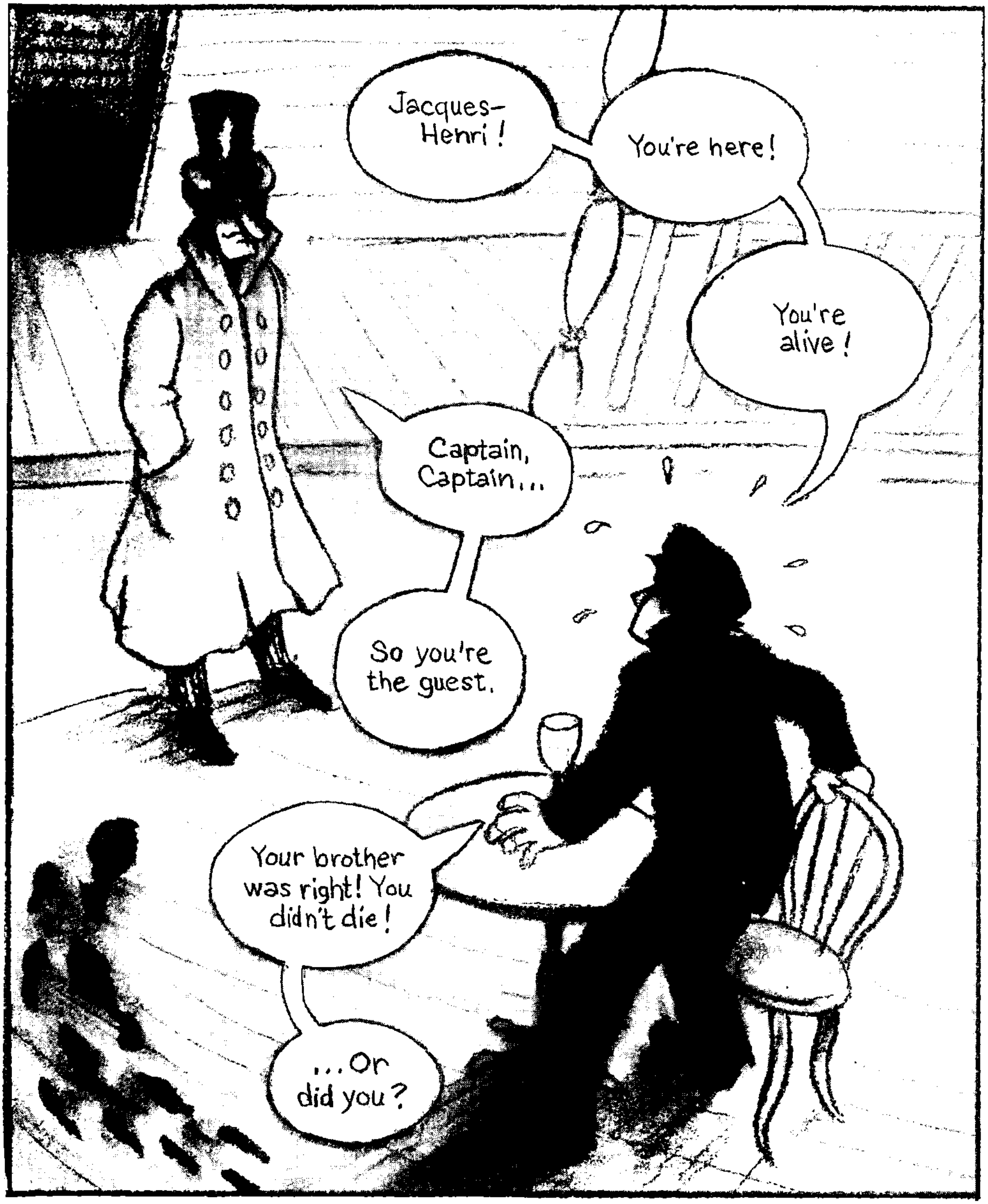
Jacques-Henri!
You're here!
You're alive!
Captain, Captain...
So you're the guest.
Your brother was right! You didn't die!
...Or did you?

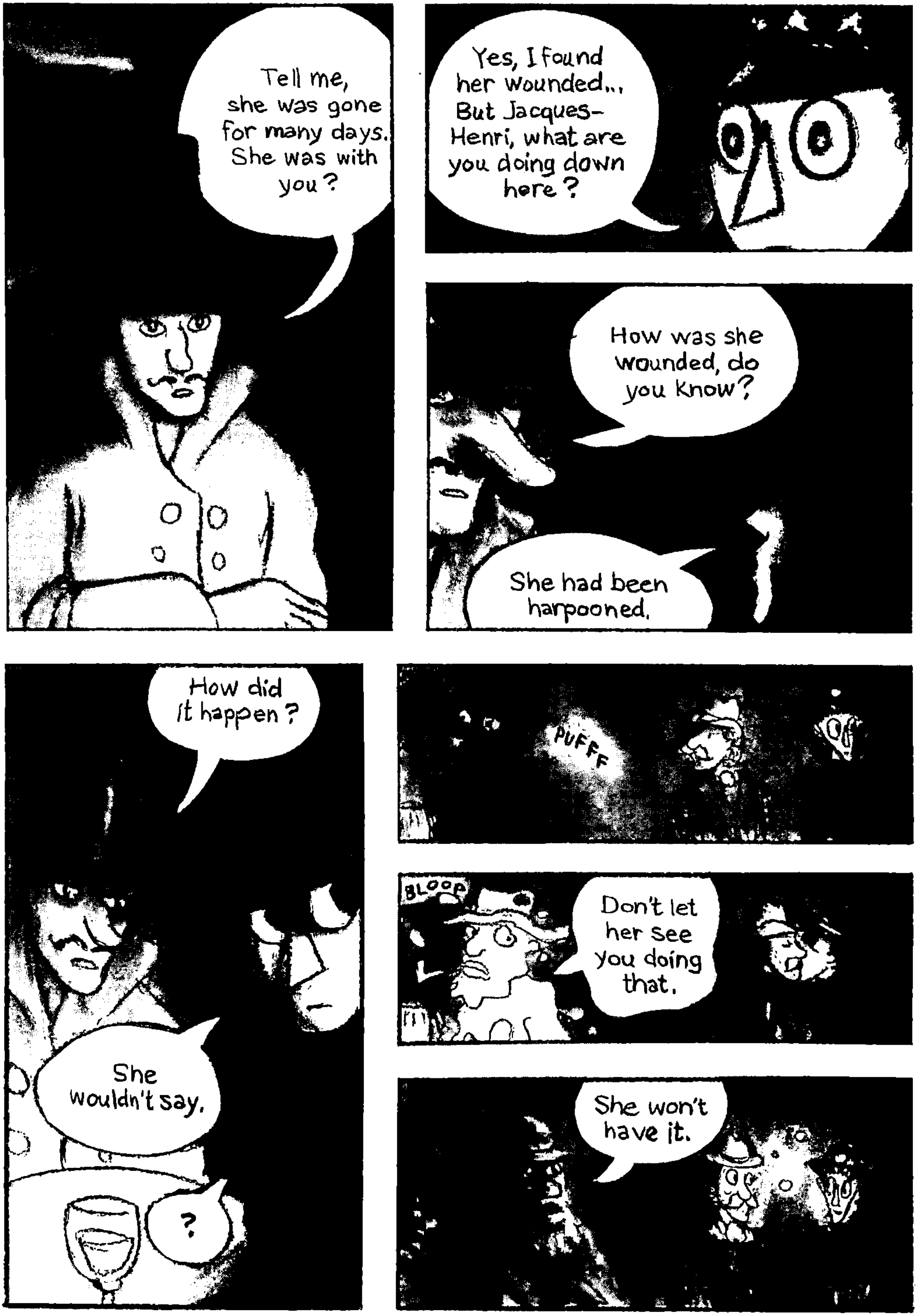
Tell me, she was gone for many days. She was with you?
Yes, I found her wounded... But Jacques-Henri, what are you doing down here?
How was she wounded, do you know?
She had been harpooned.
How did it happen?
She wouldn't say.
?
PUFFF
BLOOP
Don't let her see you doing that.
She won't have it.

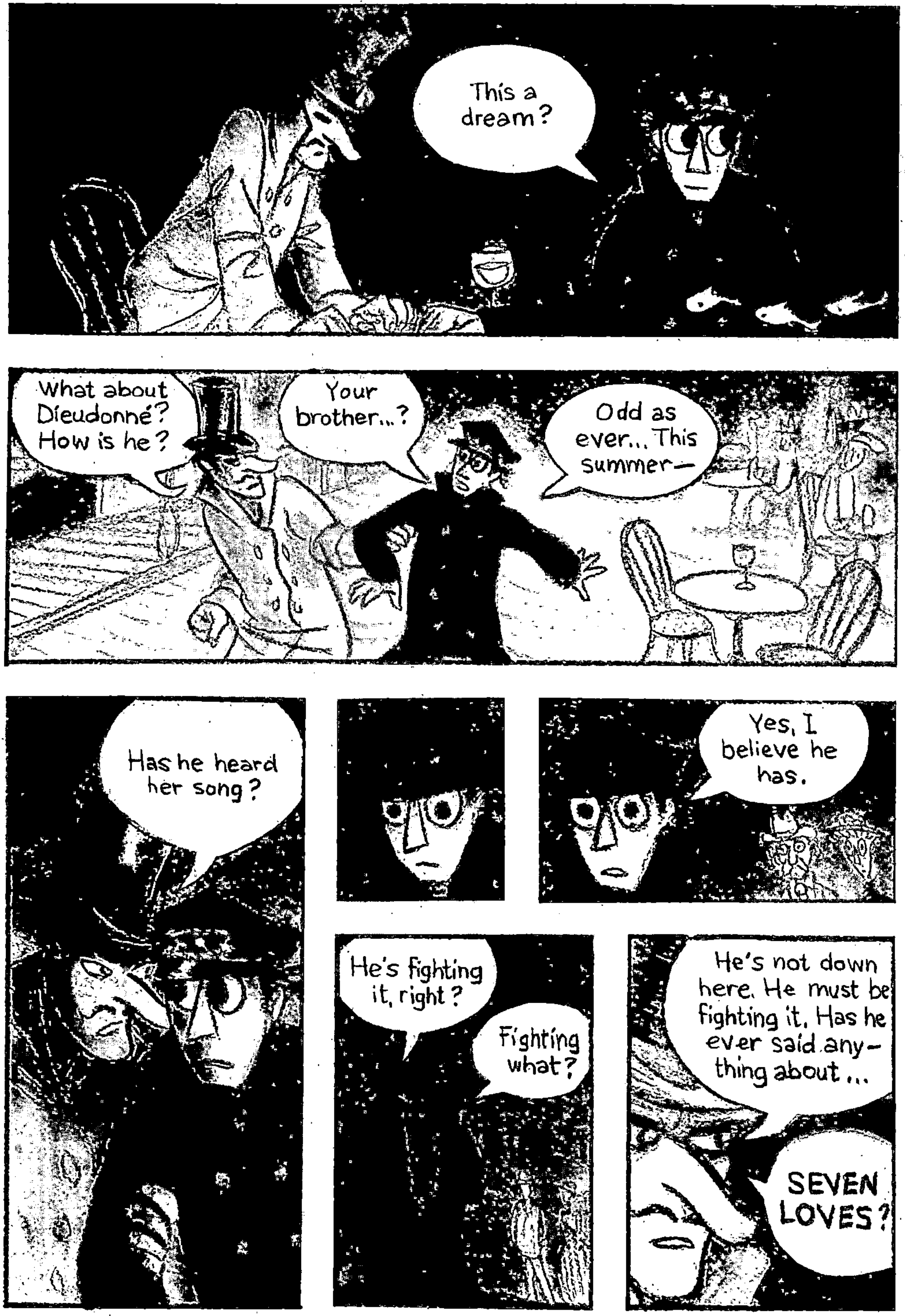
This a dream?
What about Dieudonné? How is he?
Your brother...?
Odd as ever... This summer—
Has he heard her song?
Yes, I believe he has.
He's fighting it, right?
Fighting what?
He's not down here. He must be fighting it. Has he ever said anything about...
SEVEN LOVES?

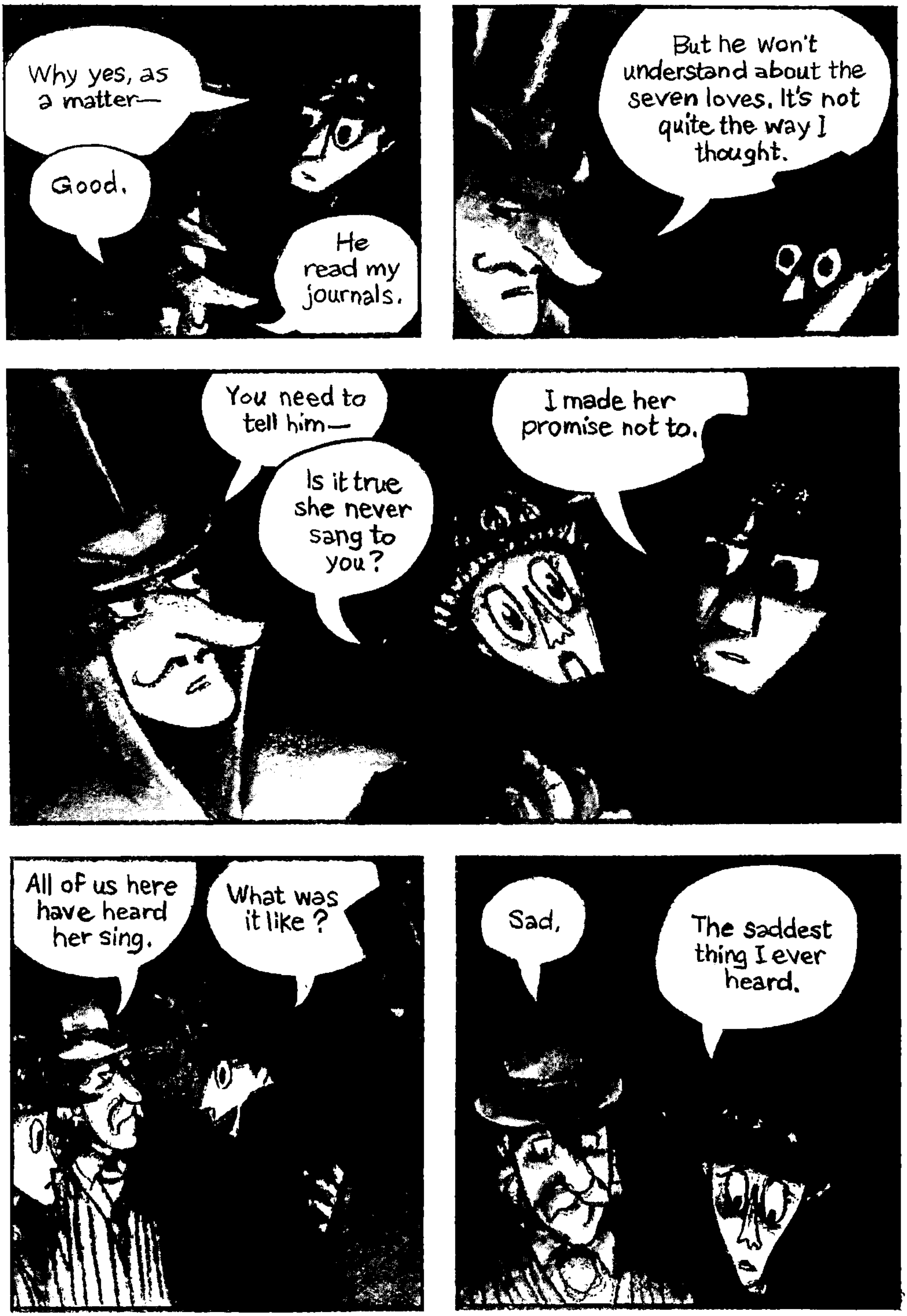

Why yes, as a matter—
Good.
He read my journals.
But he won't understand about the seven loves. It's not quite the way I thought.
You need to tell him—
Is it true she never sang to you?
I made her promise not to.
All of us here have heard her sing.
What was it like?
Sad.
The saddest thing I ever heard.

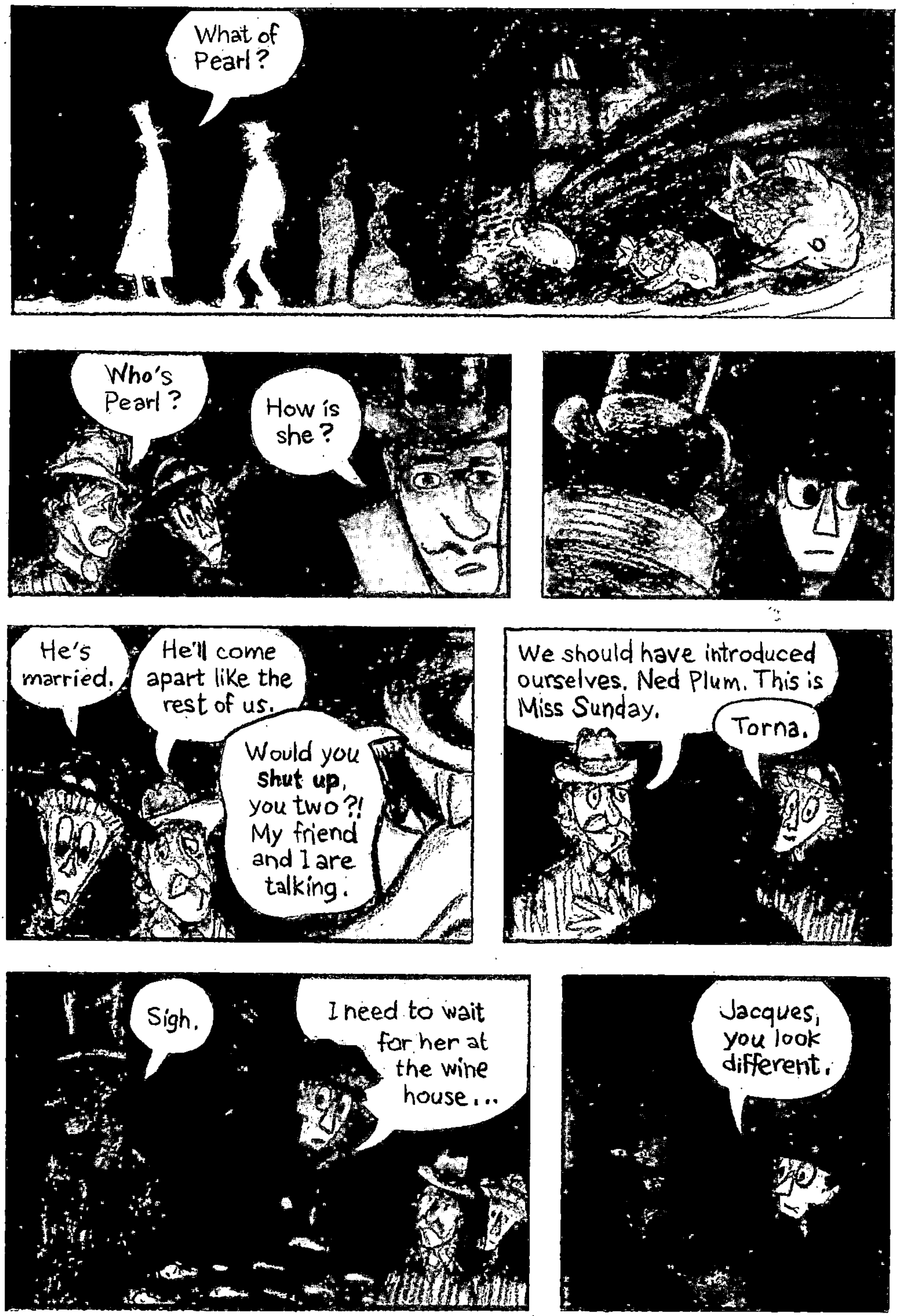
What of Pearl?
Who's Pearl?
How is she?
He's married.
He'll come apart like the rest of us.
Would you **shut up**, you two?! My friend and I are talking.
We should have introduced ourselves. Ned Plum. This is Miss Sunday.
Torna.
Sigh.
I need to wait for her at the wine house...
Jacques, you look different.

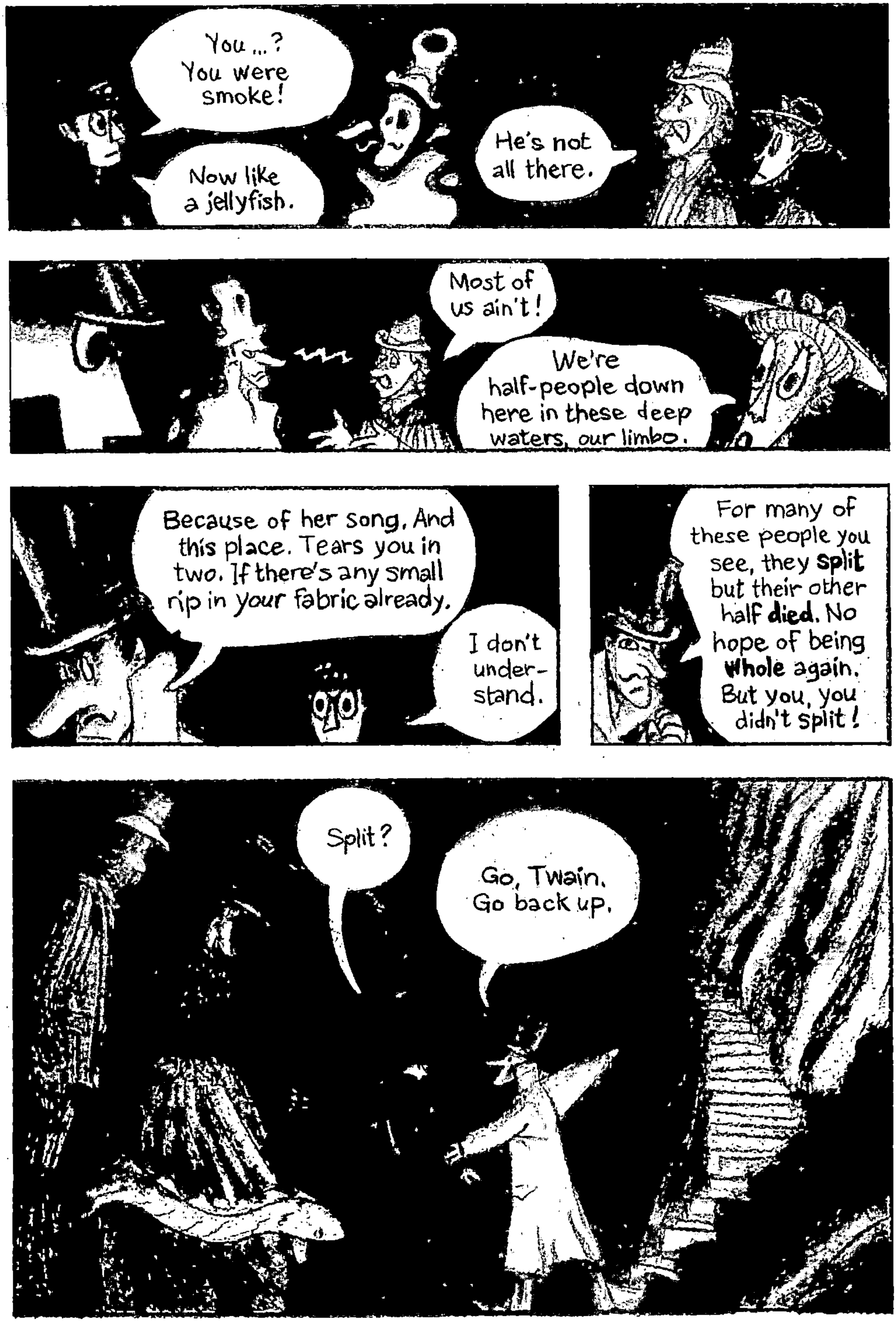
You ...? You were smoke!
Now like a jellyfish.
He's not all there.
Most of us ain't!
We're half-people down here in these deep waters, our limbo.
Because of her song. And this place. Tears you in two. If there's any small rip in *your* fabric already.
I don't under-stand.
For many of these people you see, they **split** but their other half **died**. No hope of being **whole** again. But you, you didn't split!
Split?
Go, Twain. Go back up.

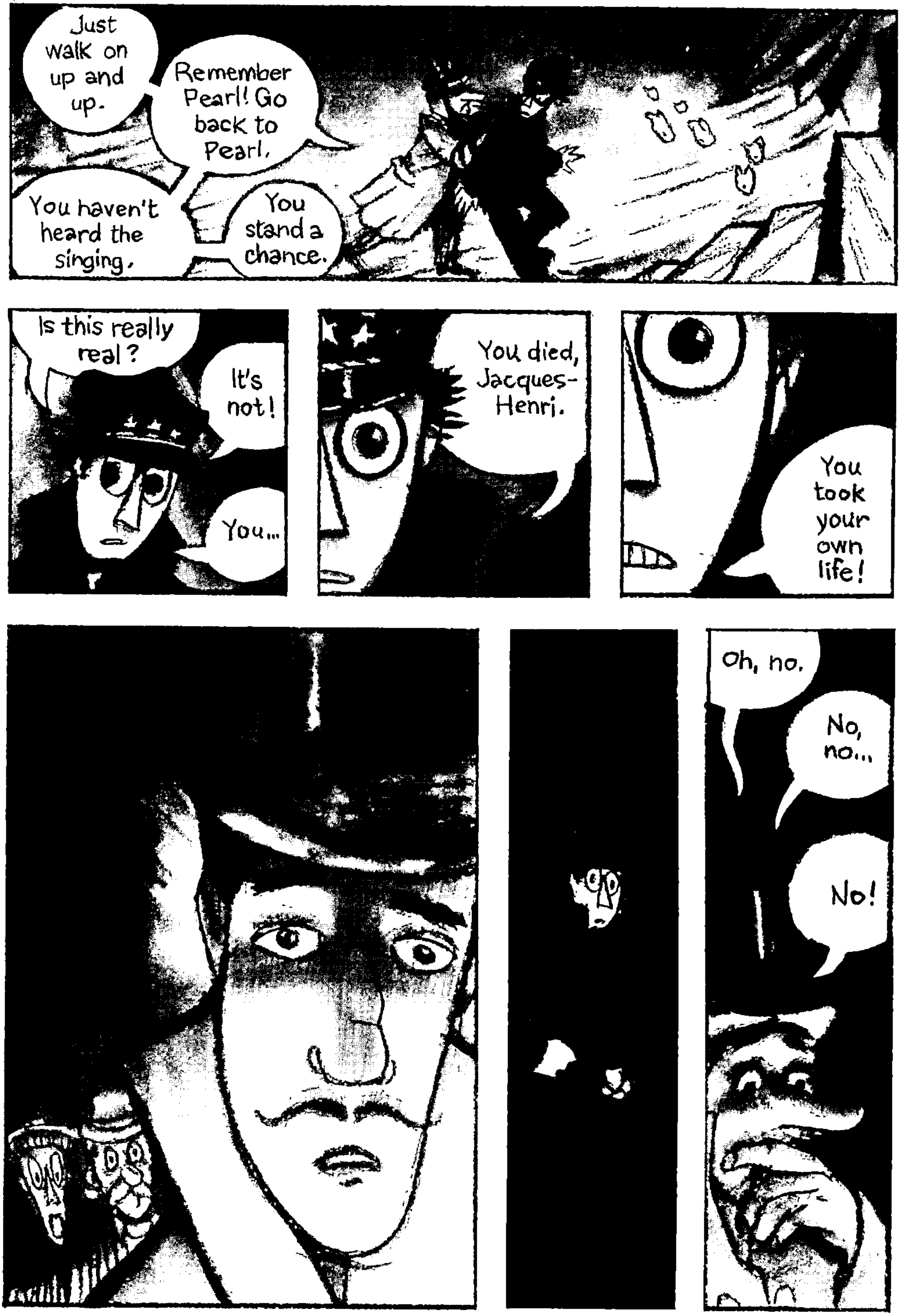

Just walk on up and up.
Remember Pearl! Go back to Pearl.
You haven't heard the singing.
You stand a chance.
Is this really real?
It's not!
You...
You died, Jacques-Henri.
You took your own life!
Oh, no.
No, no...
No!

So three's a charm. I did it this time.

"This time"...?

I killed myself! No rescue.

You had tried before?

Hm? The first time I was young. After that, my father wanted to save me from myself, and sent me to America.

"A cure of hard work," he said. It helped for a while.

The second time, that was when I thought Ella left.

Ella?

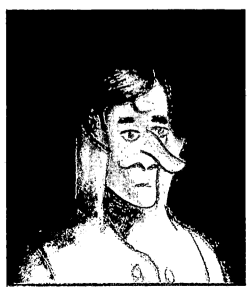

I never did tell you the whole story about Ella, did I?

Back then?

Up above?

Pt III, Chap.3

"A LADY BEGUILED"

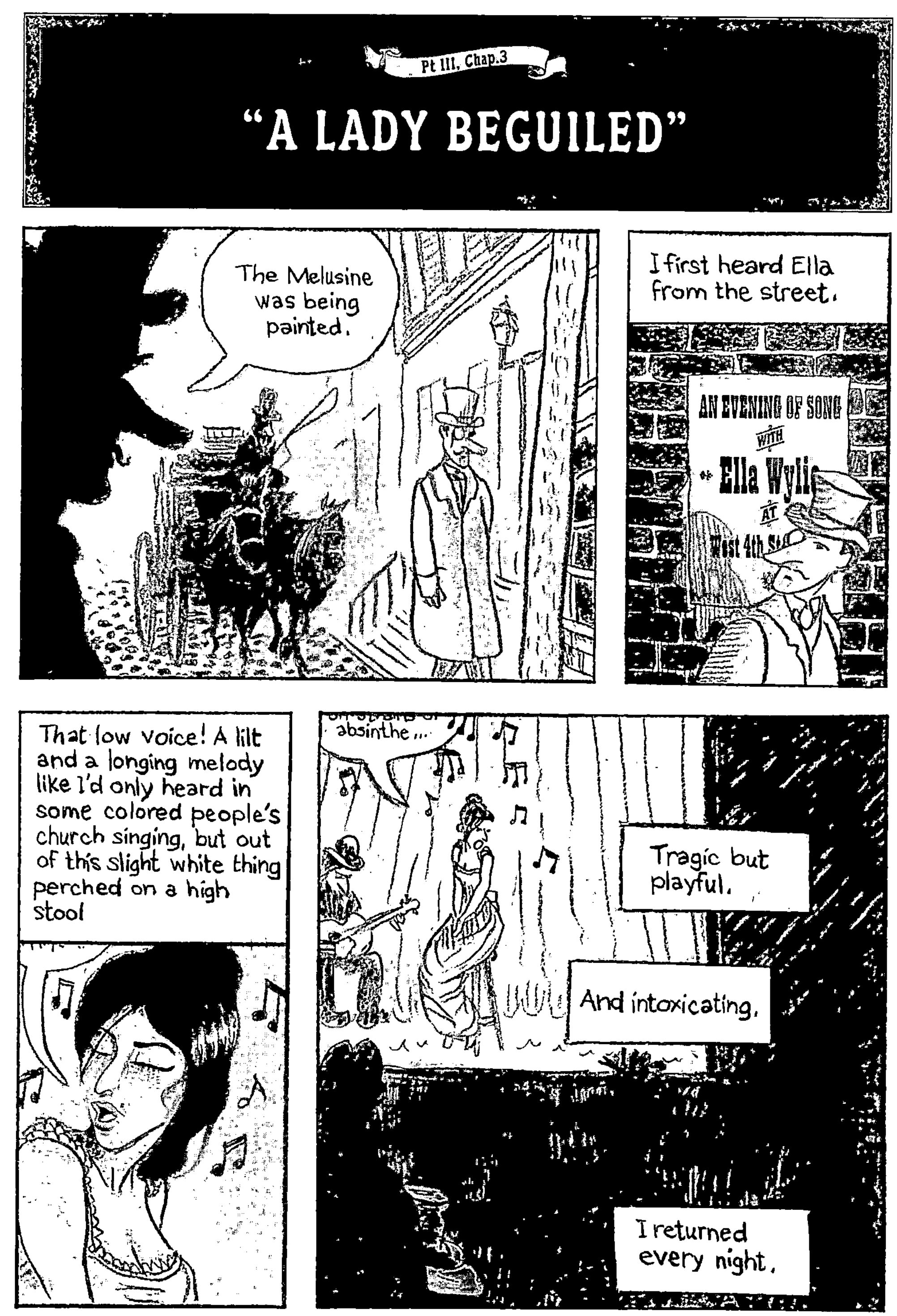
The Melusine was being painted.
I first heard Ella from the street.
AN EVENING OF SONG
WITH
Ella Wyli
AT
West 4th S
That low voice! A lilt and a longing melody like I'd only heard in some colored people's church singing, but out of this slight white thing perched on a high stool
absinthe,,,
Tragic but playful.
And intoxicating.
I returned every night.

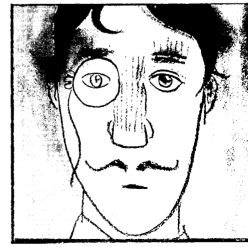

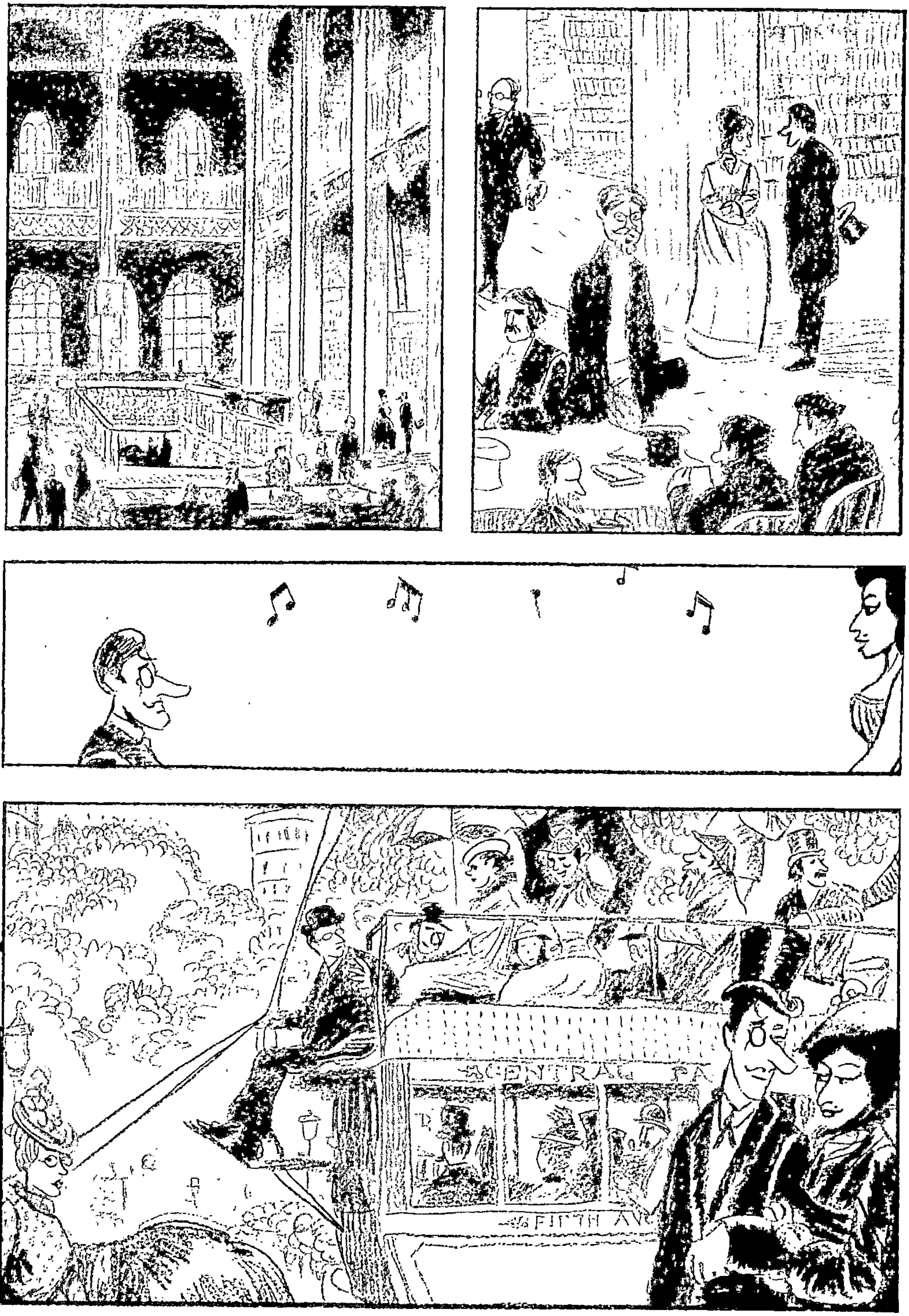
CENTRAL PA
FIFTH AV

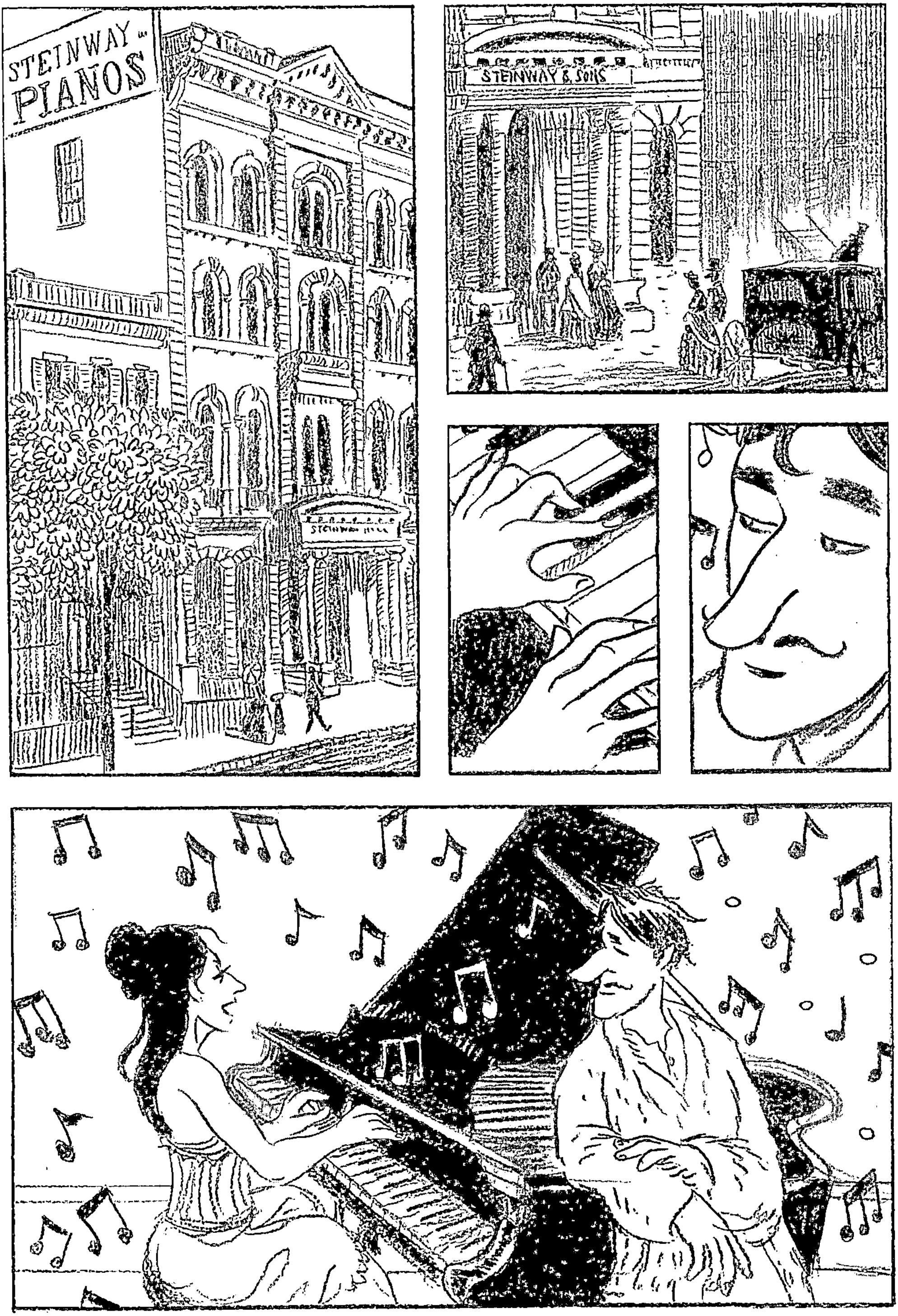
STEINWAY PIANOS
STEINWAY & SONS

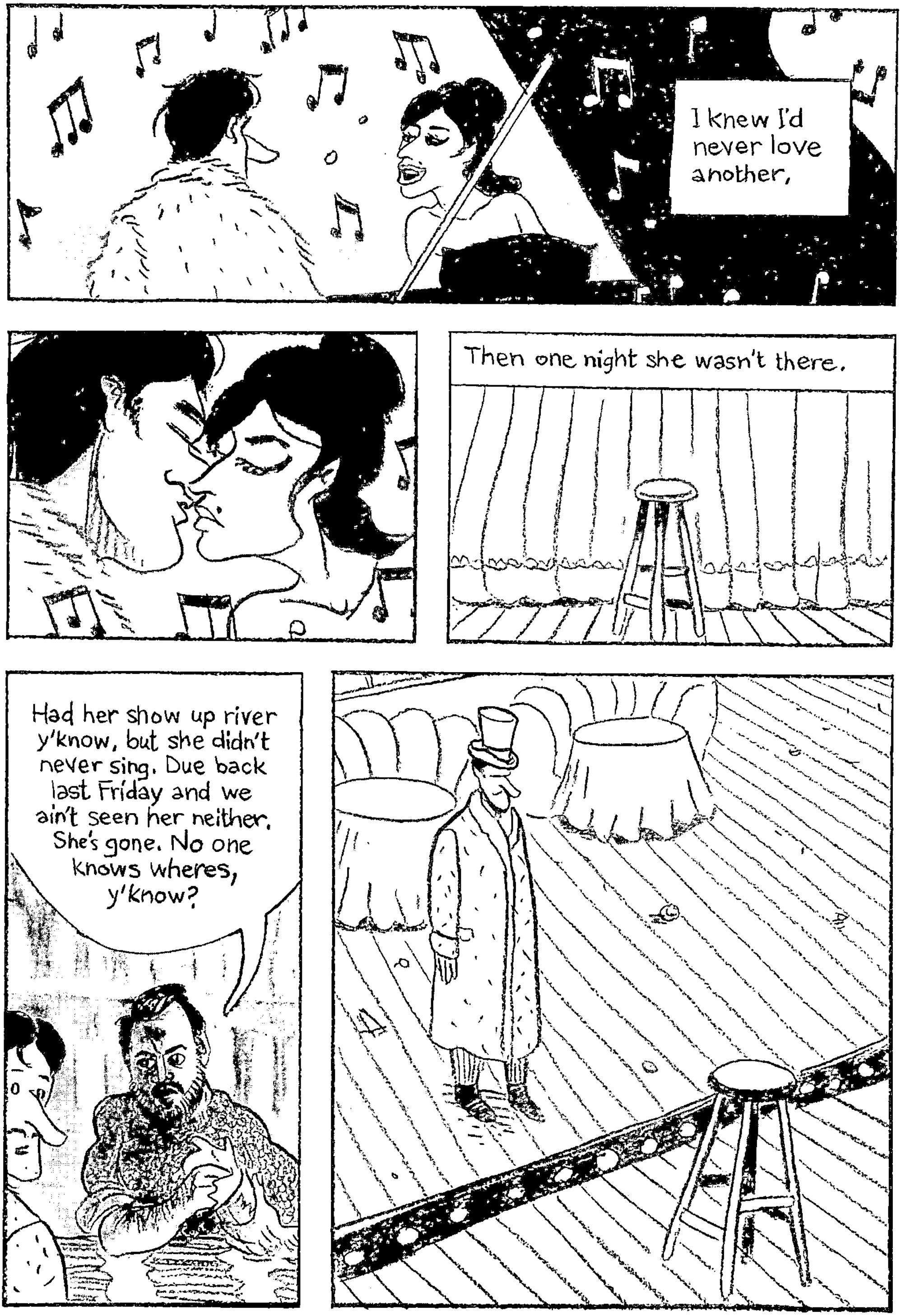
I knew I'd never love another,
Then one night she wasn't there.
Had her show up river y'know, but she didn't never sing. Due back last Friday and we ain't seen her neither. She's gone. No one knows wheres, y'know?

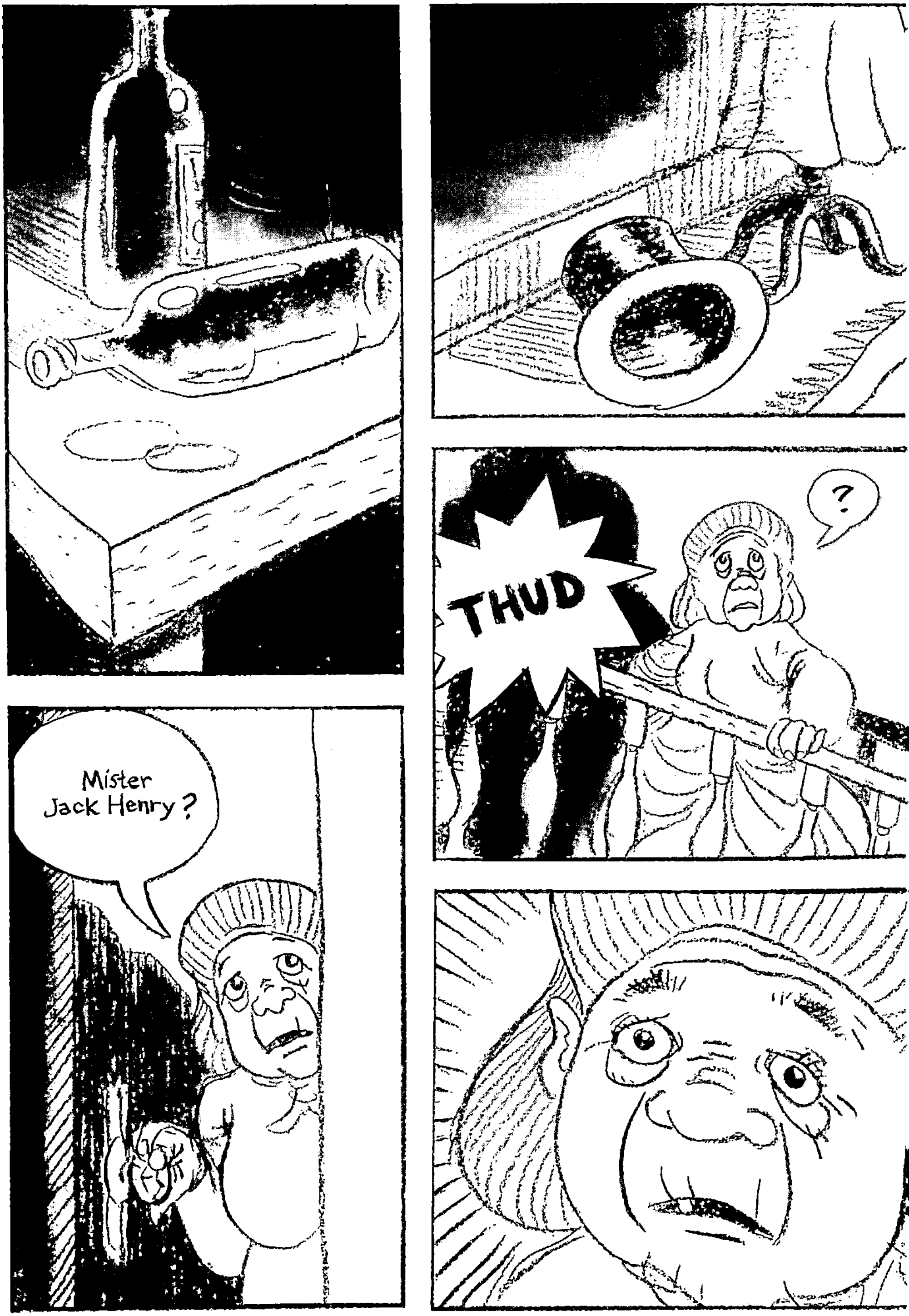
THUD
?
Mister Jack Henry?

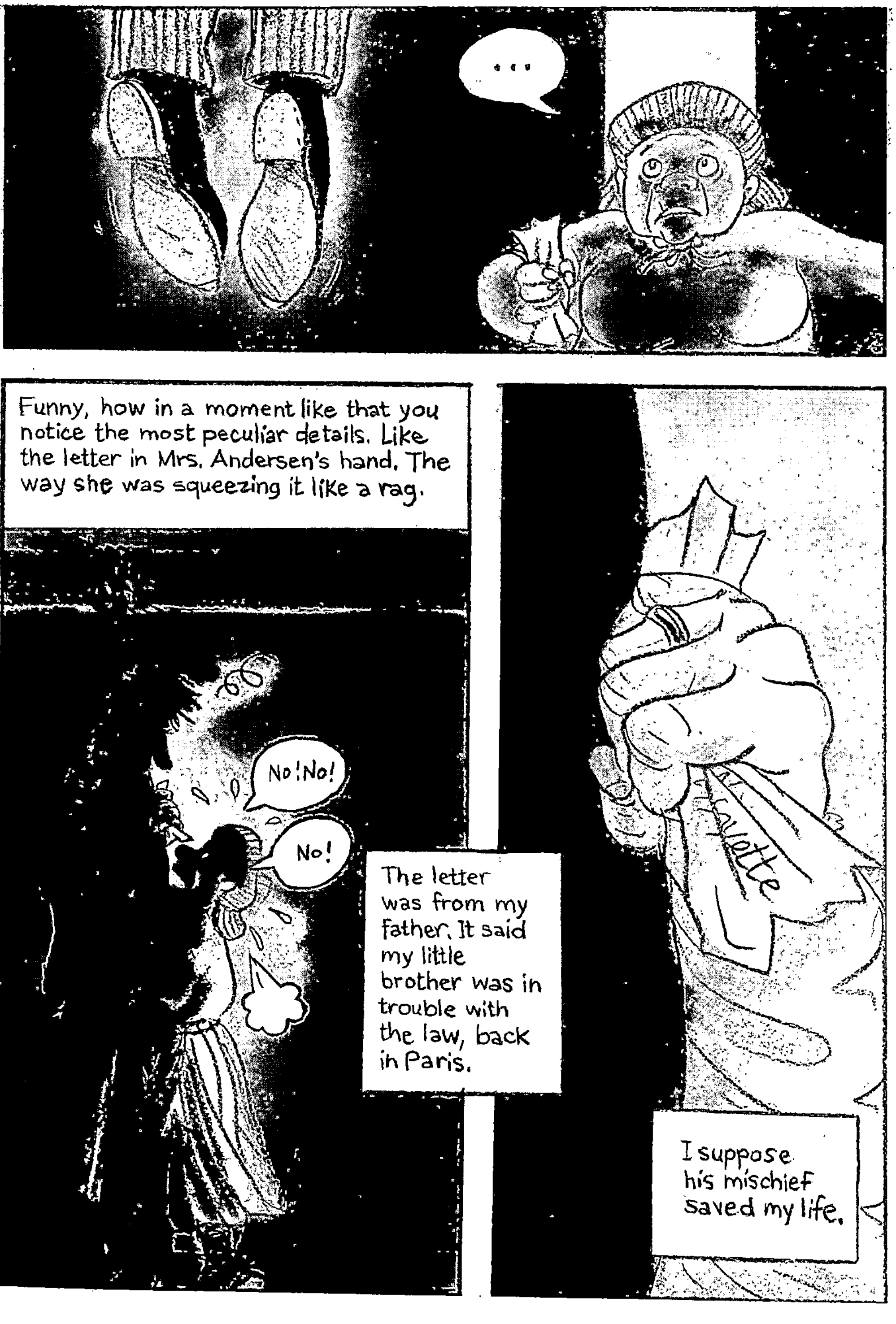
...
Funny, how in a moment like that you notice the most peculiar details. Like the letter in Mrs. Andersen's hand. The way she was squeezing it like a rag.
No! No!
No!
The letter was from my father. It said my little brother was in trouble with the law, back in Paris.
I suppose his mischief saved my life.

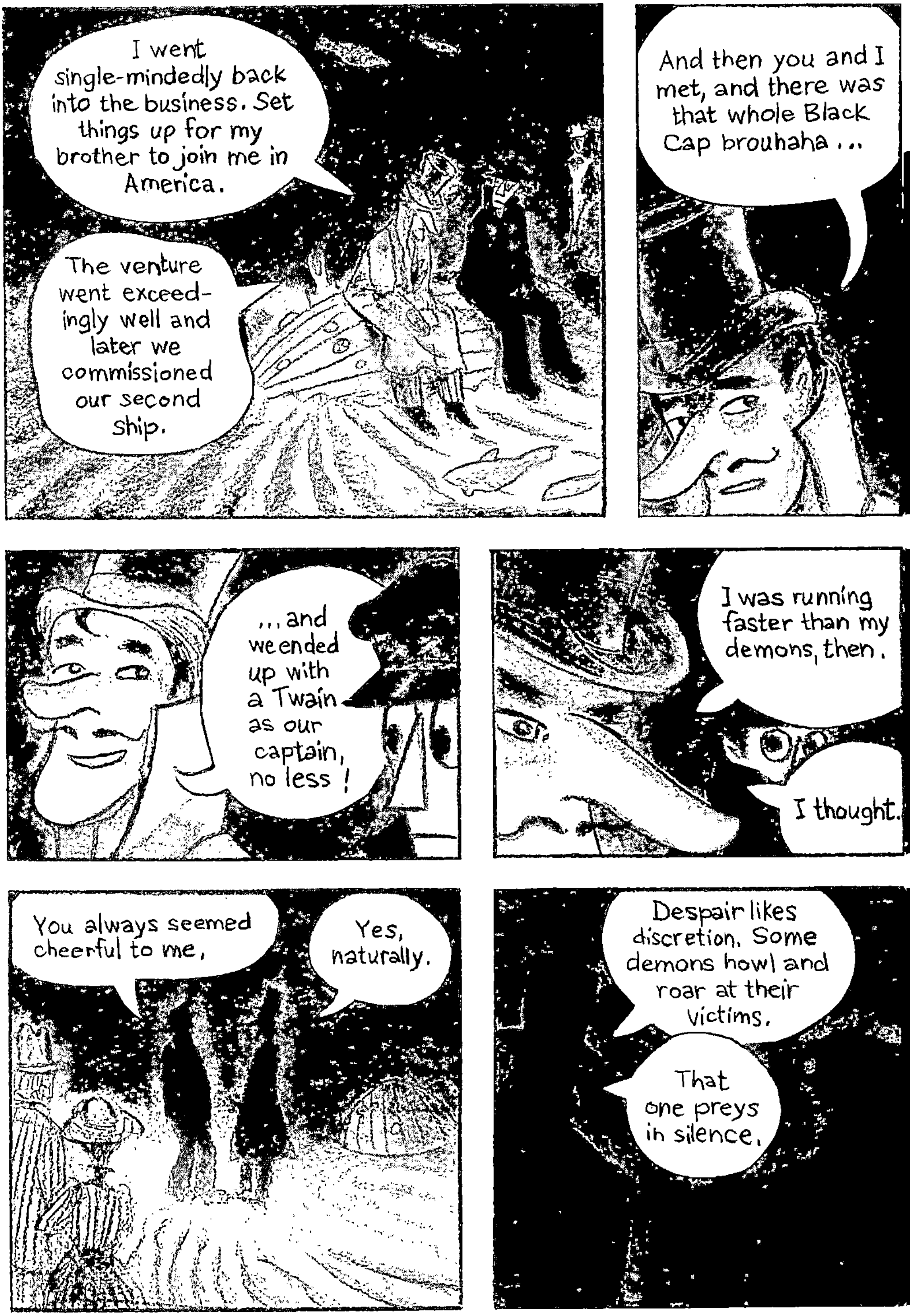
I went single-mindedly back into the business. Set things up for my brother to join me in America.
The venture went exceedingly well and later we commissioned our second ship.
And then you and I met, and there was that whole Black Cap brouhaha ...
... and we ended up with a Twain as our captain, no less!
I was running faster than my demons, then.
I thought.
You always seemed cheerful to me,
Yes, naturally.
Despair likes discretion. Some demons howl and roar at their victims.
That one preys in silence.

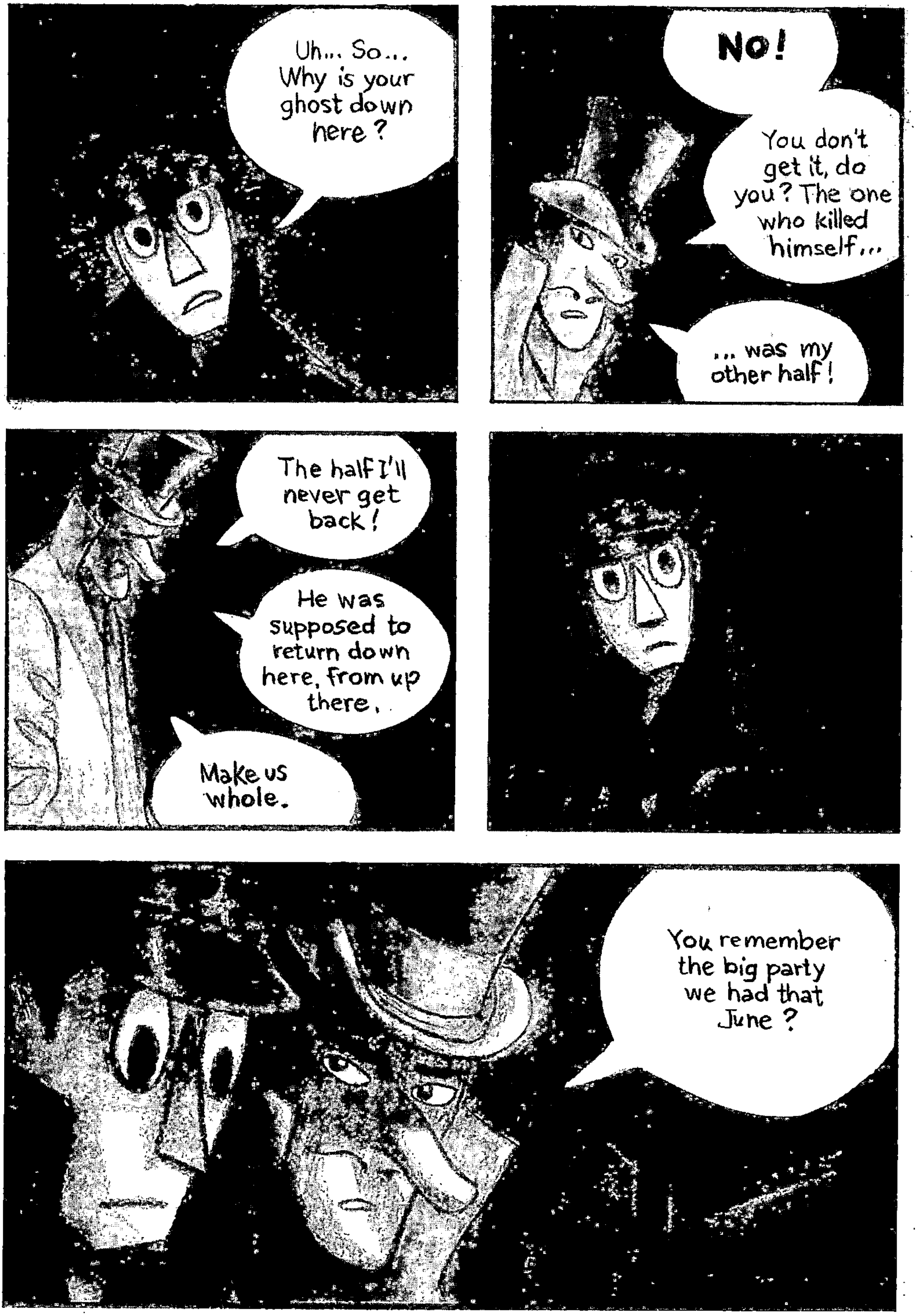

Uh... So... Why is your ghost down here?
NO!
You don't get it, do you? The one who killed himself...
... was my other half!
The half I'll never get back!
He was supposed to return down here, from up there.
Make us whole.
You remember the big party we had that June?

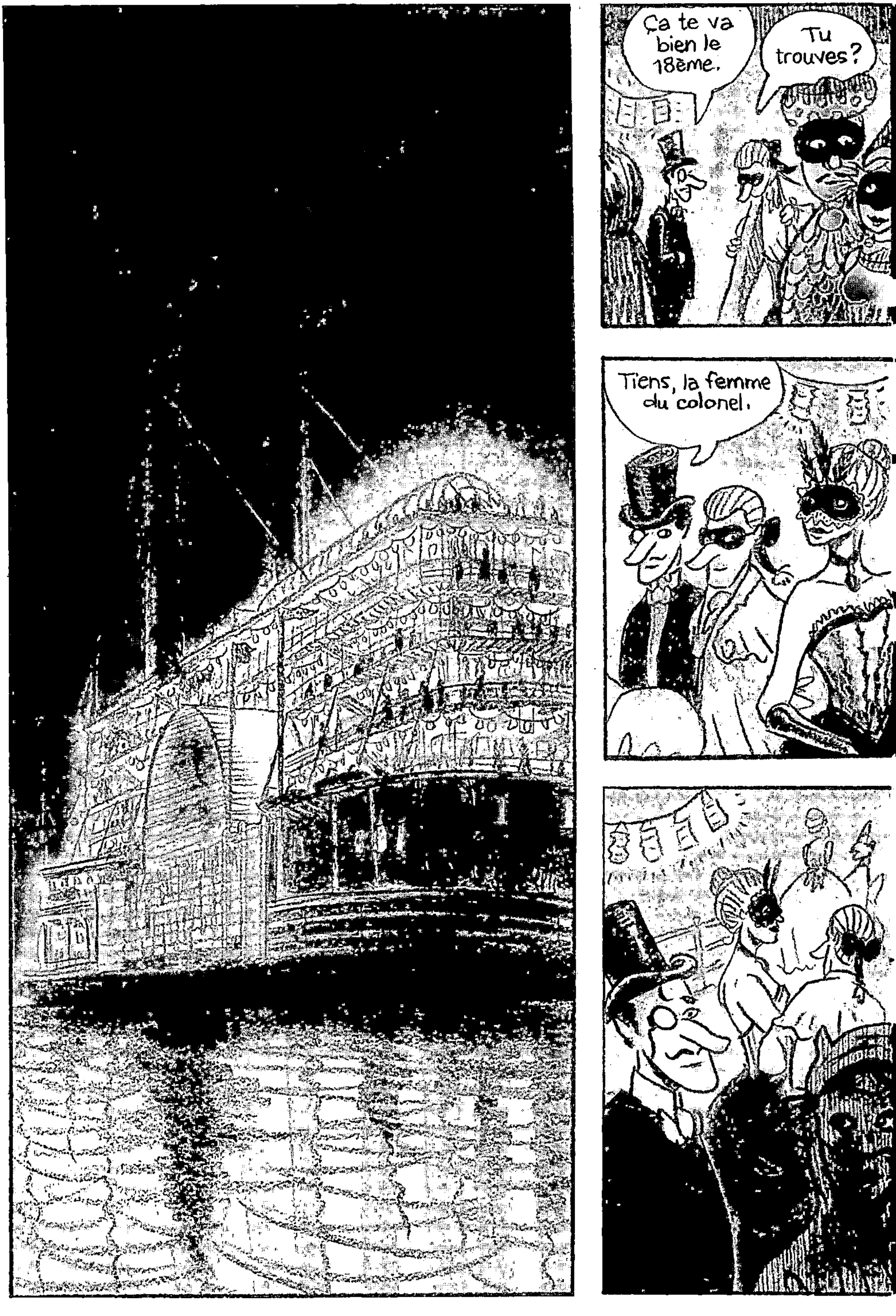
Ça te va bien le 18ème.
Tu trouves?
Tiens, la femme du colonel.

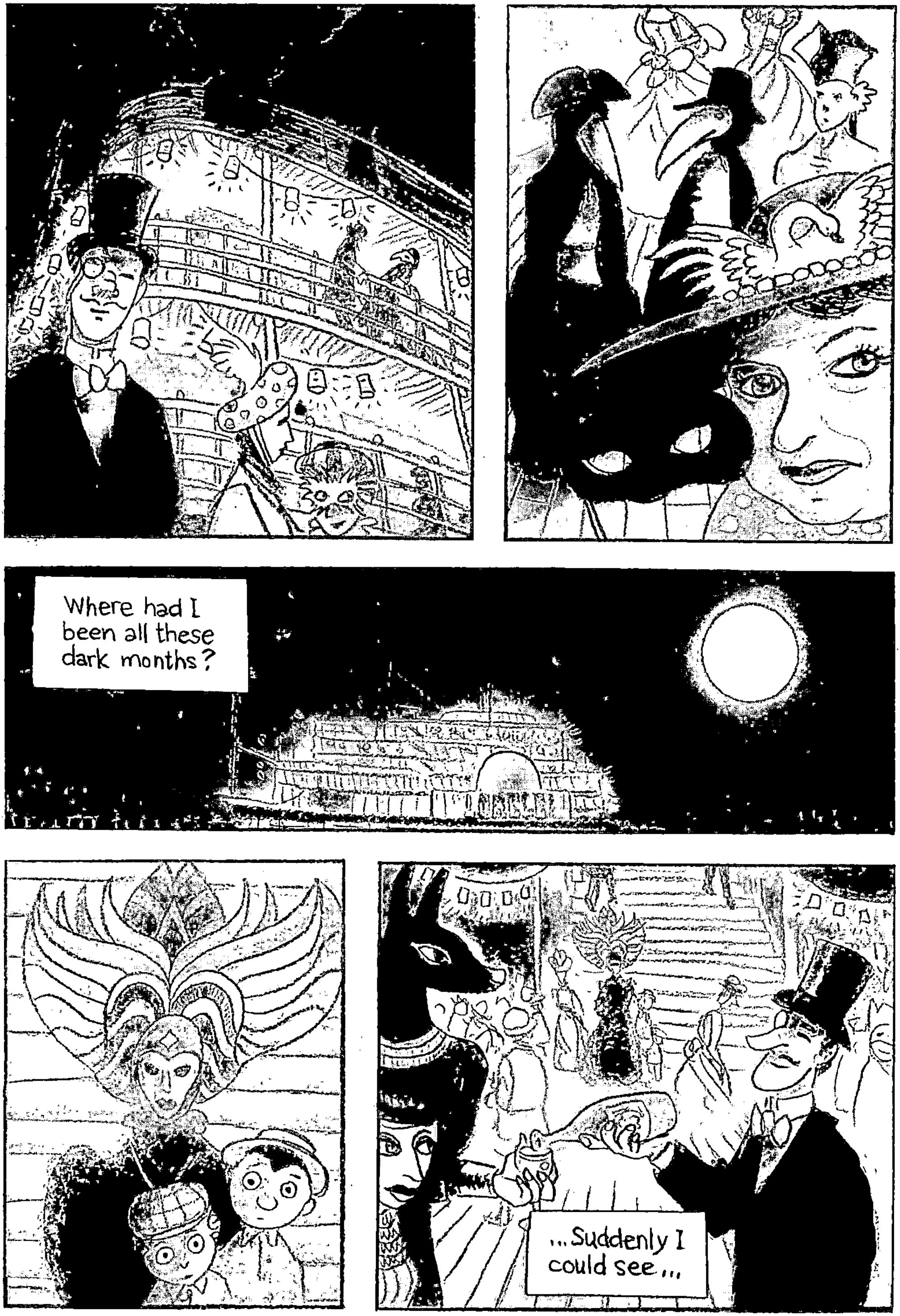
Where had I been all these dark months?
...Suddenly I could see...

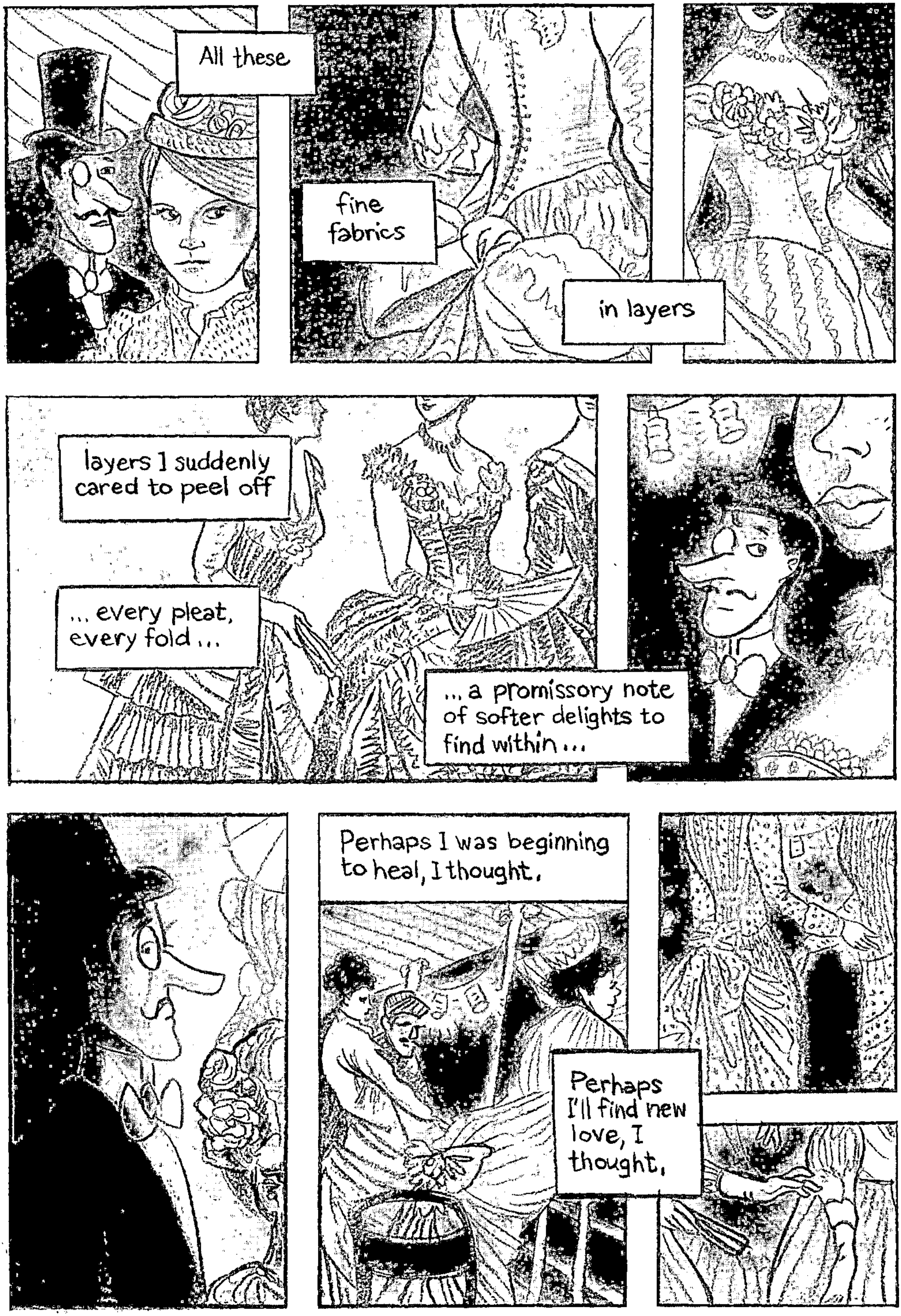
All these
fine fabrics
in layers
layers I suddenly cared to peel off
... every pleat, every fold ...
... a promissory note of softer delights to find within ...
Perhaps I was beginning to heal, I thought.
Perhaps I'll find new love, I thought.

Then suddenly . . .

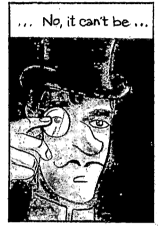

. . . No, it can't be . . .

. . . Can it . . . ?

Ah! Jacques-Henri, have you met—

SHE'S HERE!

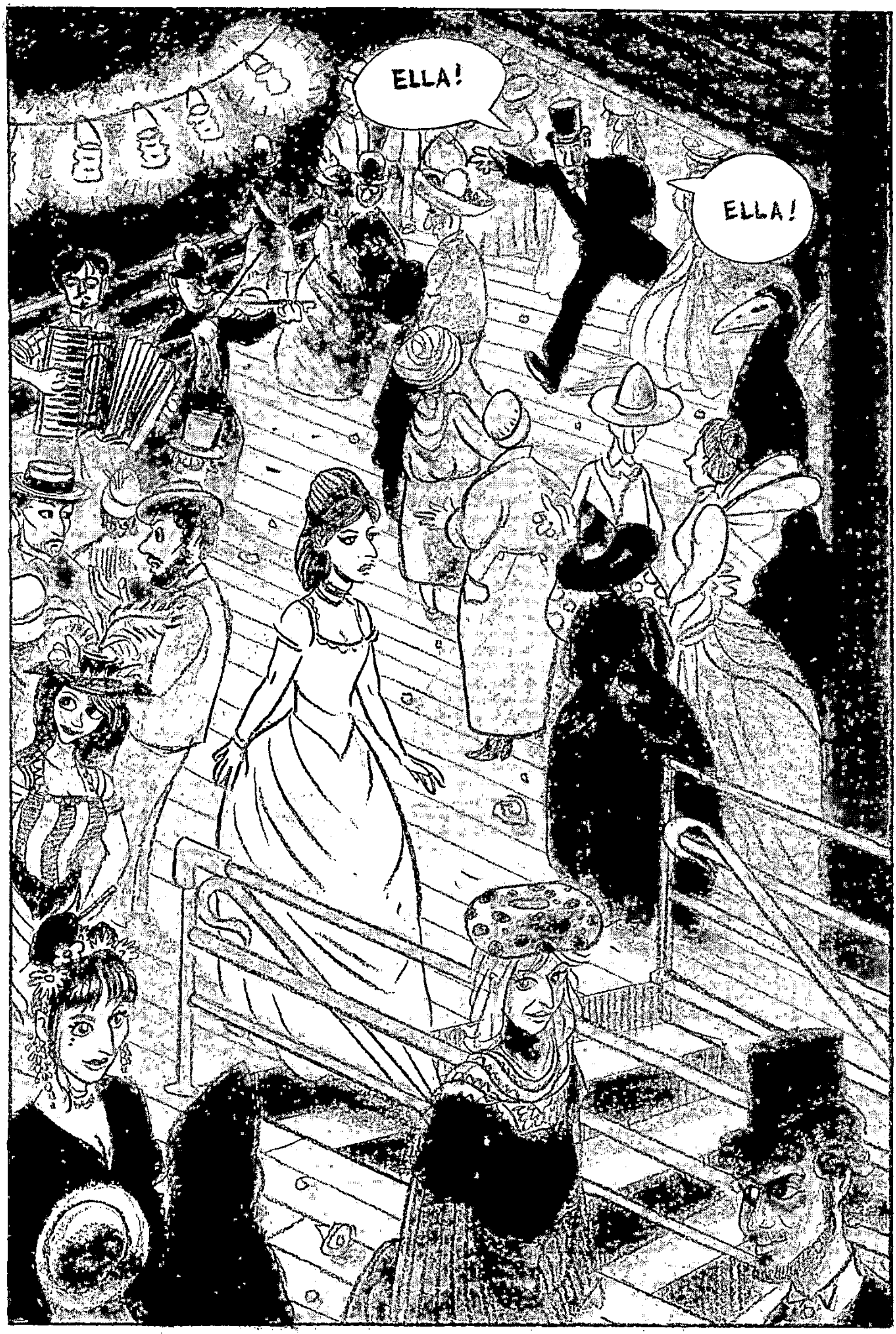
ELLA!
ELLA!

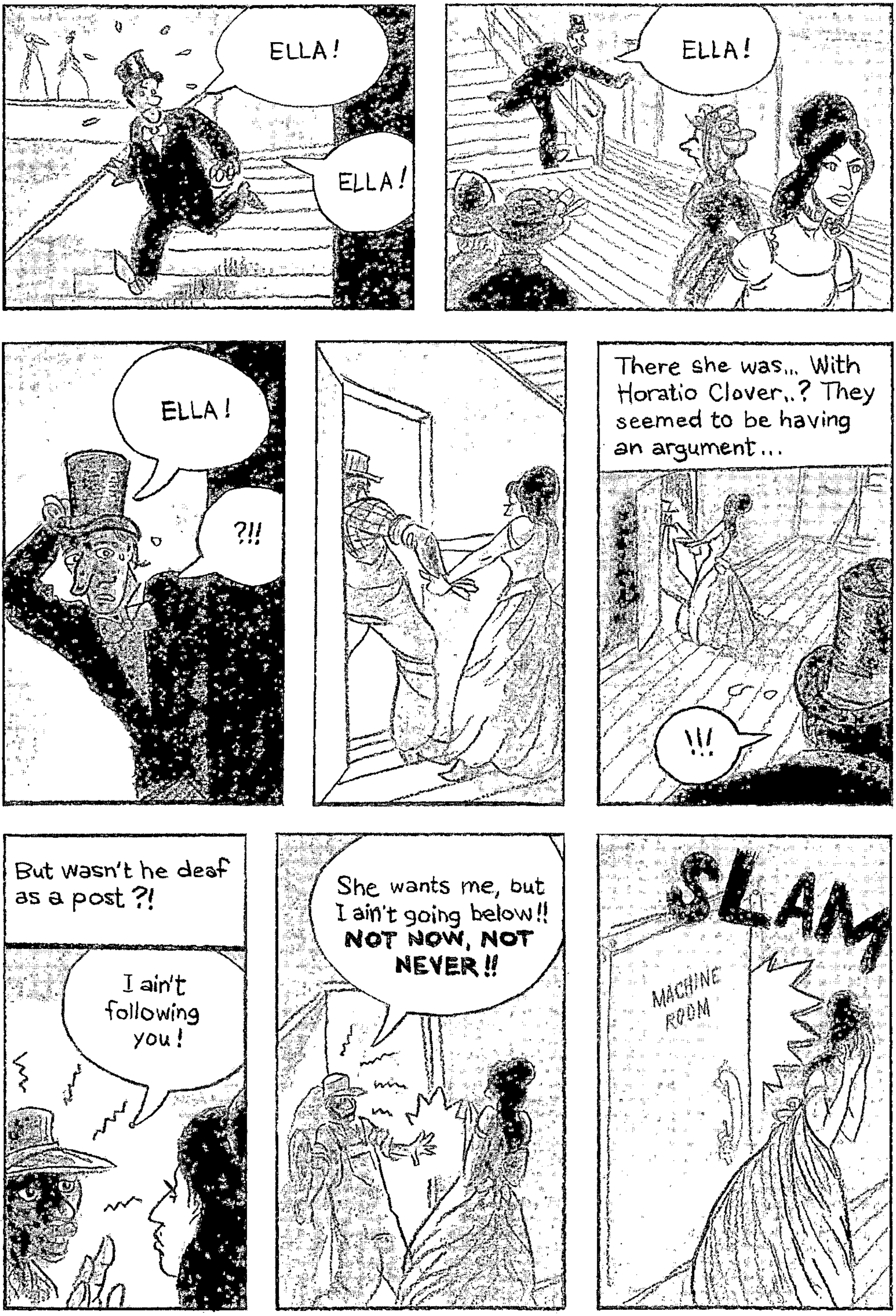
ELLA!
ELLA!
ELLA!
ELLA!
?!!
There she was... With Horatio Clover..? They seemed to be having an argument...
!!!
But wasn't he deaf as a post?!
I ain't following you!
She wants me, but I ain't going below!! NOT NOW, NOT NEVER!!
SLAM
MACHINE ROOM

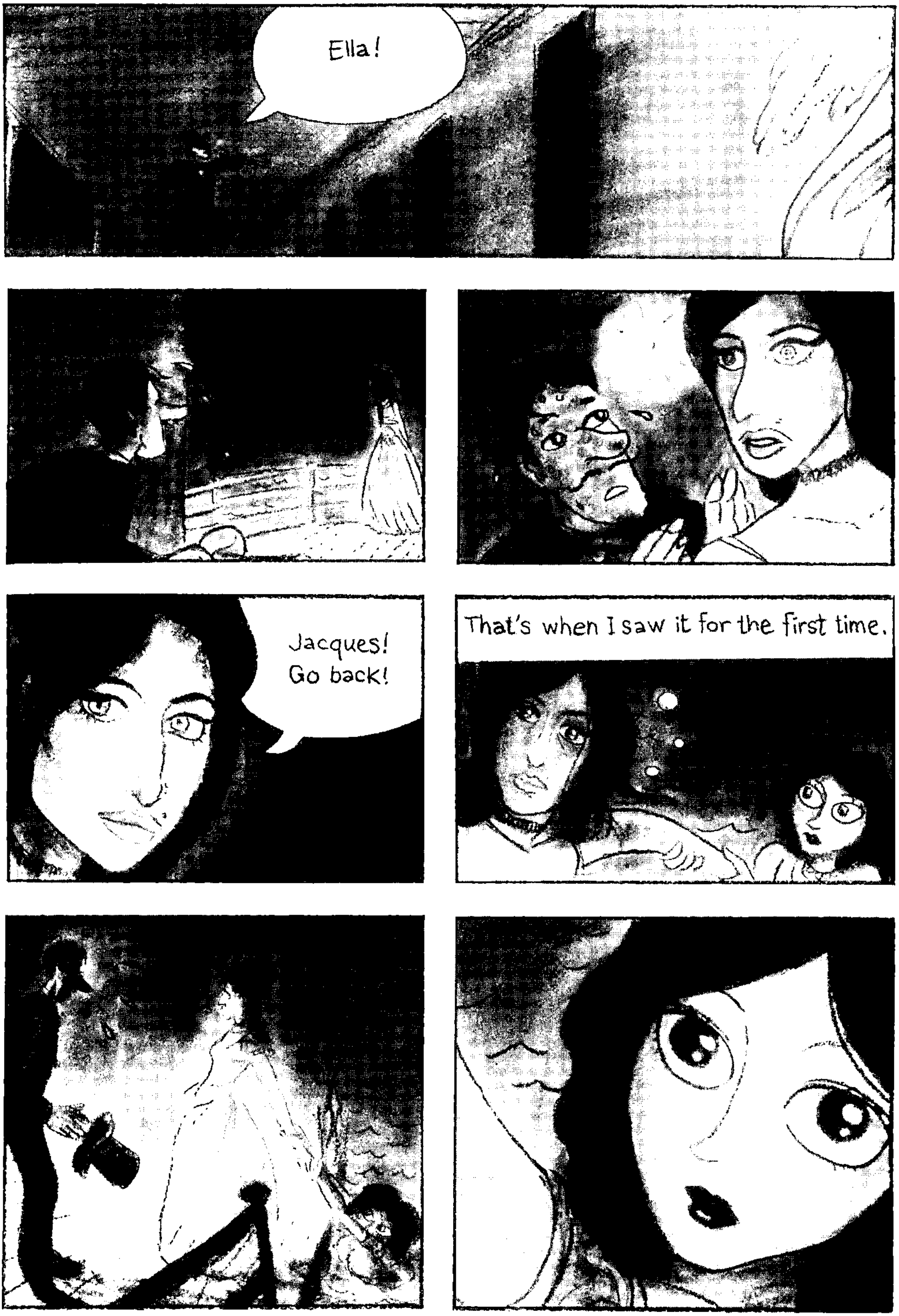
Ella!
Jacques! Go back!
That's when I saw it for the first time.

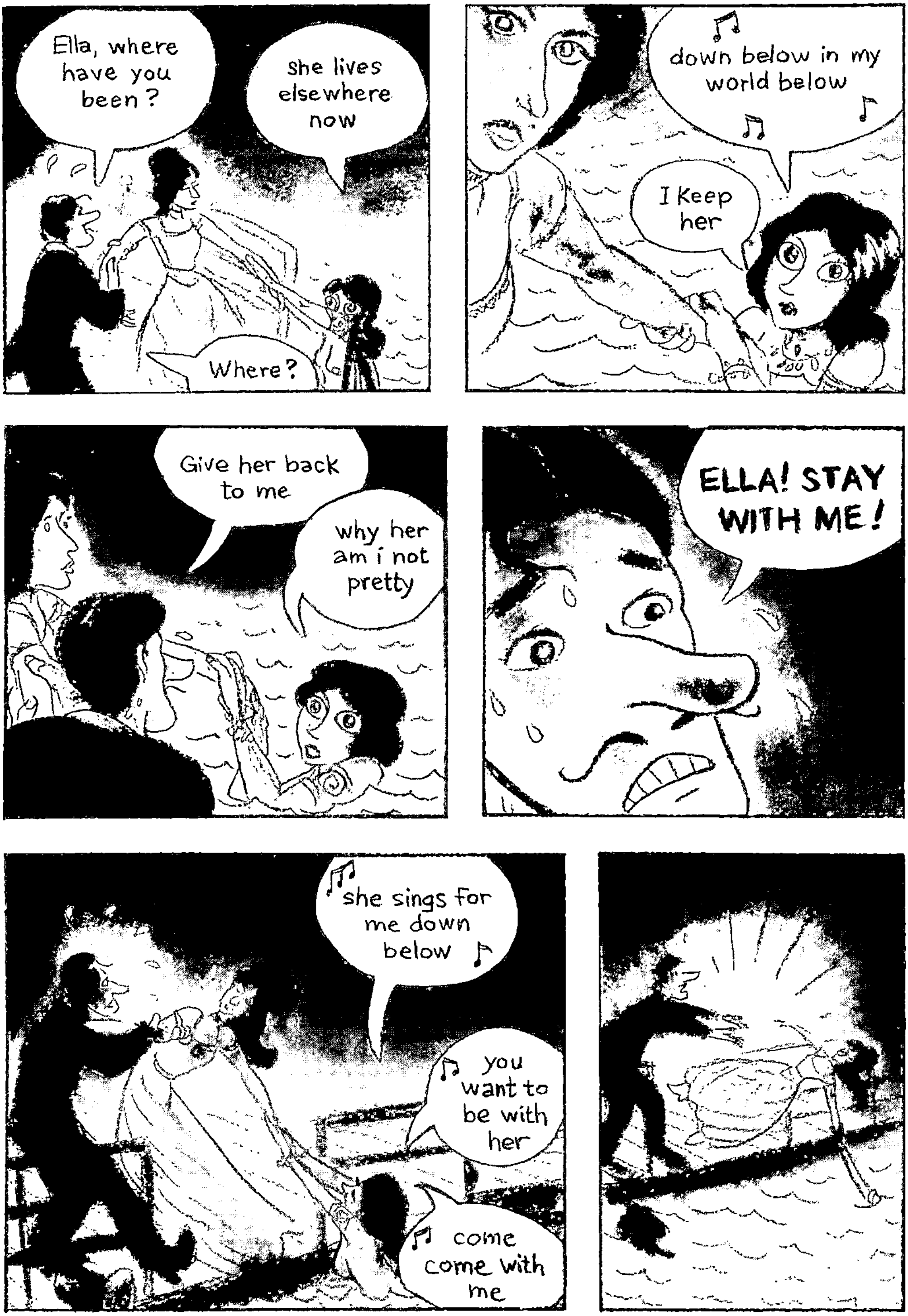
Ella, where have you been?
She lives elsewhere now
Where?
down below in my world below
I Keep her
Give her back to me
why her am i not pretty
ELLA! STAY WITH ME!
she sings for me down below
you want to be with her
come come with me

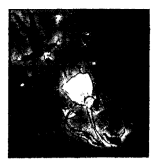

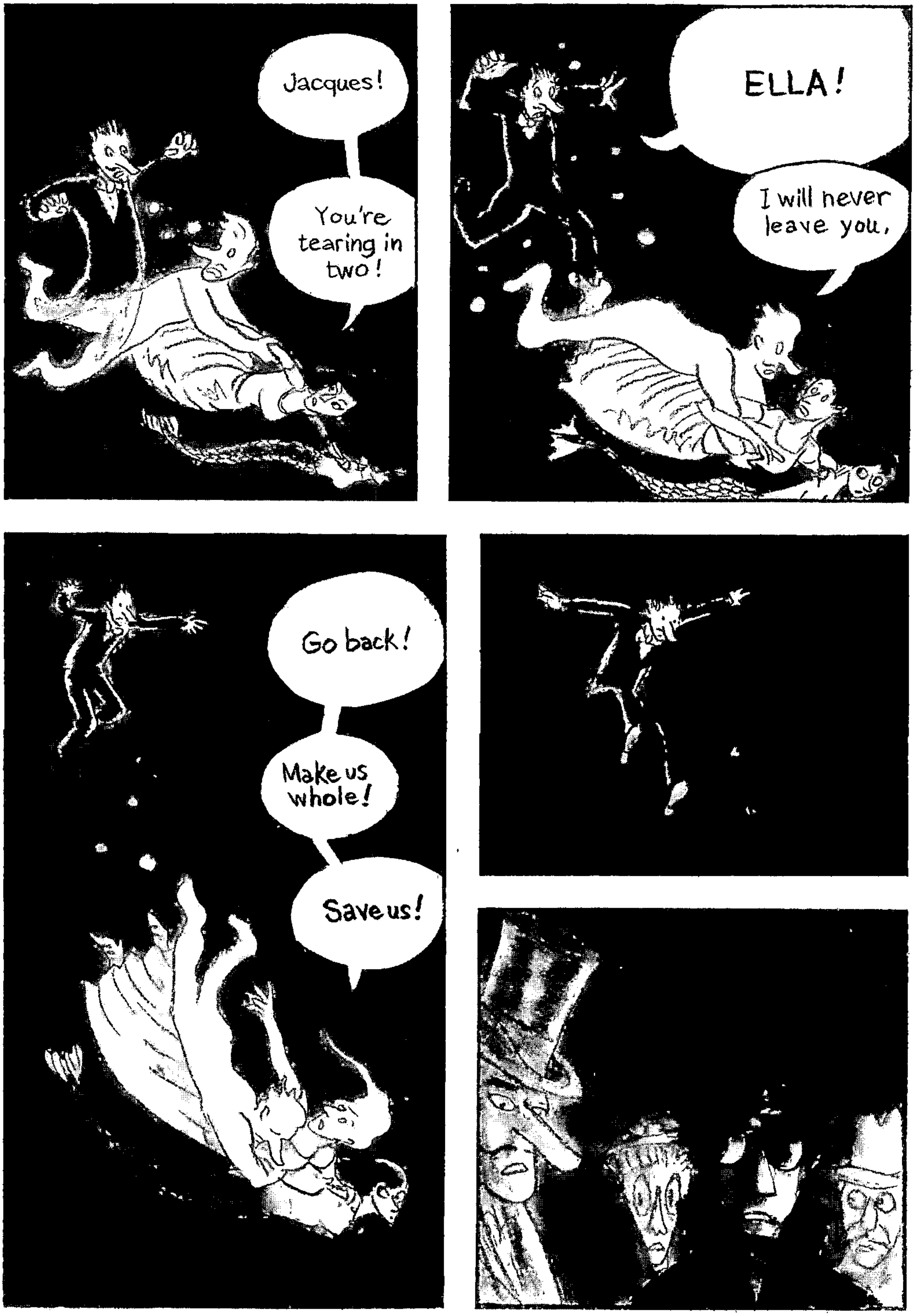
Jacques!
You're tearing in two!
ELLA!
I will never leave you,
Go back!
Make us whole!
Save us!

Months passed.

My other half must have tried to find a cure, tried to reunify us and found that he couldn't.

He must have thought all was lost. My demons caught up to him.

No one is coming for Ella and me.

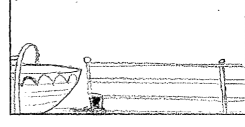

He went and killed himself?

What do you mean you tore in two?! Tore how?

It's when she sings to you. She traps a part of you here.

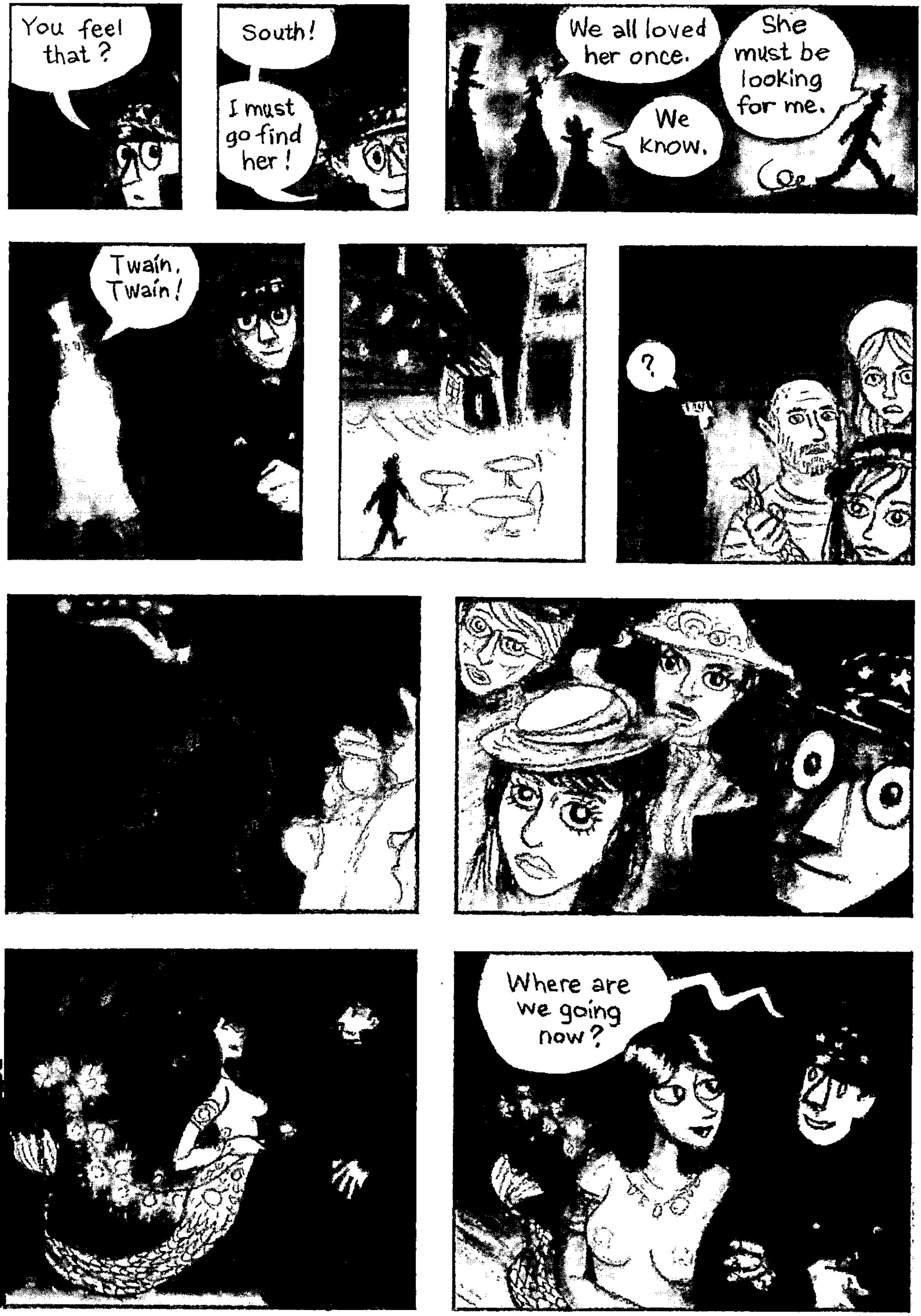
You feel that?
South!
I must go find her!
We all loved her once.
We know.
She must be looking for me.
Twain, Twain!
?
Where are we going now?

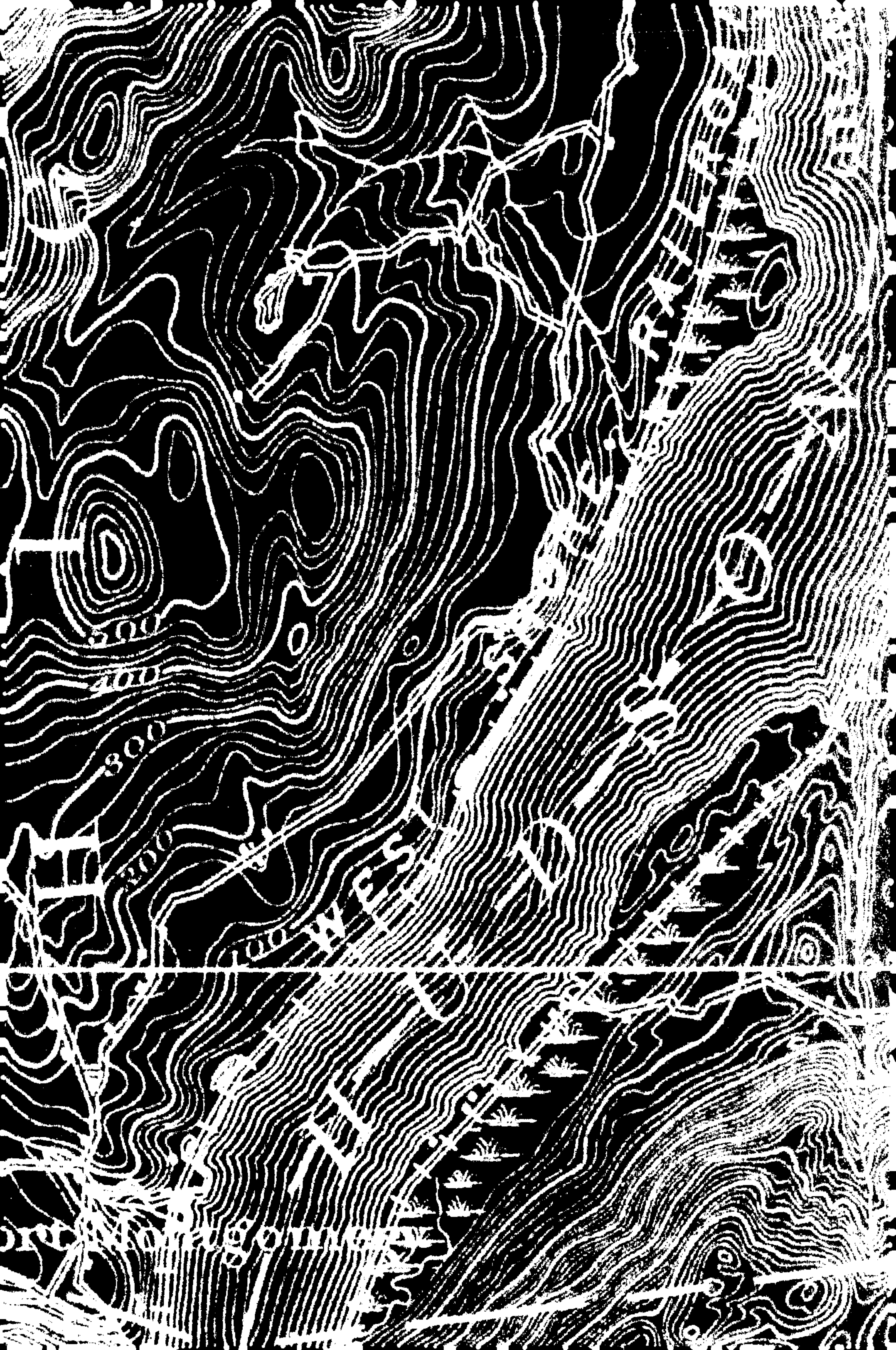
400
300
200
100

Pt III, Chap.4

"THE CHAINED HEART"

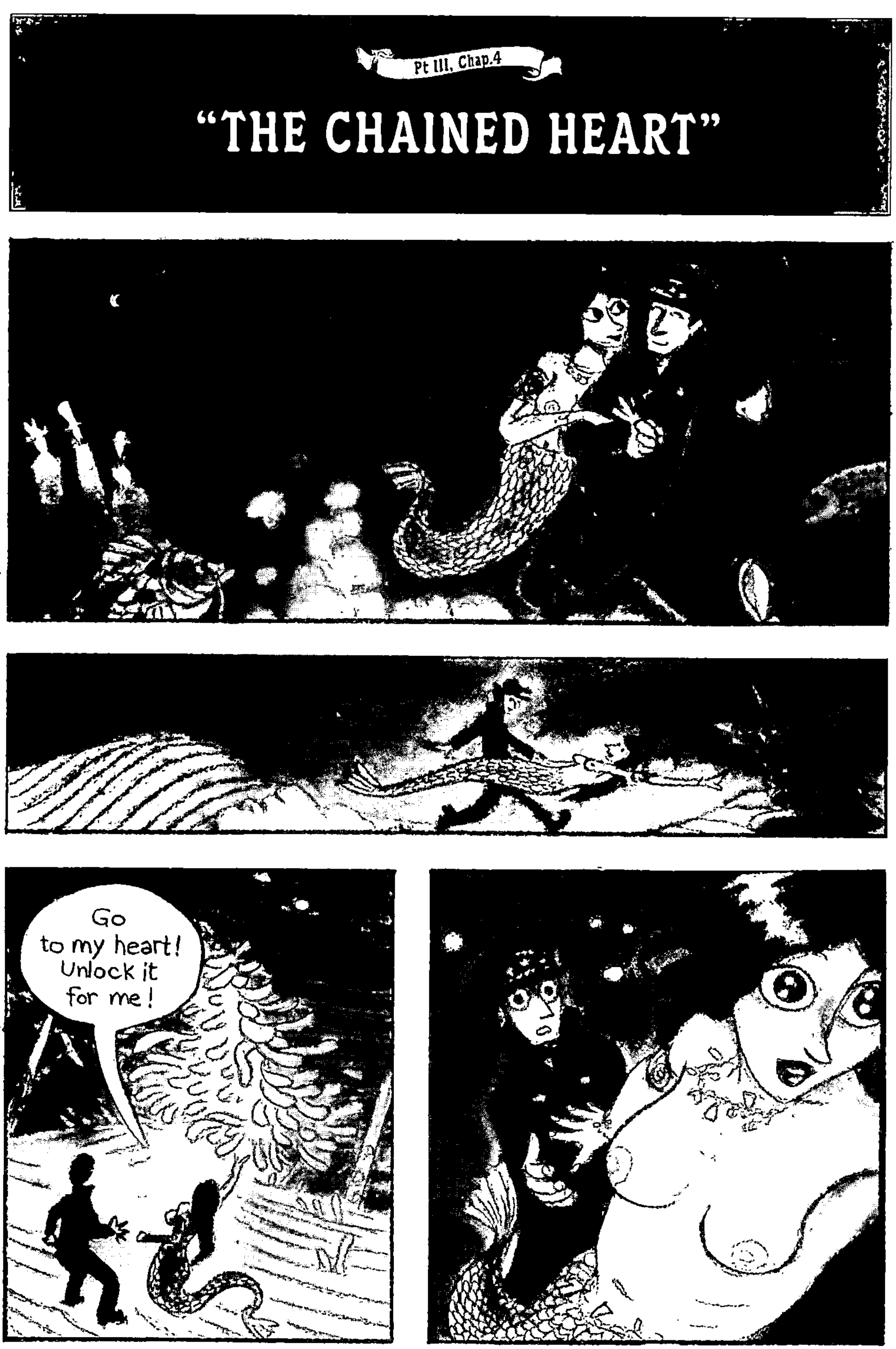
Go to my heart! Unlock it for me!

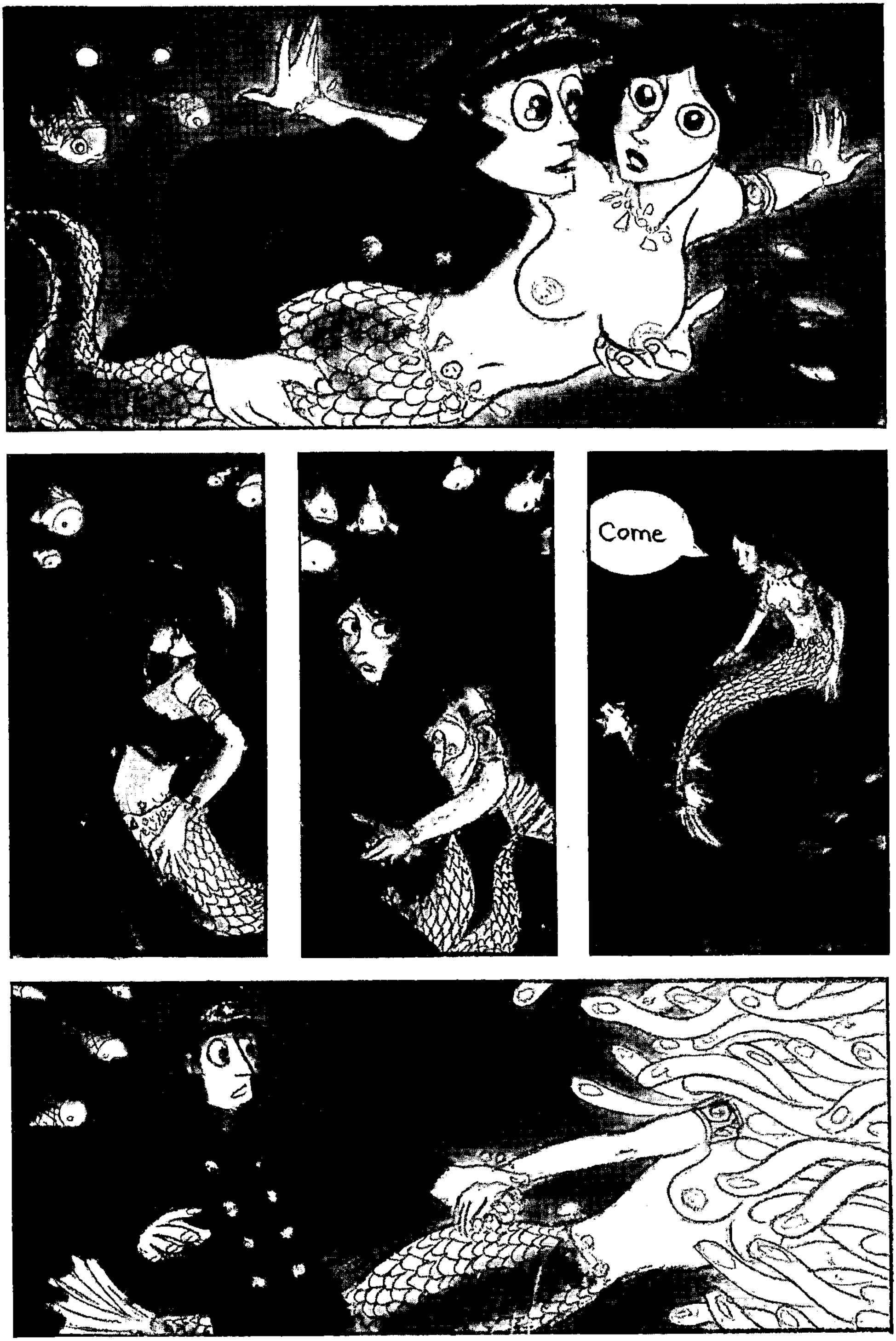
Come

I've waited so long.

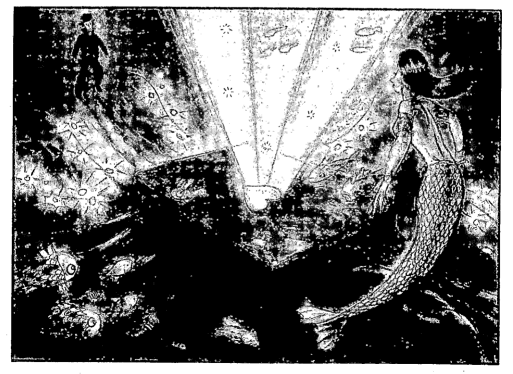

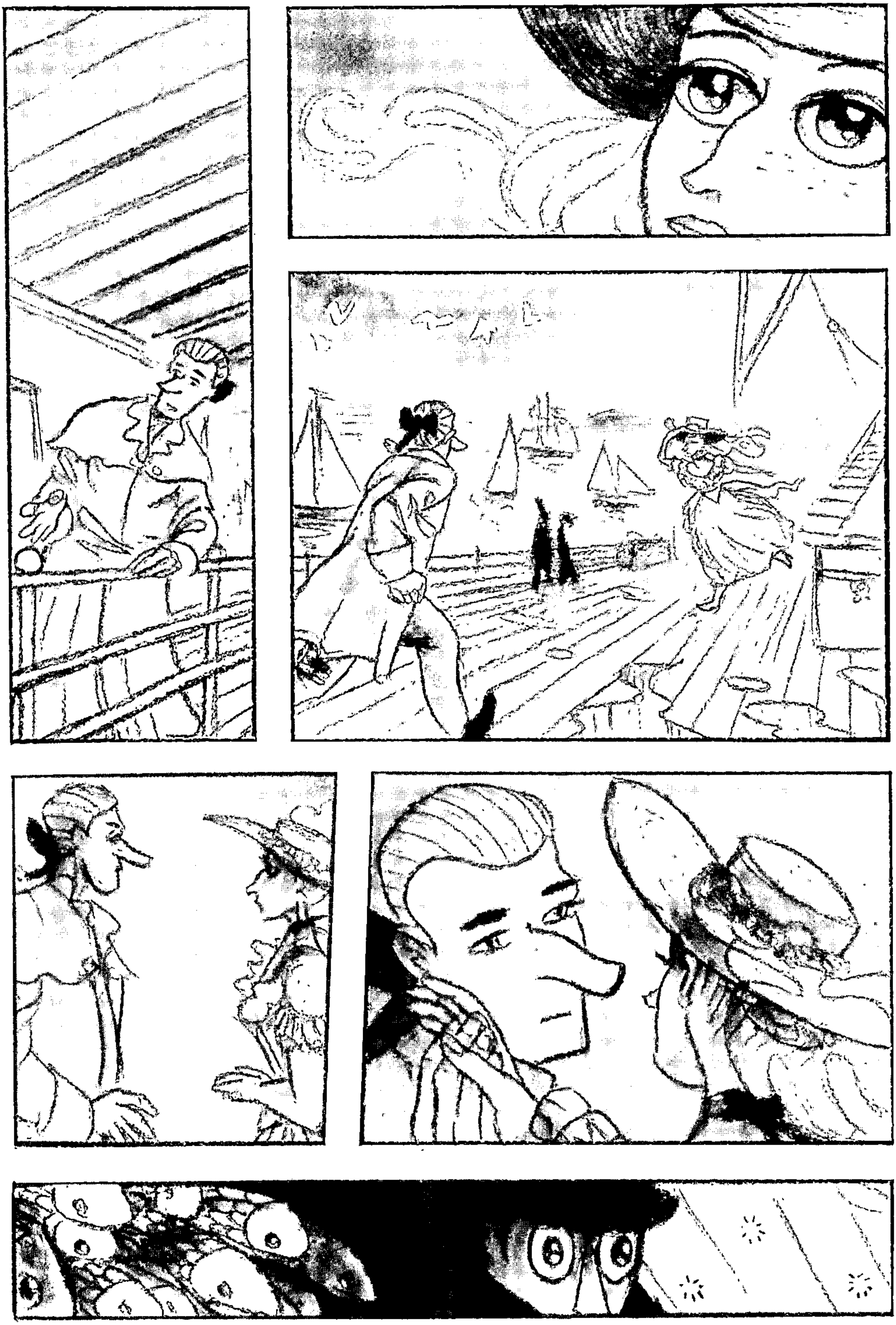

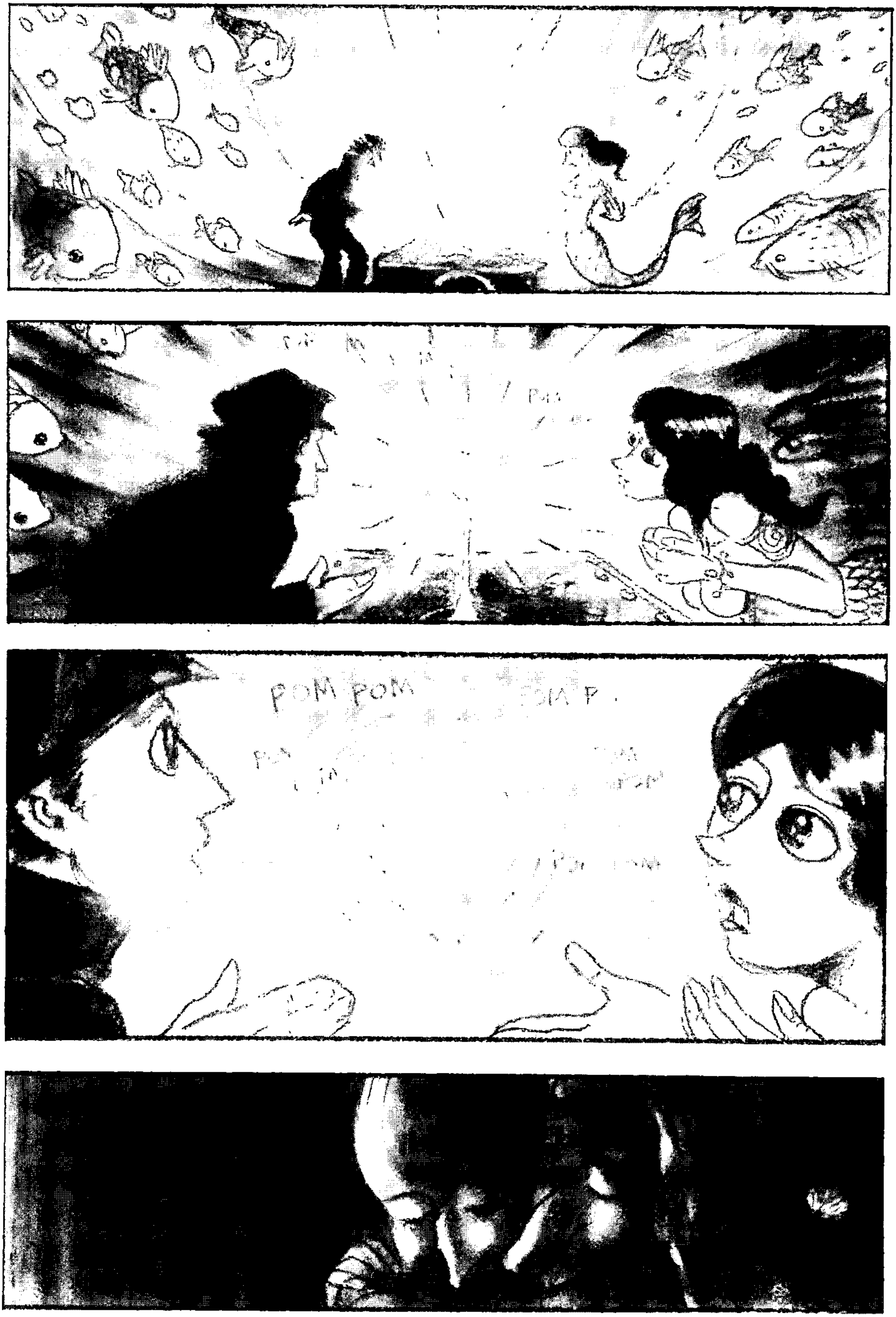
POM POM

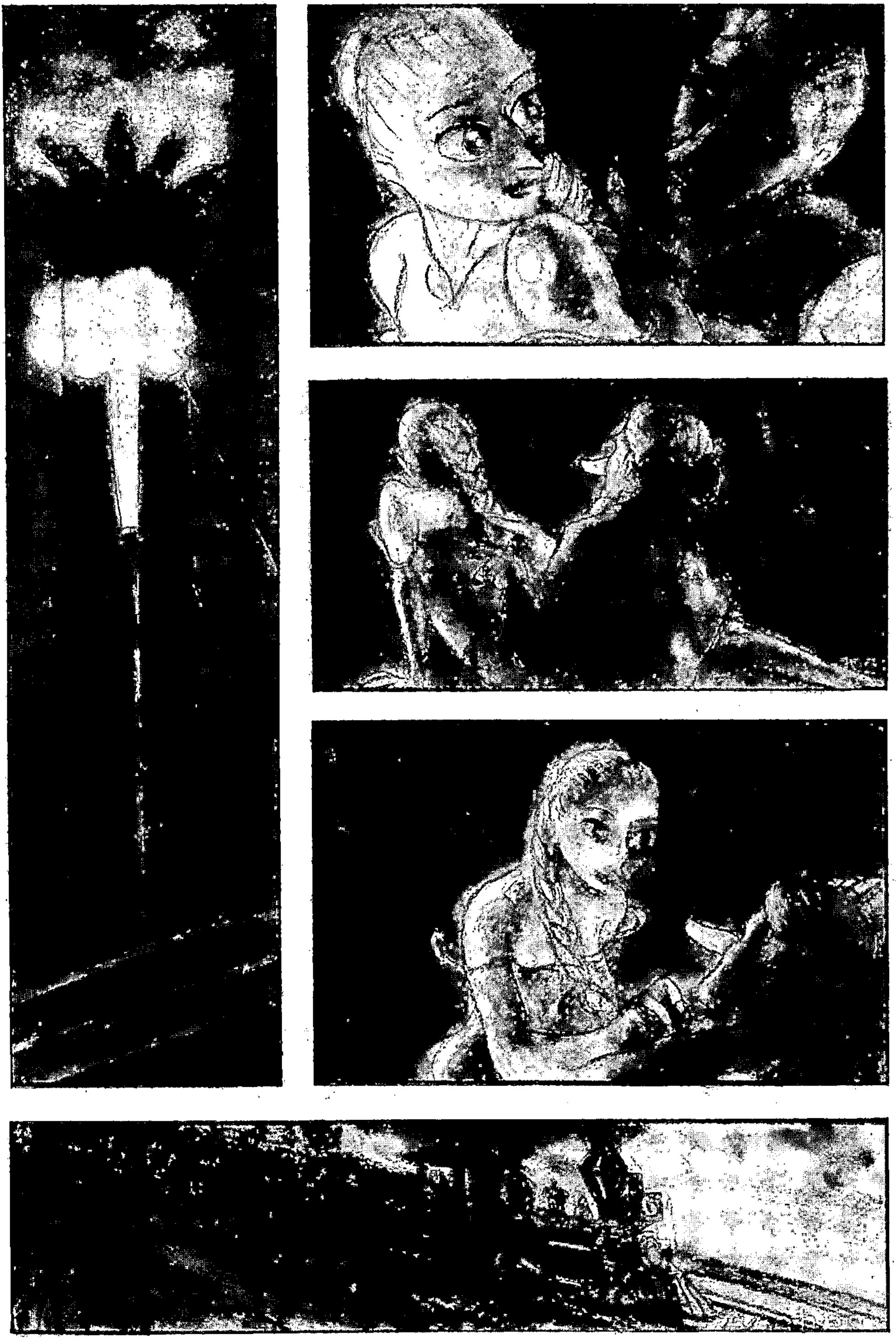

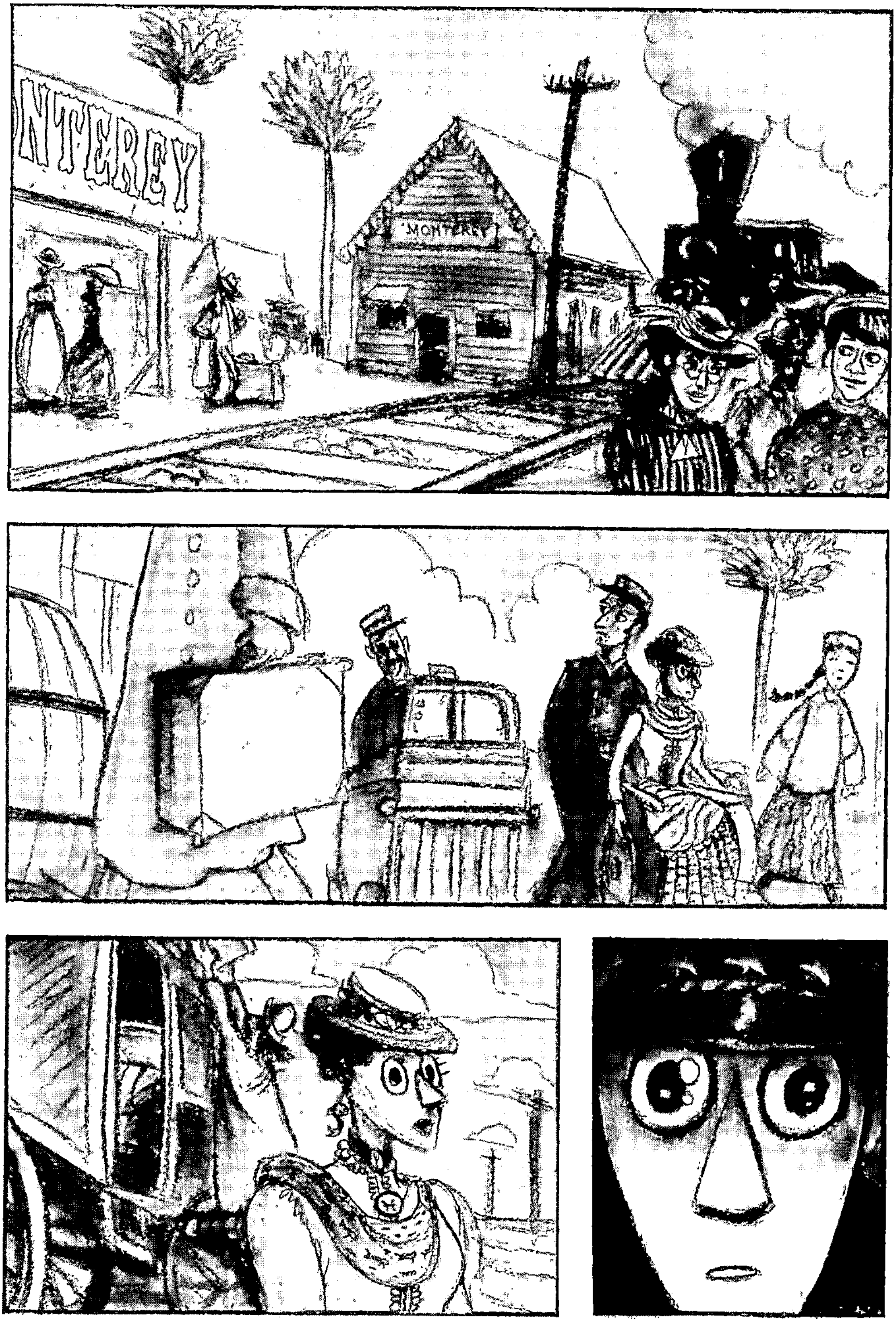
MONTEREY

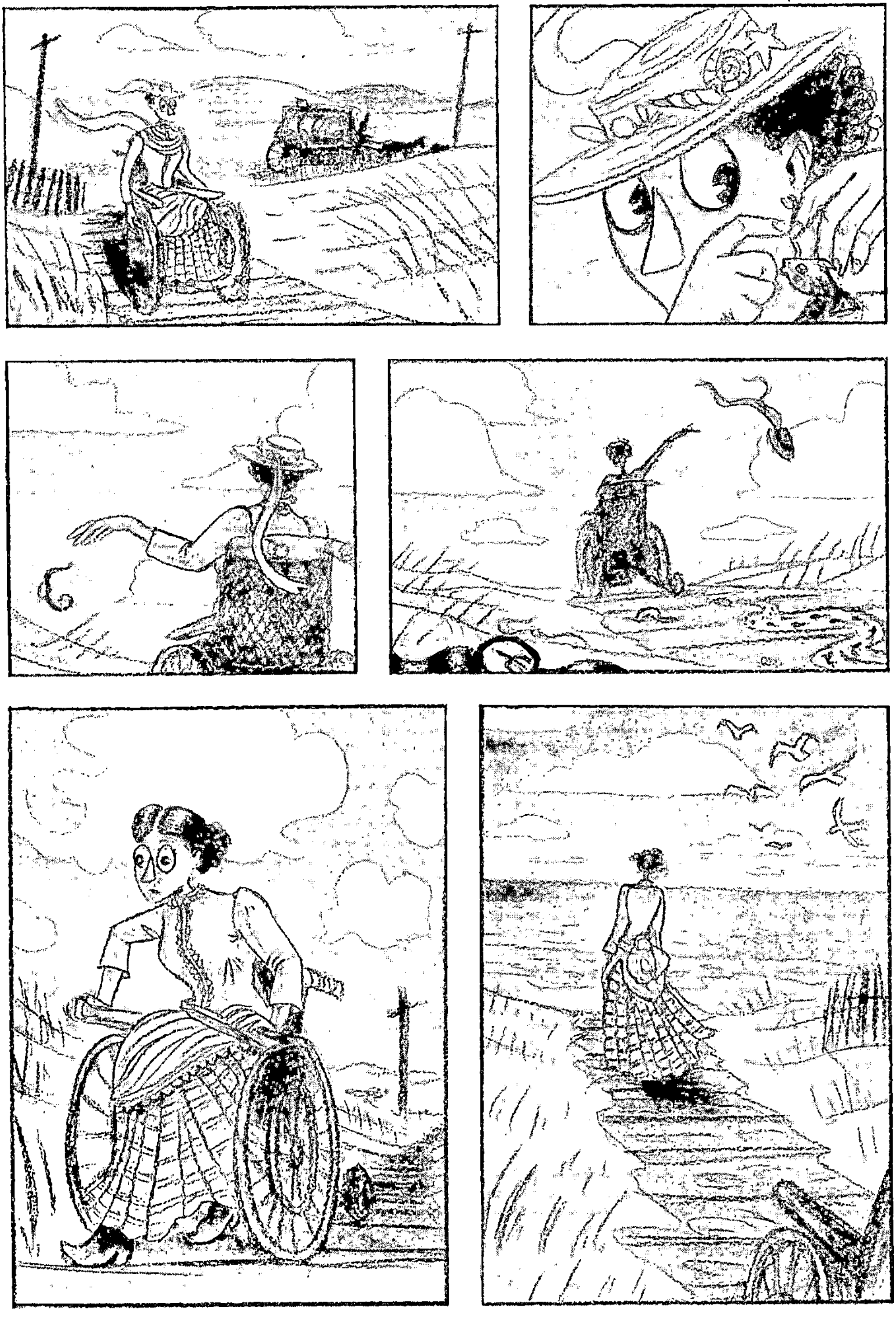

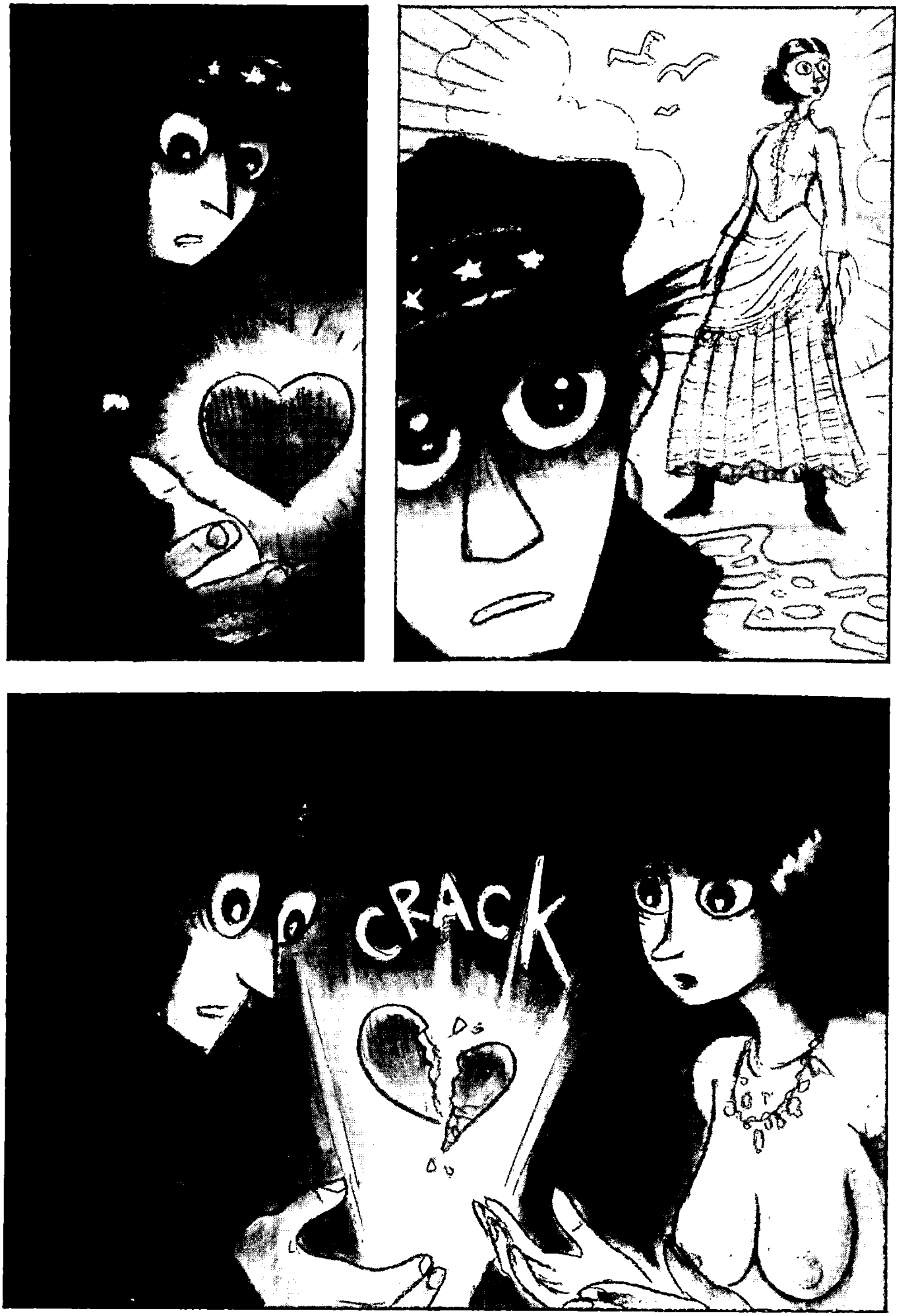
CRACK

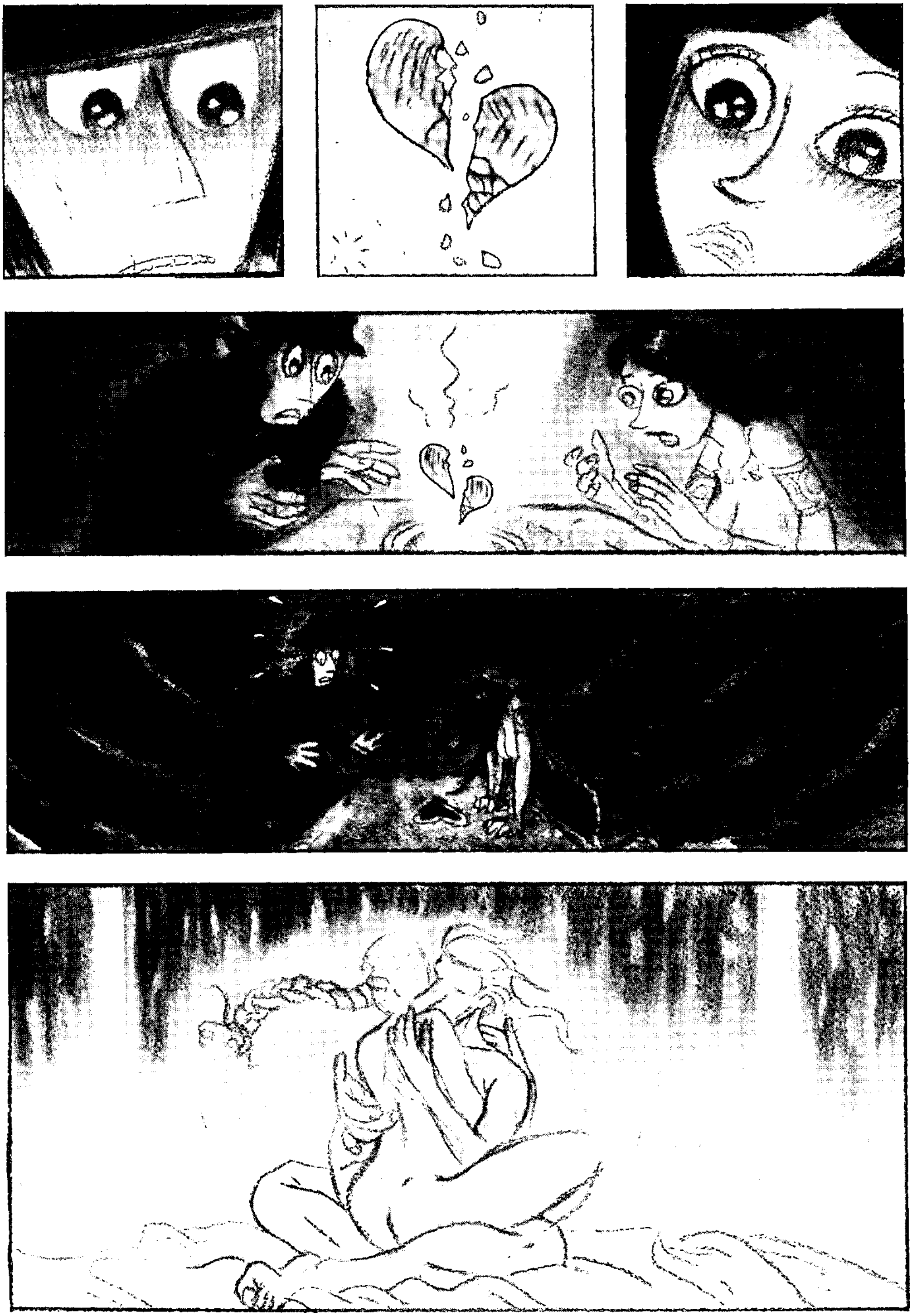

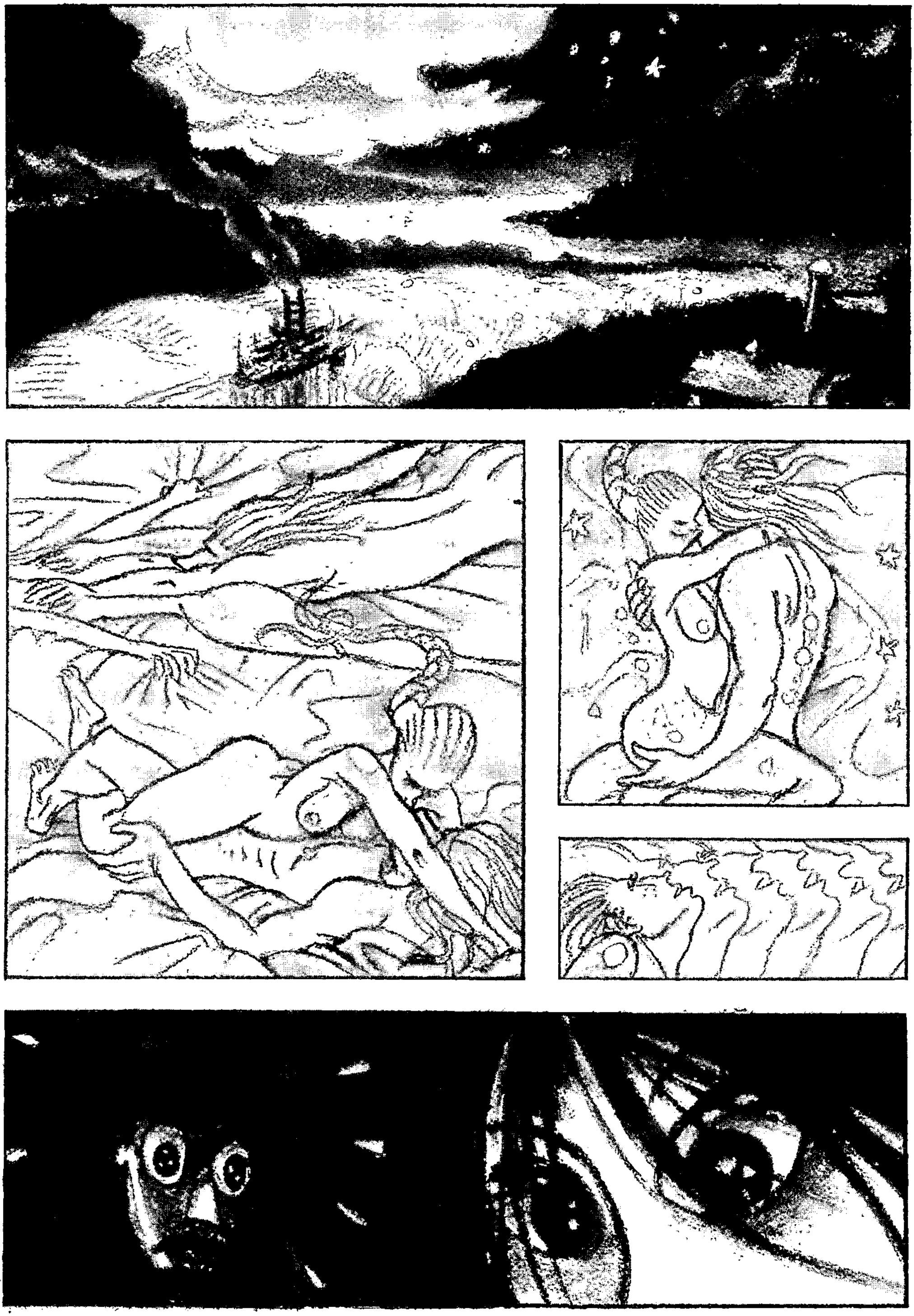

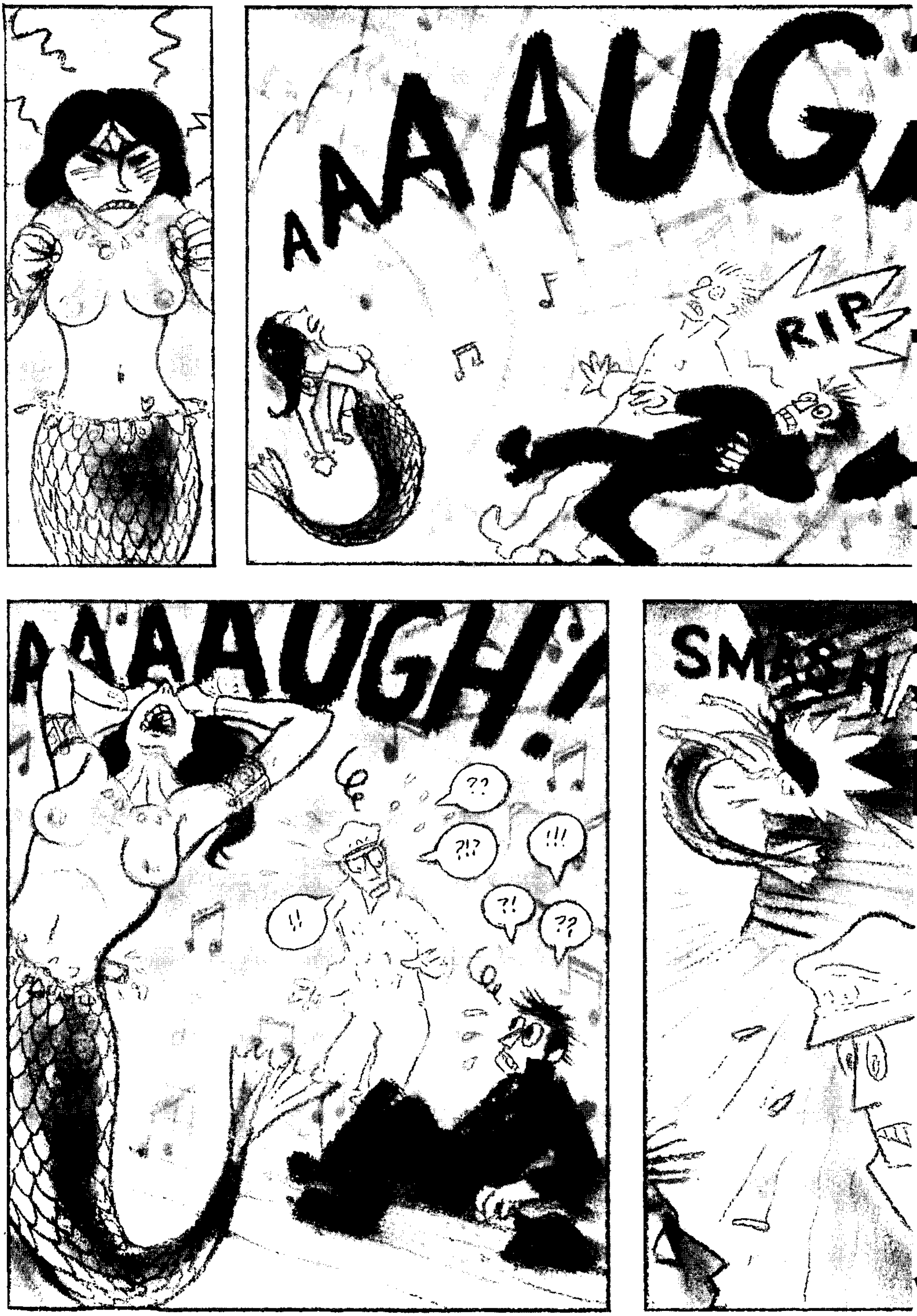
AAAAUG
RIP
AAAAUGH!
??
?!?
!!!
!!
?!
??

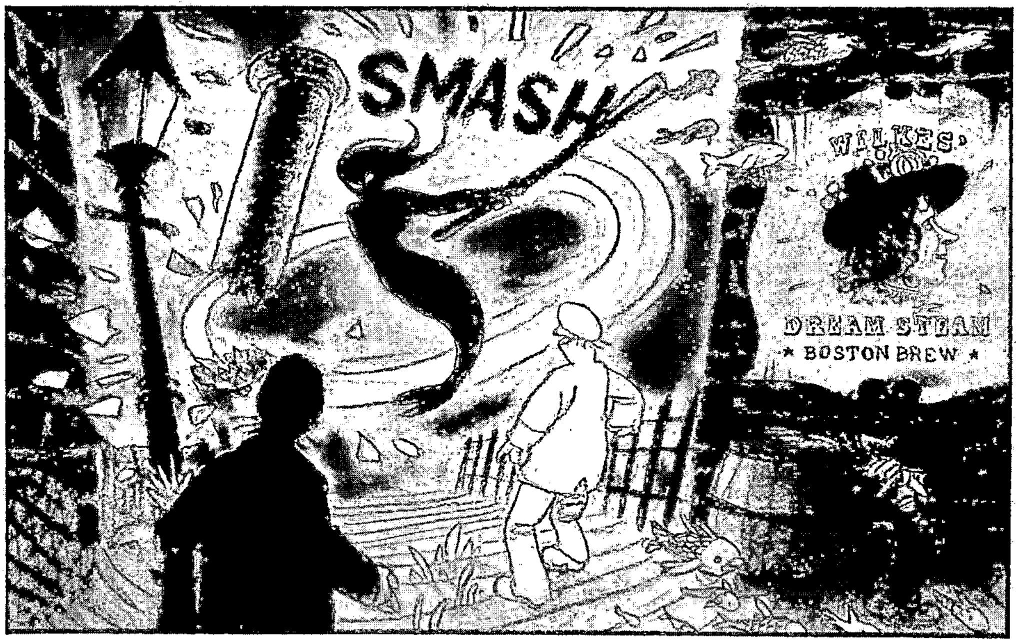
SMASH
WALKES'
DREAM STEAM
★ BOSTON BREW ★

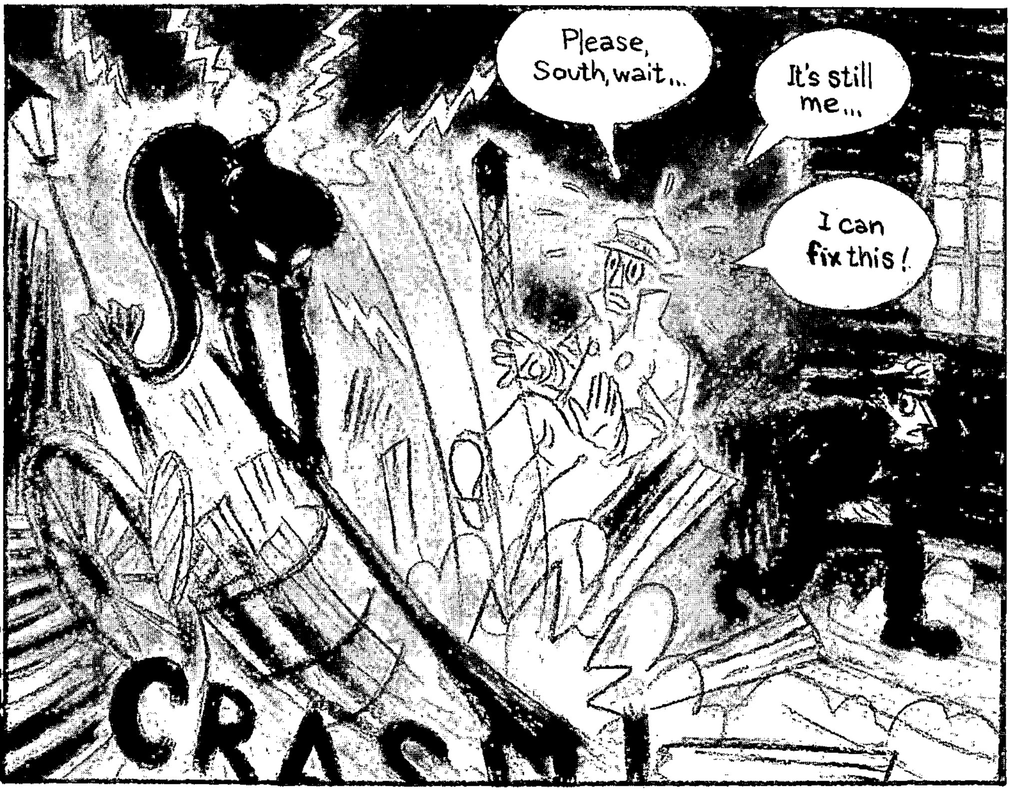
Please, South, wait...
It's still me...
I can fix this!
CRASH

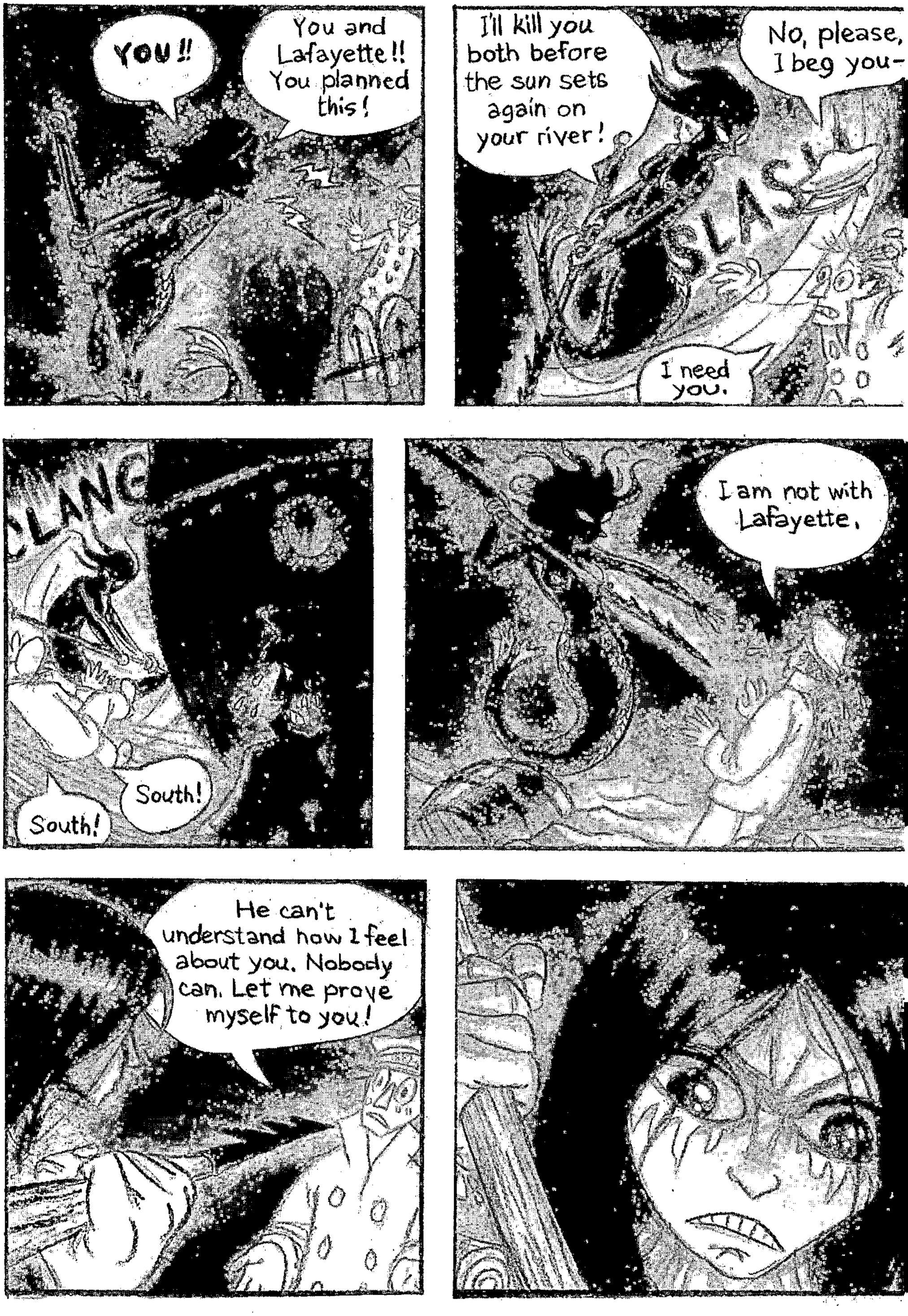
YOU!!
You and Lafayette!! You planned this!
I'll kill you both before the sun sets again on your river!
No, please, I beg you-
I need you.
CLANG
South!
South!
I am not with Lafayette,
He can't understand how I feel about you. Nobody can. Let me prove myself to you!

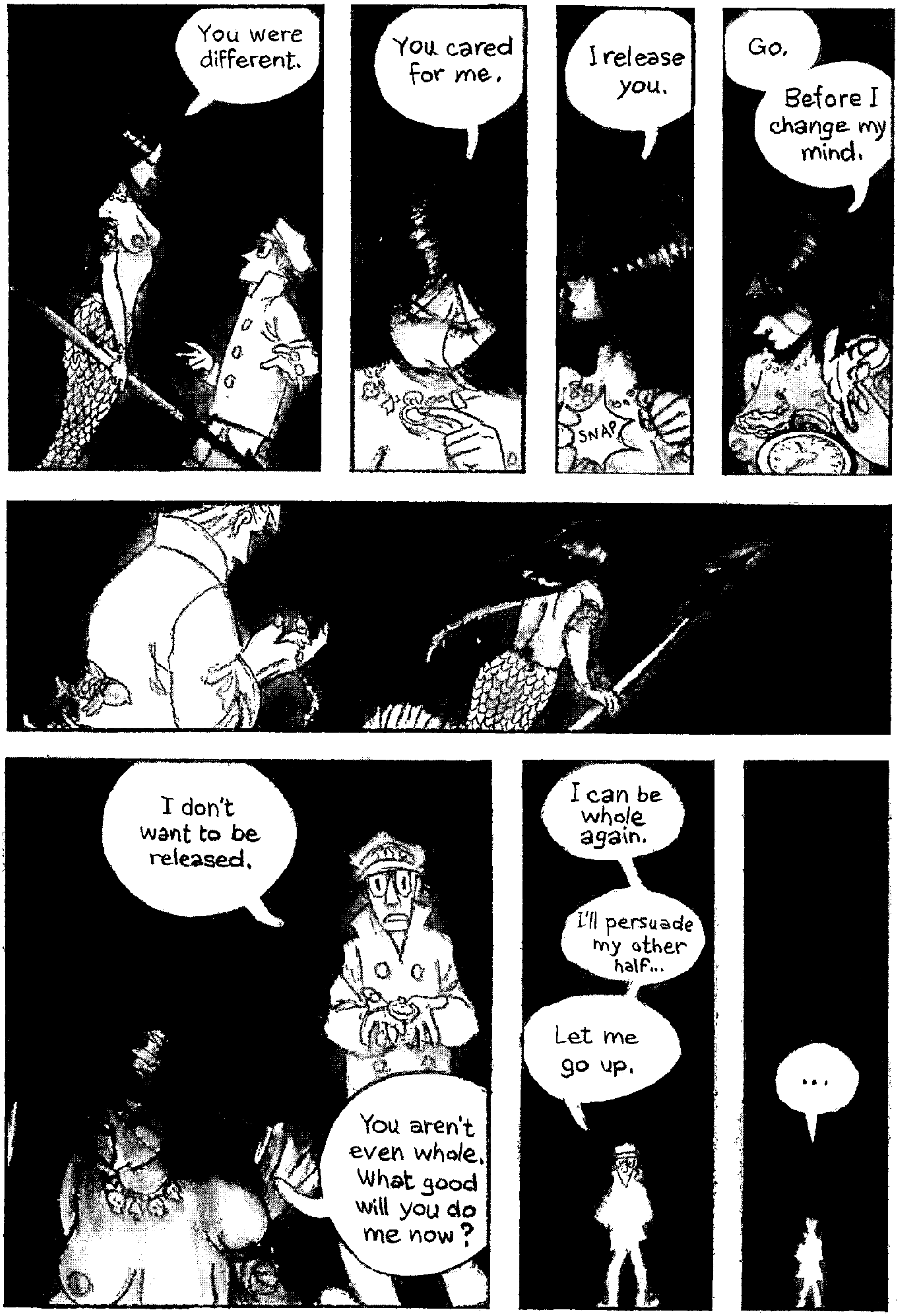
You were different.
You cared for me.
I release you.
SNAP
Go.
Before I change my mind.
I don't want to be released.
You aren't even whole. What good will you do me now?
I can be whole again.
I'll persuade my other half...
Let me go up.
...

MMER STORM

Elijah Twain

river flow
sands

C.G. Beaverton's
RETS MYSTERIES
OF THE River HUDSON

BEAVERTON
AUTHOR OF

RETS AND MYS
THE RIVER

RARE PUBLI
SEVERING CRUEL BOND

Part Four
SAILOR TWAIN

hole engine roo
Beaverton went on: ...to witness the four
physical cruelty, in our daily news... The
Tennessee lynchings are but the latest...
Have I lured you all here today under false
pretenses? No doubt many of you would
rather hear about the legends and folktales
of the Hudson, than to be outraged with
me over the latest ghastly headlines.
But how can we not be trouble
Why does cruelty sedu
Why does it have
uman fa

THE END

WEEKLY

BENEFIT FOR N.A.W.S.A.
WOMEN'S SUFFRAGE ASSOCIATION

New-York Tim

NEW-YORK, WEDNESDAY, NOVEMBER 18, 1887

FOUND GUILT
Stripped of captainc
Trial concludes in mi

STEAMBO
DISASTE
Survivors not re

HARPER'S
JOURNAL OF CIVILIZATION

Pt IV, Chap.1

"THE TWAIN SHALL MEET"

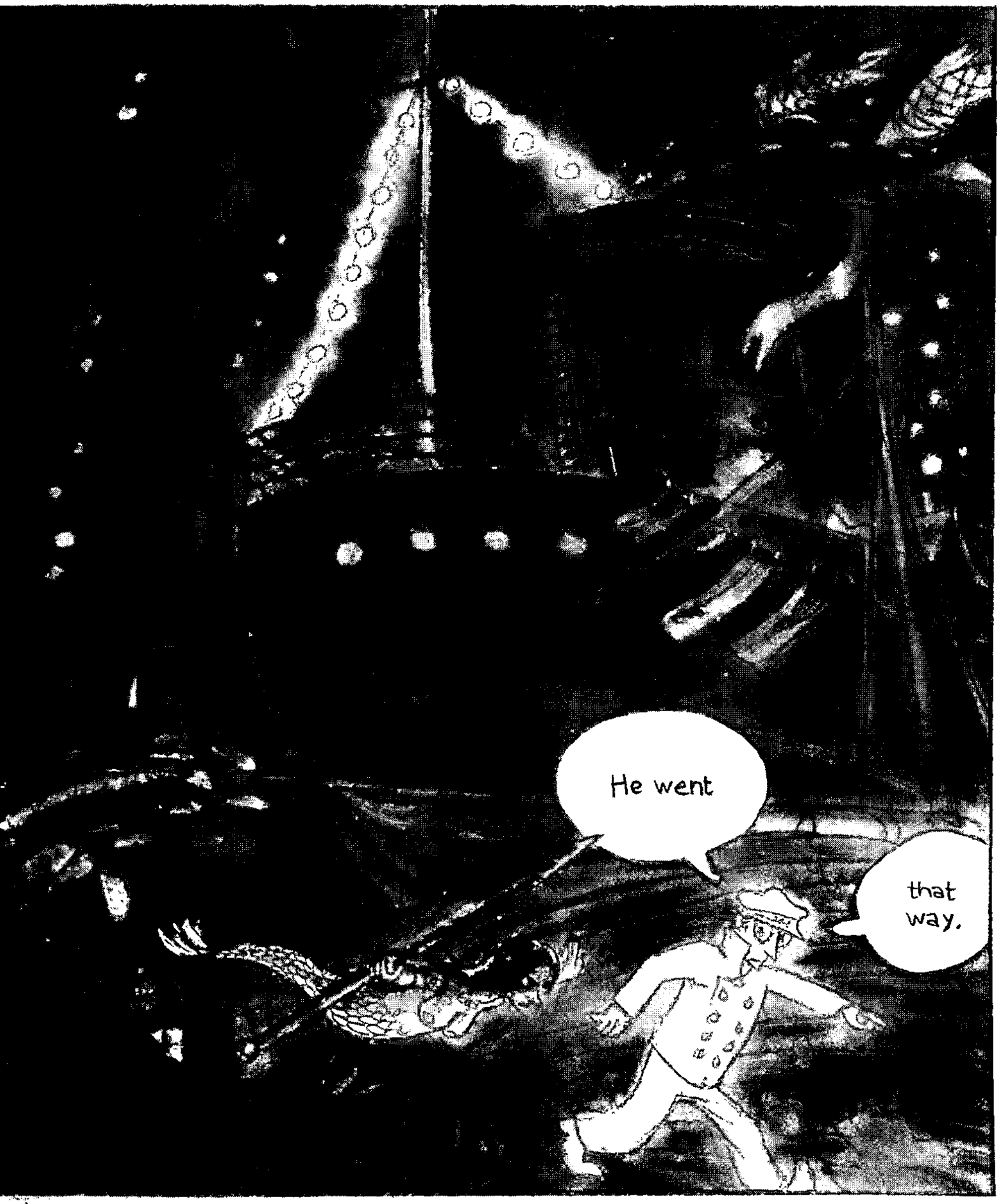
He went
that way.

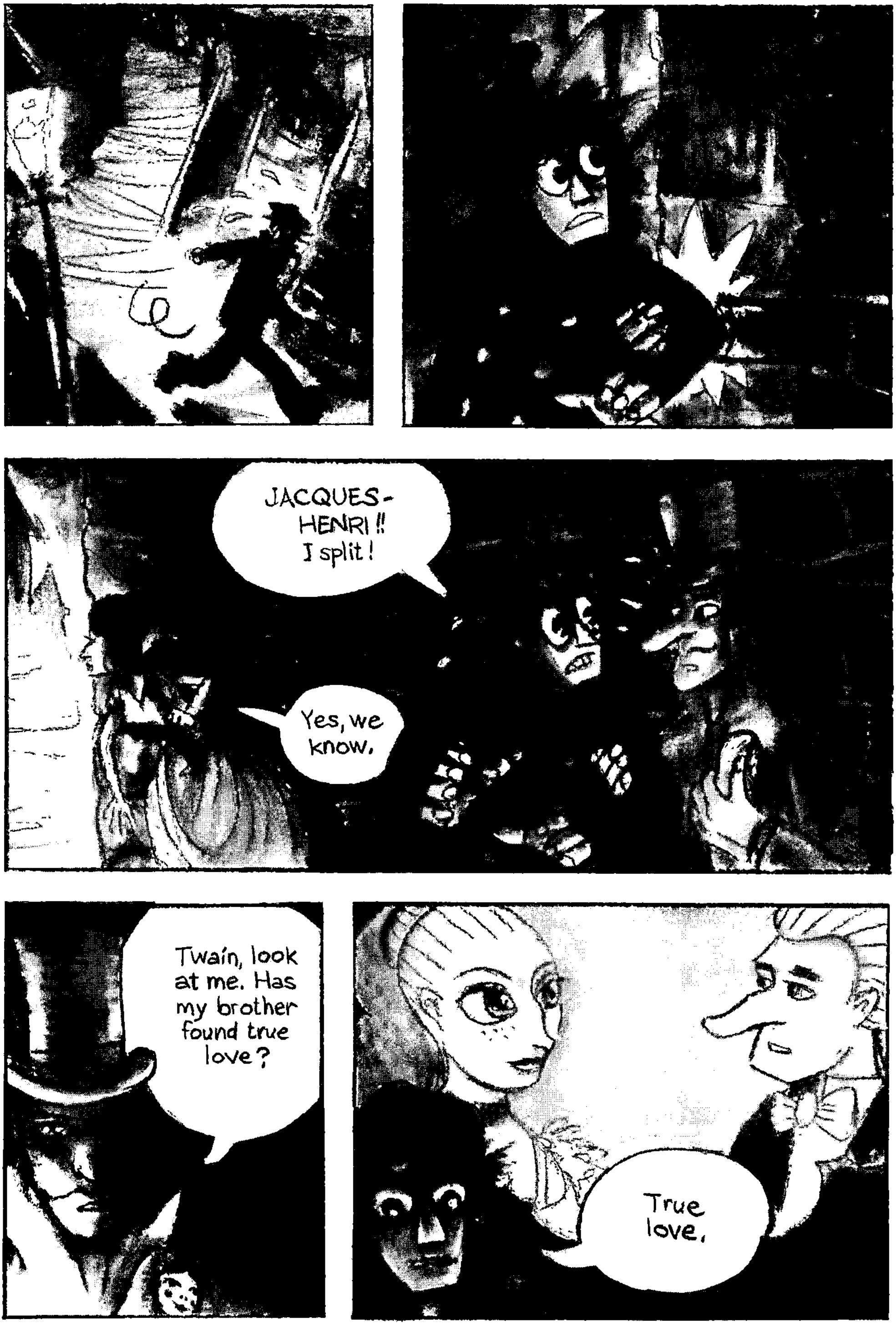
JACQUES-HENRI !! I split !
Yes, we know.
Twain, look at me. Has my brother found true love?
True love.

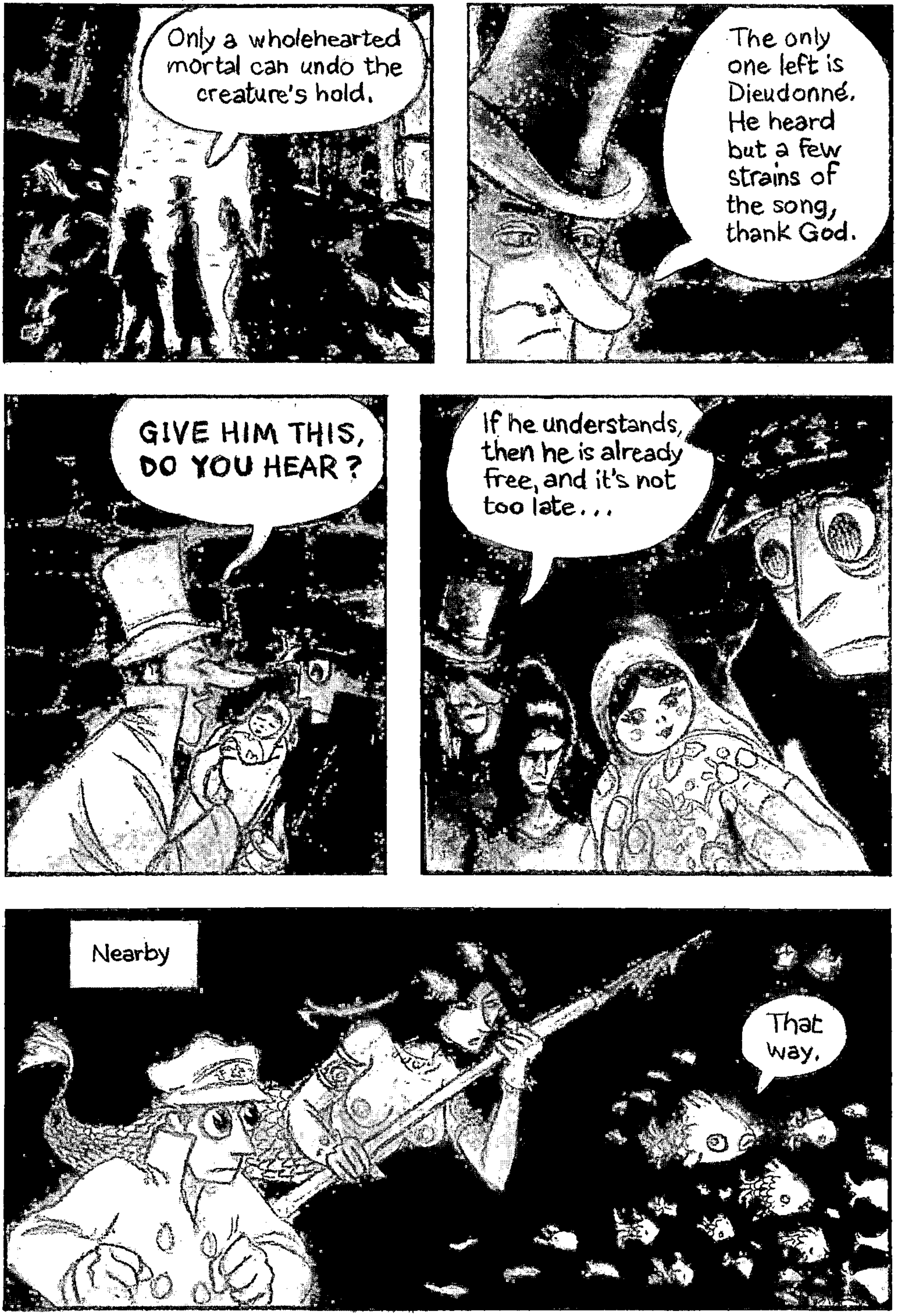
Only a wholehearted mortal can undo the creature's hold.
The only one left is Dieudonné. He heard but a few strains of the song, thank God.
GIVE HIM THIS, DO YOU HEAR?
If he understands, then he is already free, and it's not too late...
Nearby
That way.

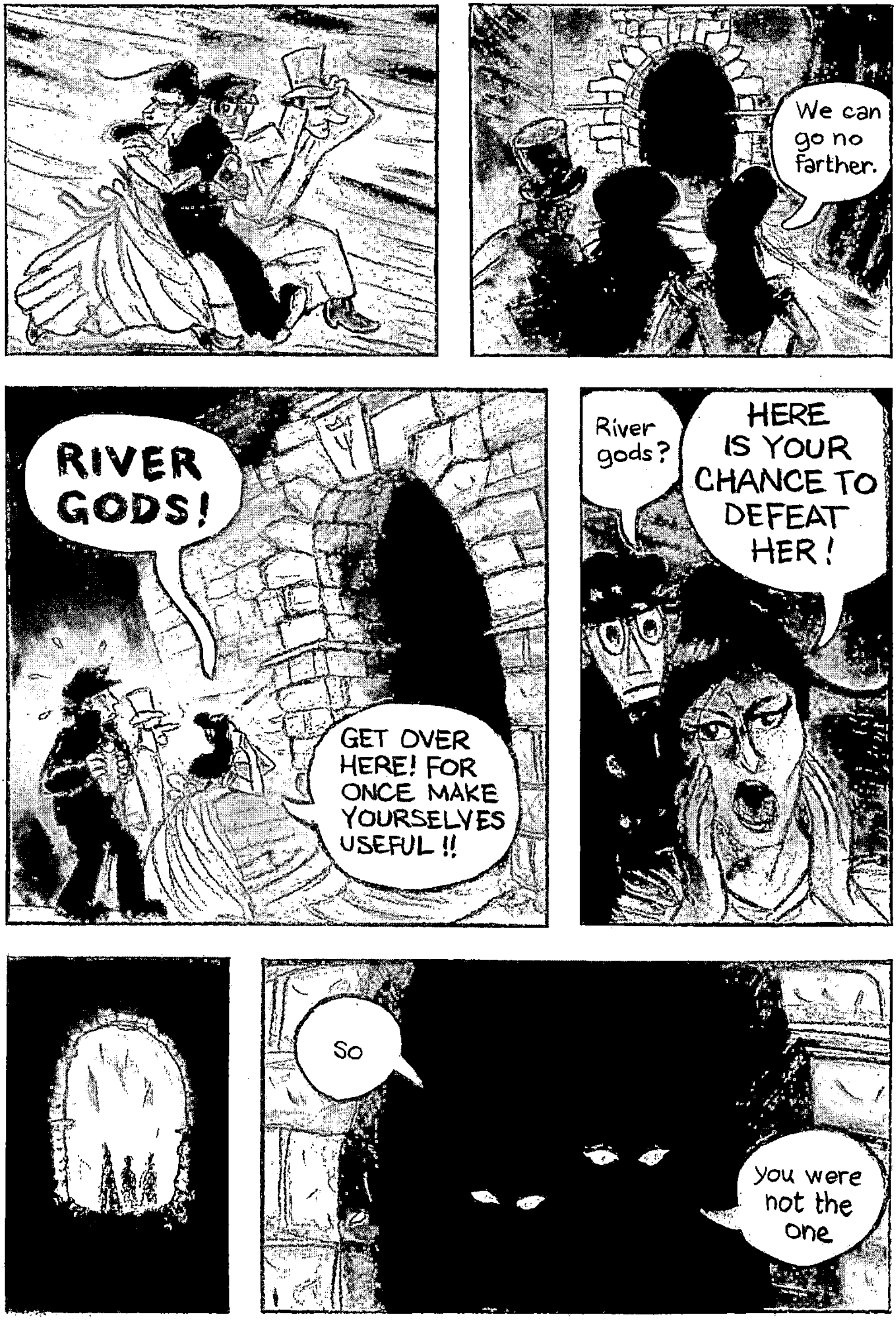
We can go no farther.
RIVER GODS!
GET OVER HERE! FOR ONCE MAKE YOURSELVES USEFUL!!
River gods?
HERE IS YOUR CHANCE TO DEFEAT HER!
So
you were not the one

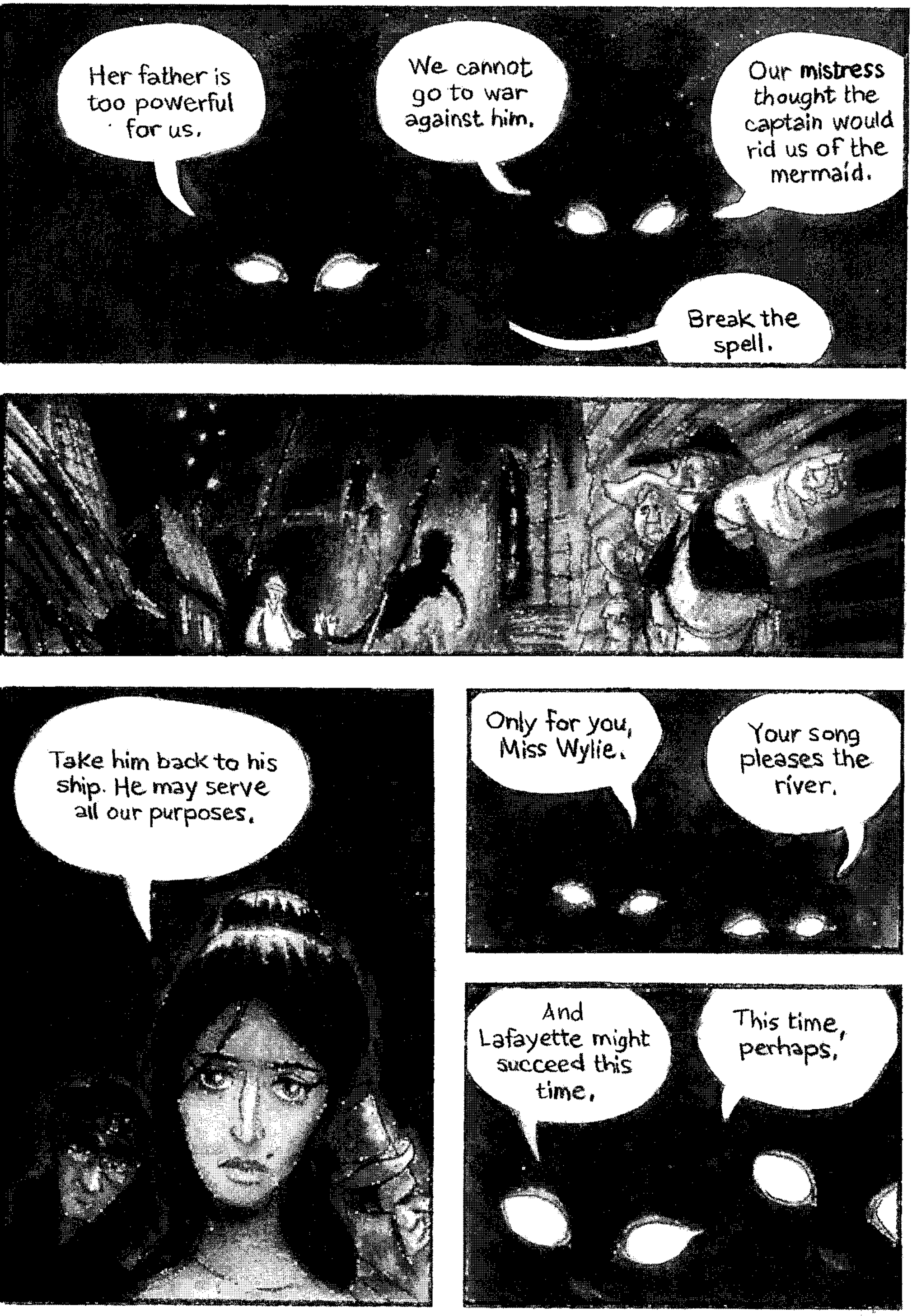
Her father is too powerful for us.
We cannot go to war against him.
Our mistress thought the captain would rid us of the mermaid.
Break the spell.
Take him back to his ship. He may serve all our purposes.
Only for you, Miss Wylie.
Your song pleases the river.
And Lafayette might succeed this time.
This time, perhaps.

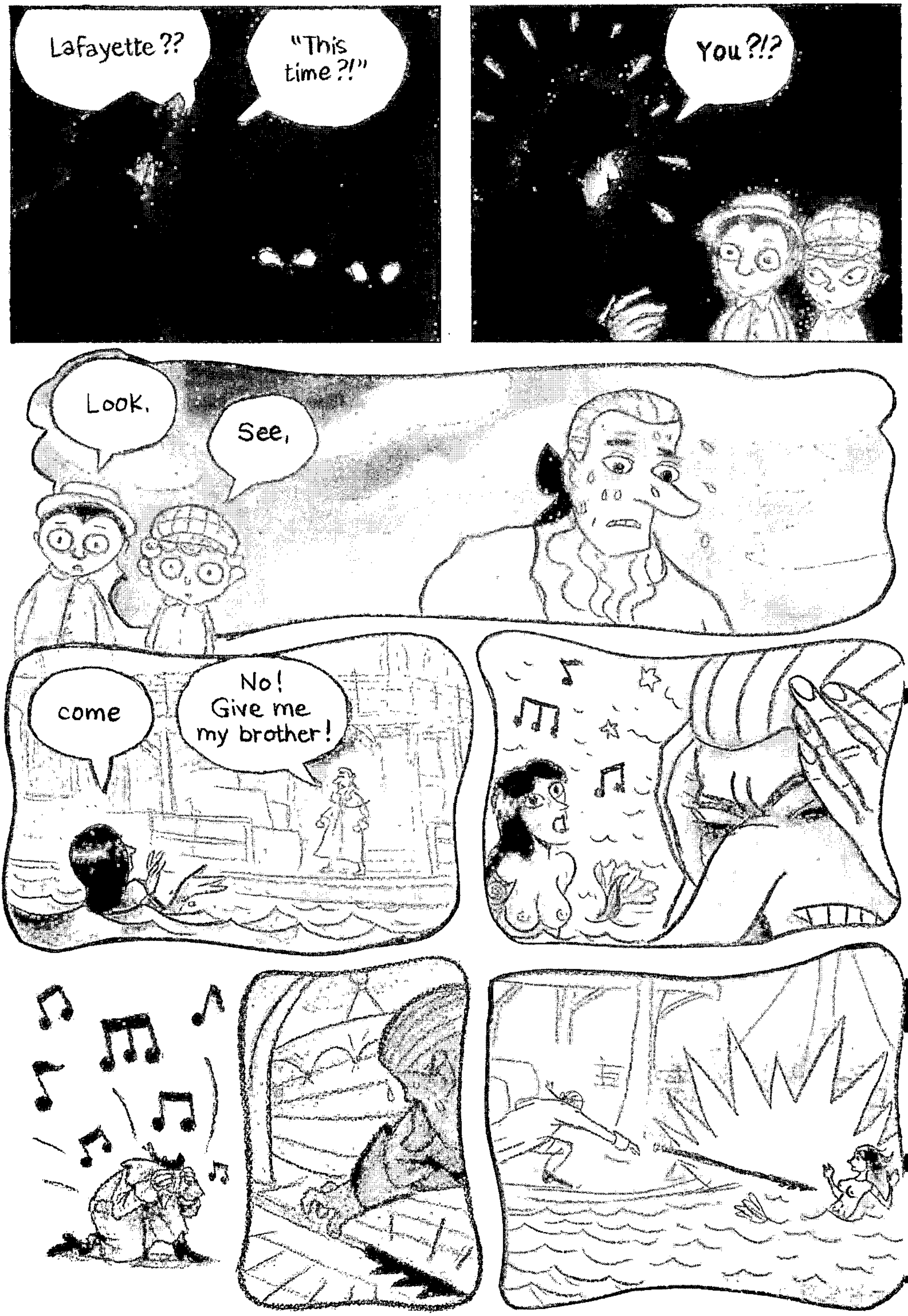
Lafayette??
"This time?!"
You?!?
Look,
See,
come
No!
Give me
my brother!

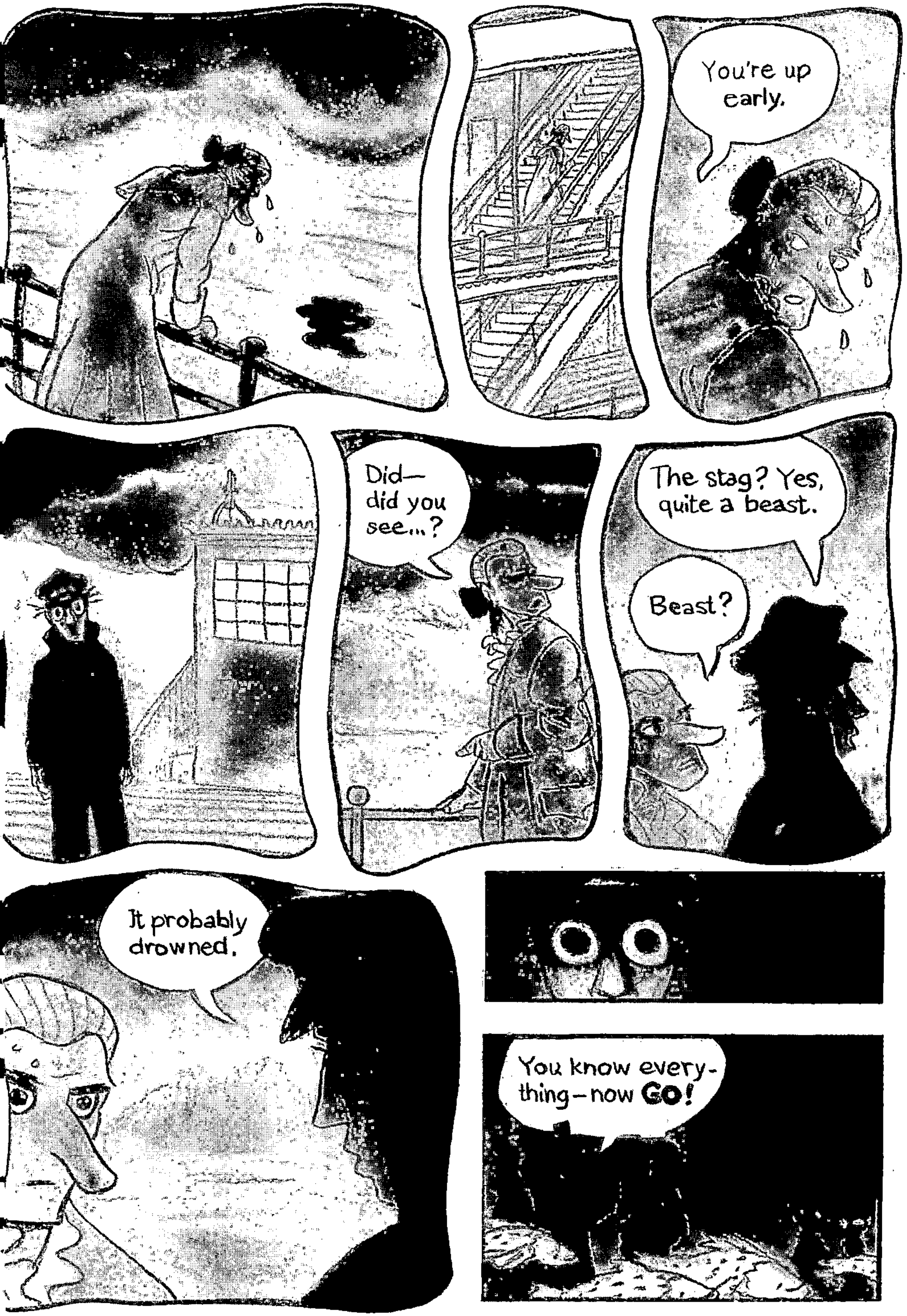
You're up early.
Did— did you see...?
The stag? Yes, quite a beast.
Beast?
It probably drowned.
You know every-thing—now **GO**!

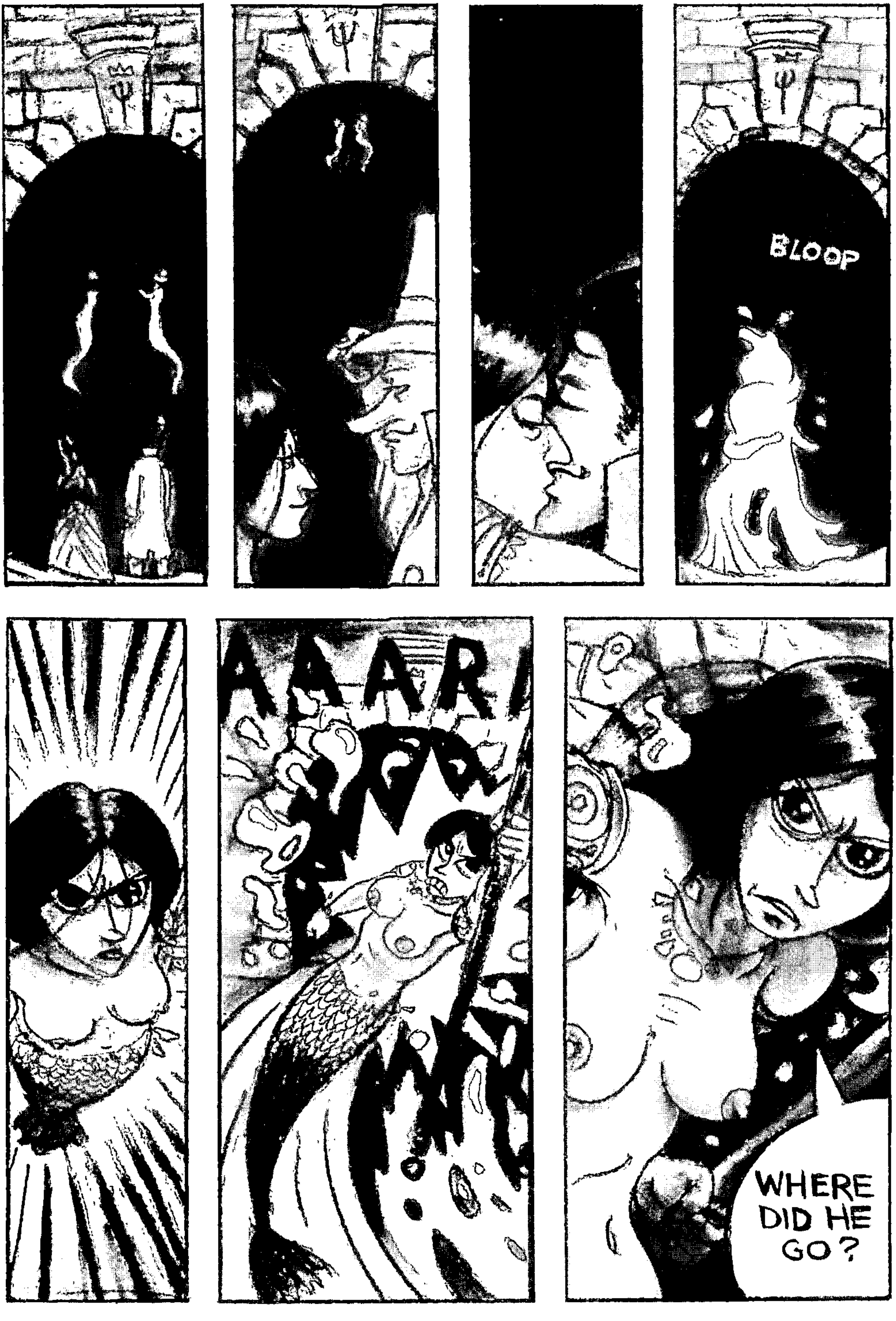
BLOOP
AAAR
WHERE DID HE GO?

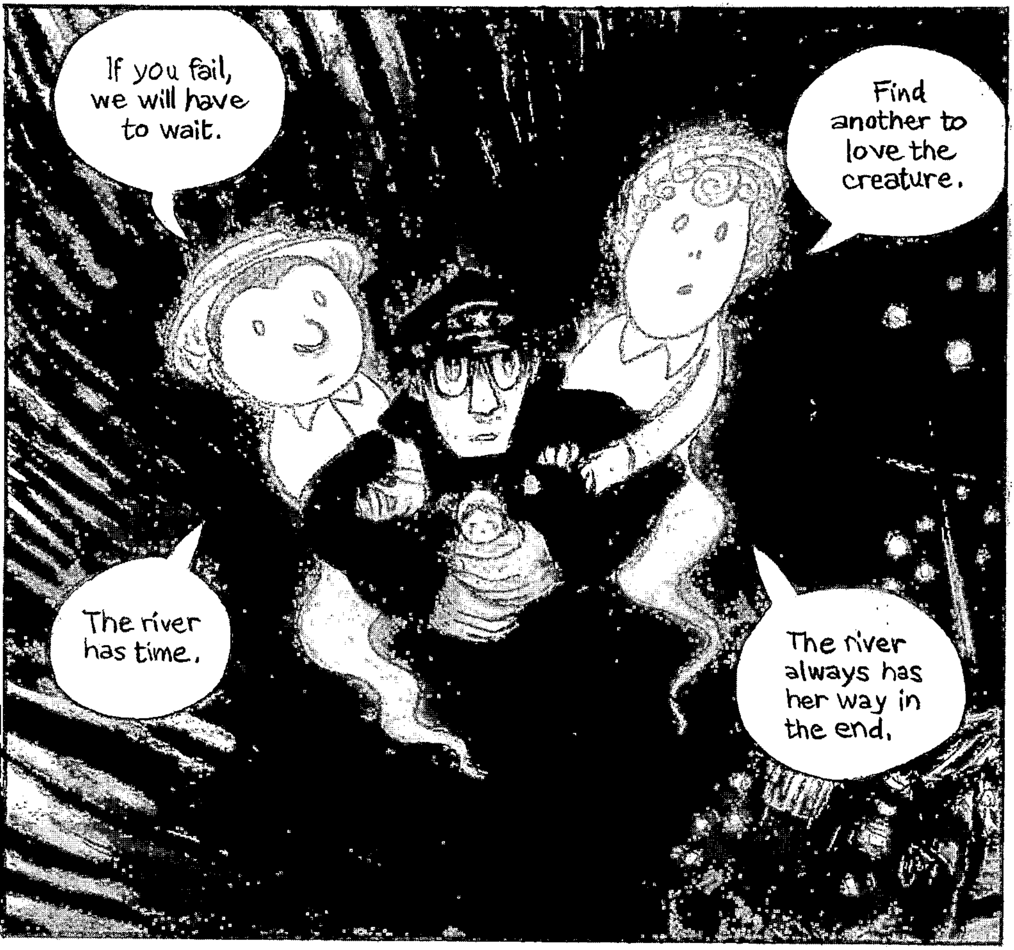
If you fail, we will have to wait.
Find another to love the creature.
The river has time.
The river always has her way in the end.

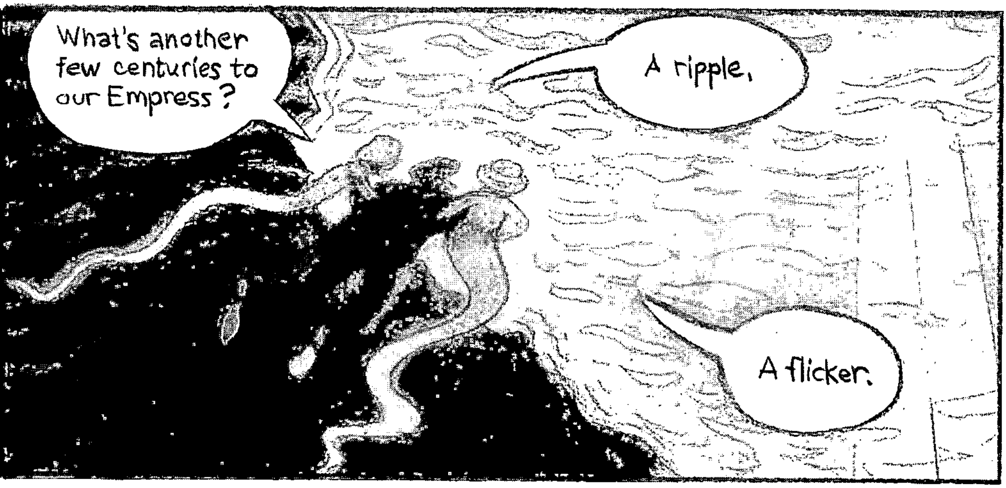
What's another few centuries to our Empress?
A ripple.
A flicker.

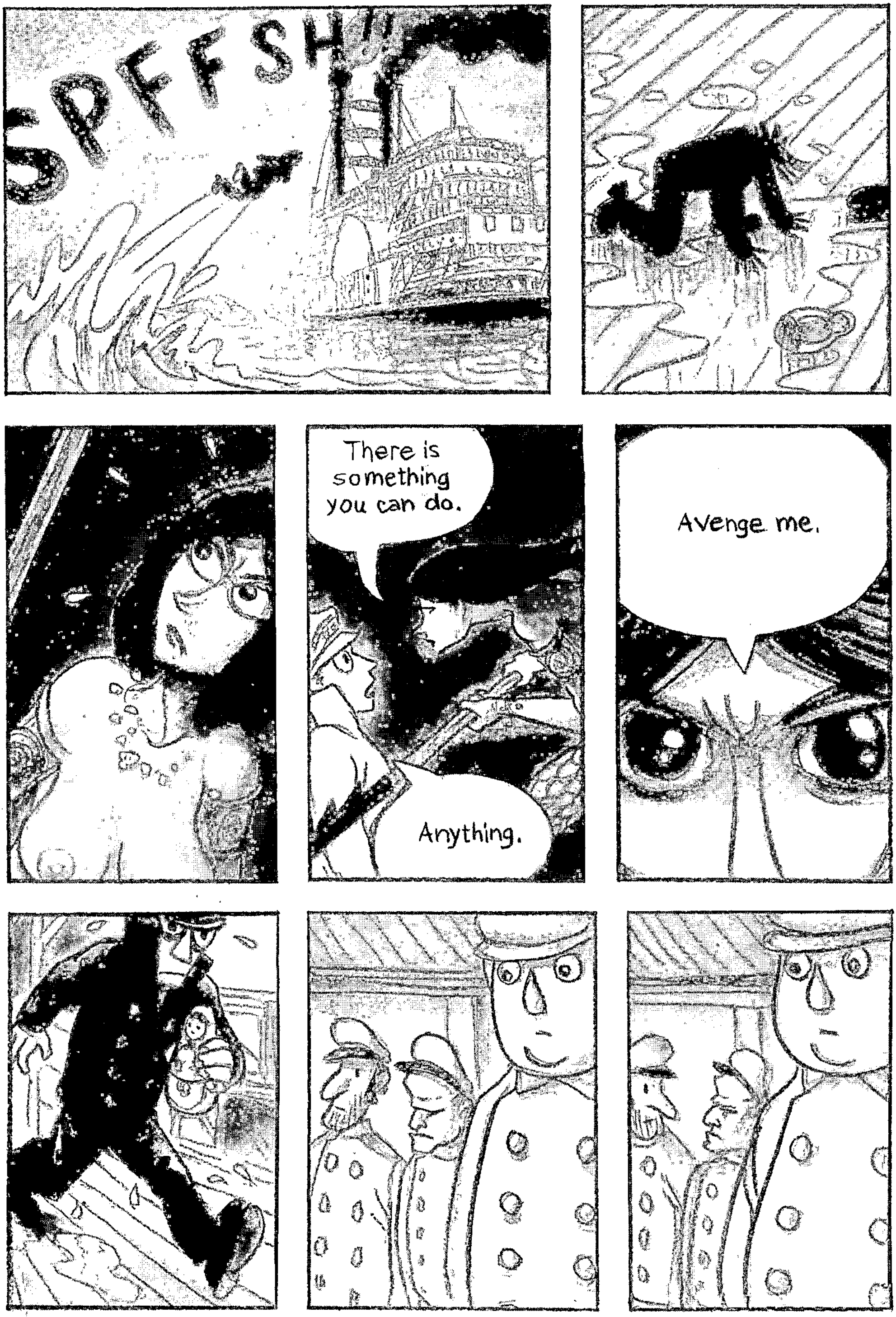
SPFFSH!!
There is something you can do.
Anything.
Avenge me.

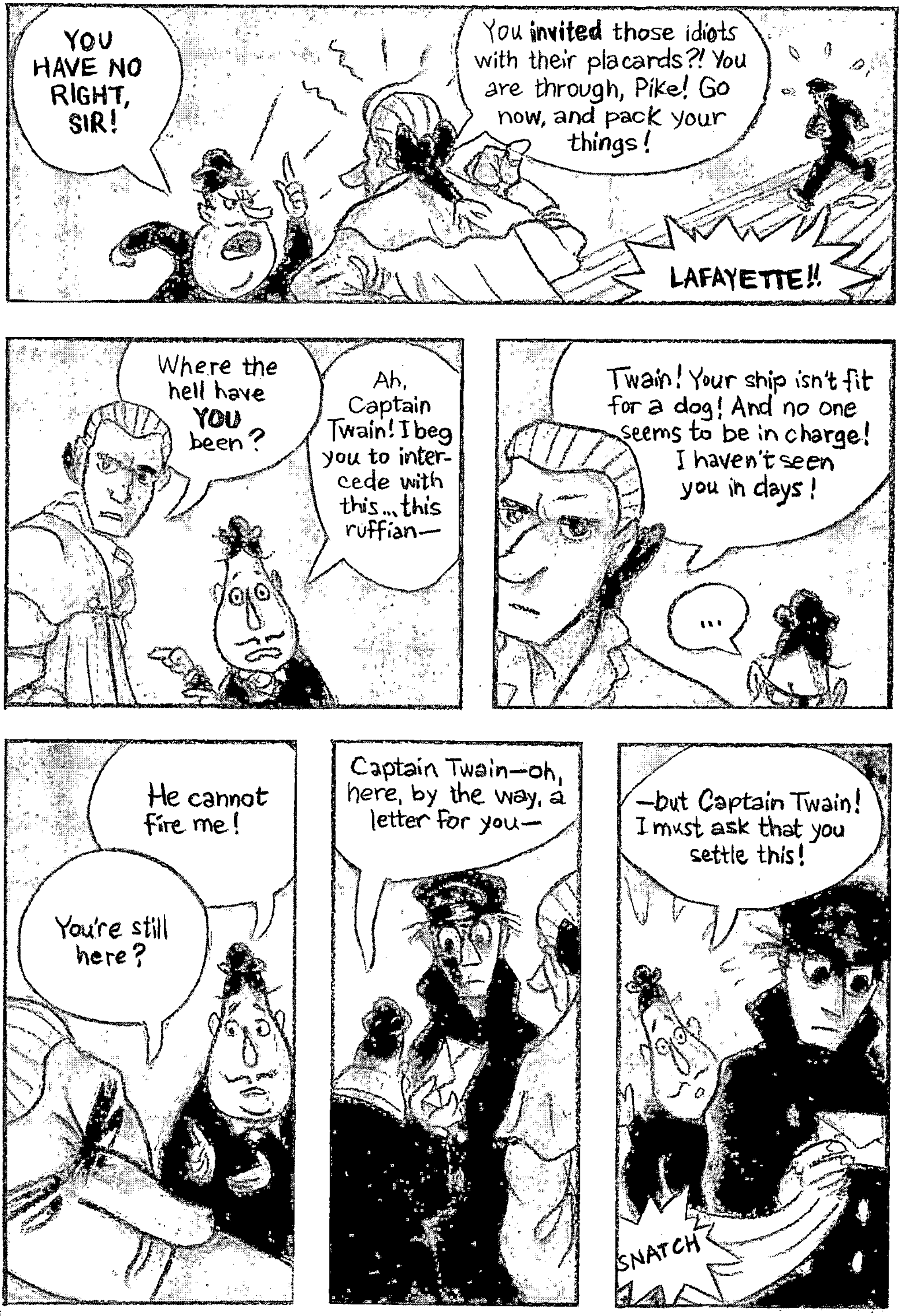
YOU HAVE NO RIGHT, SIR!
You invited those idiots with their placards?! You are through, Pike! Go now, and pack your things!
LAFAYETTE!!
Where the hell have YOU been?
Ah, Captain Twain! I beg you to intercede with this... this ruffian—
Twain! Your ship isn't fit for a dog! And no one seems to be in charge! I haven't seen you in days!
...
He cannot fire me!
You're still here?
Captain Twain—oh, here, by the way, a letter for you—
—but Captain Twain! I must ask that you settle this!
SNATCH

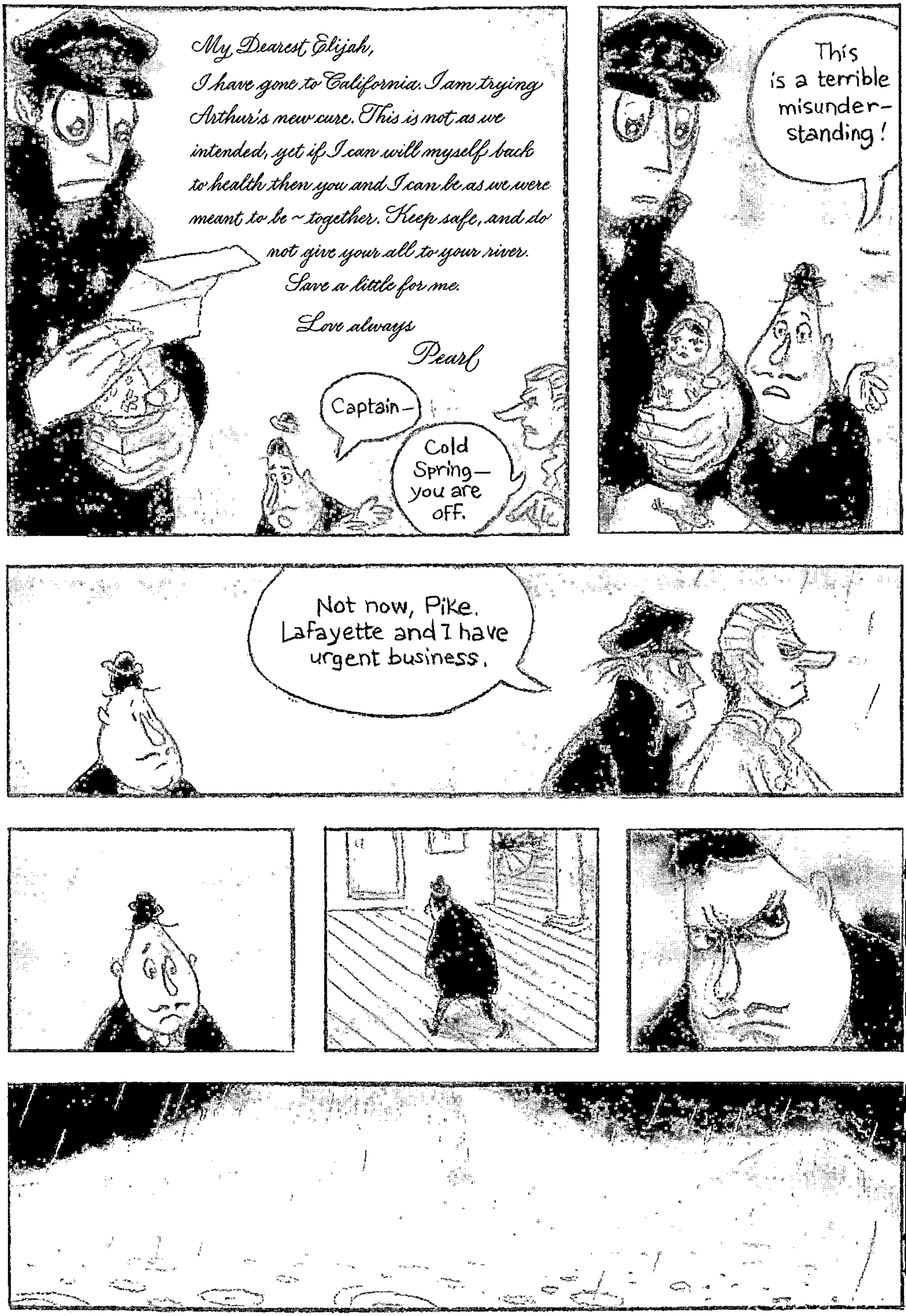
My Dearest Elijah,
I have gone to California. I am trying Arthur's new cure. This is not as we intended, yet if I can will myself back to health then you and I can be as we were meant to be ~ together. Keep safe, and do not give your all to your river. Save a little for me.
Love always
Pearl
Captain—
Cold Spring— you are off.
This is a terrible misunderstanding!
Not now, Pike. Lafayette and I have urgent business.

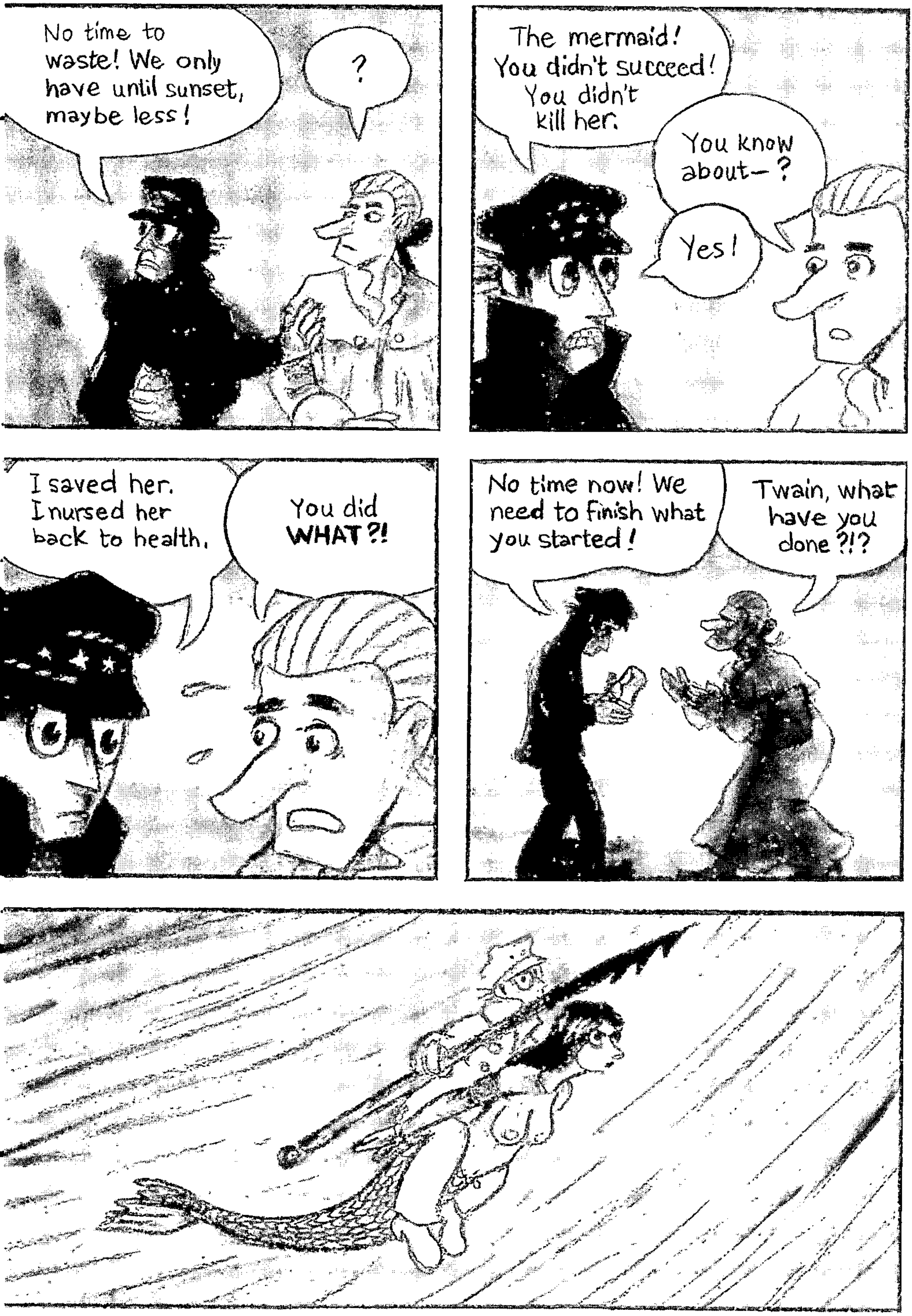
No time to waste! We only have until sunset, maybe less!
?
The mermaid! You didn't succeed! You didn't kill her.
You know about—?
Yes!
I saved her. I nursed her back to health.
You did WHAT?!
No time now! We need to finish what you started!
Twain, what have you done?!?

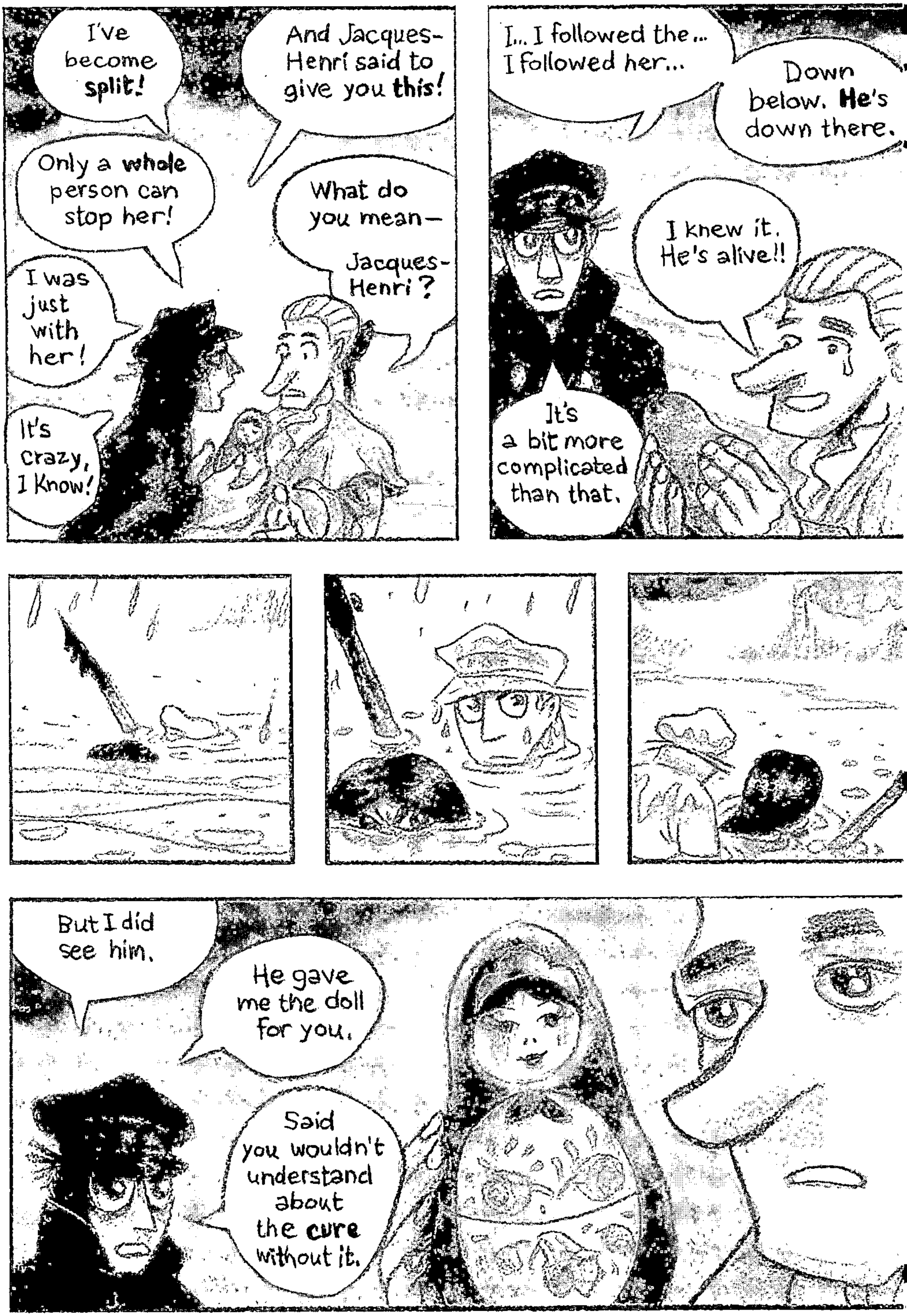
I've become split!
And Jacques-Henri said to give you this!
Only a whole person can stop her!
What do you mean—
Jacques-Henri?
I was just with her!
It's crazy, I know!
I... I followed the... I followed her...
Down below. He's down there.
I knew it. He's alive!!
It's a bit more complicated than that.
But I did see him.
He gave me the doll for you.
Said you wouldn't understand about the cure without it.

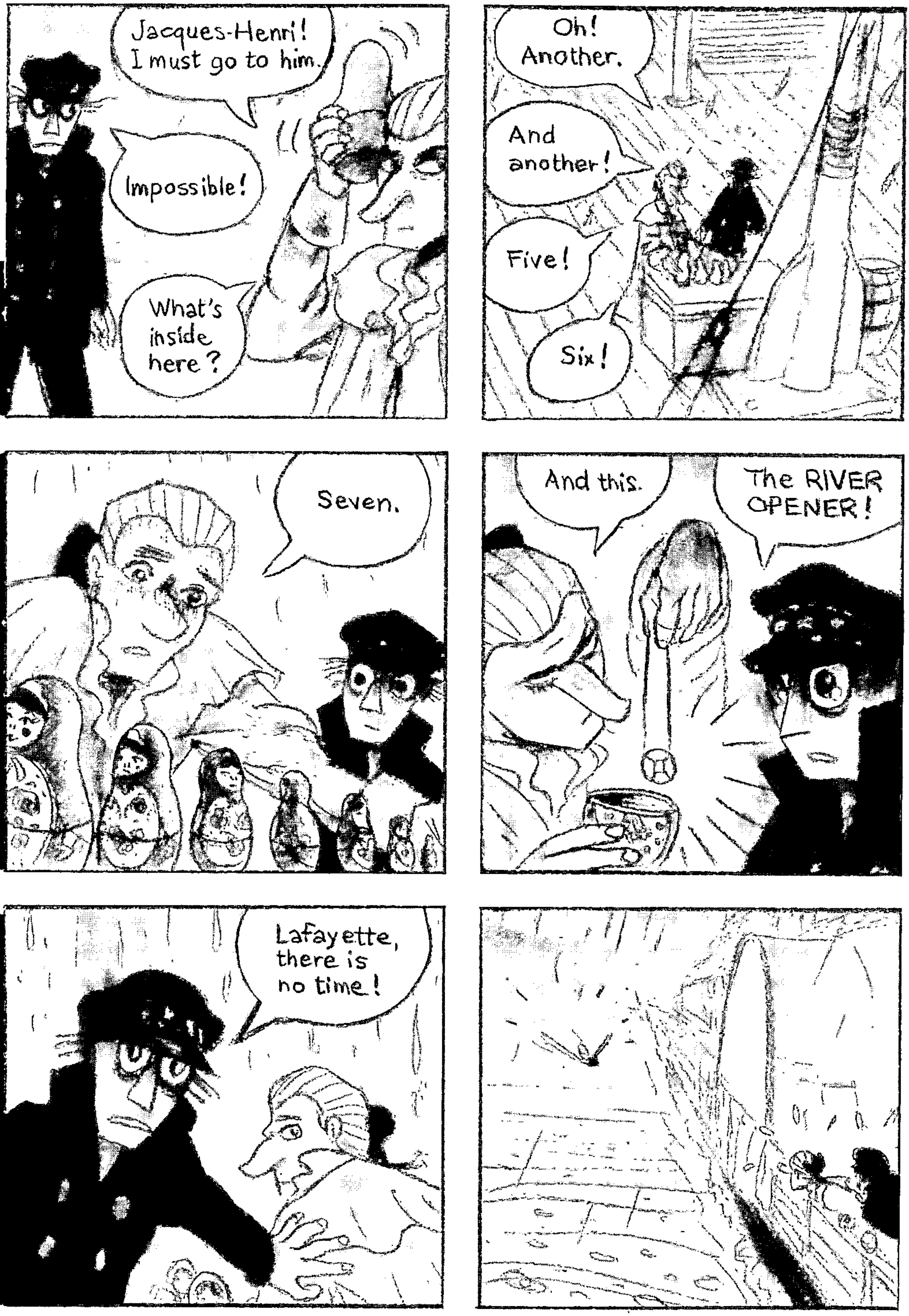
Jacques-Henri! I must go to him.
Impossible!
What's inside here?
Oh! Another.
And another!
Five!
Six!
Seven.
And this.
The RIVER OPENER!
Lafayette, there is no time!

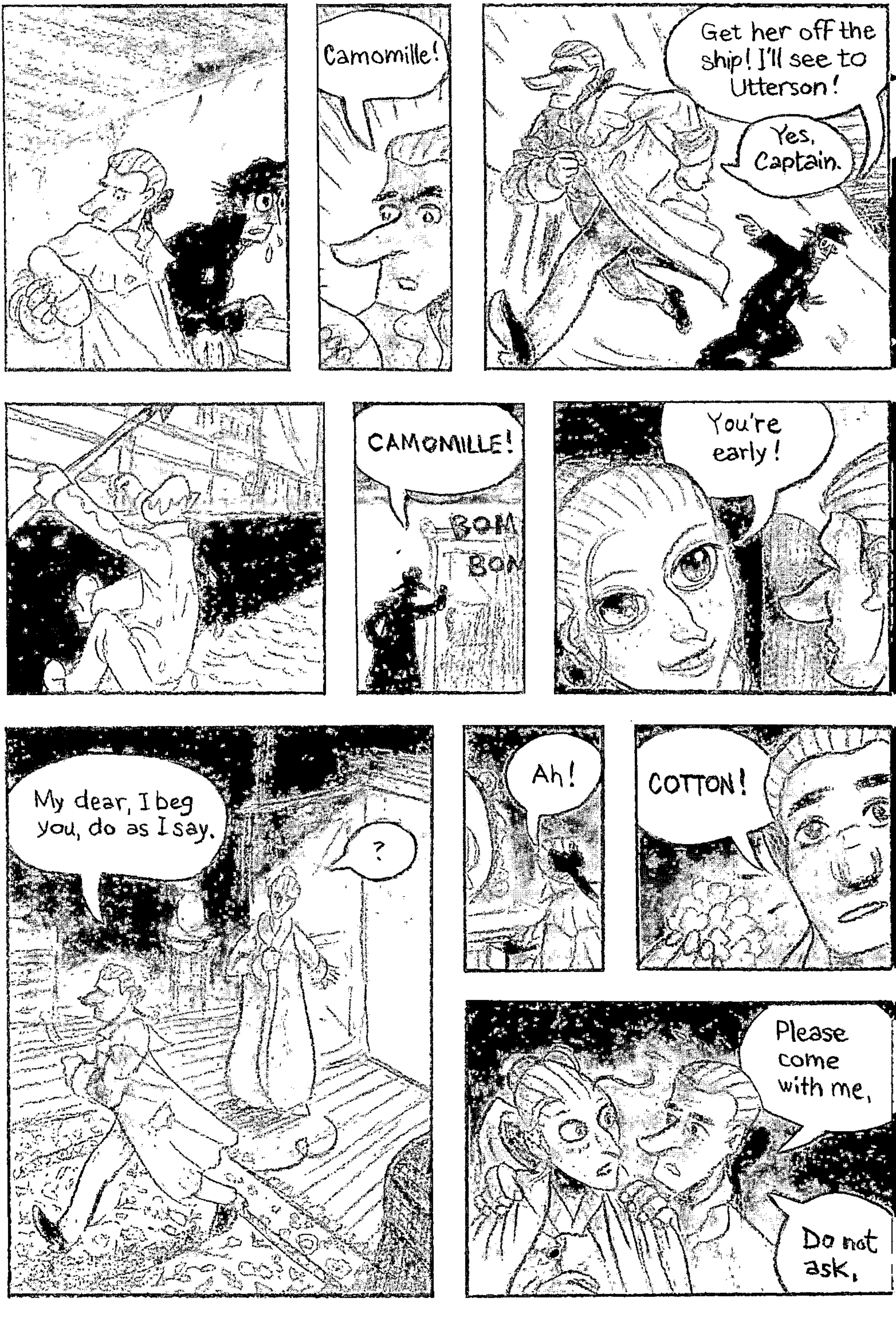
Camomille!
Get her off the ship! I'll see to Utterson!
Yes, Captain.
CAMOMILLE!
BOM BOM
You're early!
My dear, I beg you, do as I say.
?
Ah!
COTTON!
Please come with me.
Do not ask.

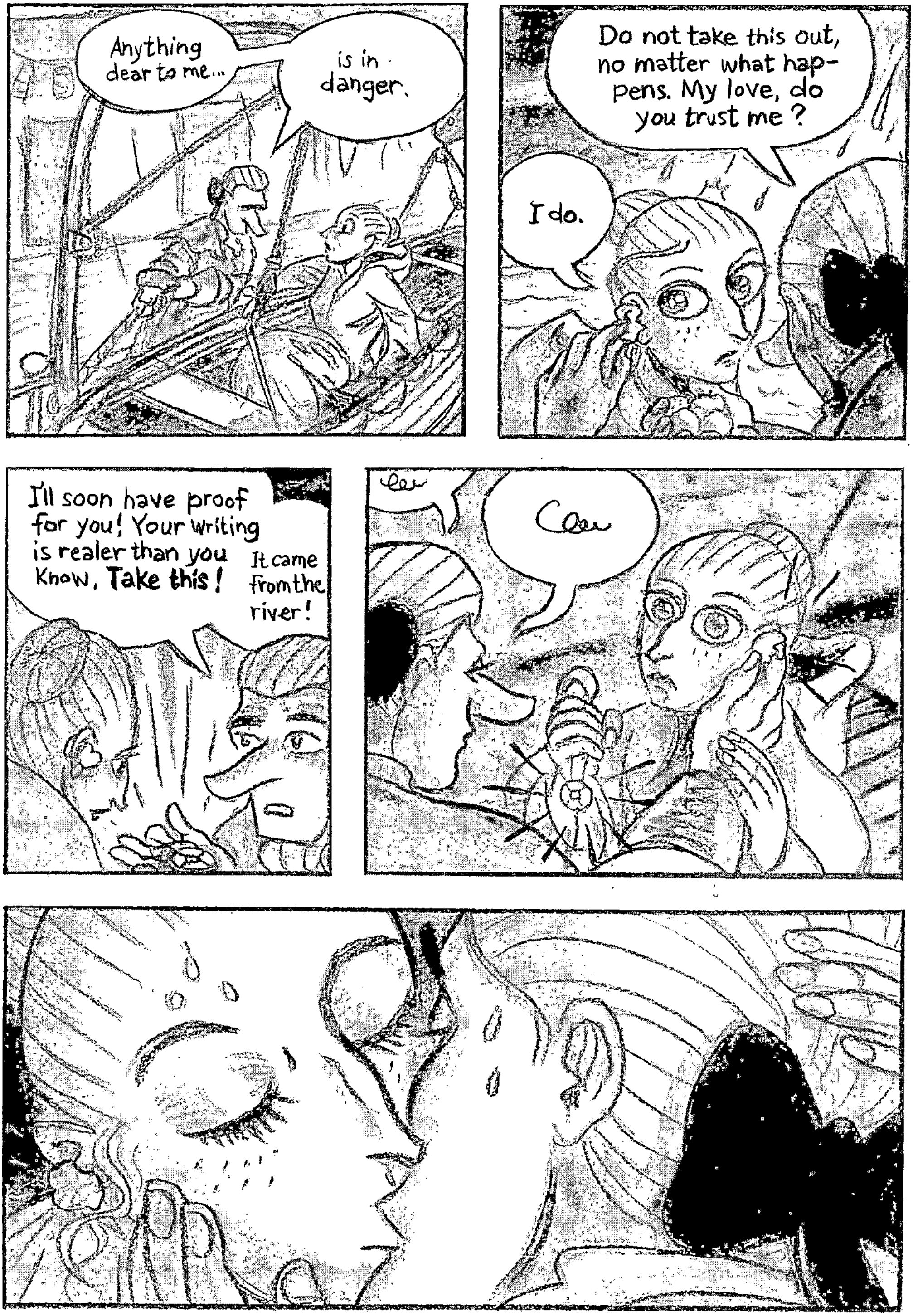
Anything dear to me...
is in danger.
Do not take this out, no matter what hap-pens. My love, do you trust me?
I do.
I'll soon have proof for you! Your writing is realer than you Know. **Take this!**
It came from the river!

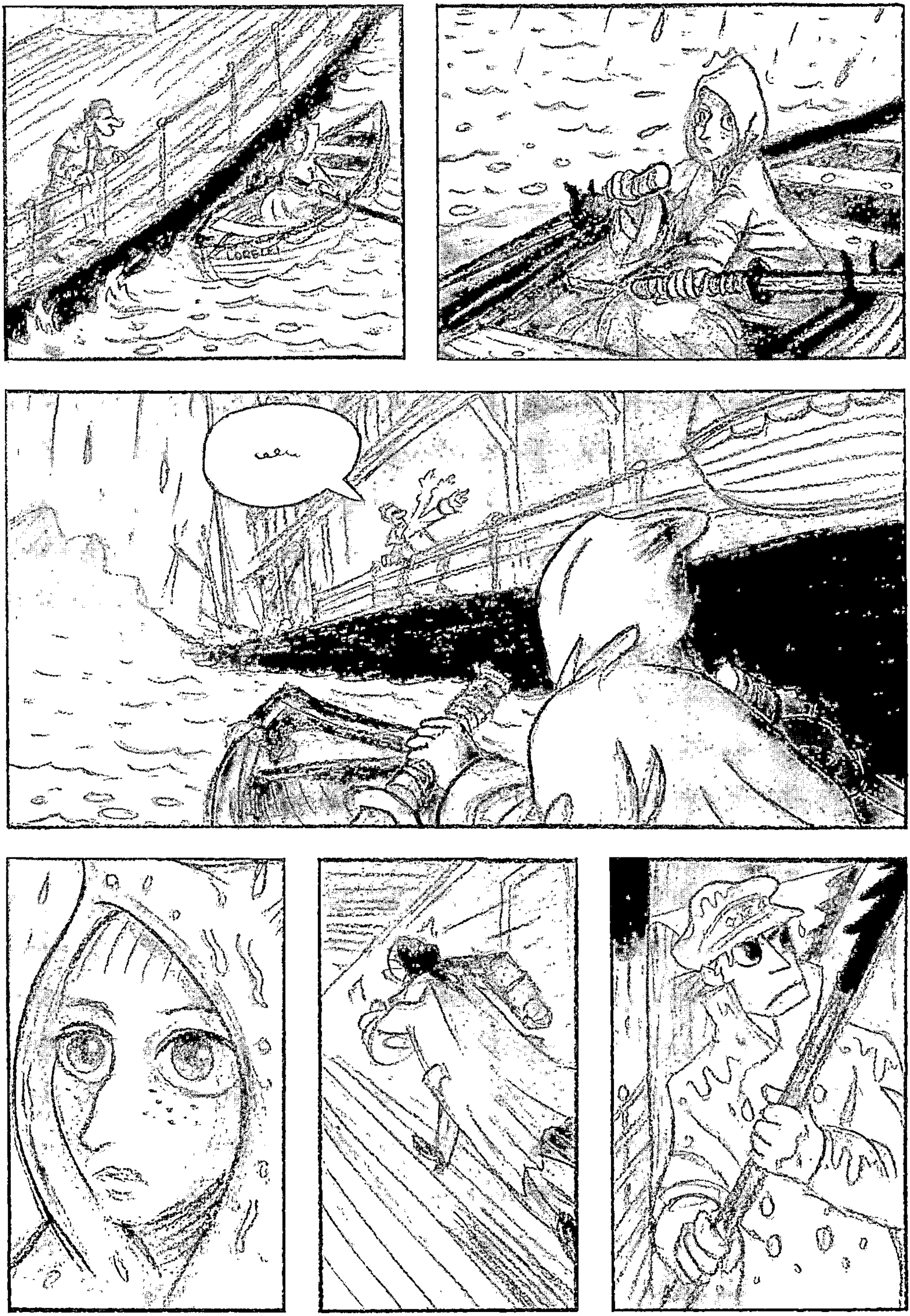
LORELEI

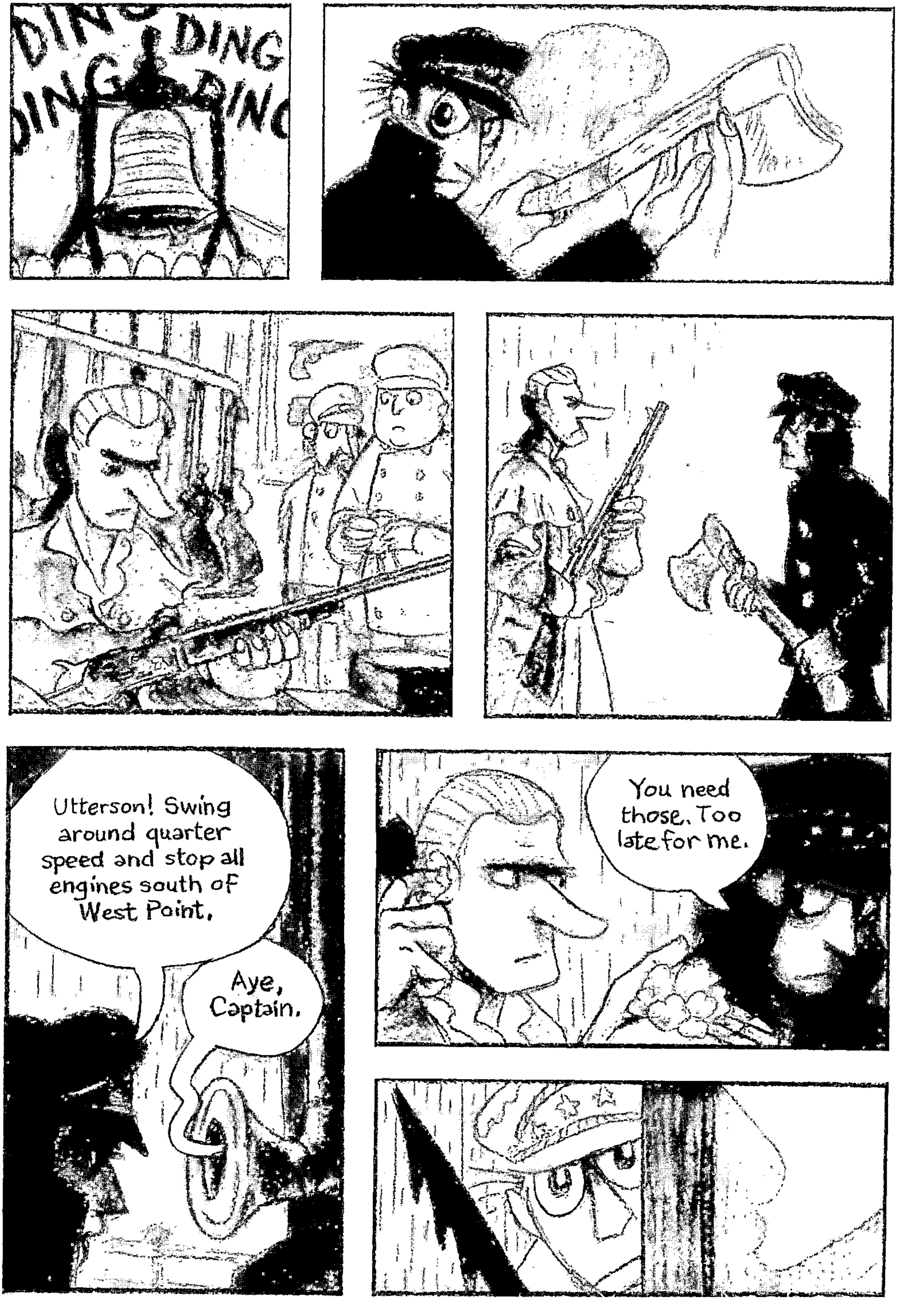
DING DING
DING DING
Utterson! Swing around quarter speed and stop all engines south of West Point.
Aye, Captain.
You need those. Too late for me.

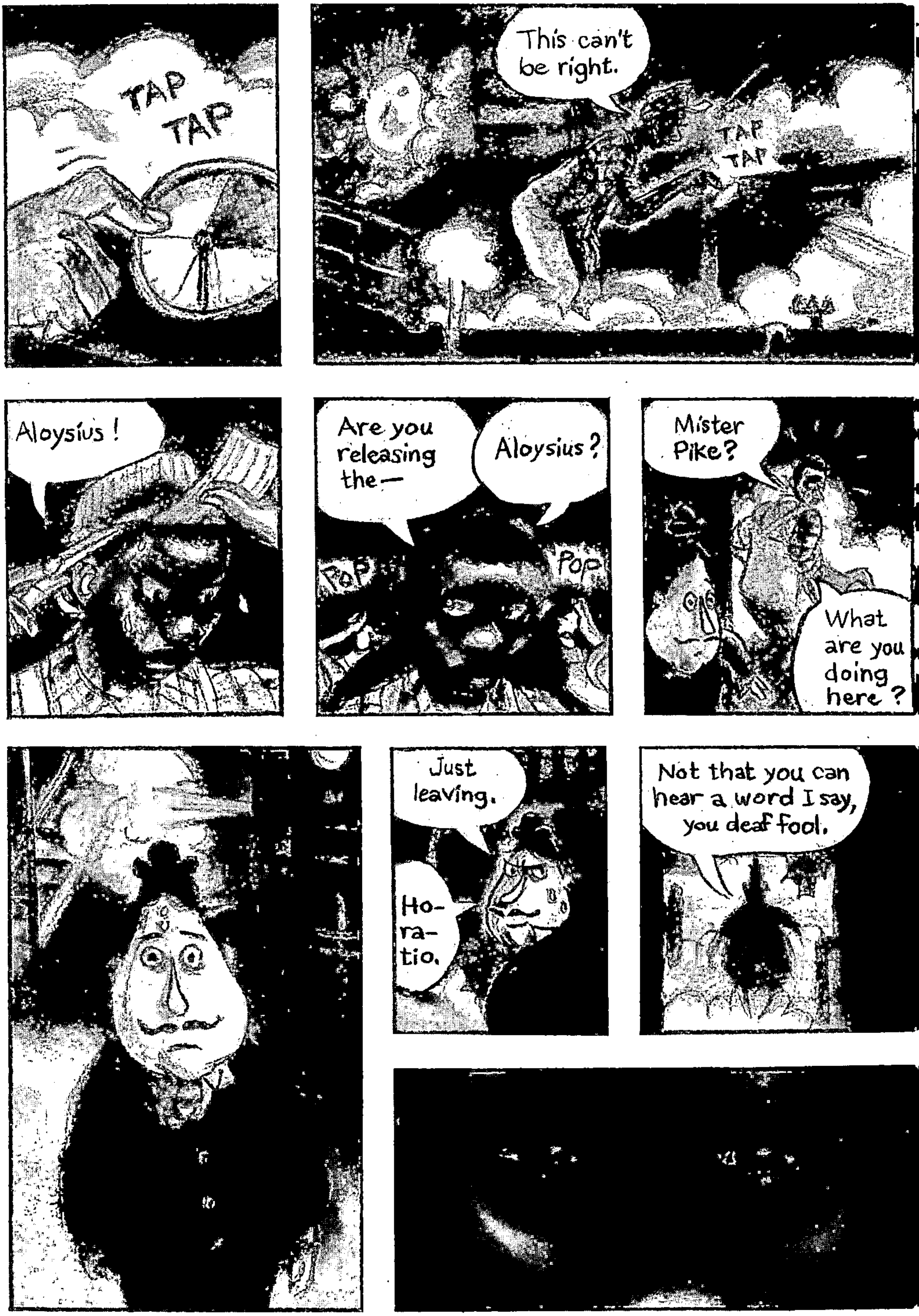
TAP
TAP
This can't be right.
TAP
TAP
Aloysius!
Are you releasing the—
Aloysius?
POP
POP
Mister Pike?
What are you doing here?
Just leaving.
Ho-ra-tio.
Not that you can hear a word I say, you deaf fool.

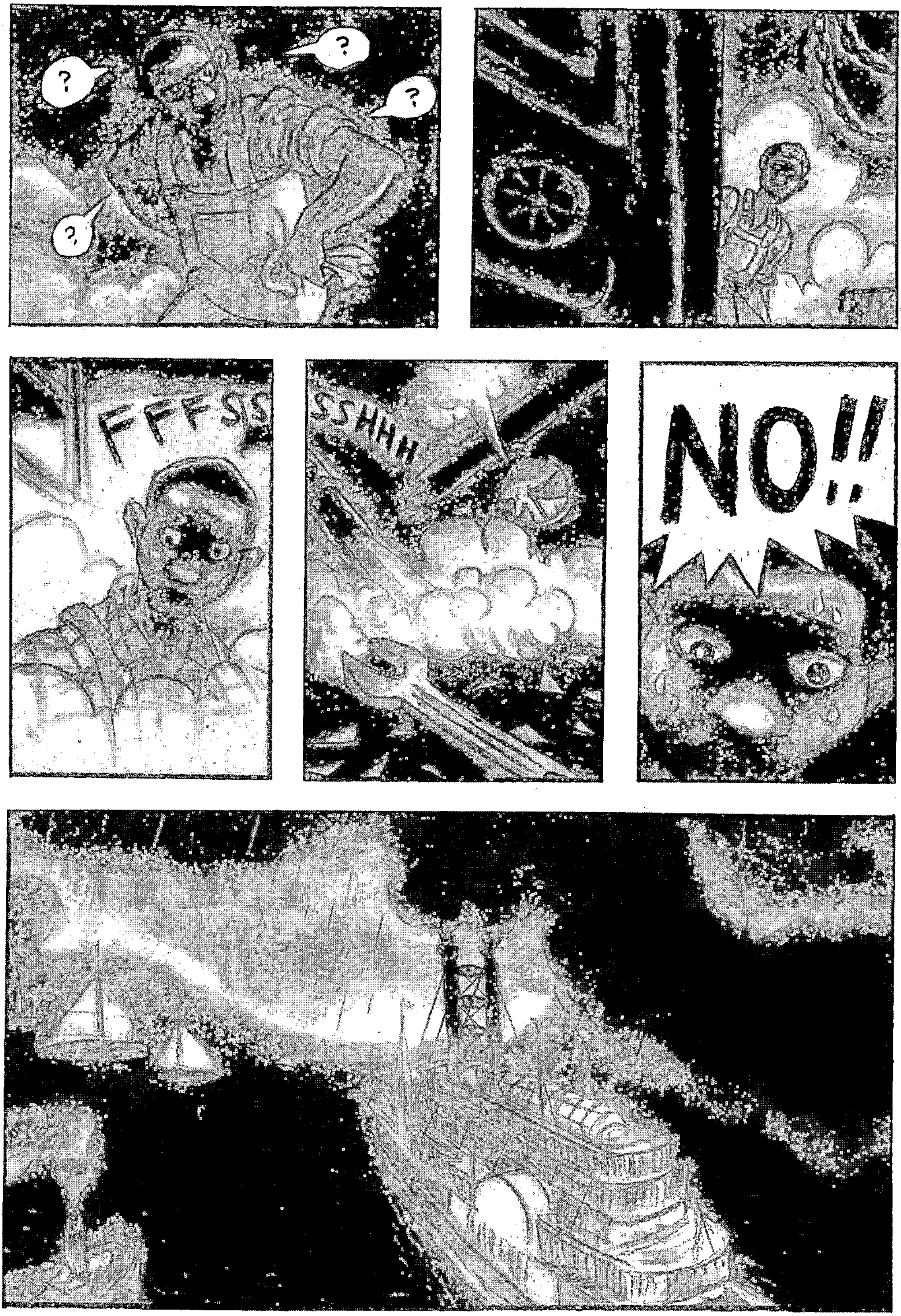
?
?
?
?
FFFSSS
SSHHH
NO!!

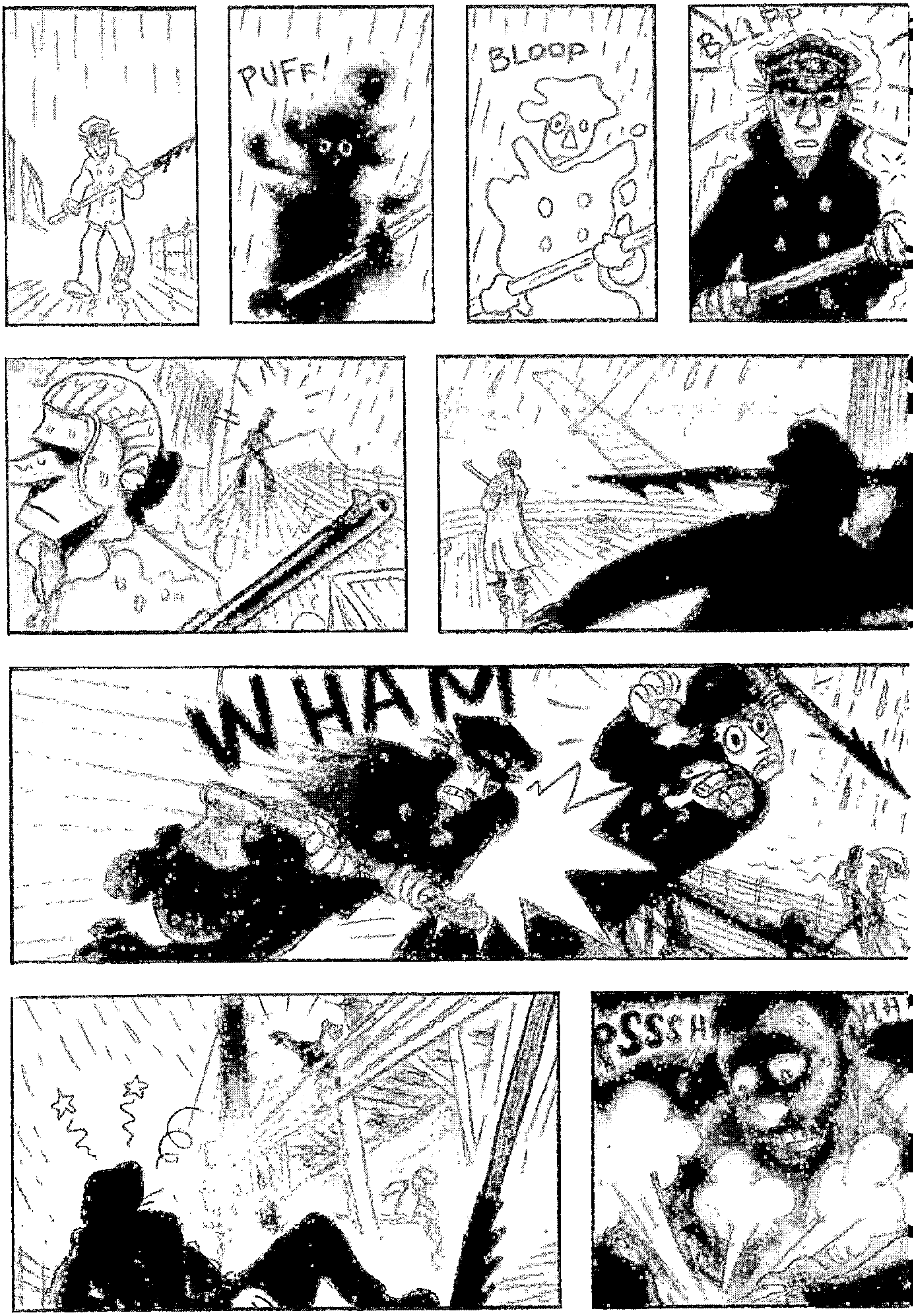
PUFF!
BLOOP
BLIPP
WHAM
PSSSH

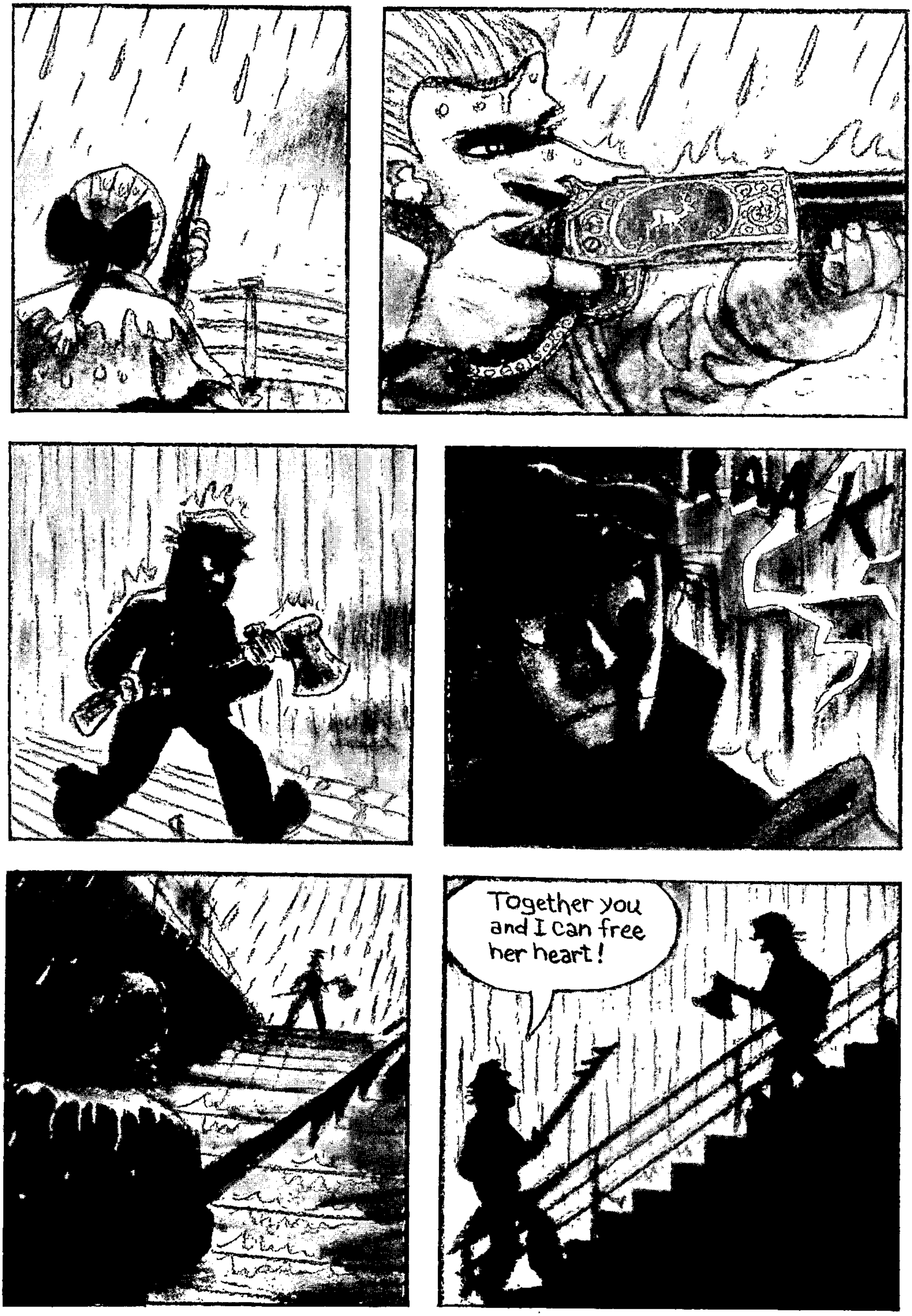
Together you and I can free her heart!

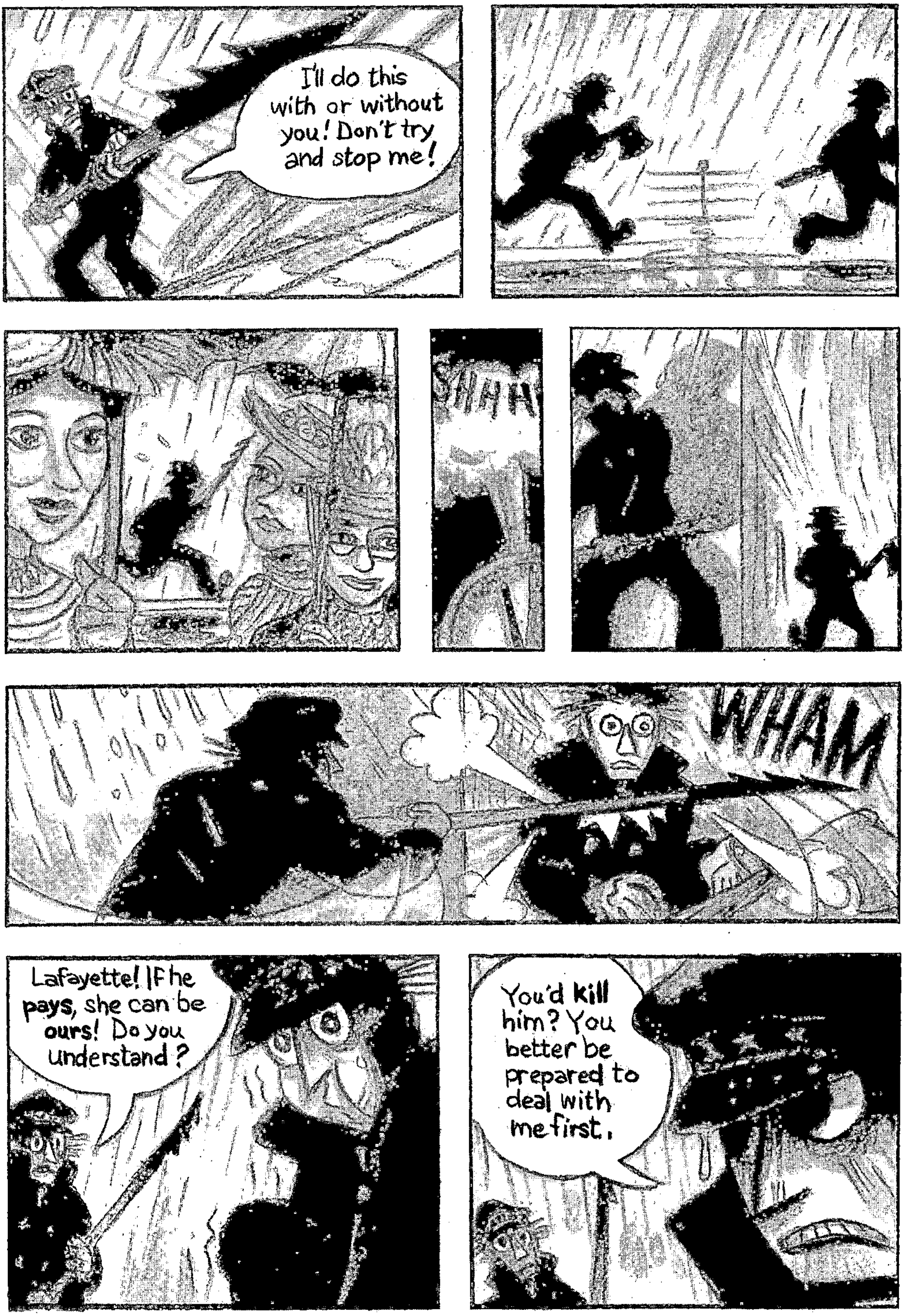

I'll do this with or without you! Don't try and stop me!
SHHH
WHAM
Lafayette! If he **pays**, she can be **ours**! Do you understand?
You'd **kill** him? You better be prepared to deal with me first.

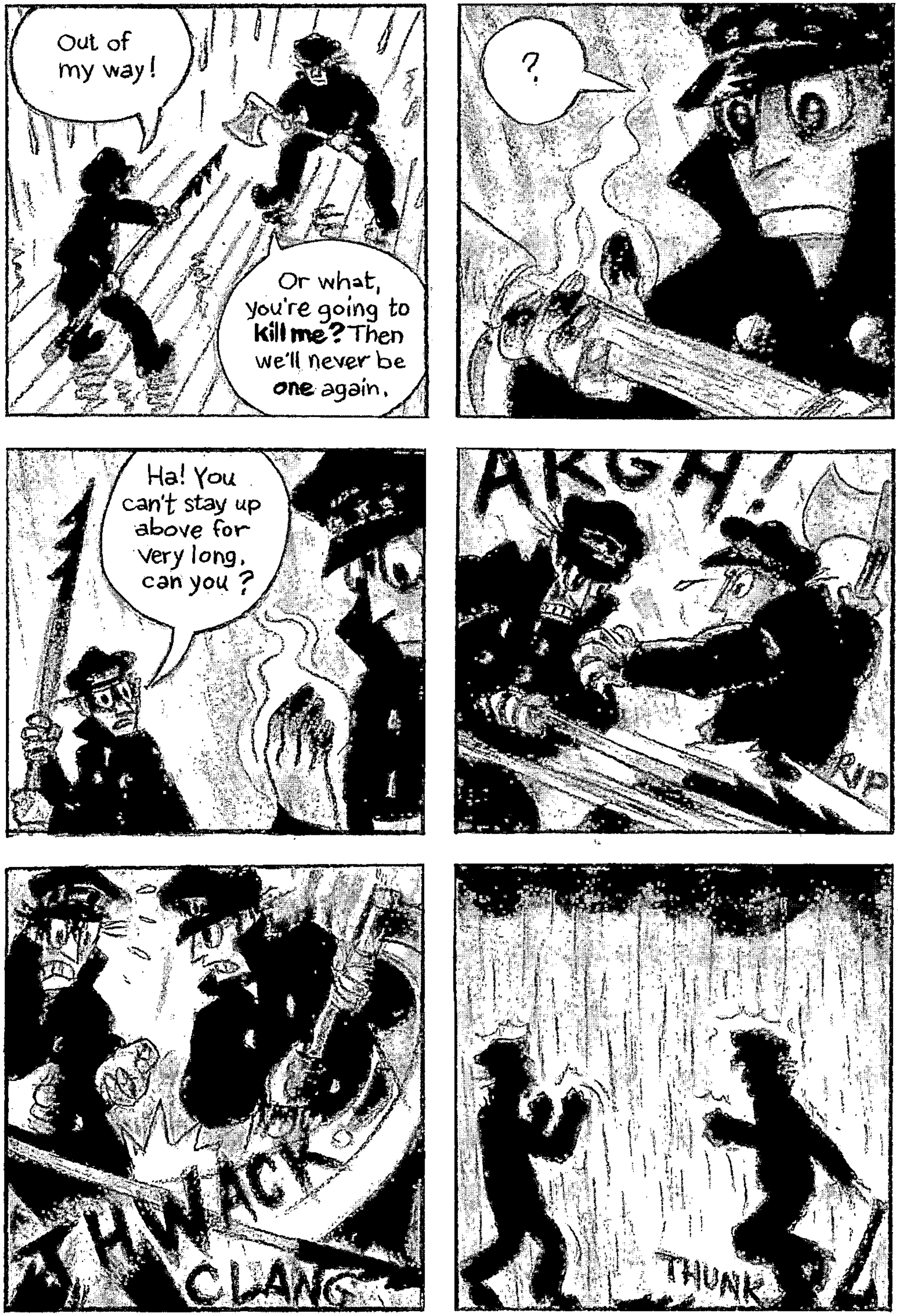
Out of my way!
Or what, you're going to **kill me?** Then we'll never be **one** again.
?
Ha! You can't stay up above for very long, can you?
ARGH!
RIP
THWACK
CLANG
THUNK

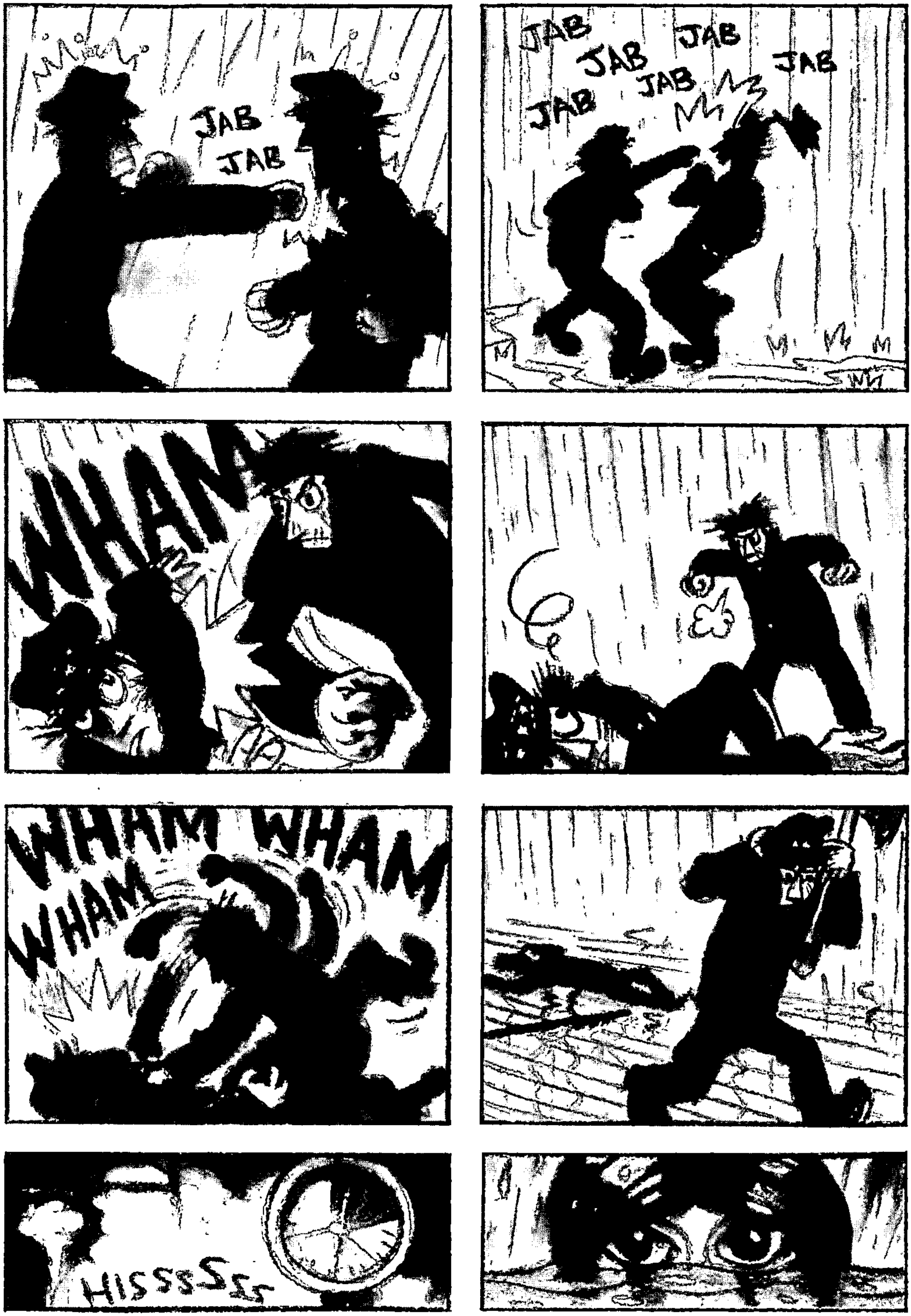
JAB
JAB
JAB
JAB
JAB
JAB
JAB
JAB
WHAM
WHAM WHAM
WHAM
HISSSSSS

Pt IV, Chap.2

"THE SIREN'S WRATH"

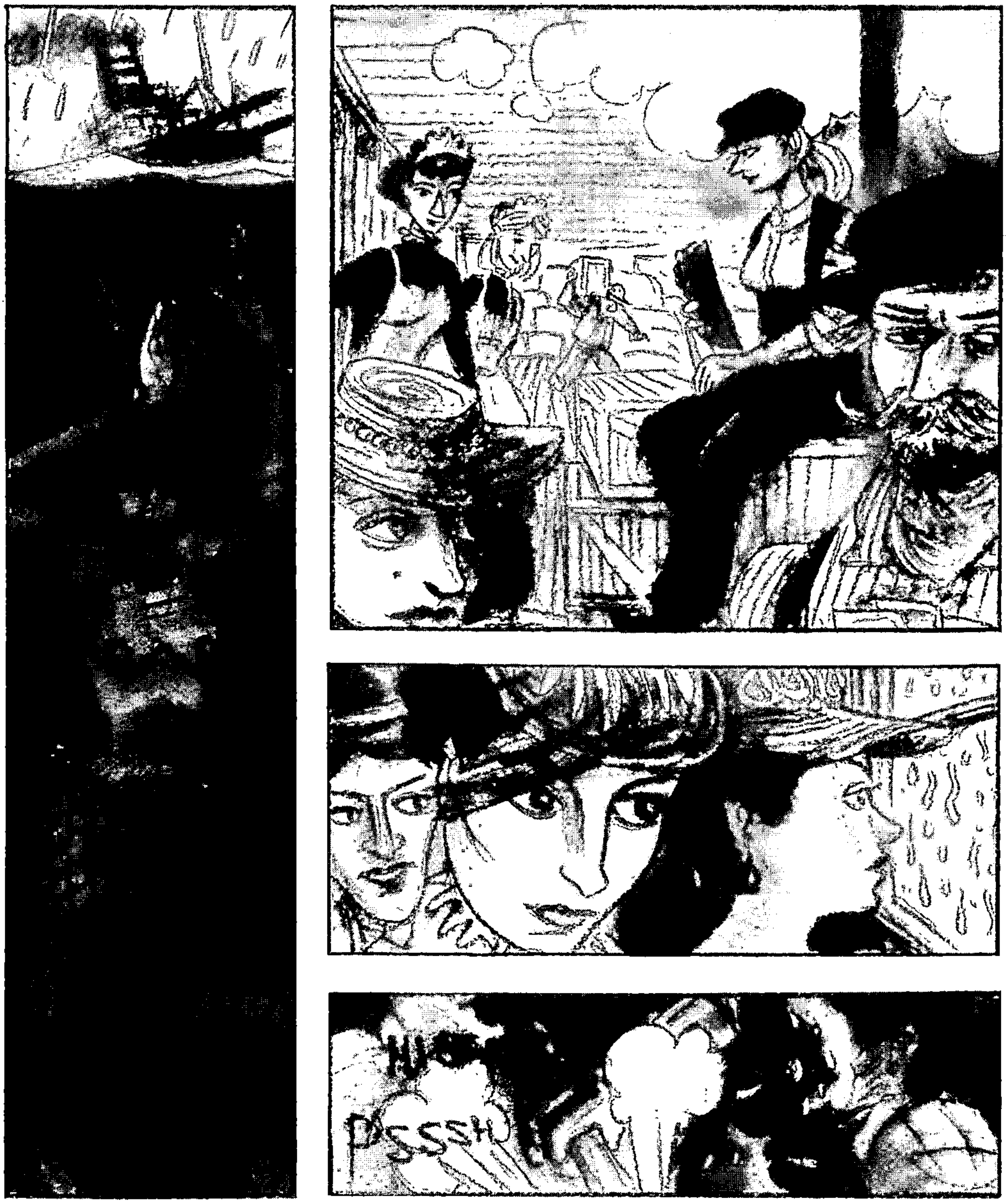
PSSSH

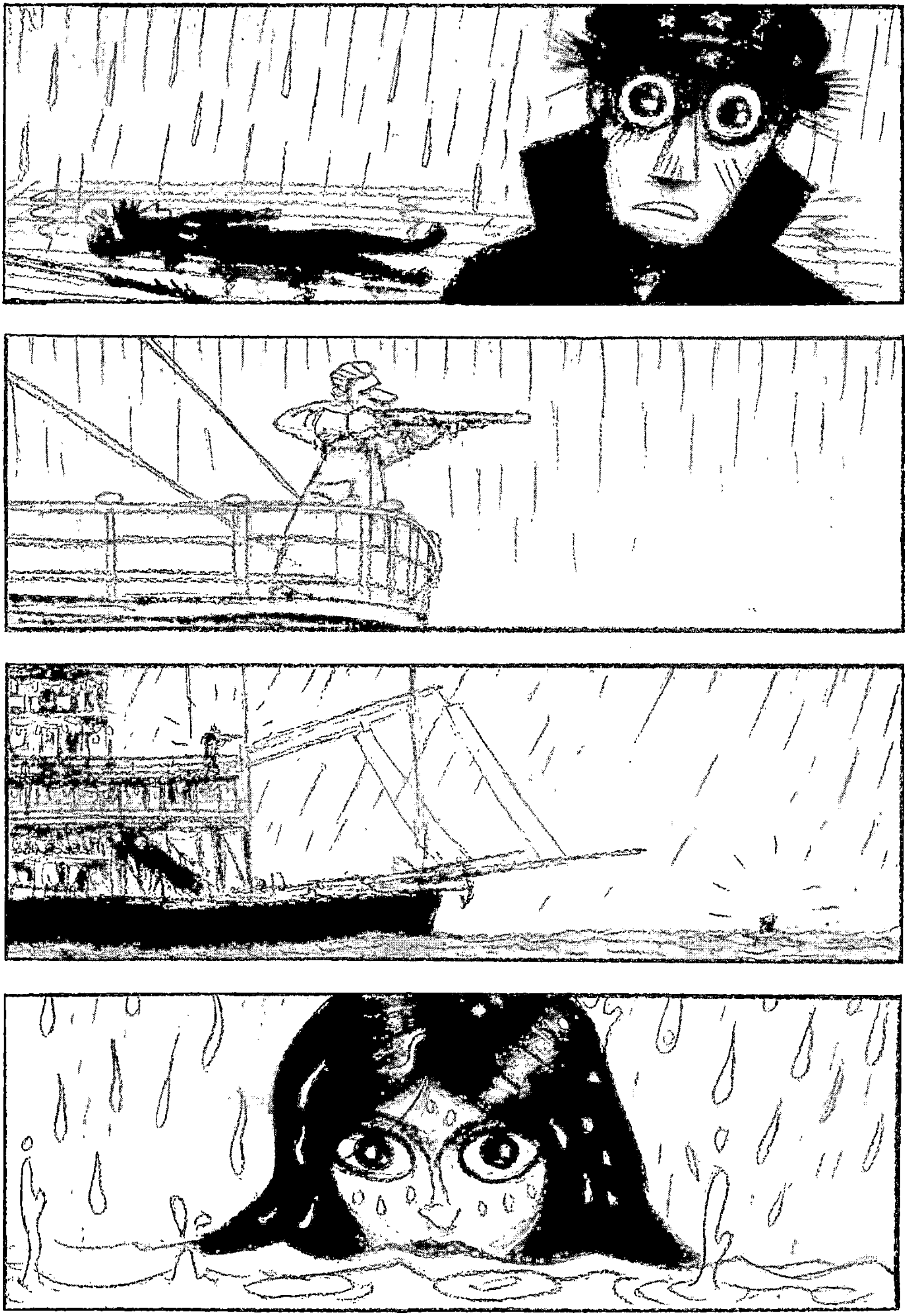

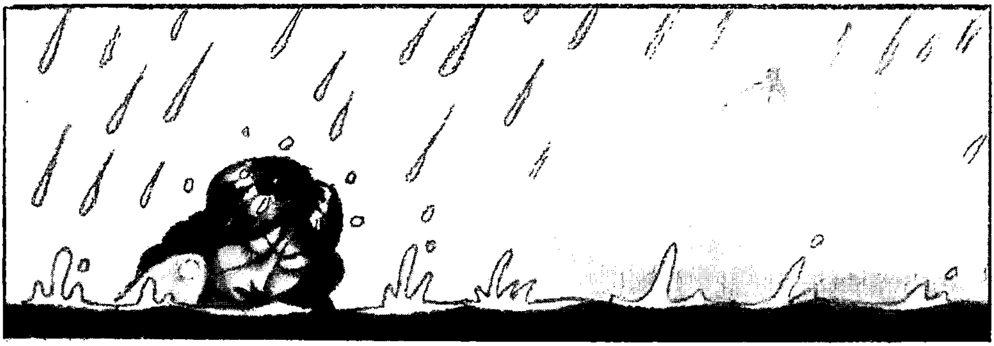

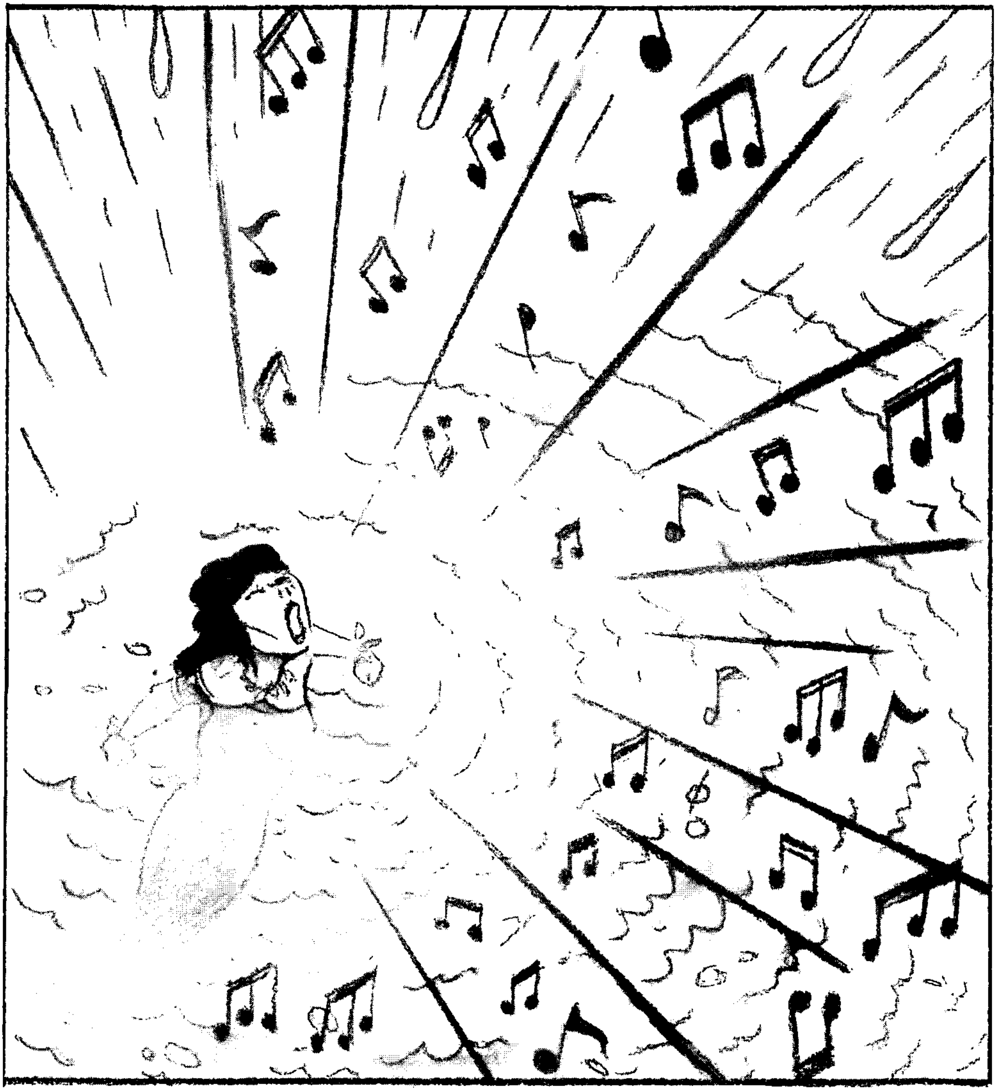

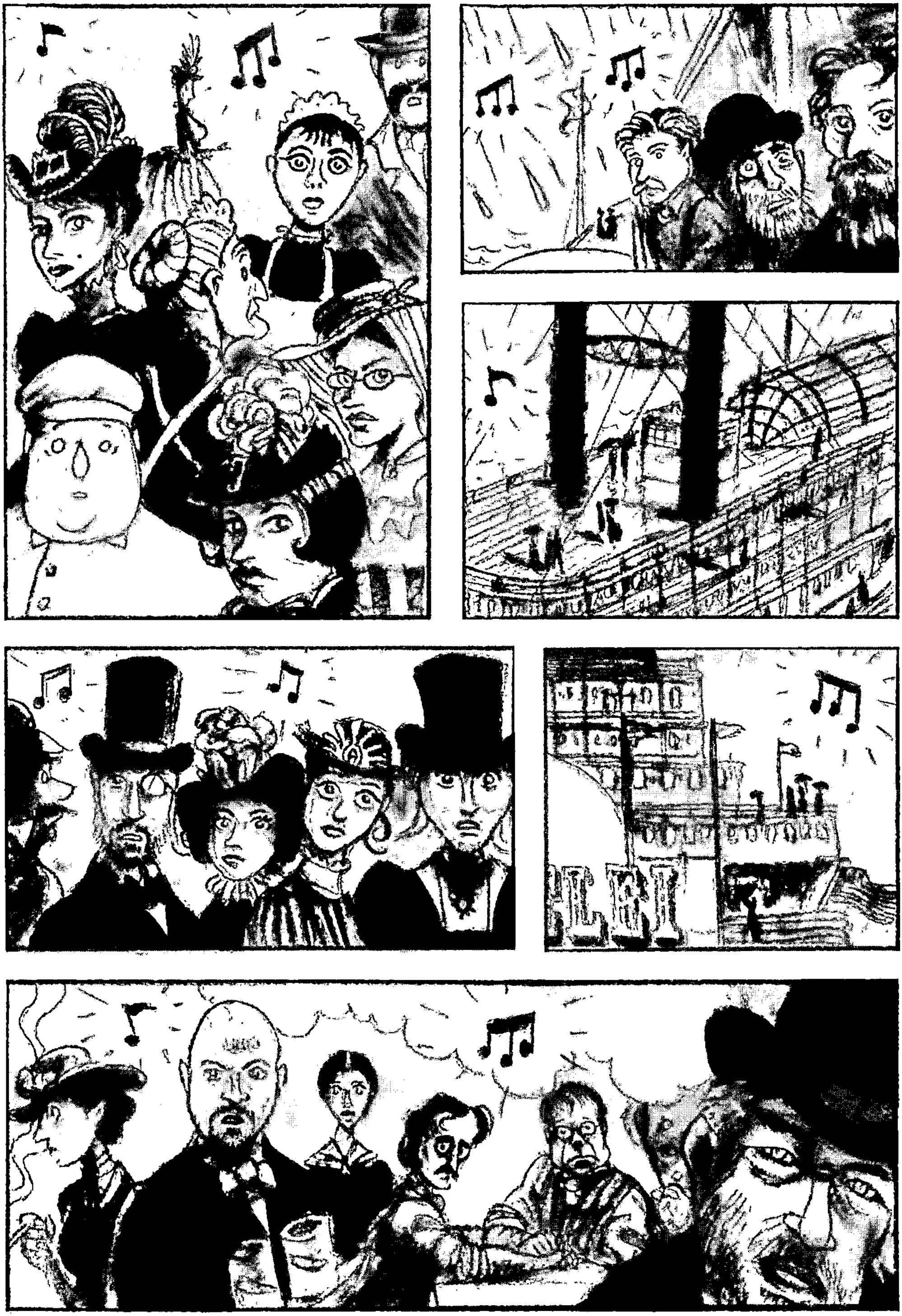

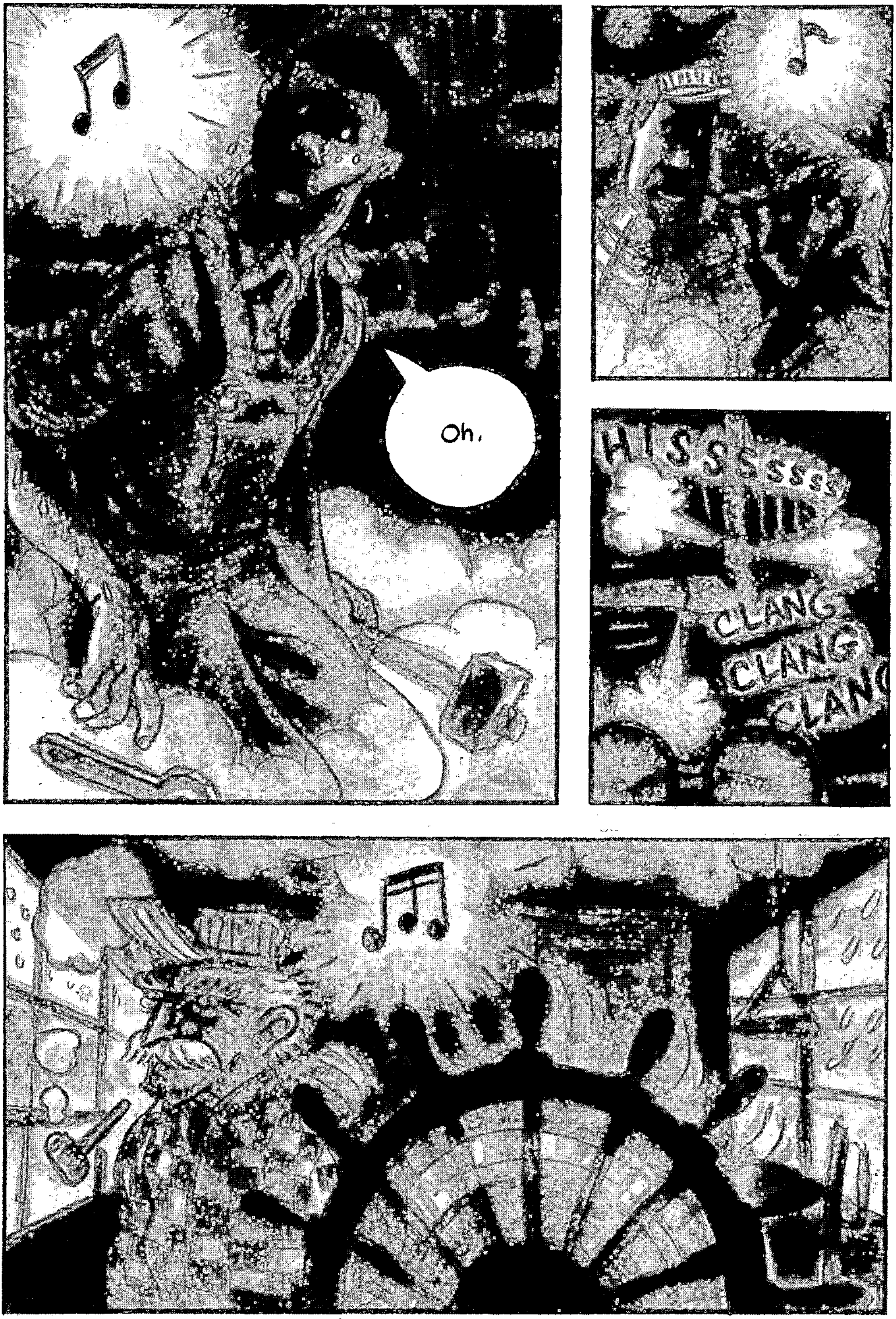
Oh.
HISSSSSS
CLANG
CLANG

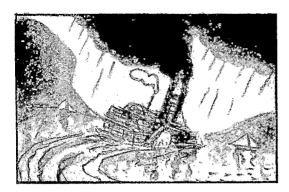

What is he waiting for?

His bullets are useless against her.

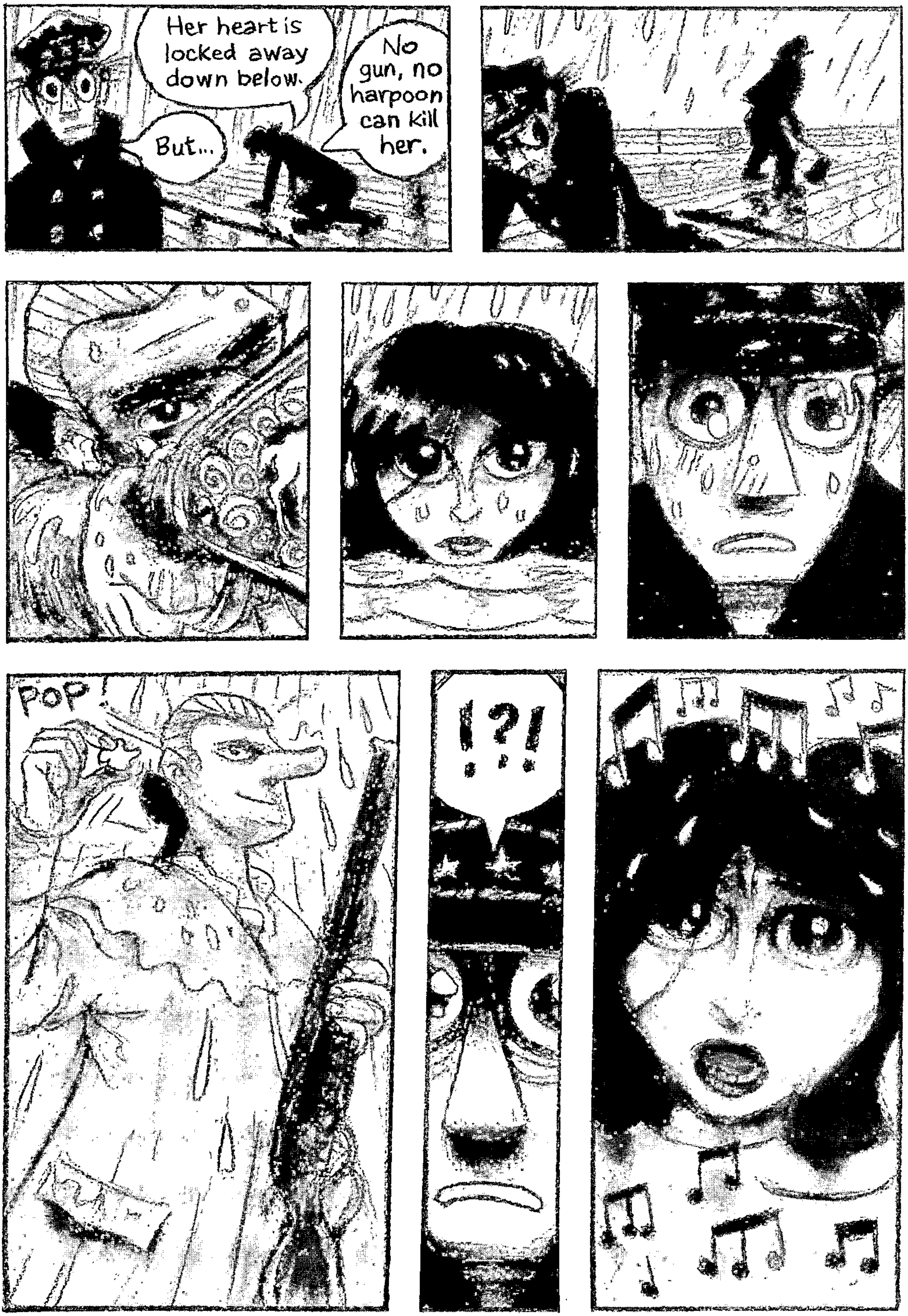
Her heart is locked away down below.
But...
No gun, no harpoon can kill her.
POP!
!?!

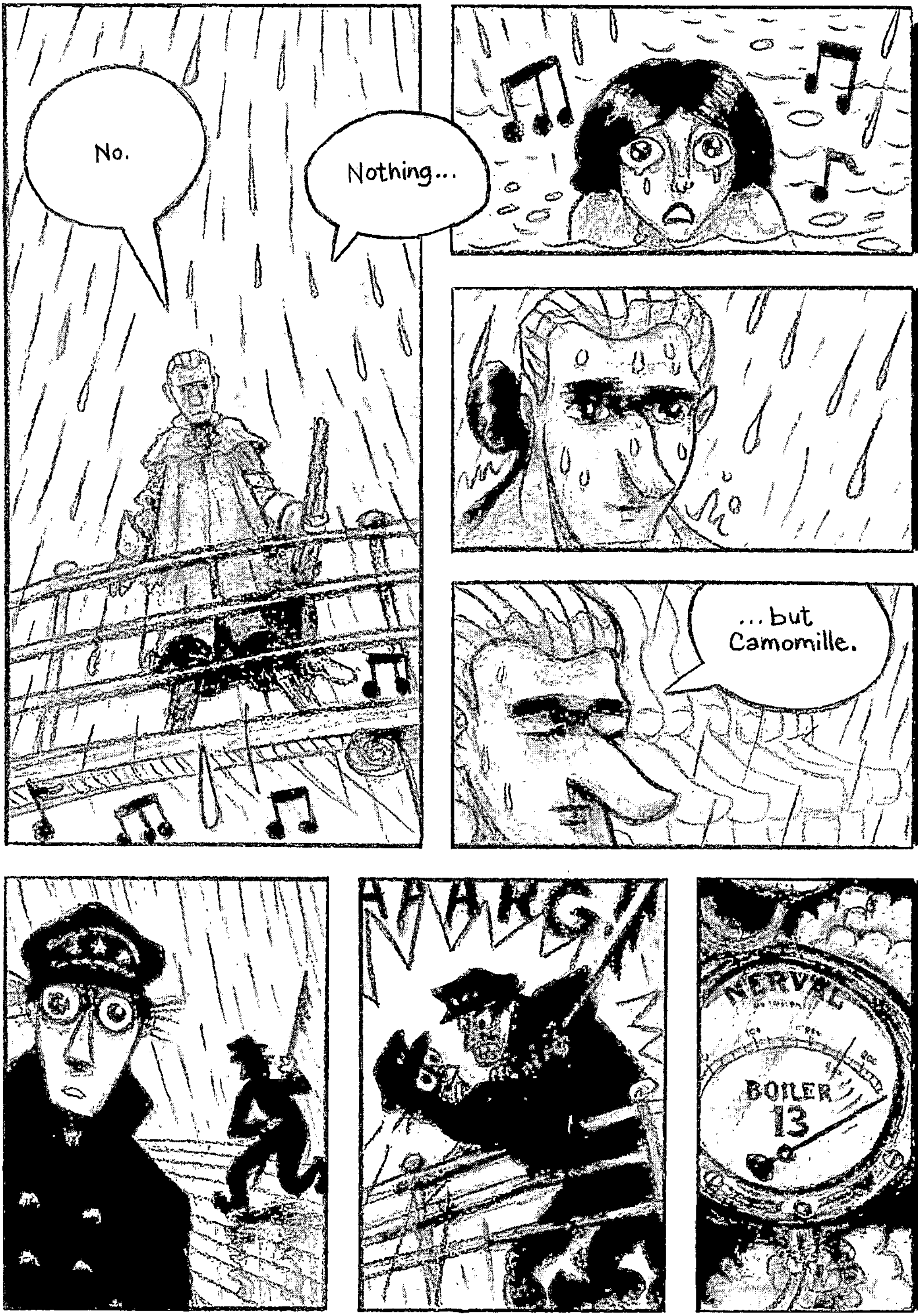
No.
Nothing...
...but Camomille.
AARG!!
NERVAL
BOILER
13

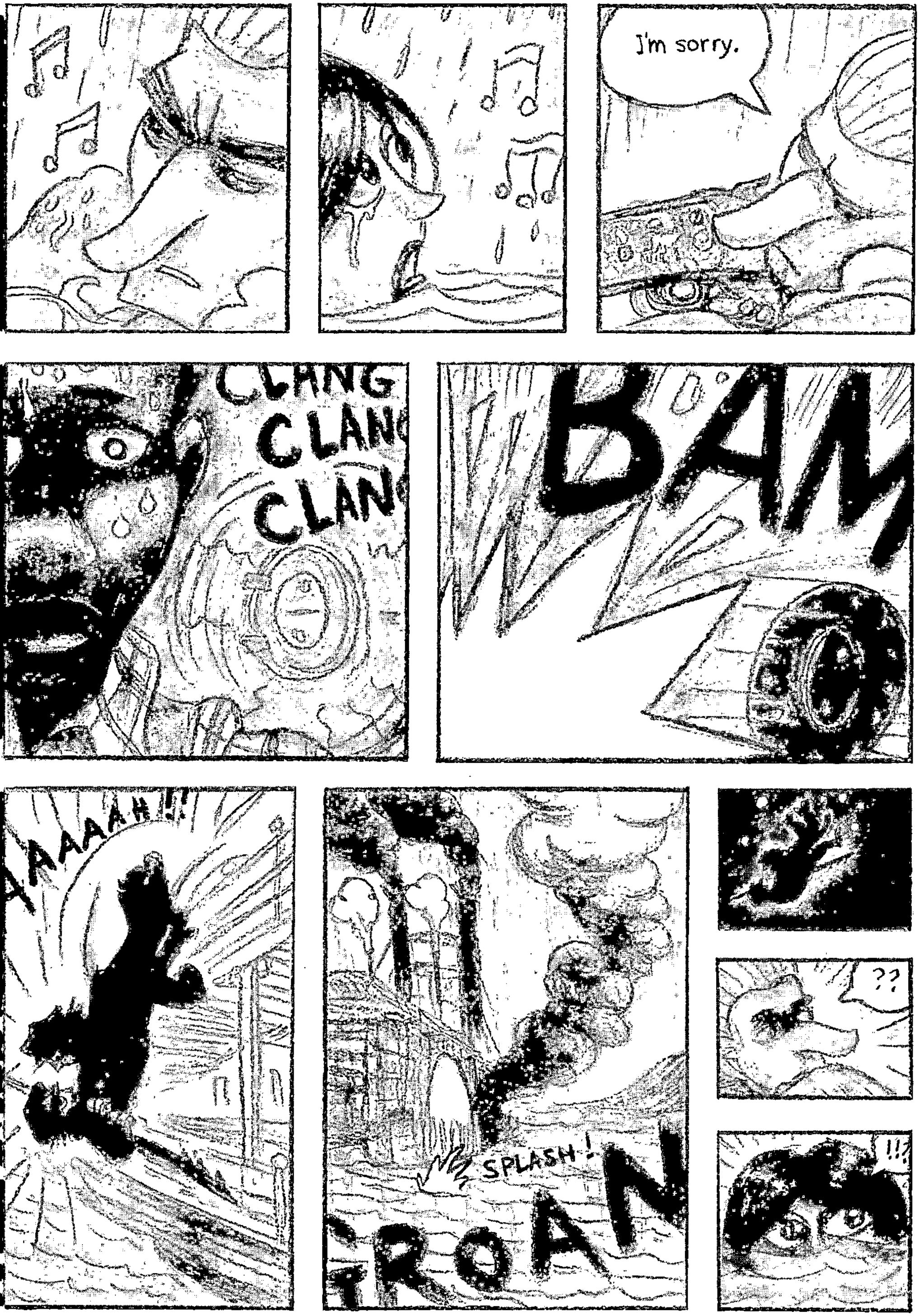
I'm sorry.
CLANG
CLANG
CLANG
BAM
AAAAAH!!
SPLASH!
TROAN
??
!!?

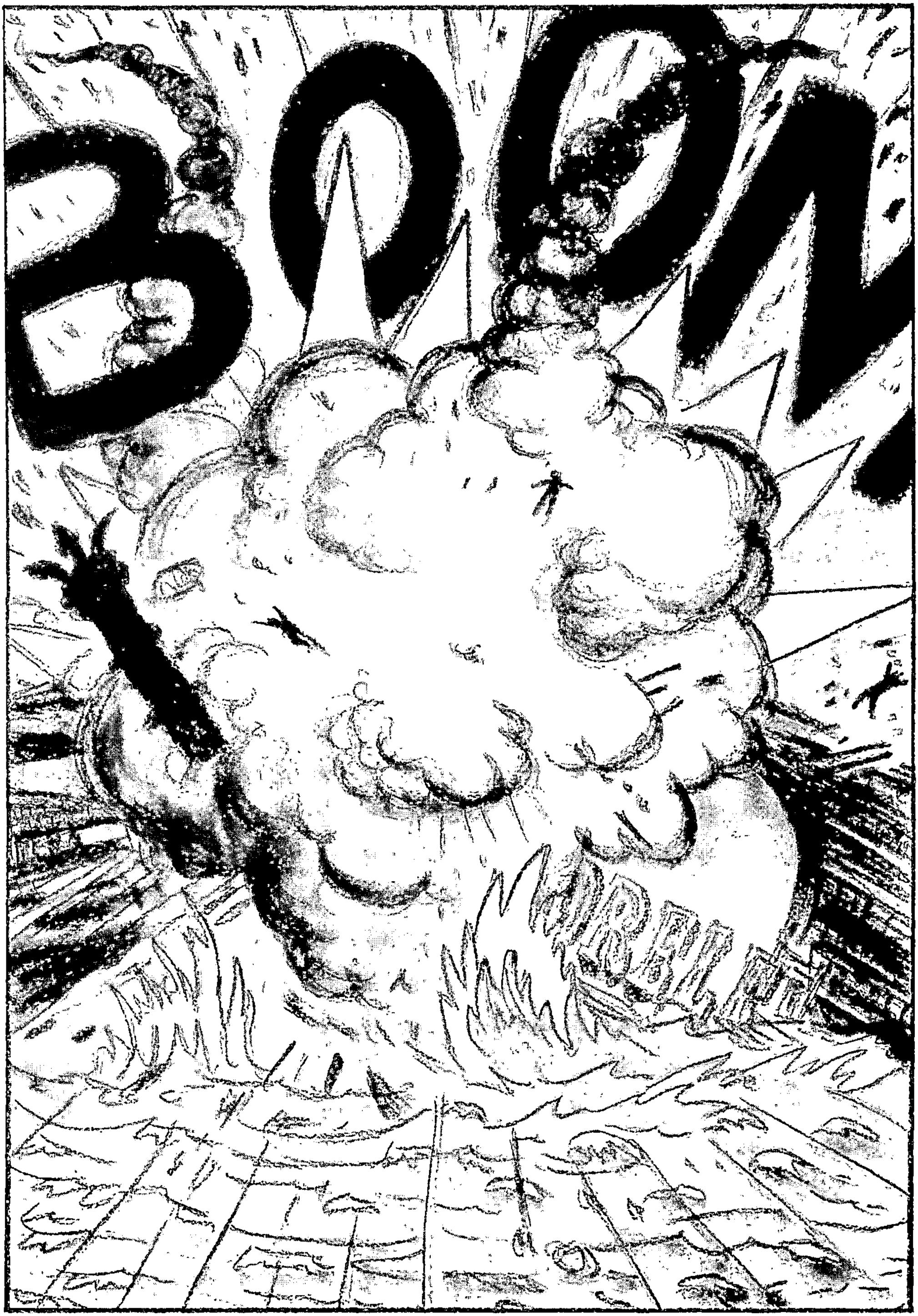
BOOM

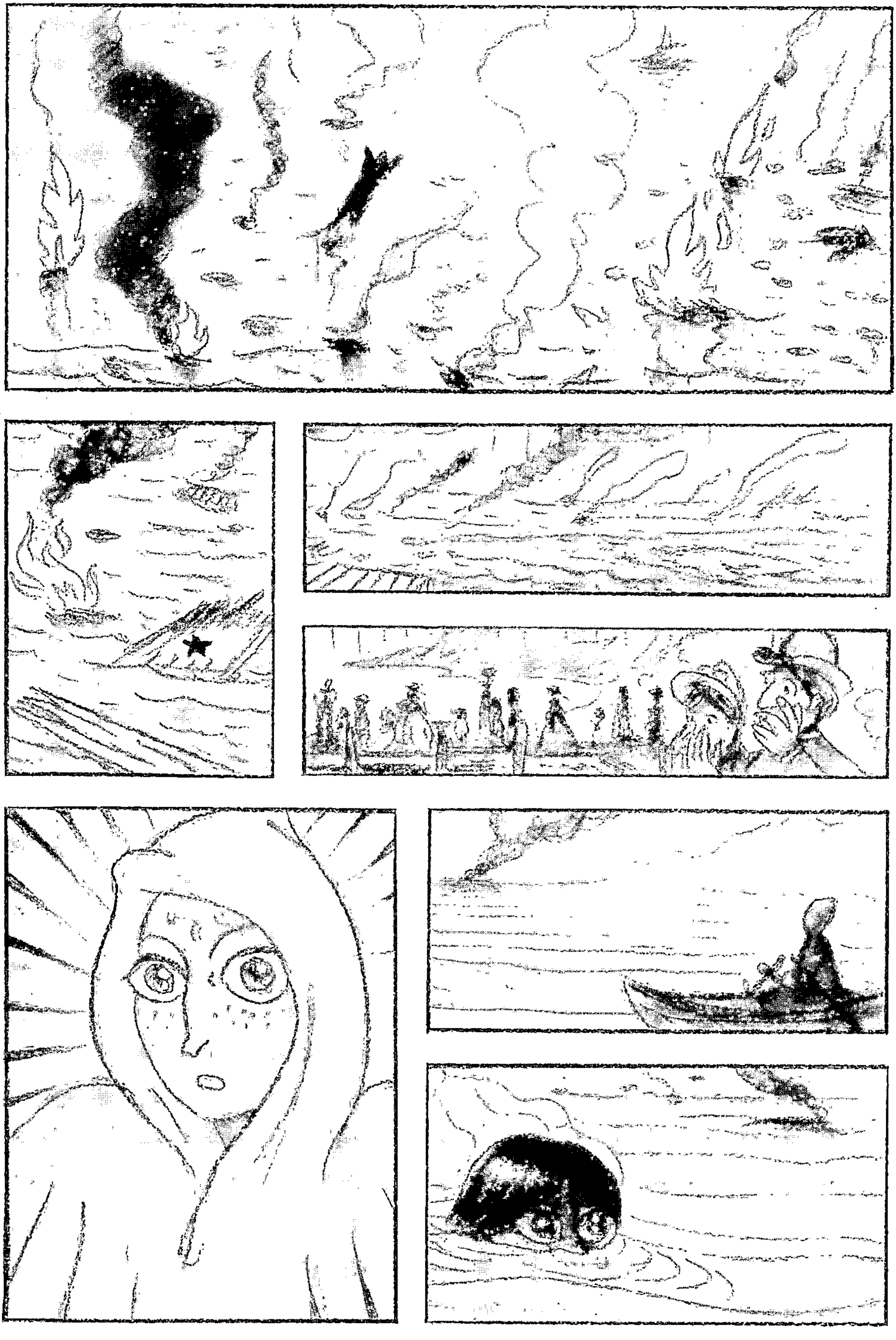

CODA

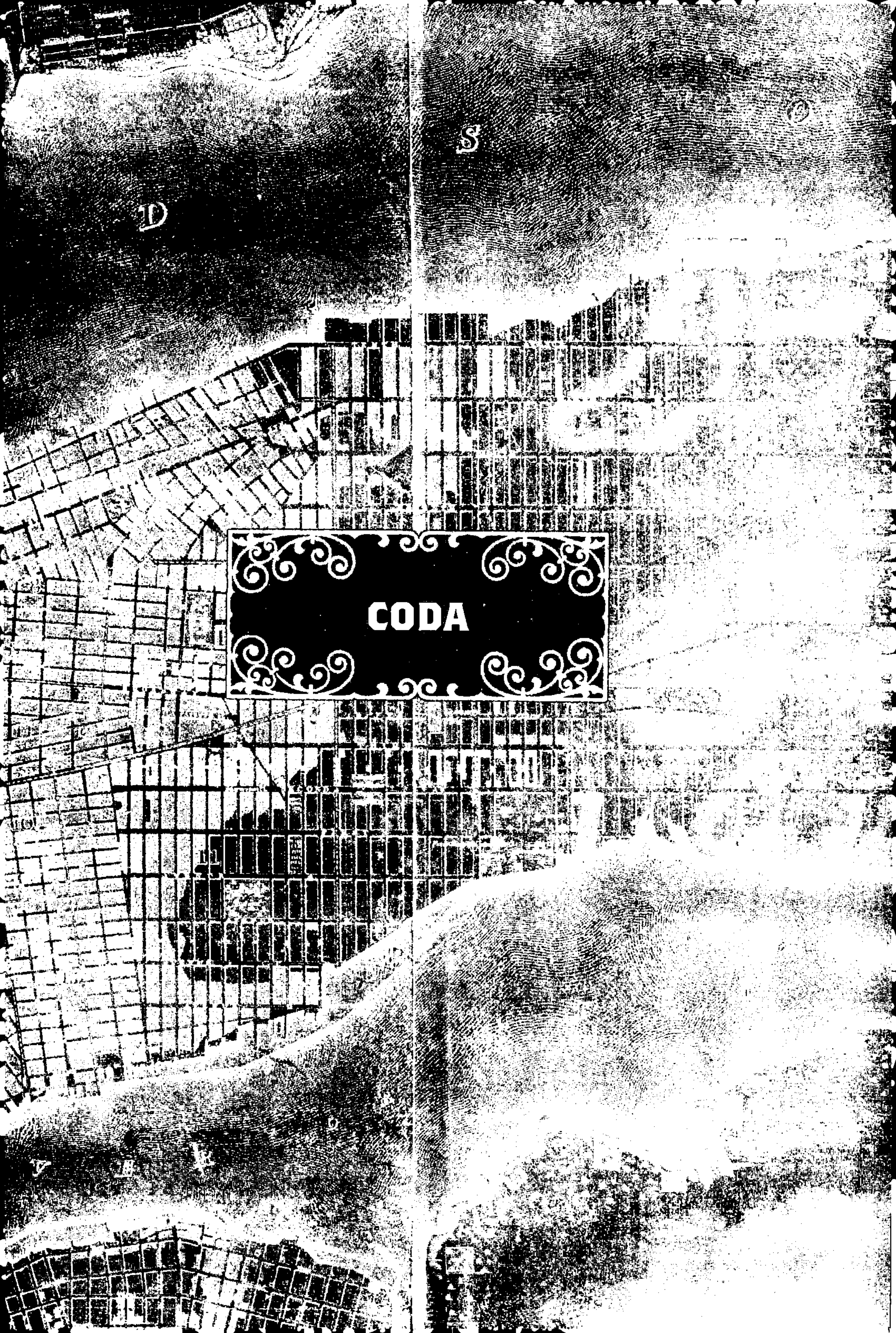

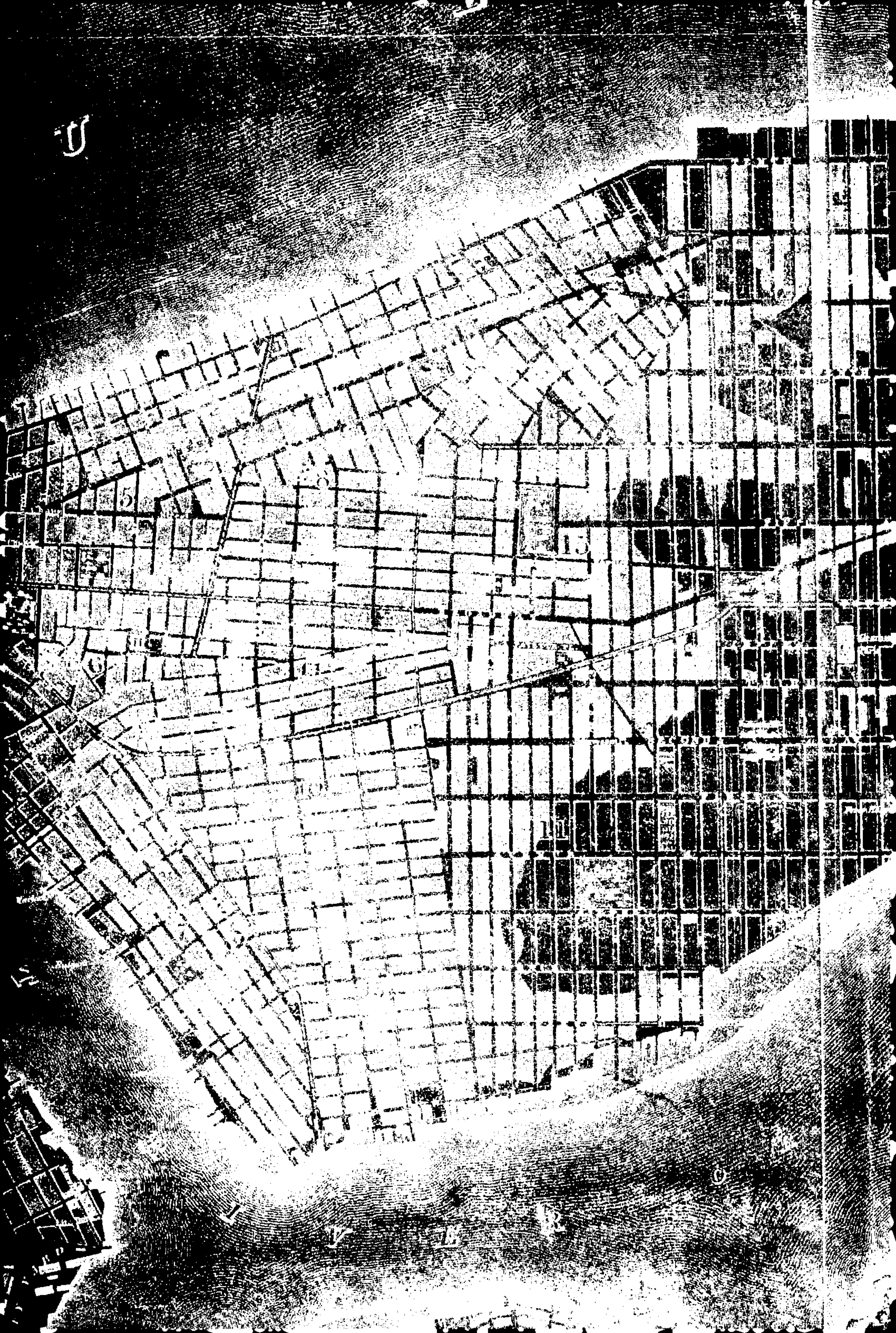

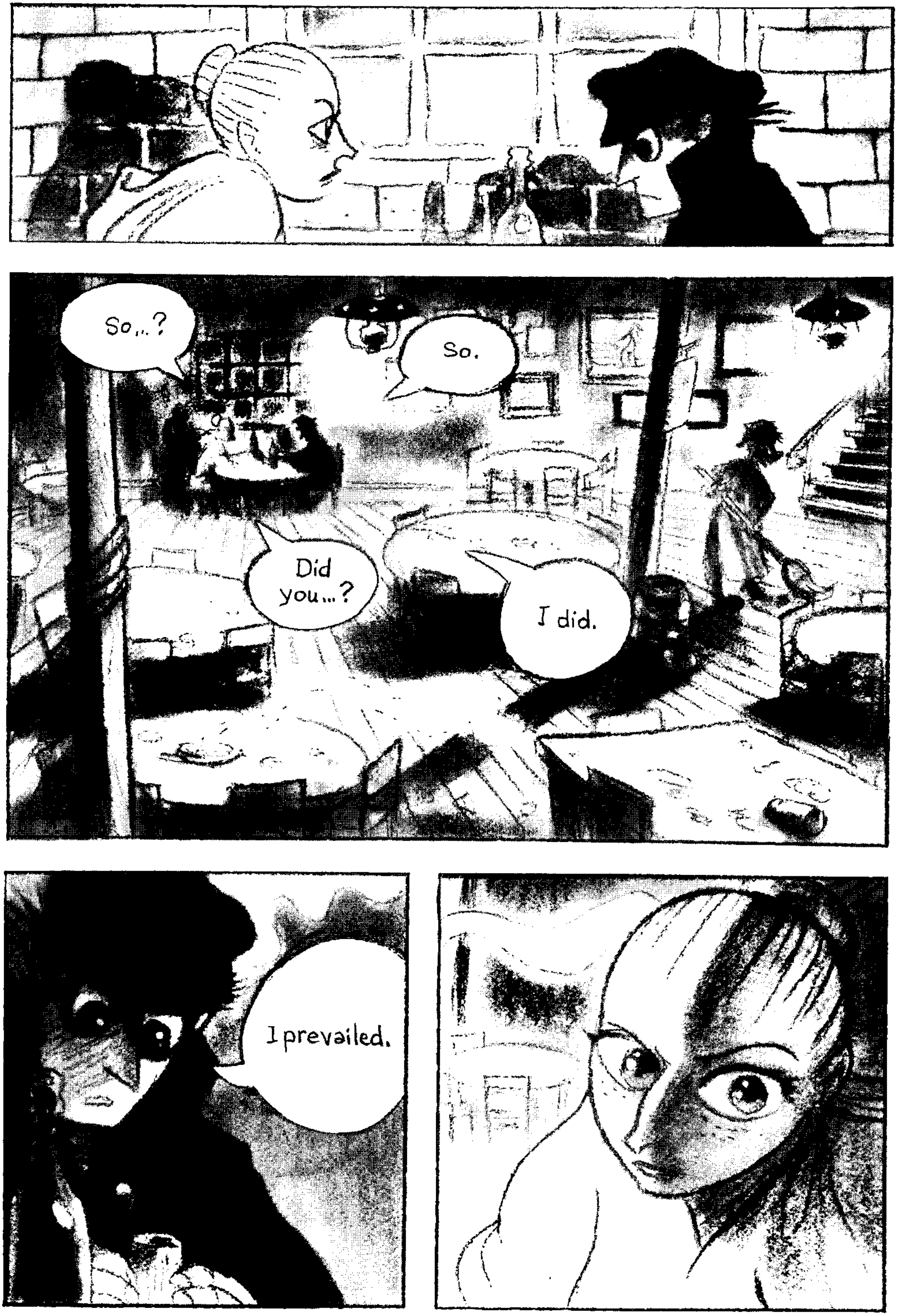
So...?
So.
Did you...?
I did.
I prevailed.

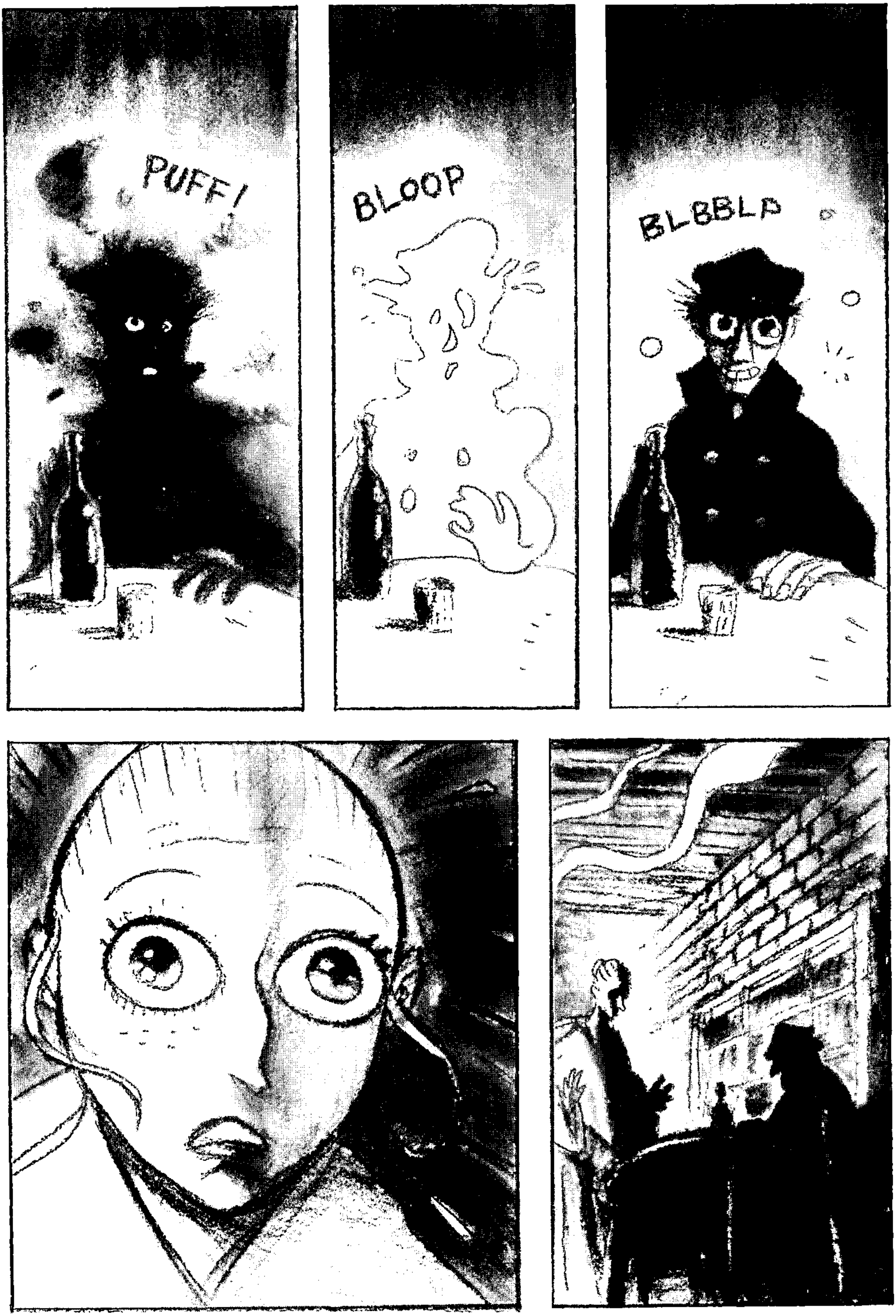
PUFF!
BLOOP
BLBBLP

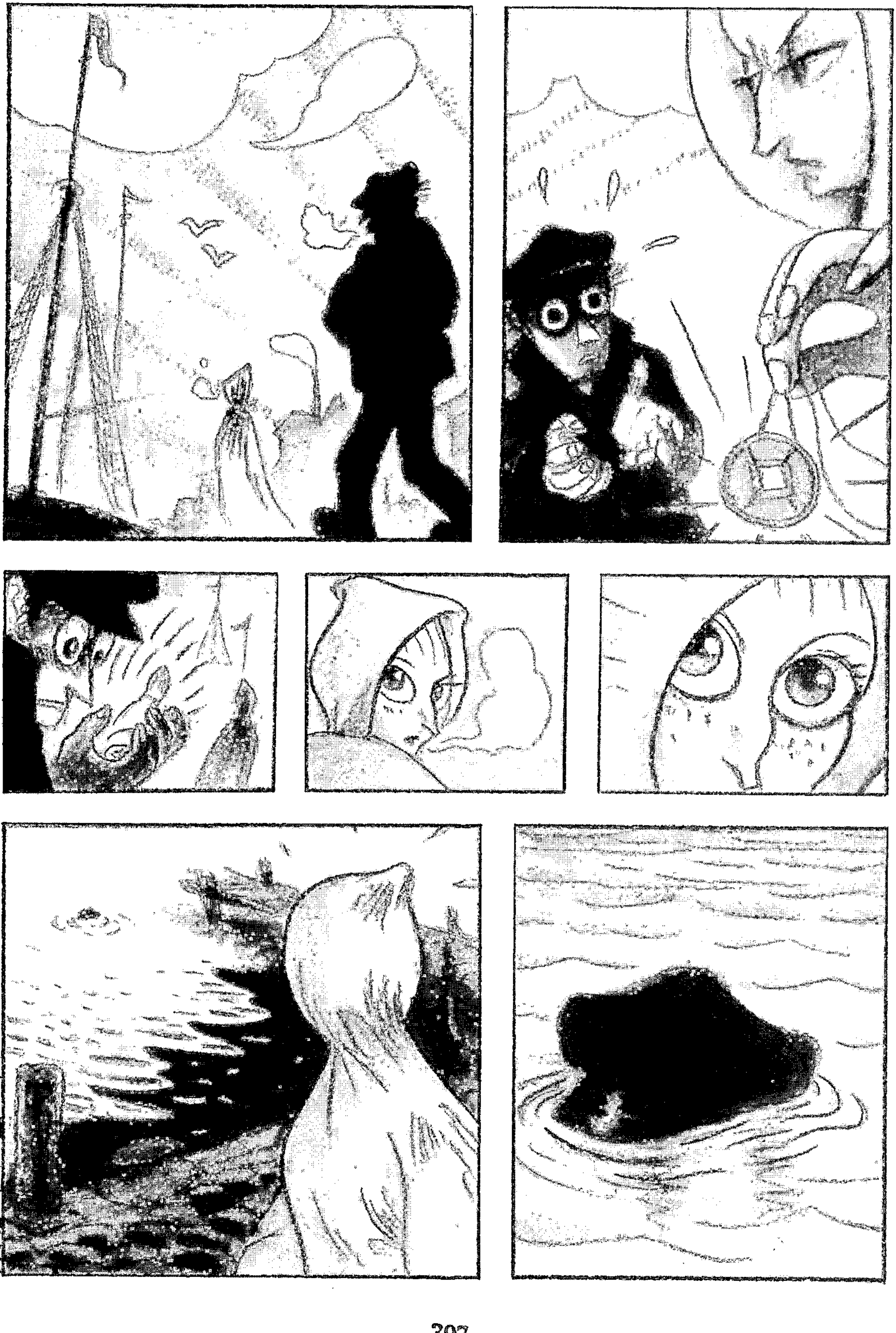

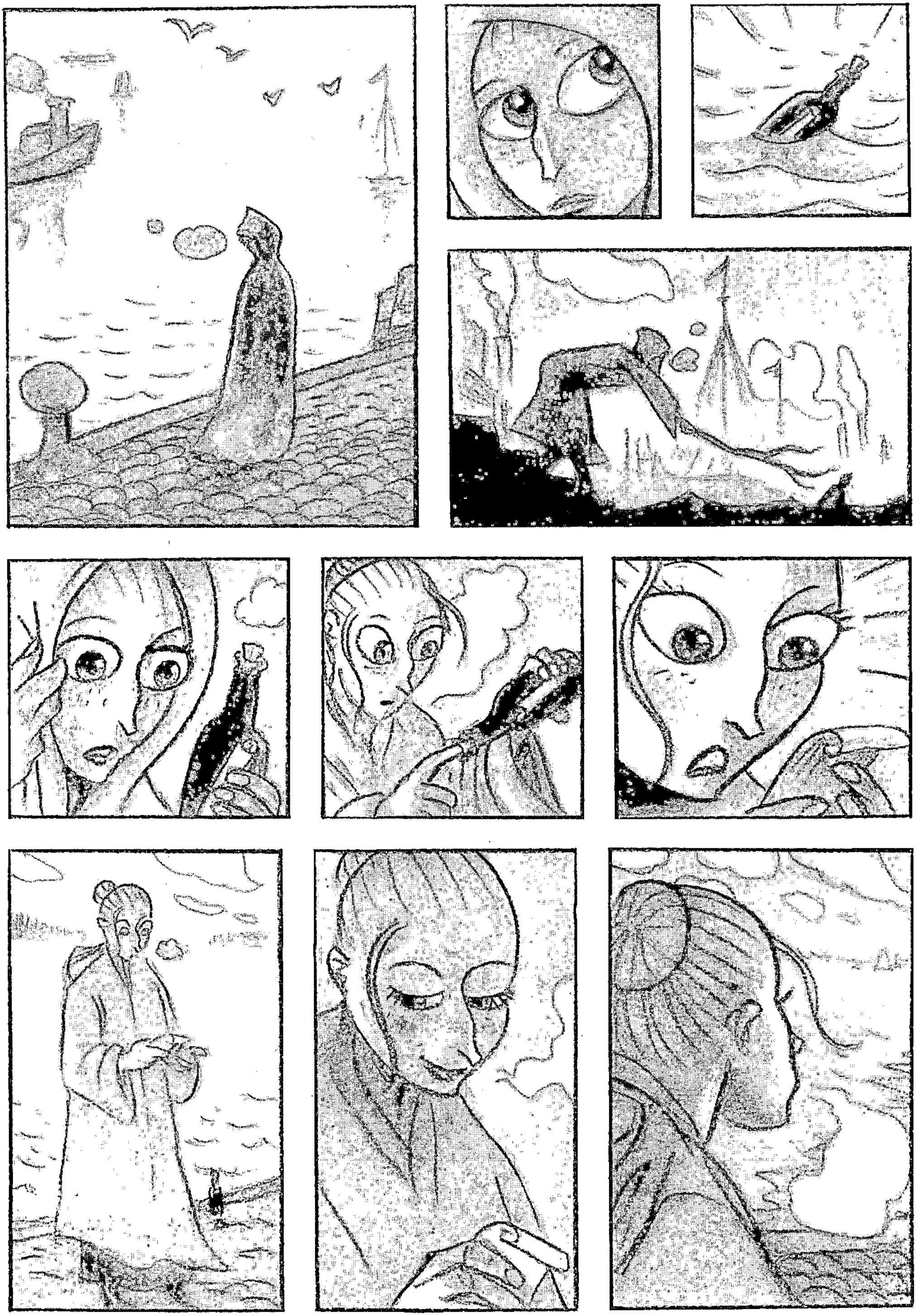

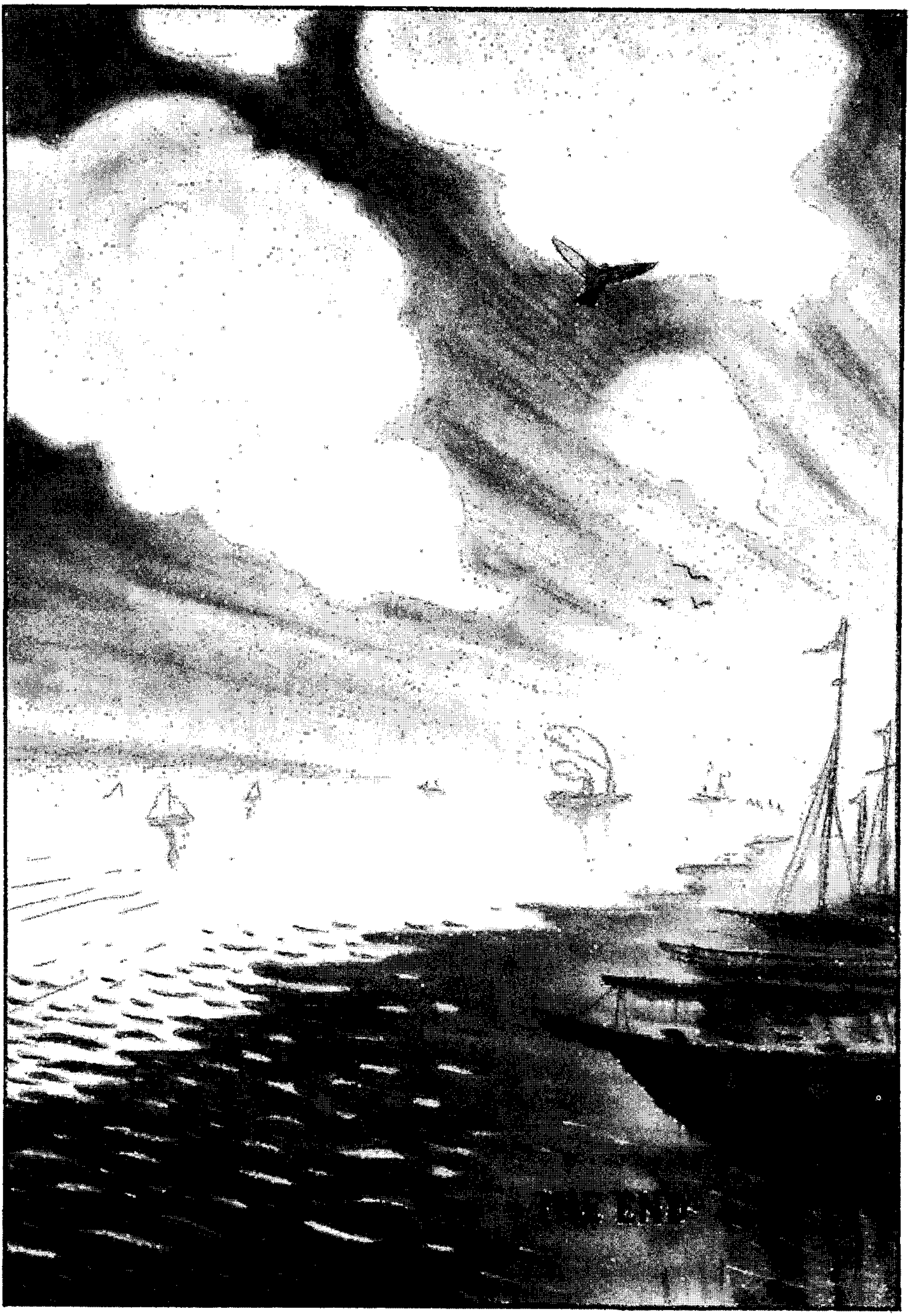

THANK YOU

My dearest Siena, for the paths we haven't taken.

Tanya McKinnon, for your brilliant and relentless partnership.

Alexis Siegel, mon ami, mon frère, et Sonia, ma petite soeur bien aimée.

Simon Boughton, for your trust and many insights.

Colleen Venable, Calista Brill, Gina Gagliano, Jill Freshney, Alexa Villanueva

Jon Yaged, John Sargent
Lora Fountain, Holly Hunnicutt

Richard Simon, Victoria Sanders

Thierry Laroche, Muriel Chabert, Nicolas Leroy, Caroline Moreau, Raphaël Ventura, and the whole team at Gallimard

Special thanks Joann Sfar

Fellow Twainers! How can I thank you for the weeks and months spent with you in fog and rain aboard the *Lorelei*! I never knew so many friends would join what is normally a lonesome journey.

Extra thanks for help on the Old English, Italian, and Russian: Anne Maclachlan, Filippo Baccino, Lyudmila Kapustina, Konstantin Svist, and Alexey Zaytsev.

Thank you, Pete Seeger and his mighty sloop *Clearwater* and its entire crew, in particular Nina Sanders and Catherine Stankowski.

Susan Kriete and Jillian Pazereckas at the magnificent New York Historical Society

The mighty Matt Knutzen at the New York Public Library's Maps Division

Allison Hourcade of RockLove, for creating the Sailor Twain jewelry!

Joe Monti, for reading a dreadful early script and research help on New York folklore.

Katherine Ramos and Mariana Cardier, partners in crime
Kelly Maguire, web ninja extraordinaire
Joe DiStefano and Andrea Blasich
Evelyn Kriete
Tor.com and HeroesandHeartbreakers.com
Casey Gonzalez

Don and Karen Steinmetz
Jonathan Kruk, for his passion and knowledge of all things Hudson.

Professor Paul Kane at Vassar, for leading me to the river's great poetry.

CREDITS

Pages 62–65: *Sailors of the Firmament* © Laura Senechal. Used by kind permission of the song's author.

Page 219: Valery and Lafayette share *In Cabin'd Ships at Sea*, by Walt Whitman.

Maps on chapter breaks are from nineteenth century surveys courtesy of the U.S.G.S. and Colton's 1836 Topographical Map of New York City is from the David Rumsey Historical Map Collection.

Page 364: Pearl's letter, calligraphy by Jennifer King. *Lorelei* letterhead created by Lissi Erwin, based on steamboat stationery of the late nineteenth century.

First Second
New York & London

Copyright © 2012 by Mark Siegel

Published by First Second
First Second is an imprint of Roaring Brook Press, a division of Holtzbrinck Publishing Holdings Limited Partnership
175 Fifth Avenue, New York, New York 10010
All rights reserved

Distributed in the United Kingdom by Macmillan Children's Books, a division of Pan Macmillan.

Cataloging-in-Publication Data is on file at the Library of Congress.

ISBN 978-1-59643-636-7

First Second books are available for special promotions and premiums.
For details, contact: Director of Special Markets, Holtzbrinck Publishers.

Book design by Colleen AF Venable
Printed in the United States of America

First edition 2012
1 3 5 7 9 10 8 6 4 2